Laurel Nakadate

Laurel Nakadate 365 Days: A Catalogue of Tears

HATJE CANTZ

The Weeping Breviary
Rick Moody

Excepting the crocodile, whose tears were long thought to be a strategy for luring in sympathetic prey, there is no animal but the human animal who weeps, and none that weeps regularly, and none that weeps to express keen feeling, and none that weeps to express remorse, and none that weeps to comfort itself to sleep. And so it's fair to think of the human animal as the weeping animal. Let's leave aside the special cases. Let's leave aside those who inadvertently weep when eating, having recently recovered from Bell's palsy. (It's true!) Let's leave aside those who appear to need to weep when appearing on television cameras so as to lend seriousness to their politics. Let's leave aside the weeping Japanese women who are catering to a Japanese porn fetish. (It's true! Japanese weeping porn!)

Let's leave aside even those who weep *gratefully*, as this too is specialized, and less common, when you get right down to it, than weeping in which the weeper is sad, forlorn, regretful, lost, lonely, bereft, grief-stricken, adrift, or full of pity for the suffering of others. Sadder tears are commoner, because sadder experiences are more routine than those in which we are surfeited with gratitude.

Laurel Nakadate's "365 Days: A Catalogue of Tears" provides an abundance of substantiation for the argument that forlornness is the commonest of feelings, the most human of feelings in this our weeping animal, for it purports to catalogue an entire year, 2010, in which the artist wept *every single day* and managed in the process, somehow, to turn on a camera and to shoot herself performing this elemental task. Every day. Just as if she were flossing her teeth, getting out of bed, eating, brushing her hair, or getting dressed (though it is true, on the basis of the photographs, that sometimes Nakadate wept *before* or *without* getting dressed). Weeping, in this narrative account, is a daily activity for Laurel Nakadate, because forlornness and brokenness and grief and loss are daily activities, and the one leads to the other for the weeping animal, the day leads inexorably to weeping, and weeping, further, is the marker for the passage of each diurnal interval.

What, you might ask, do 365 photographs of a young woman weeping mean? What does weeping on this scale *mean*? What, effectively, does *constant* weeping mean? What does weeping at the drop of a hat mean? Weeping in buckets? What do buckets of tears mean? And do they have to *mean* something, or can they just be? Like a bend in the river? For an artist who courted notoriety by videotaping herself dancing and performing with men she met on the street, and who thus took risks, who reveled in a certain amount of risk-taking, and who in the execution allowed herself to be re-engineered into an object of fantasy for these lonely persons, the weeping photos are indisputably a dramatic transition, a new subject, with substantially different resonances. The Nakadate of the earlier work is an exhibitionist who, nonetheless, has mixed emotions about being the fetish object and about the power of photography to turn subject into fetish, and fetish into power nexus, but who relishes the energy thrown up by mixed feelings. The earlier Nakadate implicates the audience in the ritual consumption of fetish, invites male viewers to get closer to their own shame, and, in the process, collaborates with the lonely persons who people her videos, coming in this way to *know them*. She gathers in their inmost difficulties, in the process feeling what there is to feel—even as the camera leaves all contradictions in place, woman fetishized/woman empowered, beauty celebrated/homeliness celebrated, loss idealized/loss transcended, photography as documentary medium/photography as medium of constructed reality, and so on.

The artist of "365 Days," on the other hand, is an artist who has stripped away the collaborators and the apparatus, until what remains is the pathos associated with the work and not much else. In "365 Days" the artist, the fetish, the feeling, and the aftermath of the image are all simultaneous, the feeling of being a woman, the feeling of being an object, the feeling of making art about these feelings, the feeling of art itself, these are apparent in the reifications and limitations of the photograph, so that the image and the aftermath of the image do a dance of simultaneities. *I am showing you myself, and I despair of your reaction to this image, which is not myself,* the photos remark, or *Don't watch, or else I will cry, which really ought to embarrass you*, or, *This is intimate, and you should not be seeing it, and you are ruining it by seeing it*, all of these dilemmas worth weeping over—if you are a weeping animal—and this construction of paradoxes, this reveling in contradiction, in the contradiction at the heart of documentation, is made again and again and again by Nakadate in this weeping year, in ways labored, premeditated, and absolutely on the fly, while many other things were (to speak factually) taking place (a movie was being finished, an art exhibition was being mounted, classes were being taught), so that the photographs are excisions from the year in question, and a selection of what is important in these days, an interpretation of the calendar, rather than the calendar itself.

Which raises the taxonomic questions: What kind of work is this work? Is it really photographic in the traditional sense? Is it documentary? Or is it something more? This work, I would argue, is more than photographic residue. This work is a performance, a year-long performance, mostly taking place, as it turns out, in three places: in the artist's very small apartment in Greenwich Village (in which she works especially hard, over the course of "365 Days," to find new corners, new spots, new lighting conditions, so that at the end of the journey, we feel we know intimately the modest confines of her living space, we feel we have experienced its relentless smallness), in hotels, and aboard commercial airliners. The artist, on the basis of the documentation, is in an almost constant state of flux, on jets, or in anonymous rooms, and always miserable about traveling, and since, again and again, we are thinking about the excising, about the narrative implied outside of the photographs, it's not hard to linger over the idea of the *other people on the jet* when Nakadate is busy photographing herself weeping at 1:38 a.m., somewhere over Lawrence, Kansas, let's say. Such is the project. The performance is the ritual, which is the purgation of such feelings as: sadness, forlornness, regret, loneliness, grief, or humility. And the ritual is the performance, and the performance is the work, and the performance exists because you, the audience, require it, because you too are sad, forlorn. Purgation allows artist and audience to feel better, or so Aristotle might have said. Or: purgation creates an environment in which more purgation is always necessary.

Are there aspects of the artist's biography that make it especially easy for her to weep in this way? Are there aspects of the artist's biography in 2010 that make this year an especially good weeping year? Is 2010 a better year for weeping than, say, 2008, or 2011? The ritual of "365 Days" does not include a great volume of biographical markings, nor does it explicitly reward biographical inquiry, although if one is in search of narrative, there are hints, tidbits of realism, of worldly movement, of conflict, tectonic shifting, certain landscapes that one might point to and might attempt to decode, repetitions of interiors (besides the artist's apartment), so as to construct or infer a story of the year, and, in fact, this invitation to infer implies one of the further questions about "365 Days": Why a series of photographs to document the performance rather than a series of videos? Or one continuous video? A plausible explanation would be that the artist is simply a gifted photographer, and the beauty of these bordered instants is seductive. But another explanation would adhere to the notion that the implied narrative, the fragmented narrative, makes room for the viewer, makes room for transferential exchange, and the emptying out of unwarranted biographical certainties implies that *only* the tears are memorable or important in the year 2010.

To put it yet another way: in these photos the artist is always alone. There is not another hand, not a strand of hair, not another shadow, not another human being, except in very occasional extreme distances, and there is no conversation taking place, and thus no kind words, no witticisms, to leaven the dread. There is only solitariness. We can assume that Laurel Nakadate did, in fact, have some consort with human beings in 2010, but those interactions are not part of the performance. The weeping animal is mostly alone and is best when lonely.

These are also photographs, as opposed to artistic statements in other media, because these kinds of photographs—haunted, intimate, excessively revealing, and completely isolated images of young women—are one compelling story of femininity *now*. This is the story on the Web, in millions upon millions of blogs, and Facebook pages, and online sites advocating activities both wholesome and dangerous. The bulk of these online photographs of strangers, these accounts of self, are bad, are awkward, dimly lit, haphazard, consumer-grade, hopeless, and Nakadate plays with and against this constructed femininity; she includes the *bad* photos of herself, the ones where her eyes are nearly swollen shut, where the running make-up does *not* look like what you might find in the fashion photos of the 90s; there are running noses, inflammations, unsightly grimaces, things out of focus. Nakadate likes bad images, even if she is also entirely capable of aestheticizing her weeping photographs, so that her outstretched body looks like the murder victim captured by Weegee, or so that her curled-up physique is like a deposition from the Renaissance, a Caravaggio, excepting that in this refraction Mary has breasts effulgent, as if to taunt those who would merely select for the fetish qualities of an image and who are thereby brought near to their shame. Among precursors of art history, Nakadate borrows therefore from both sacred and profane; from the performances of more recent performance art history, she also borrows—from Yoko Ono, Vito Acconci, and Marina Abramovic; from the television of recent years Nakadate borrows from the cheapness, the tawdriness of so-called *enhanced reality programming*, which is to say that this weeping happened, but the tripod was often set up and waiting beforehand, and the subject of the photos (in this case the photographer, too) invited the intrusion, despite the fact that she probably ought to have run screaming in another direction. Just like on "16 and Pregnant." Just like on "Teen Mom." Just like on "Hoarders" (the show about collecting mania). Just like on "The Biggest Loser" (weight loss as emblematic American activity).

The cataloguing of para- and intertexts above neglects, however, to remind you about the pathos, neglects to mention again that the weeping animal actually weeps, because the weeping animal cannot do otherwise, though in many cases it wishes it might. The weeping animal is felled by its sympathies, because its compassion is not evolutionarily sound, unless perhaps the weeping animal is a *mother*. The weeping animal, as in Wittgenstein's private-language argument, makes the one undeniably perceptible human utterance, the cry of pain. Though the weeping animal, in the main, is worthless to the masses of featherless bipeds because it is standing around gazing at all the disaffiliation when what it should be doing is killing and eating its antagonists, raping, pillaging, accepting government bailouts, socking away profits in offshore accounts, it is so *human*, just the same, in its frailty, its genuineness, its separateness, its estrangement.

Nakadate's year of suffering, her calendar, her breviary, is a recognition of a shared language of regret that yokes us together, therefore, and a recognition that this regret and loss are somehow beautiful, no matter how they look. The beauty is after the fact, a posteriori. Together in one place, these works by Nakadate have a lingering and brutal thrust, in the way that collections of human reiteration are always overwhelming, because the sheer amount of tears that fell, in this calendar of 2010, is enormous. Gallons perhaps. Hard to feel that we are worth all this, but Nakadate performs her tears—at us, with us, for us—nonetheless. And in the process, the aesthetic process, the personal process, the *human* process, something like redemption is introduced into this creative exchange. A sort of redemption becomes conceivable. Even likely.

365 Days:
A Catalogue
of Tears

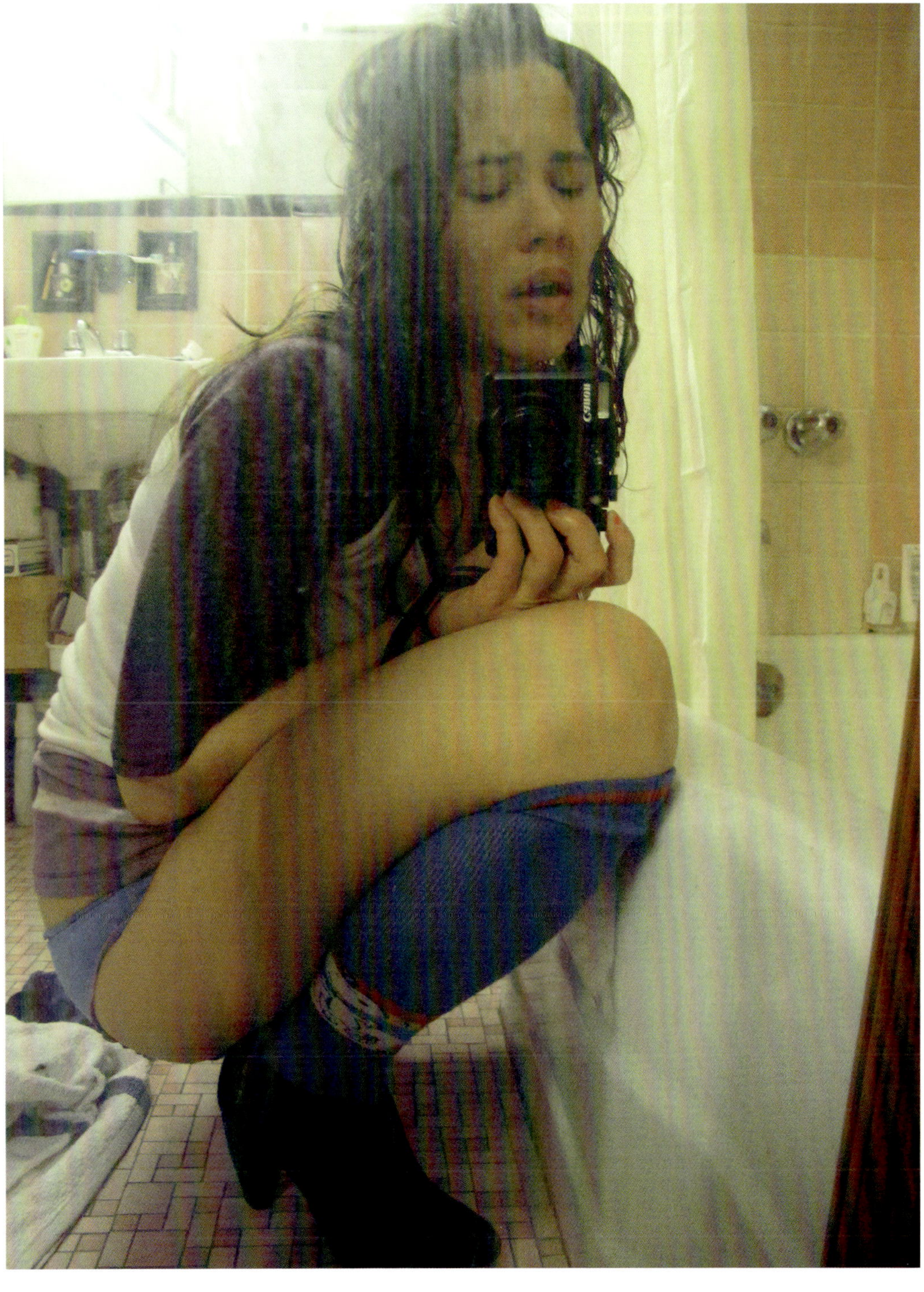

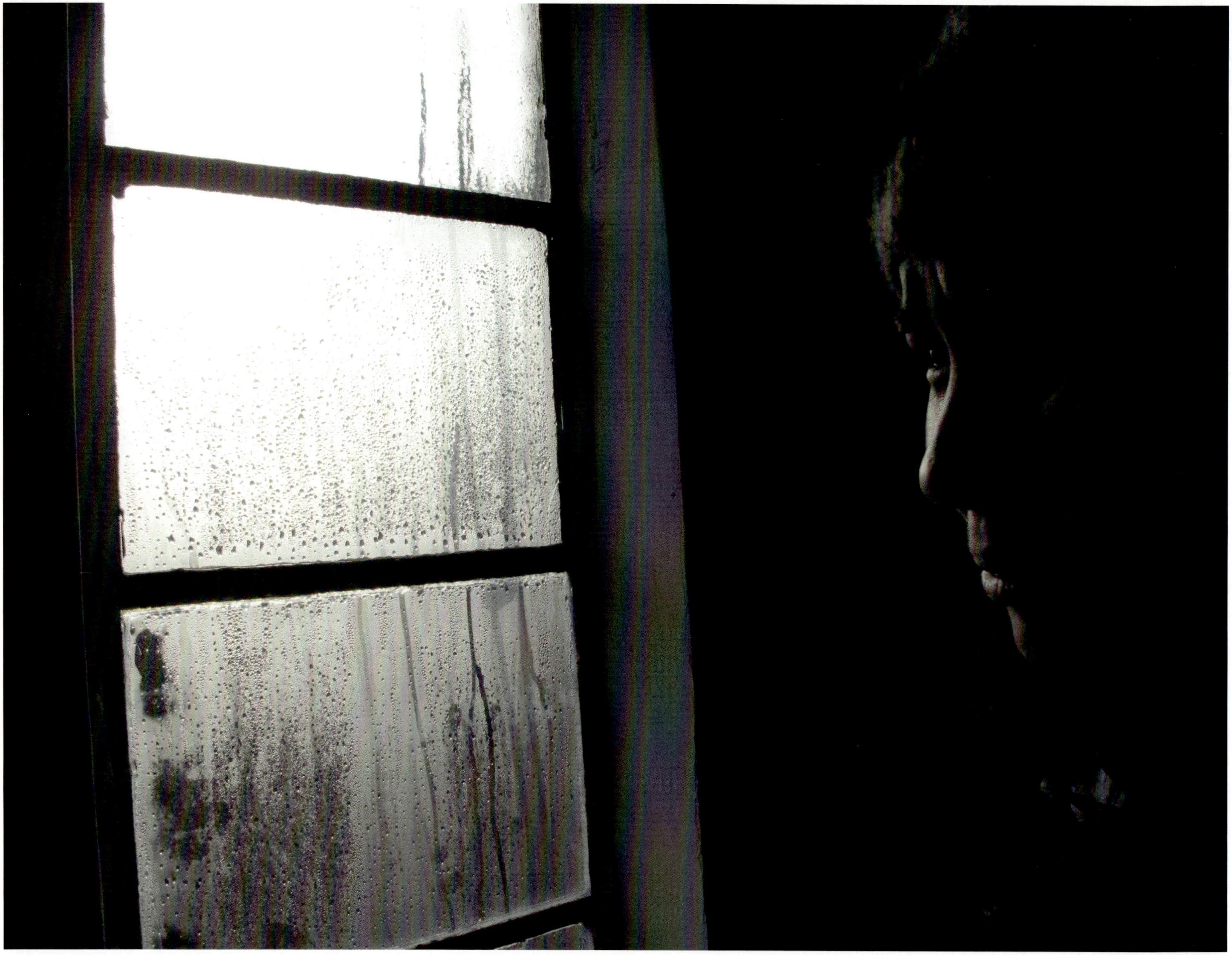

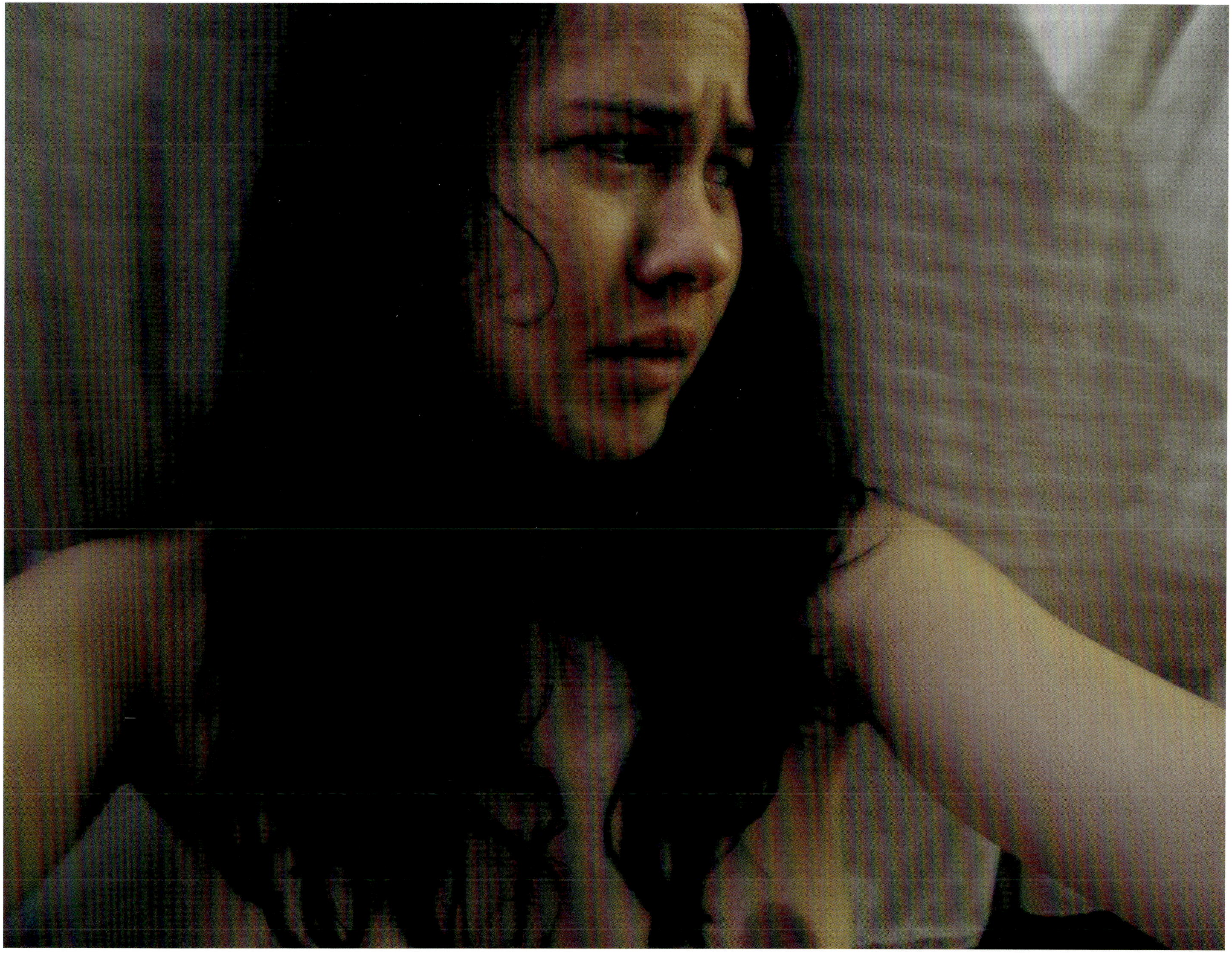

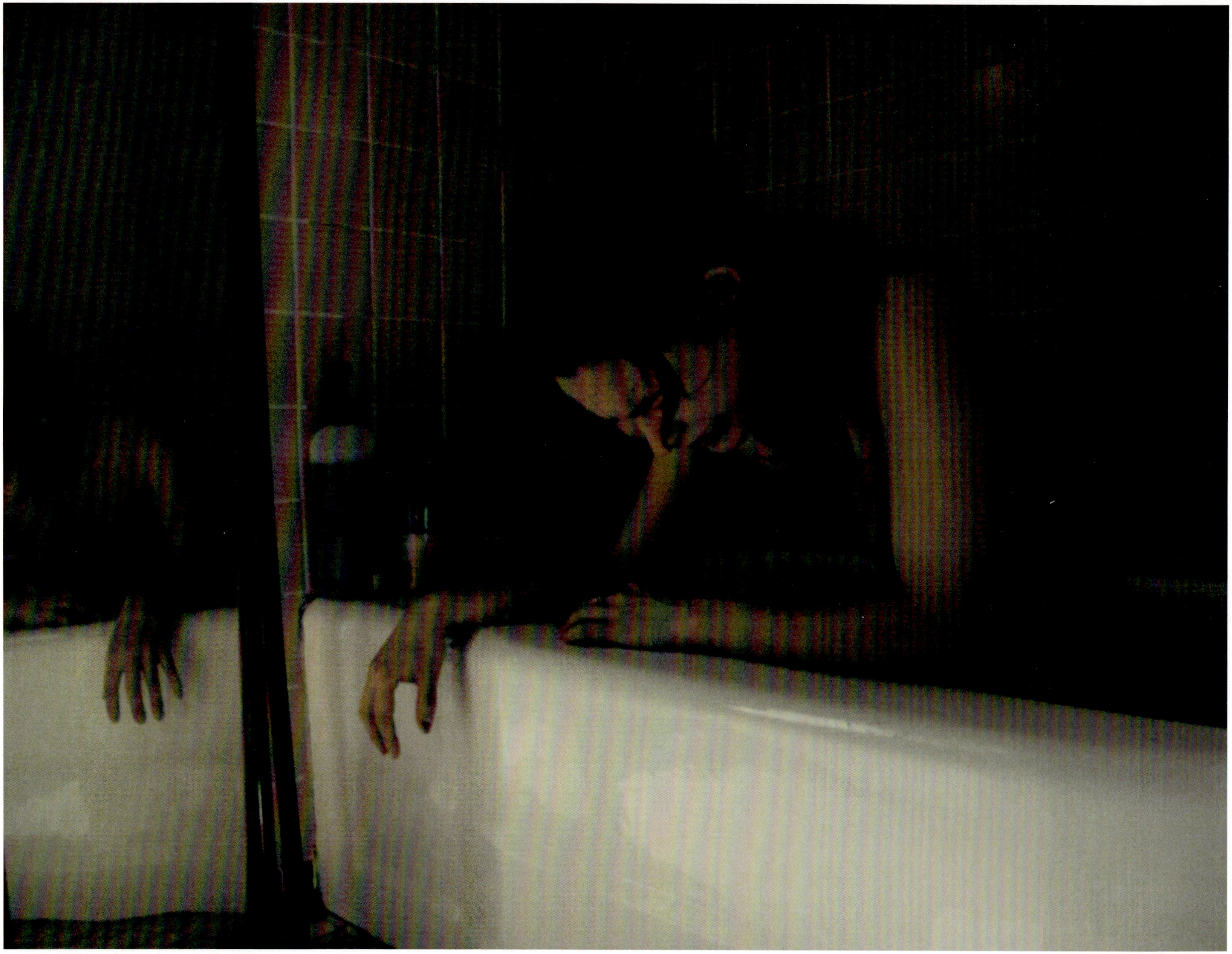

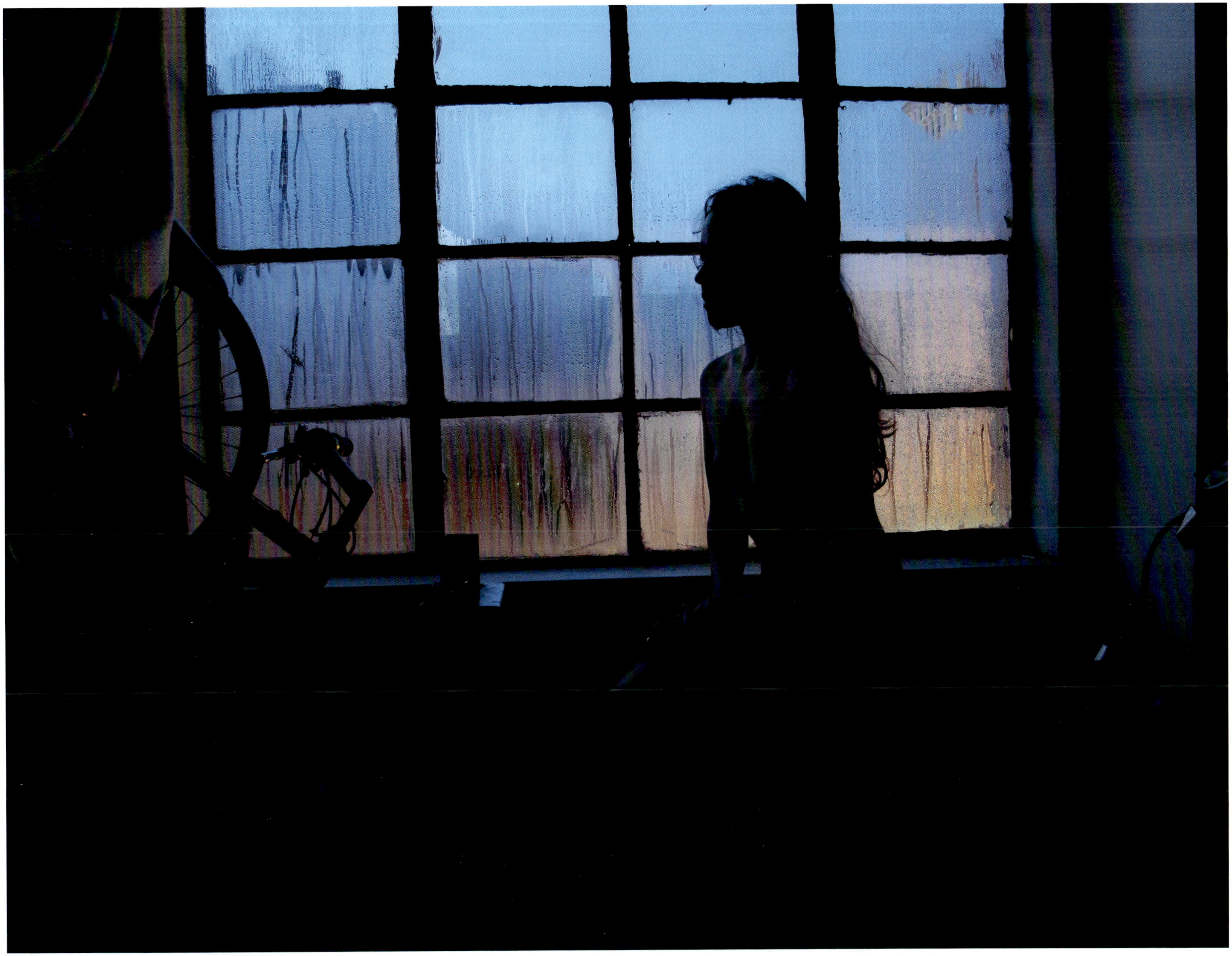

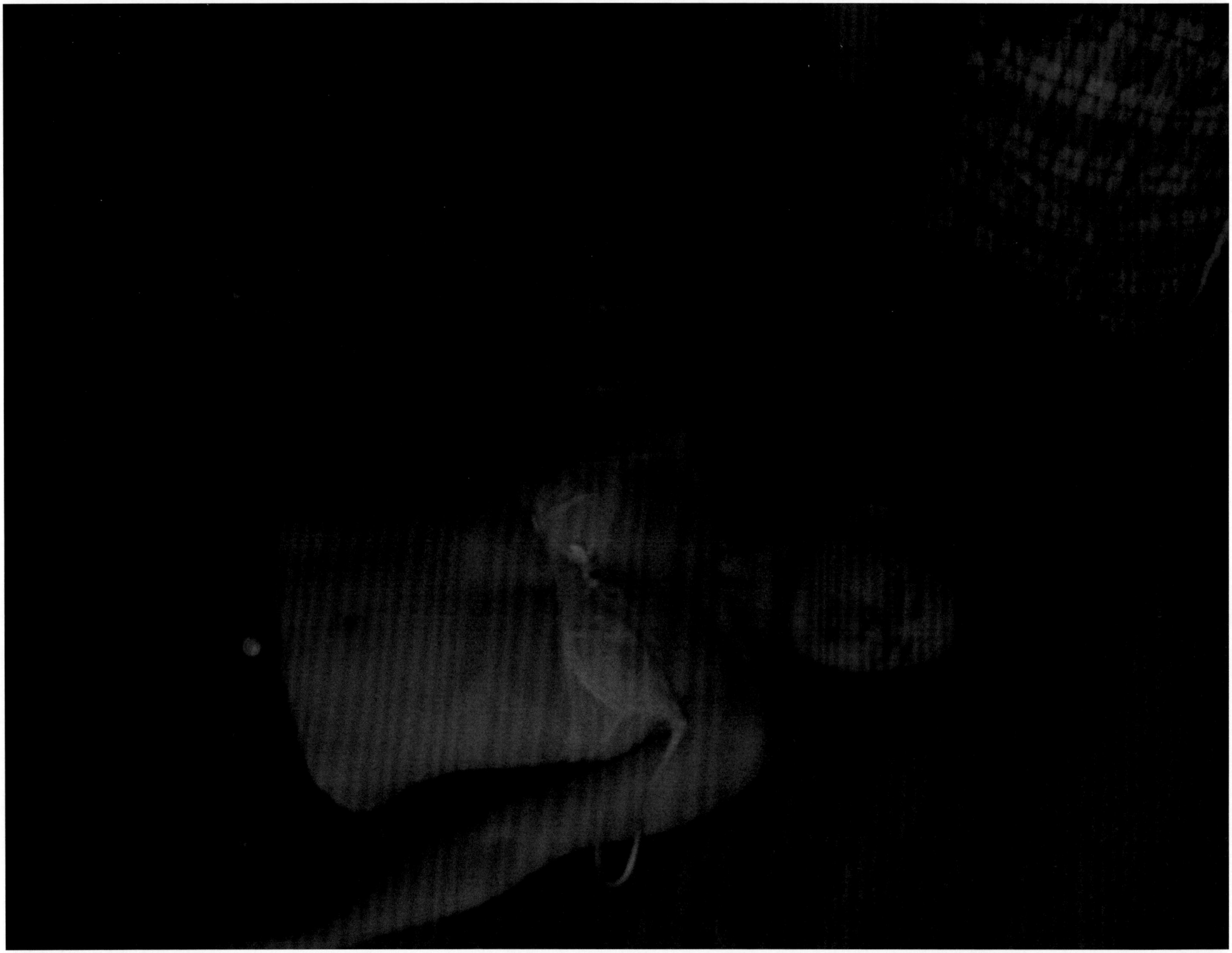

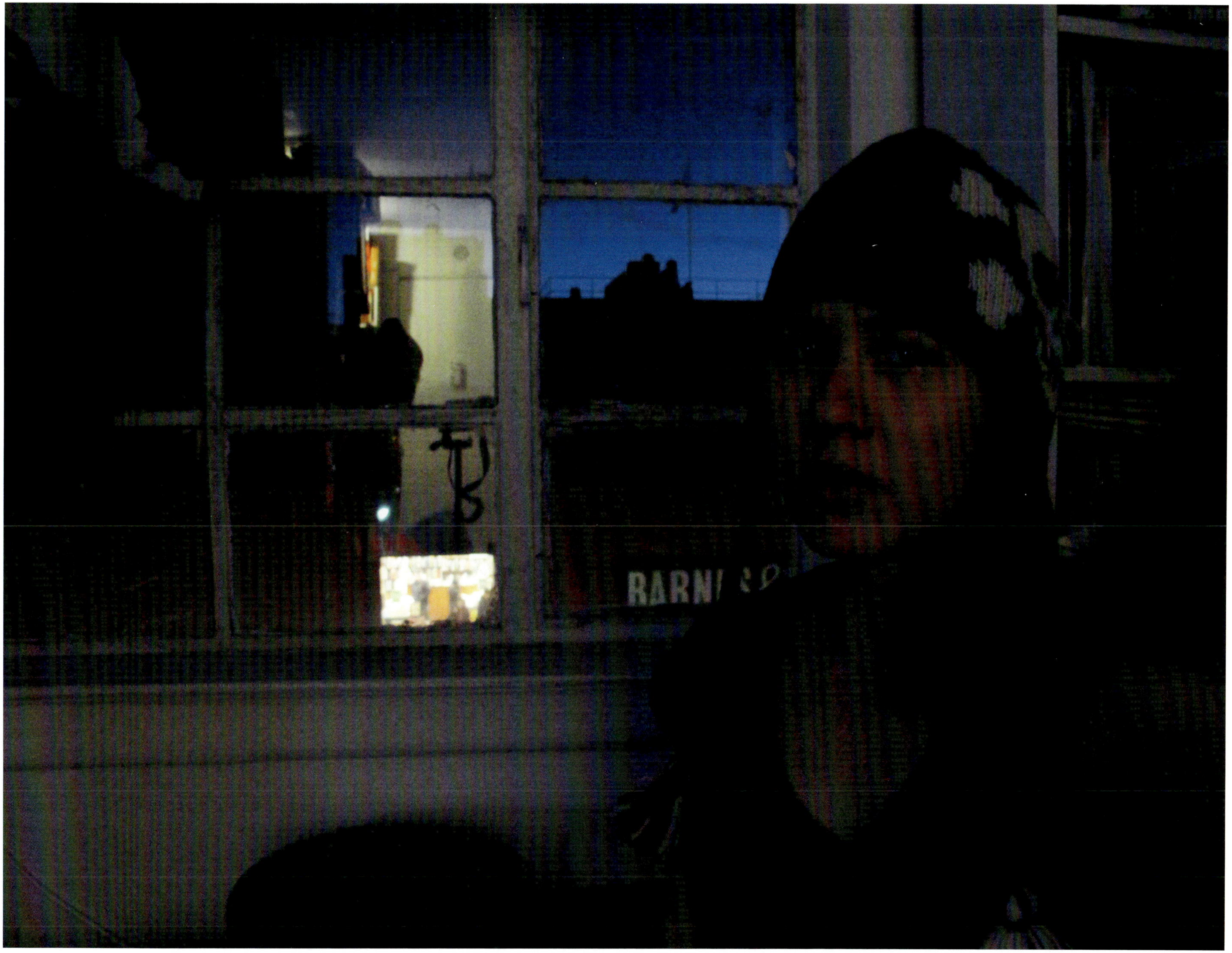

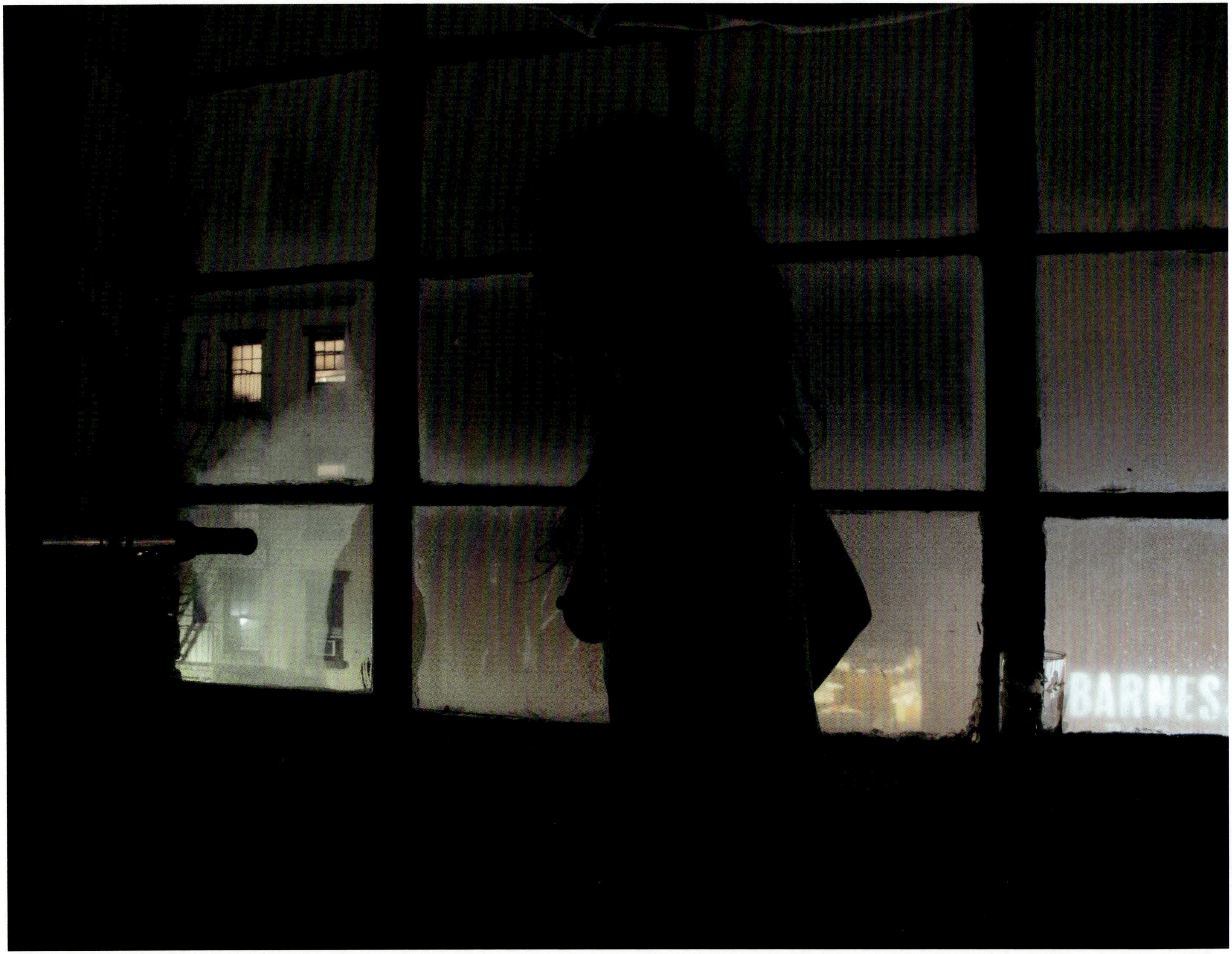
BARNES

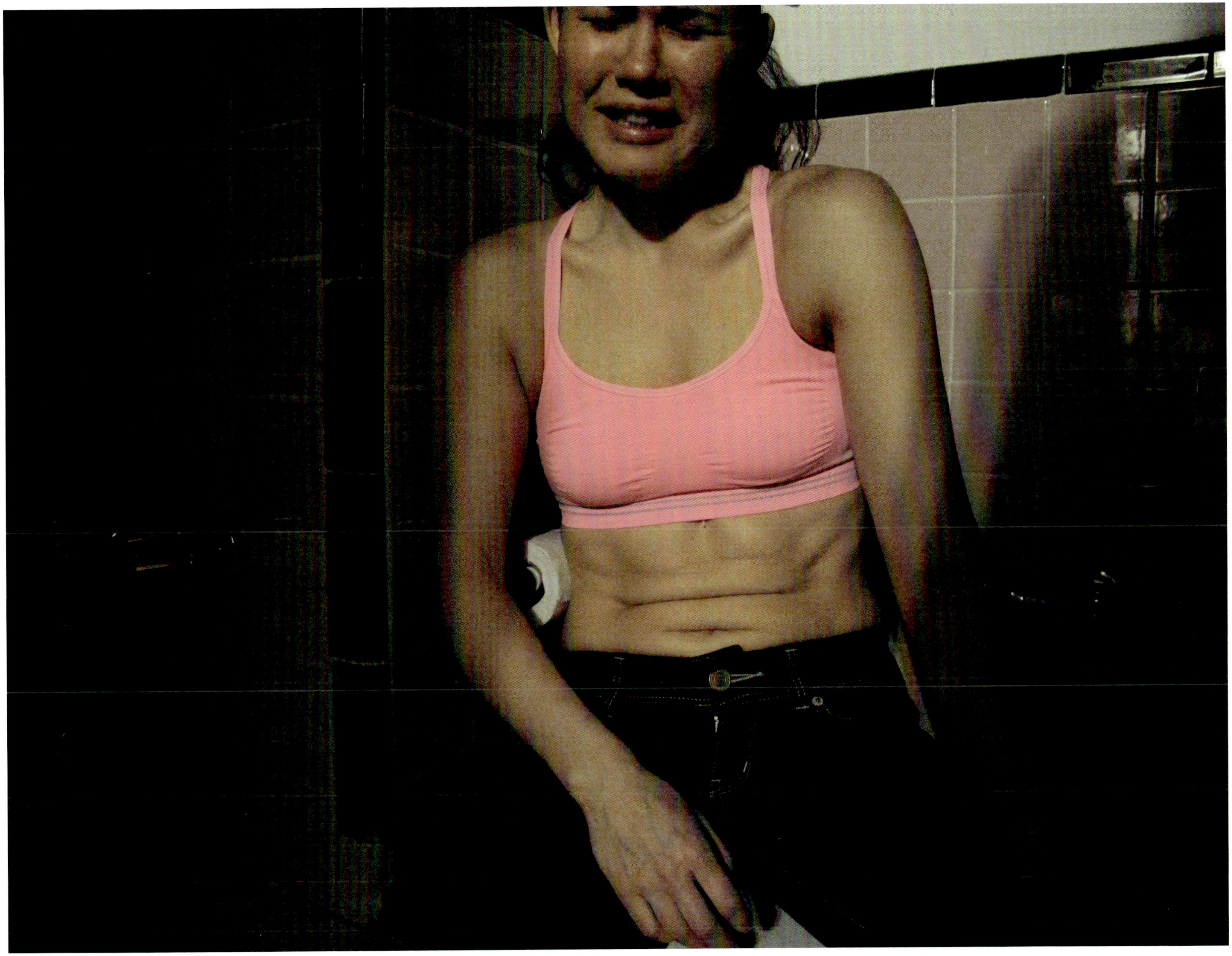

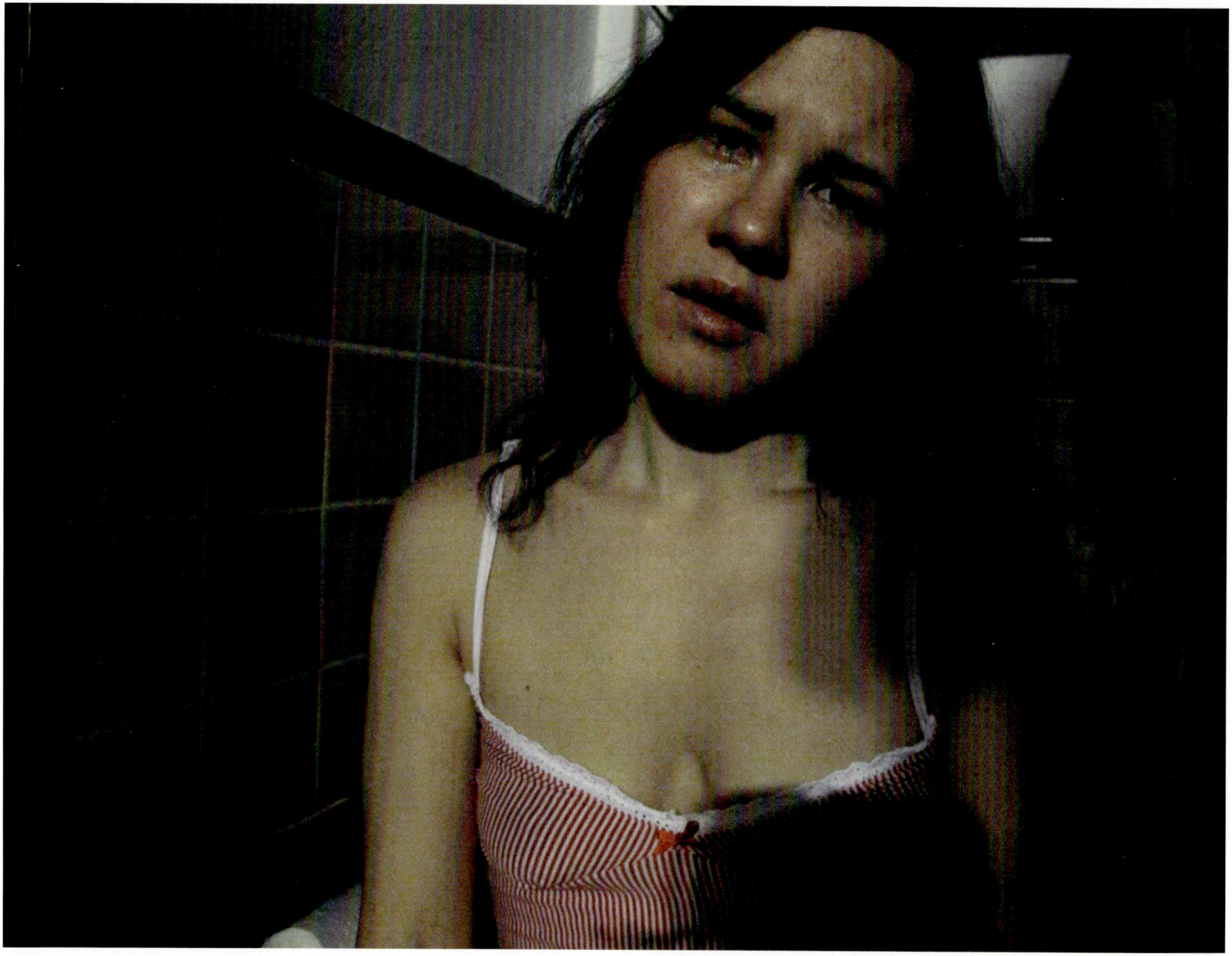

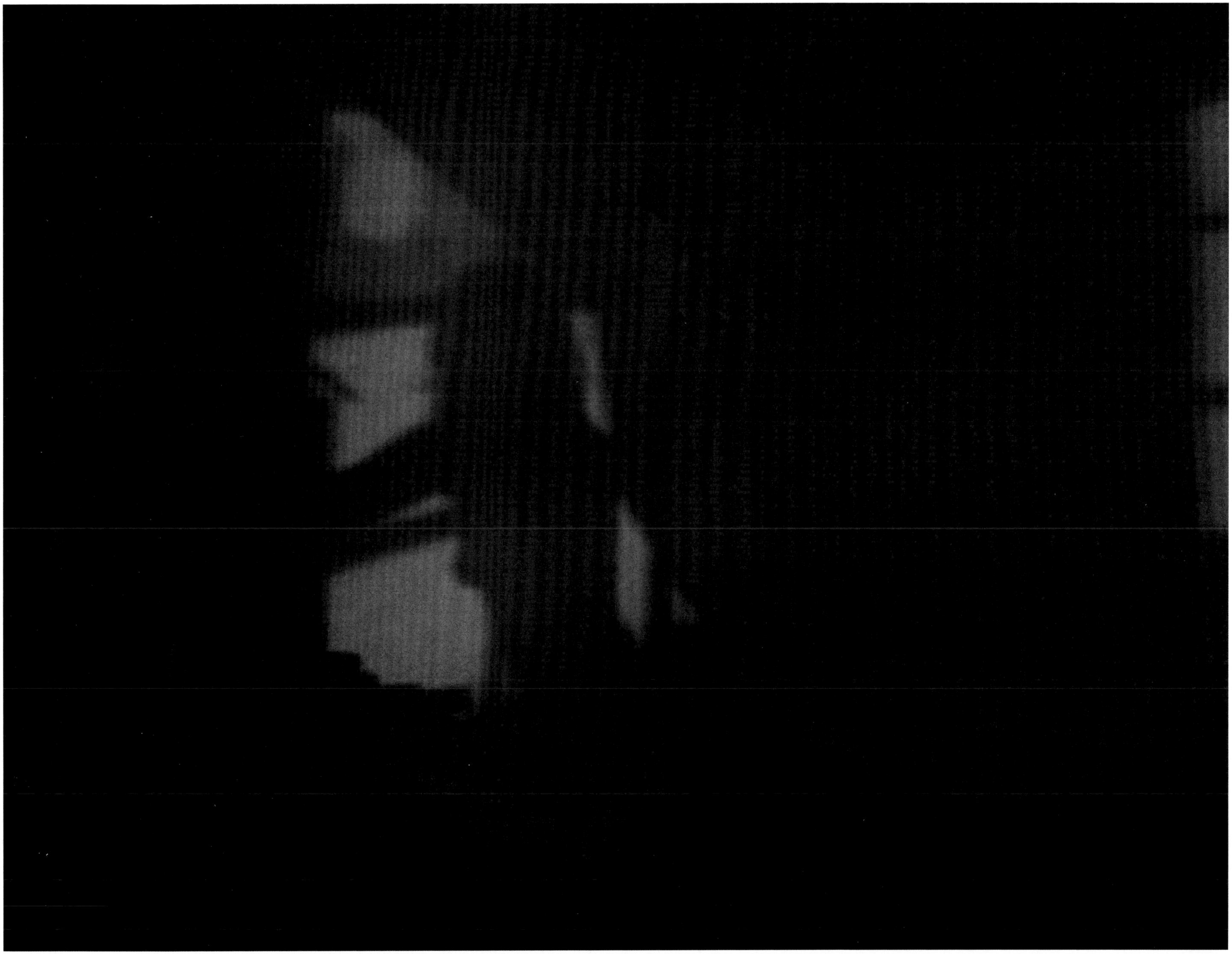

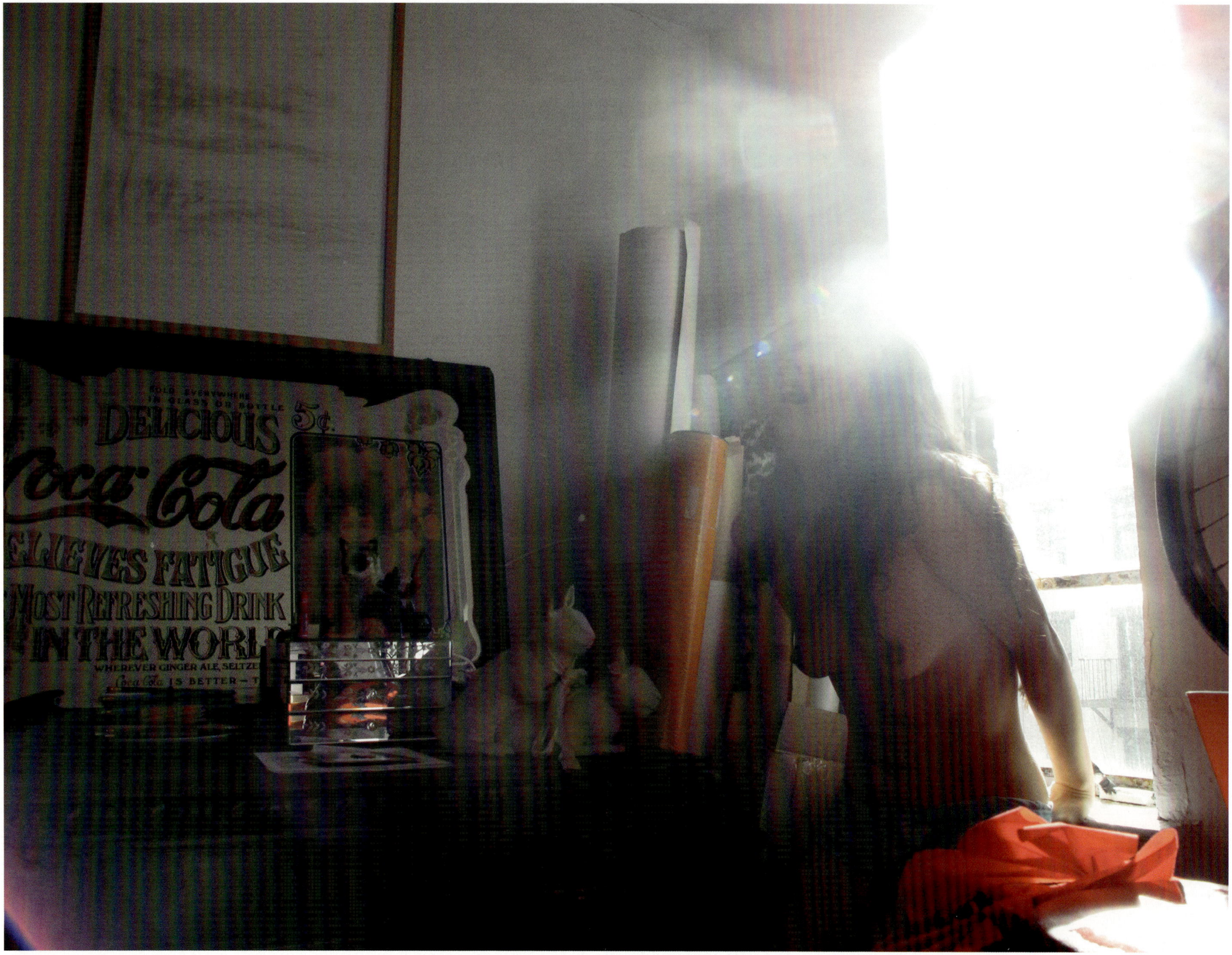
DELICIOUS
Coca-Cola
5¢
FATIGUE
MOST REFRESHING DRINK

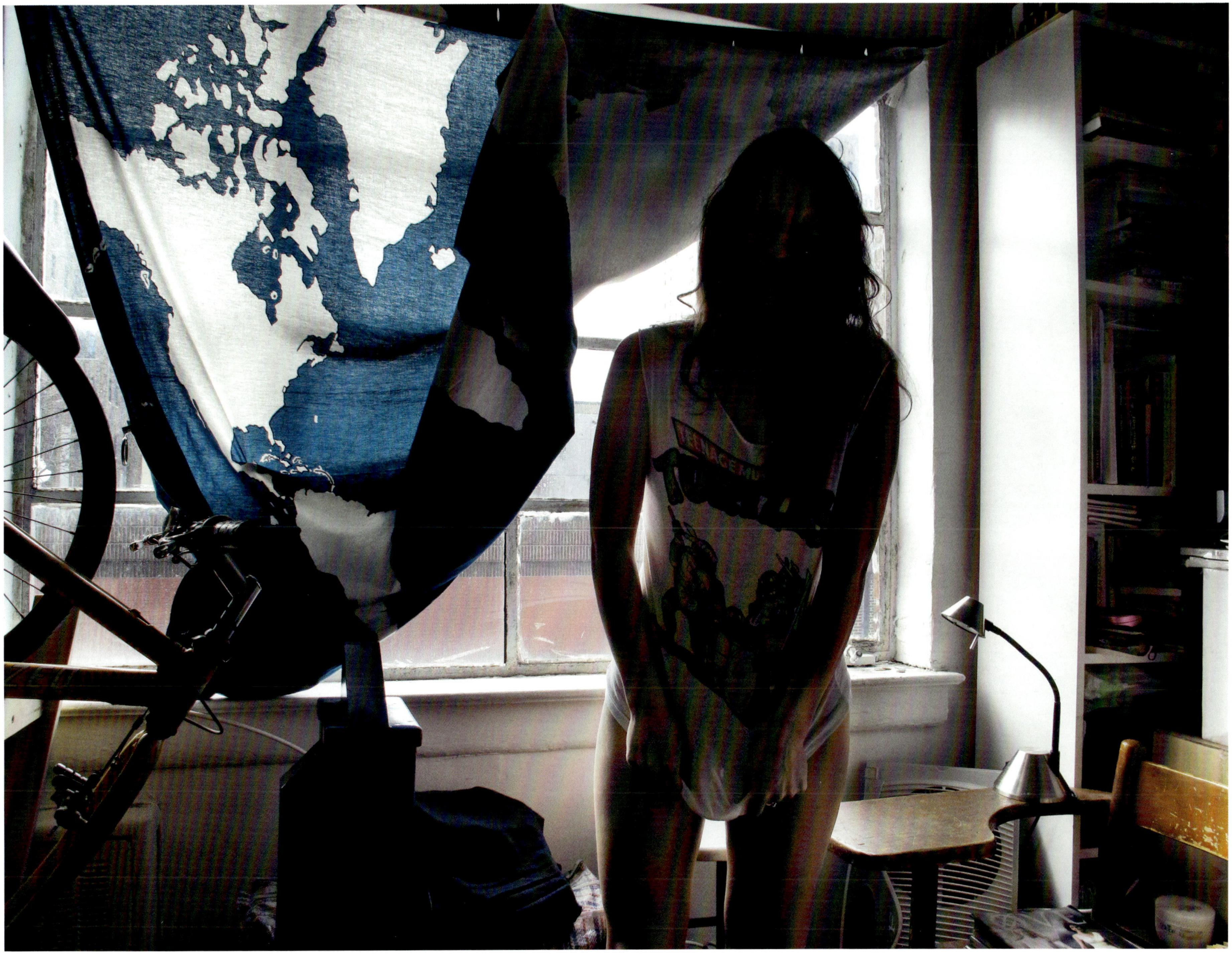

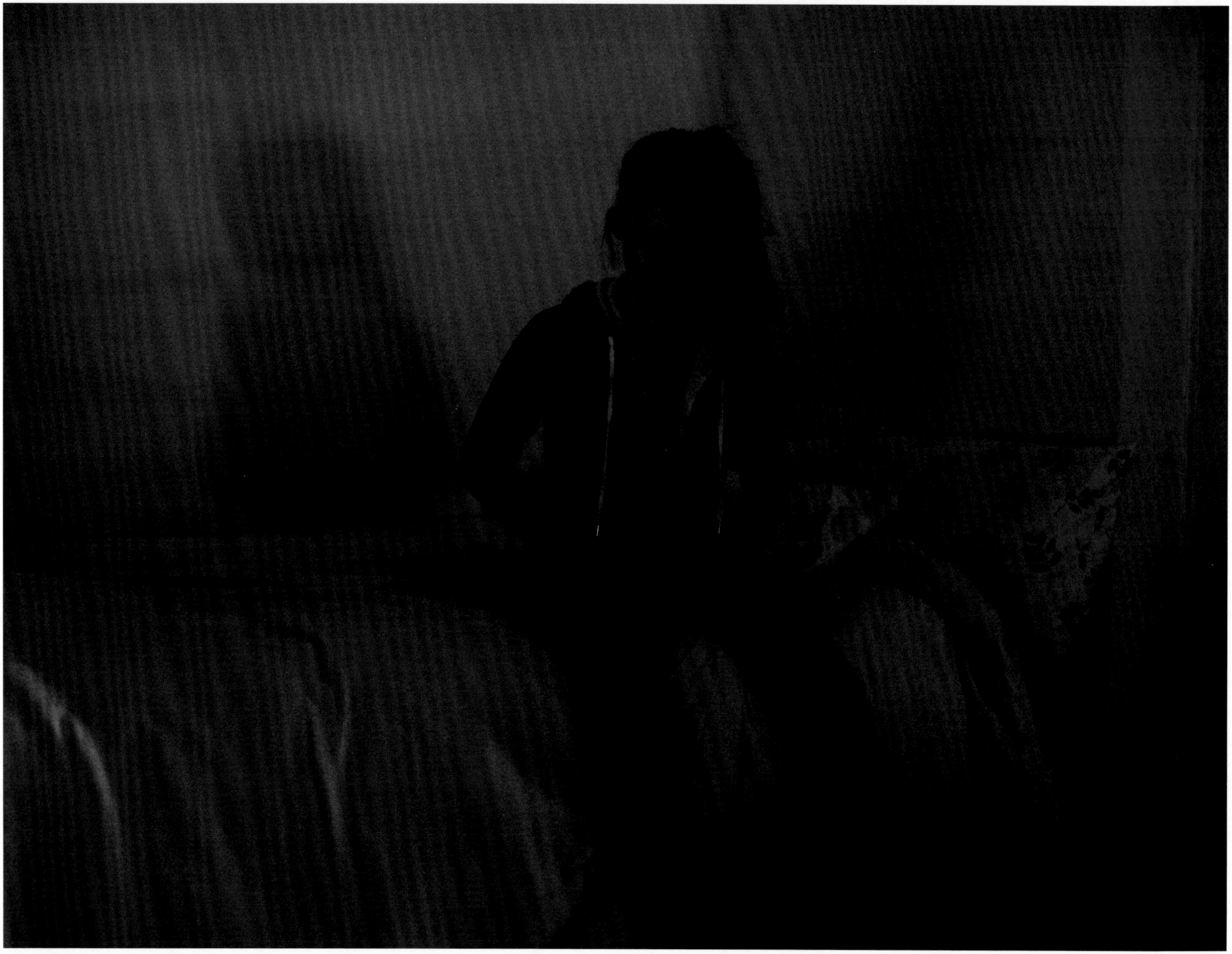

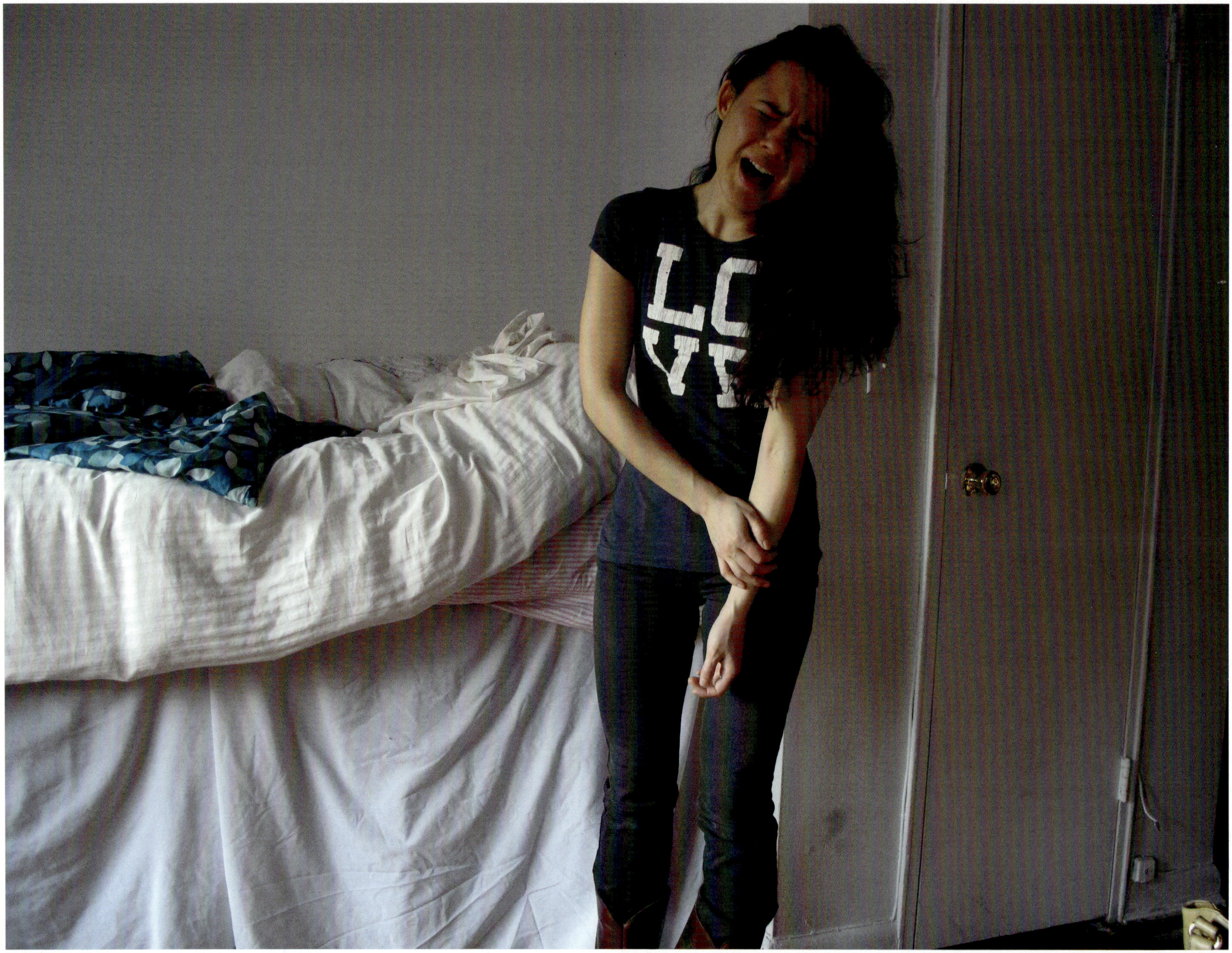

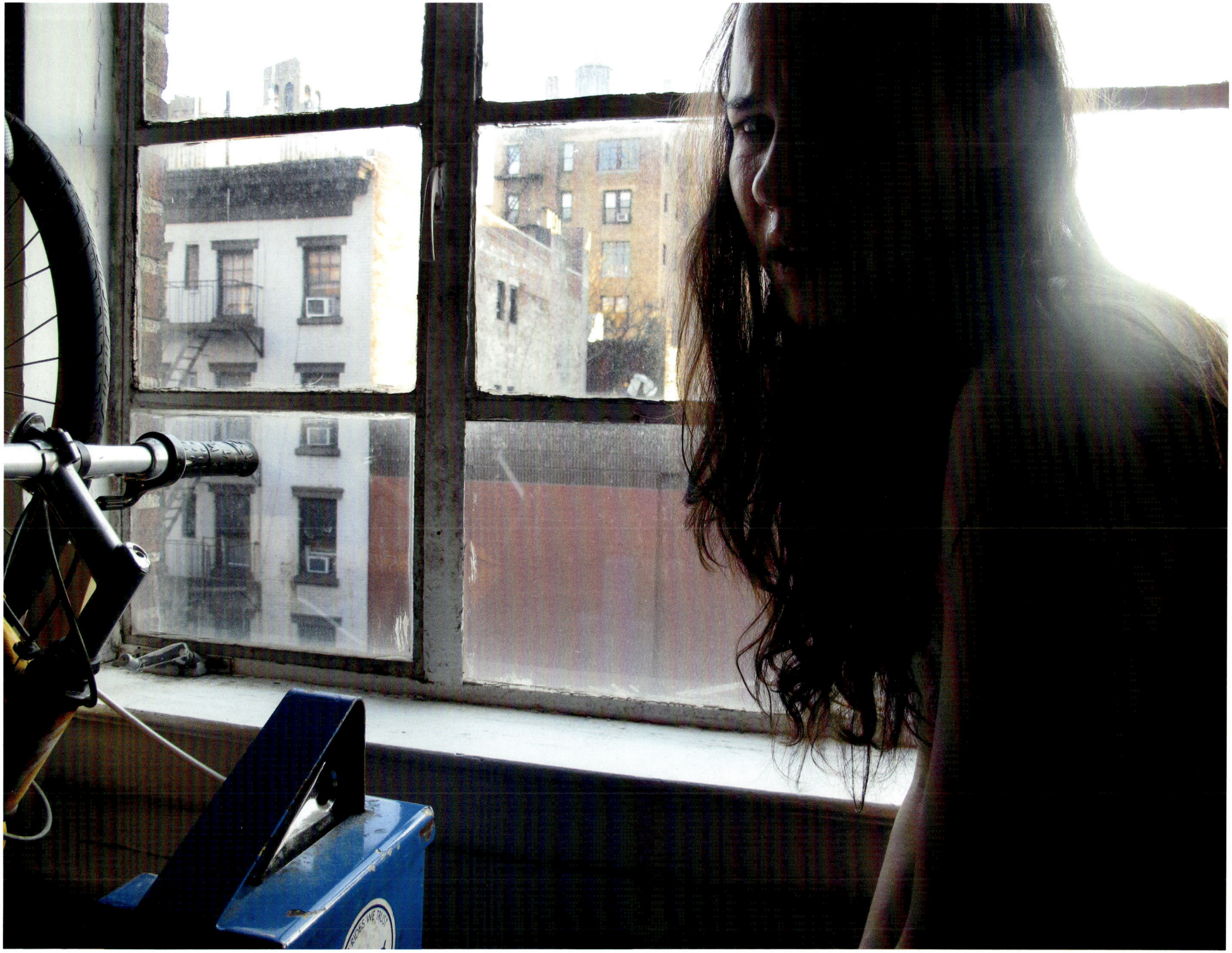

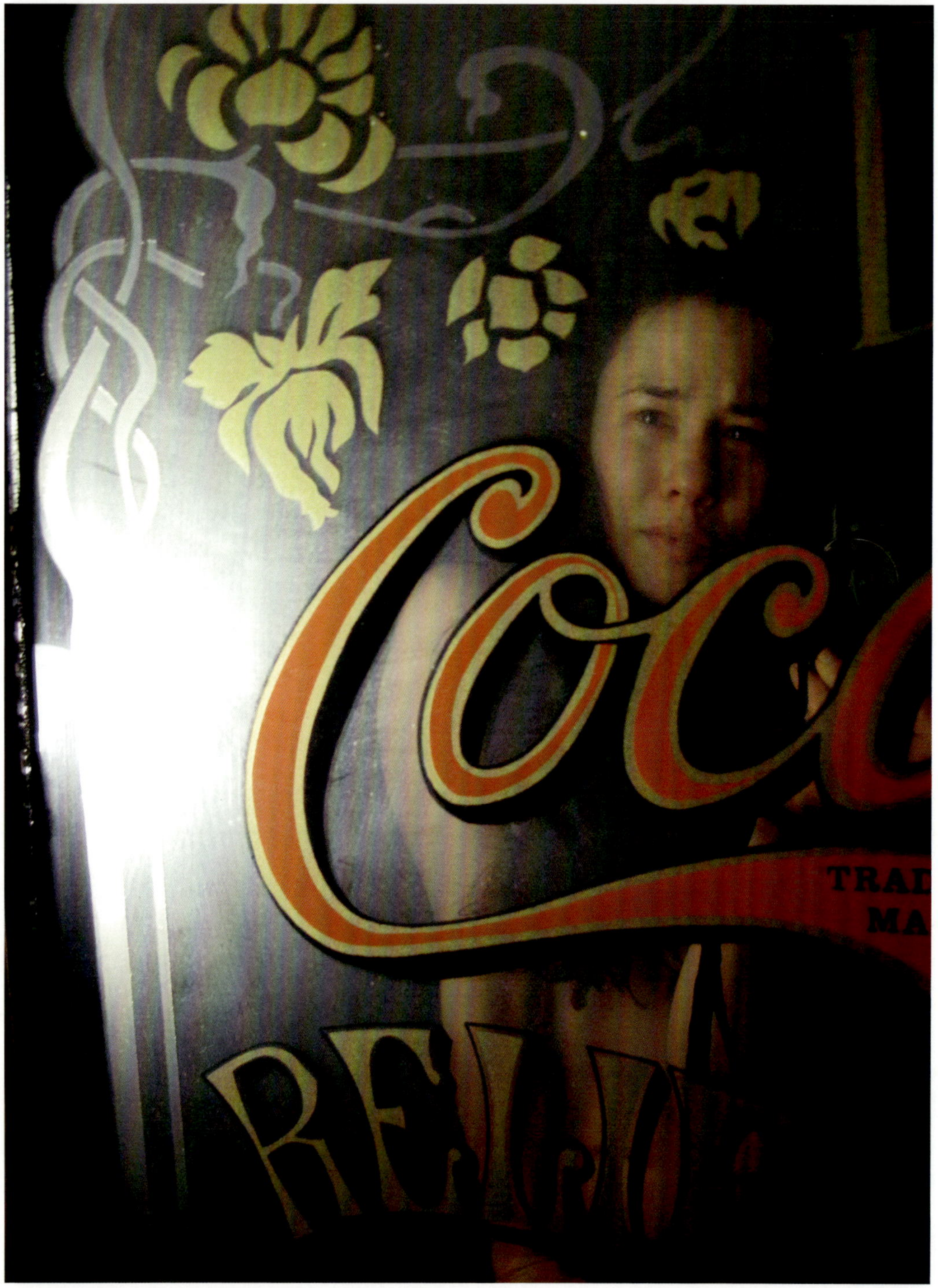

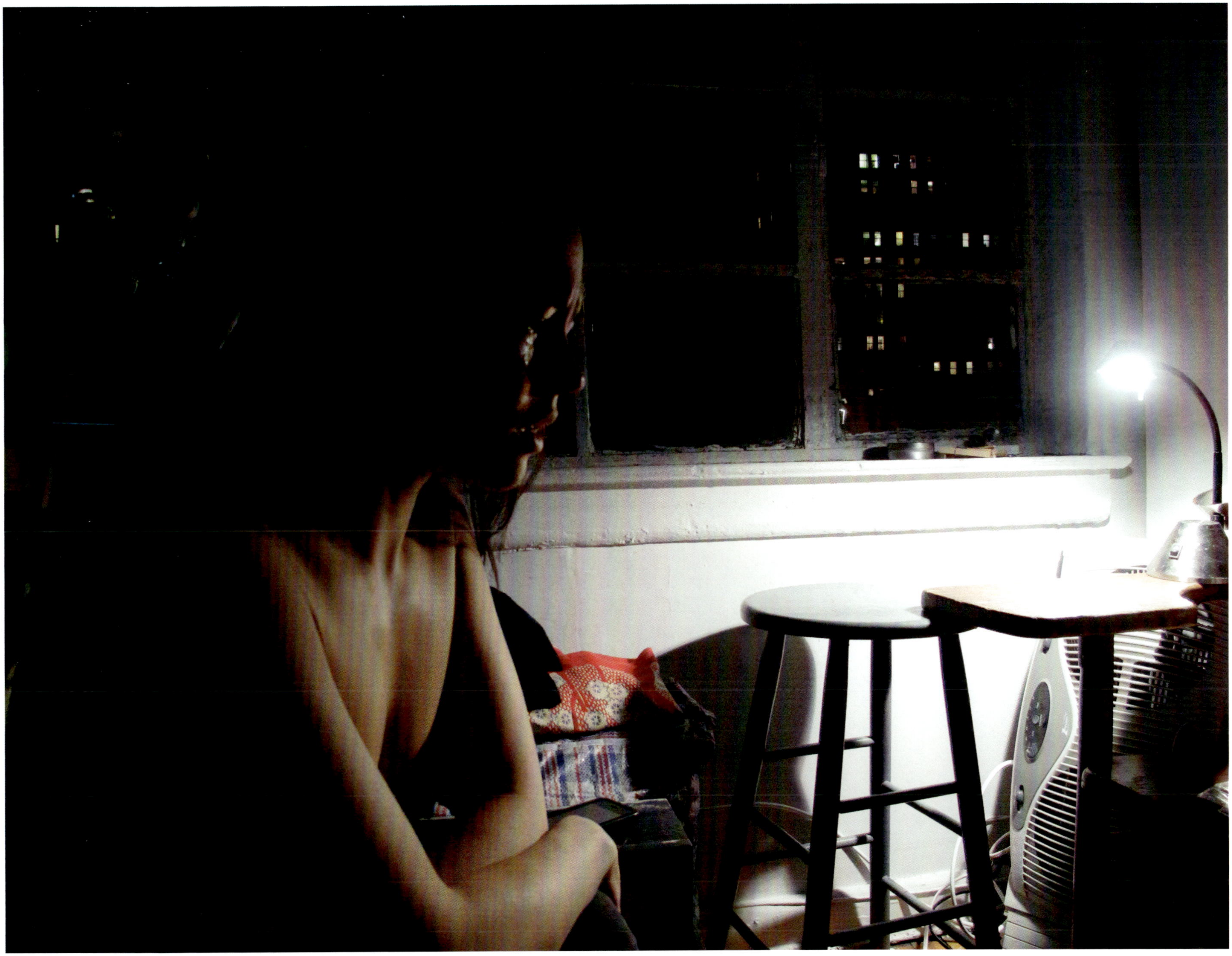

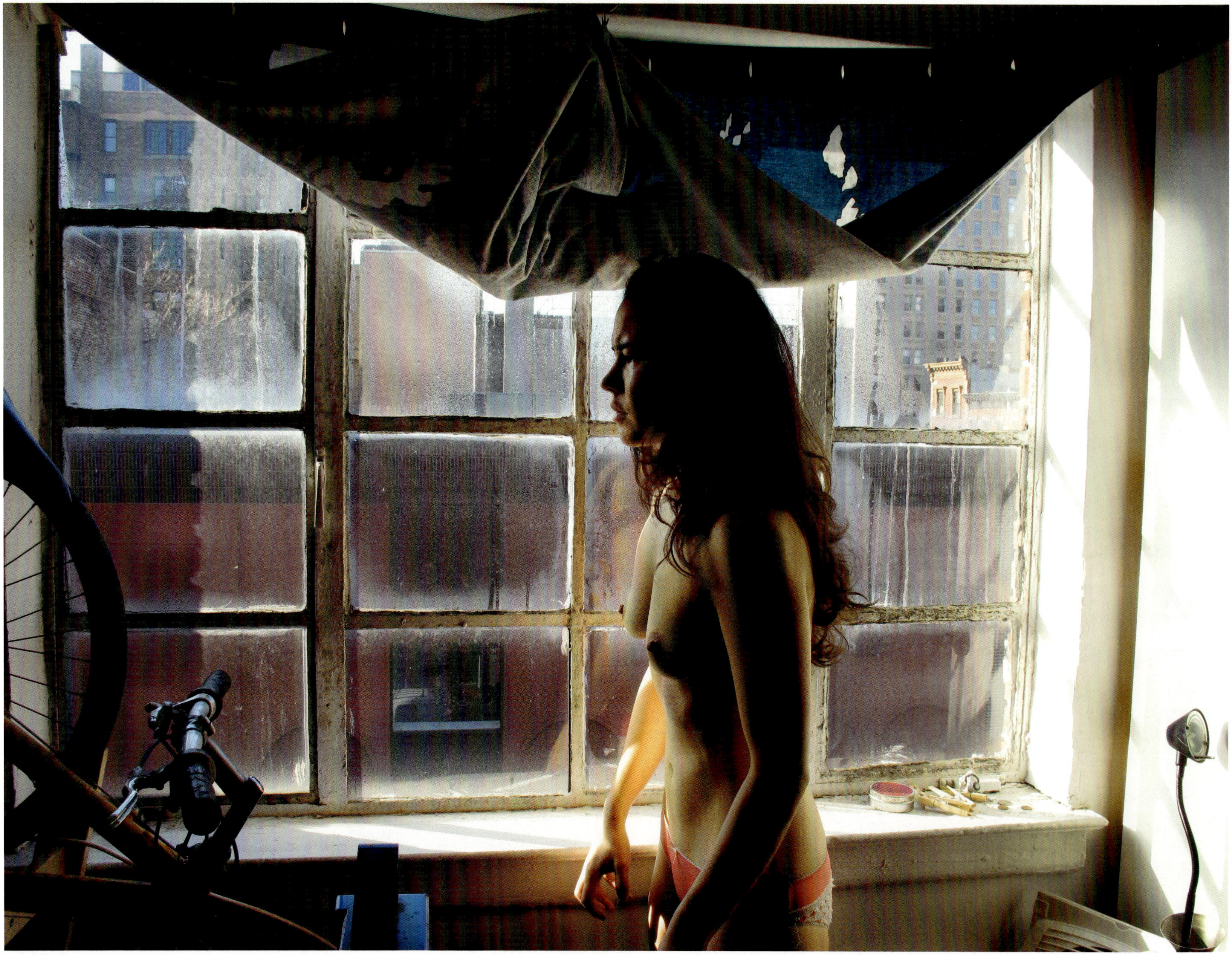

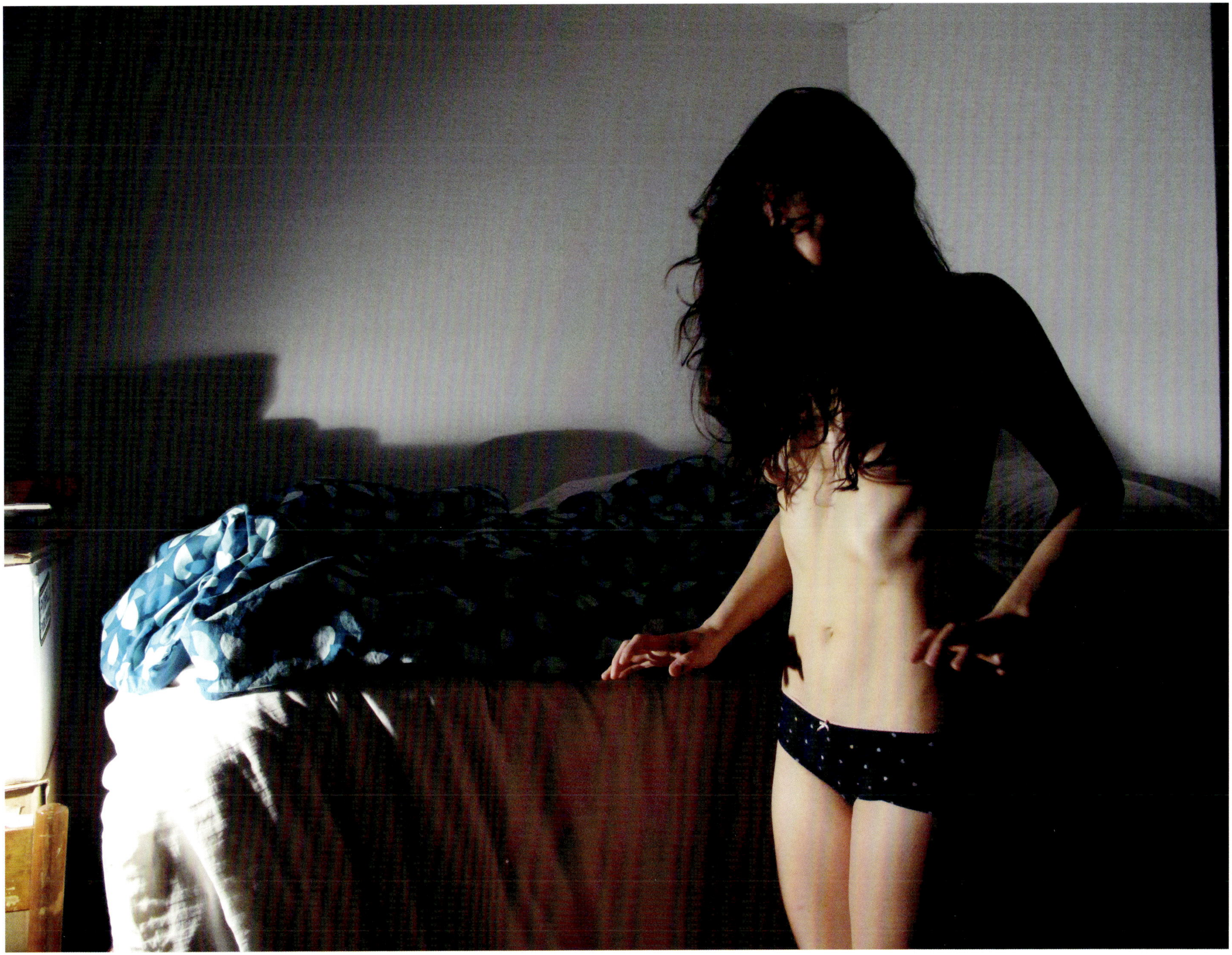

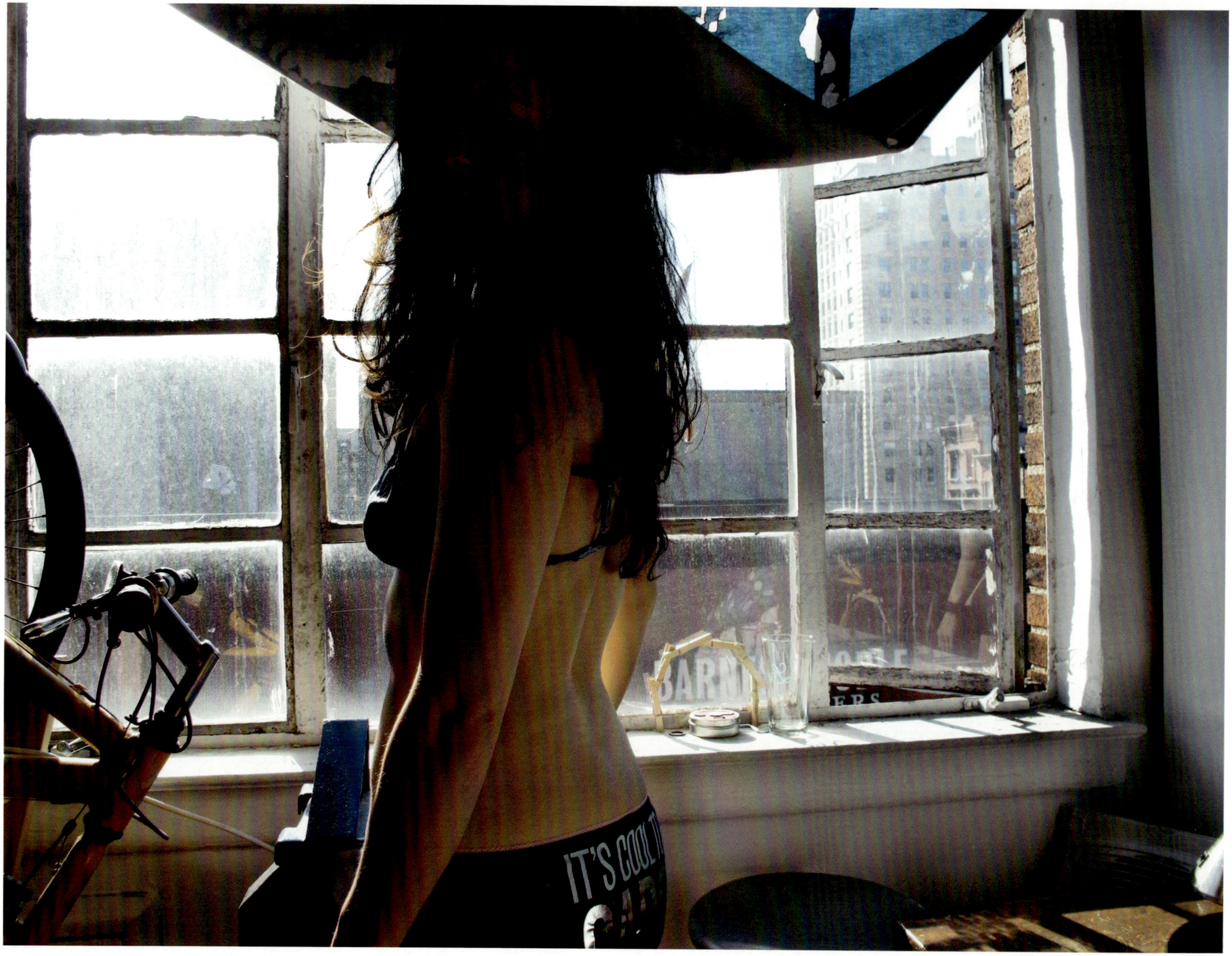
IT'S COOL

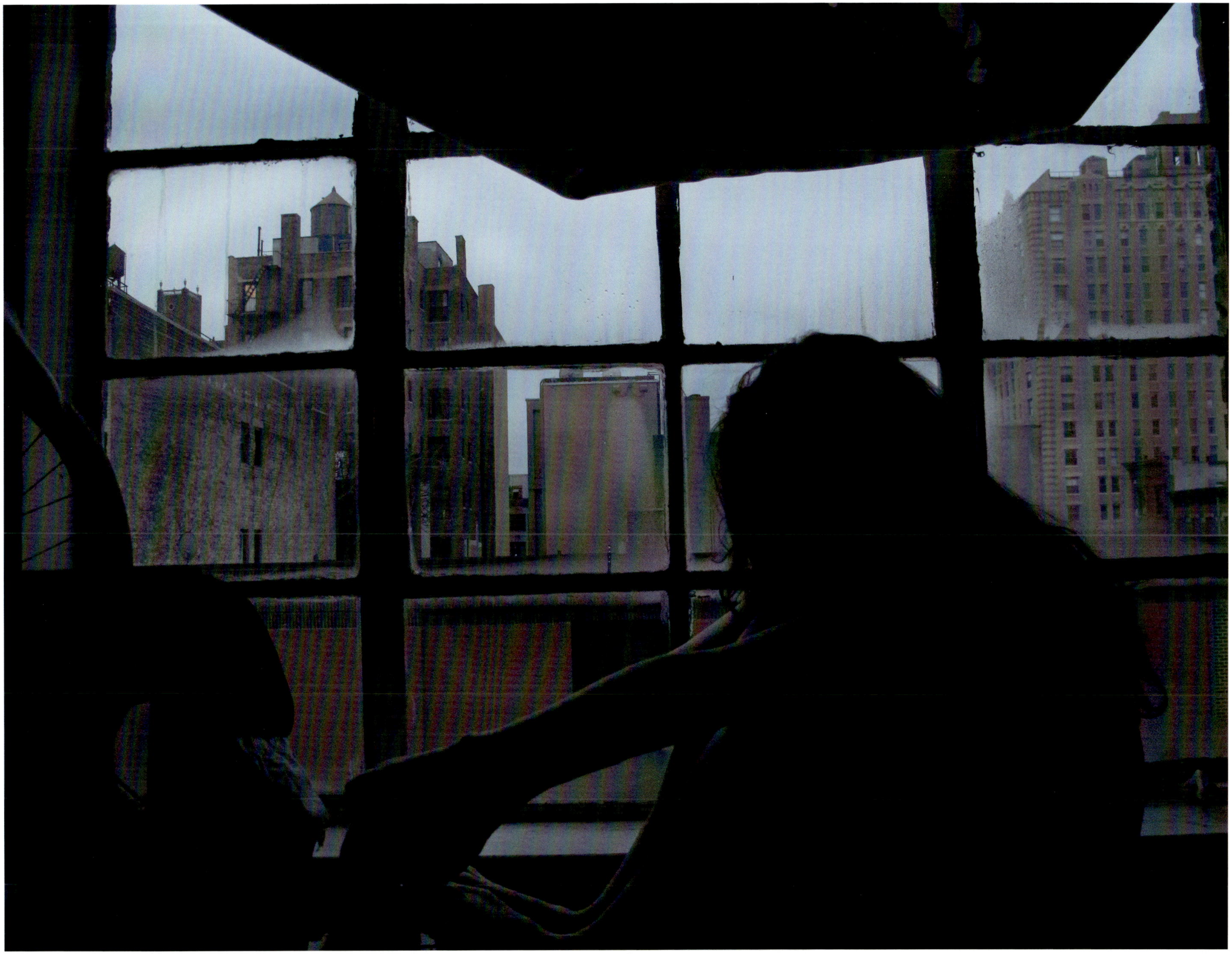

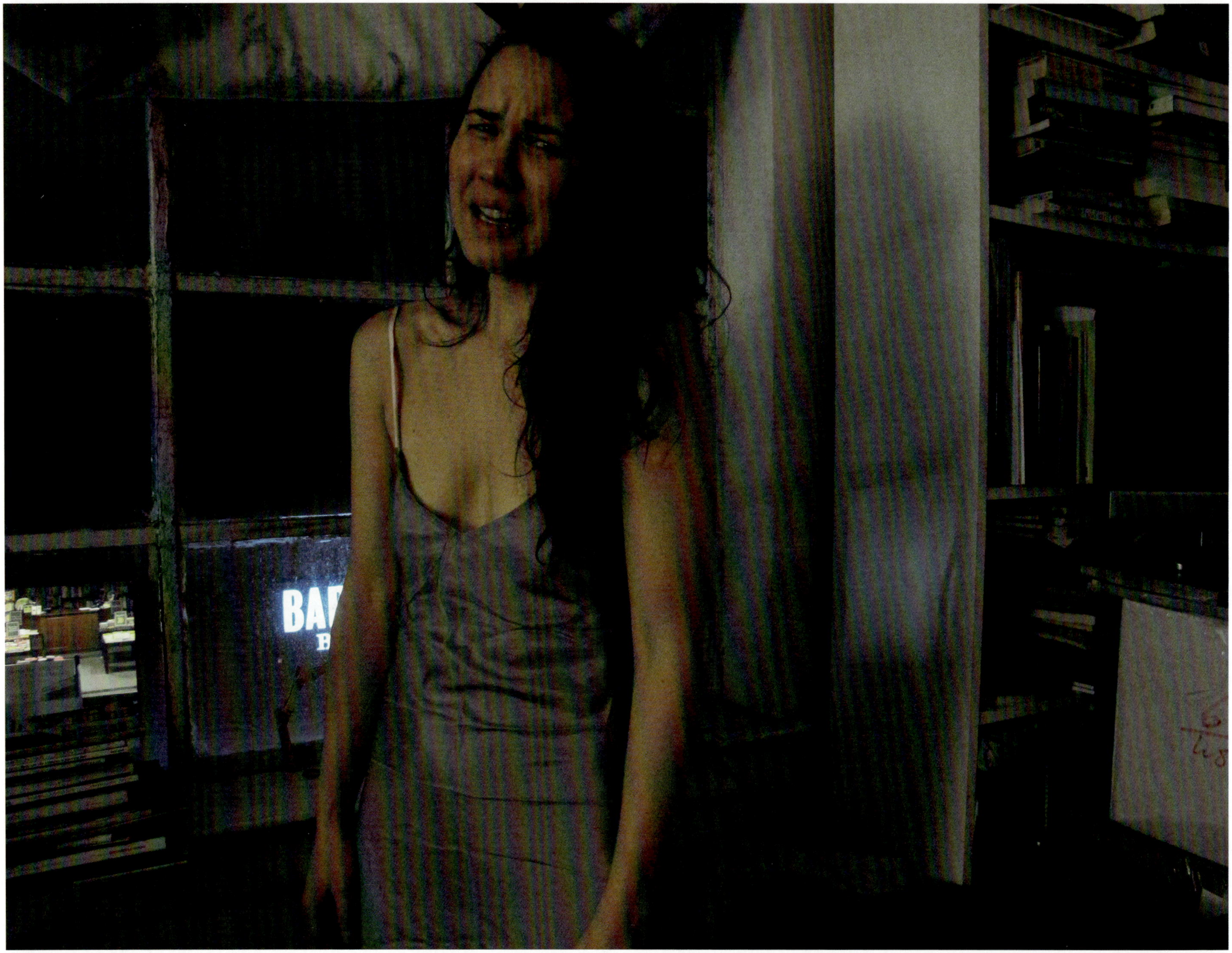

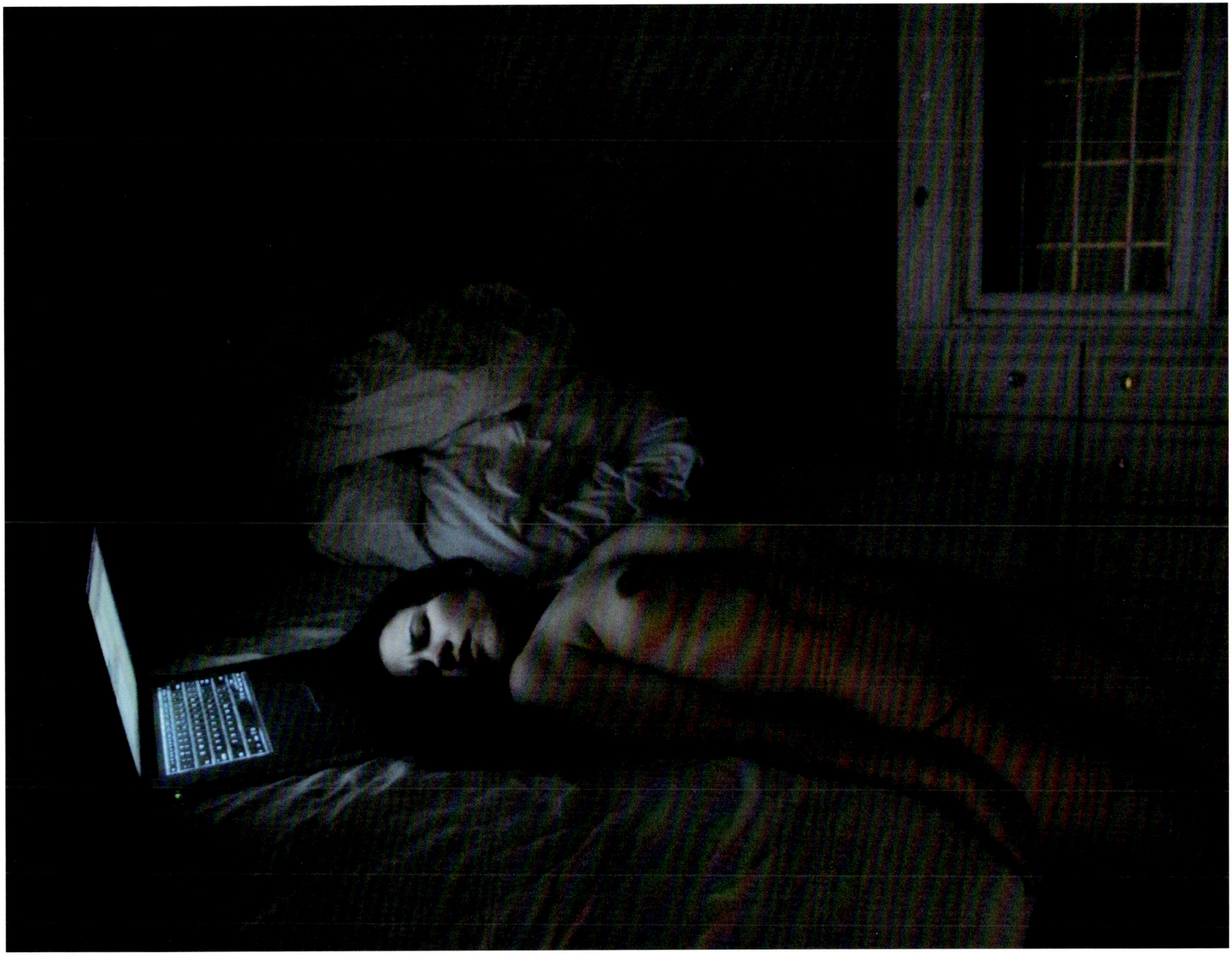

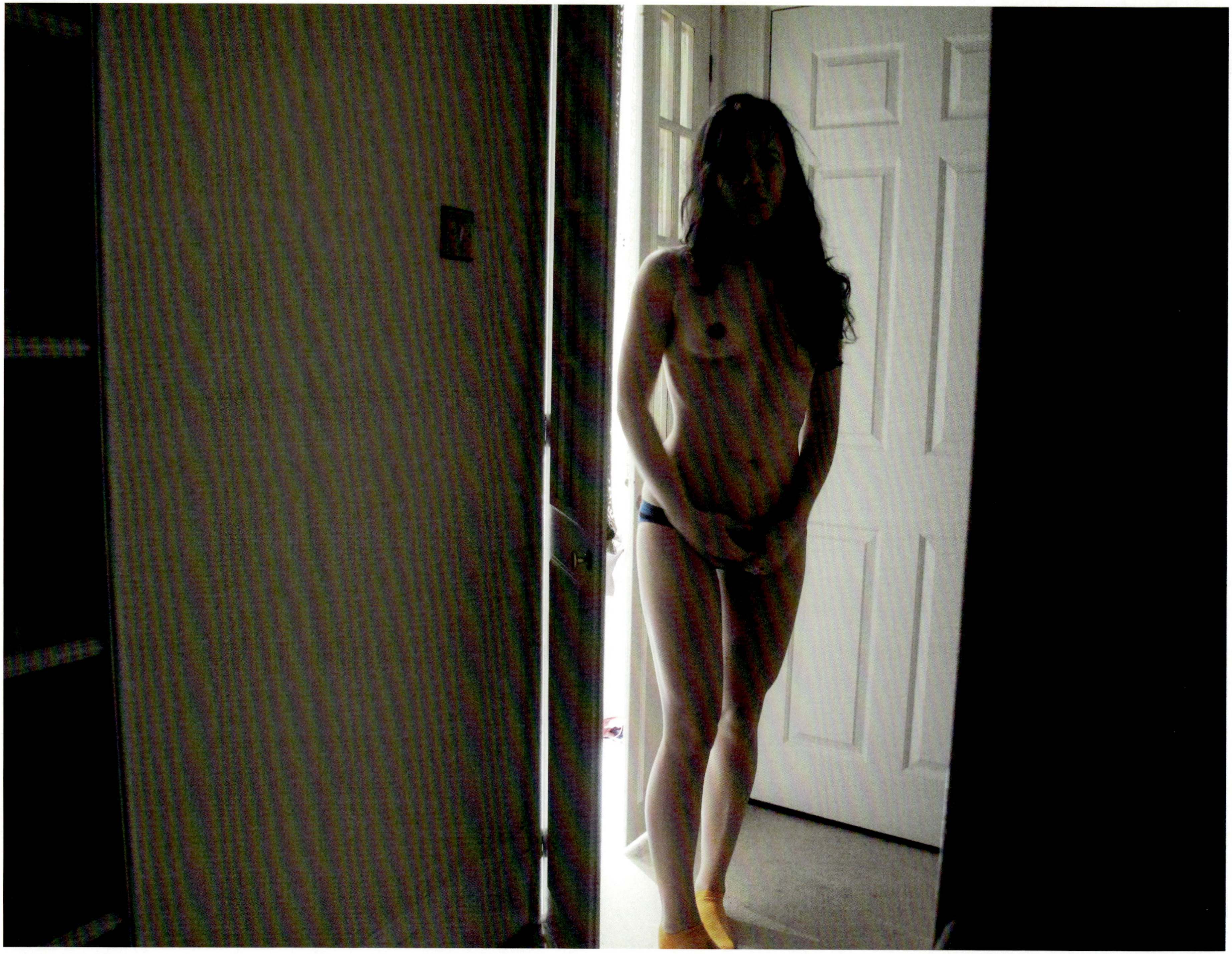

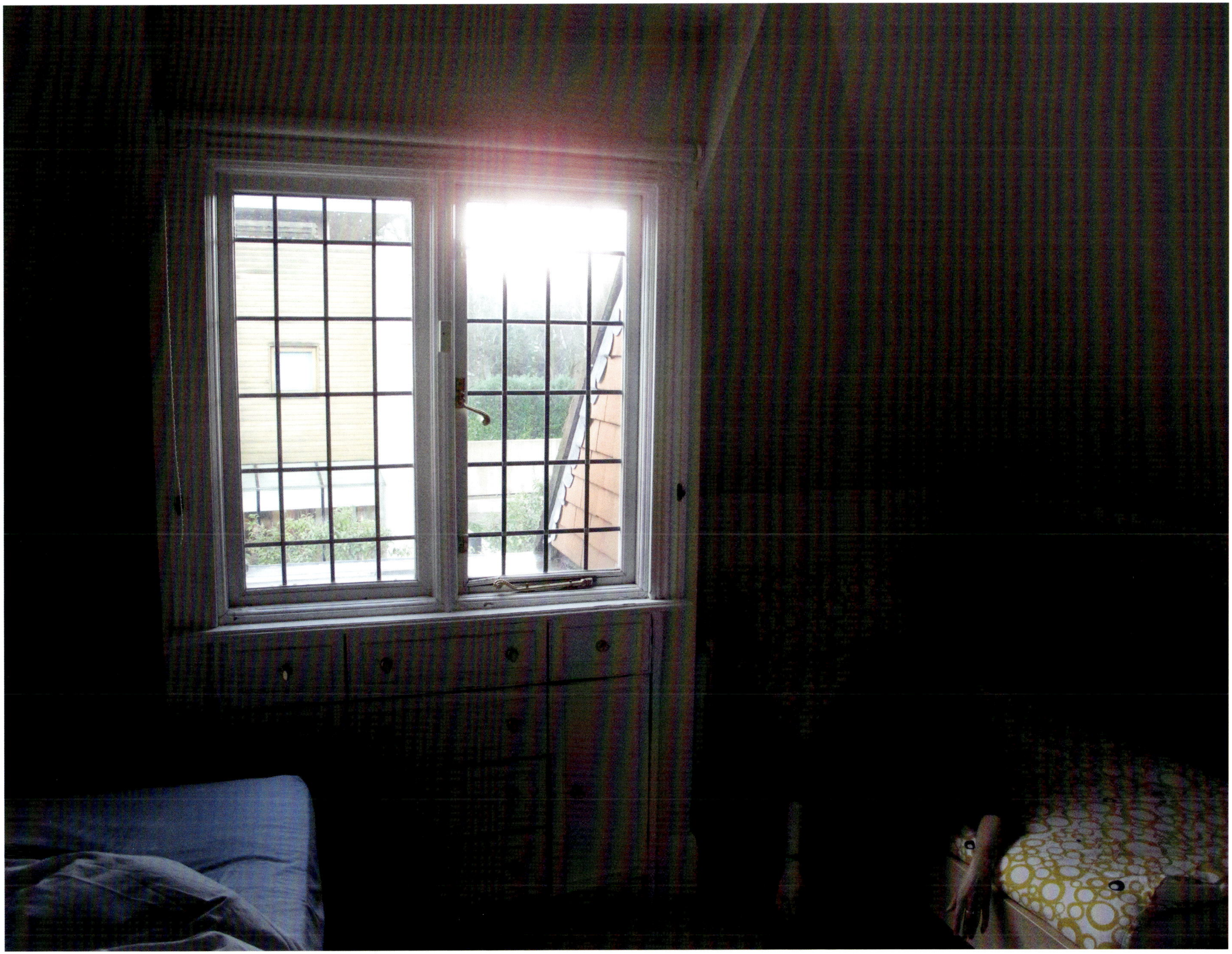

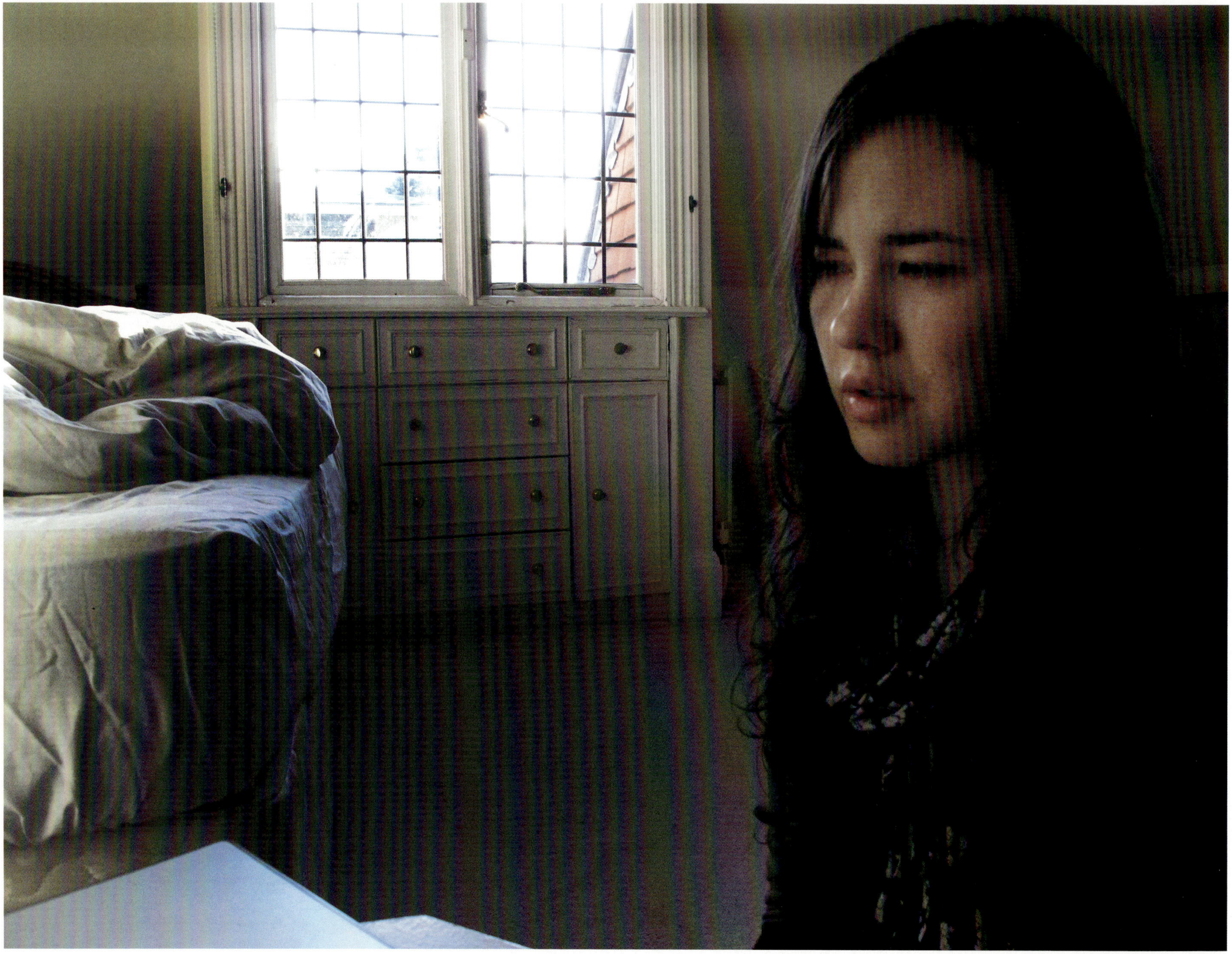

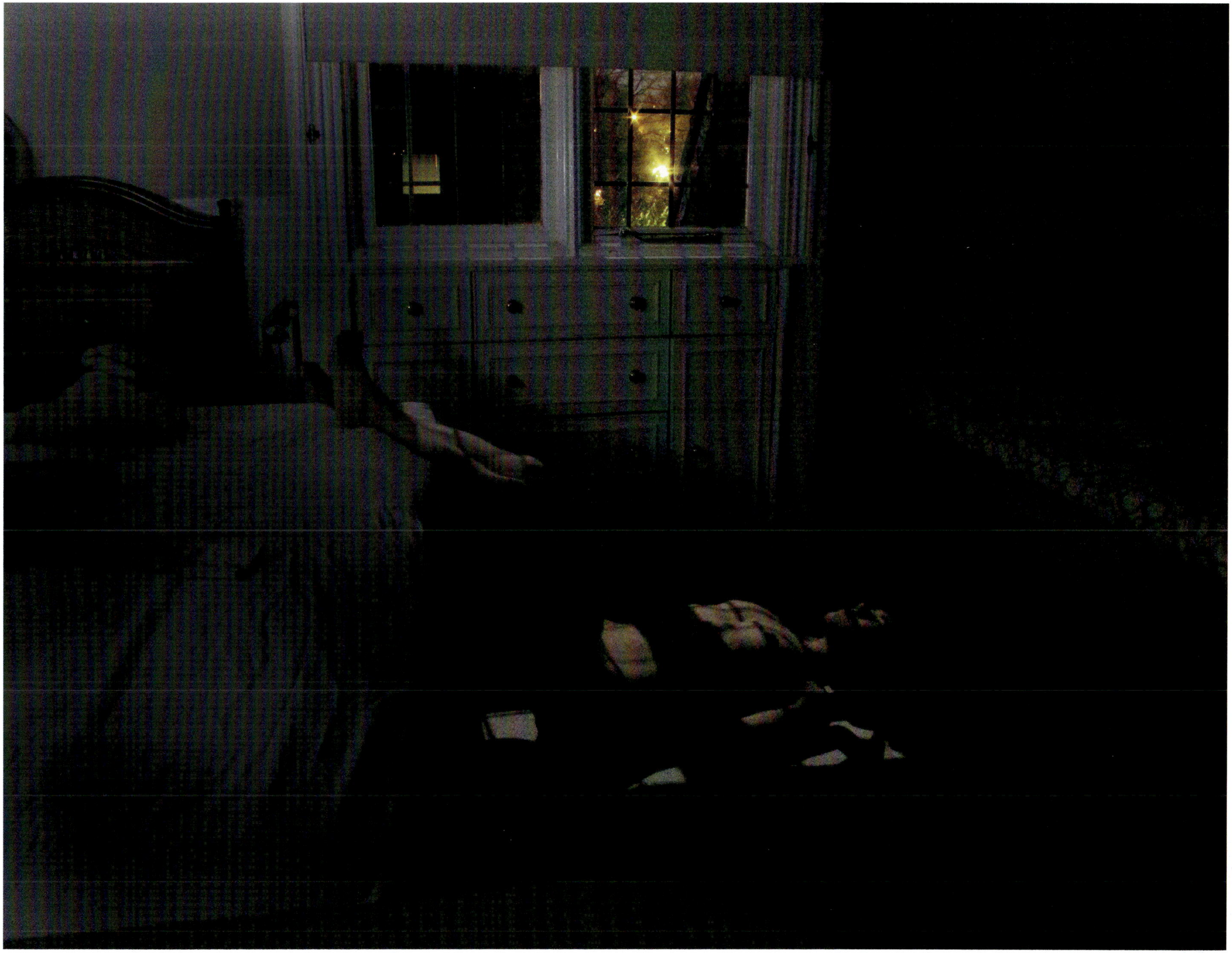

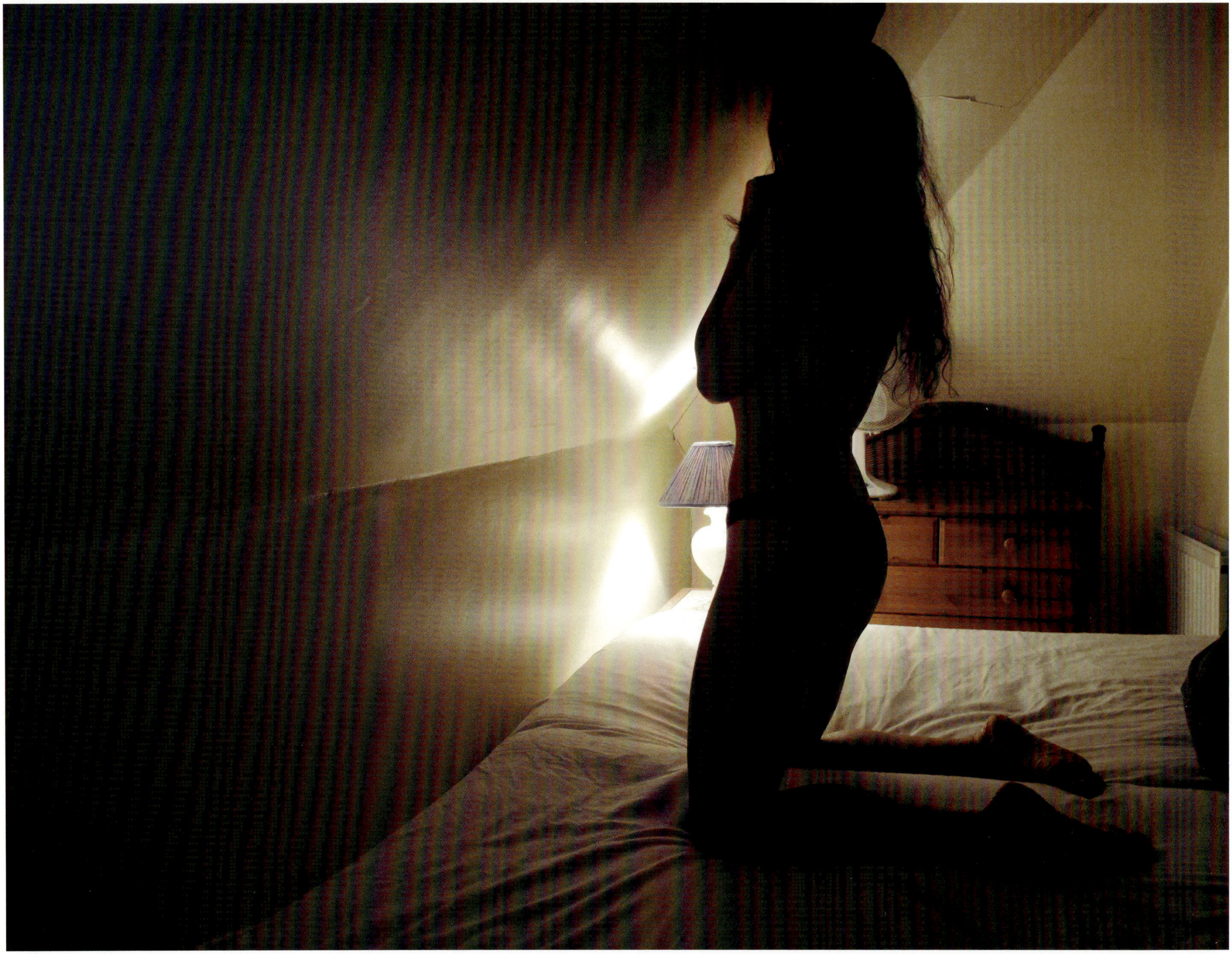

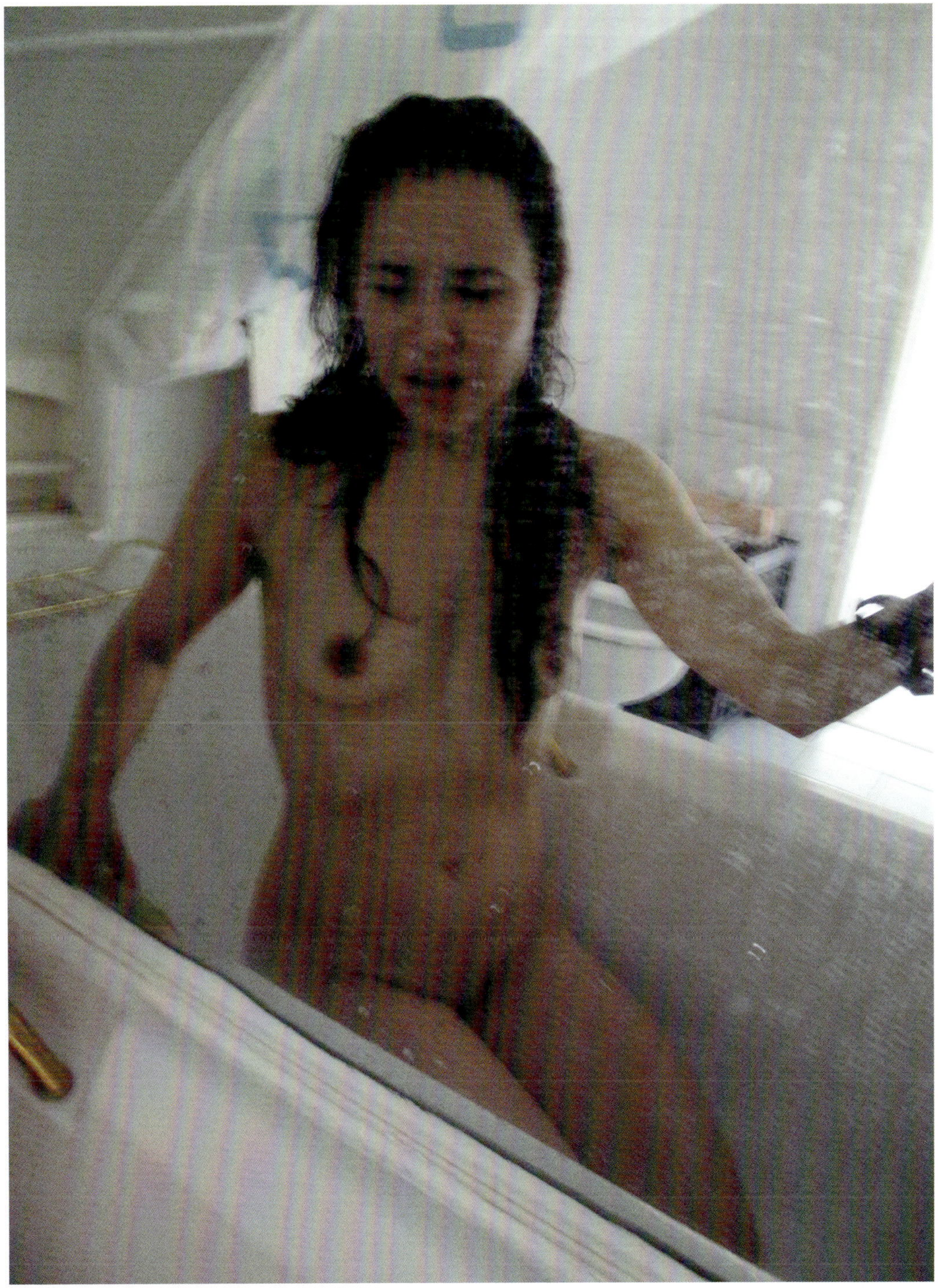

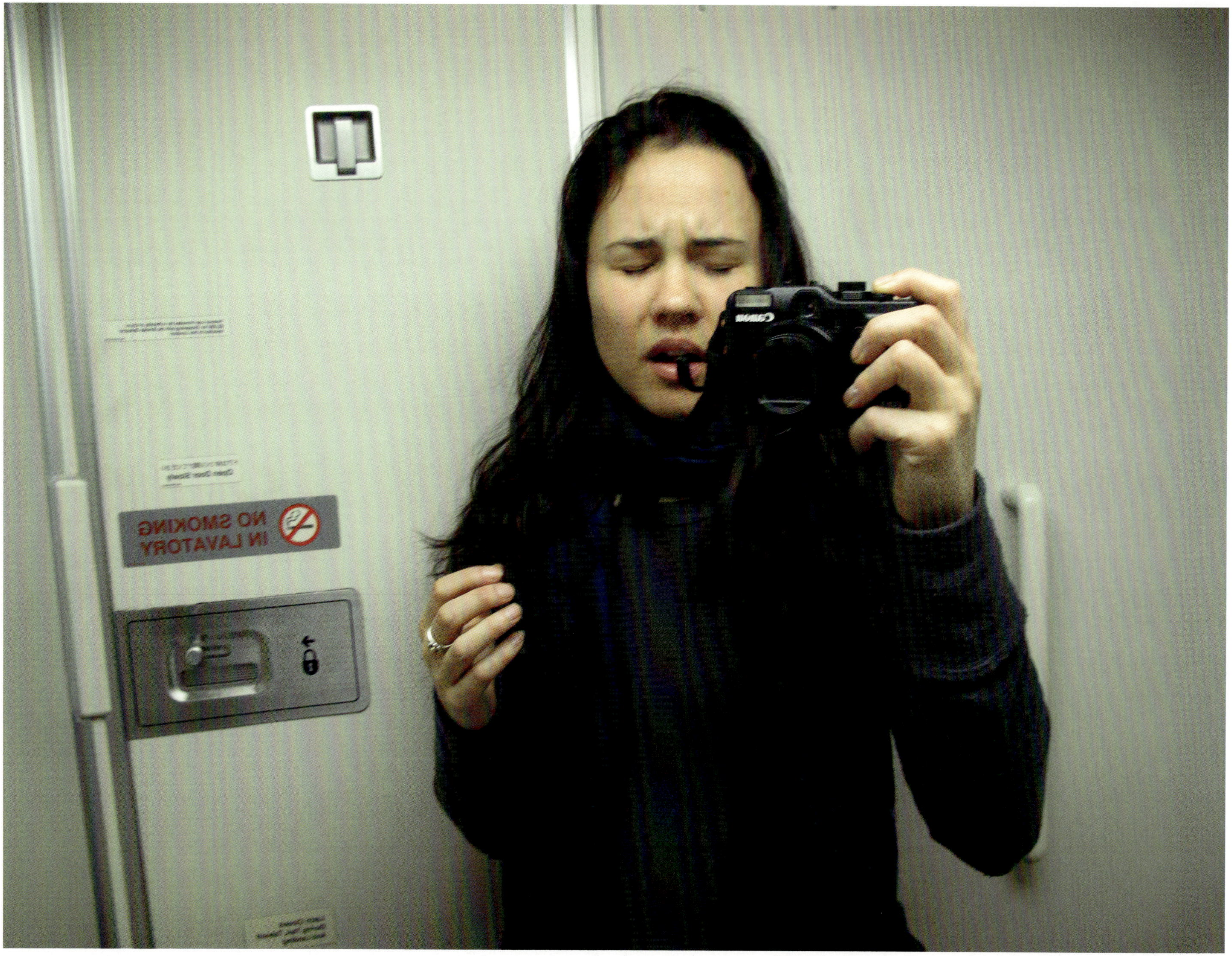
NO SMOKING
IN LAVATORY

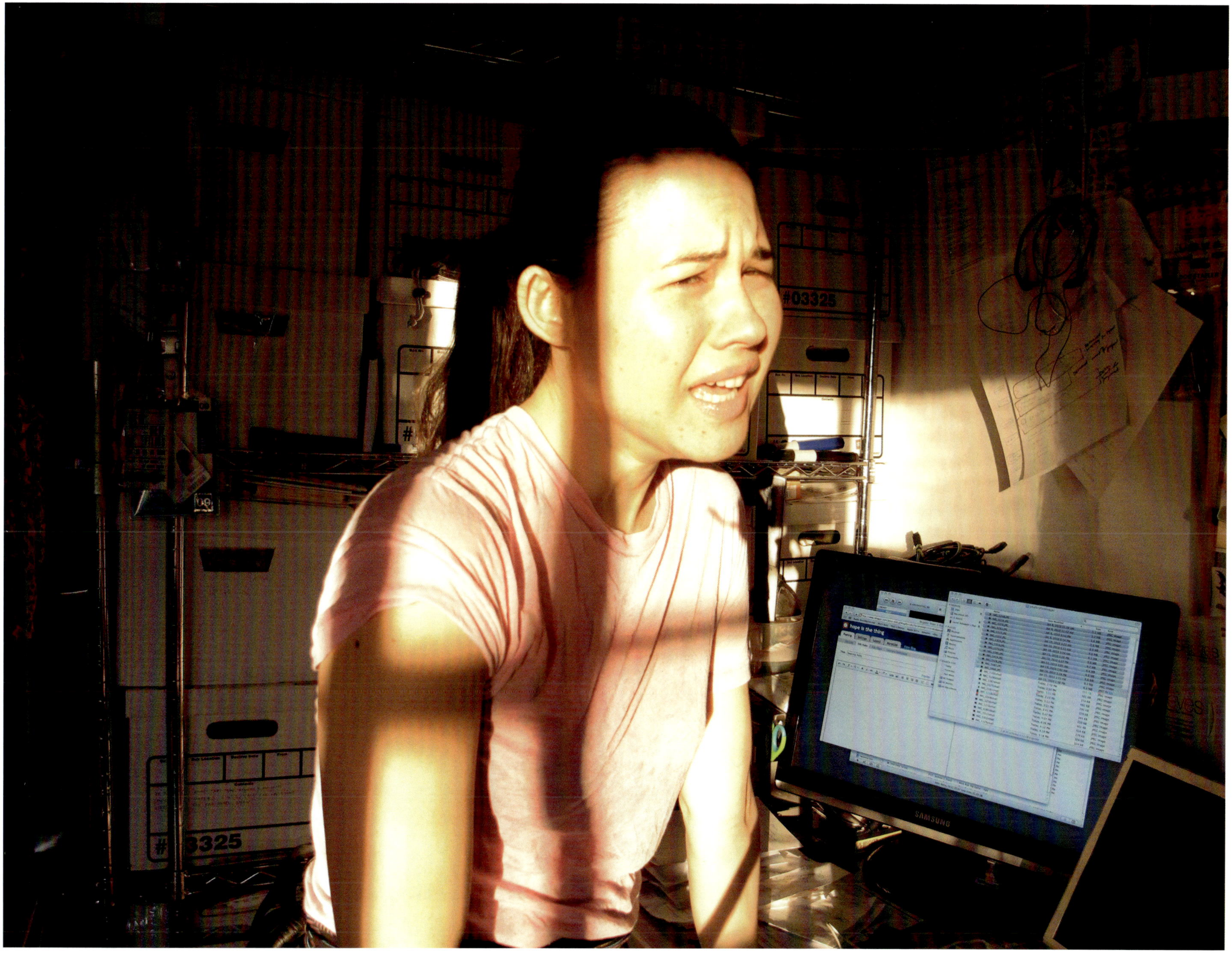
#03325
hope is the thing
SAMSUNG

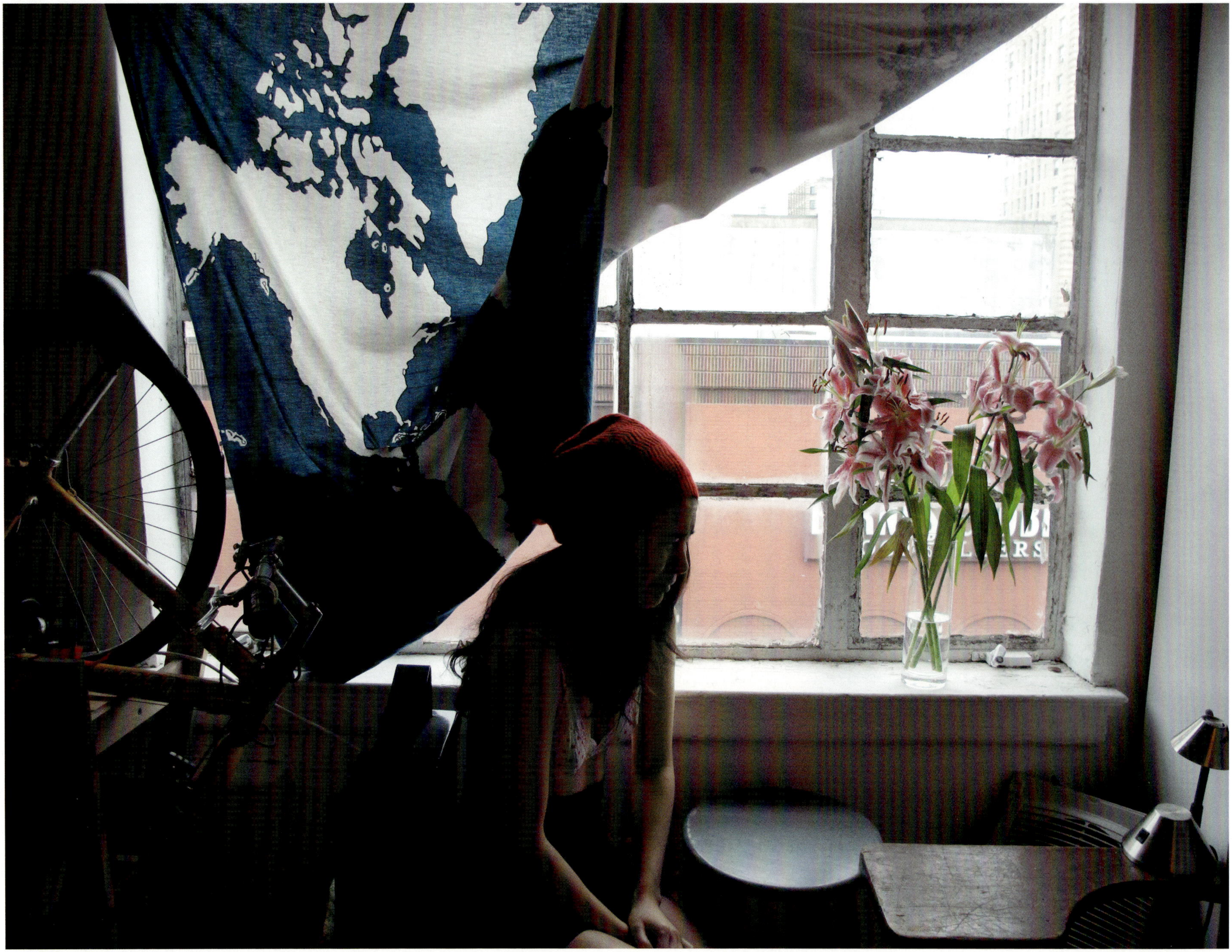

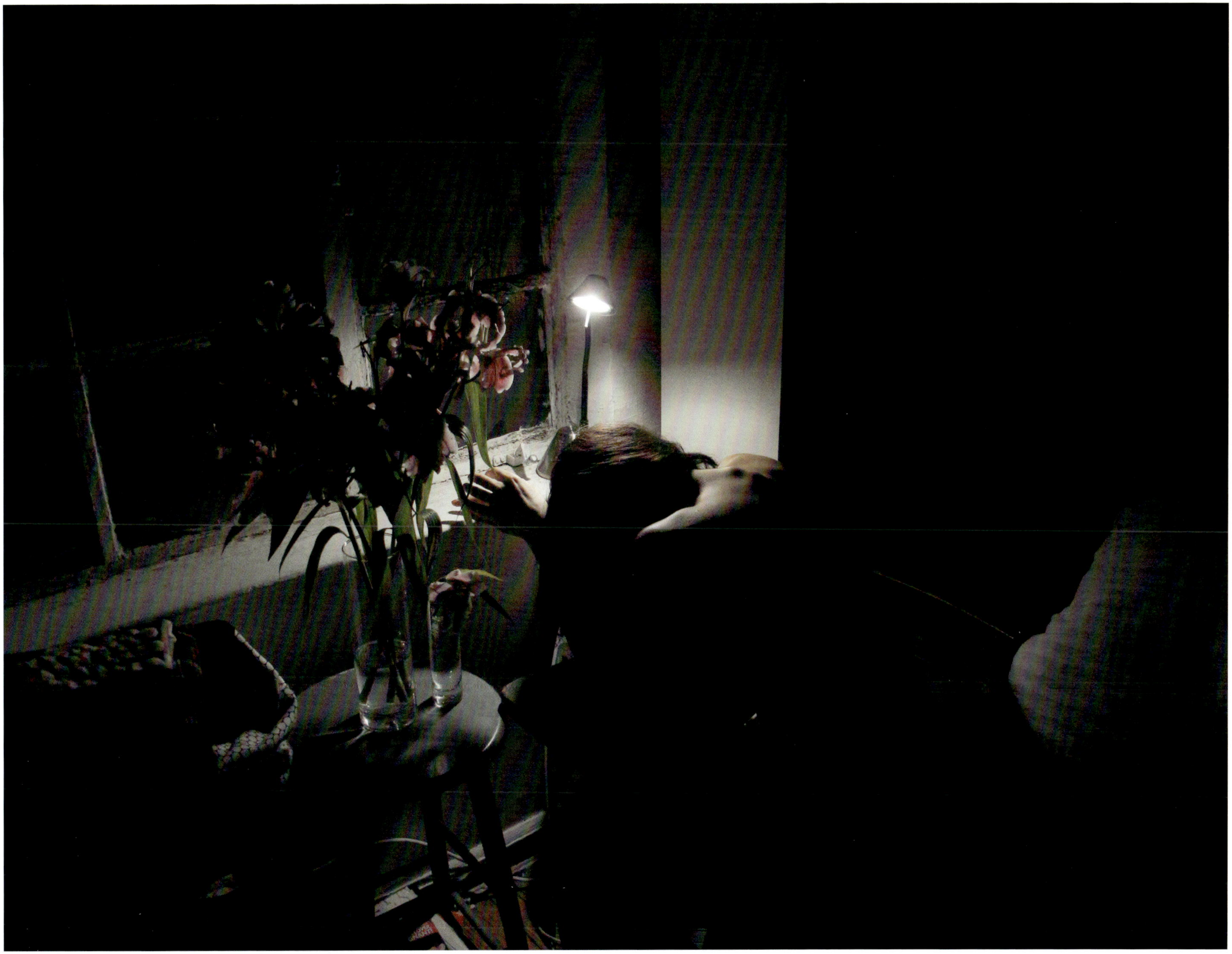

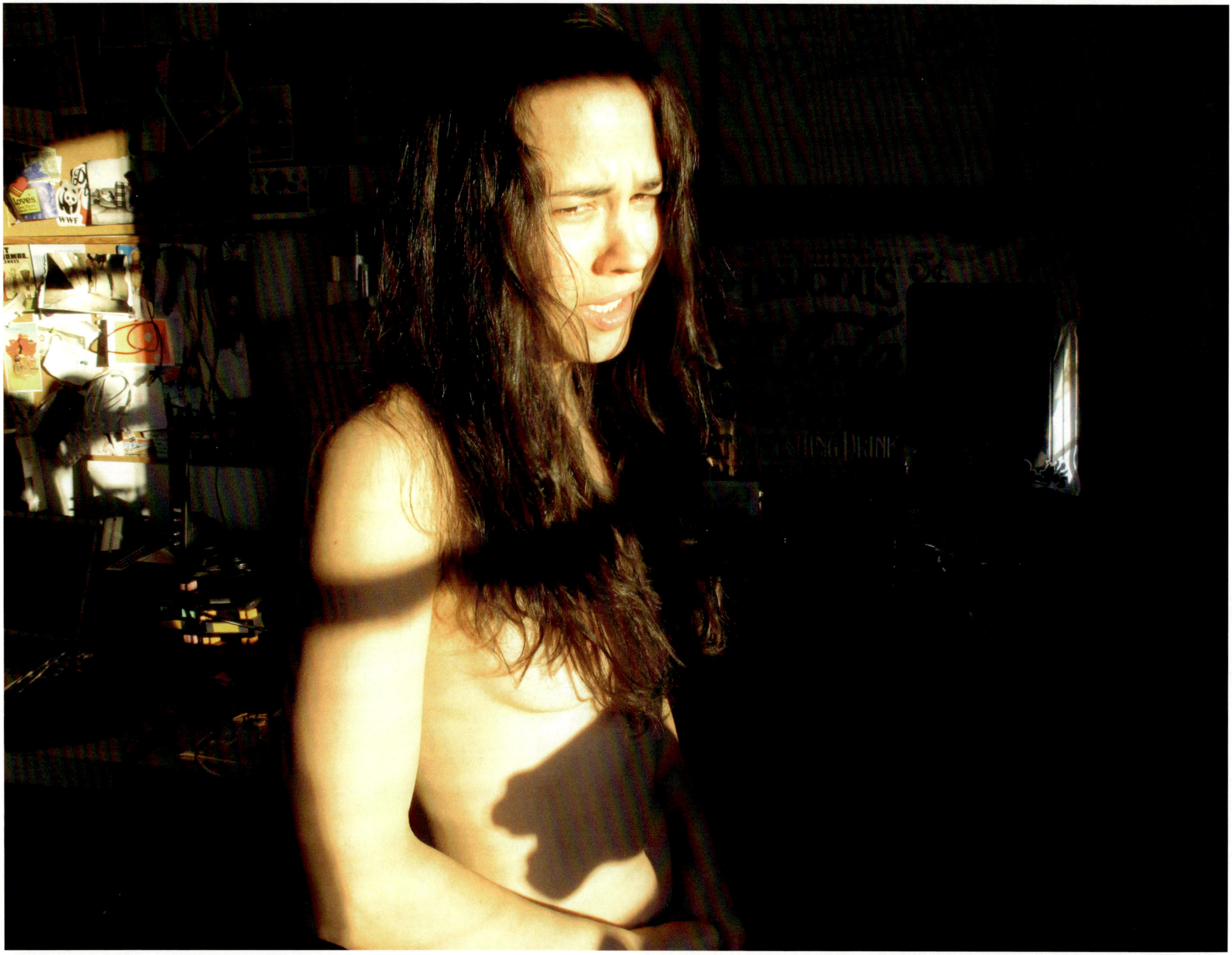
WWF

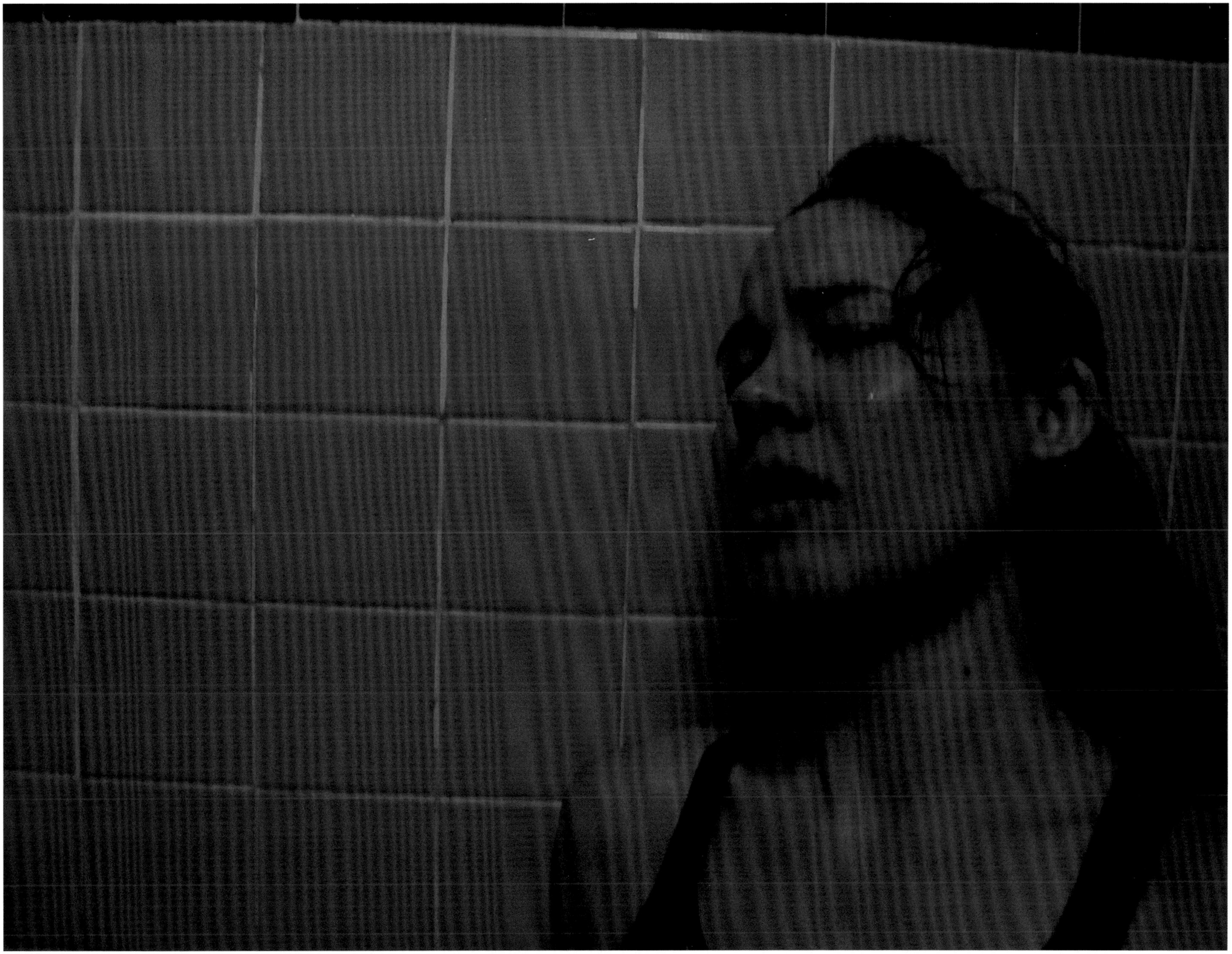

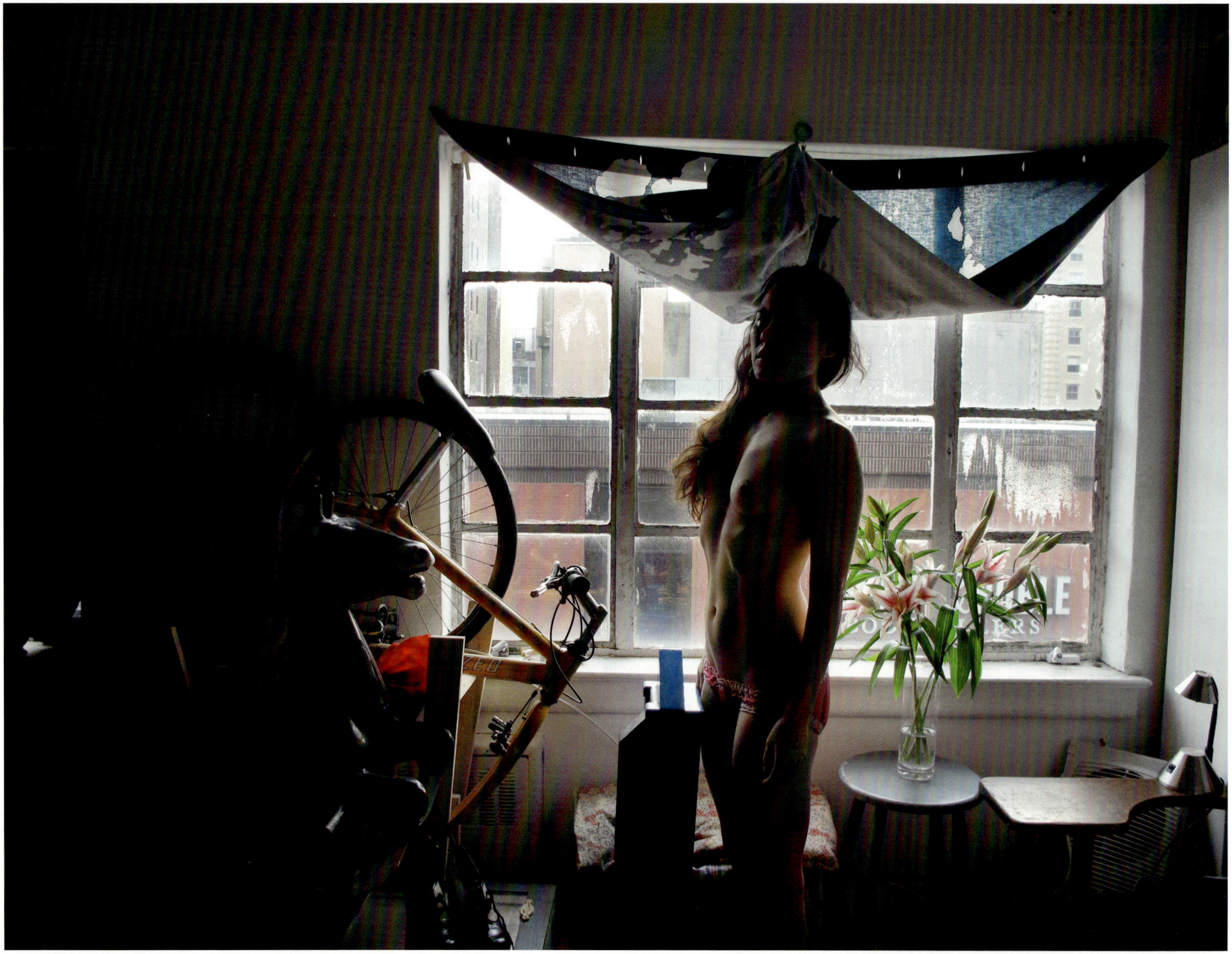

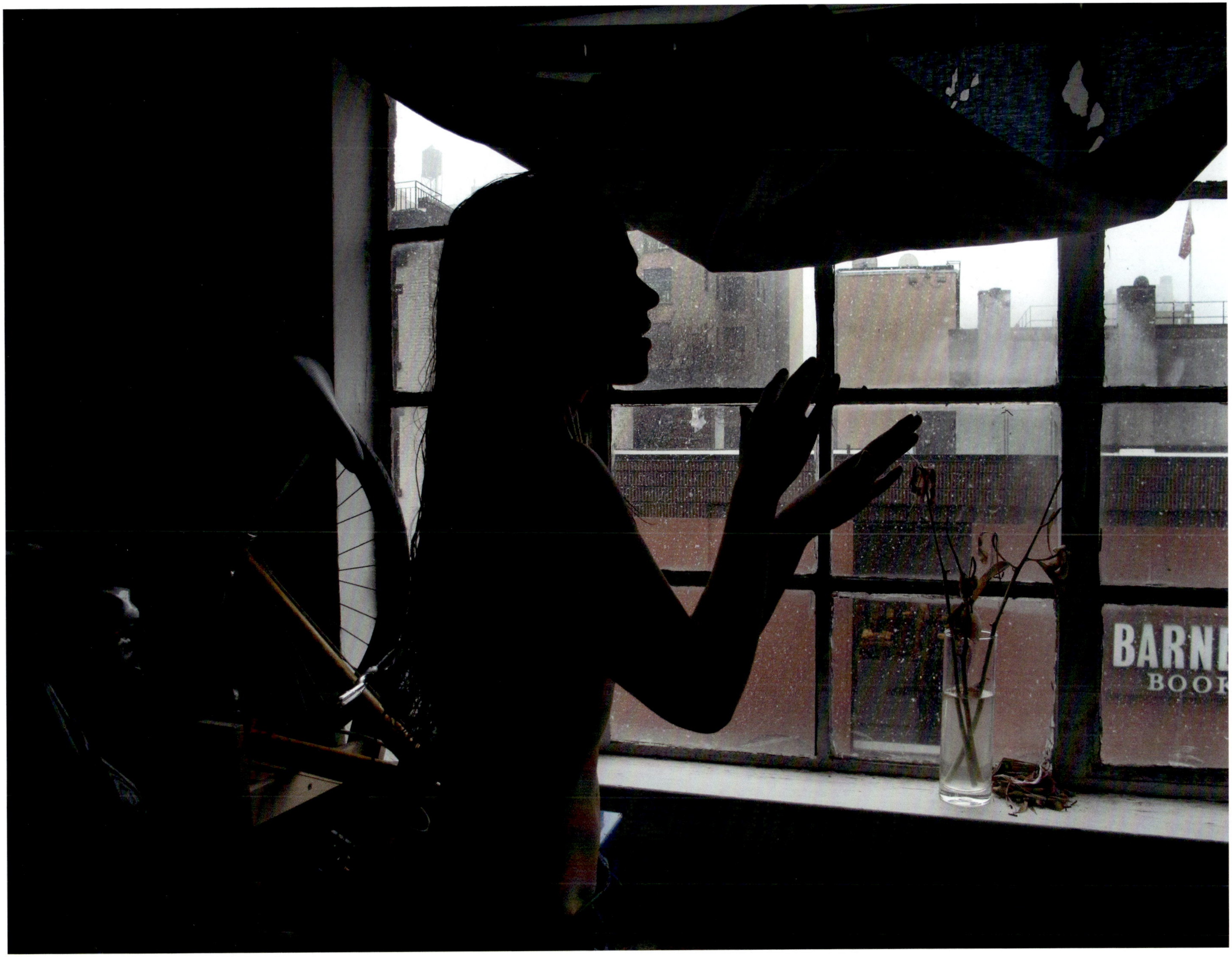
BARN
BOO

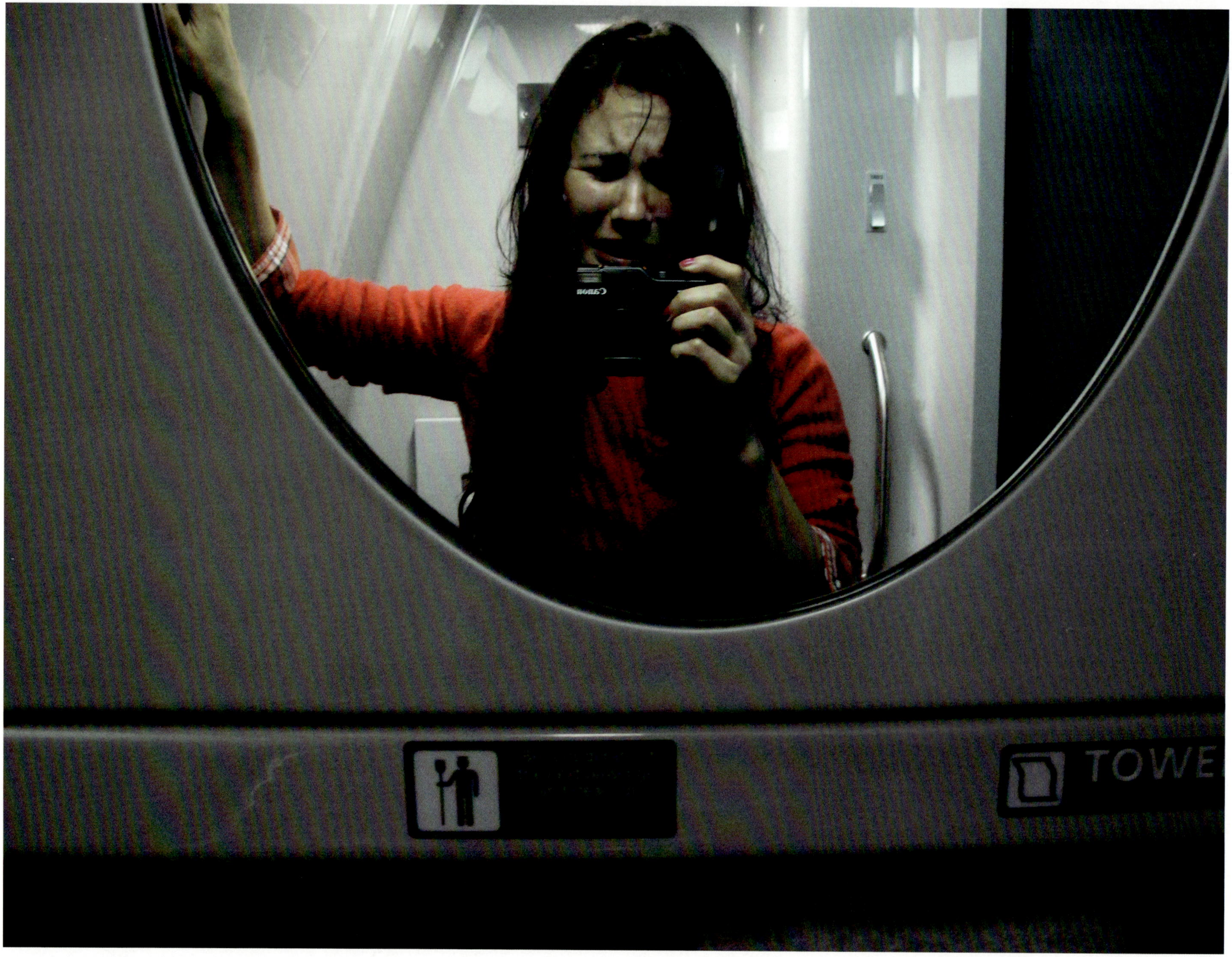
TOWE

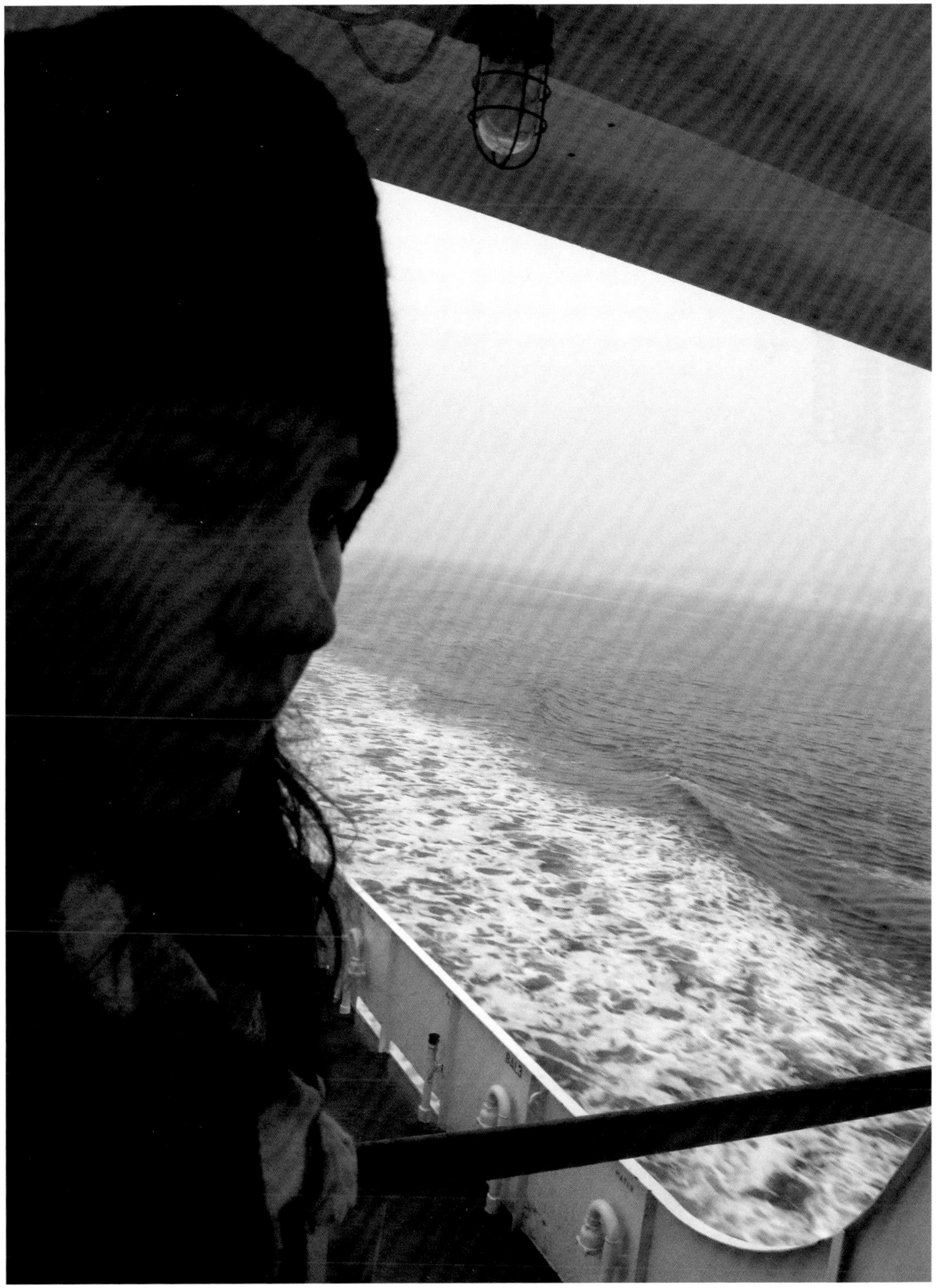

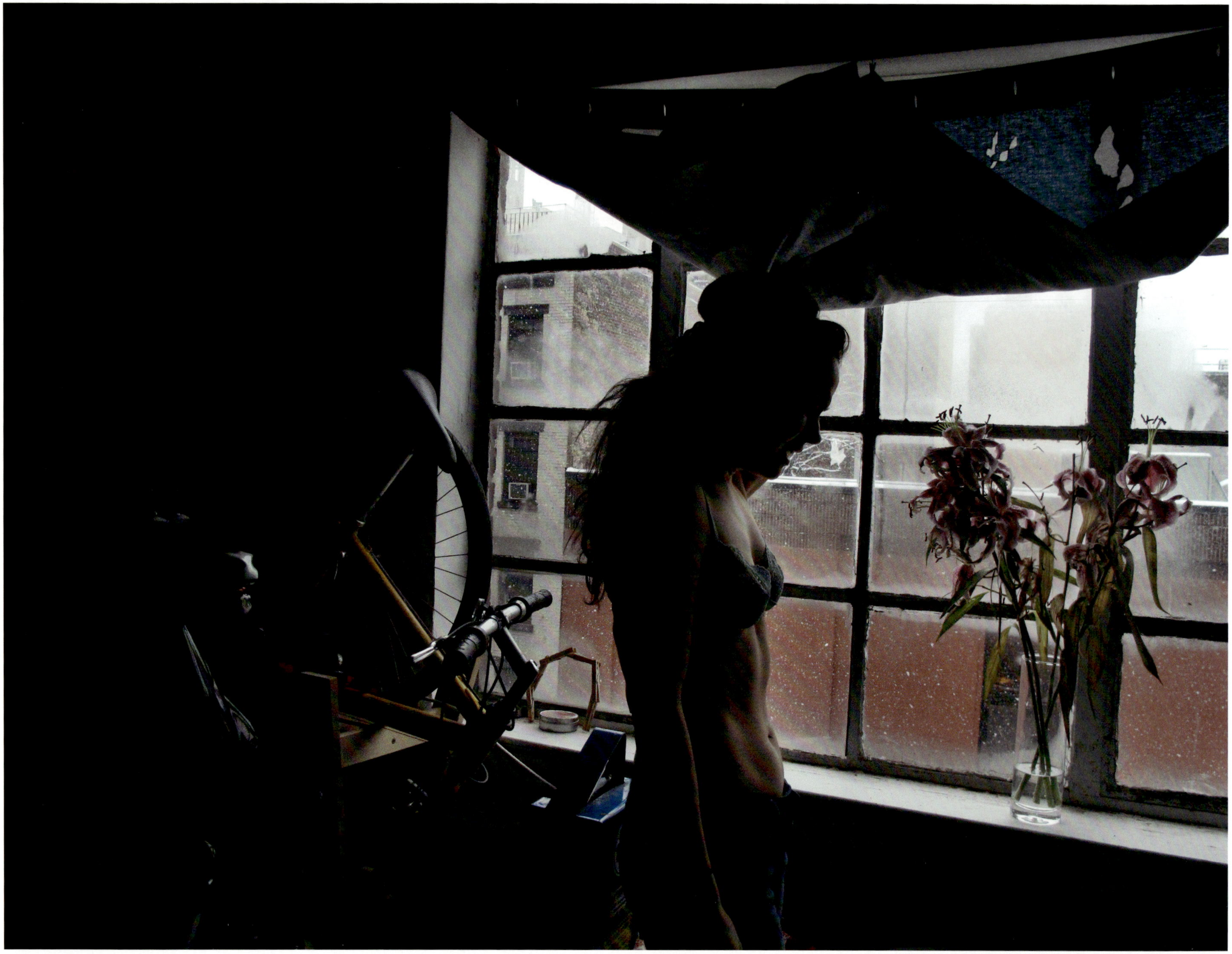

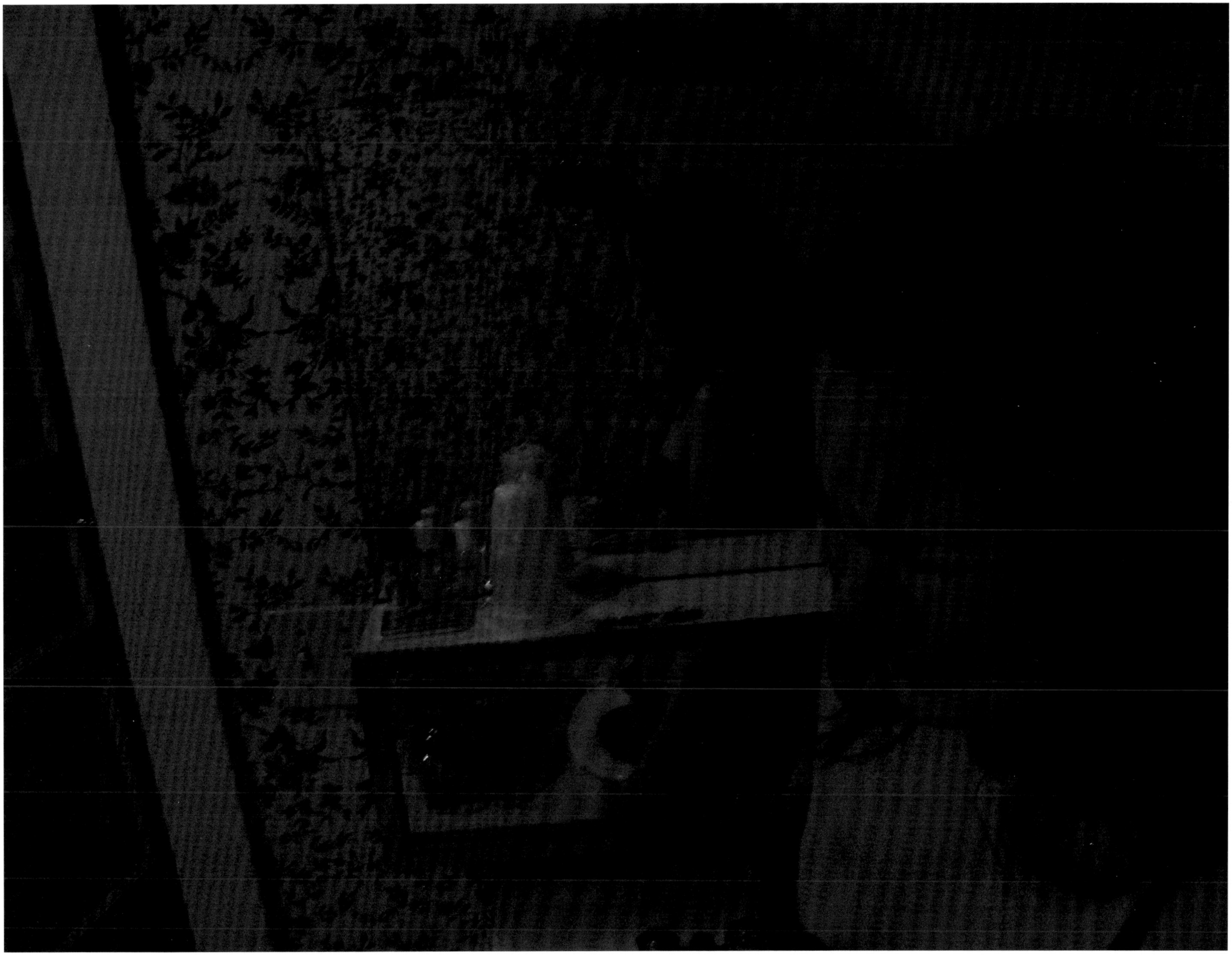

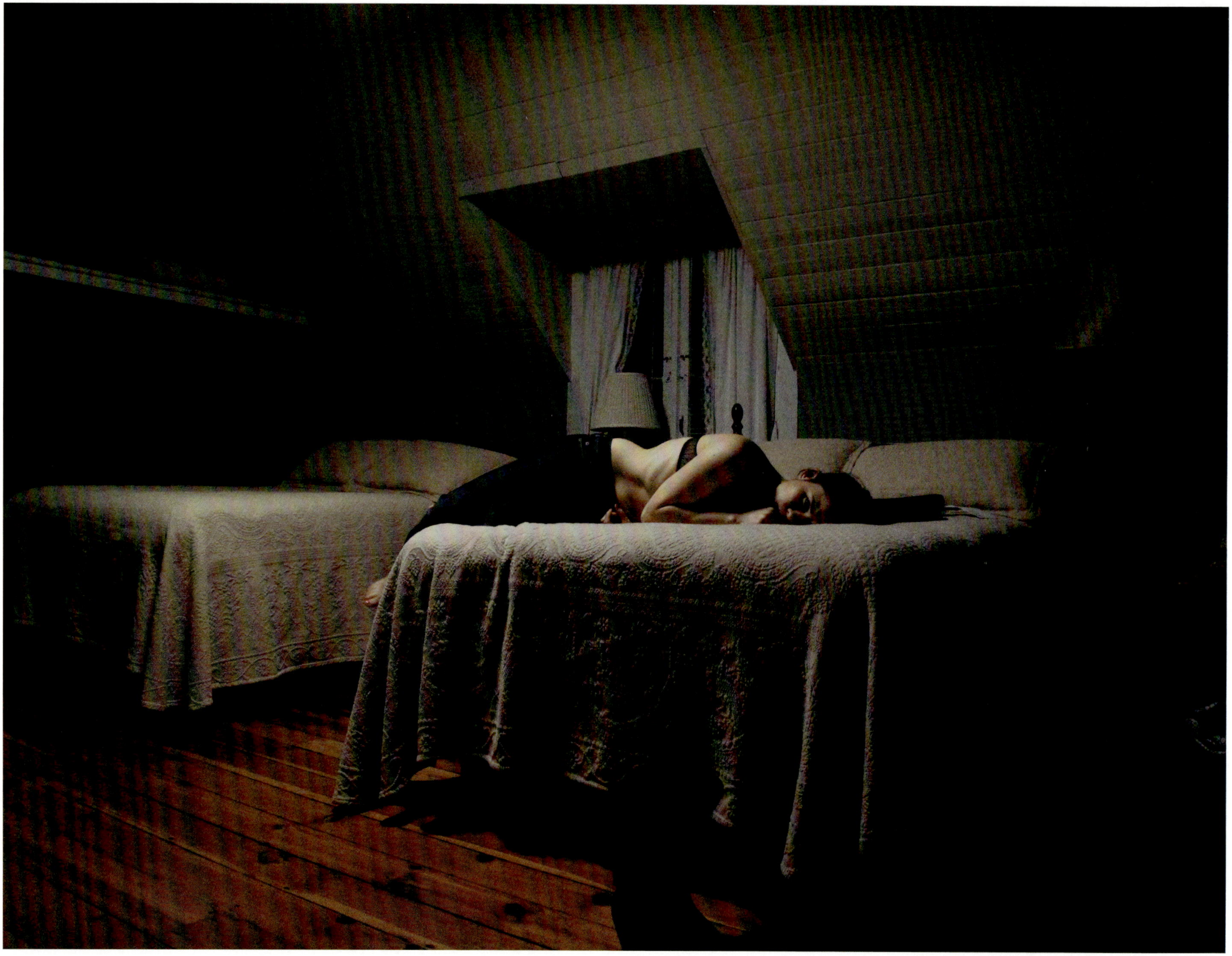

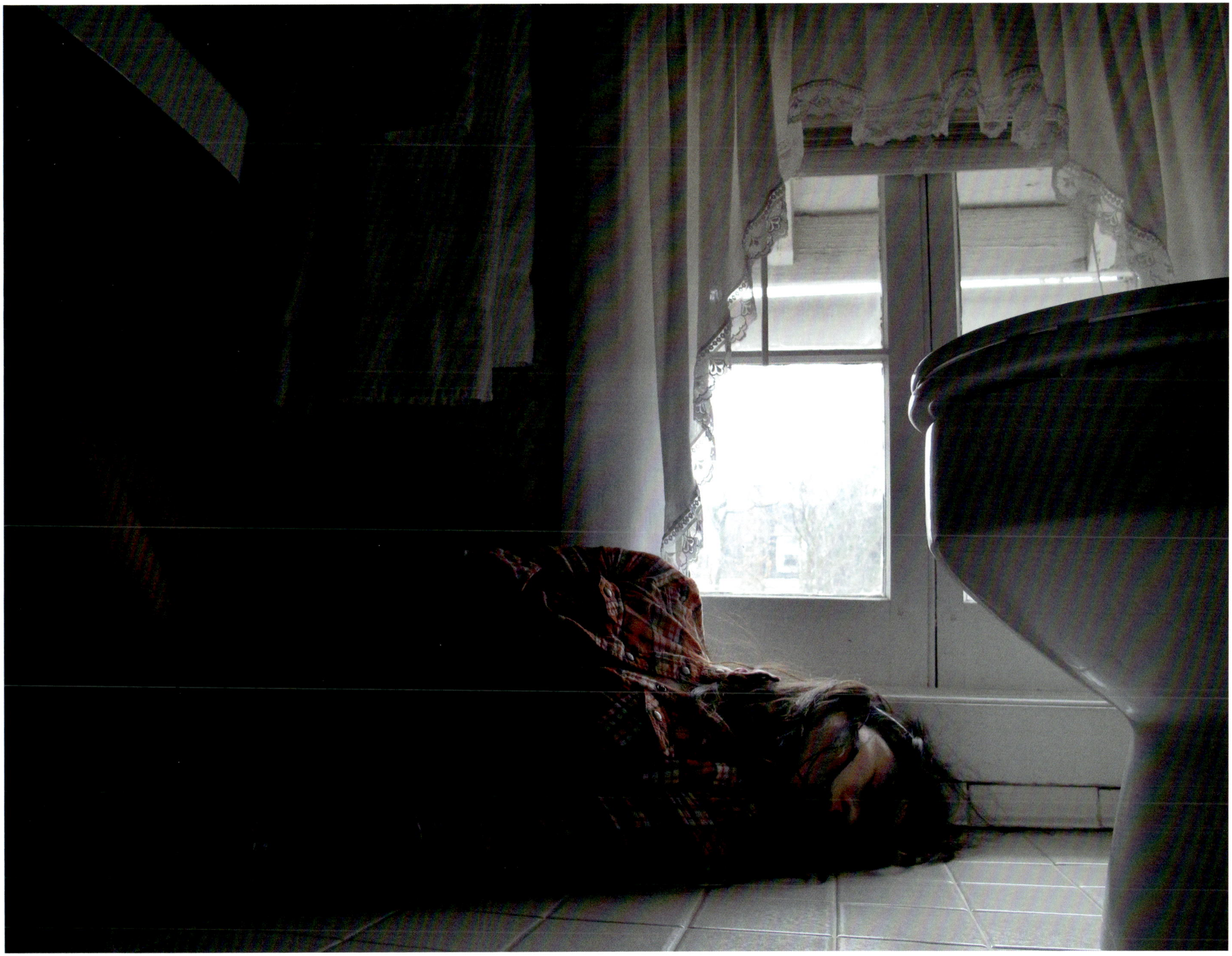

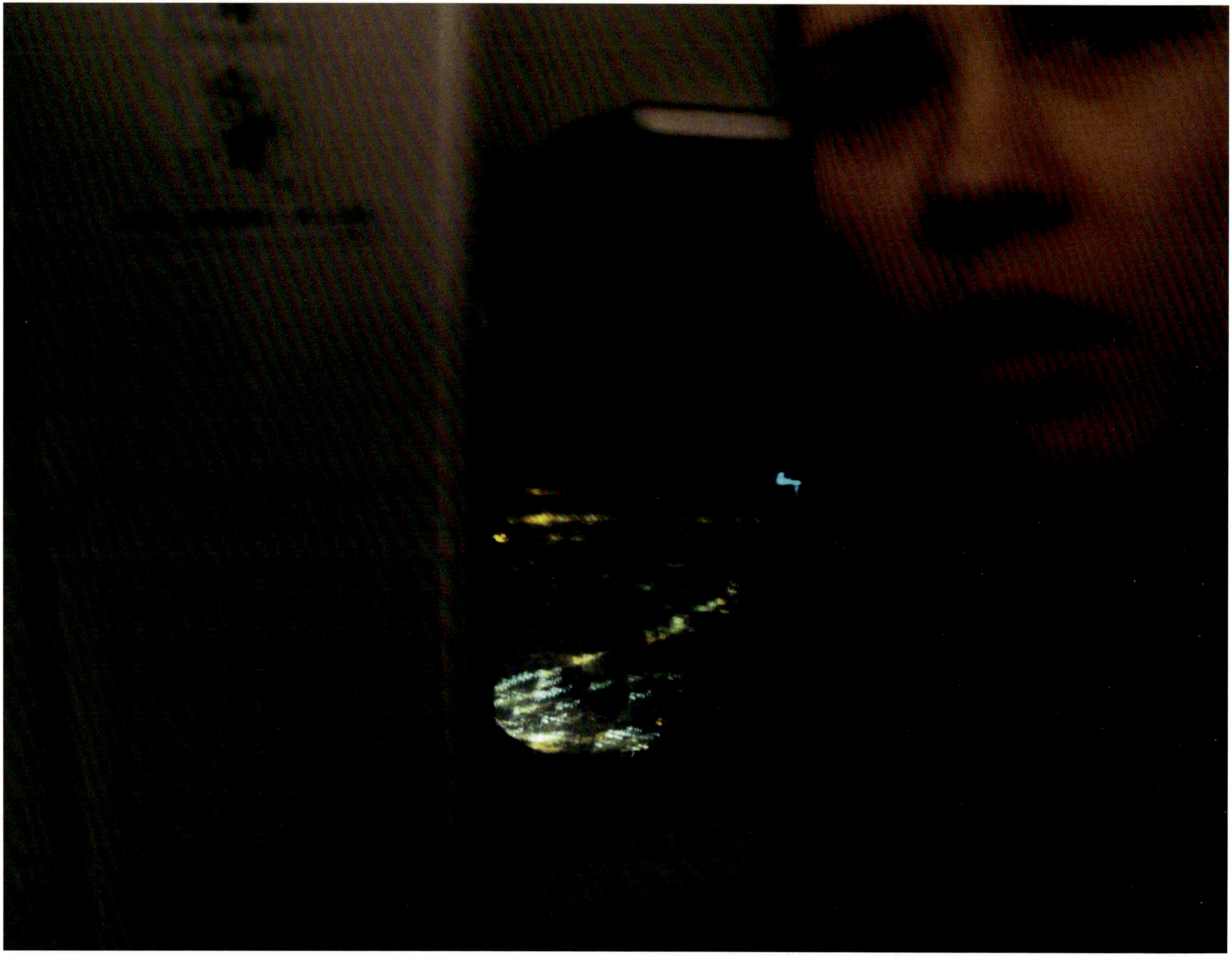

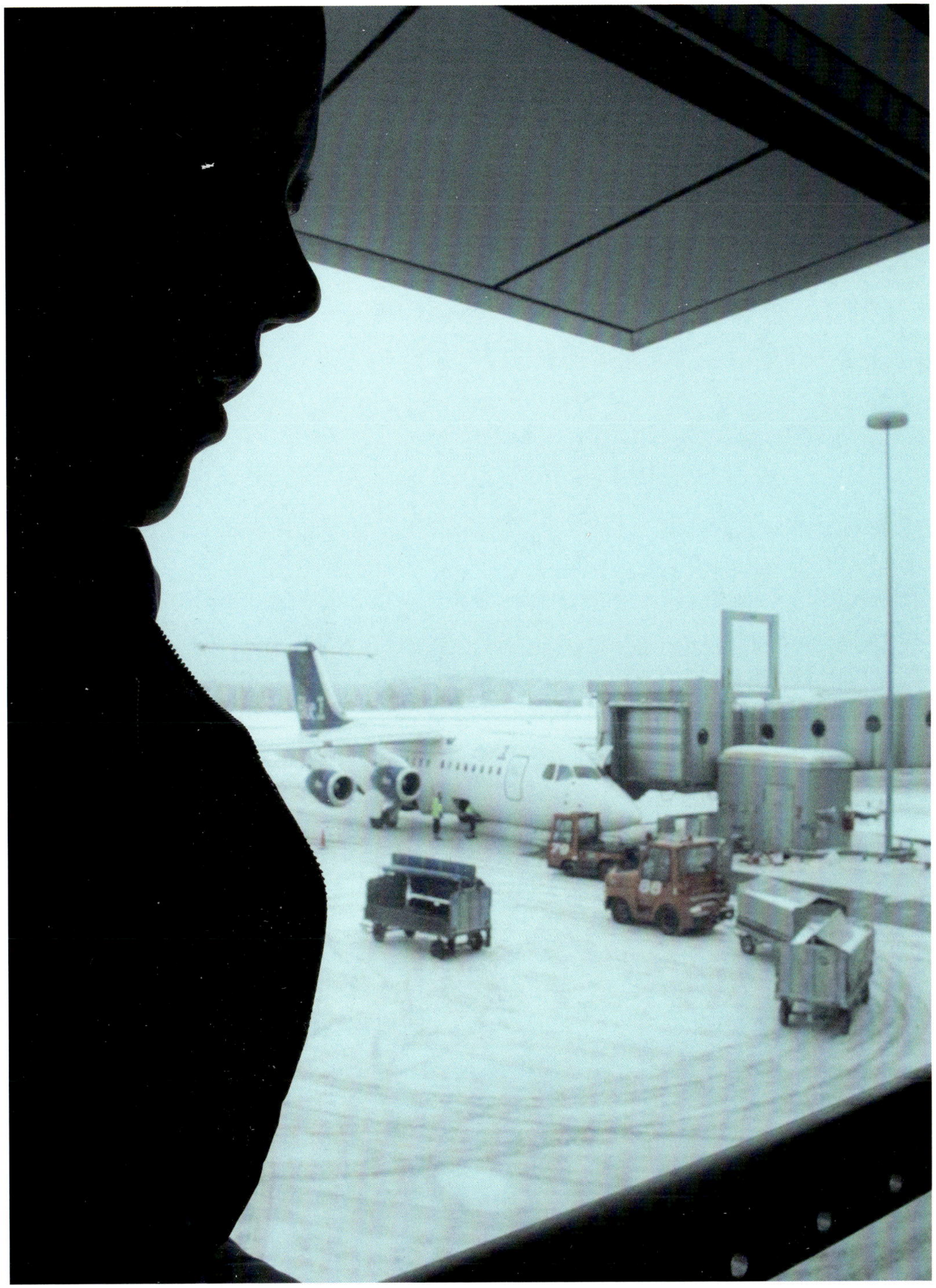

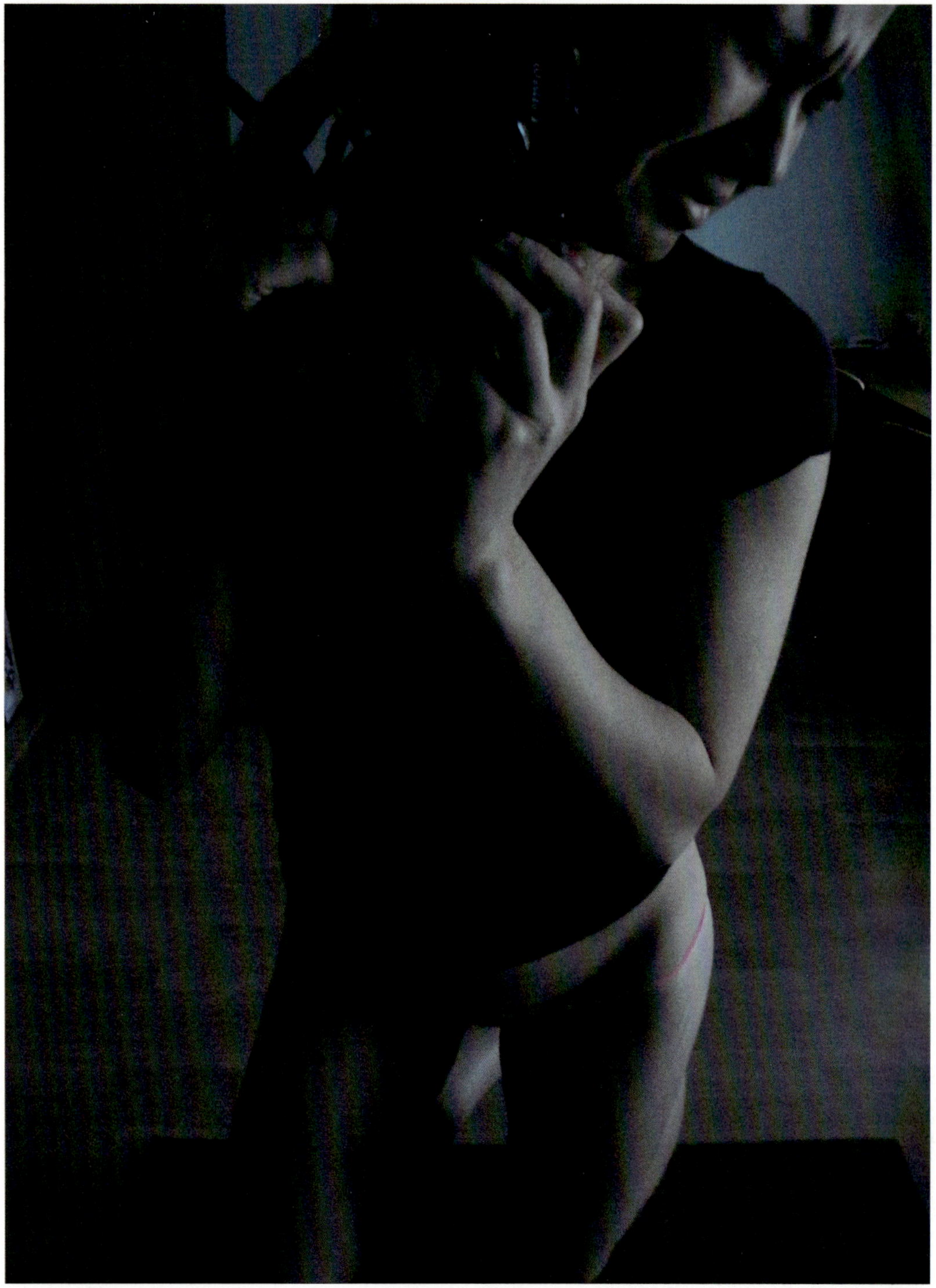

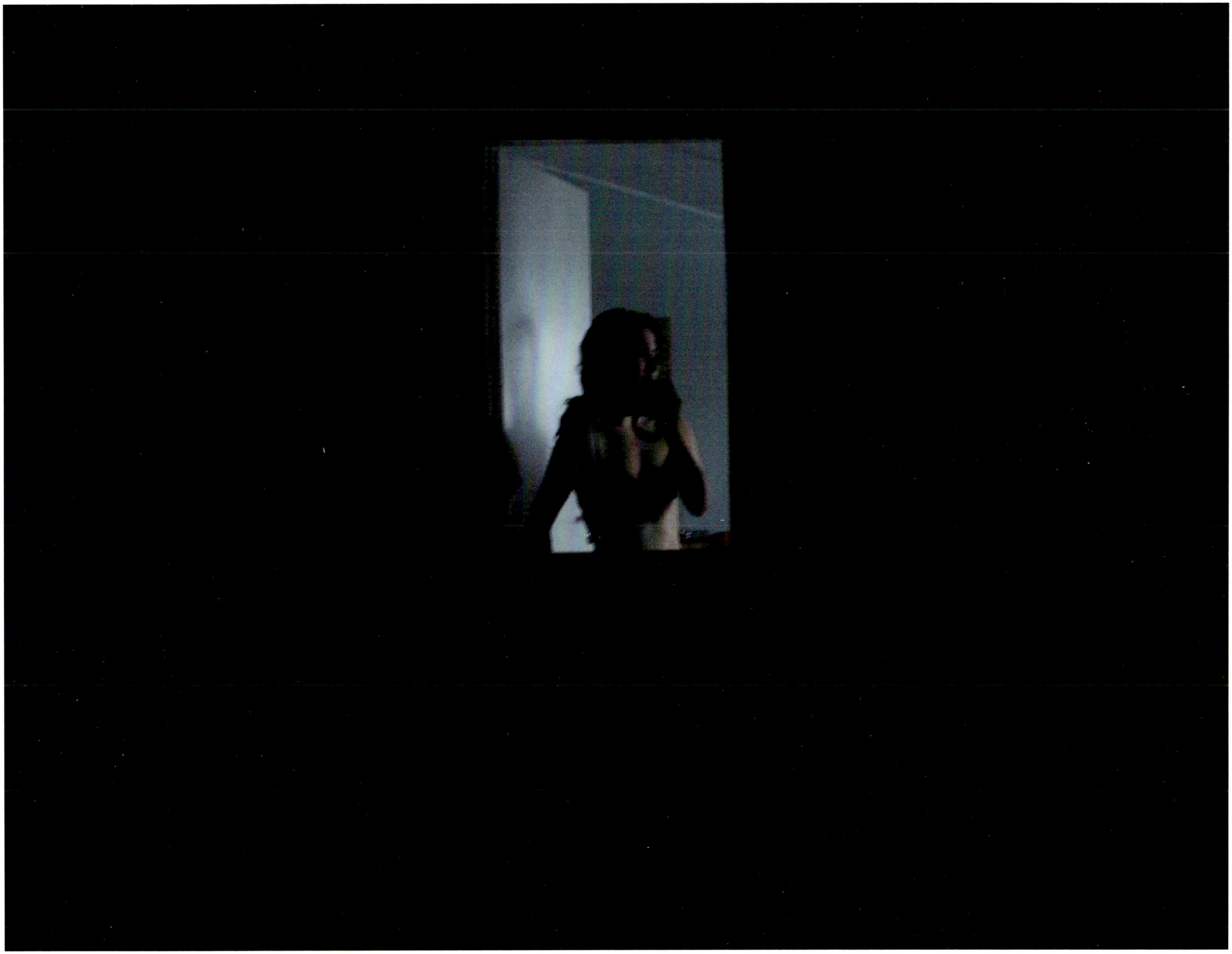

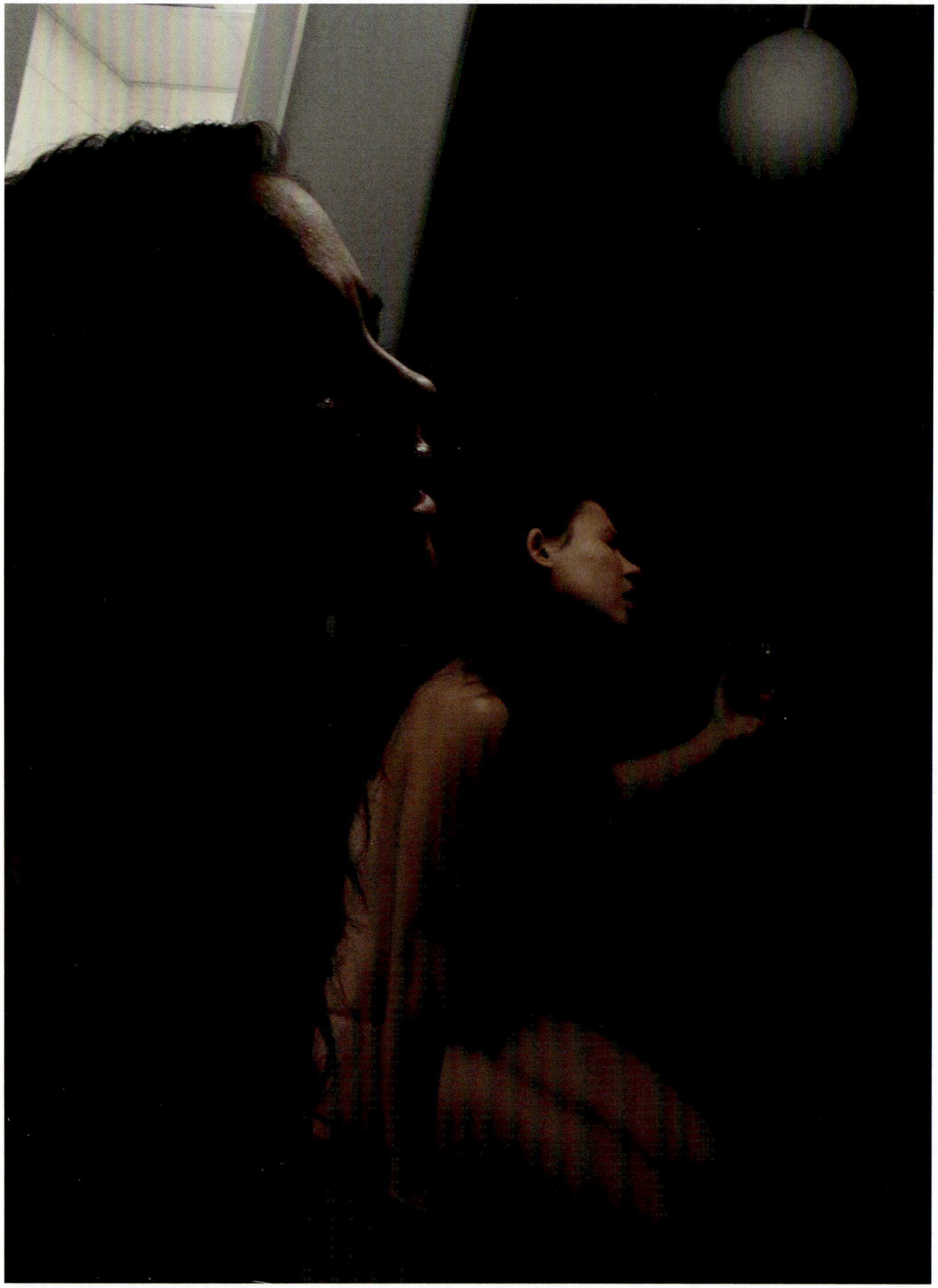

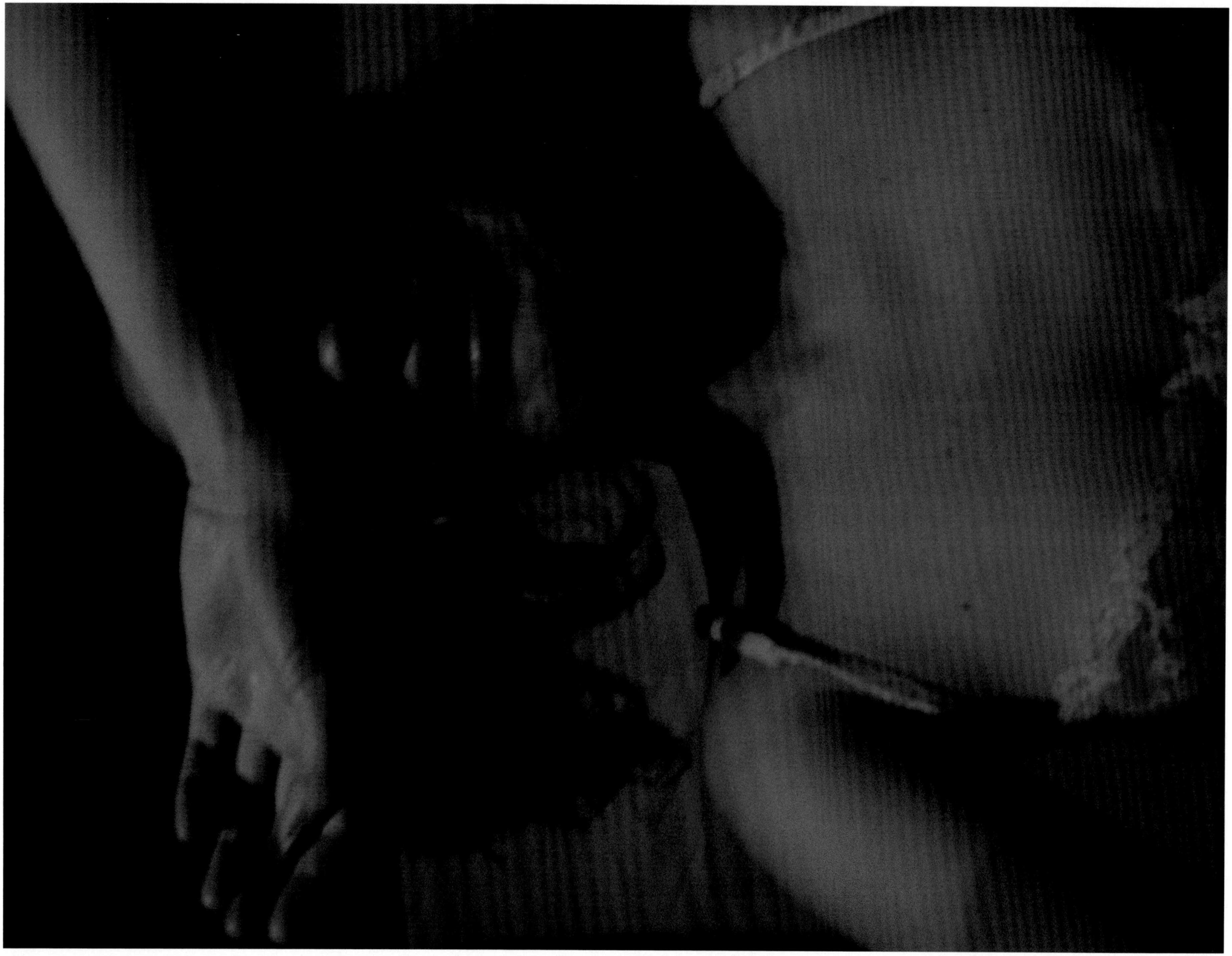

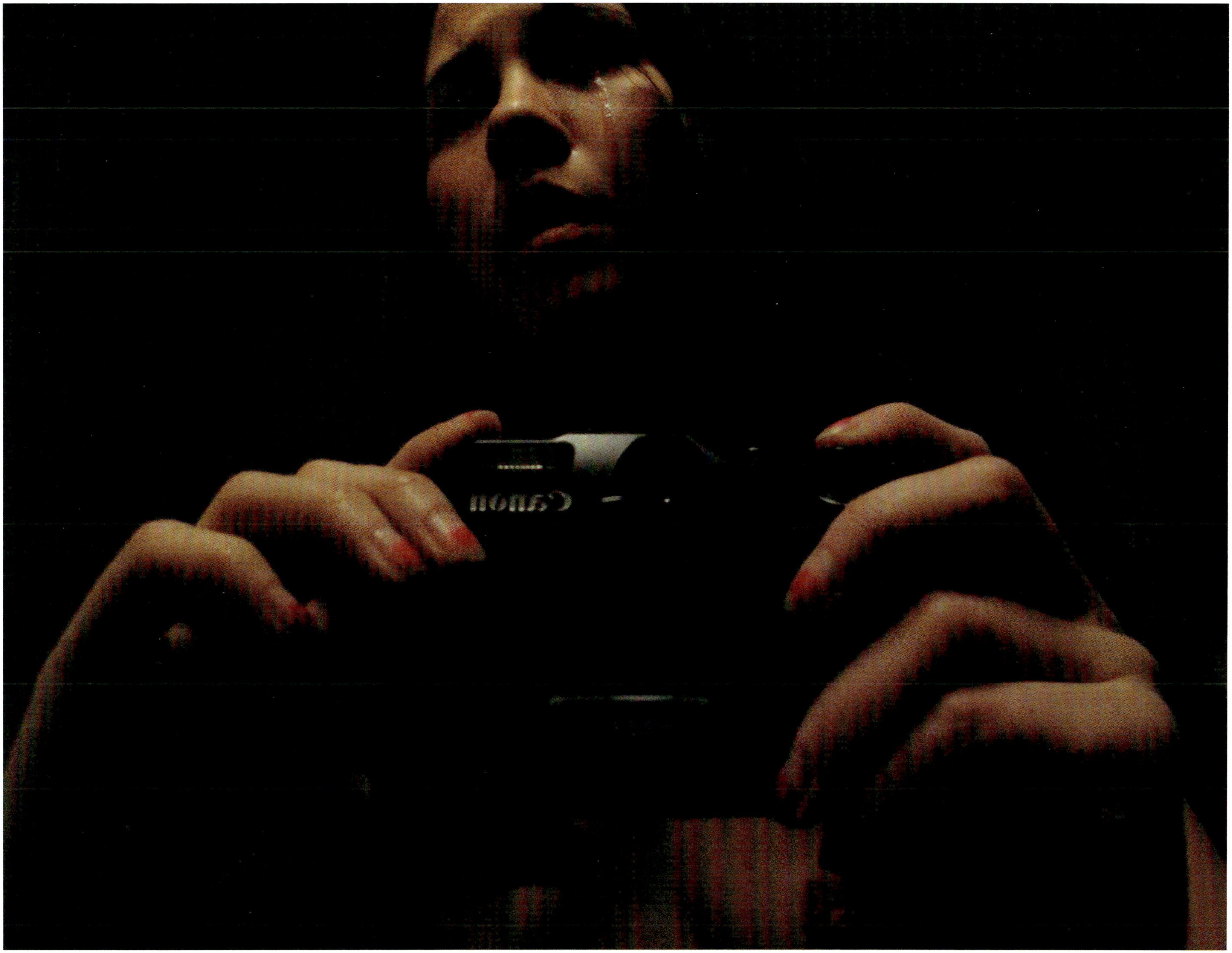

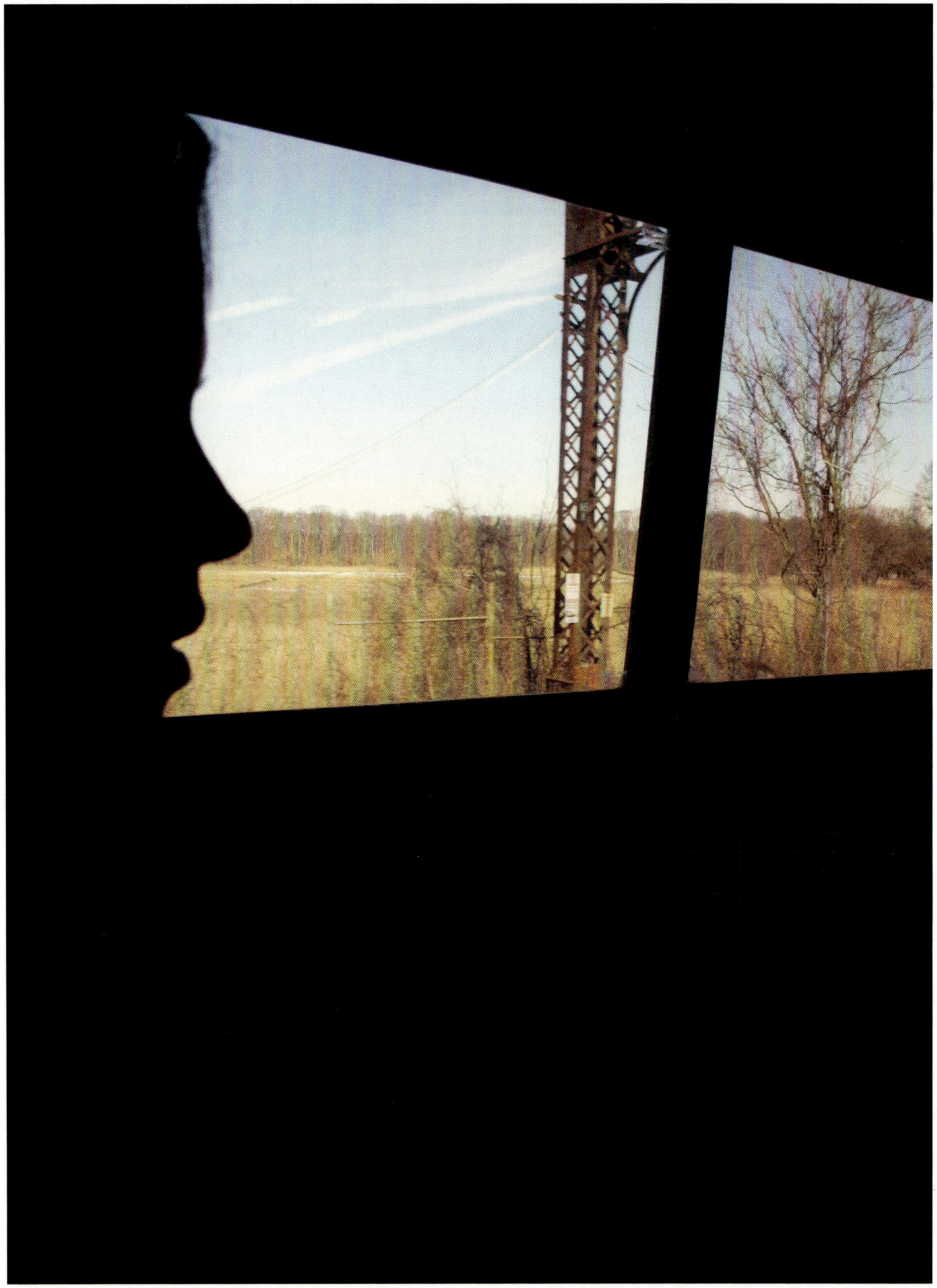

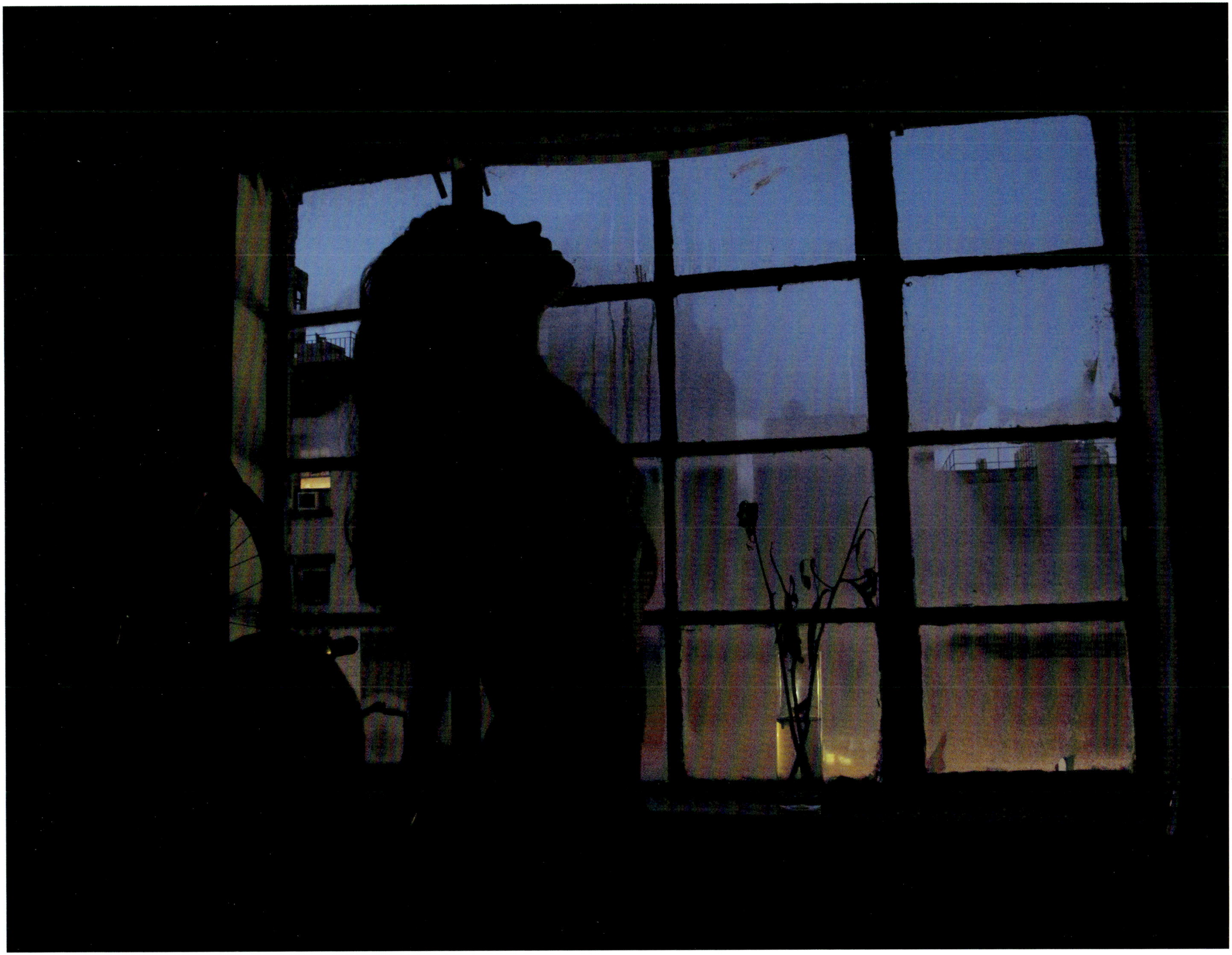

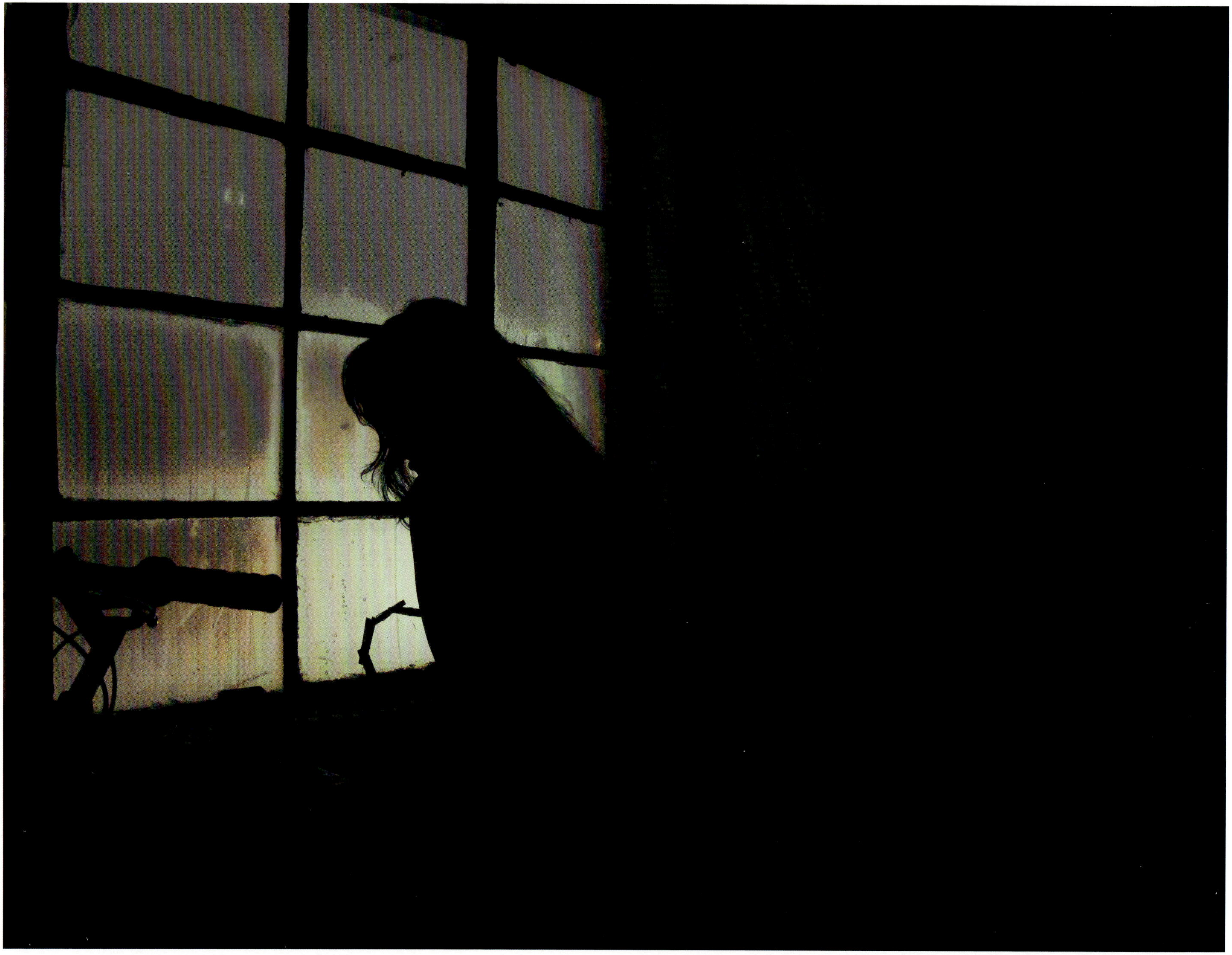

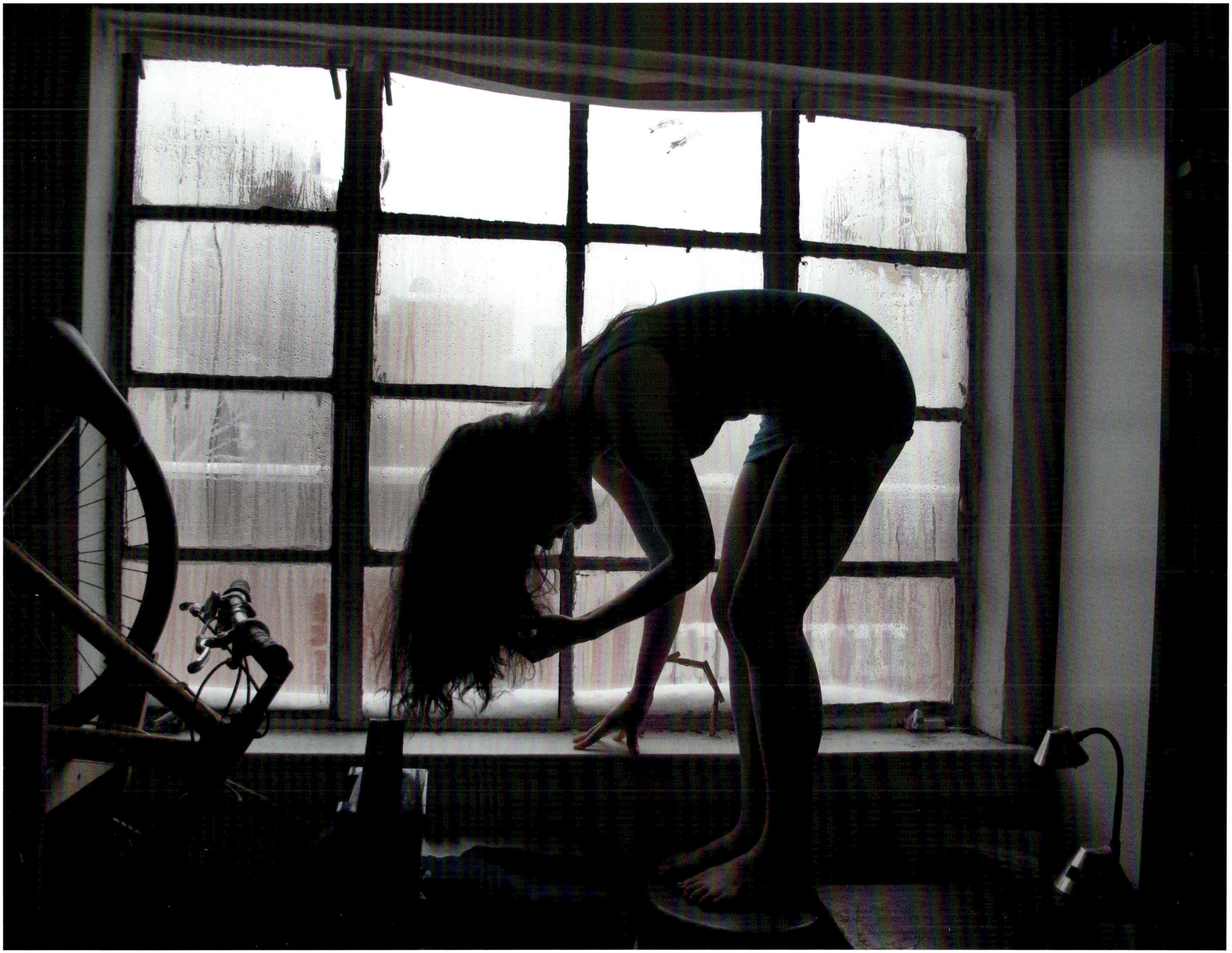

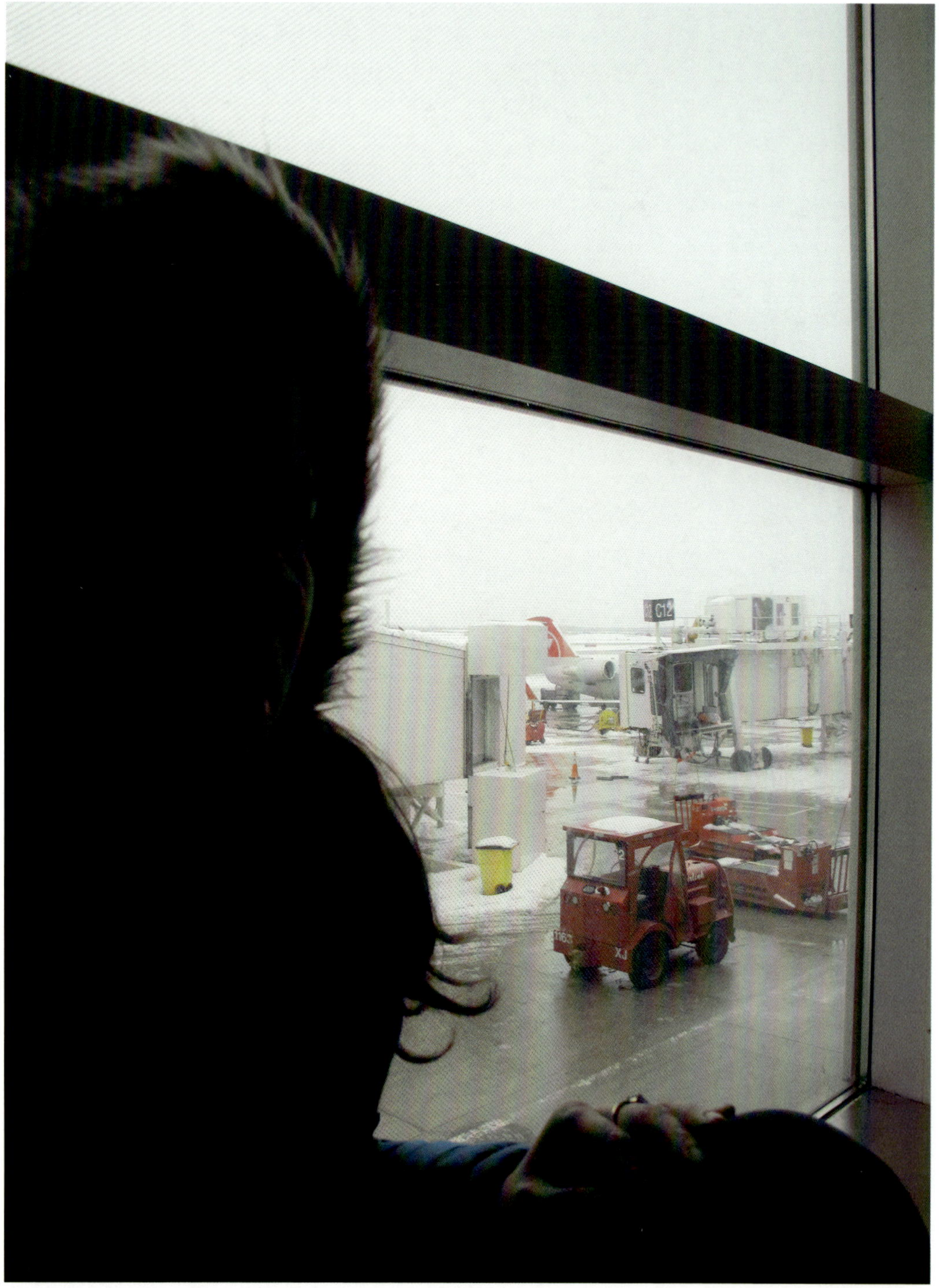
C12
XJ

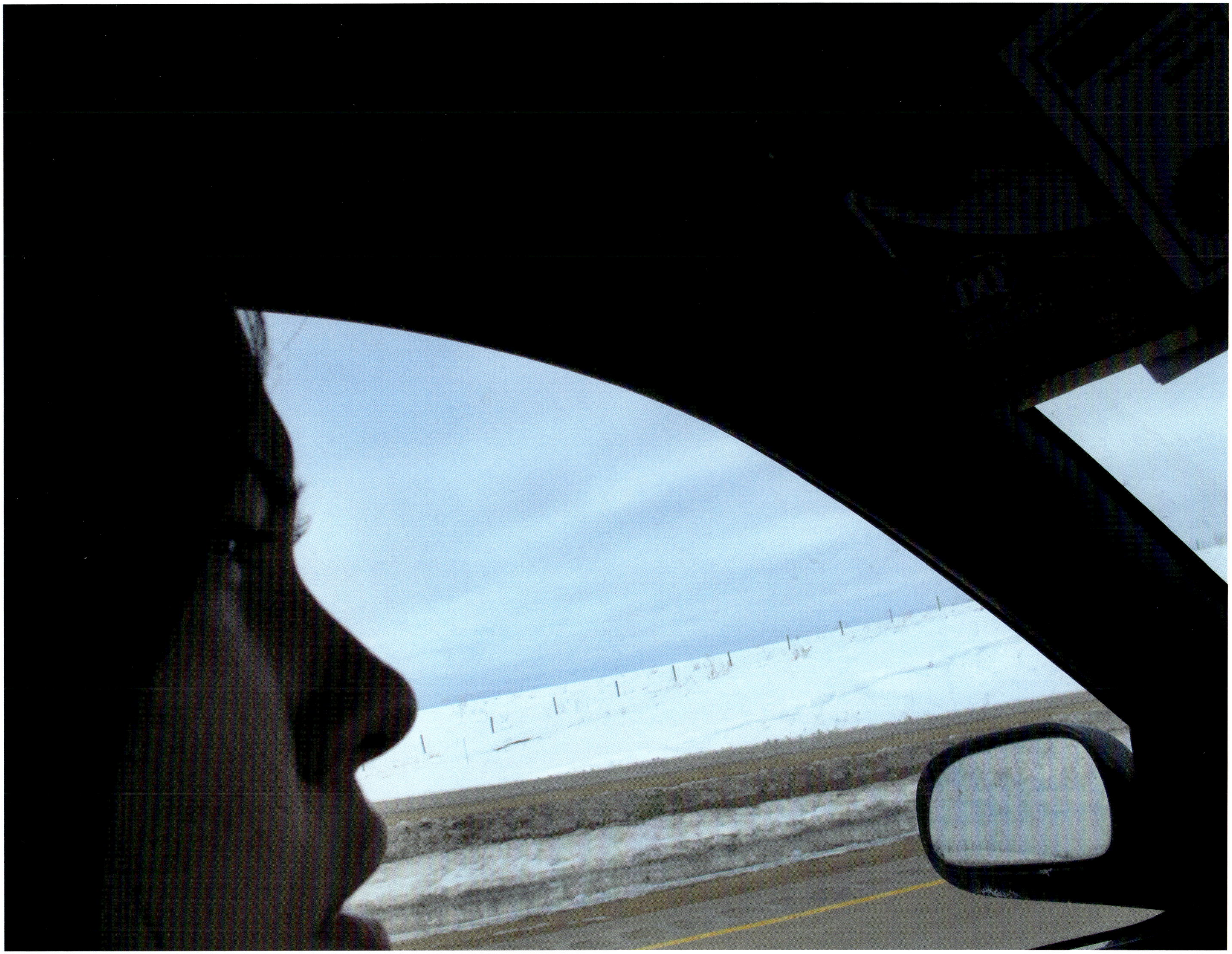

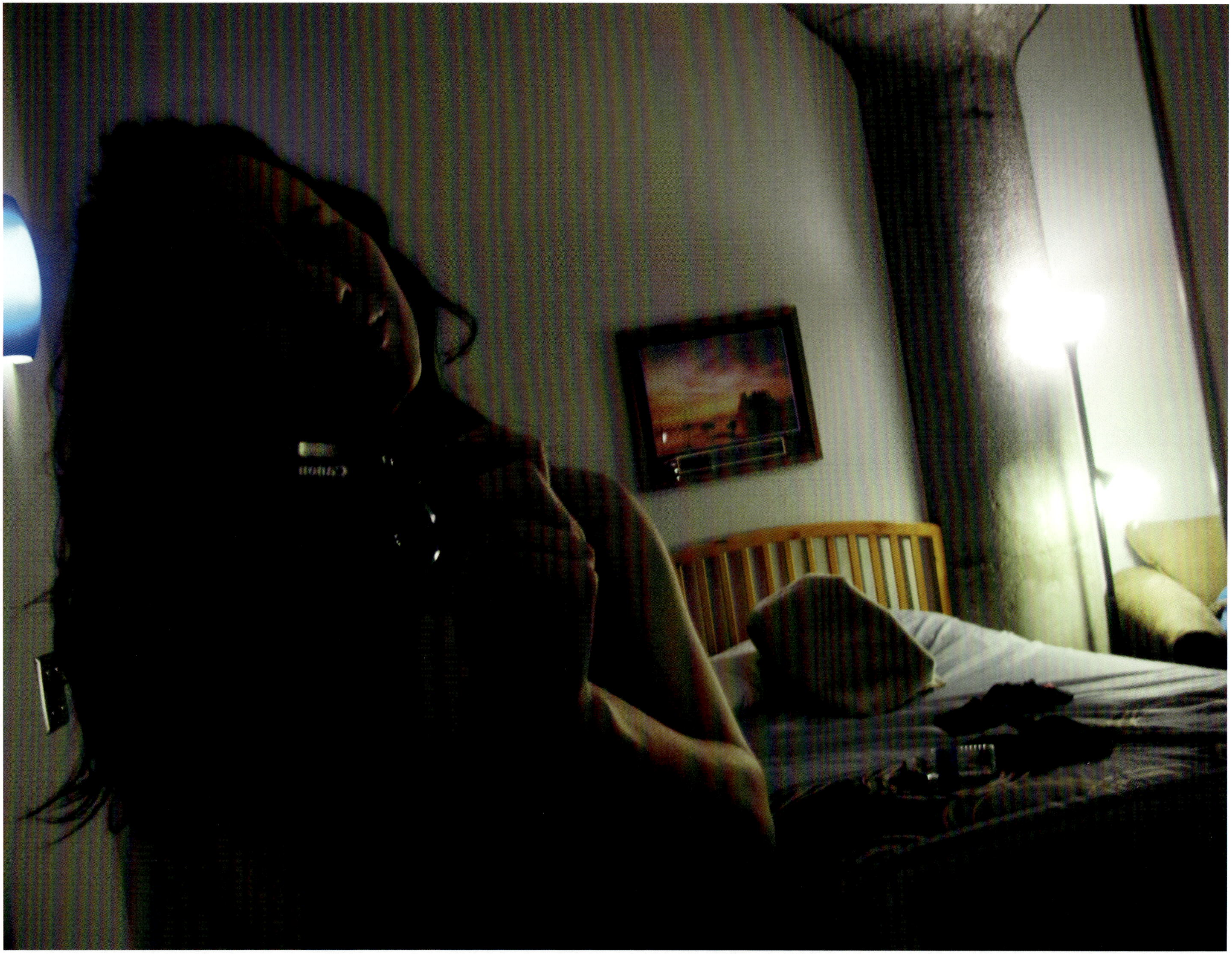

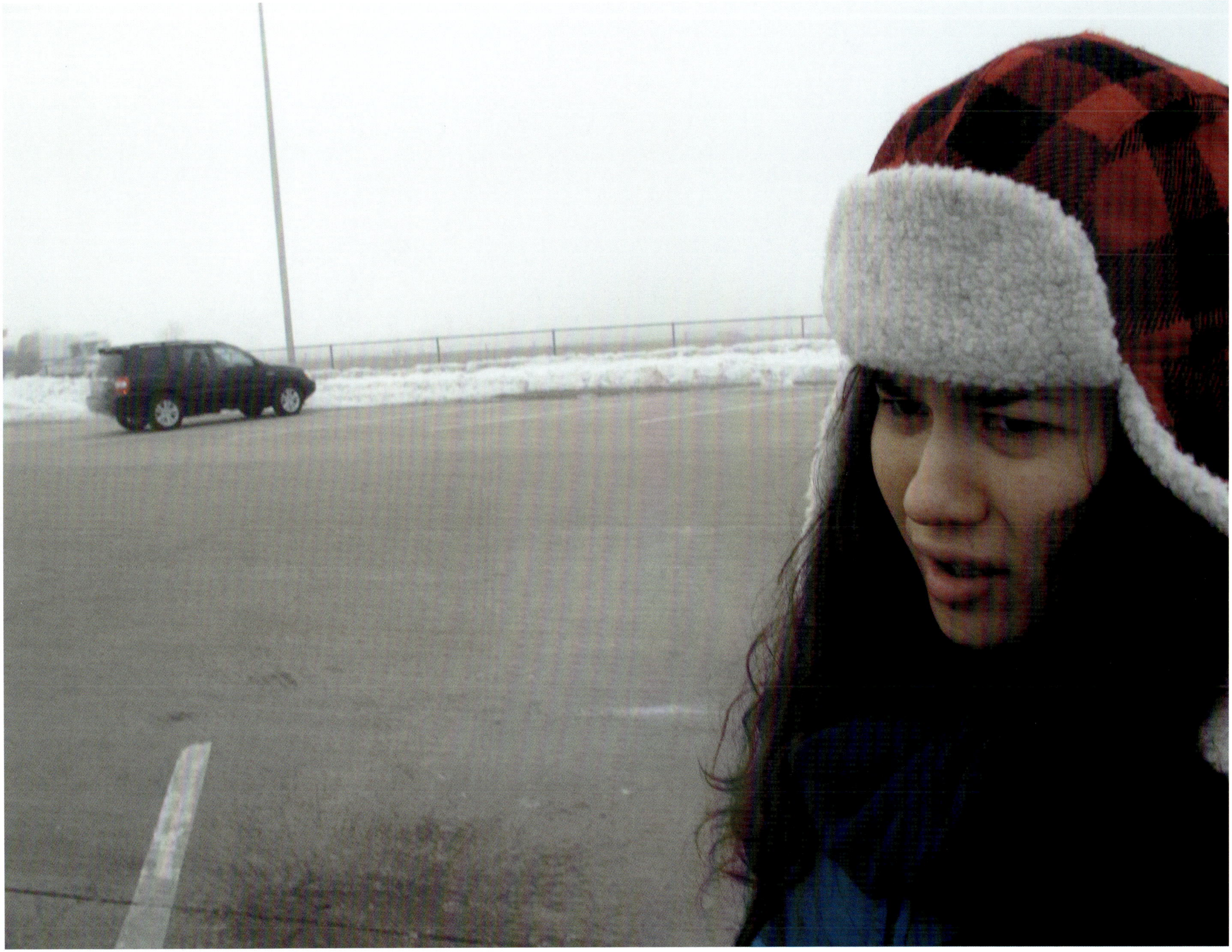

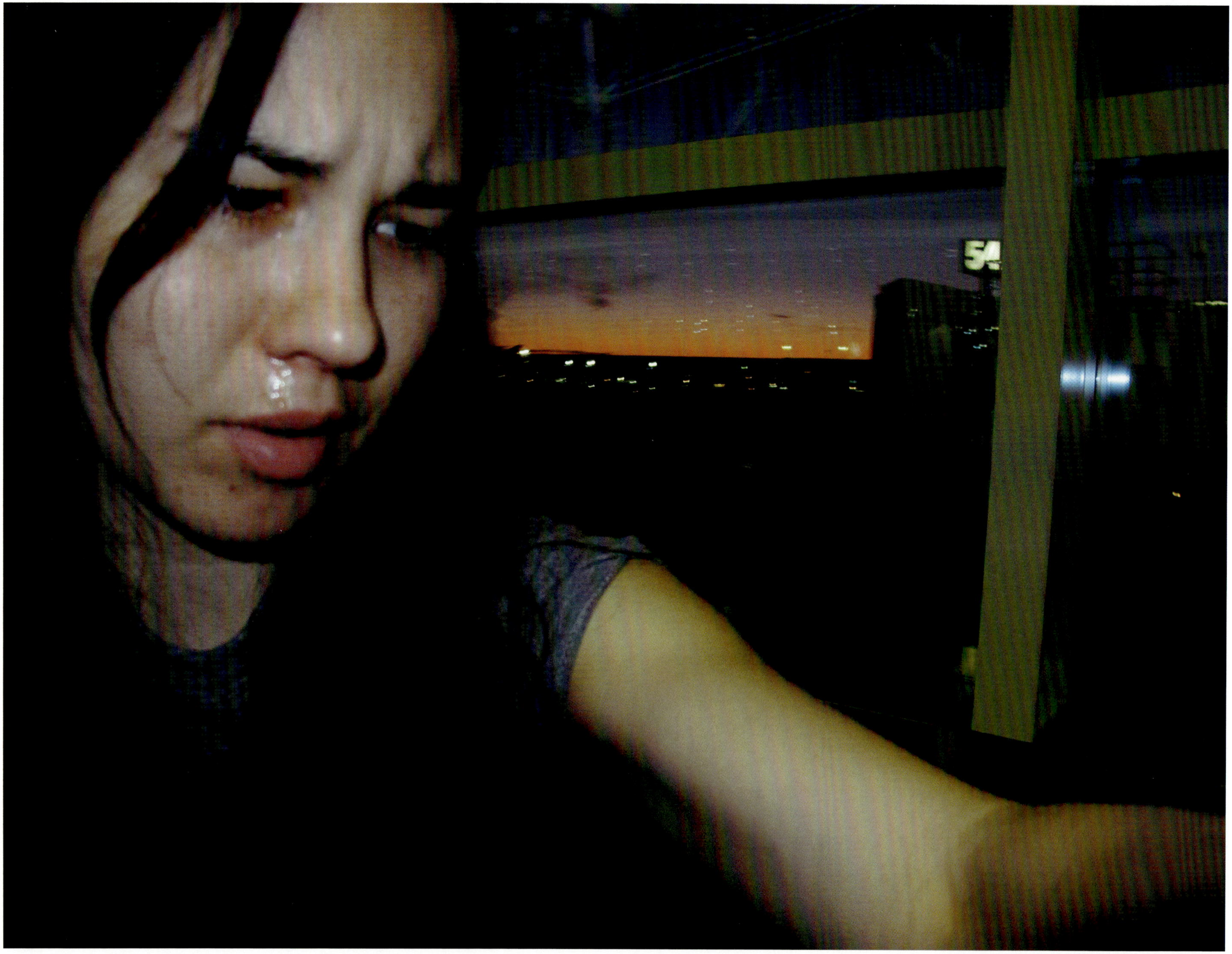

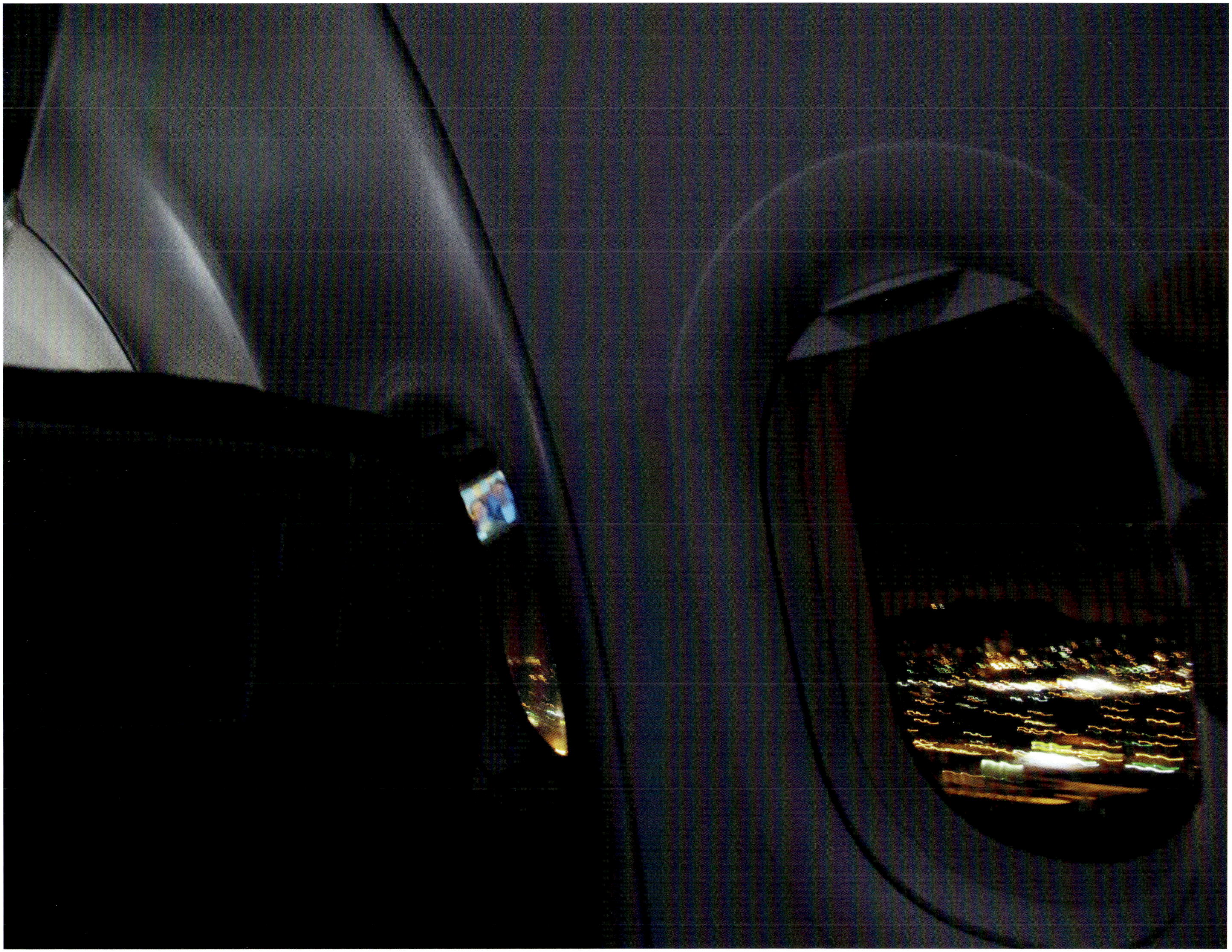

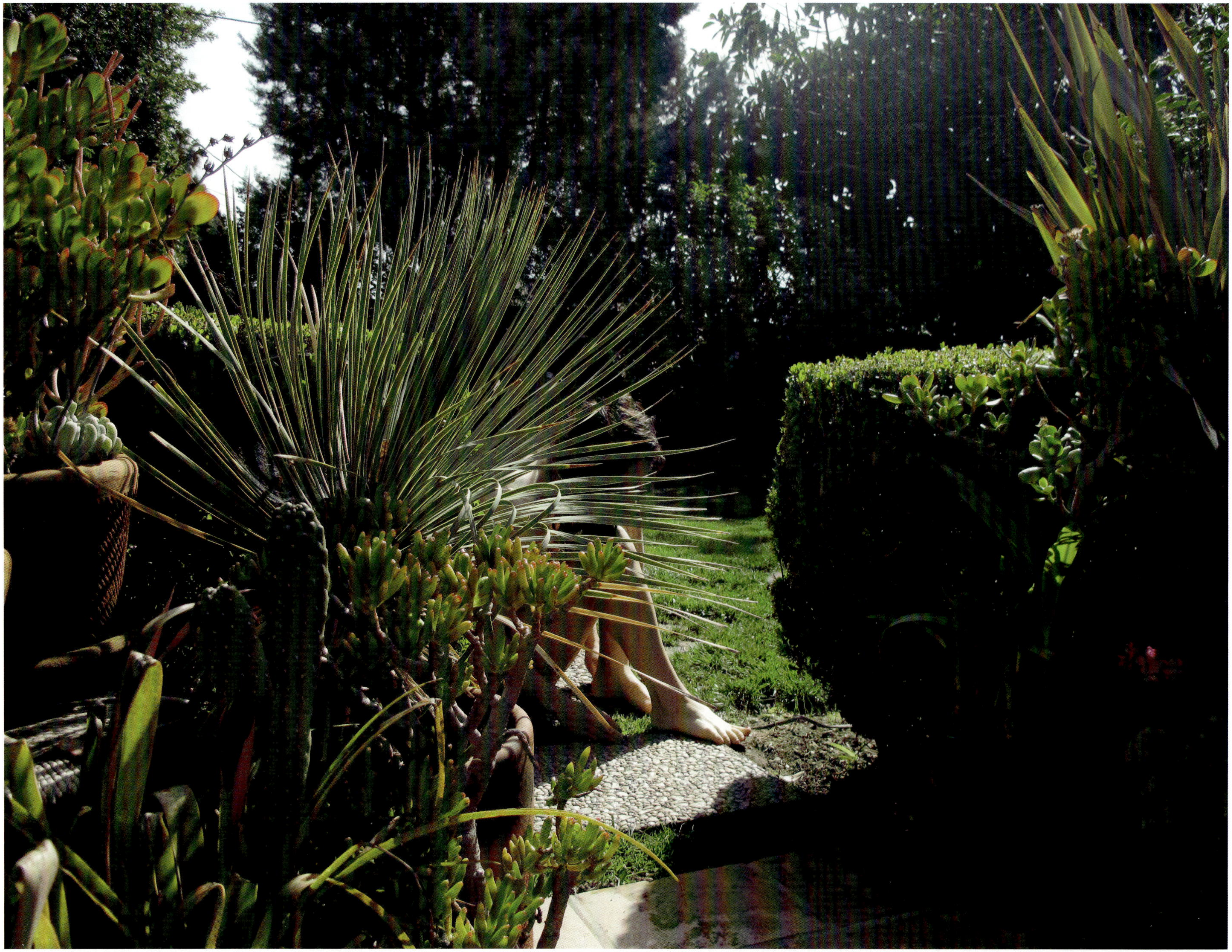

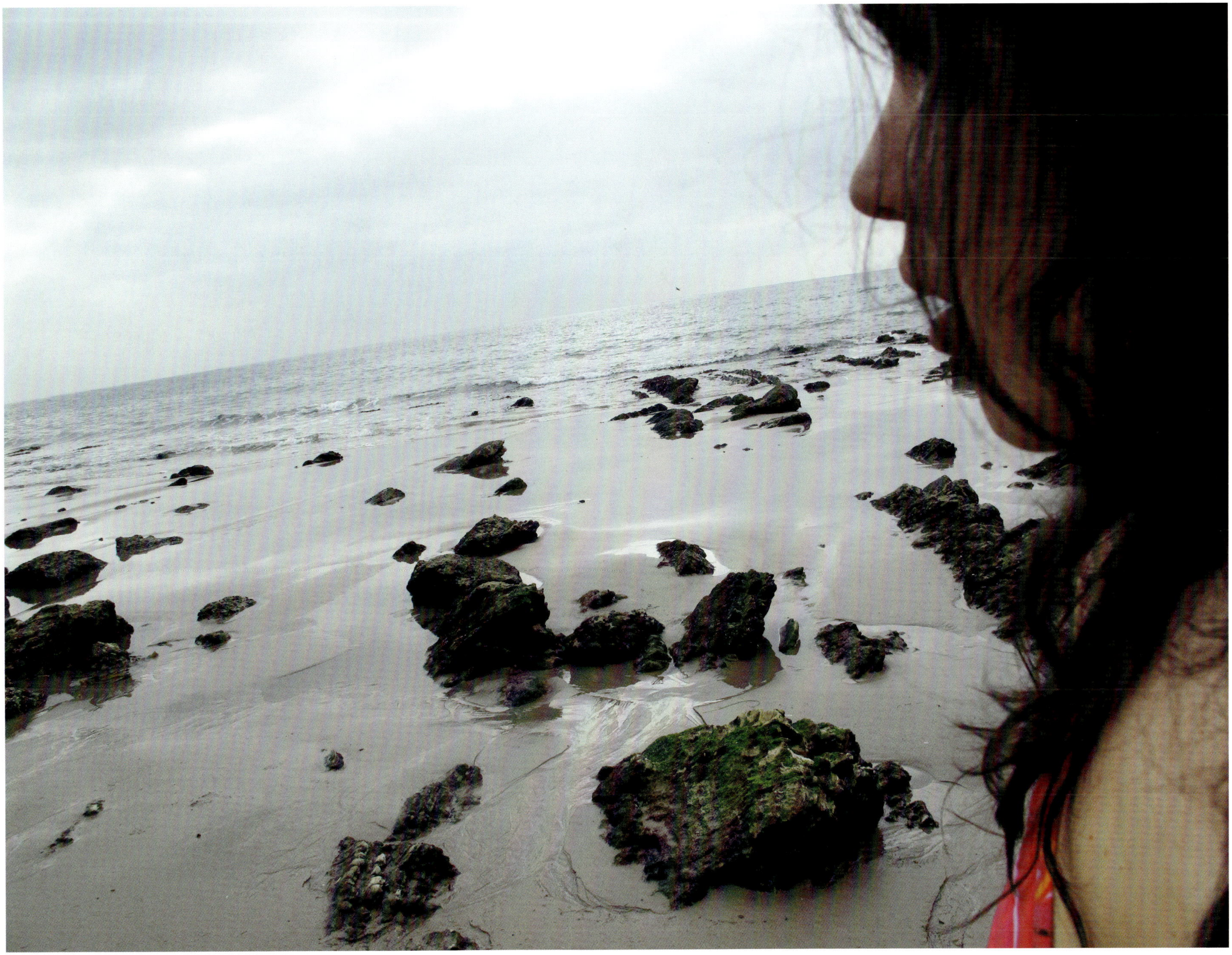

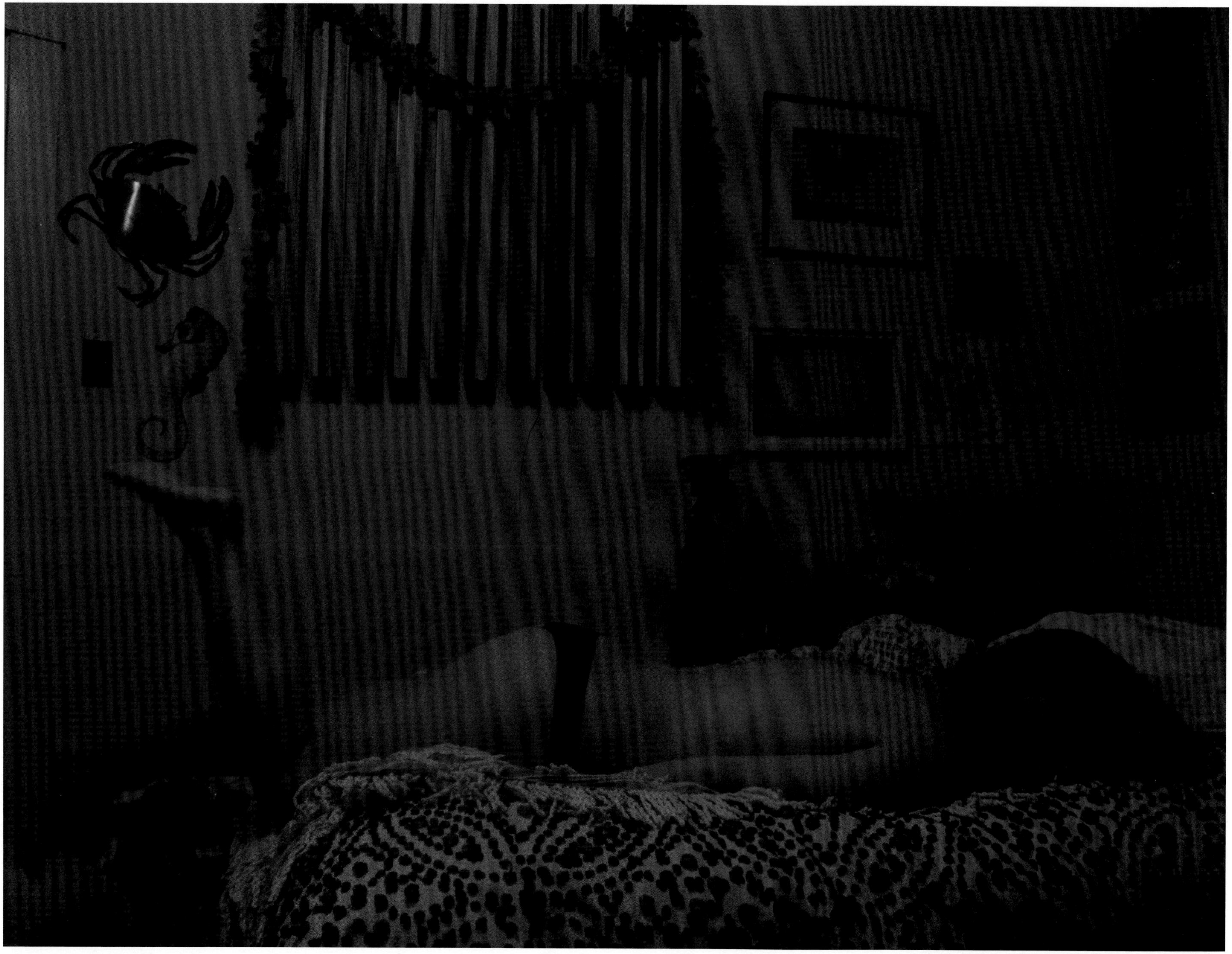

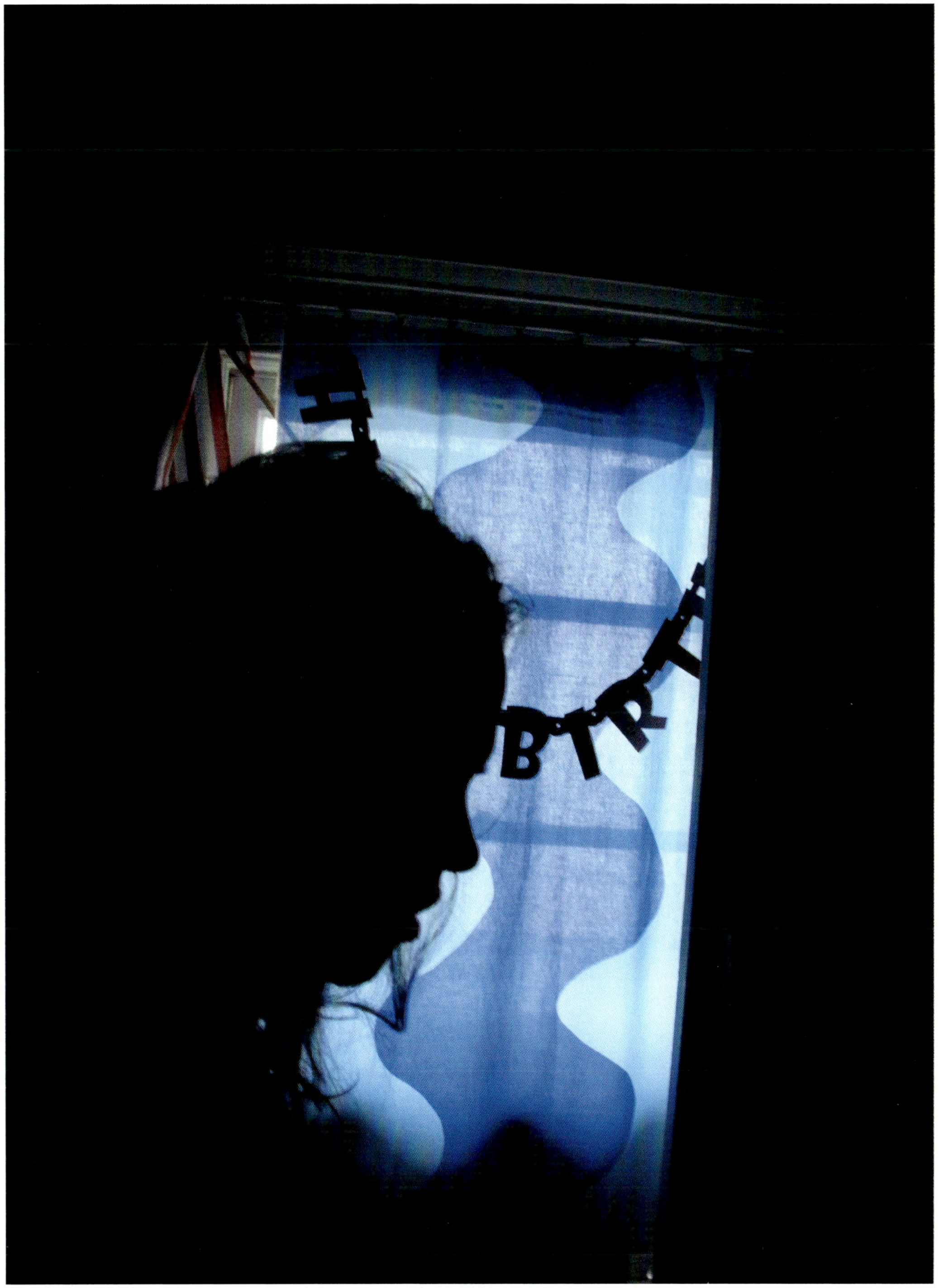

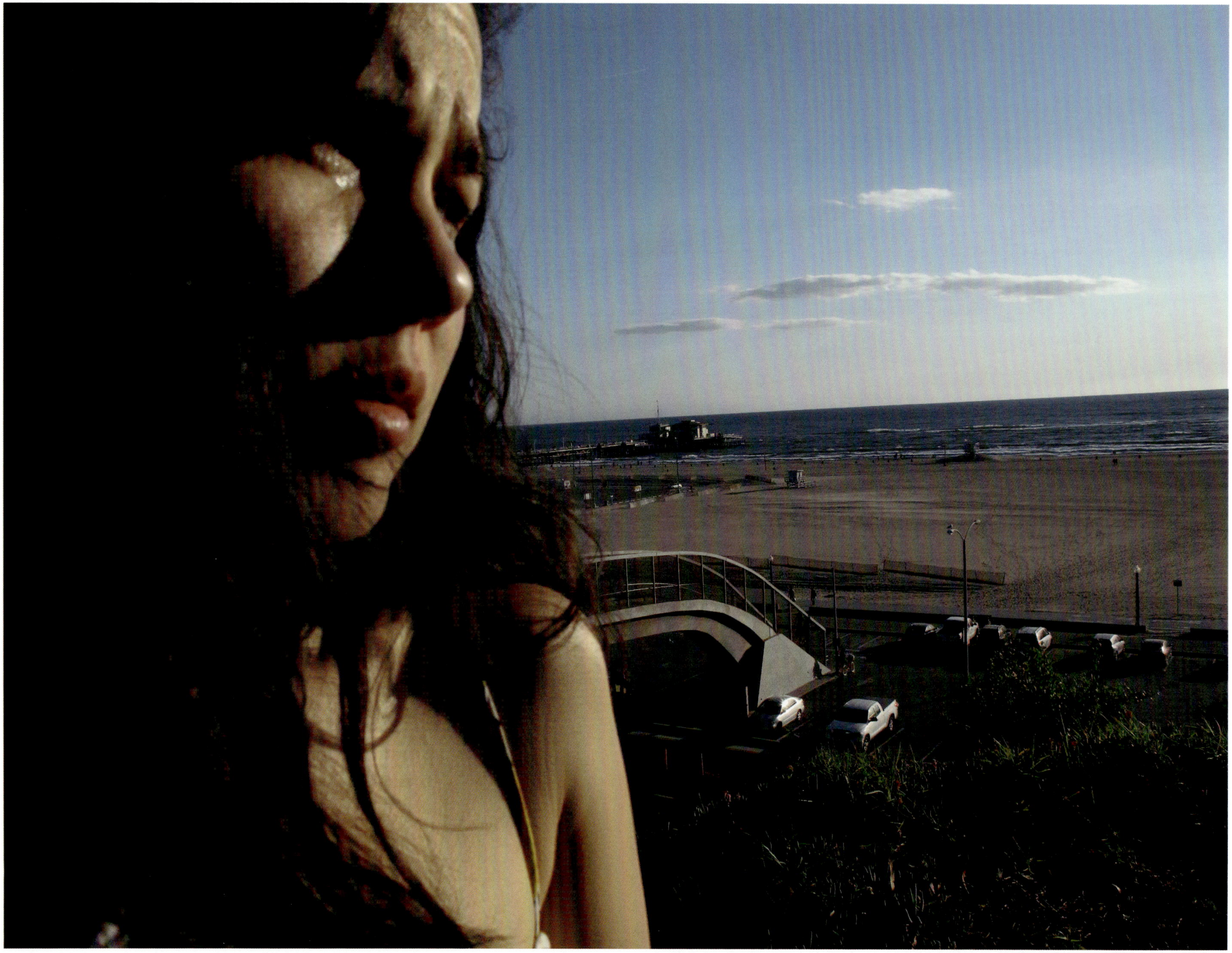

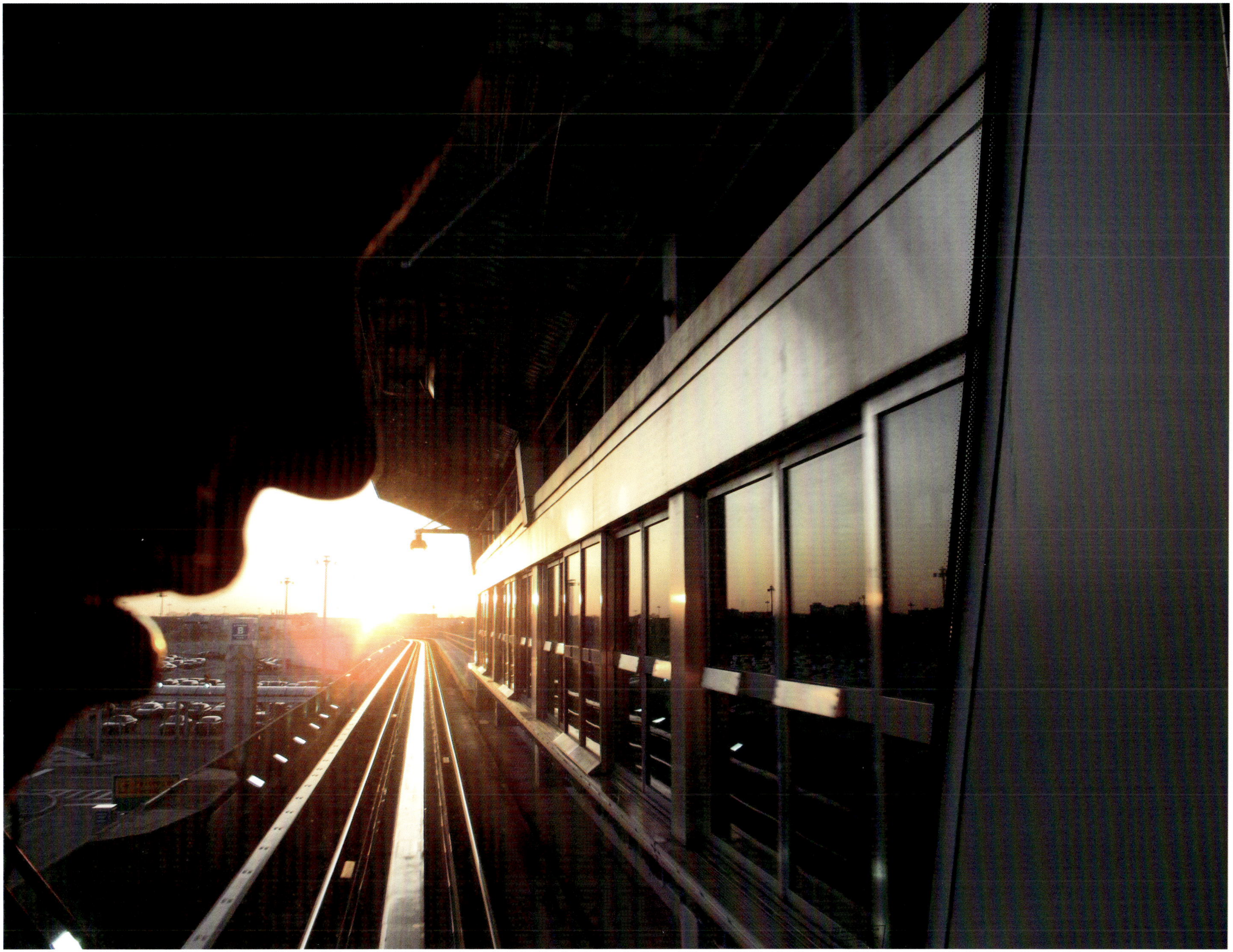

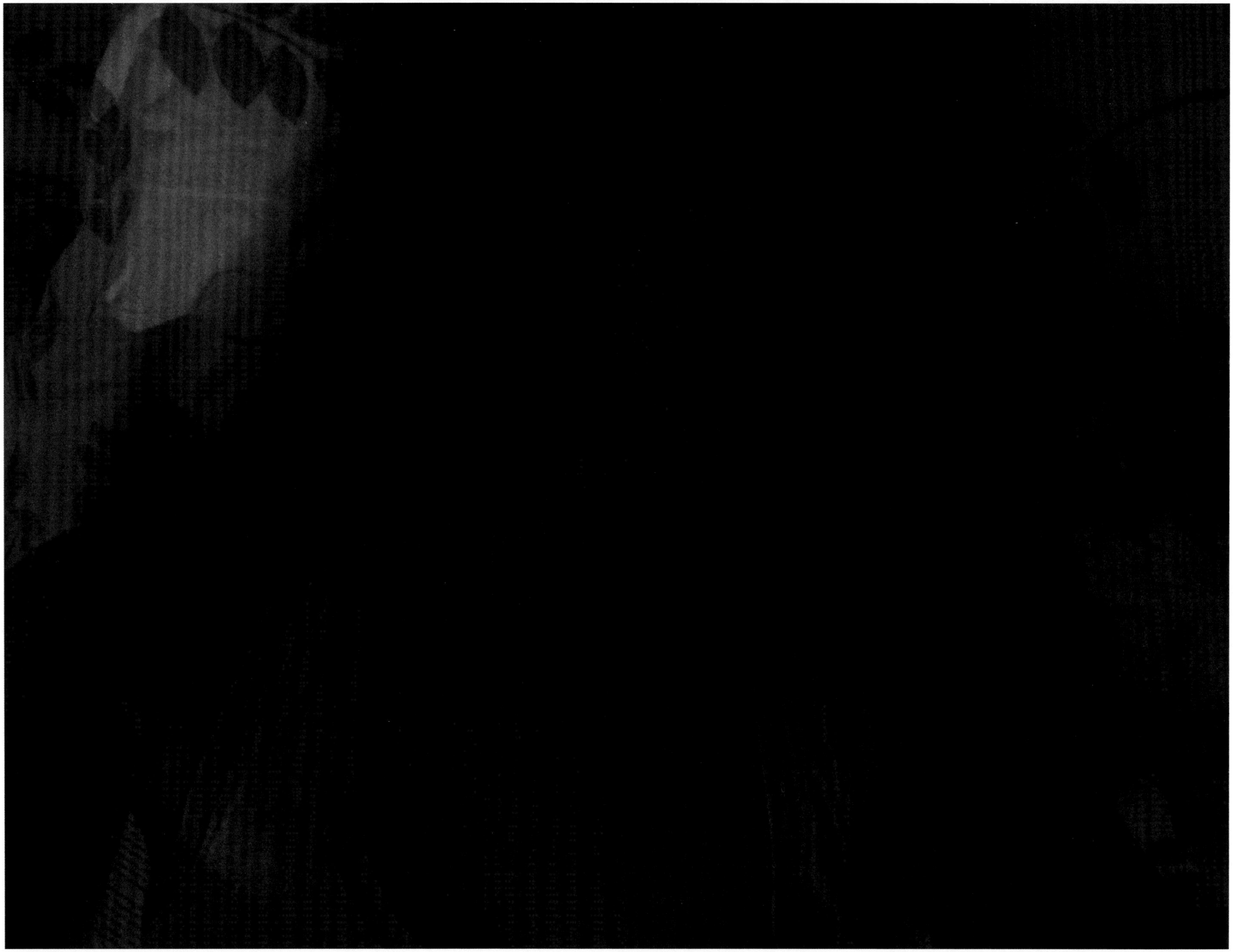

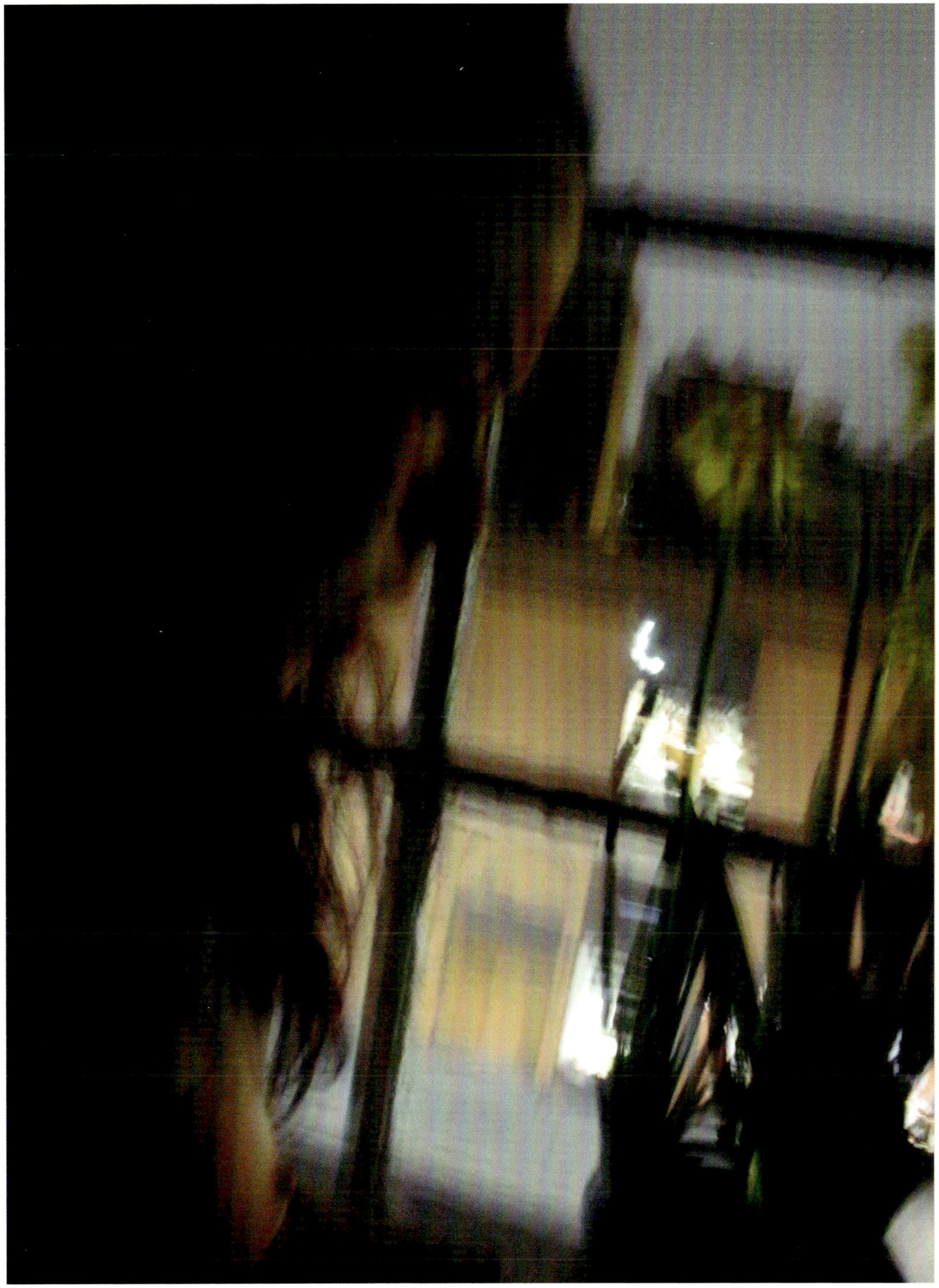

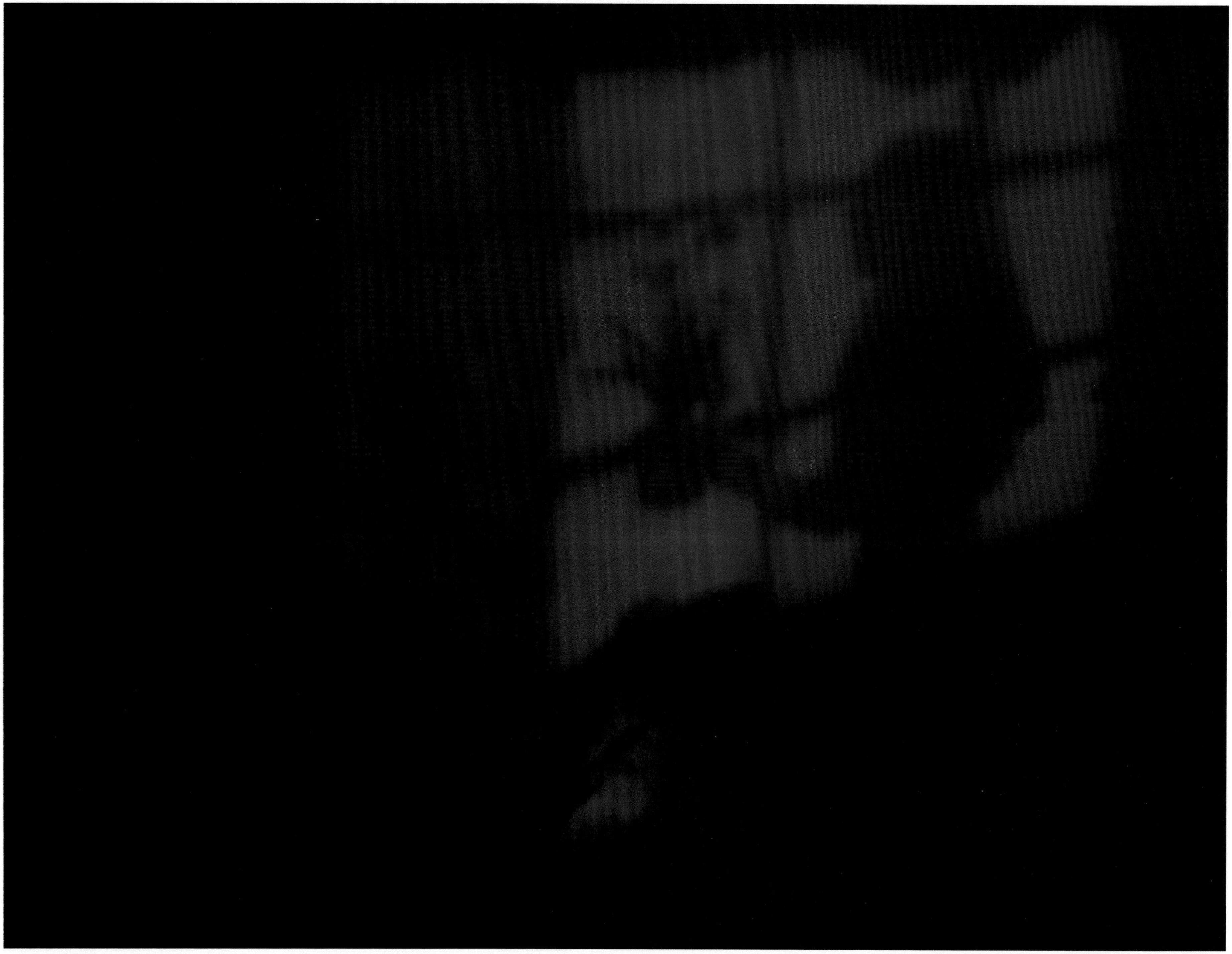

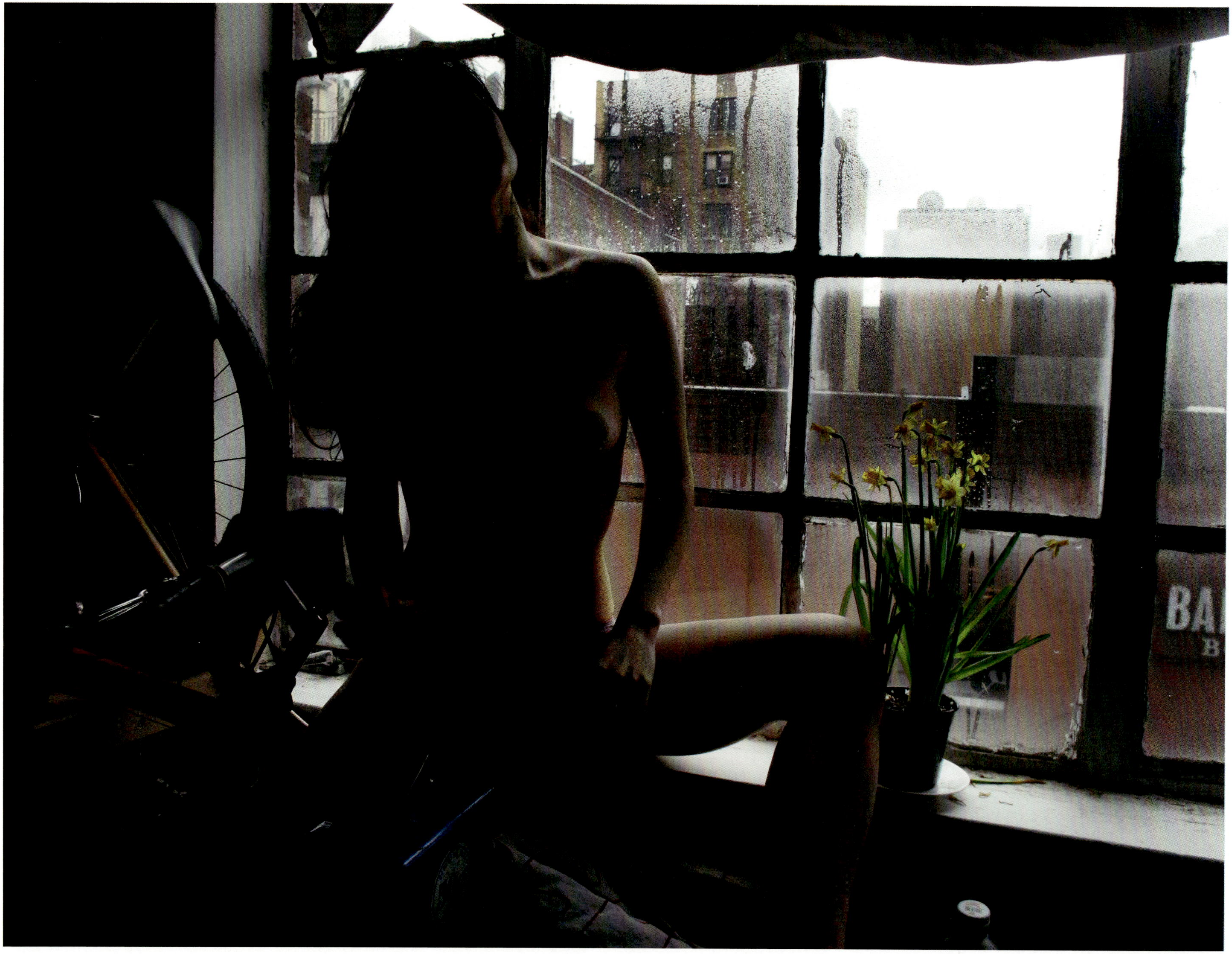

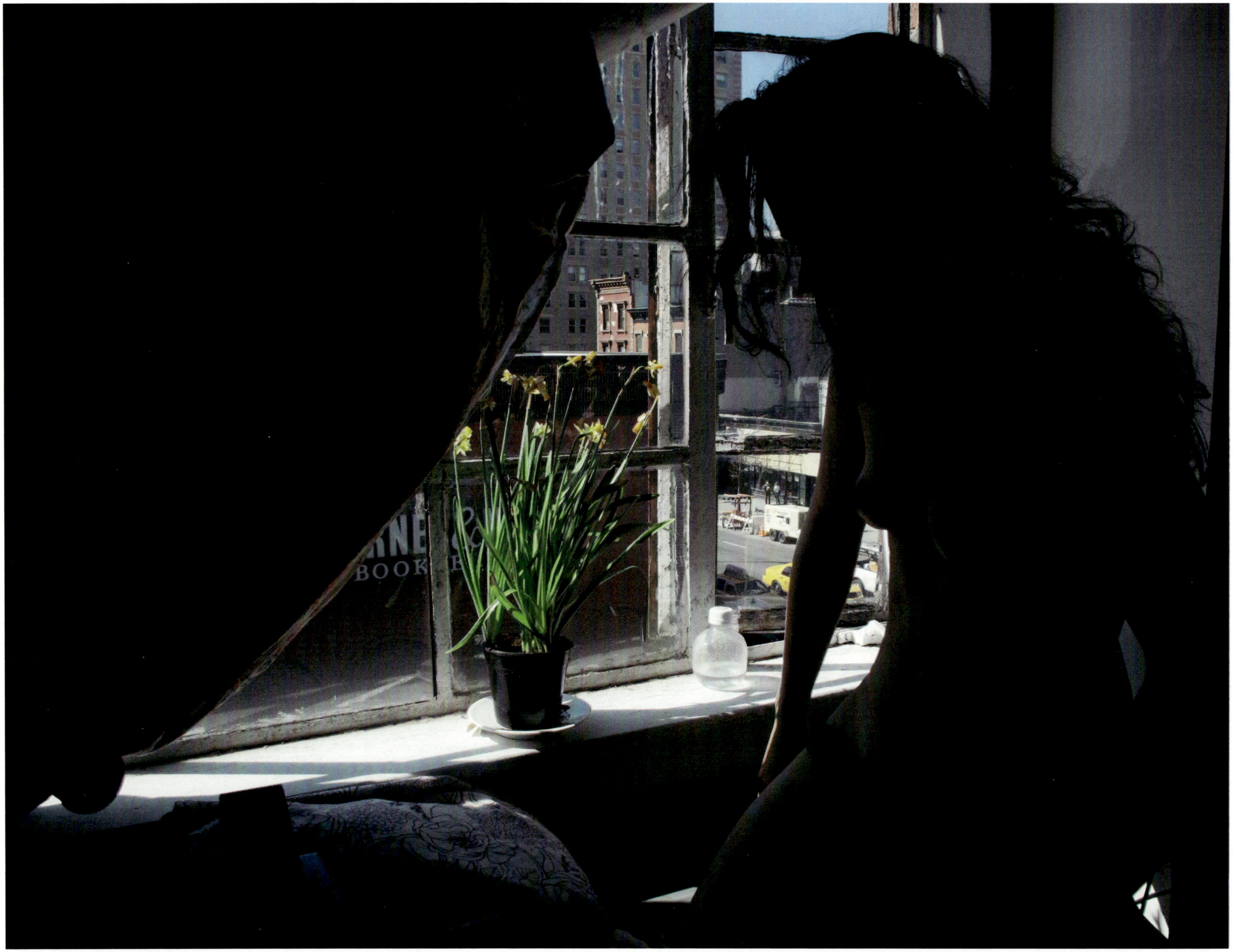

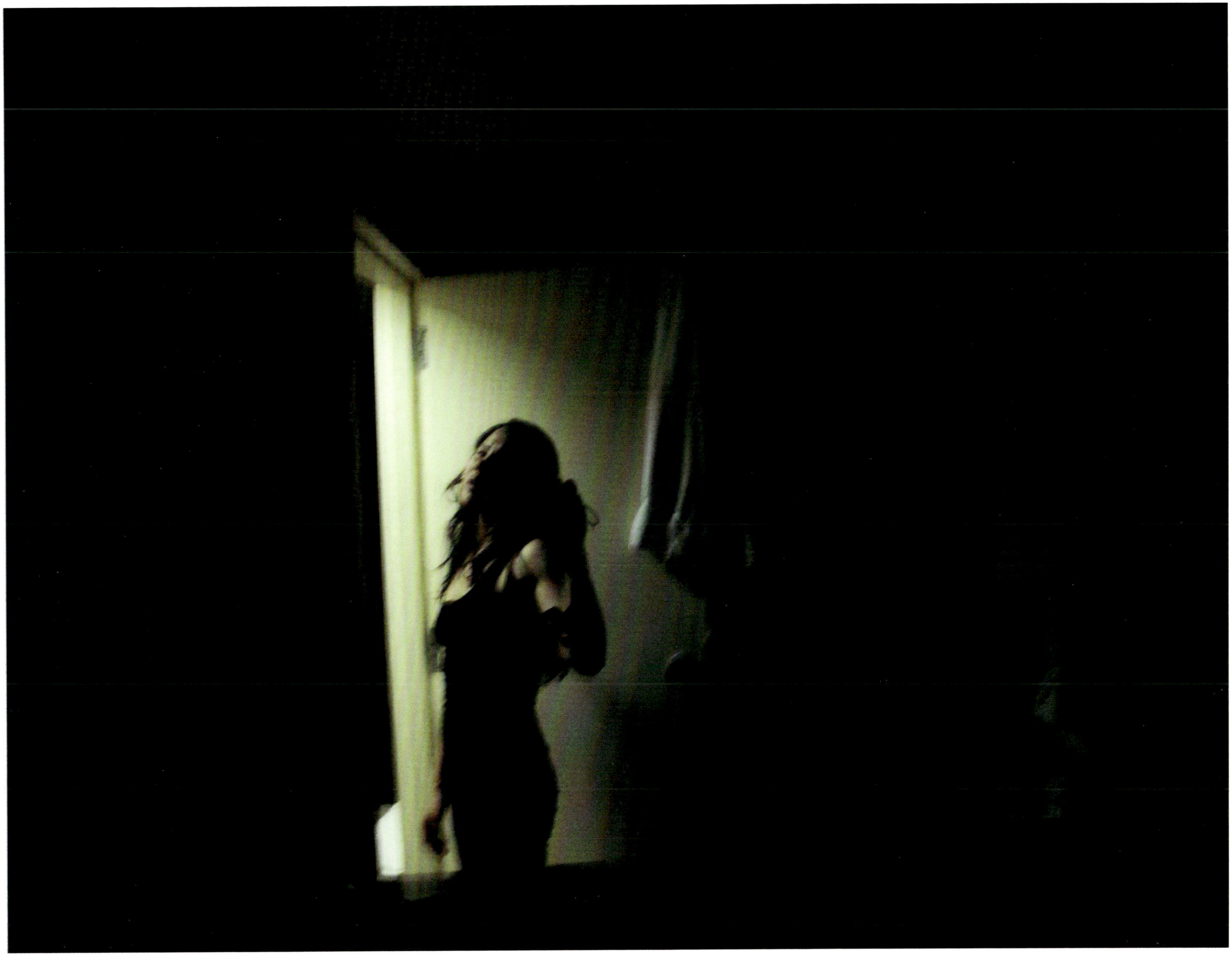

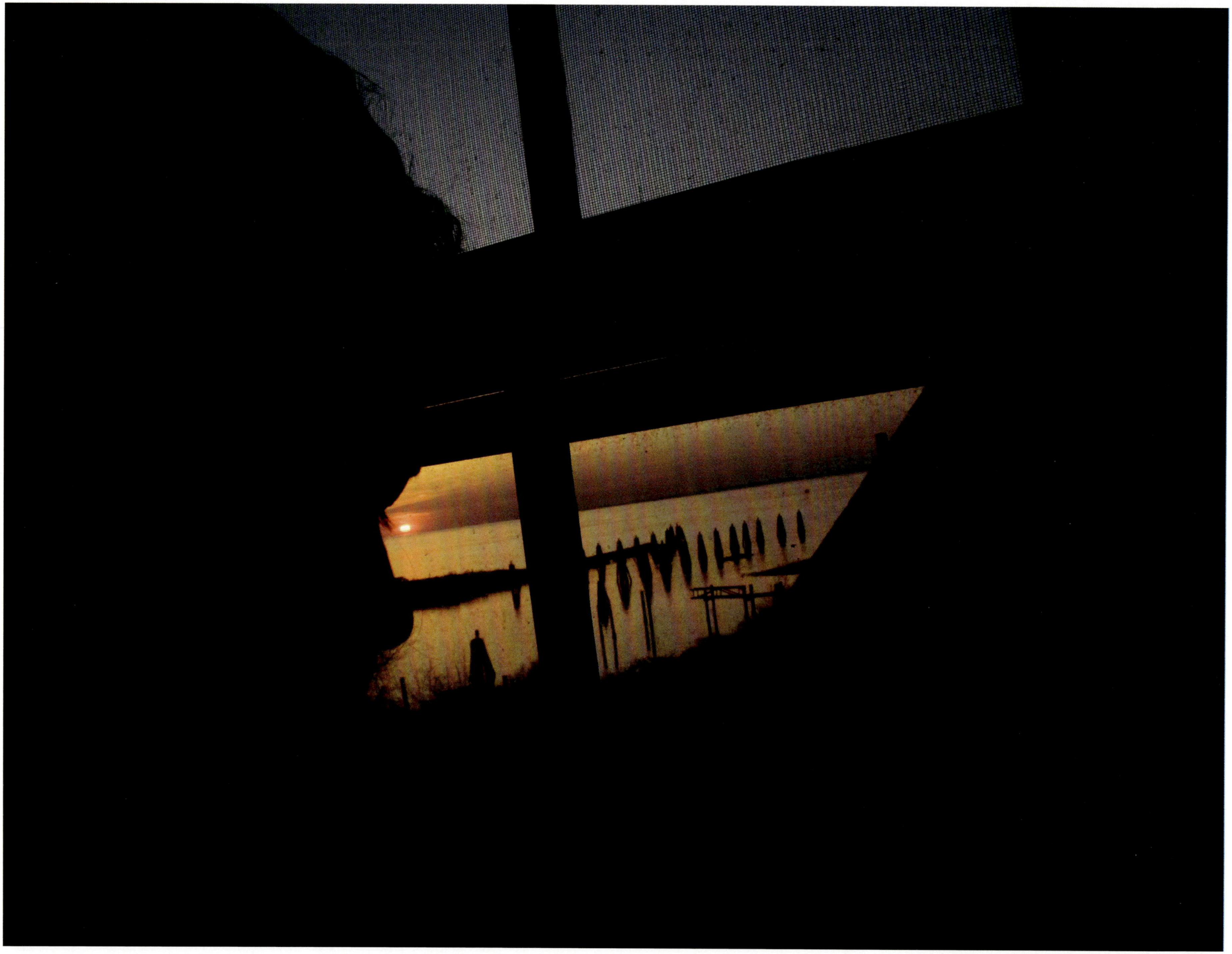

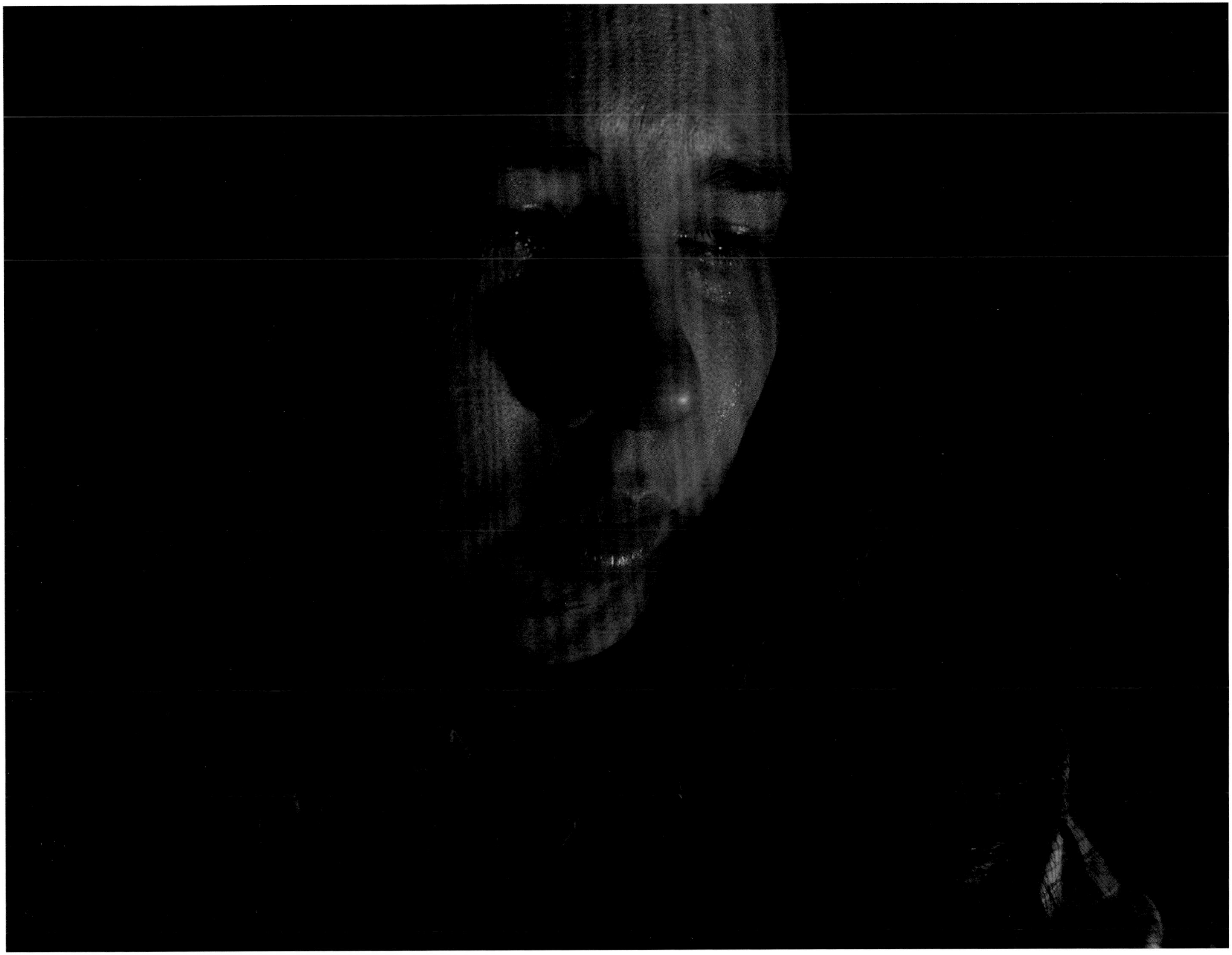

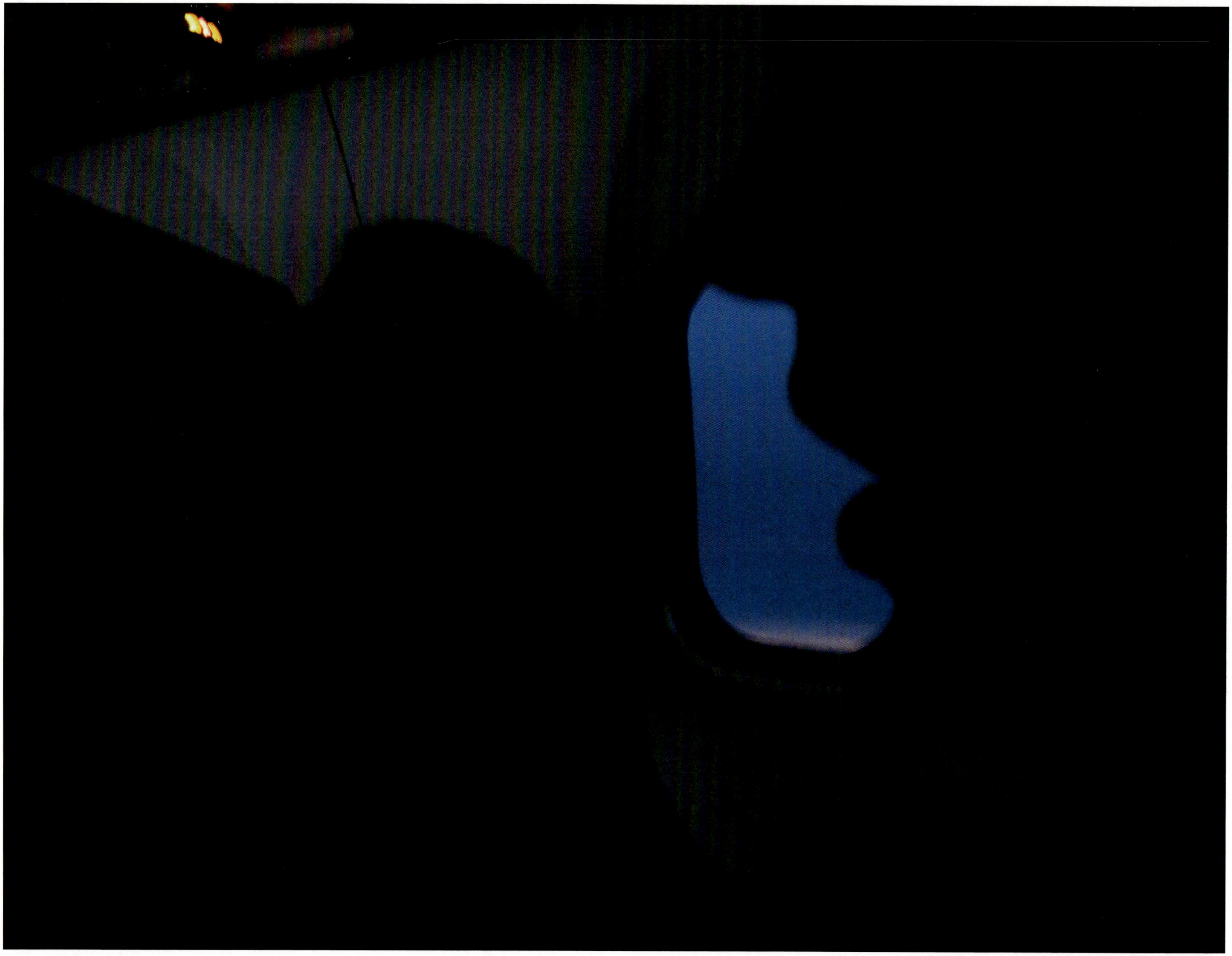

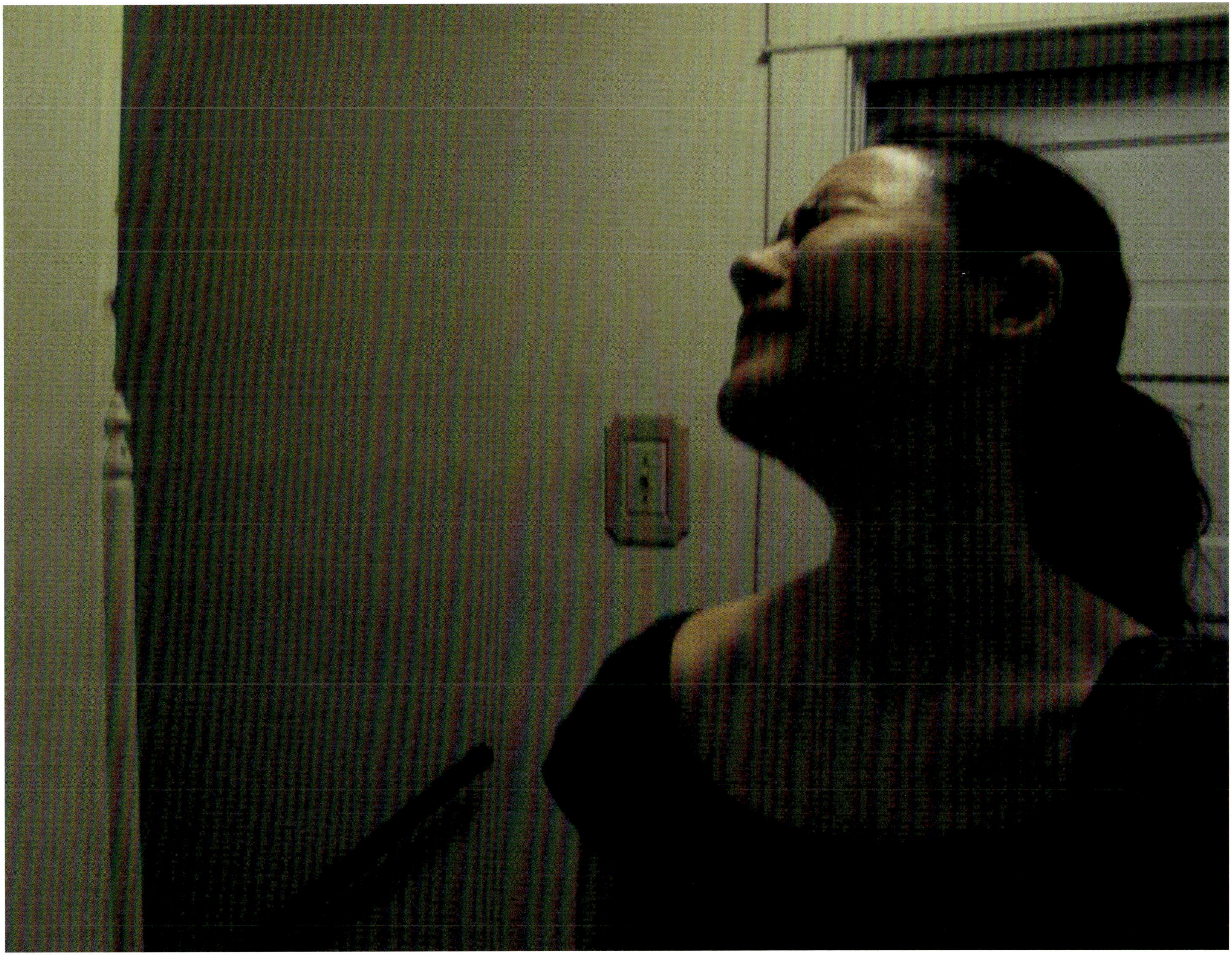

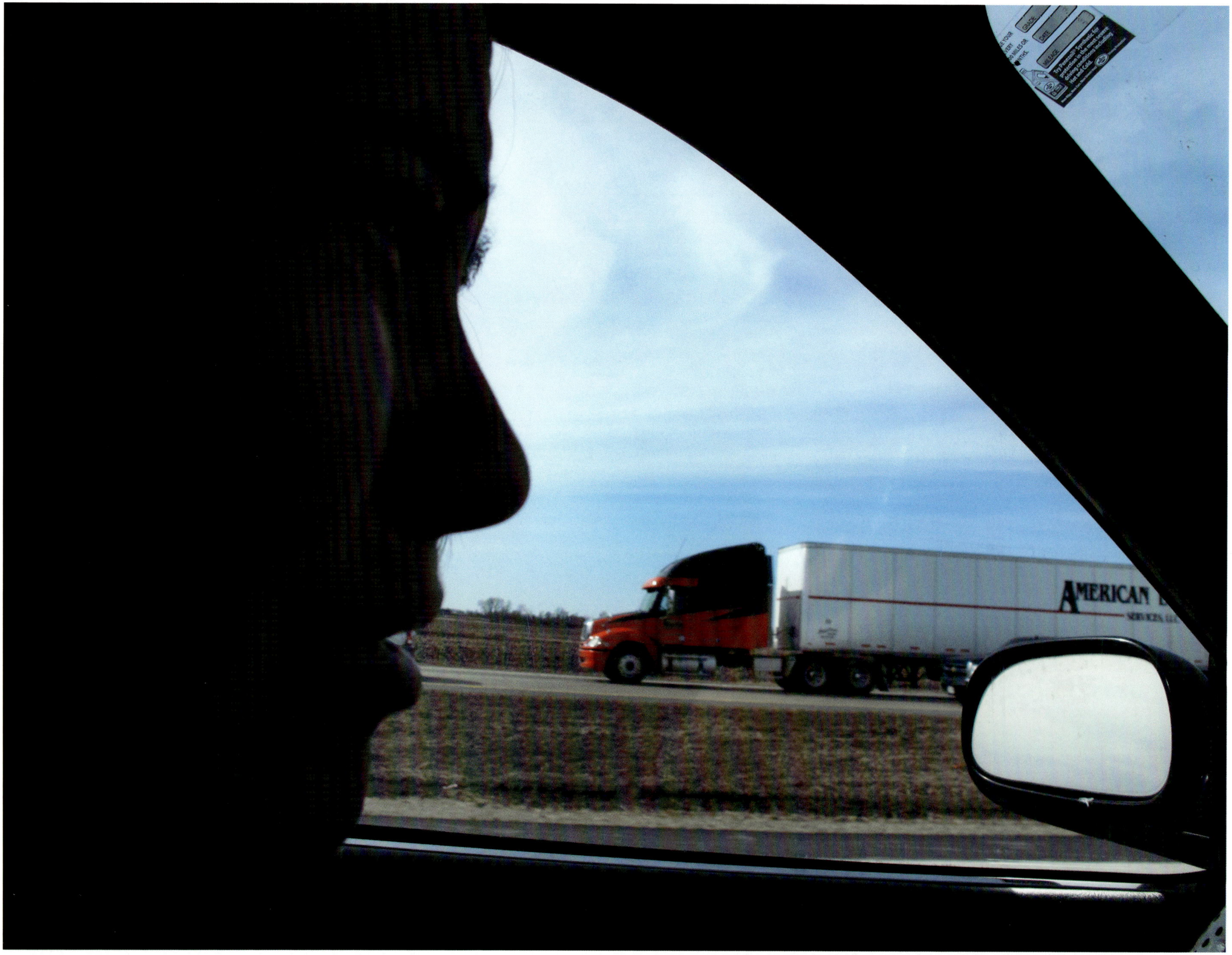
AMERICAN

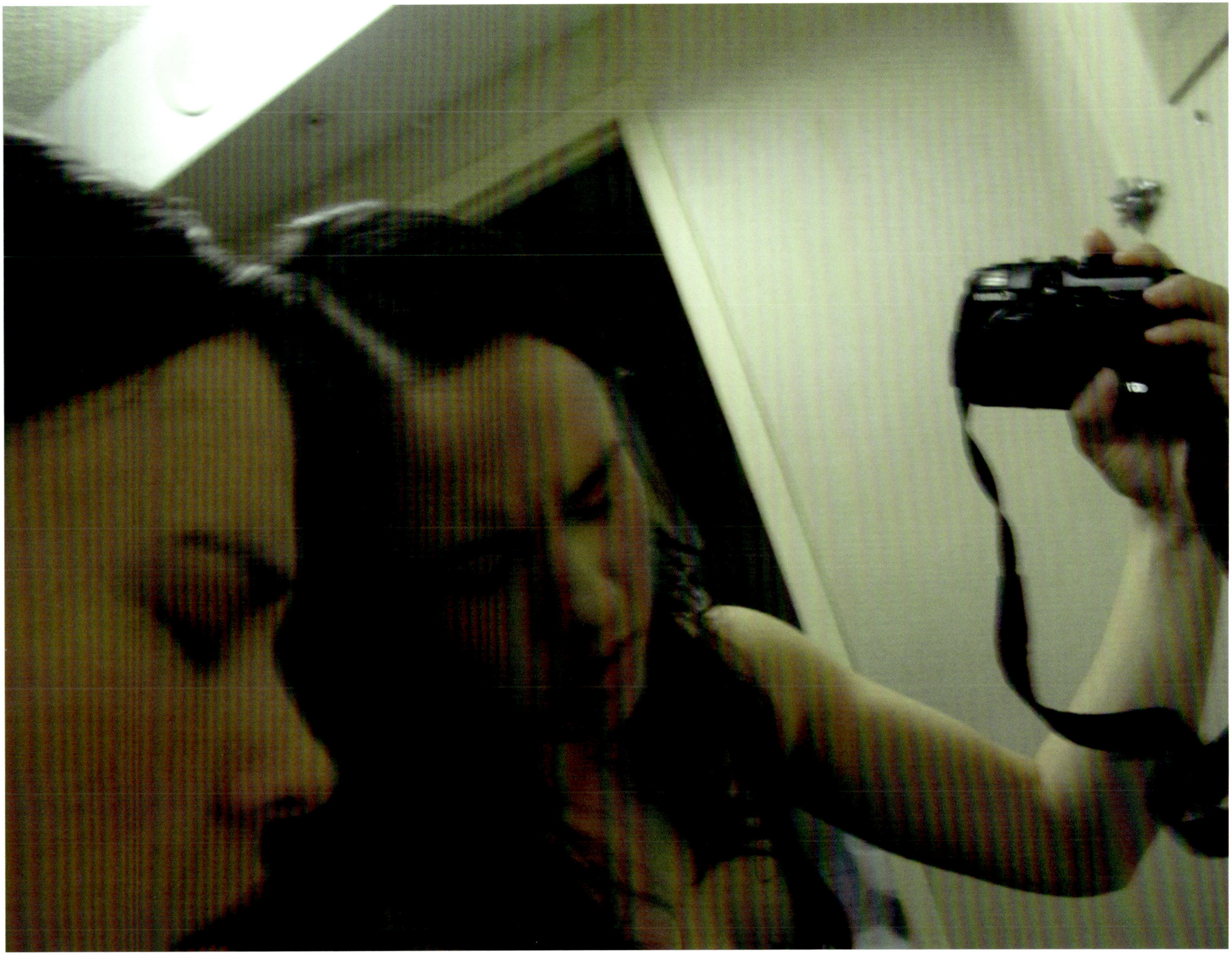

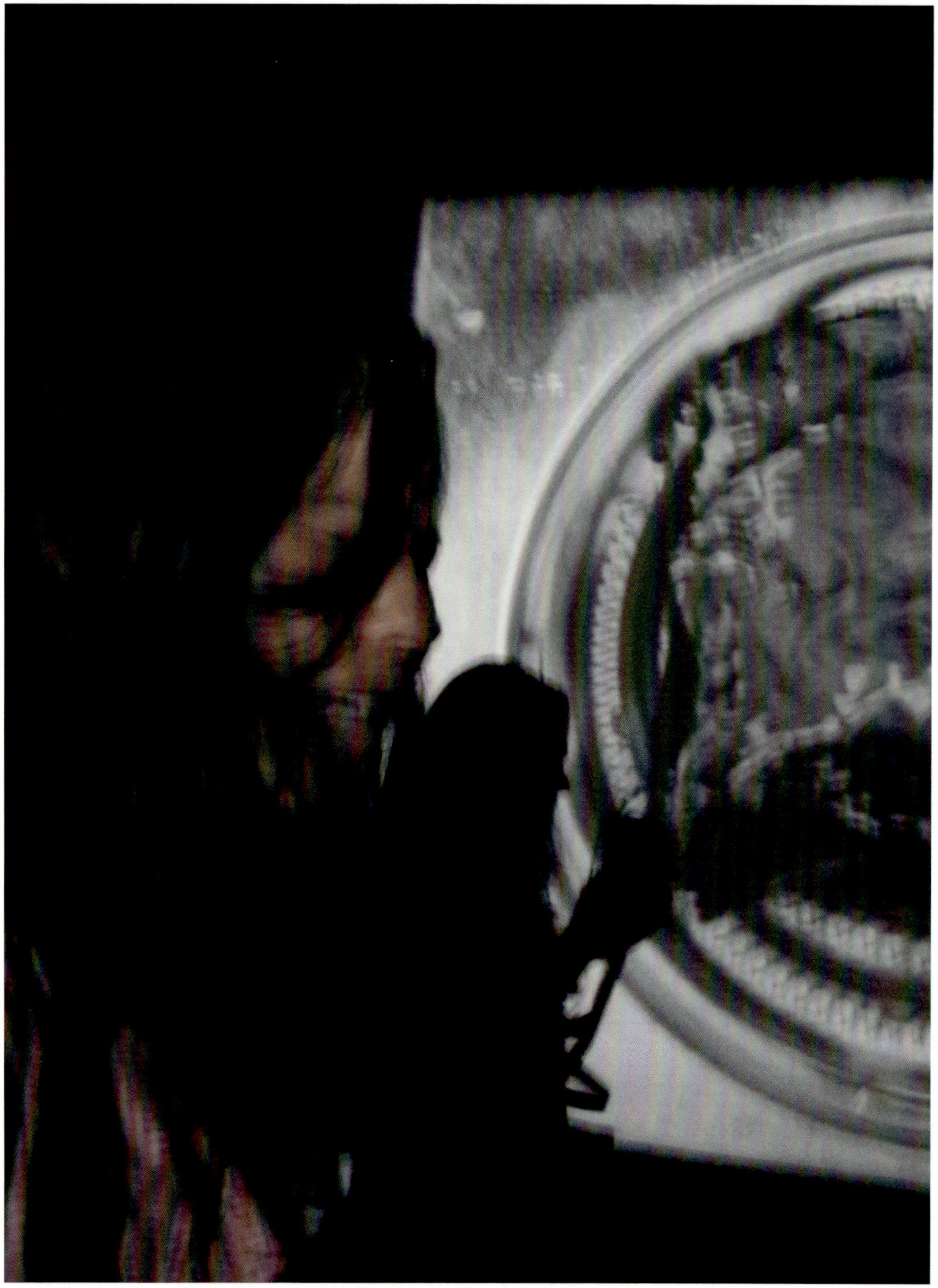

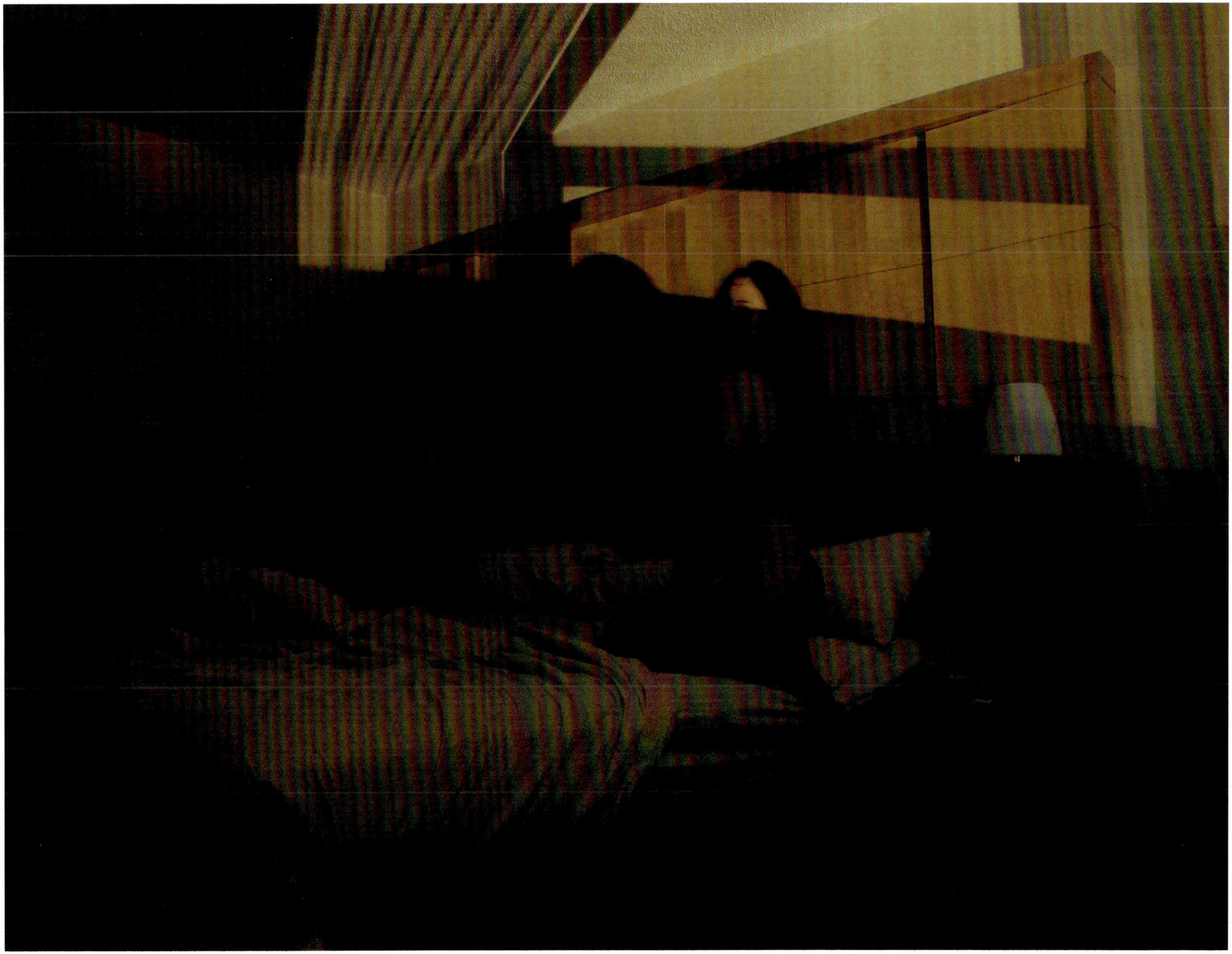

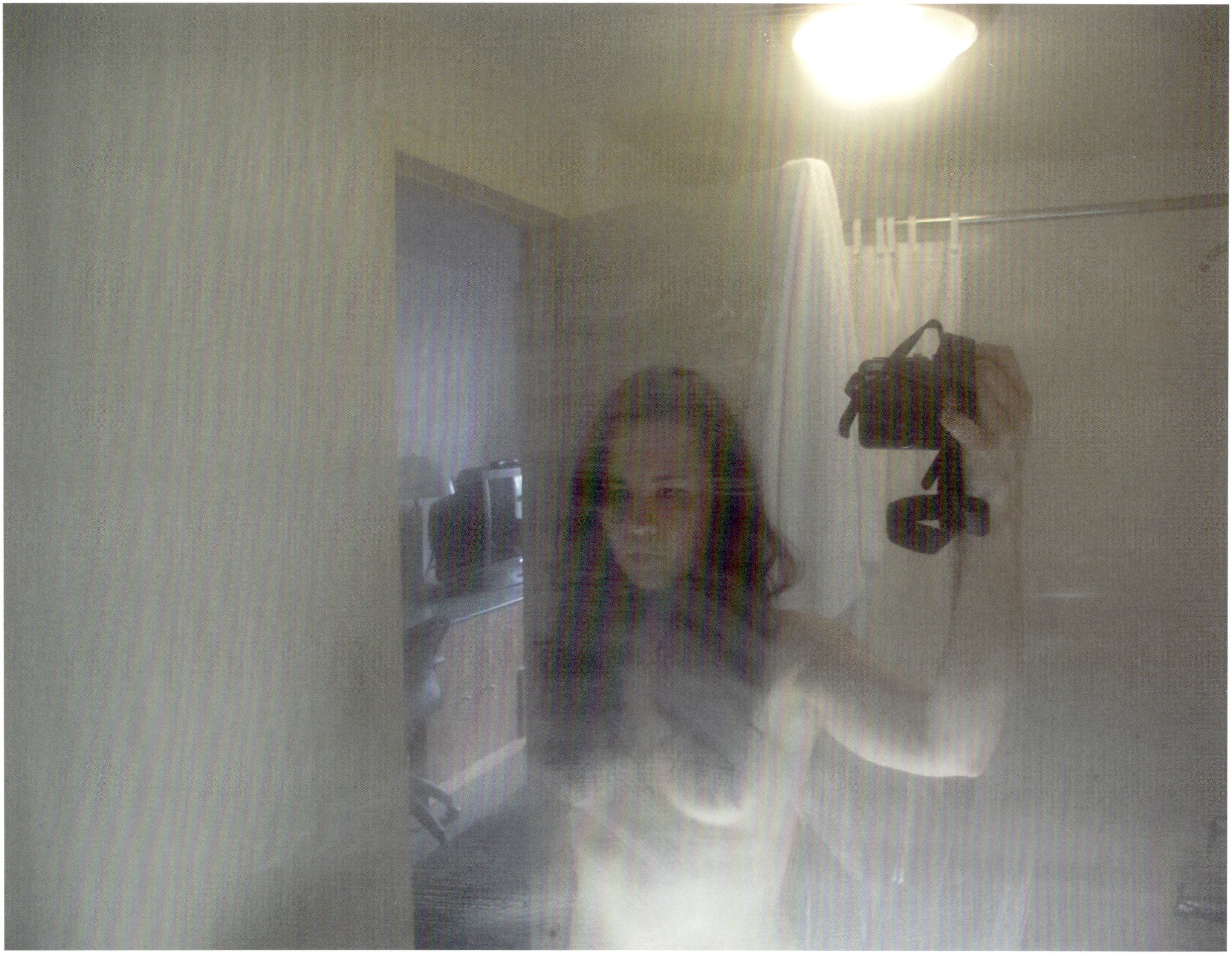

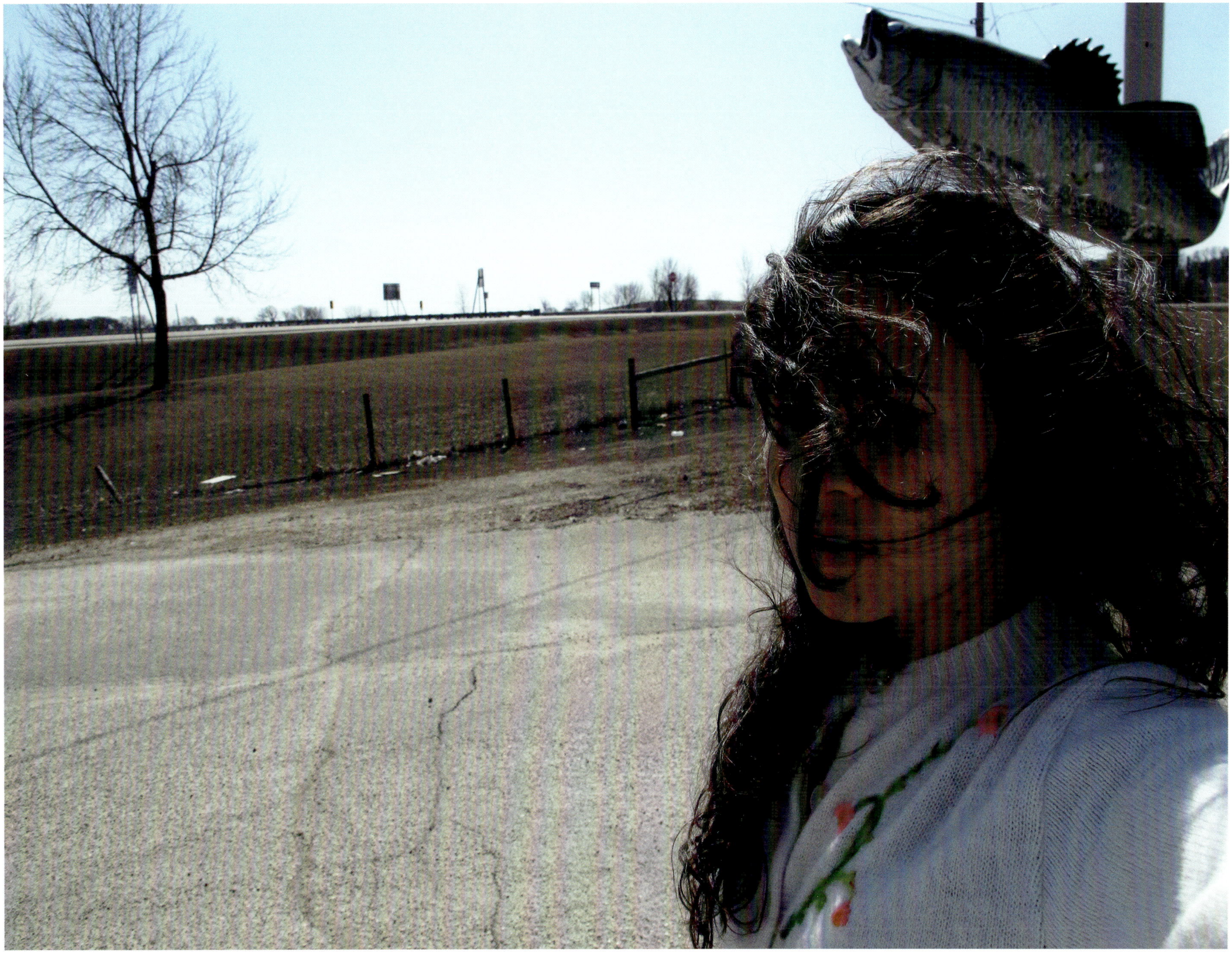

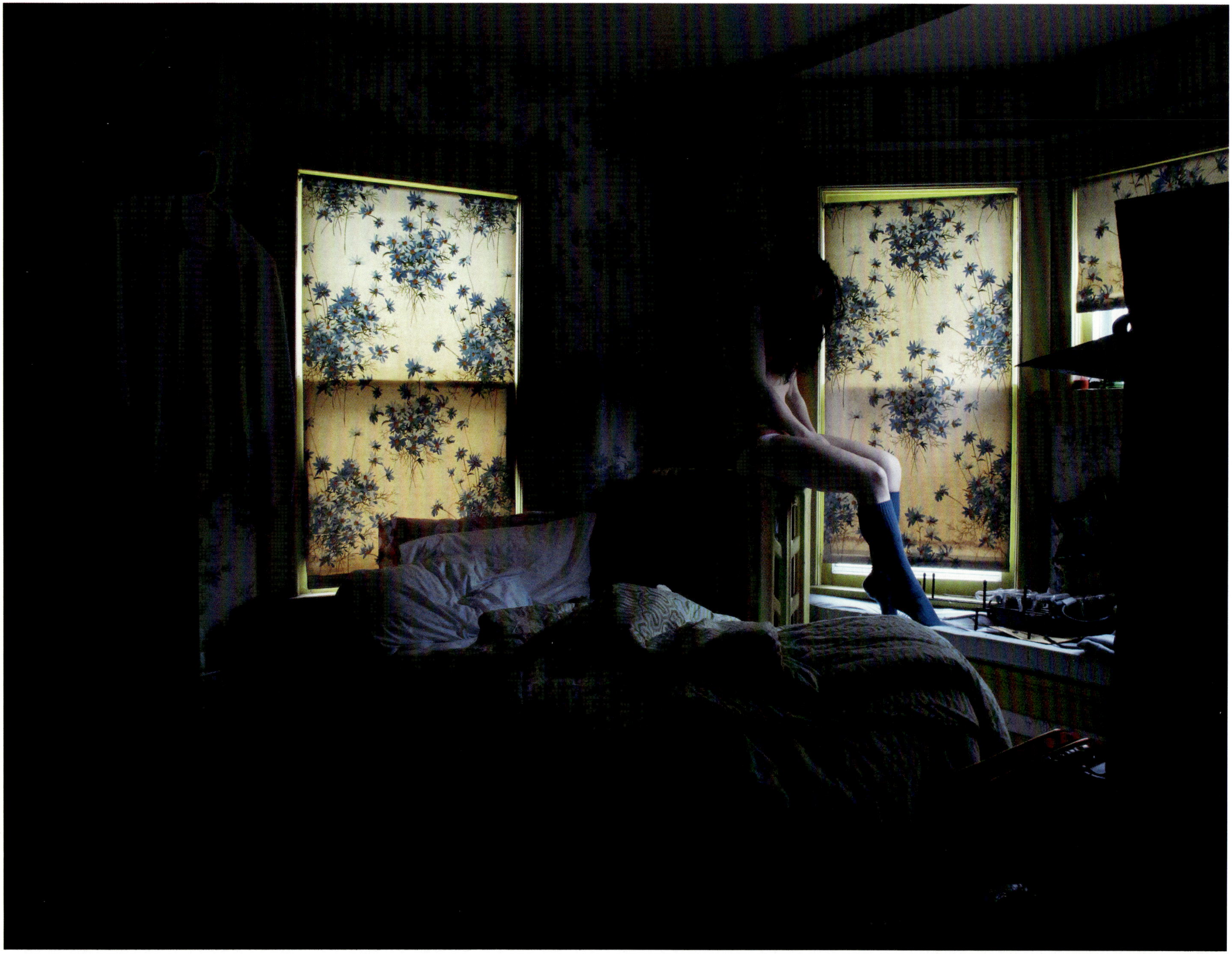

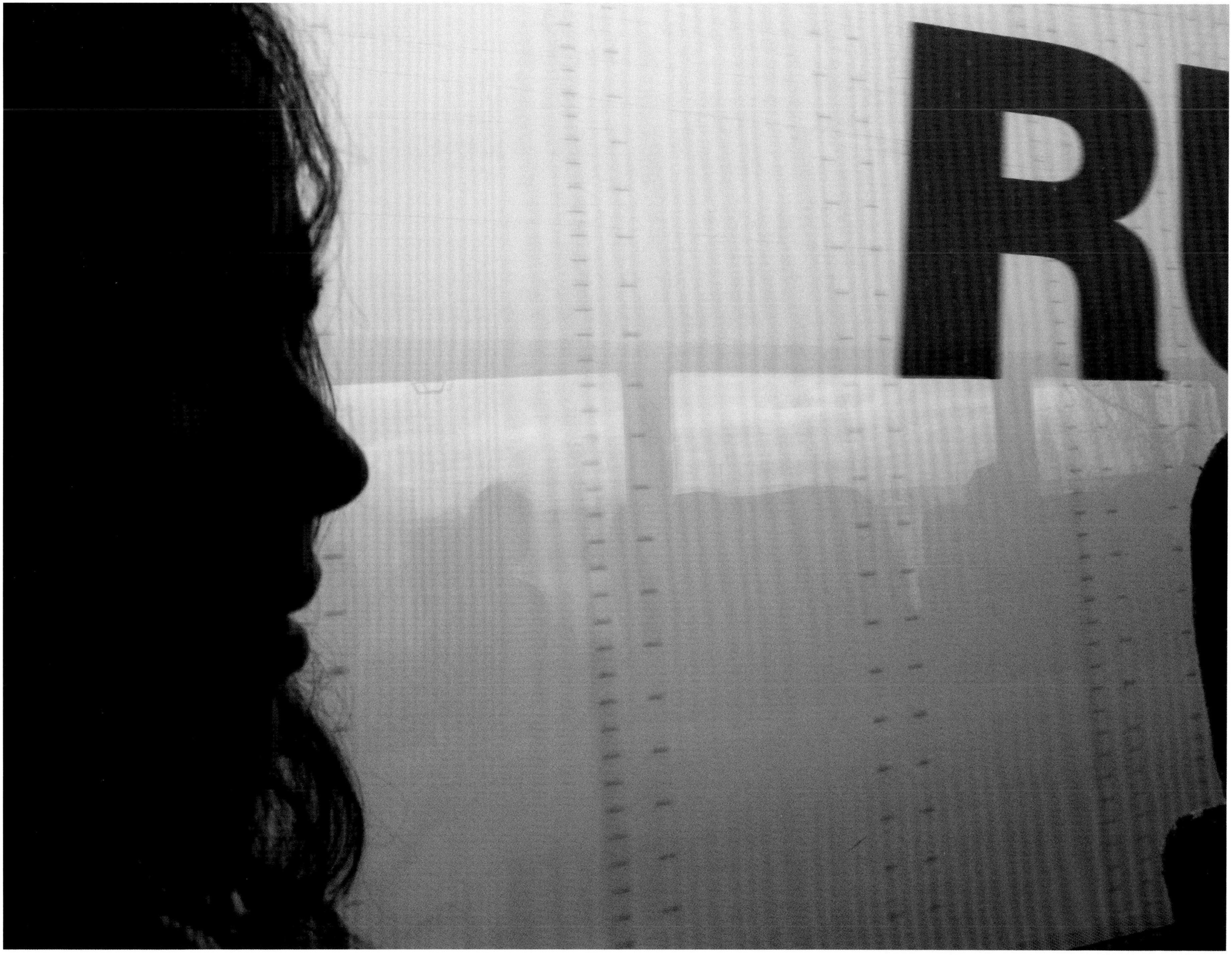

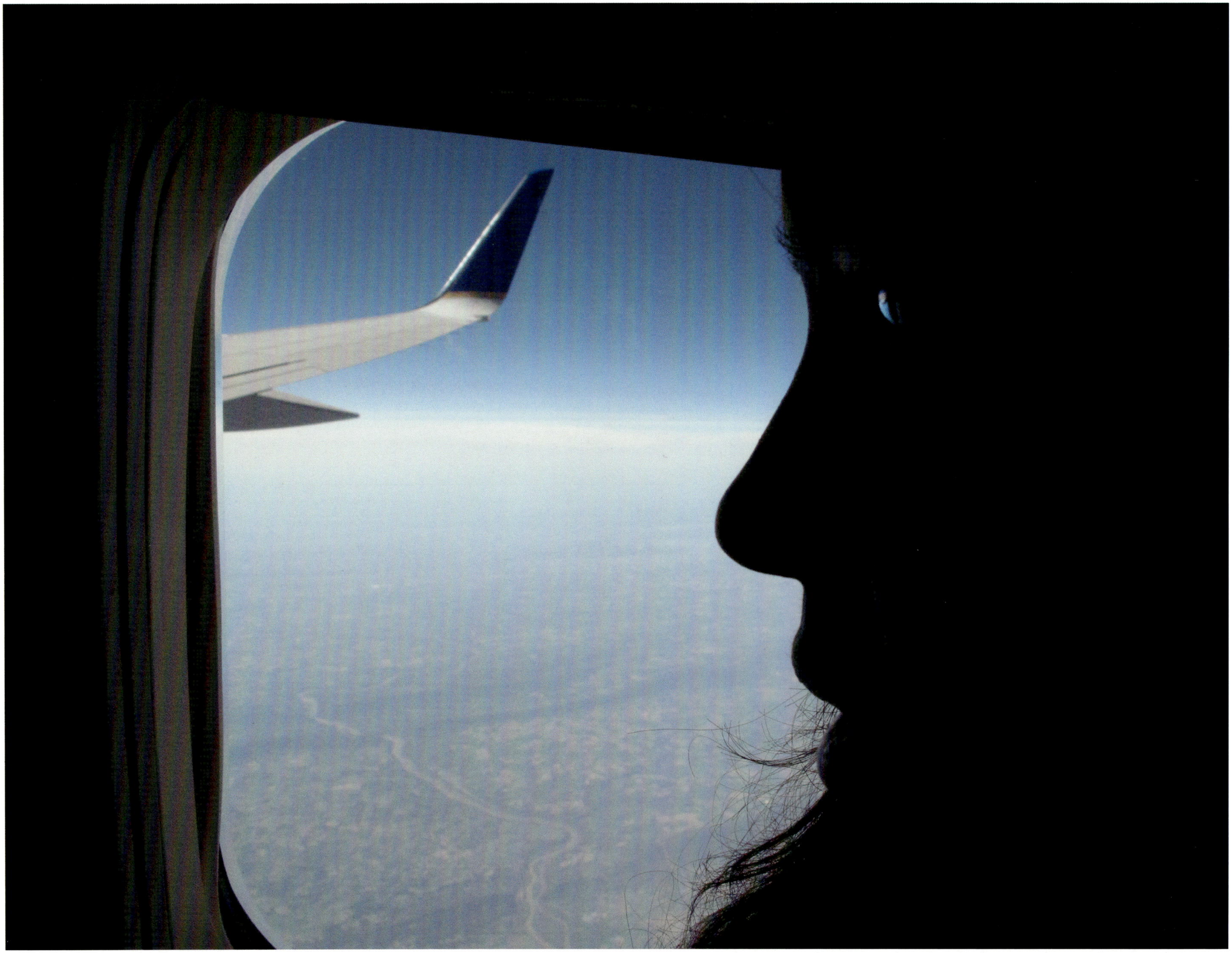

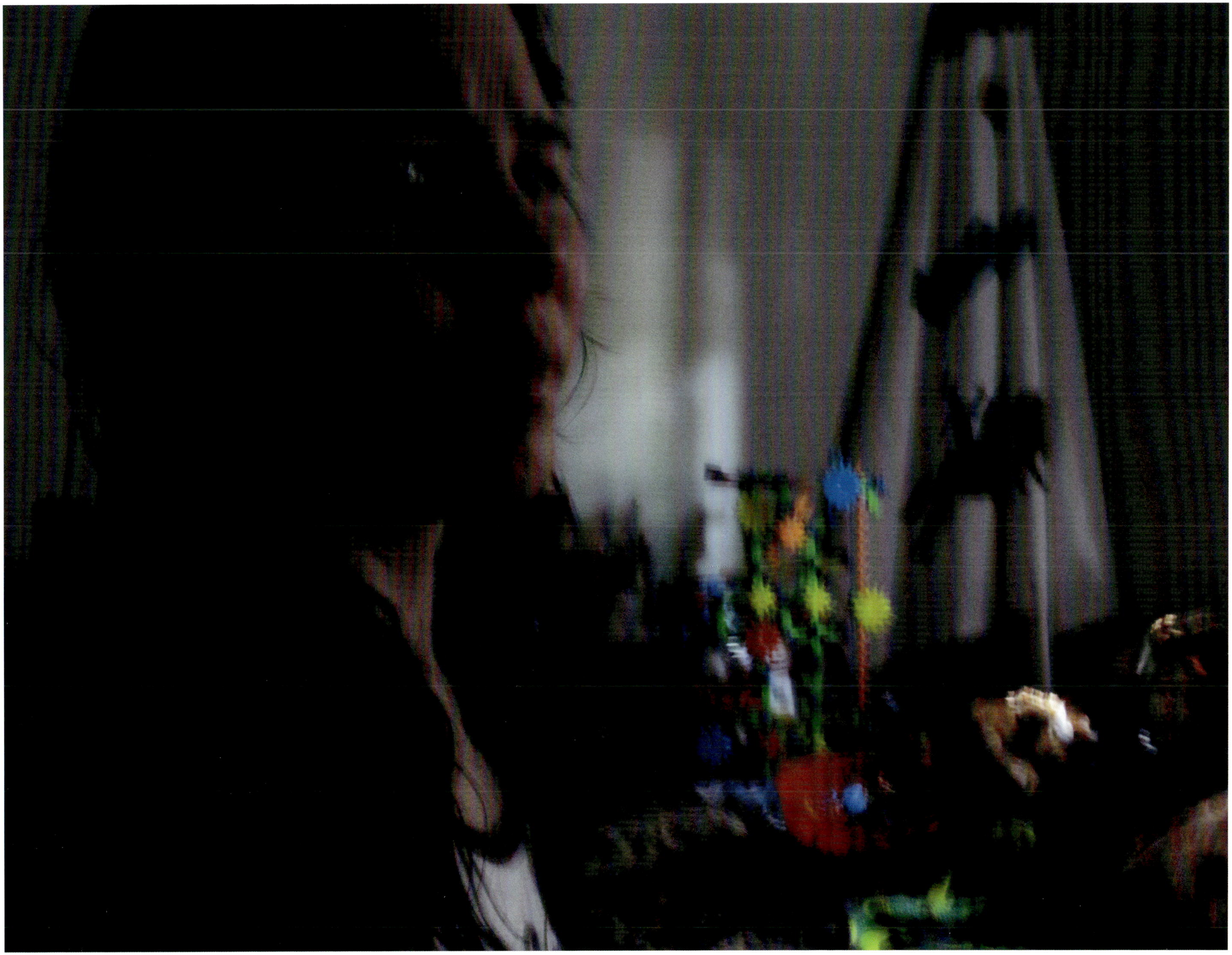

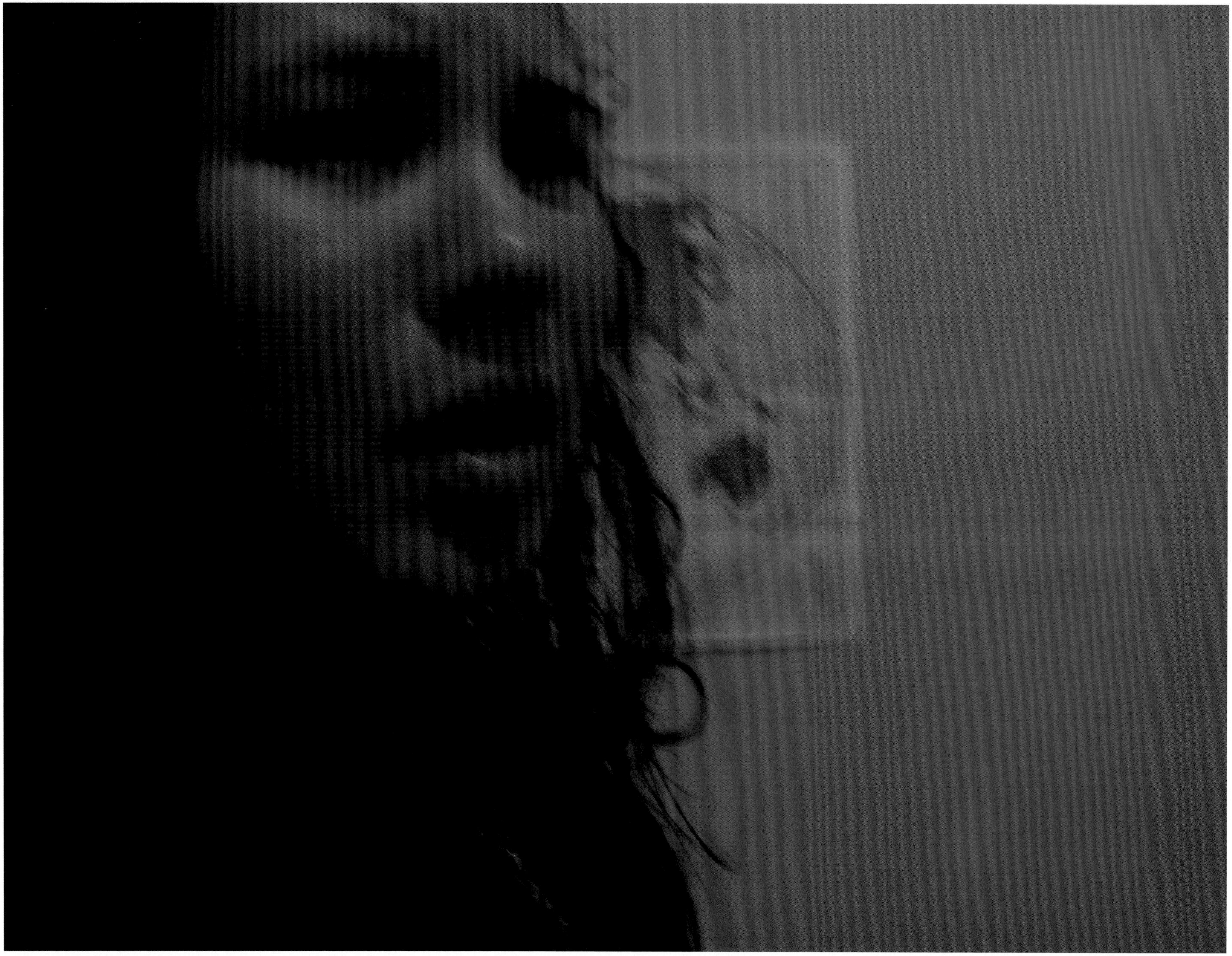

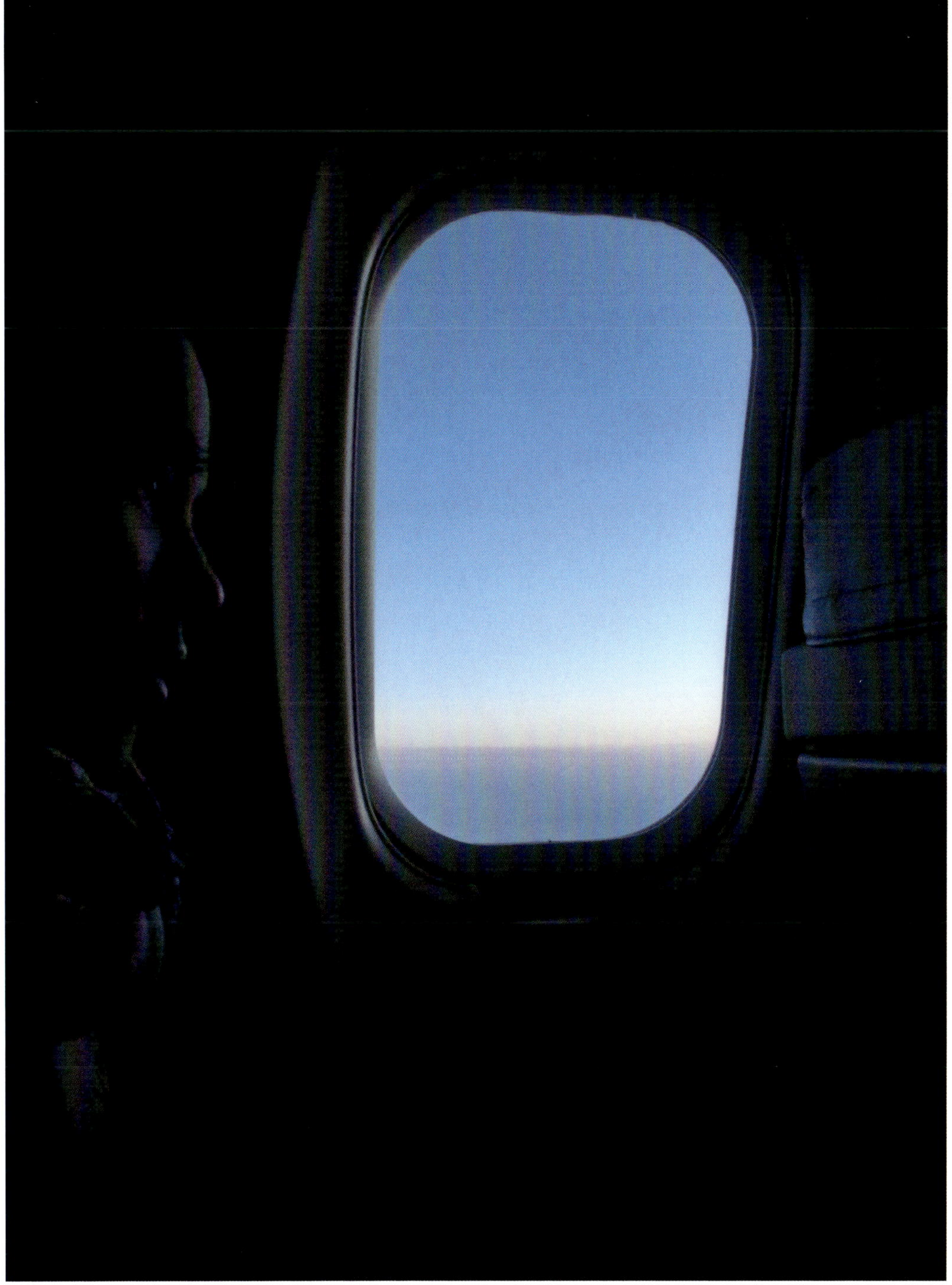

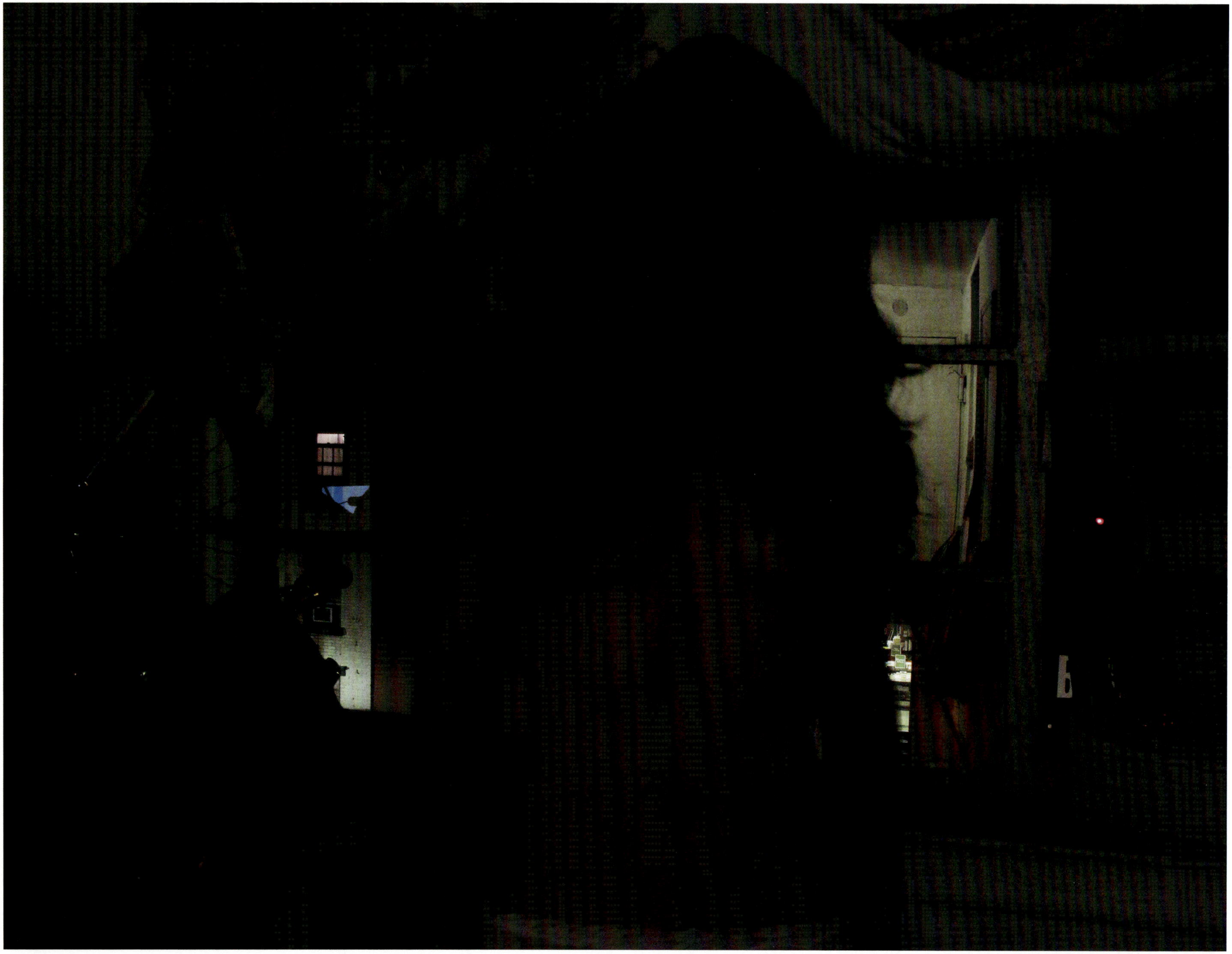

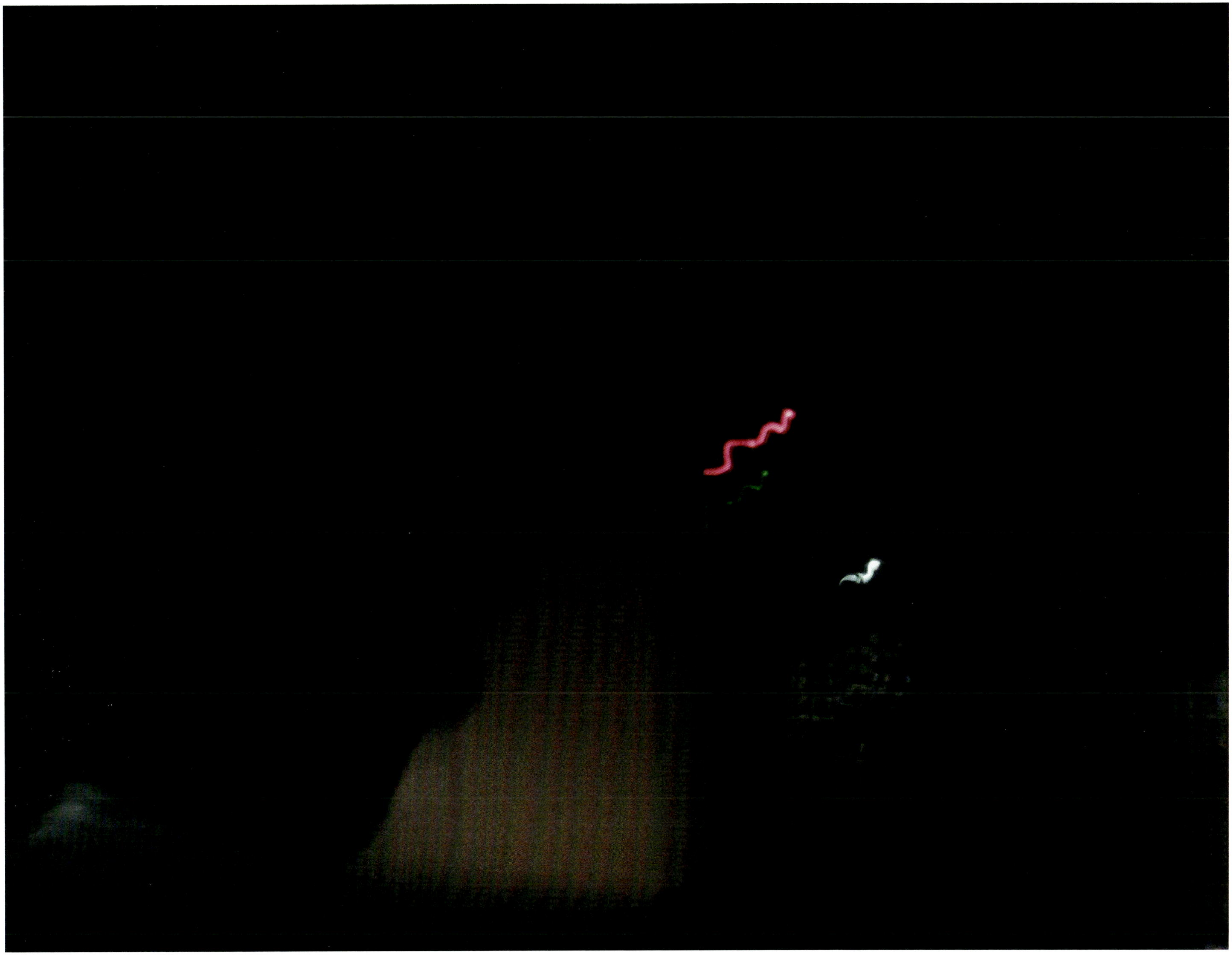

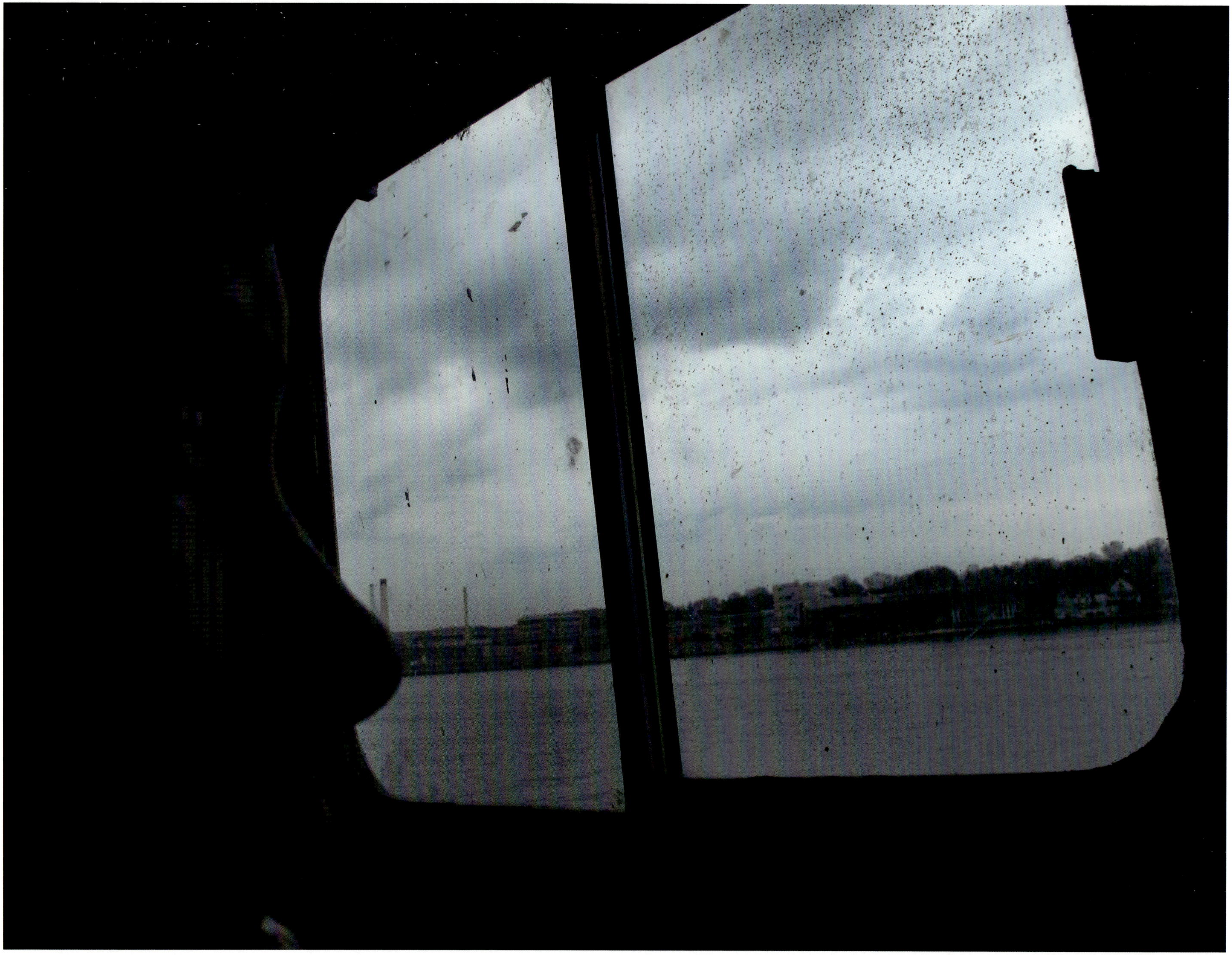

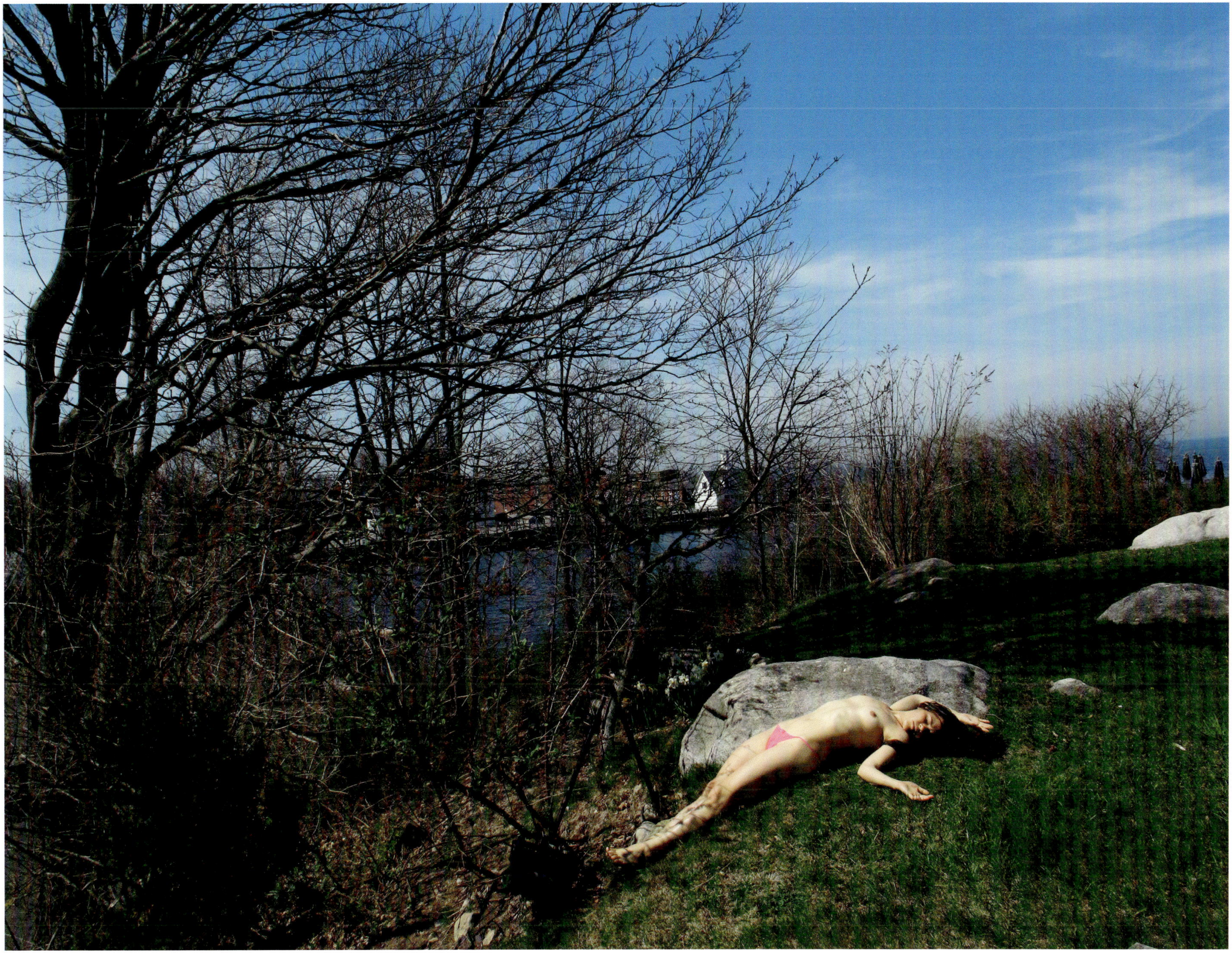

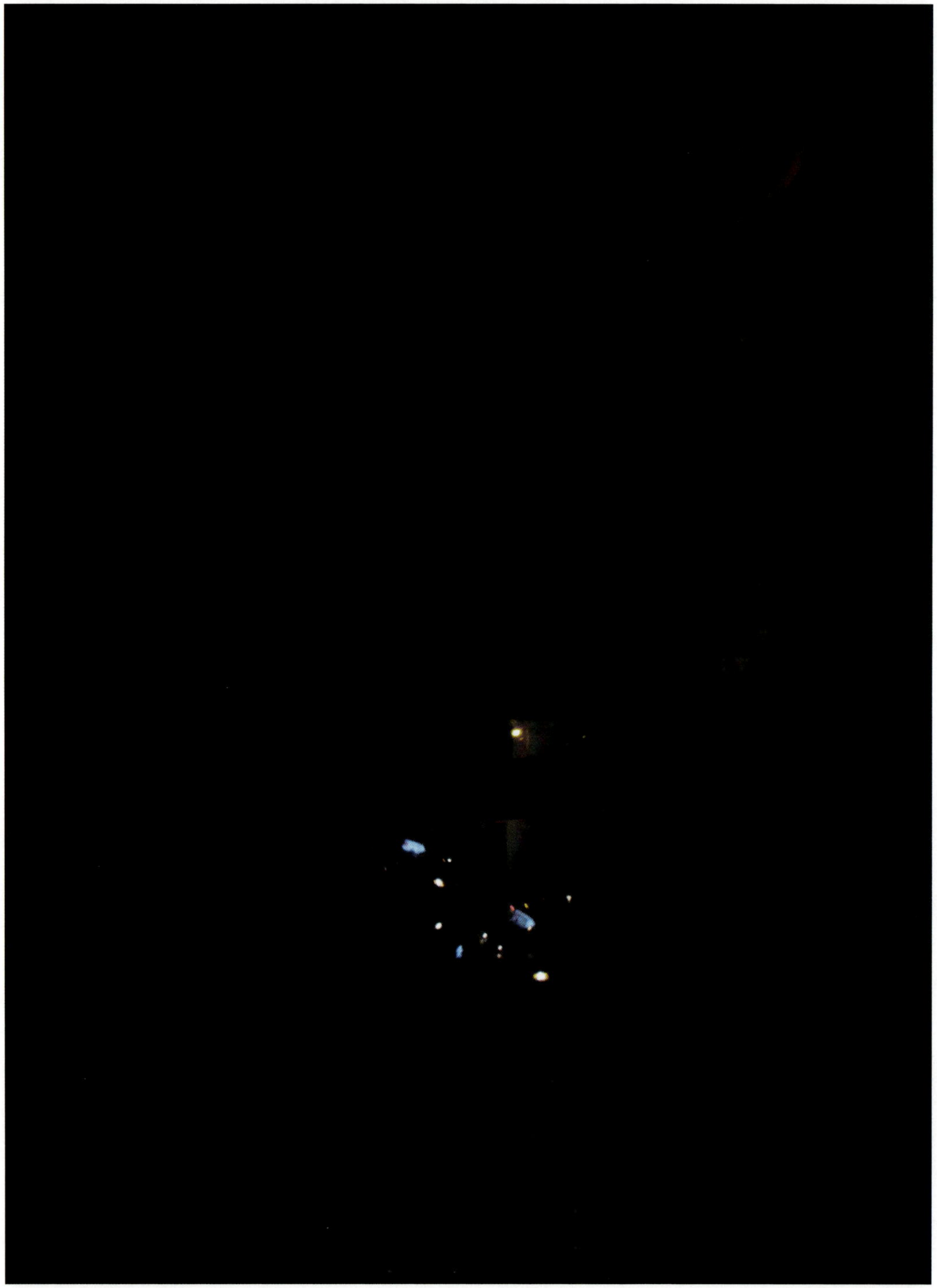

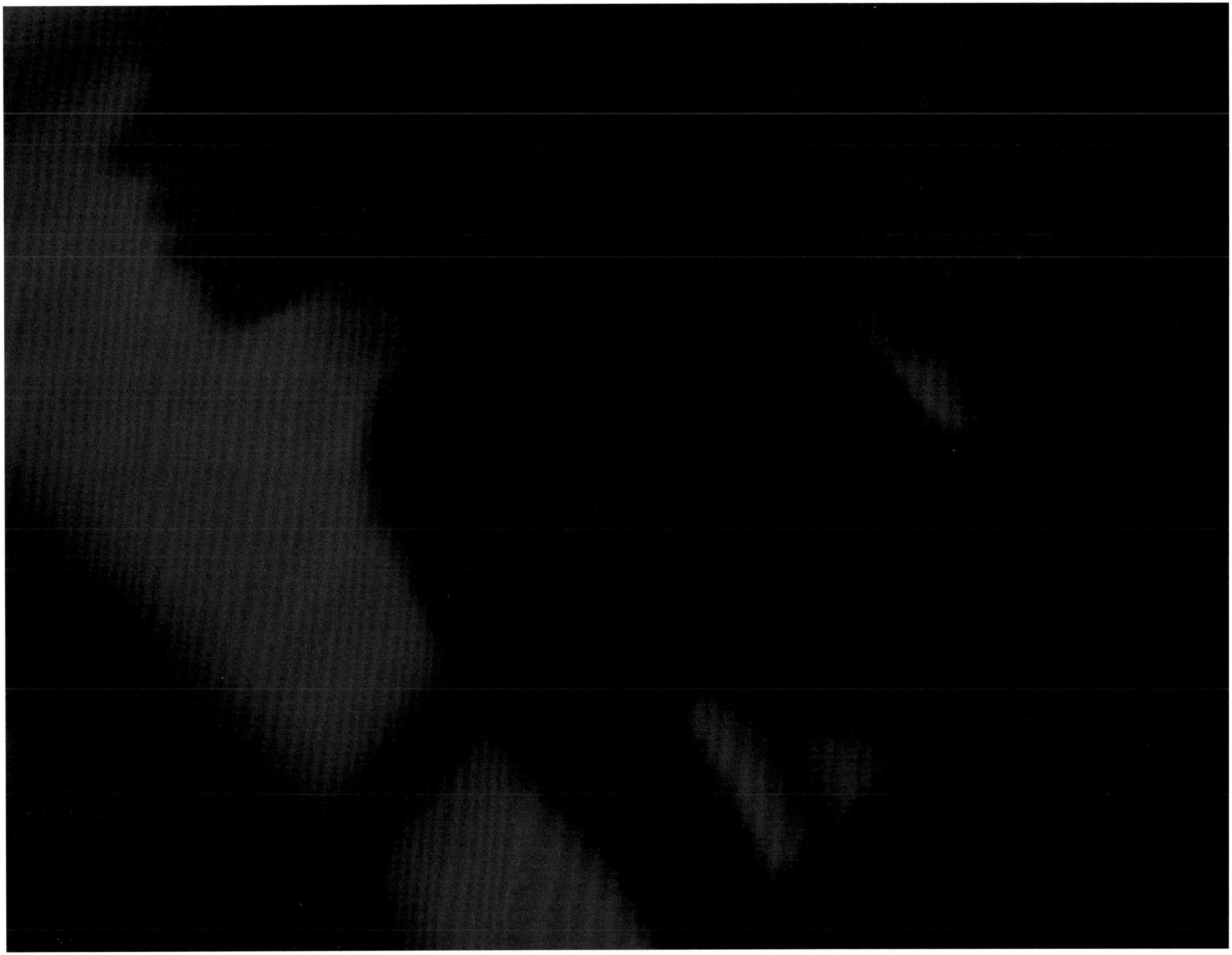

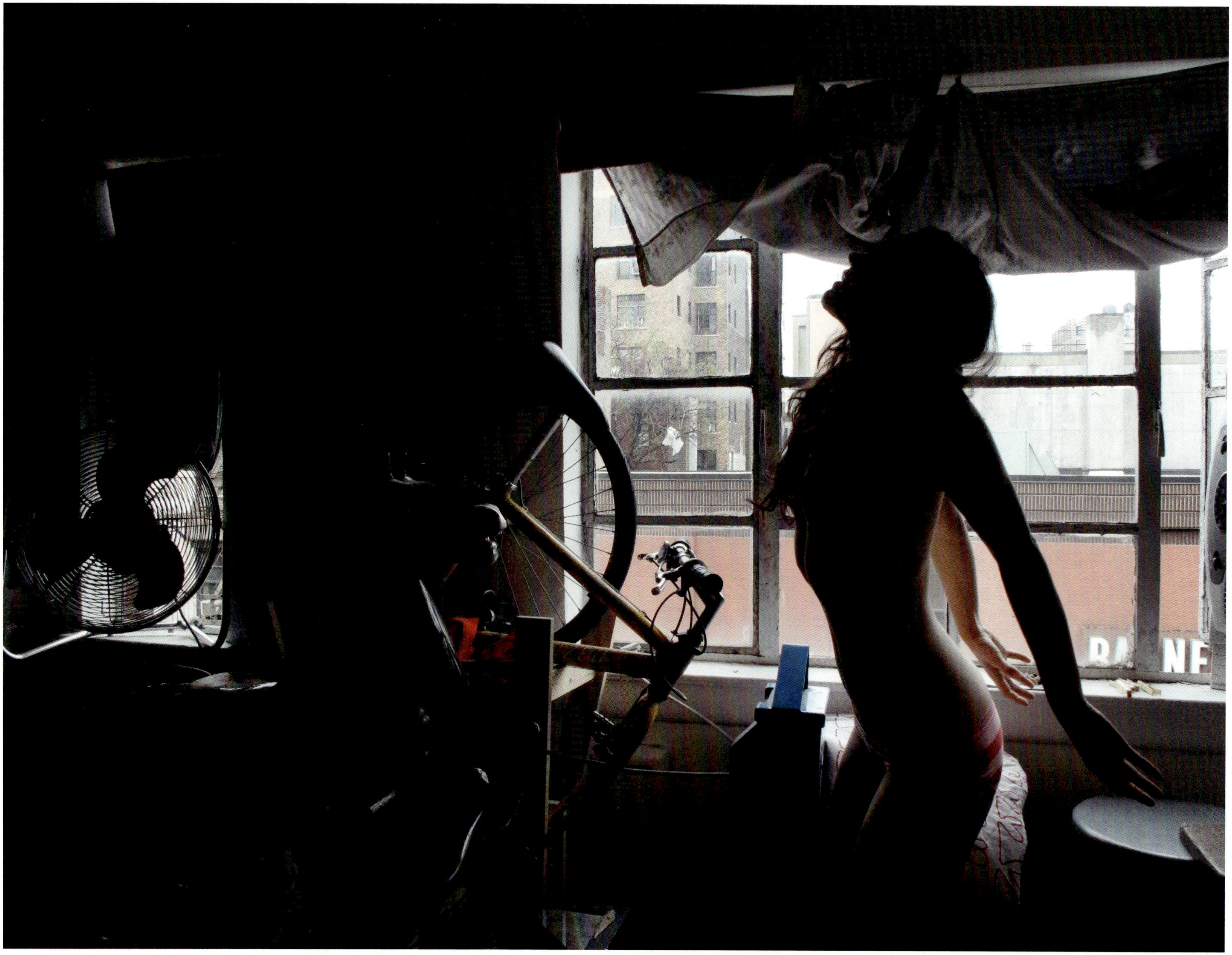

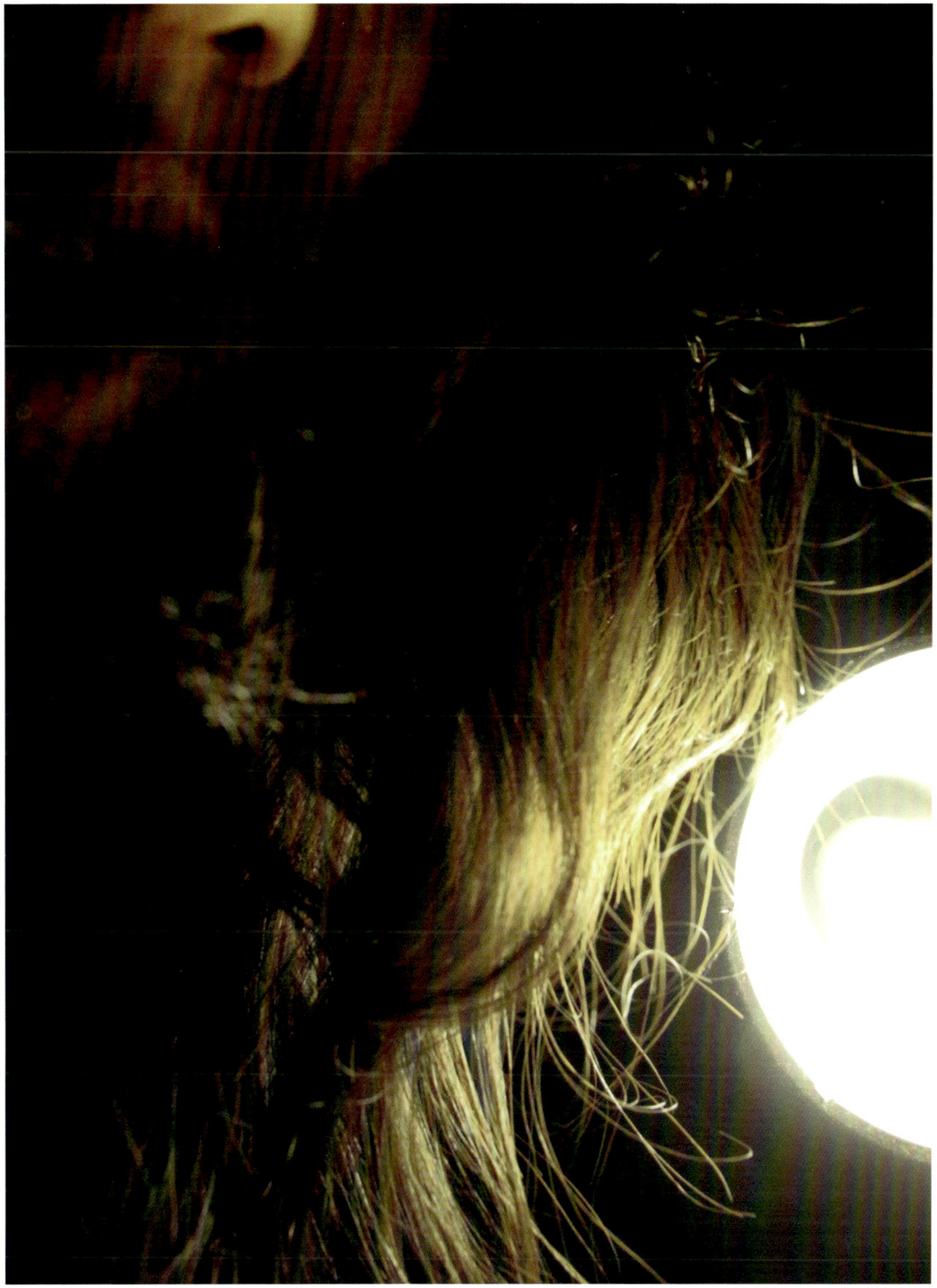

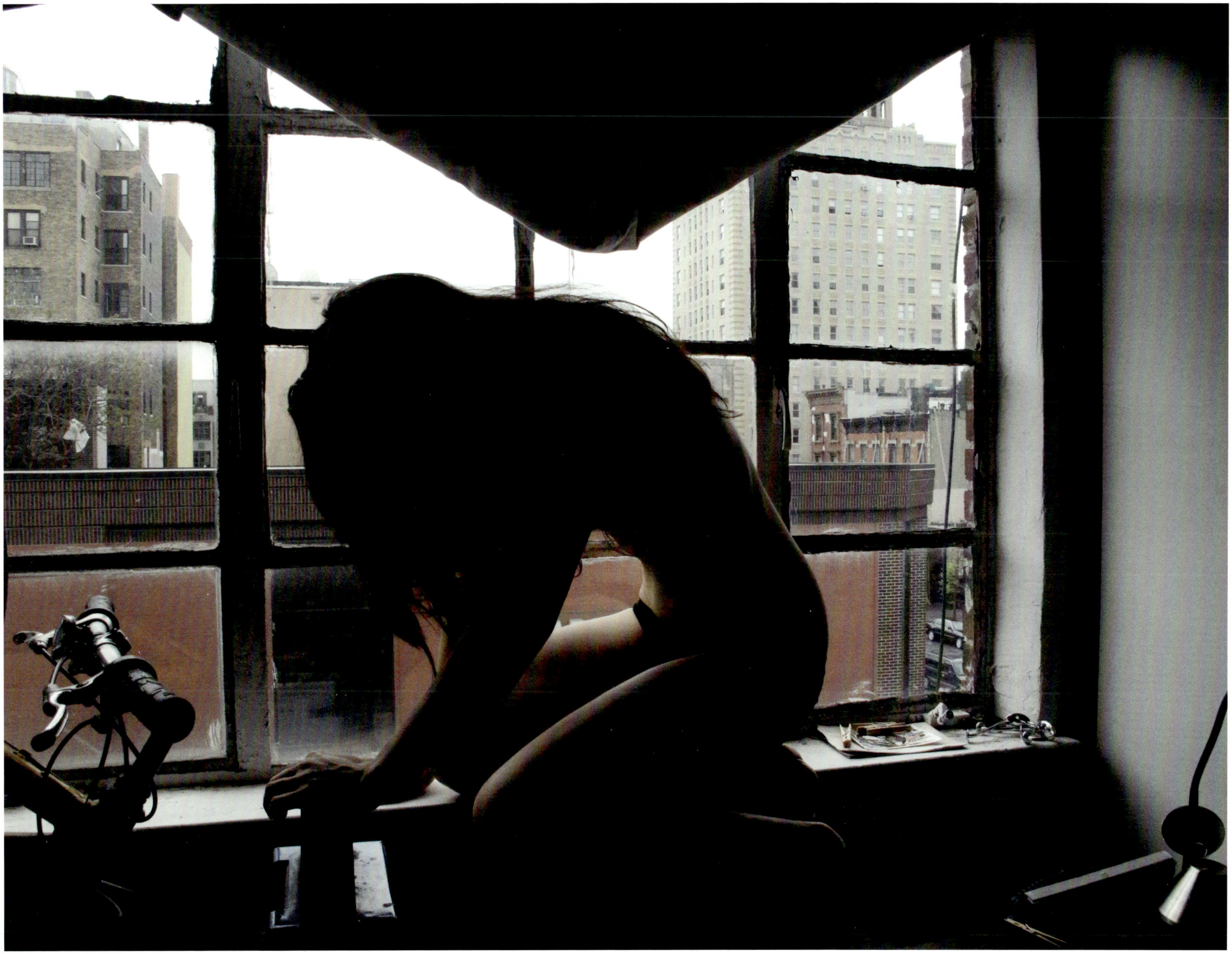

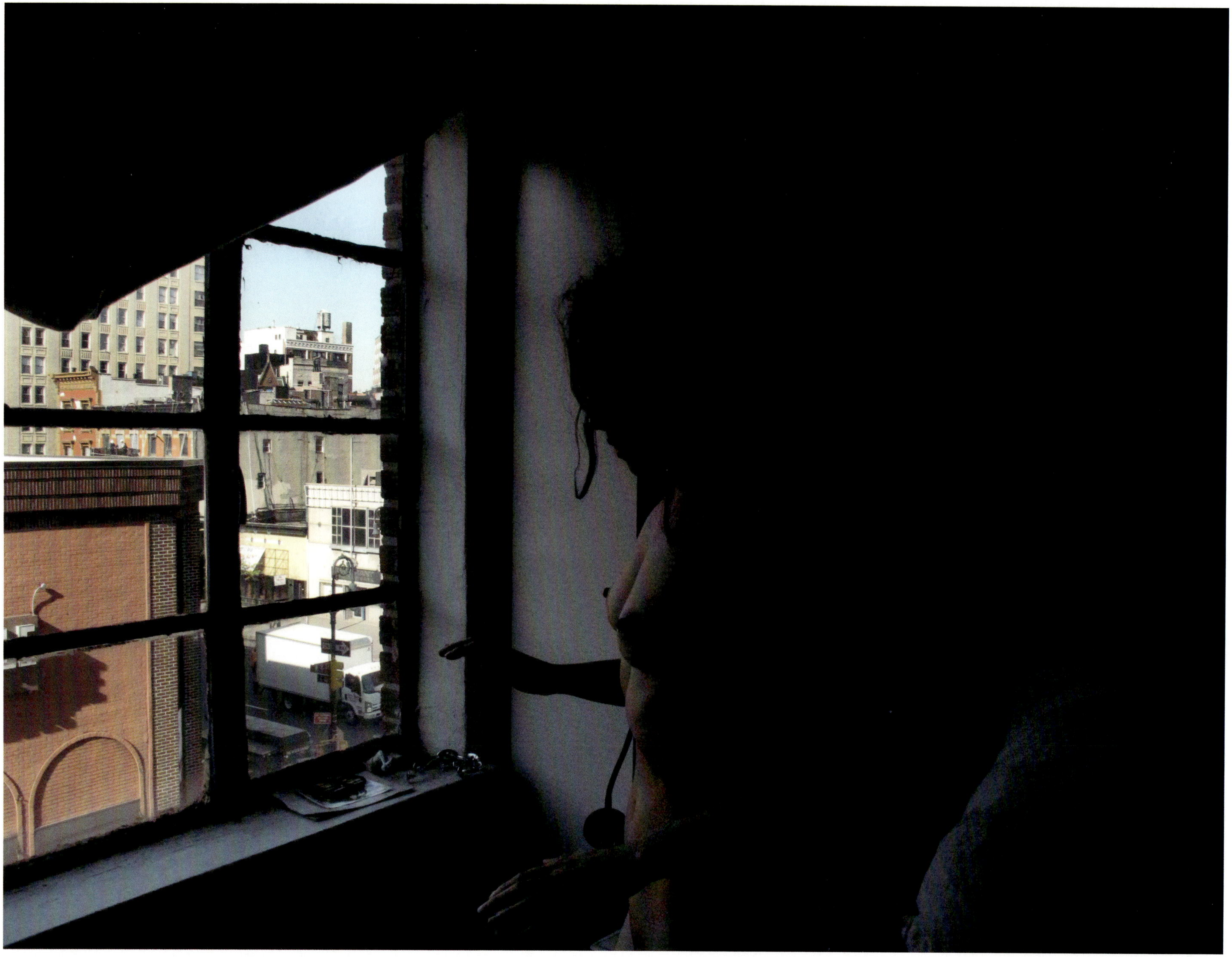

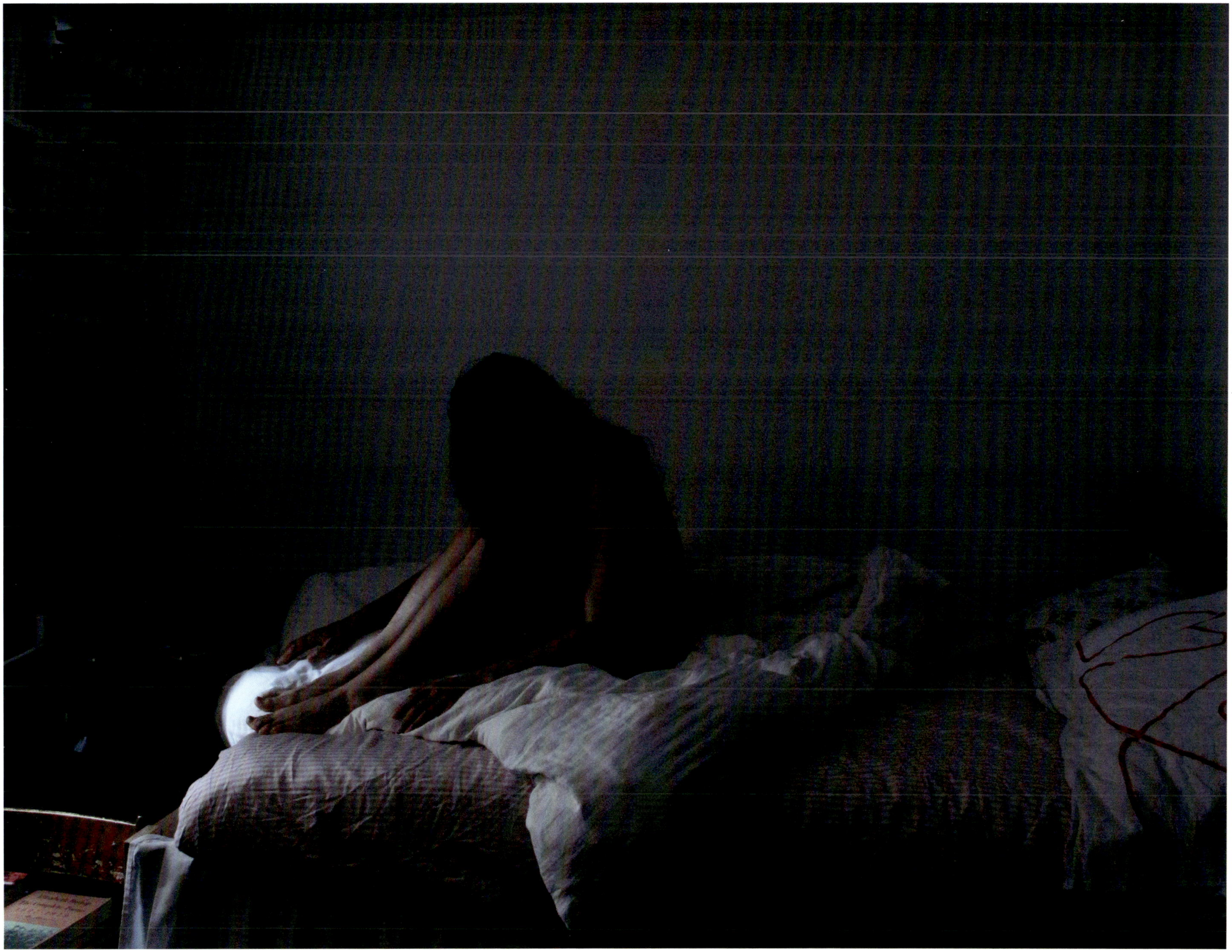

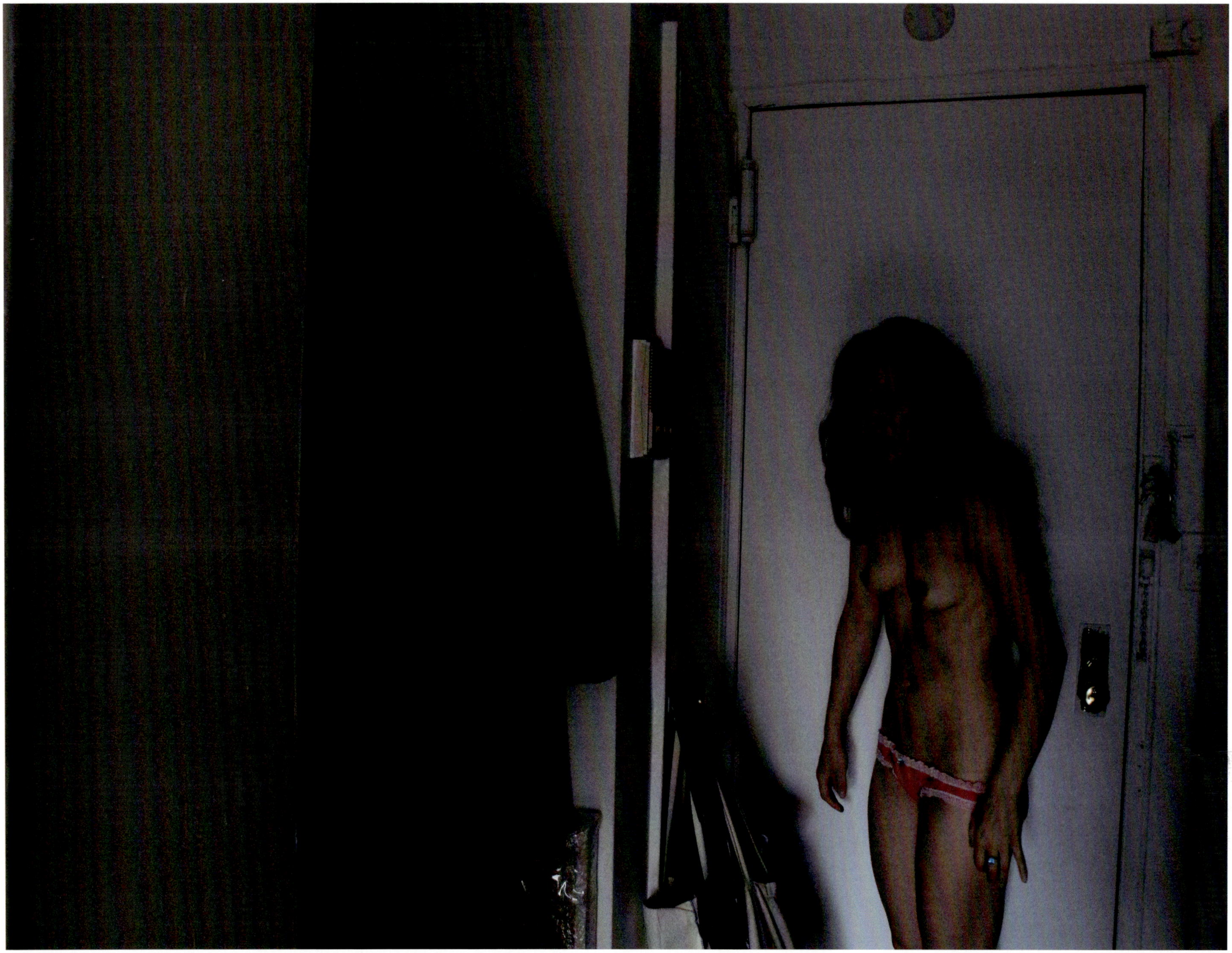

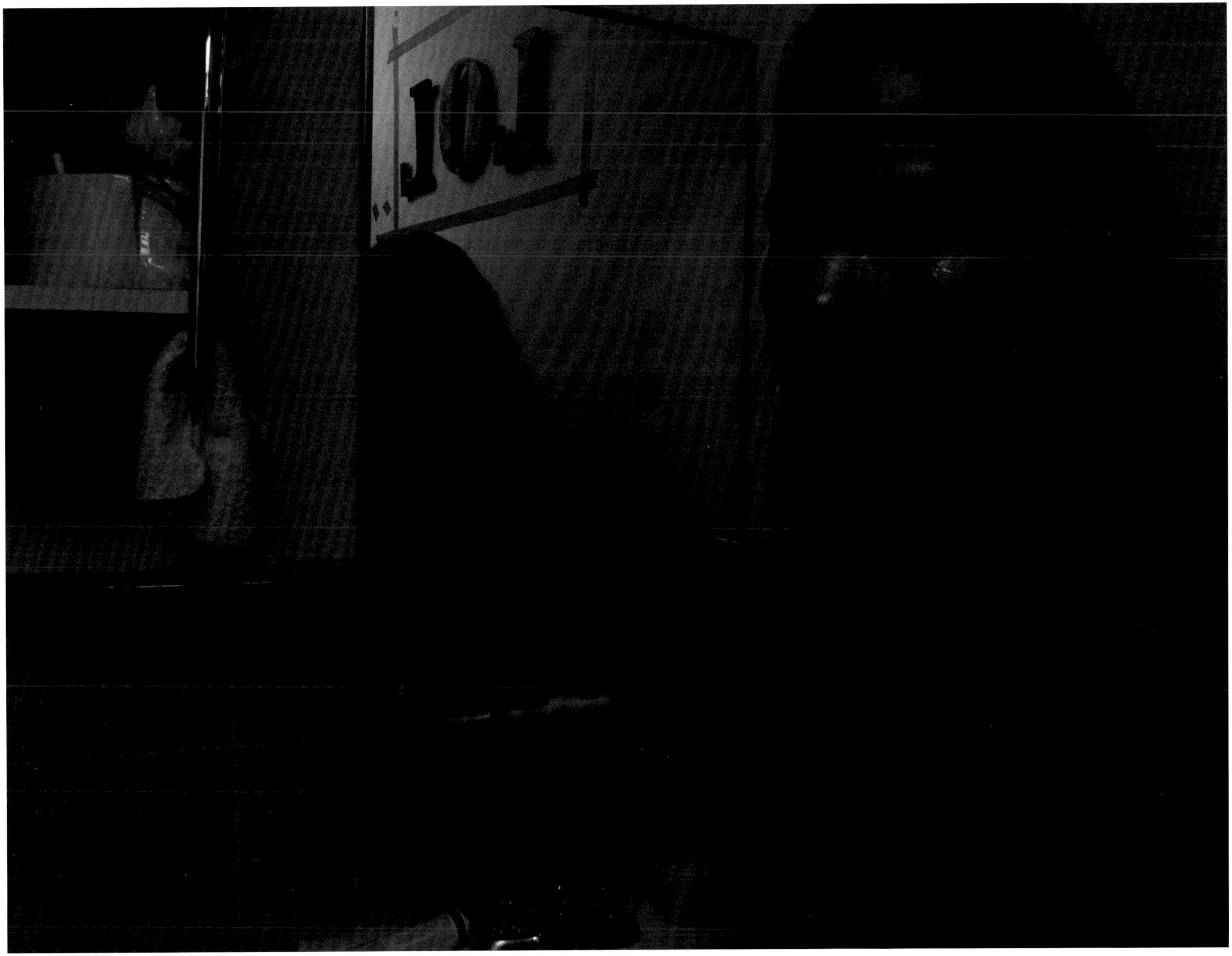

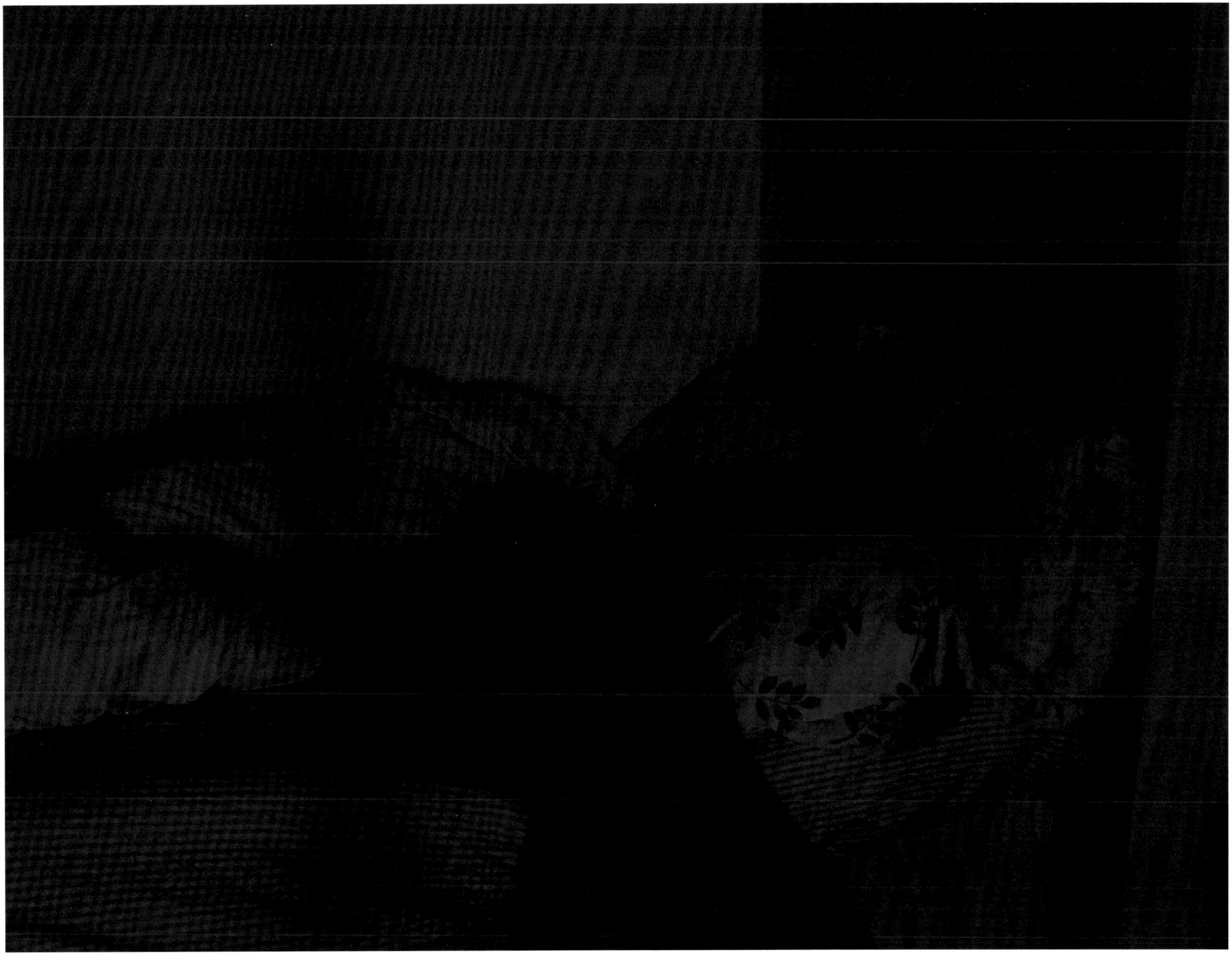

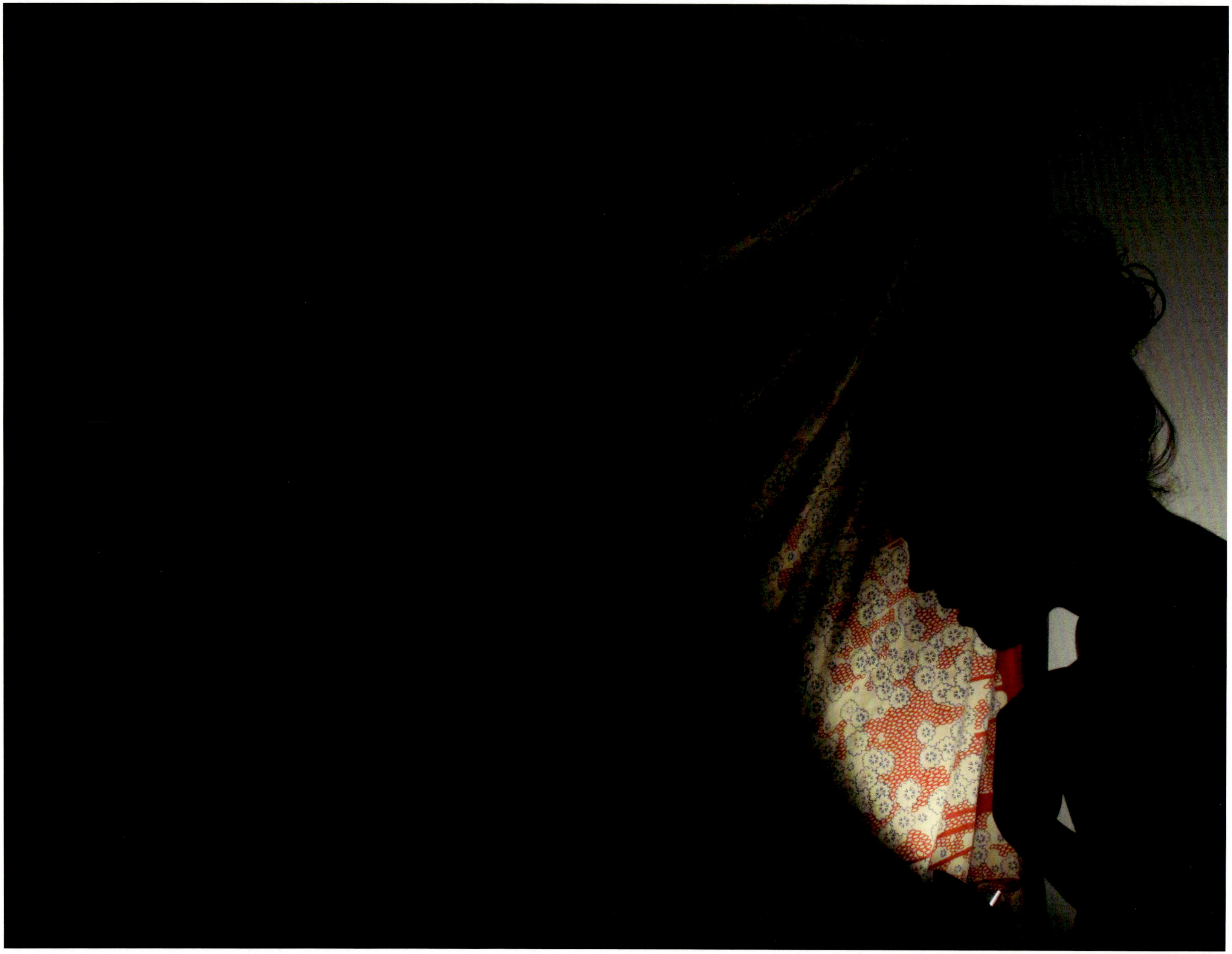

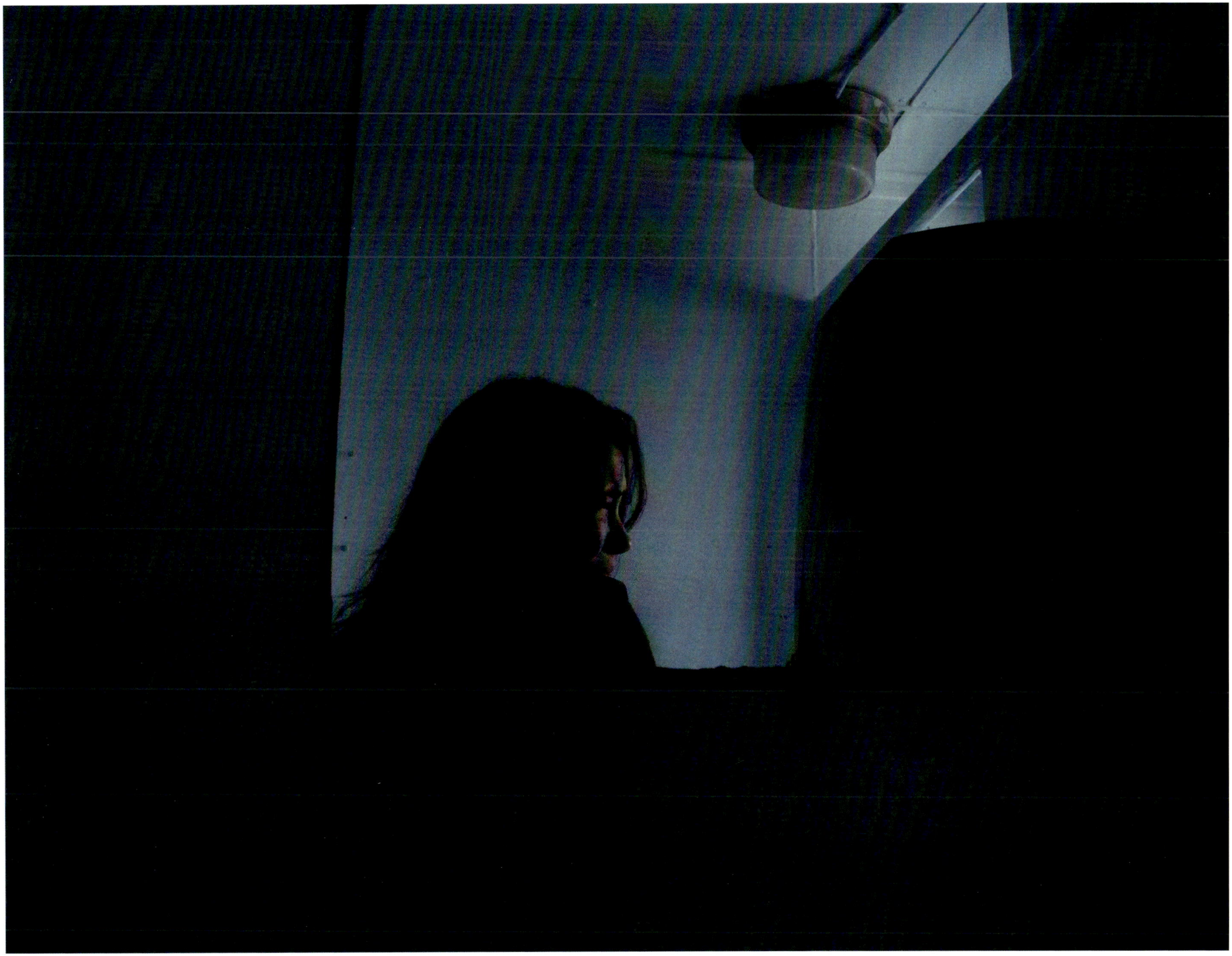

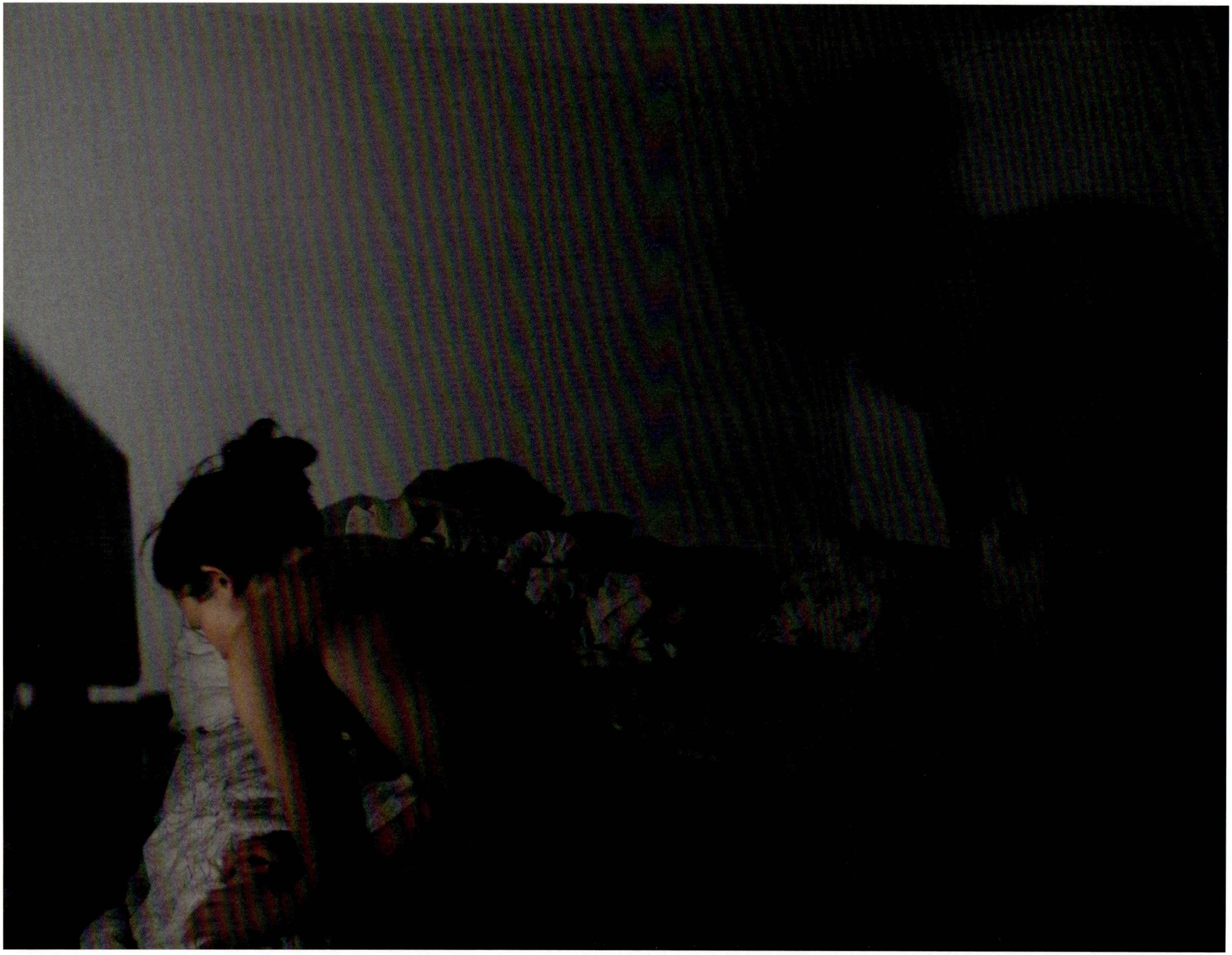

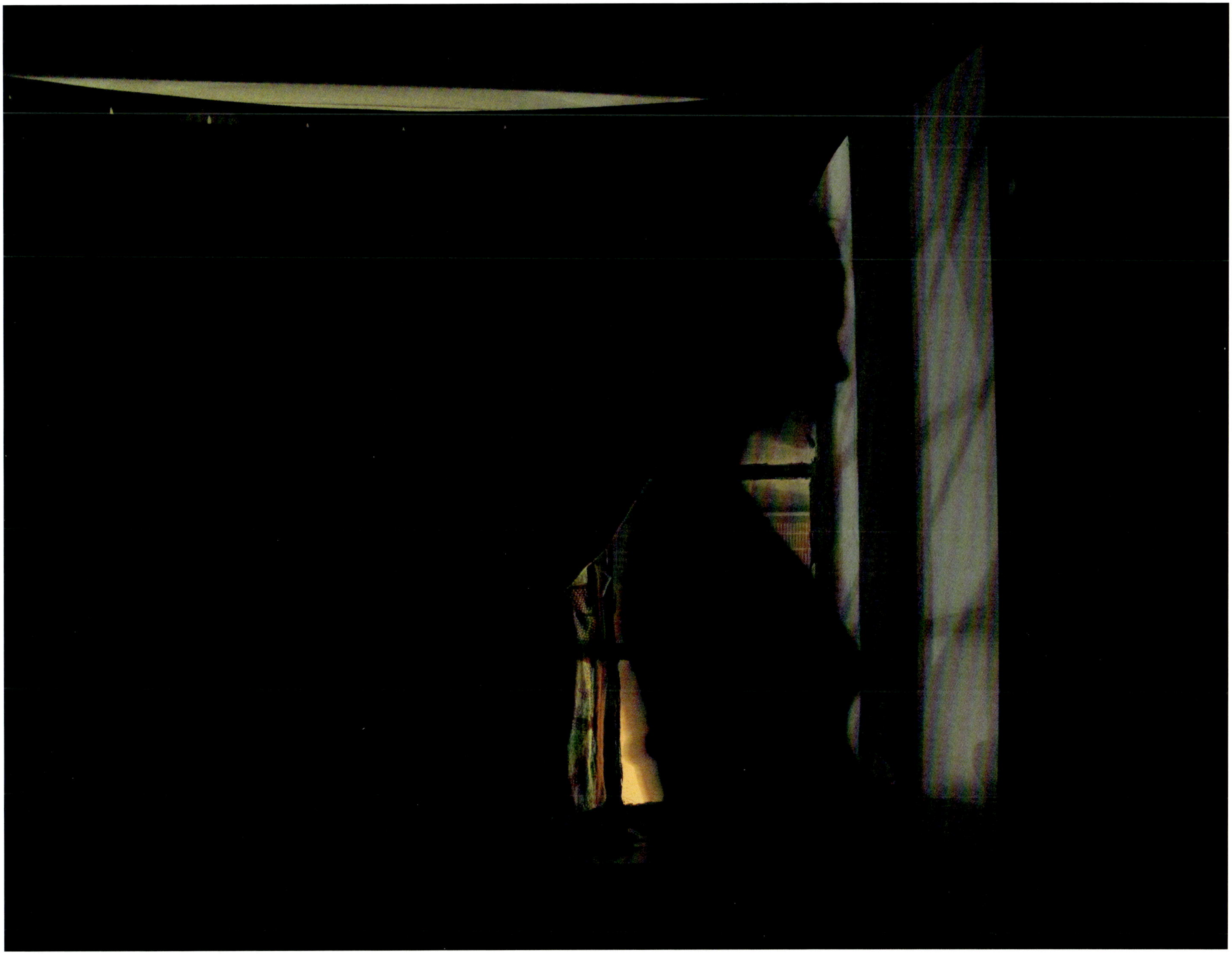

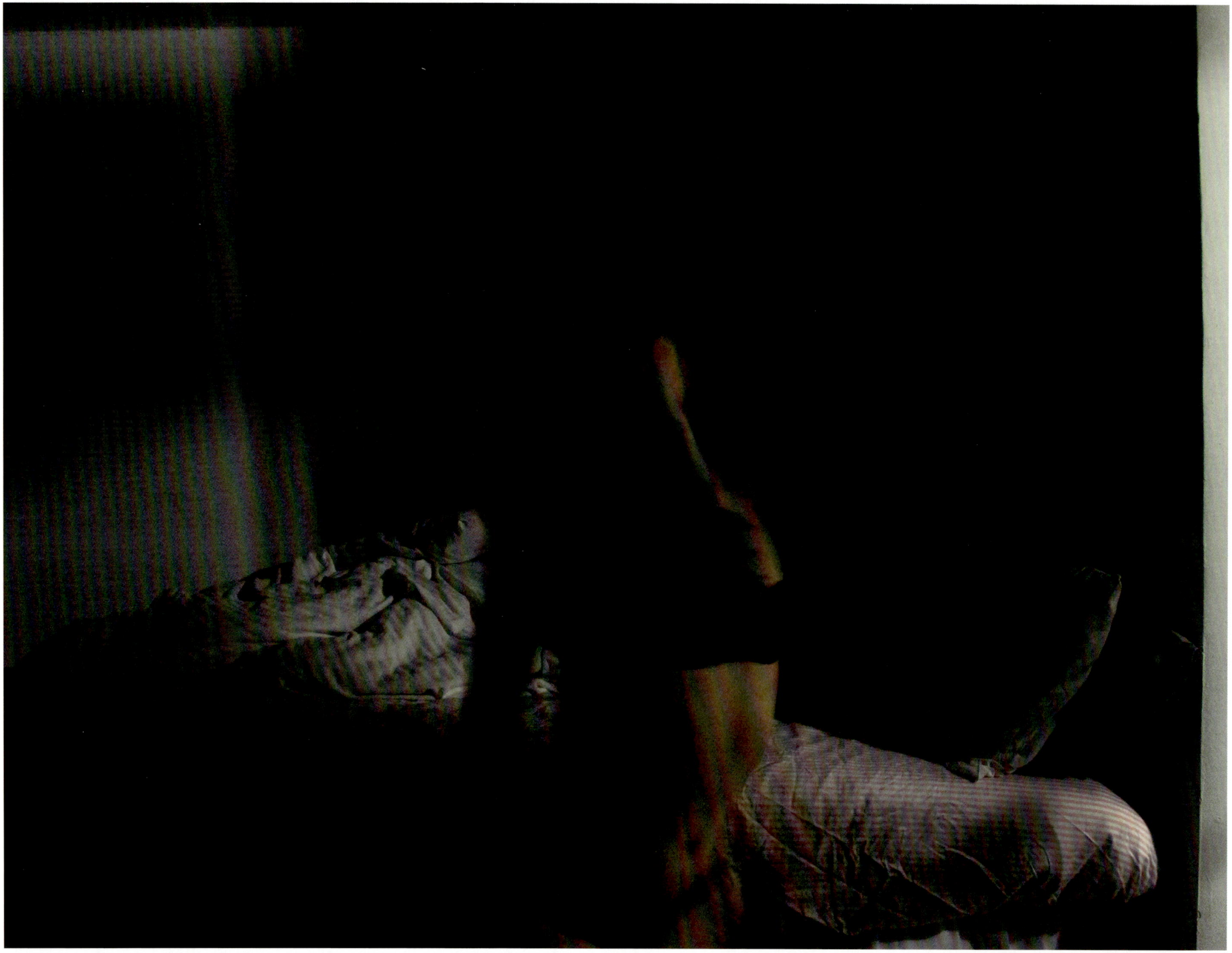

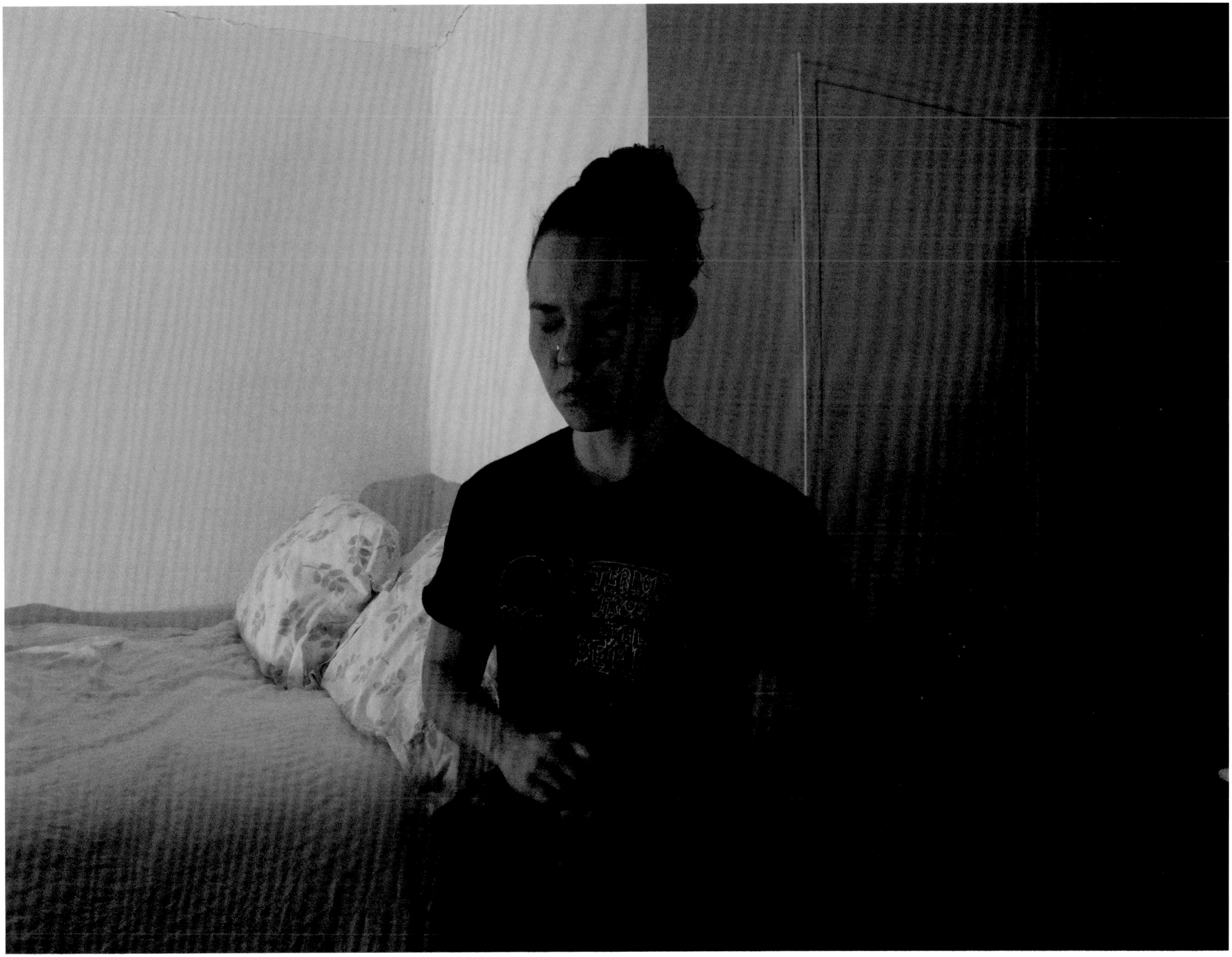

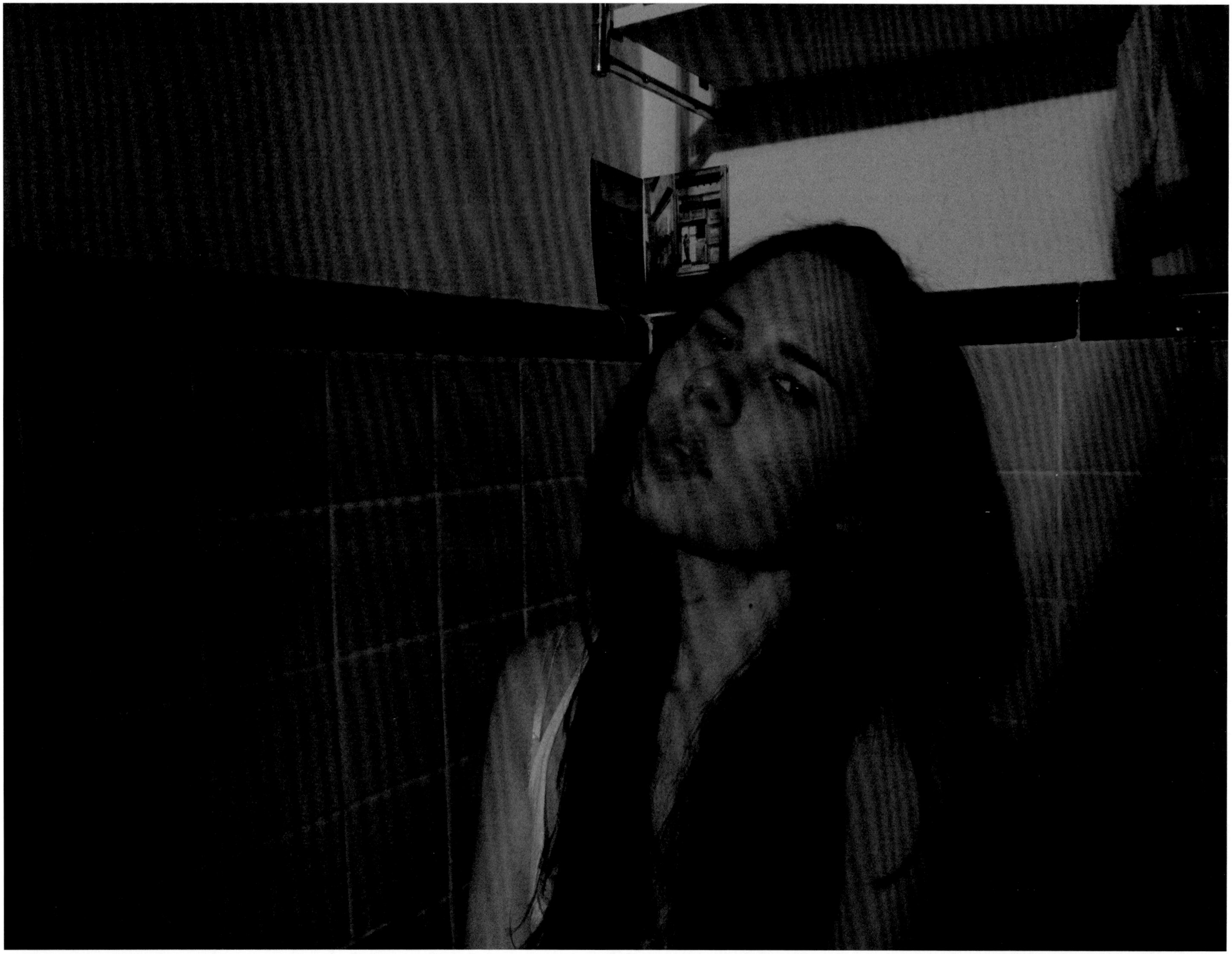

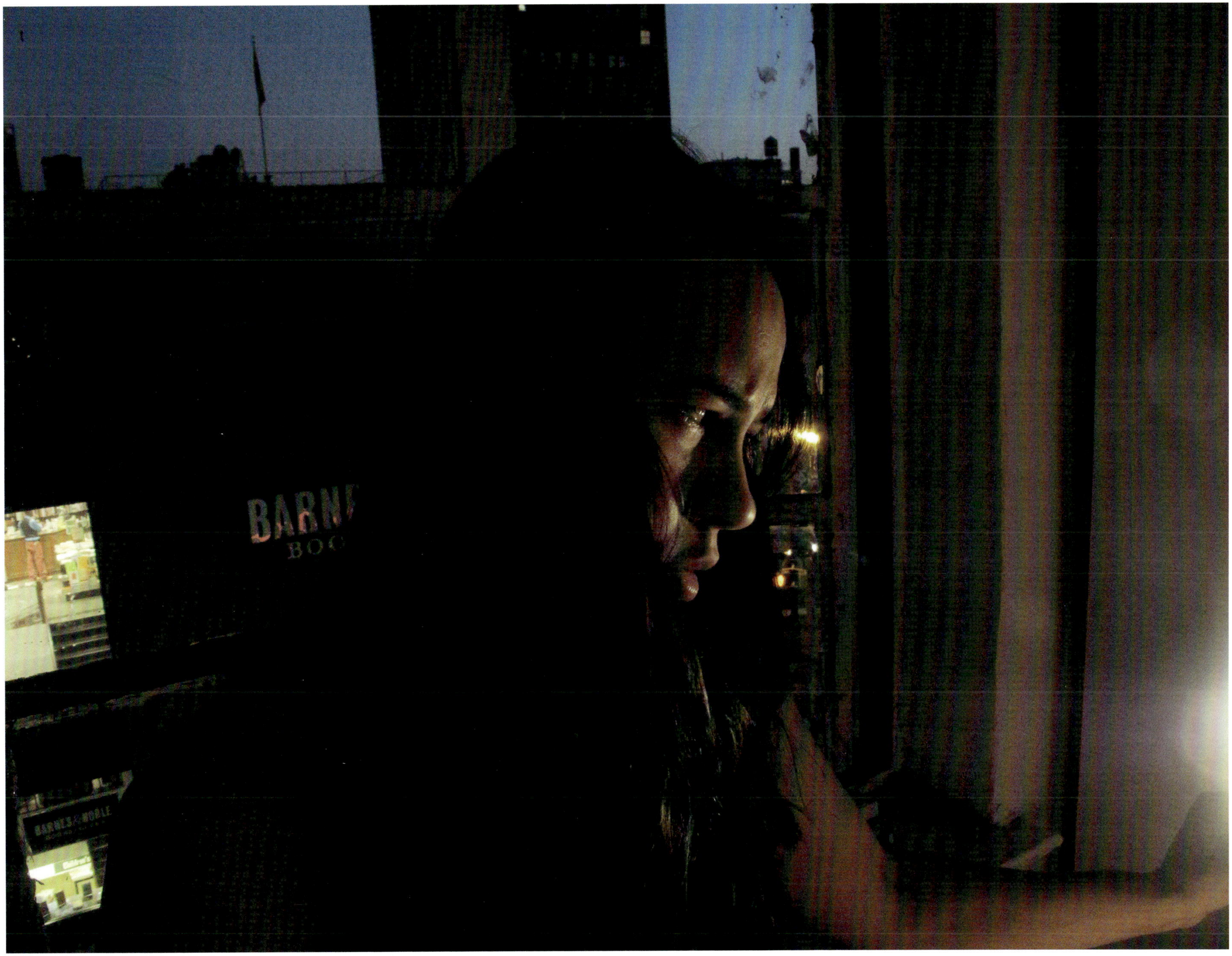

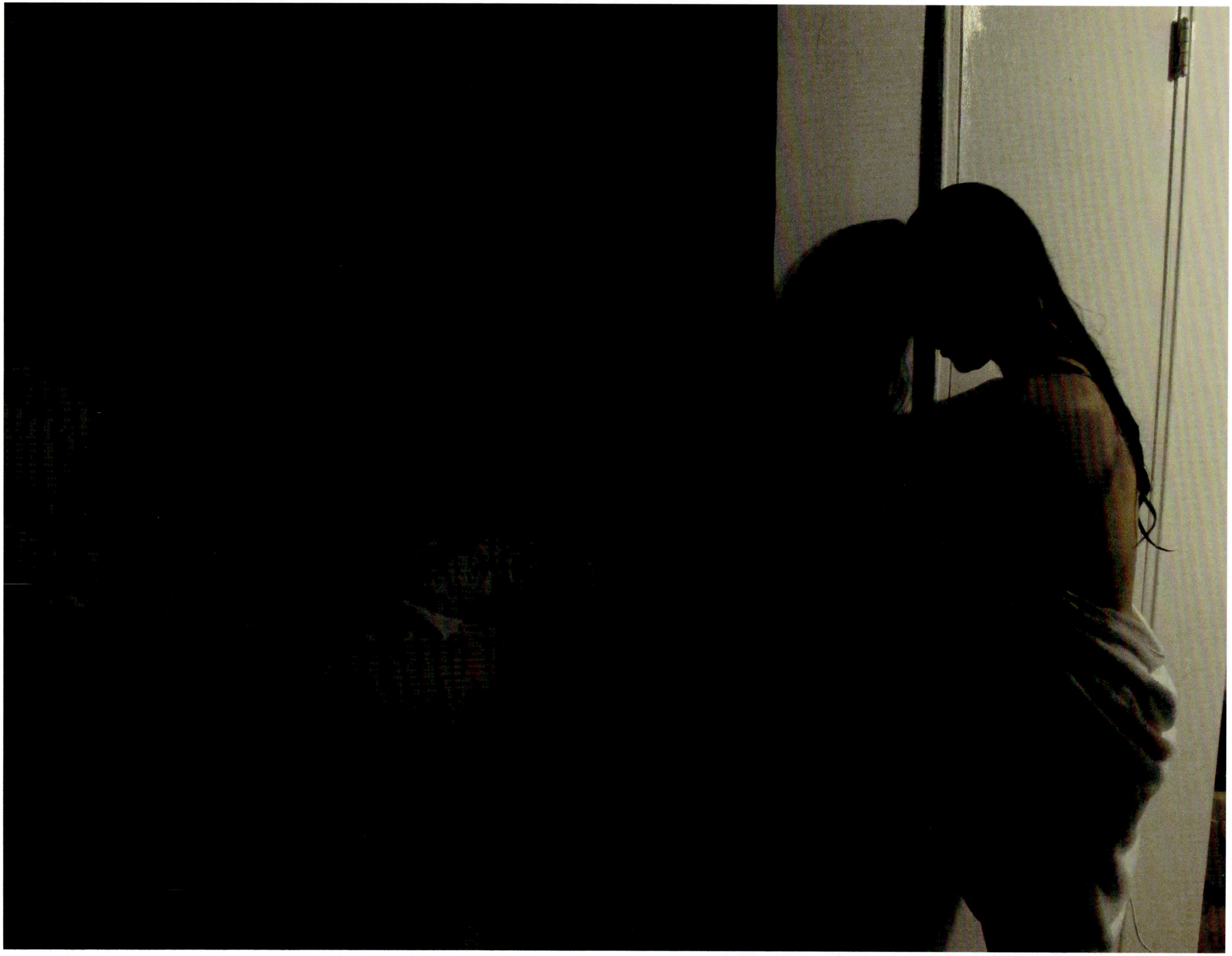

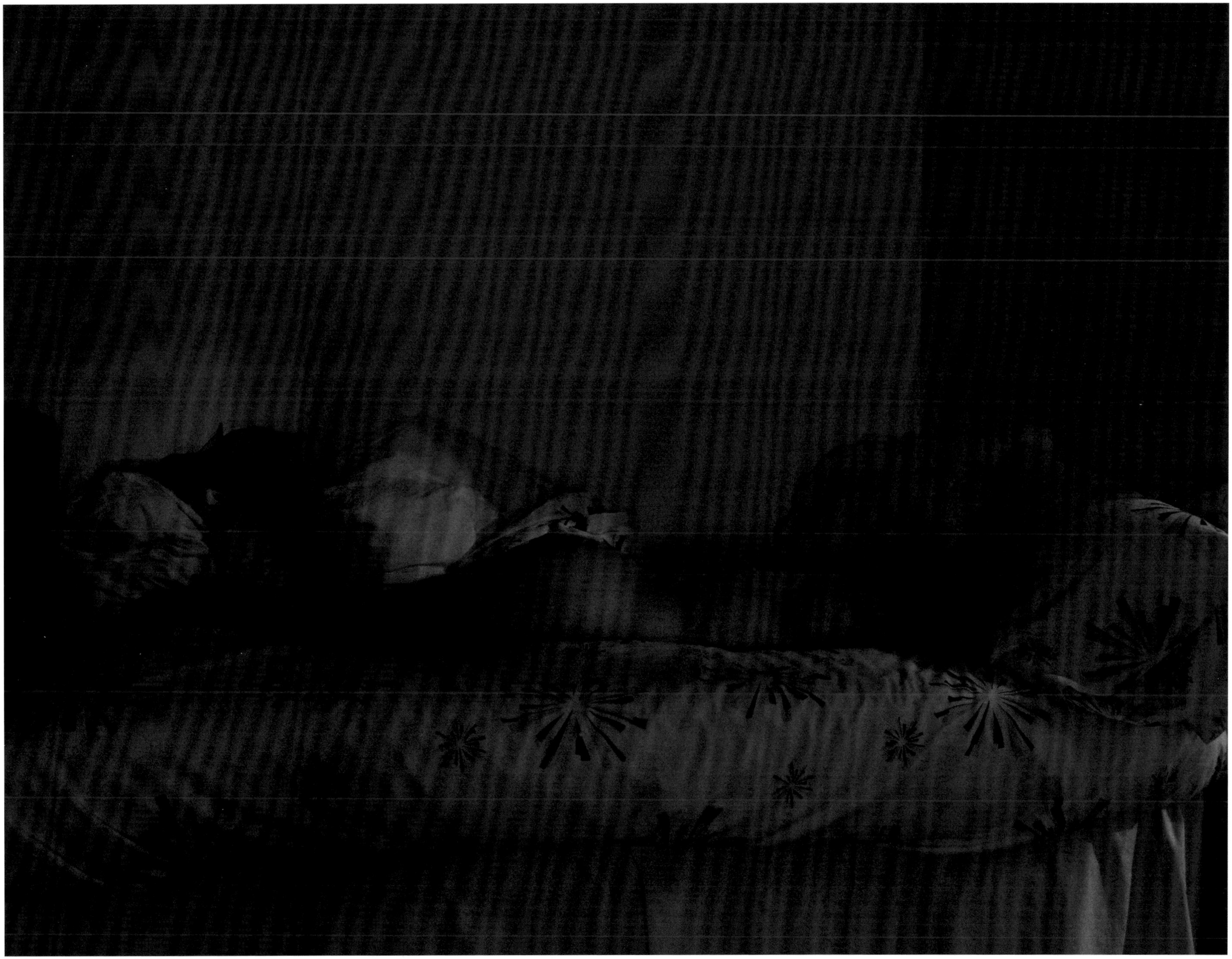

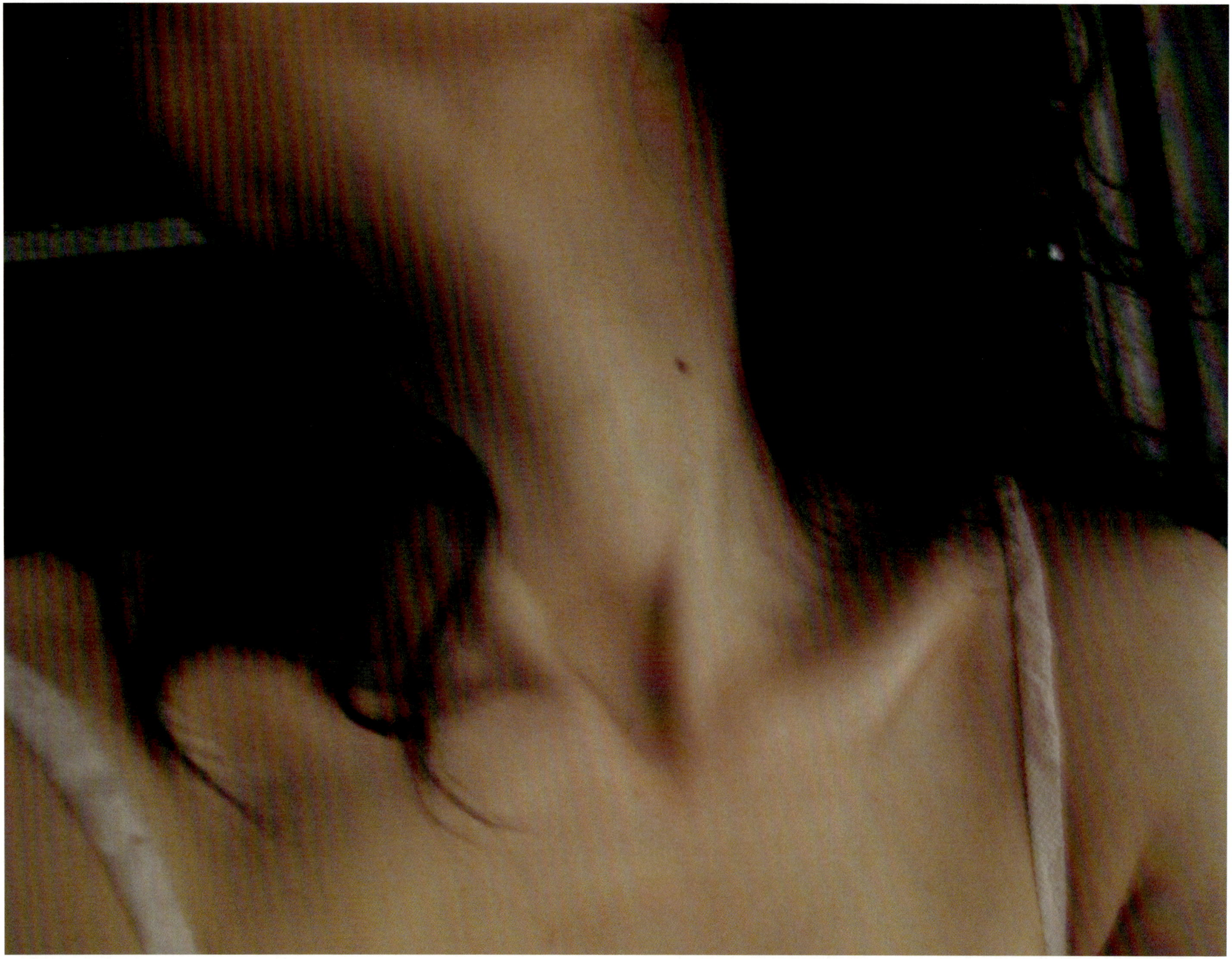

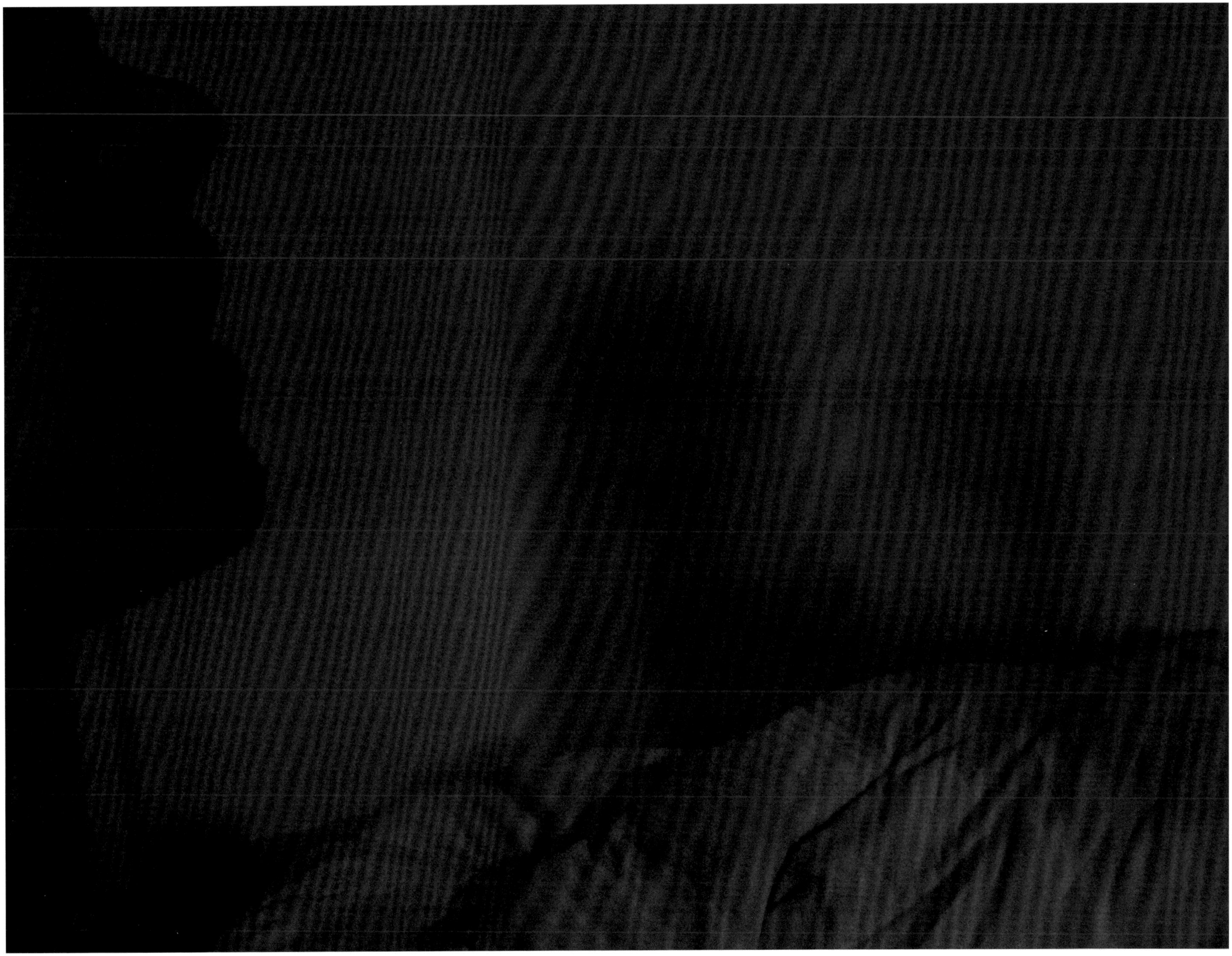

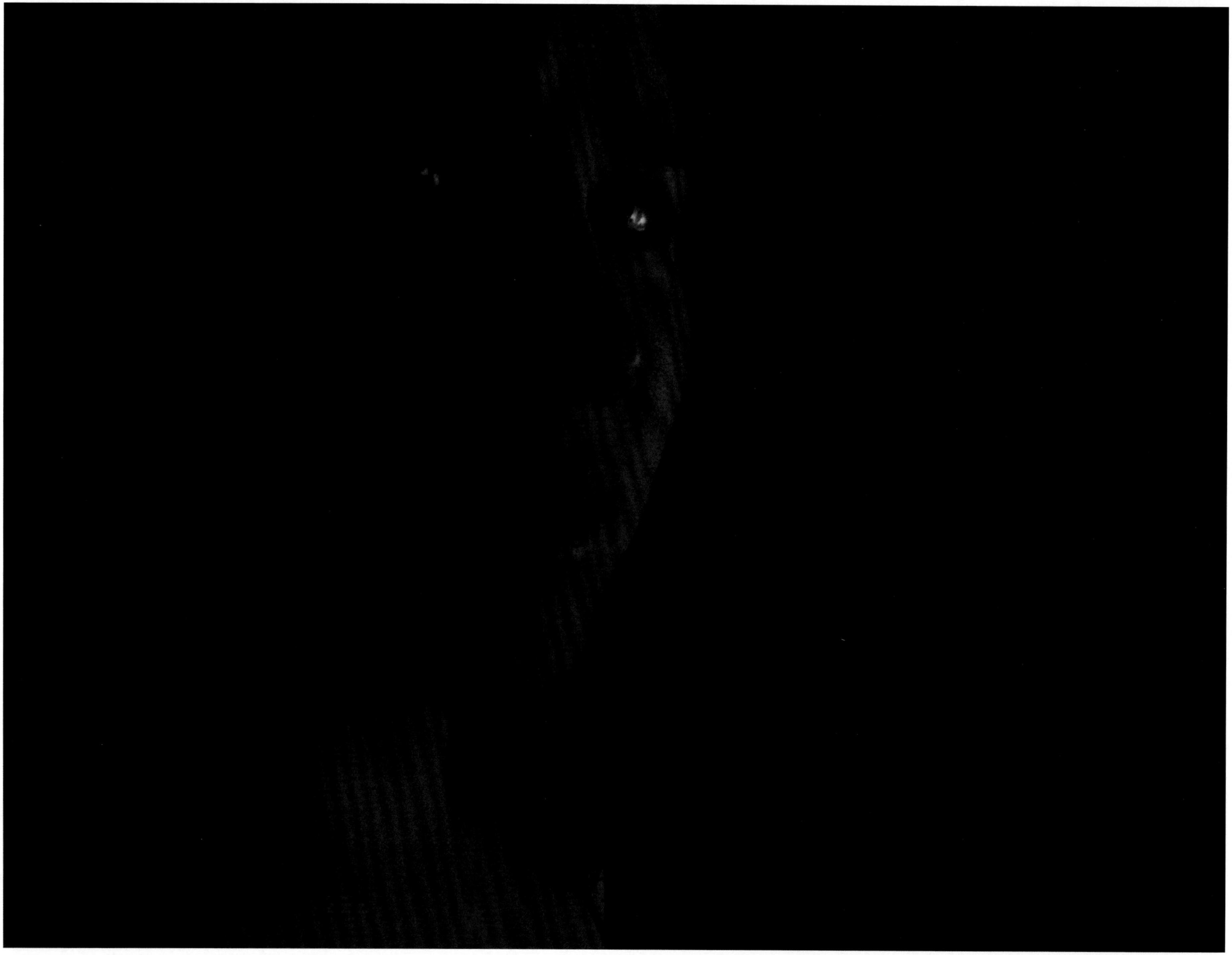

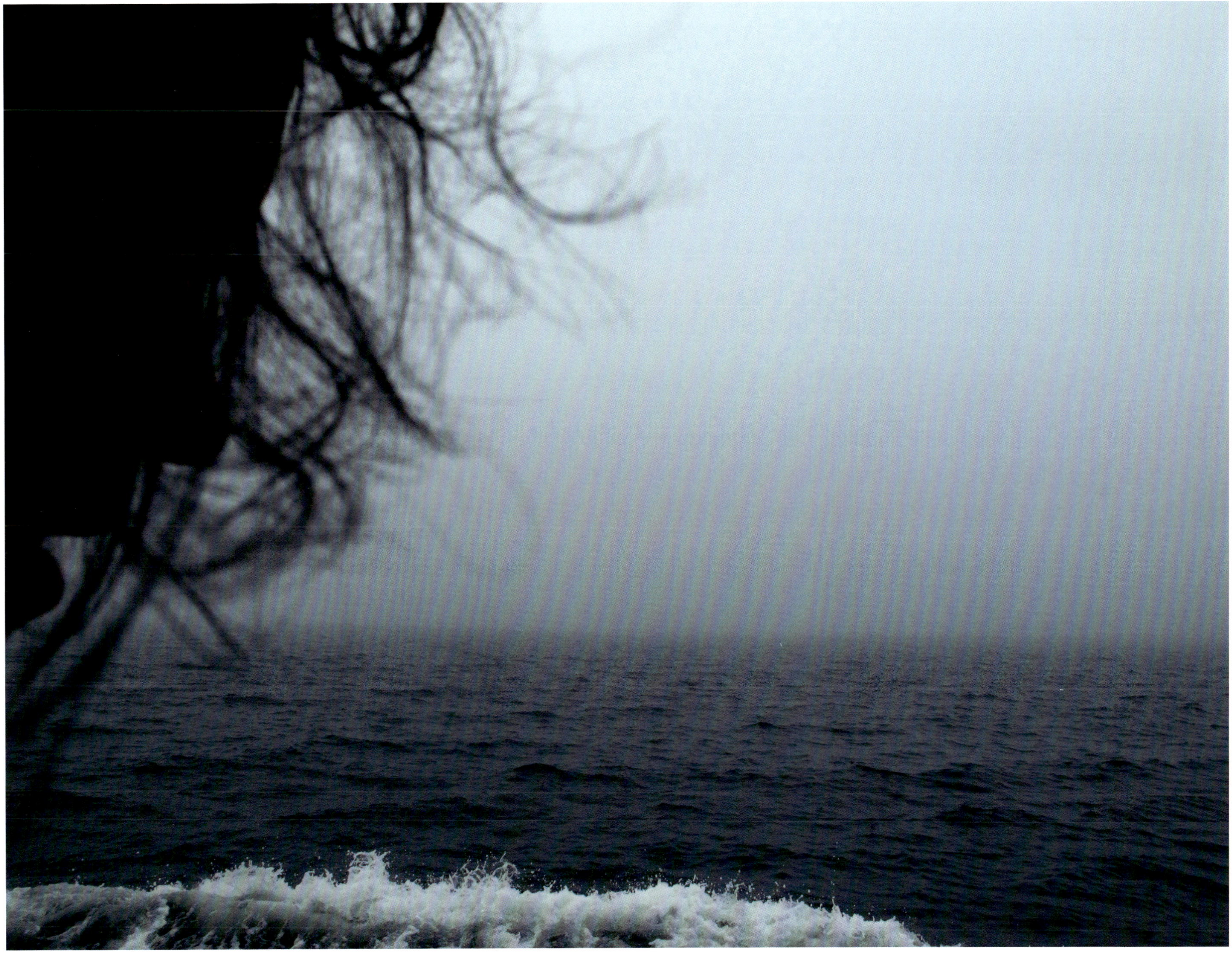

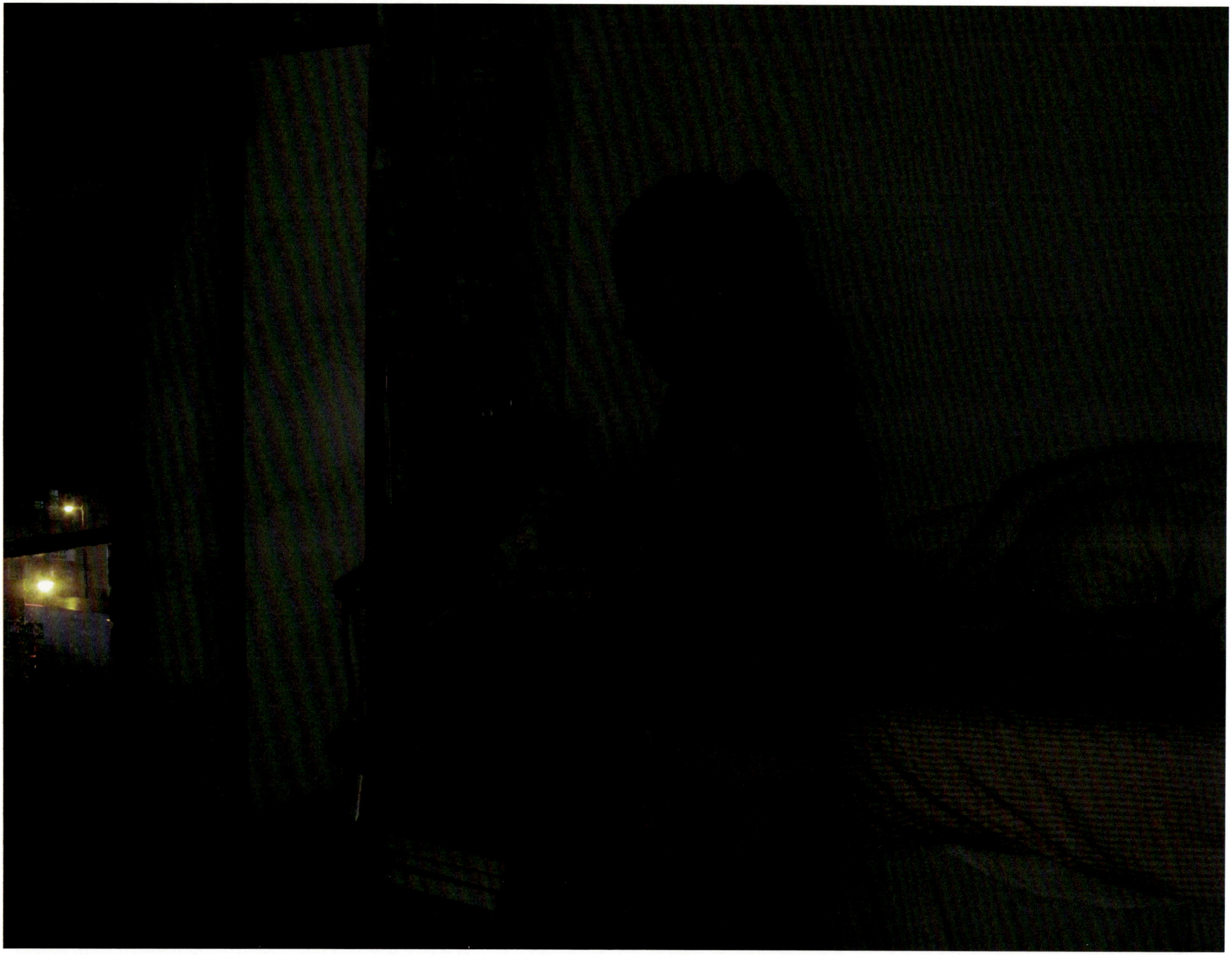

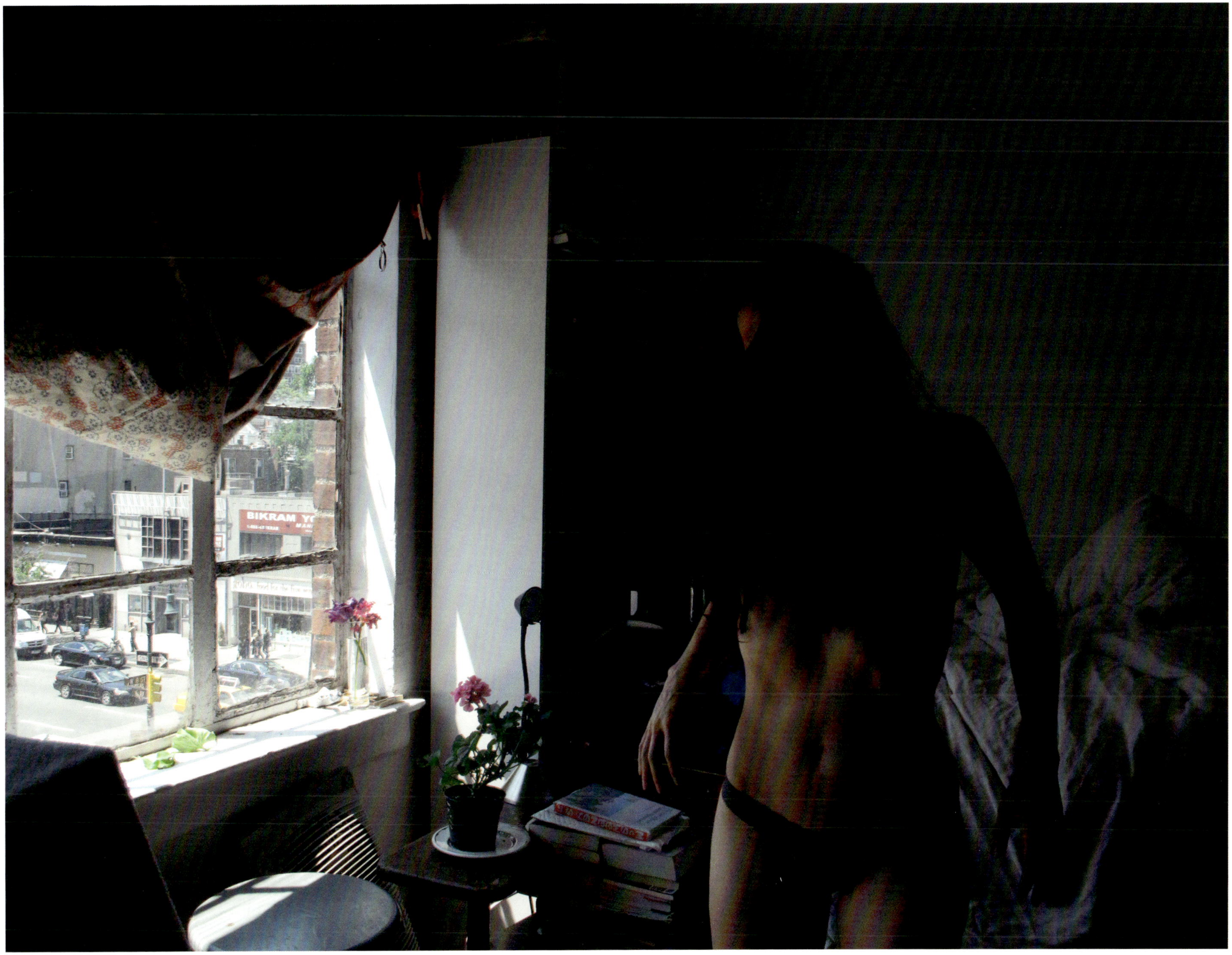
BIKRAM

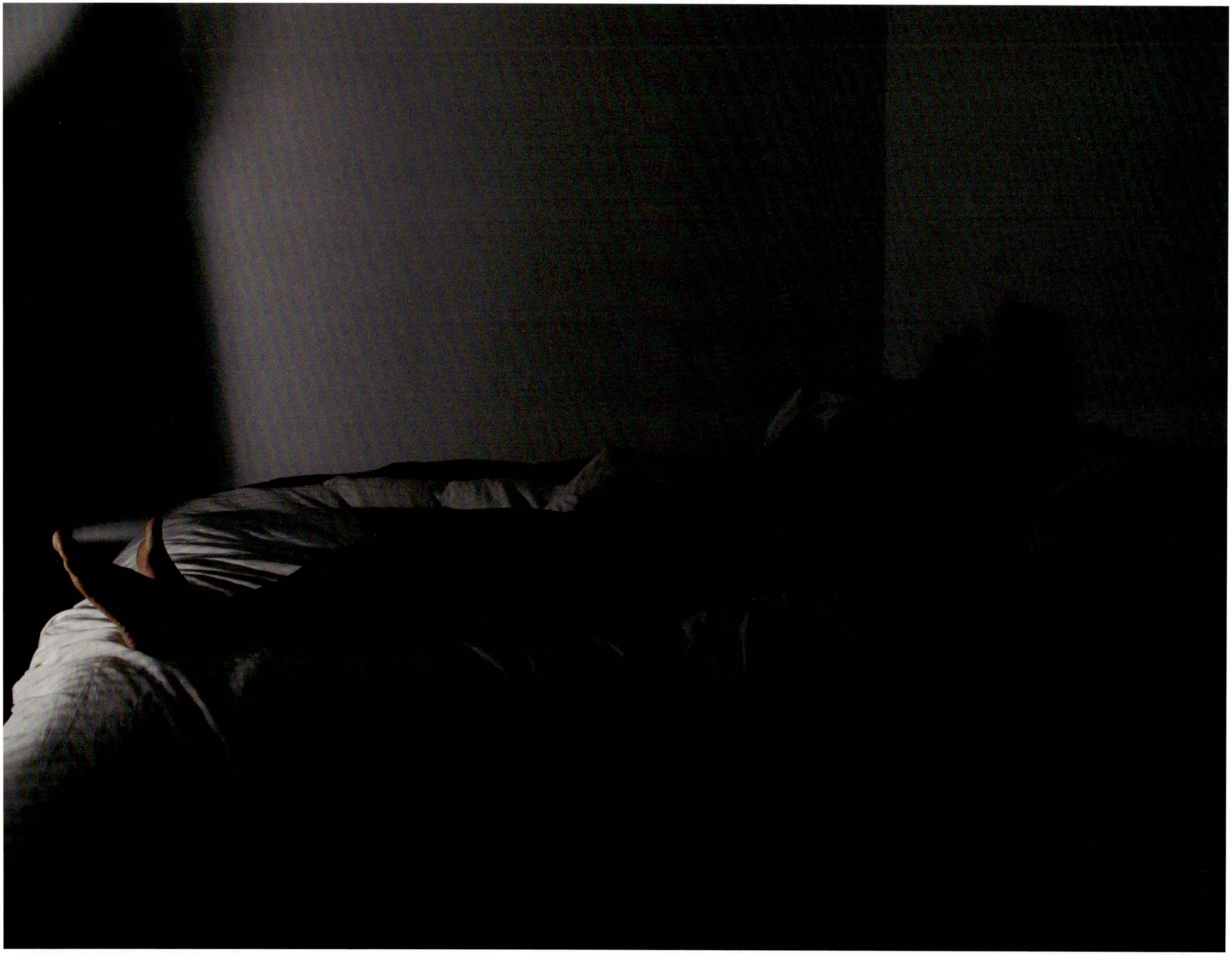

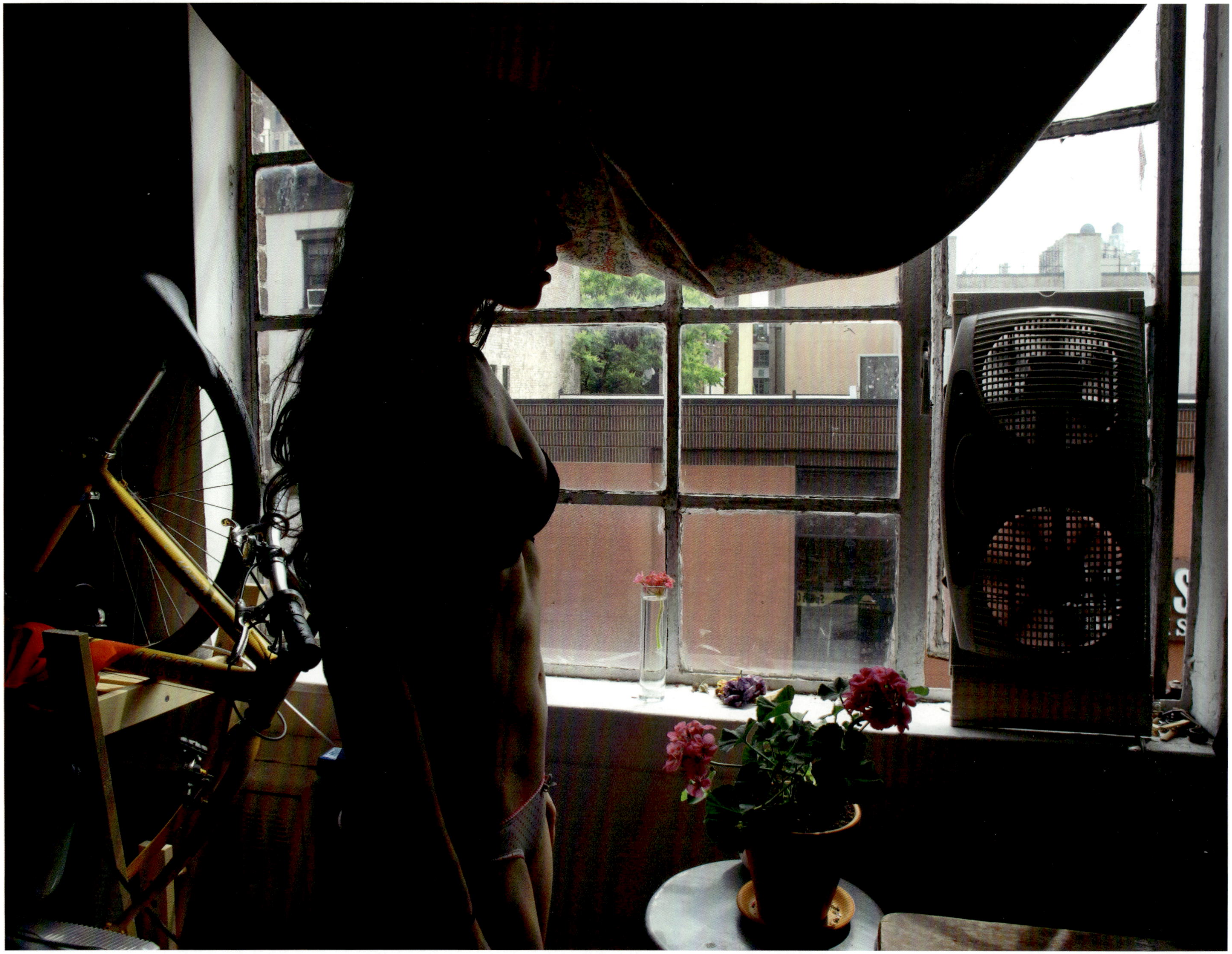

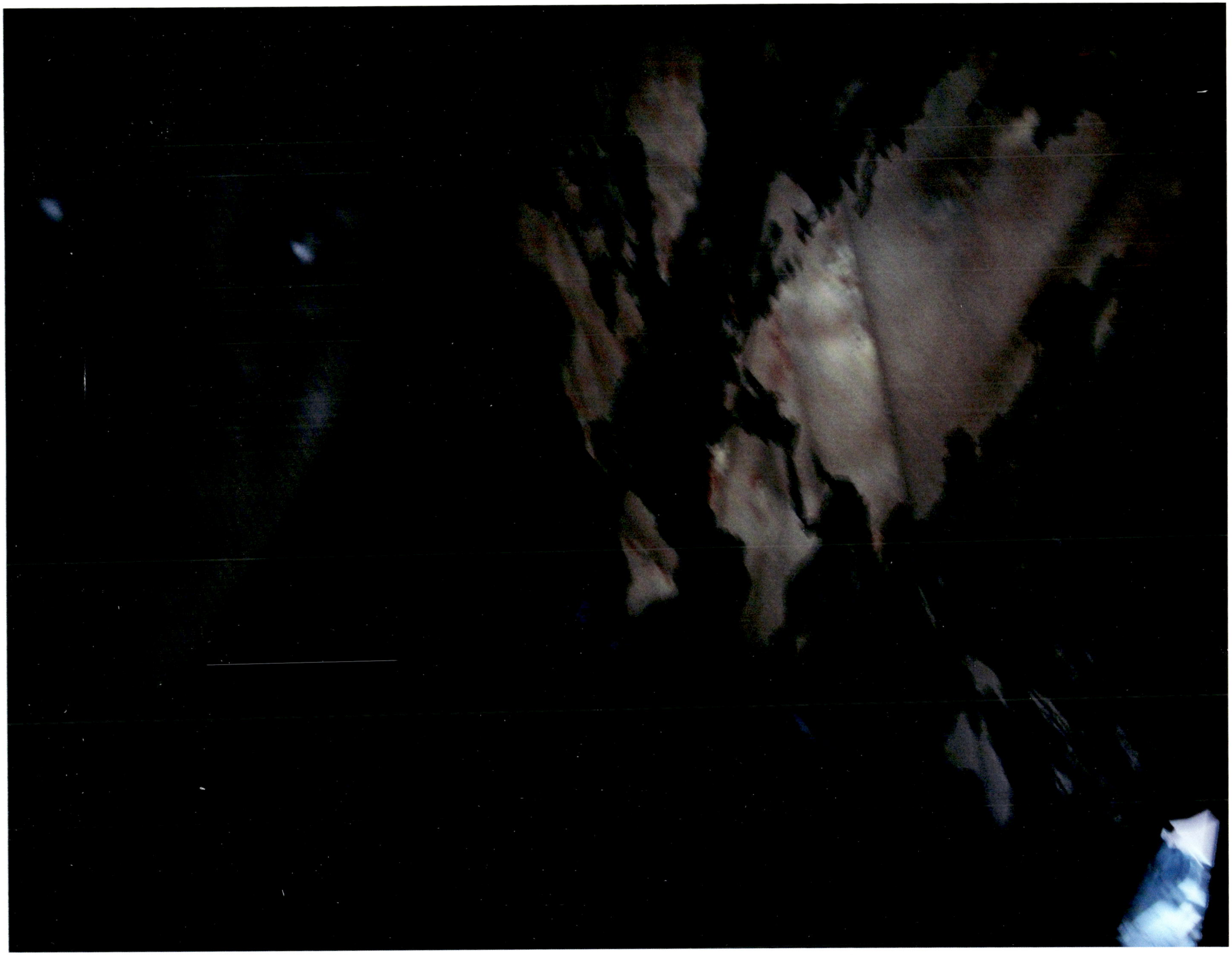

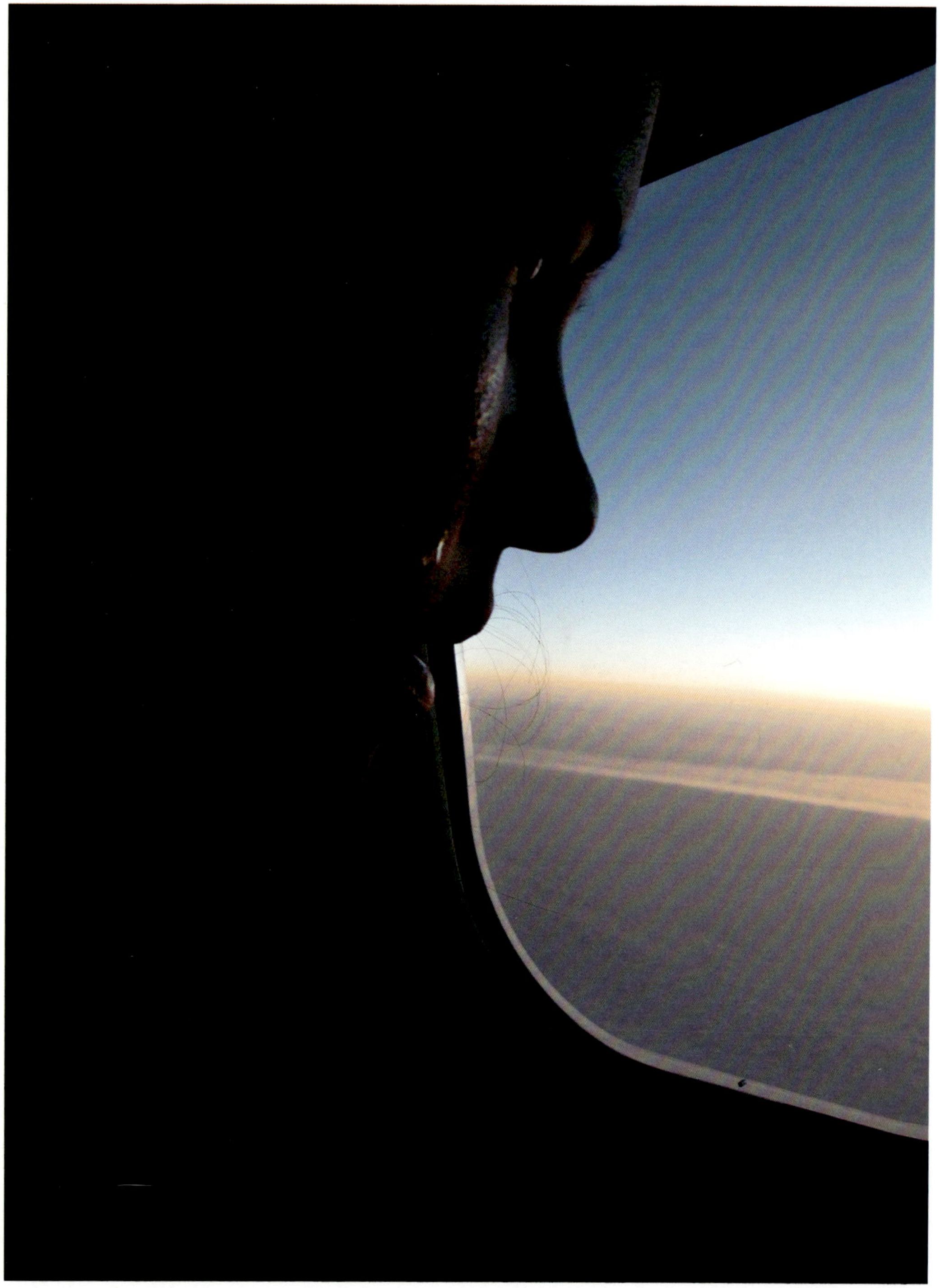

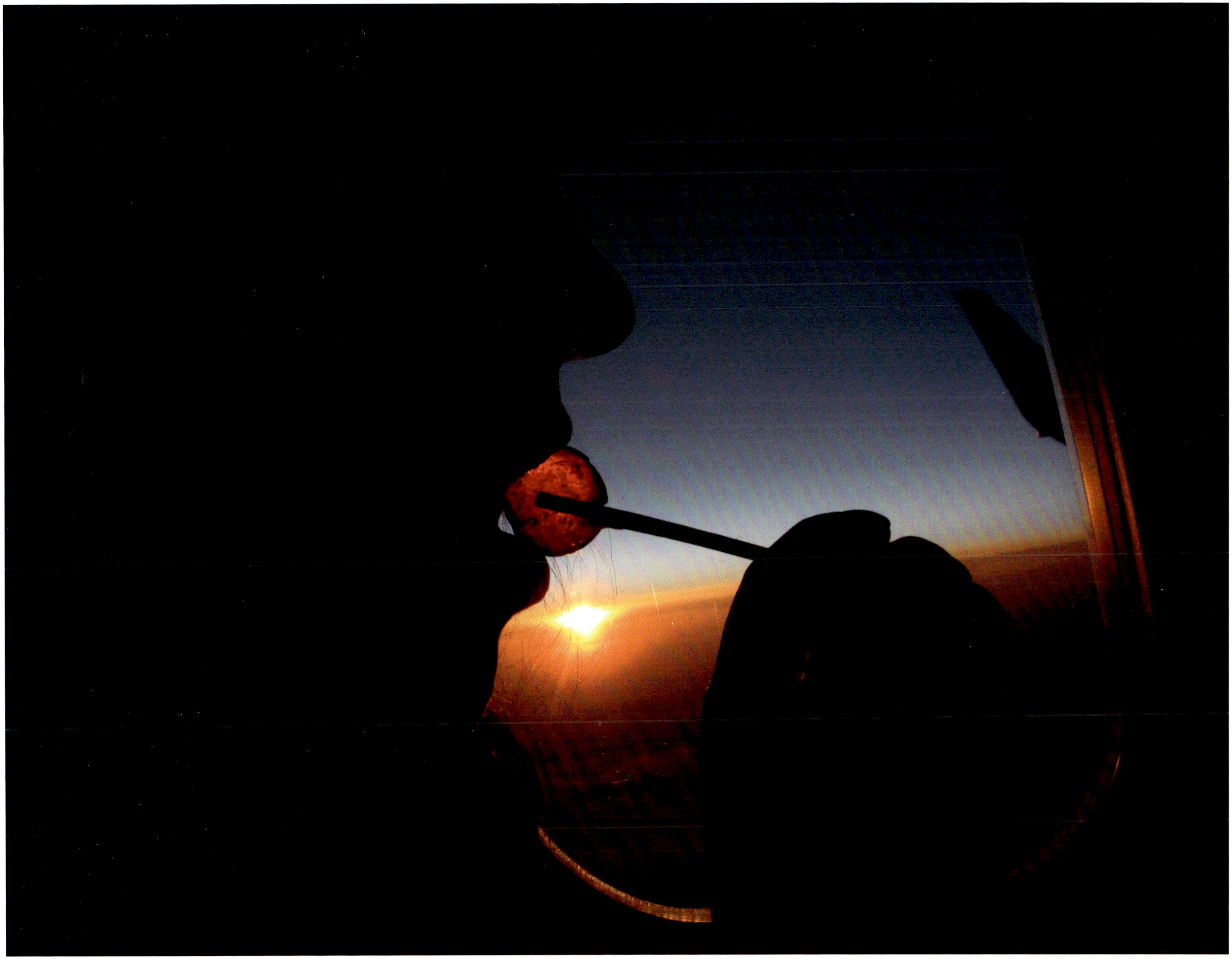

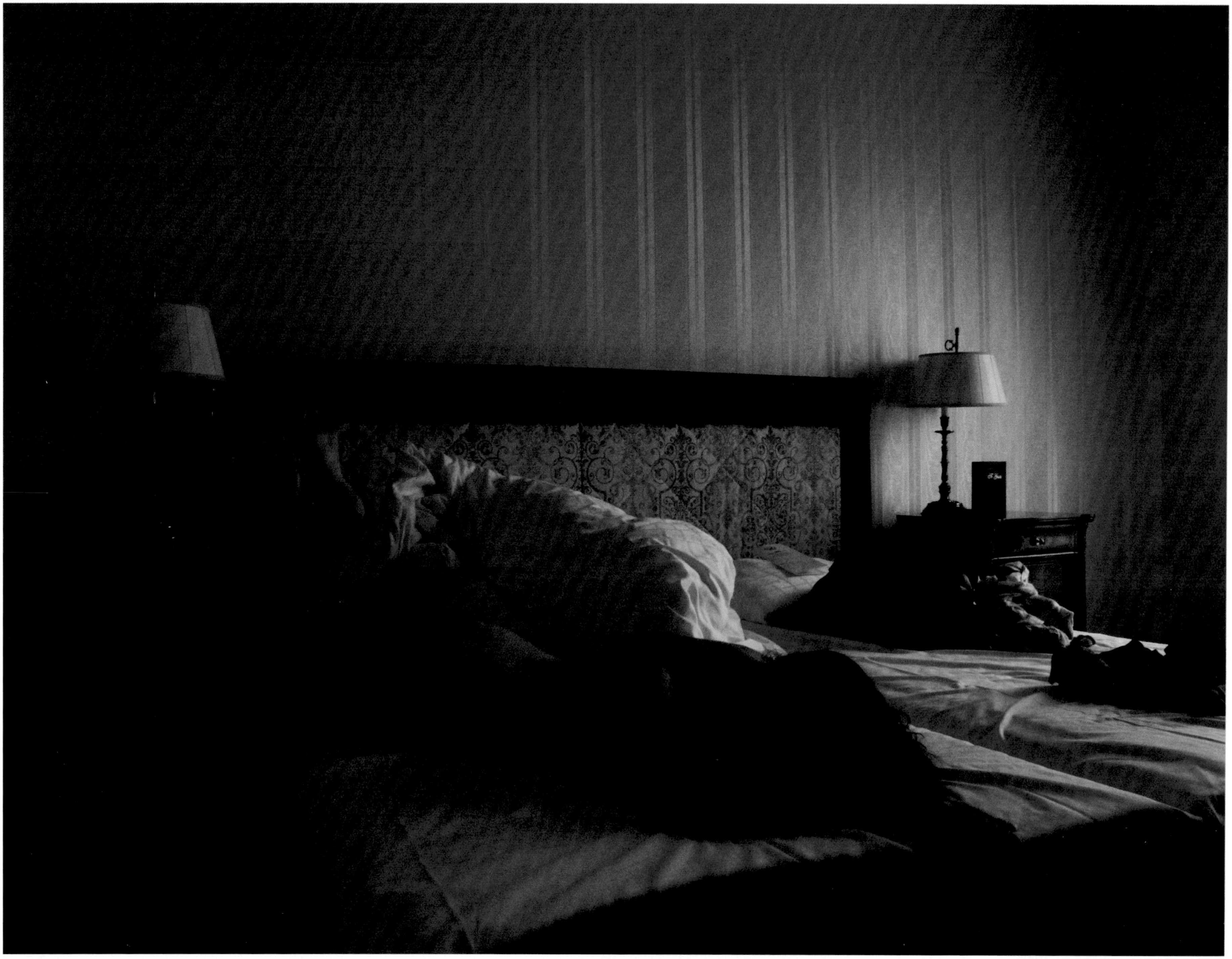

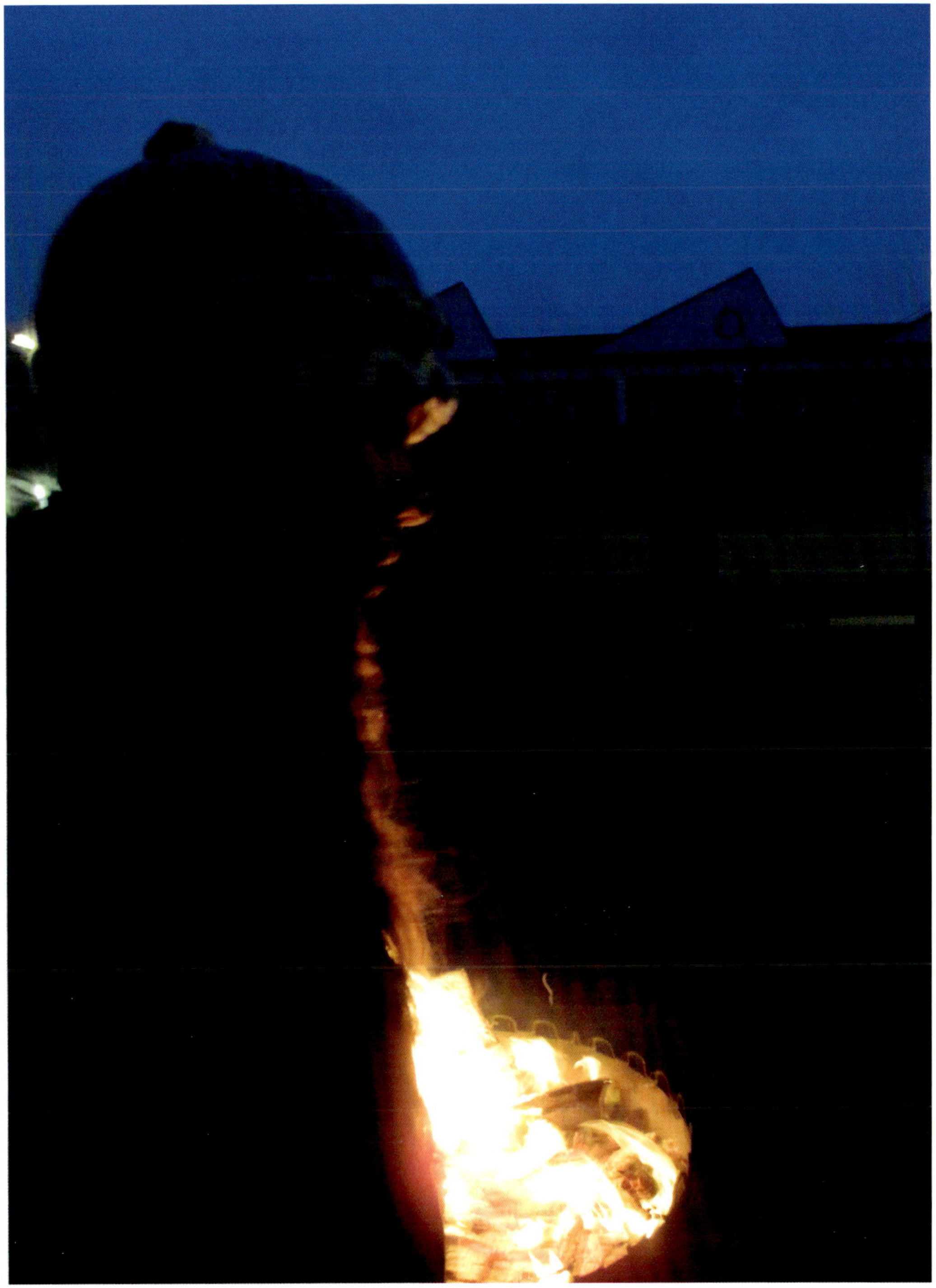

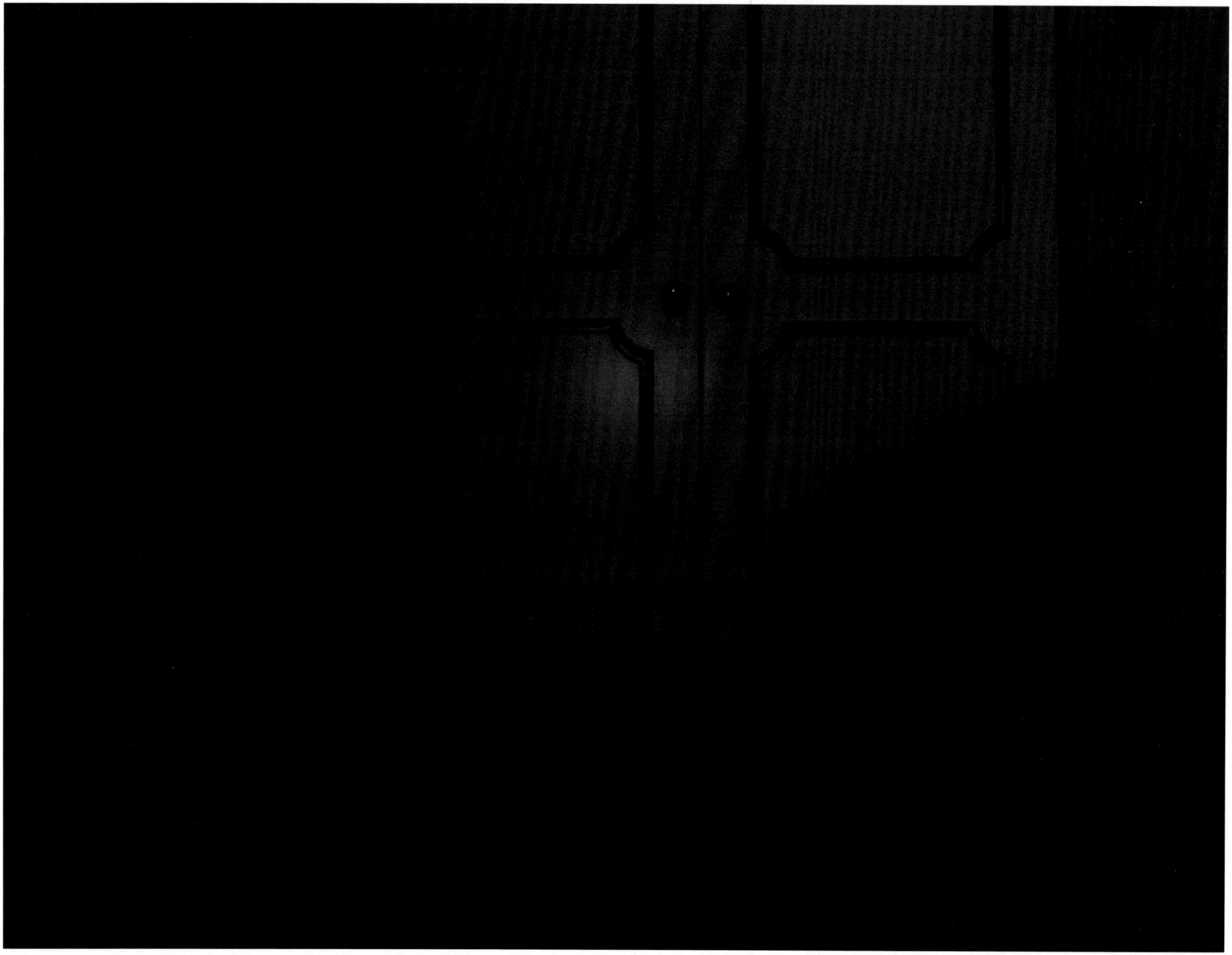

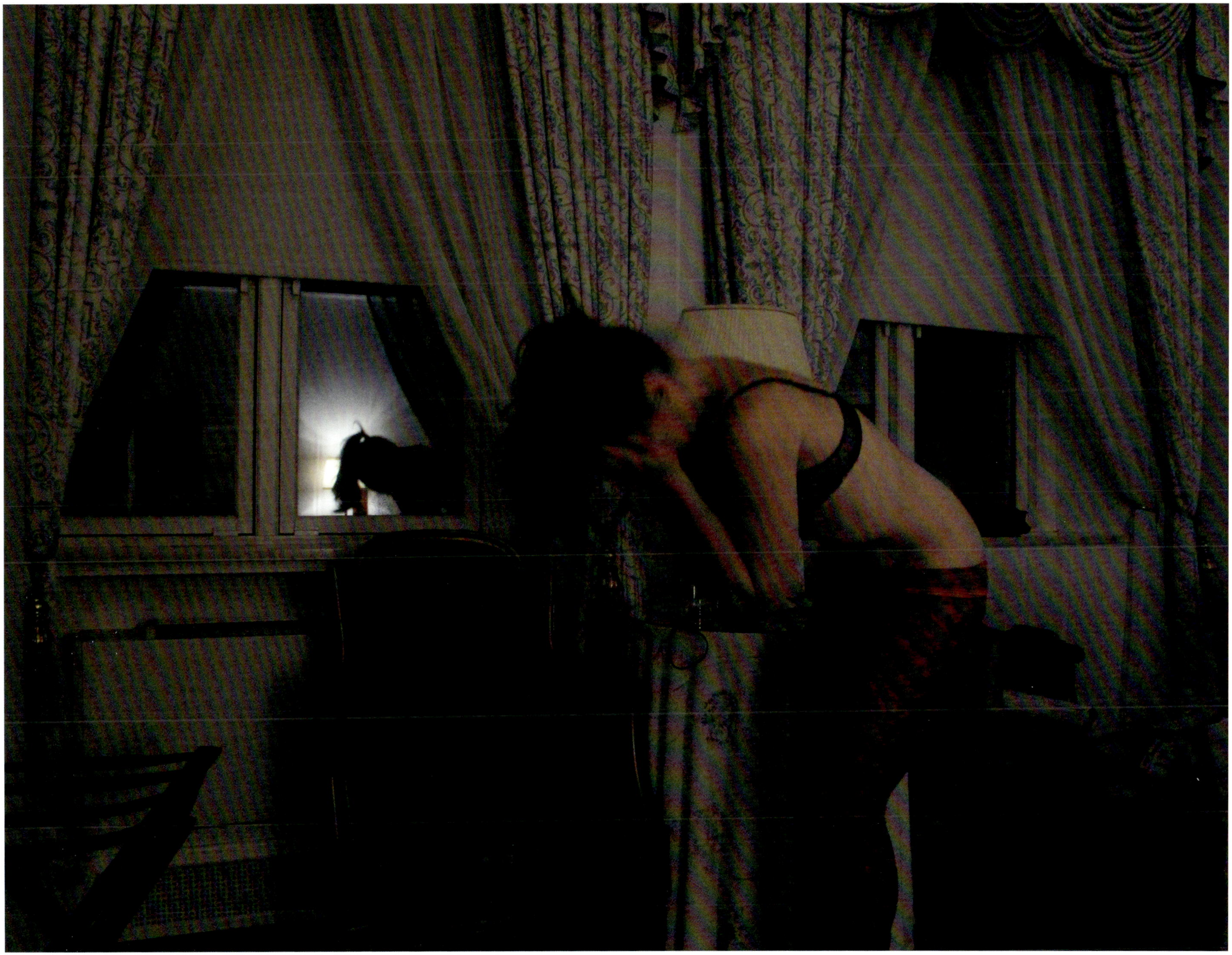

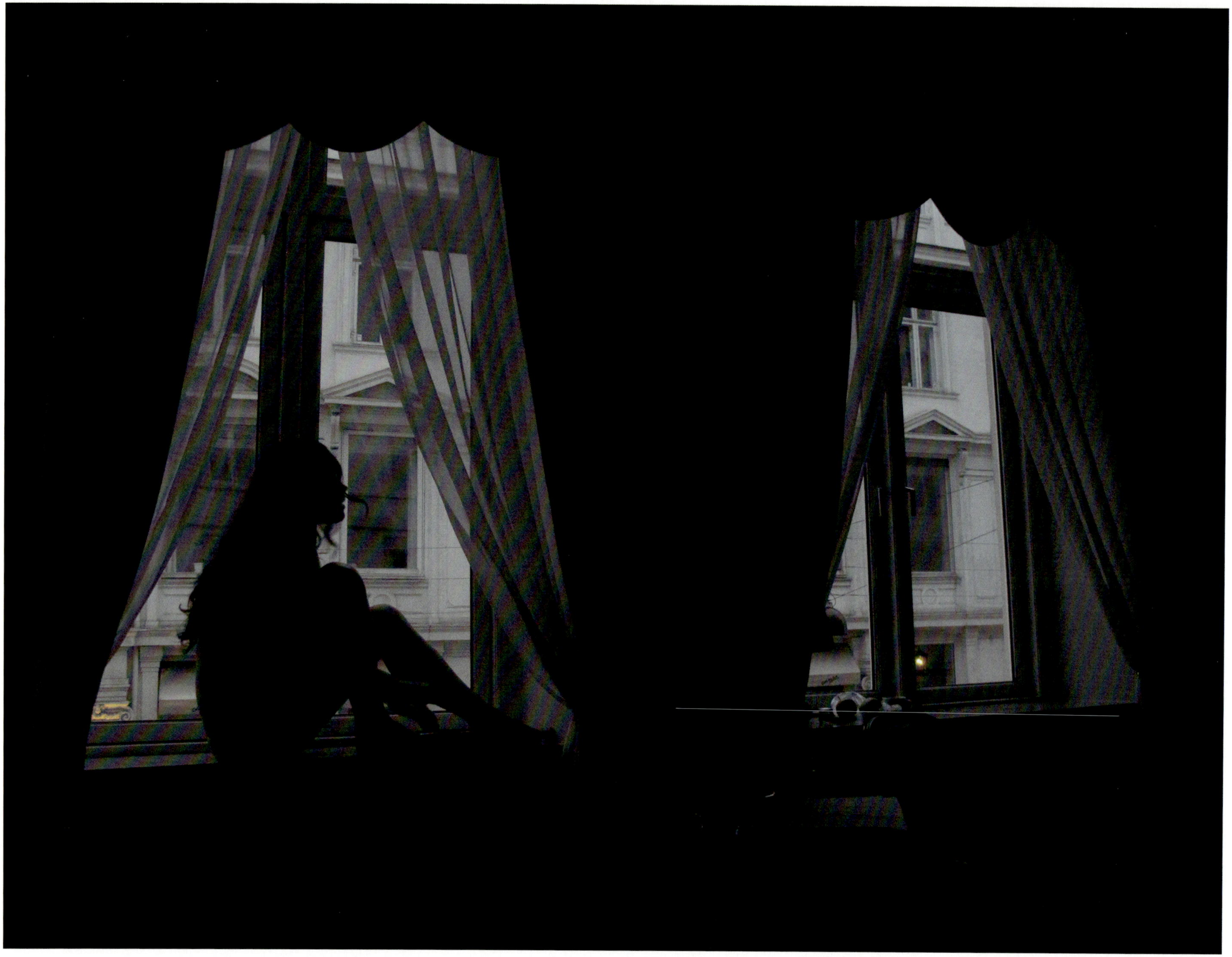

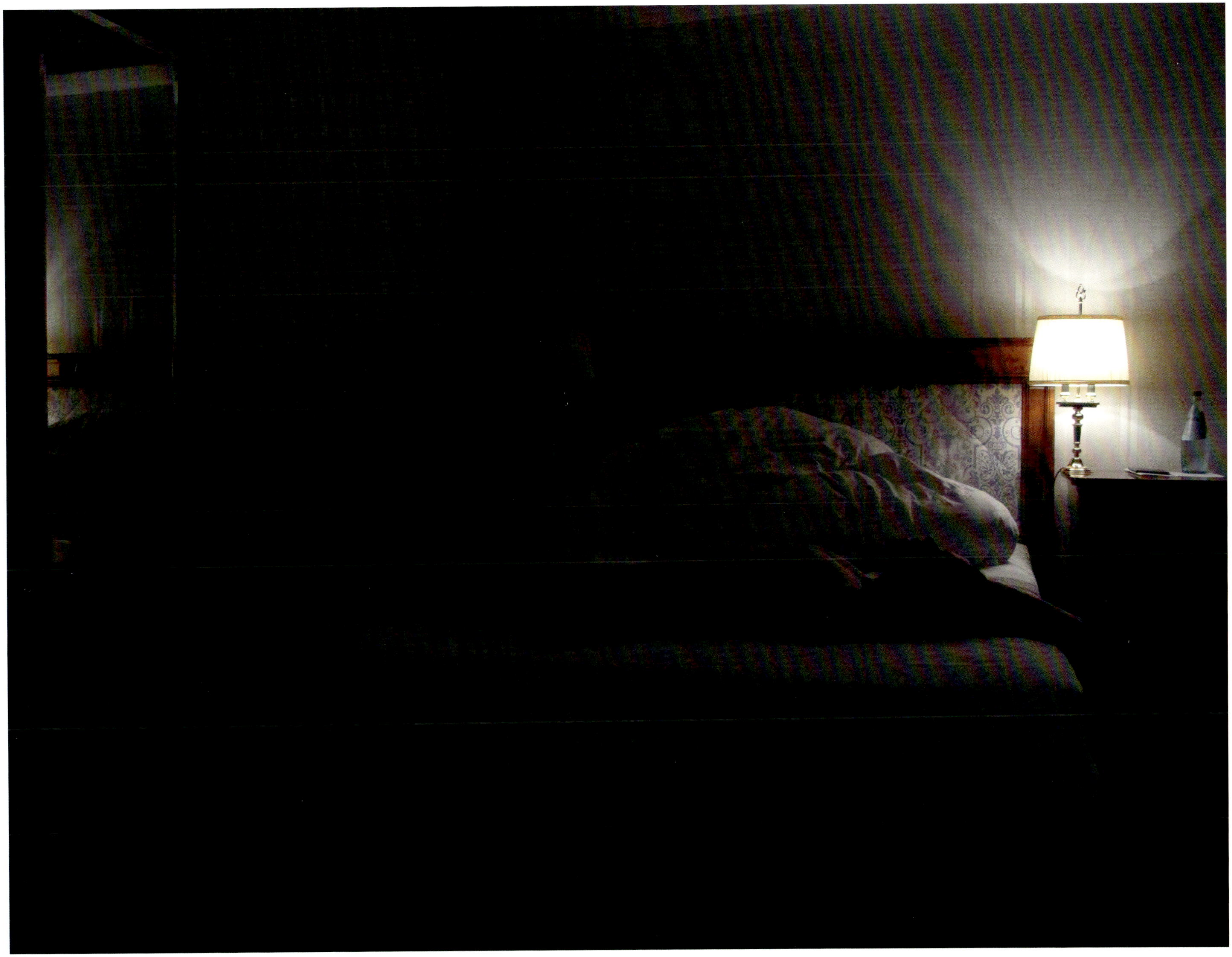

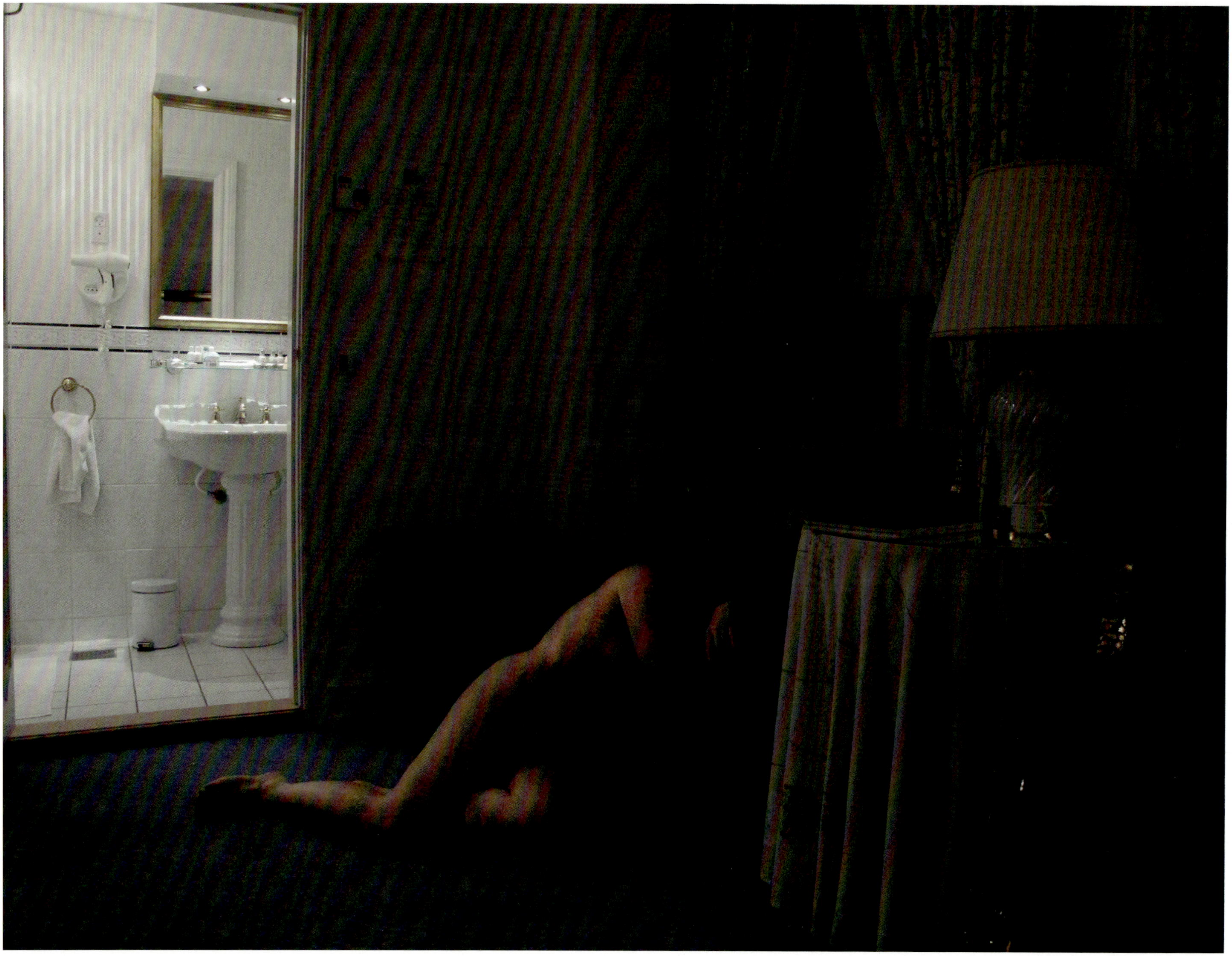

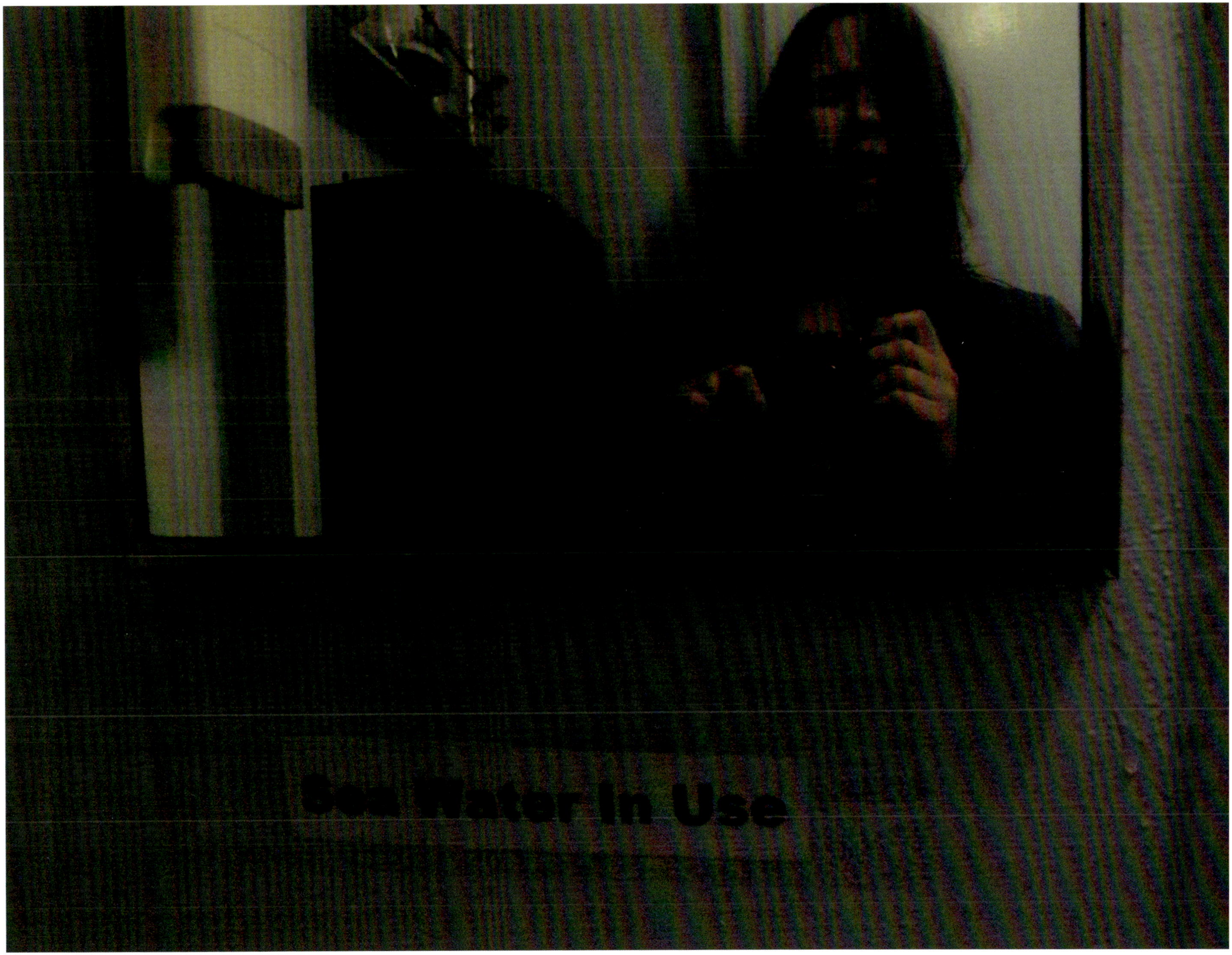
Sea Water In Use

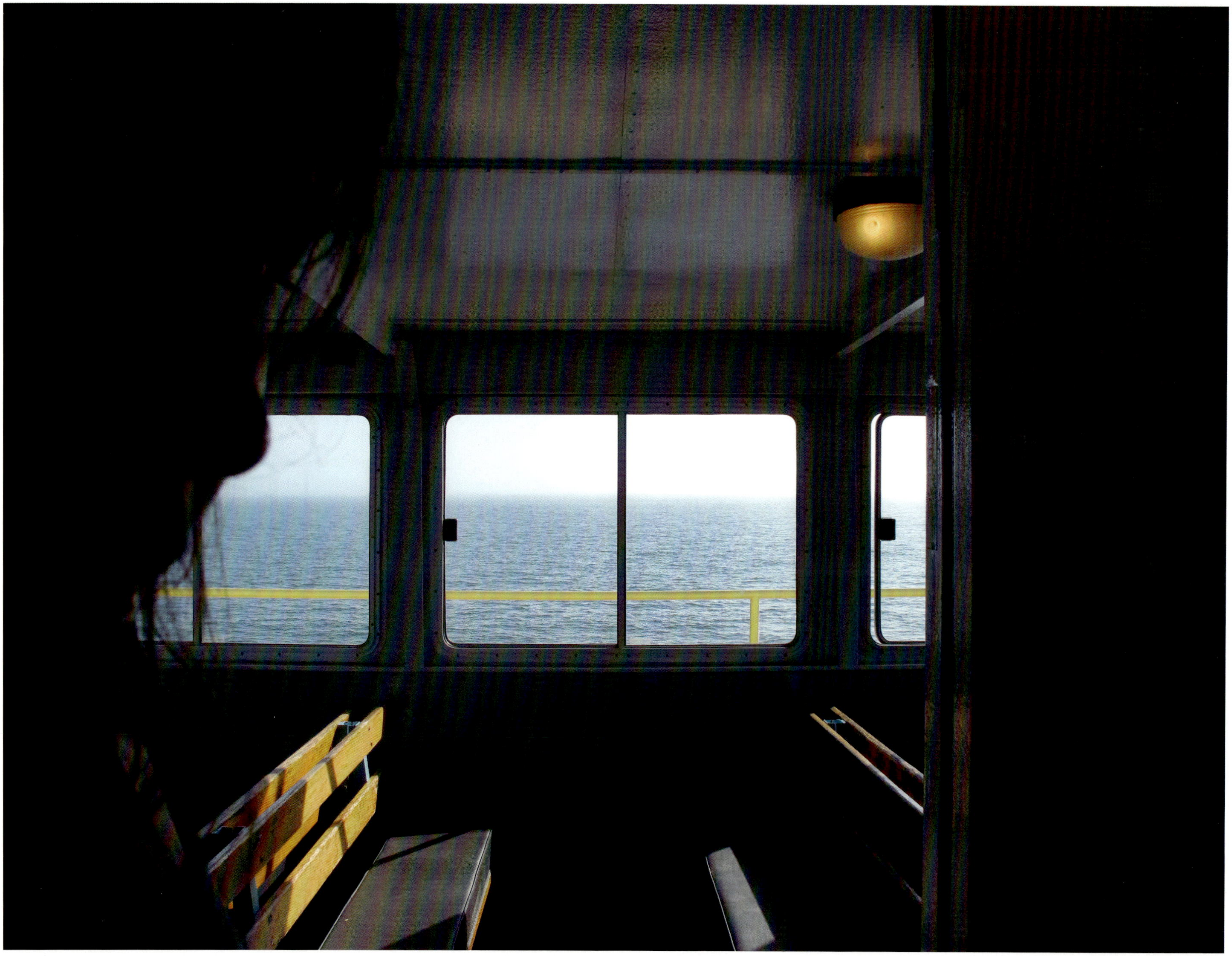

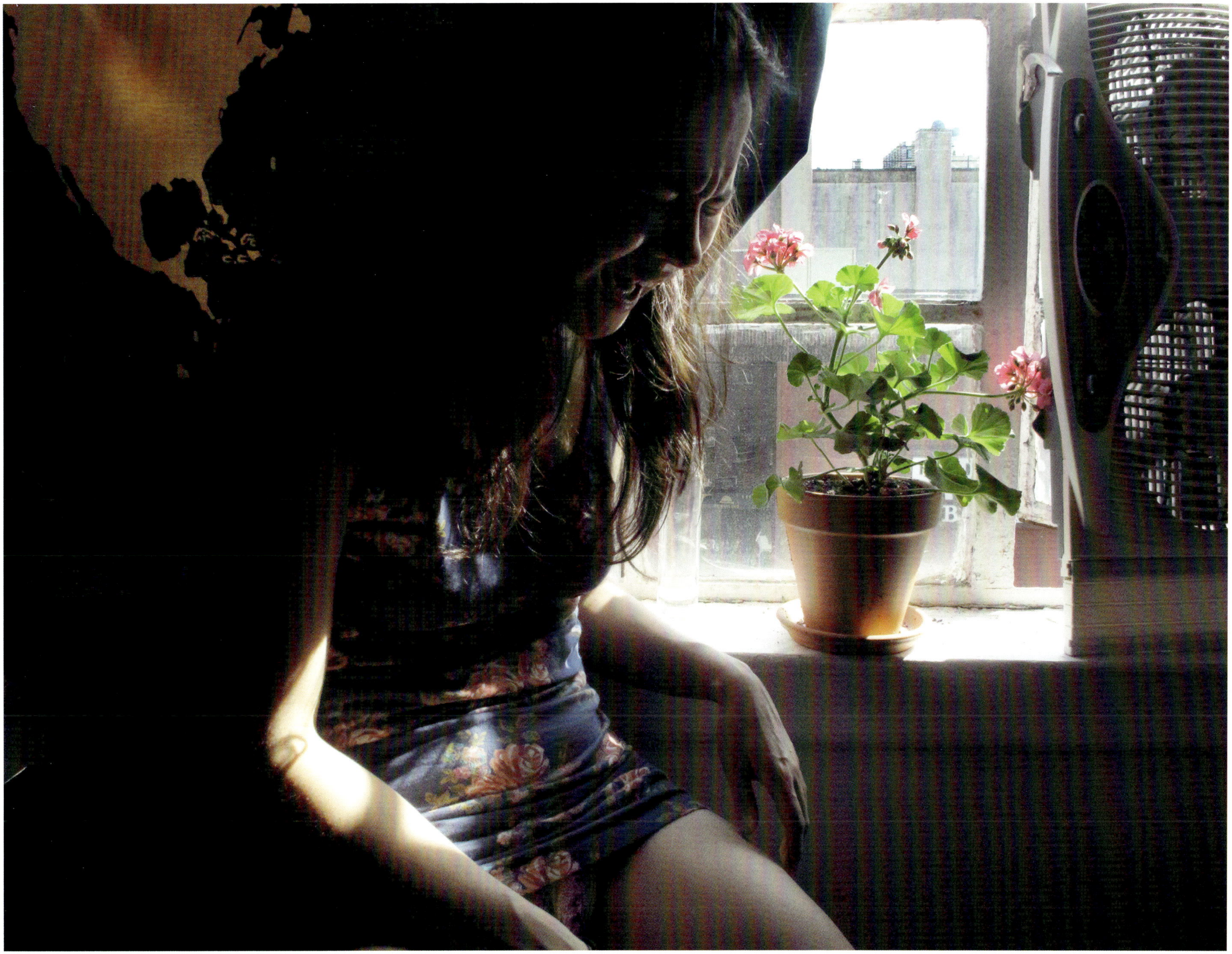

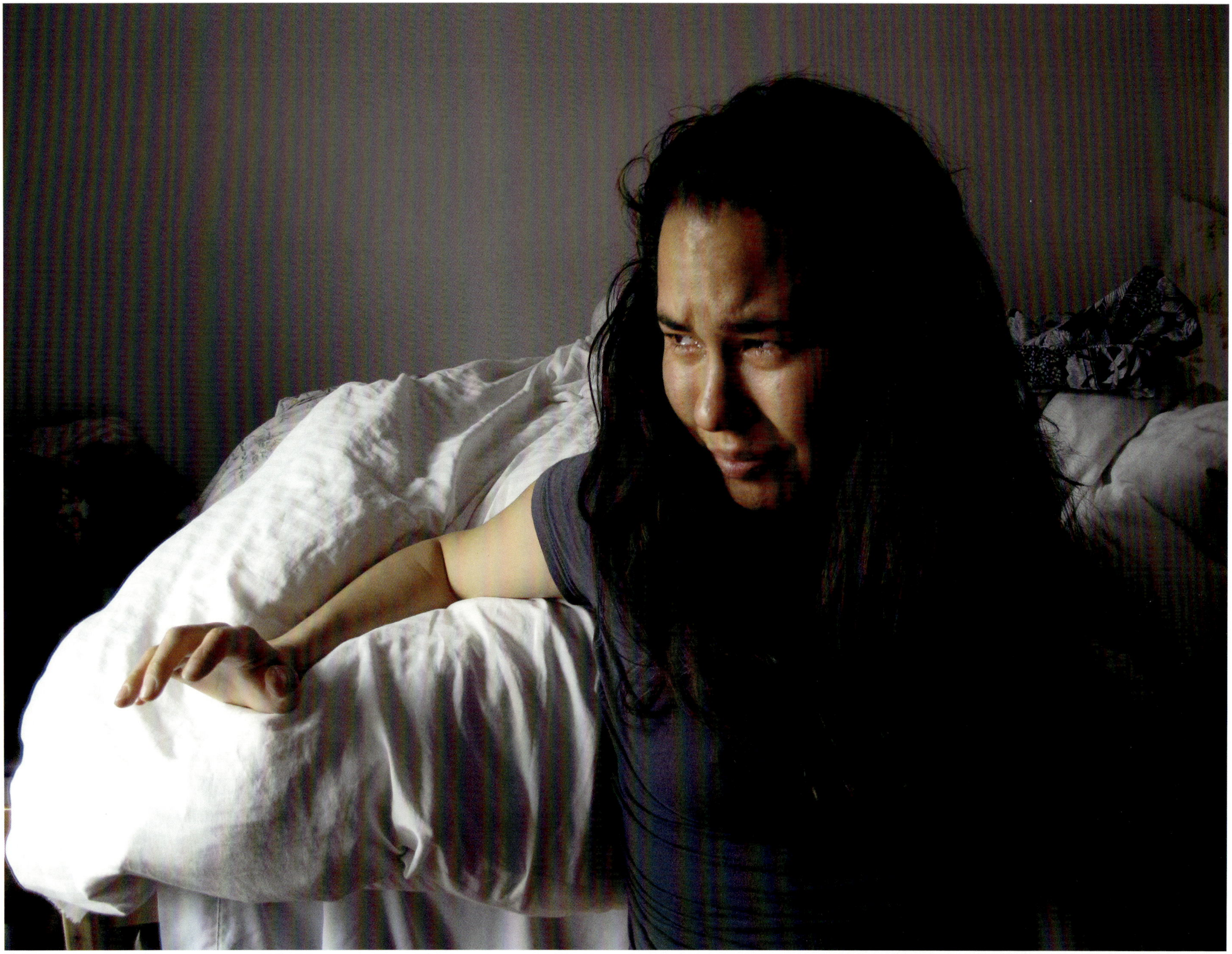

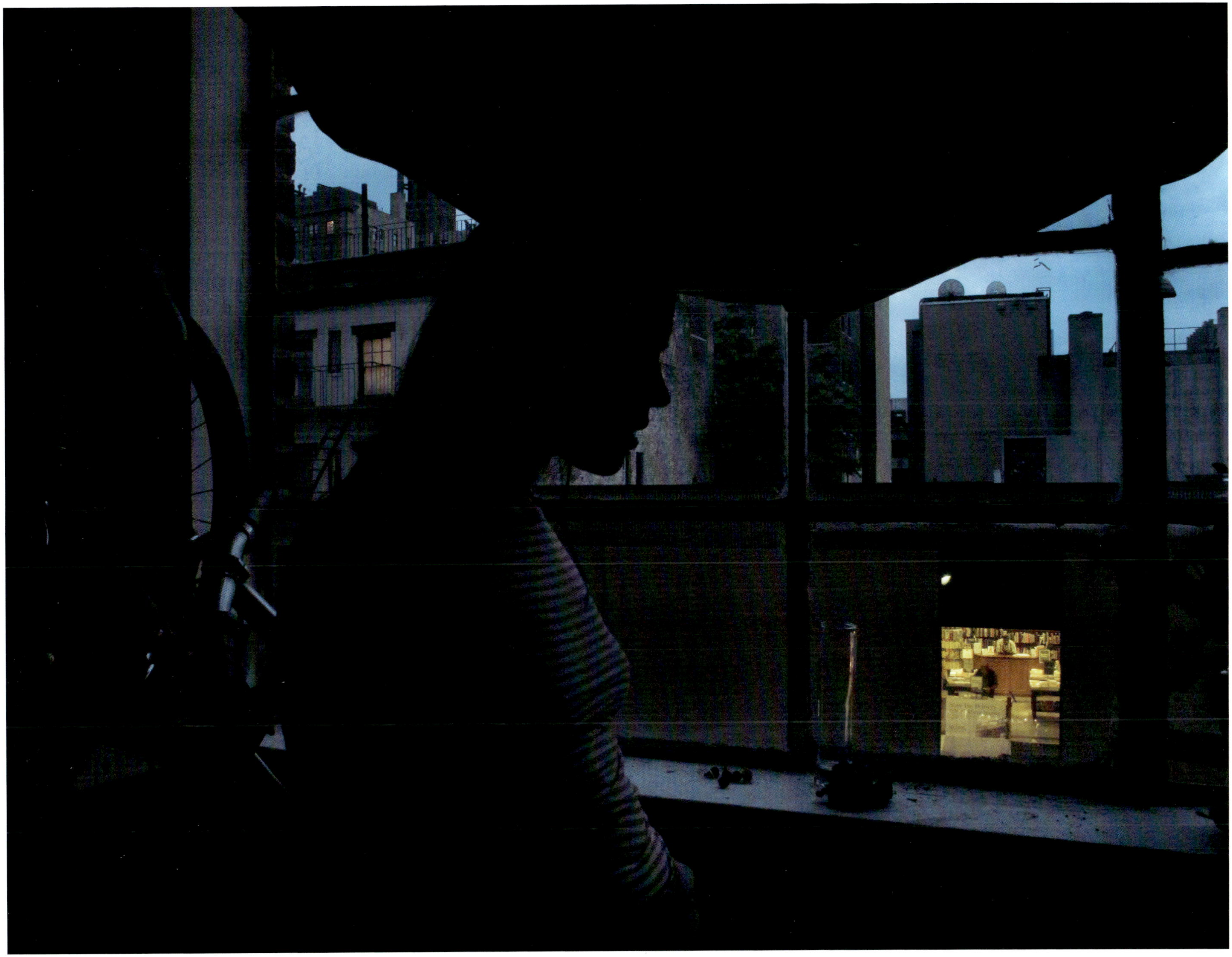

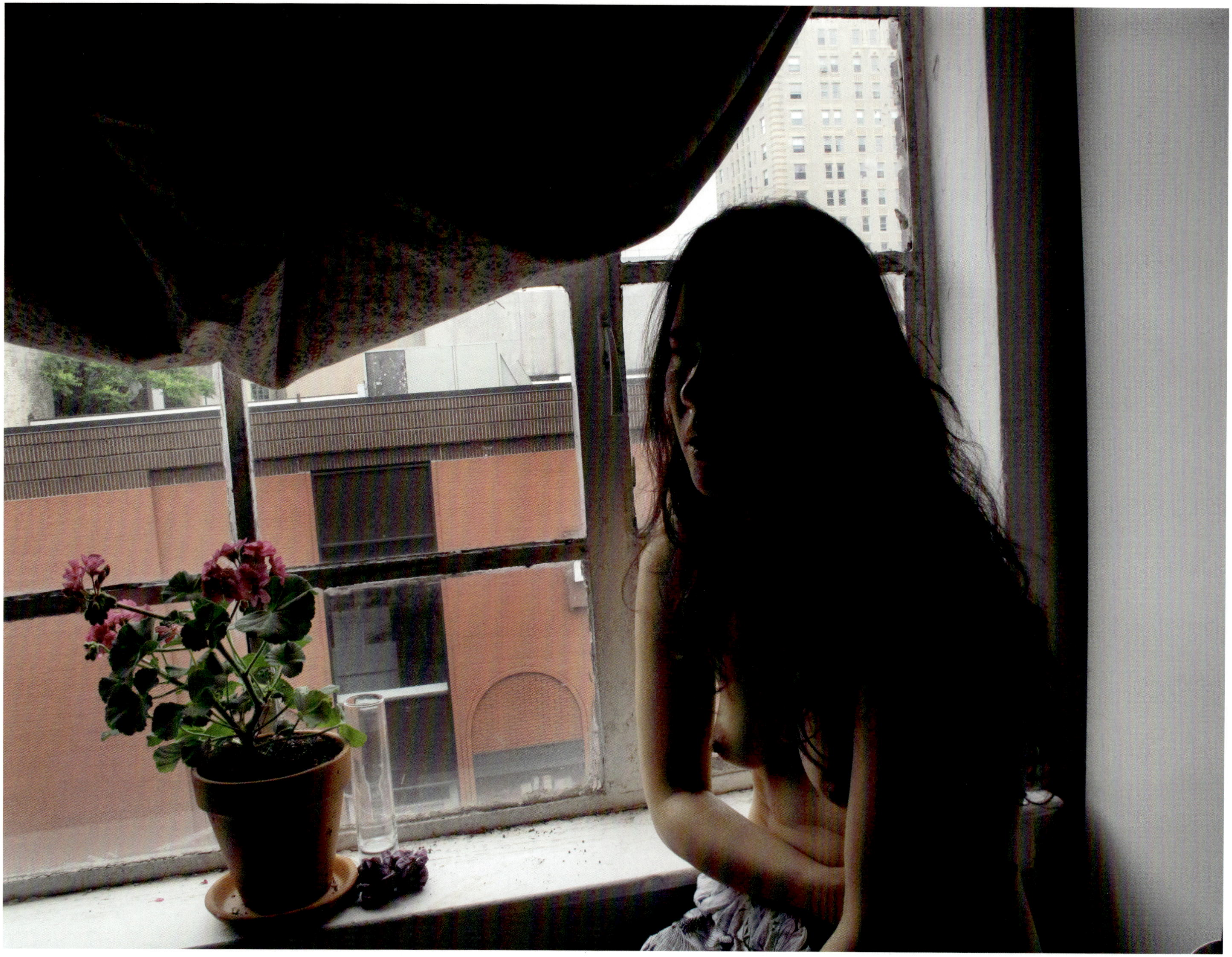

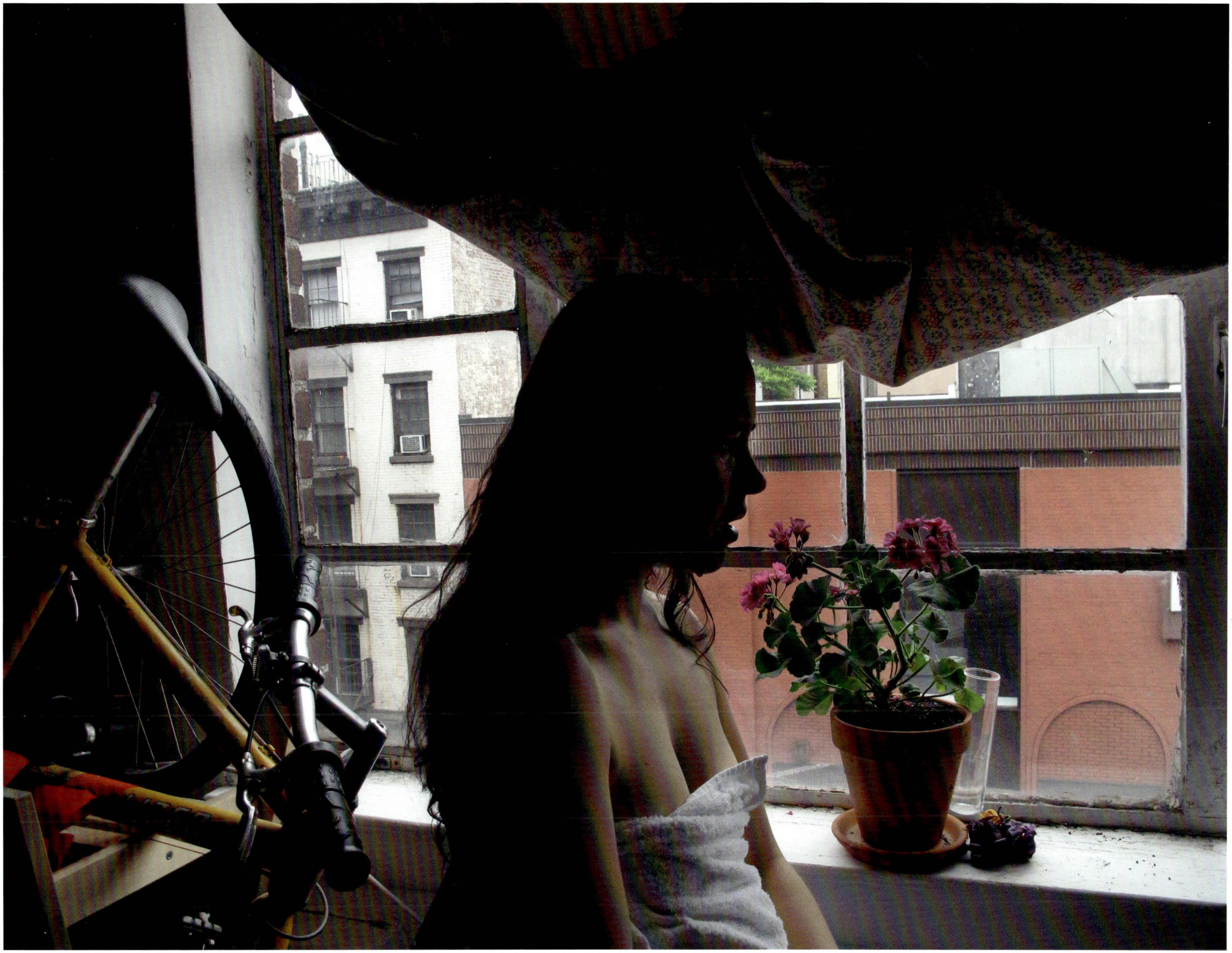

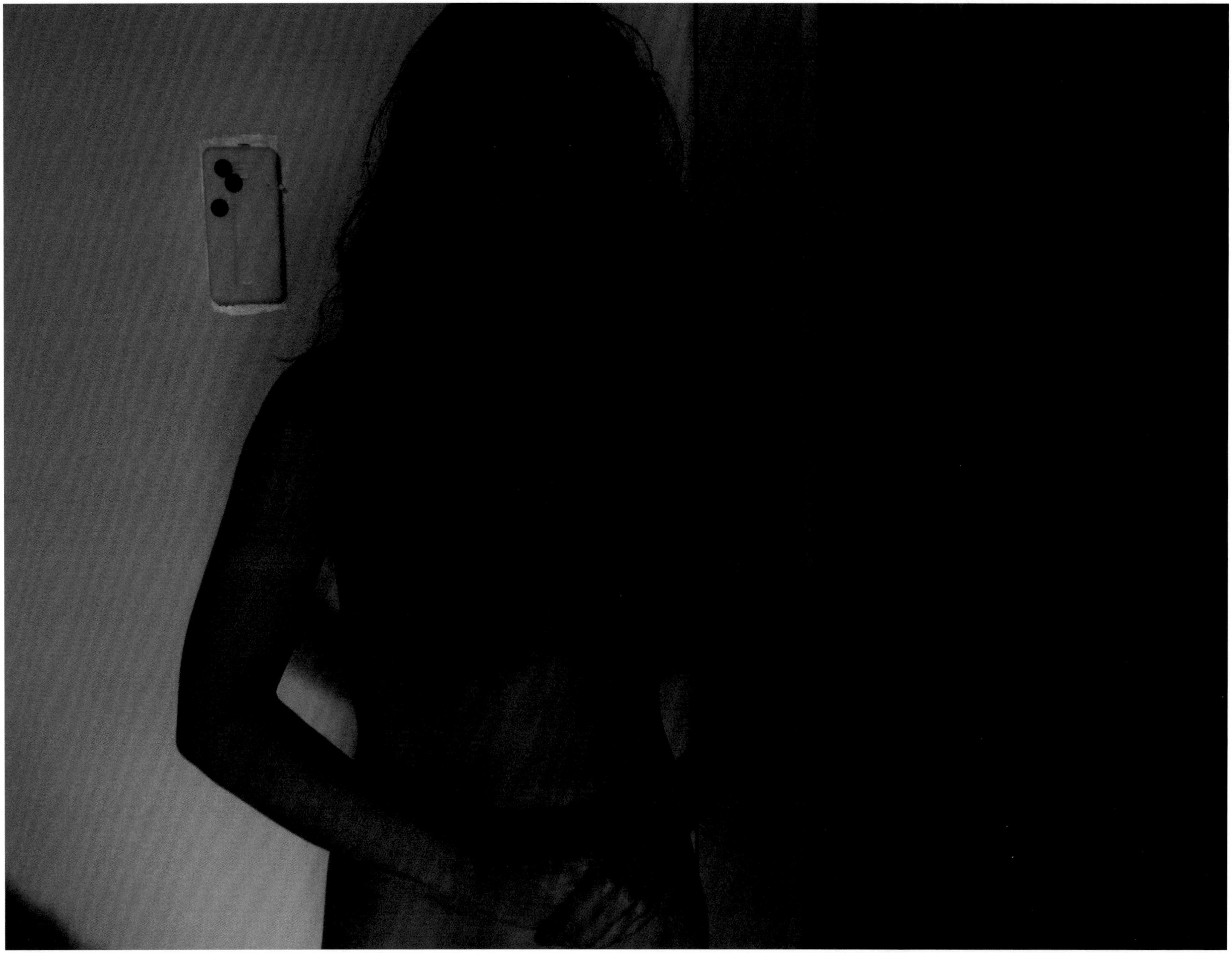

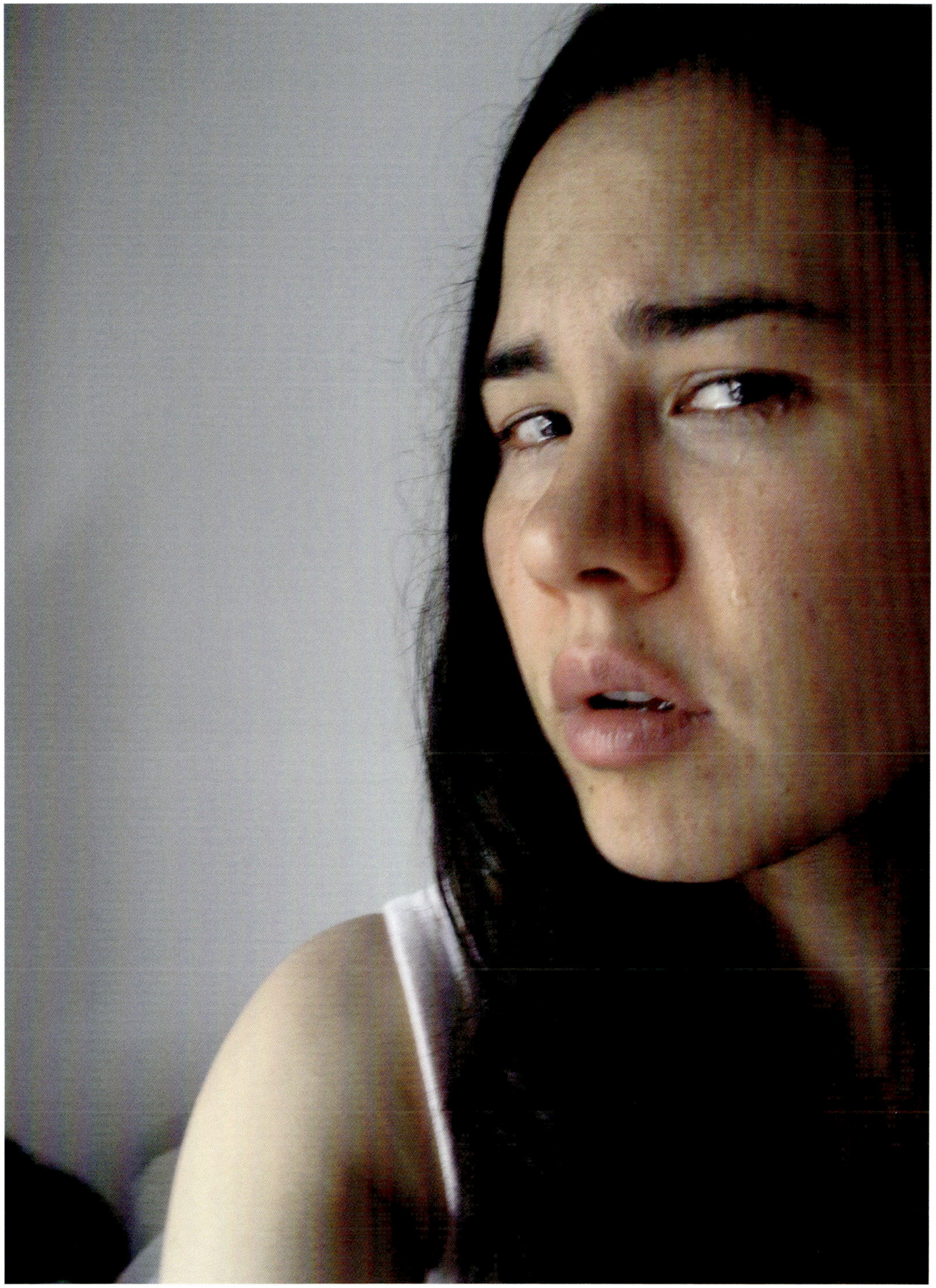

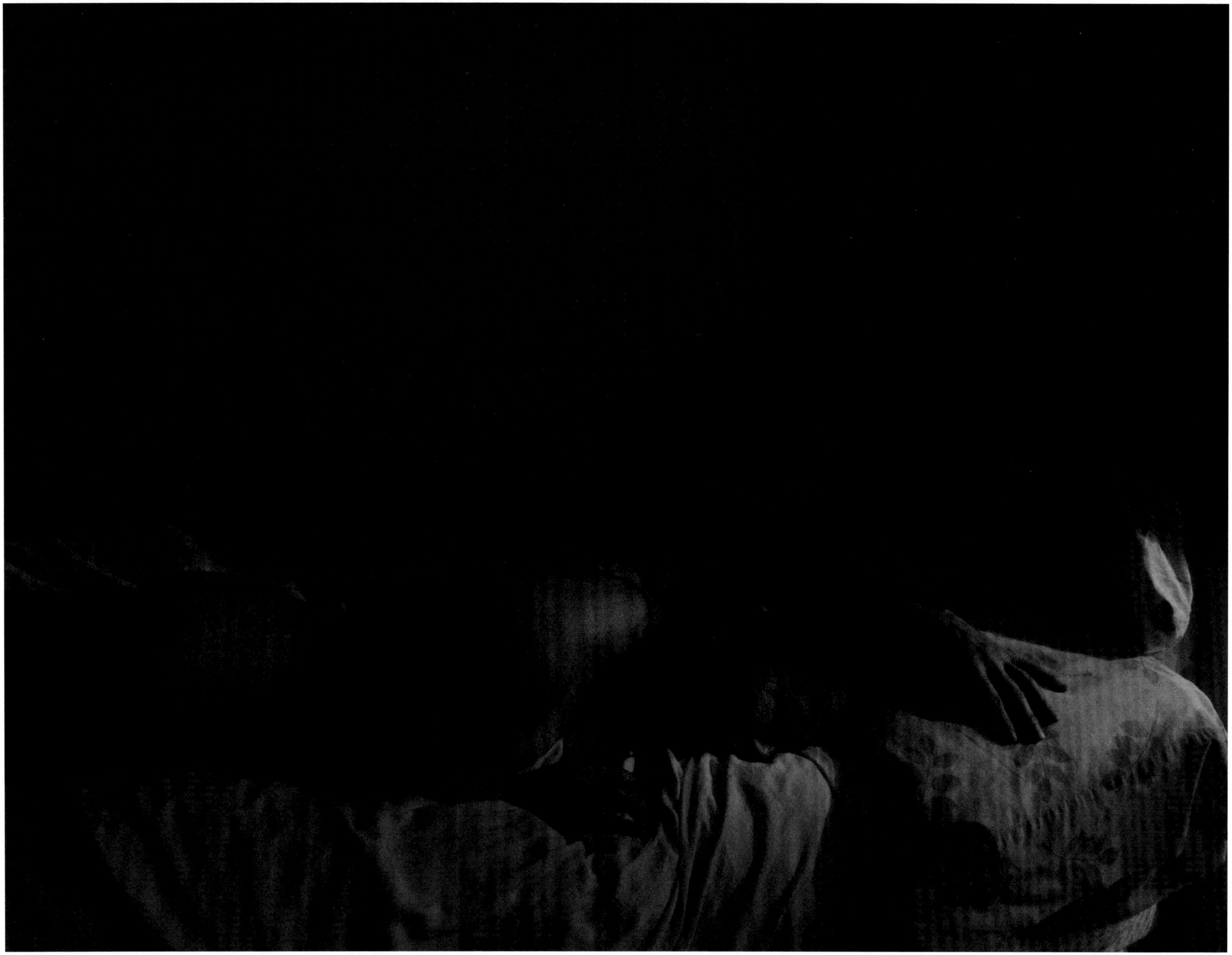

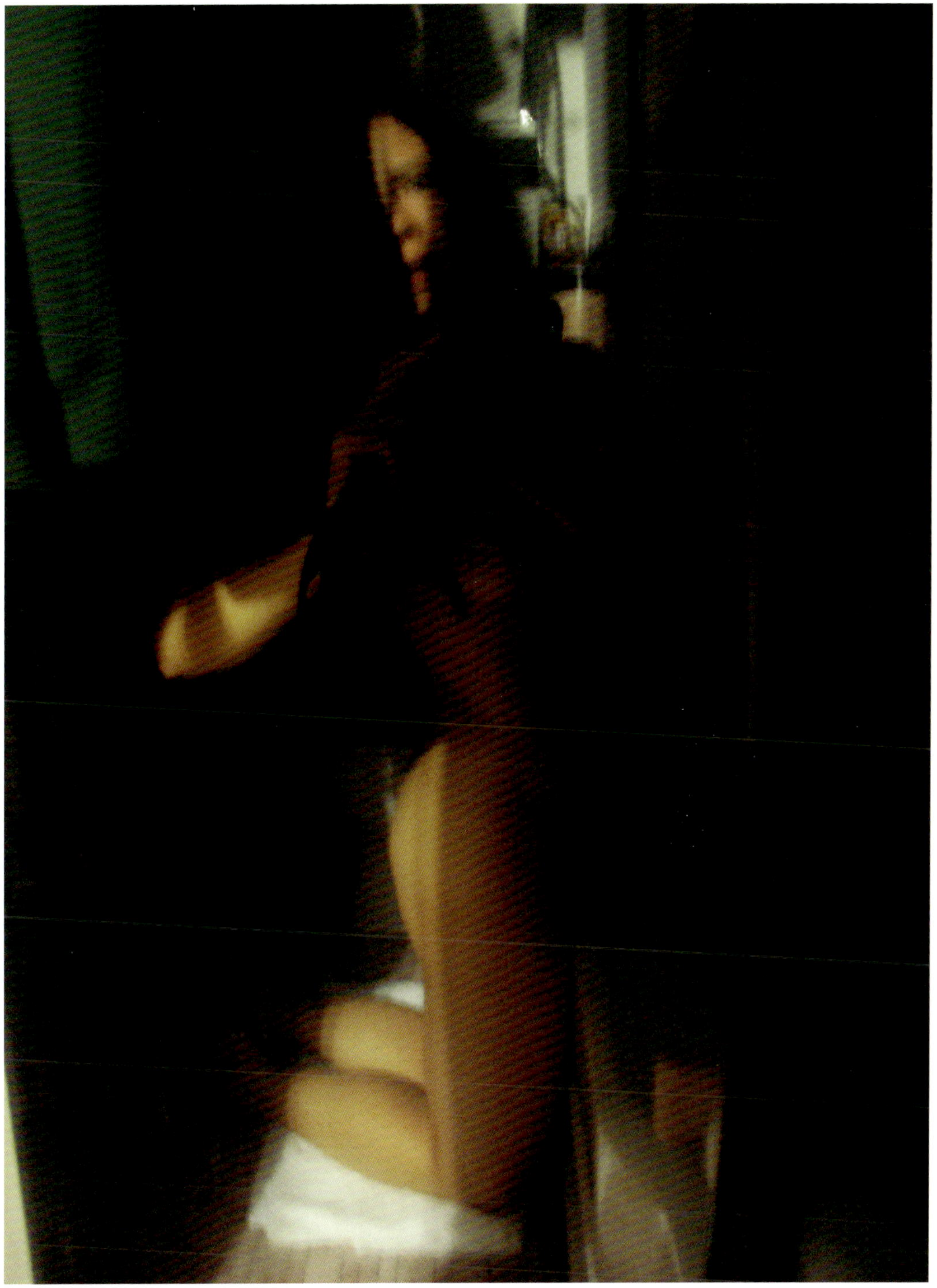

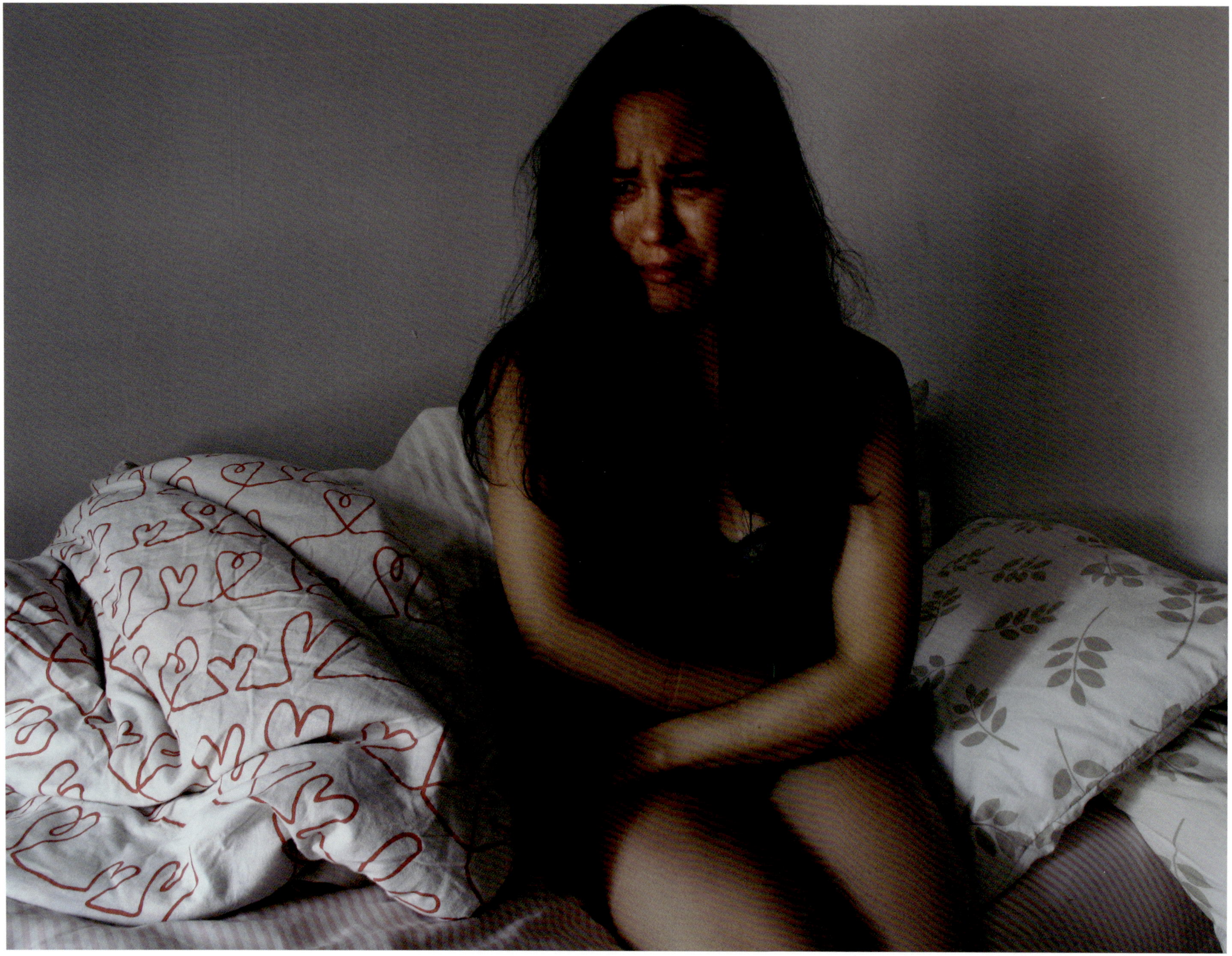

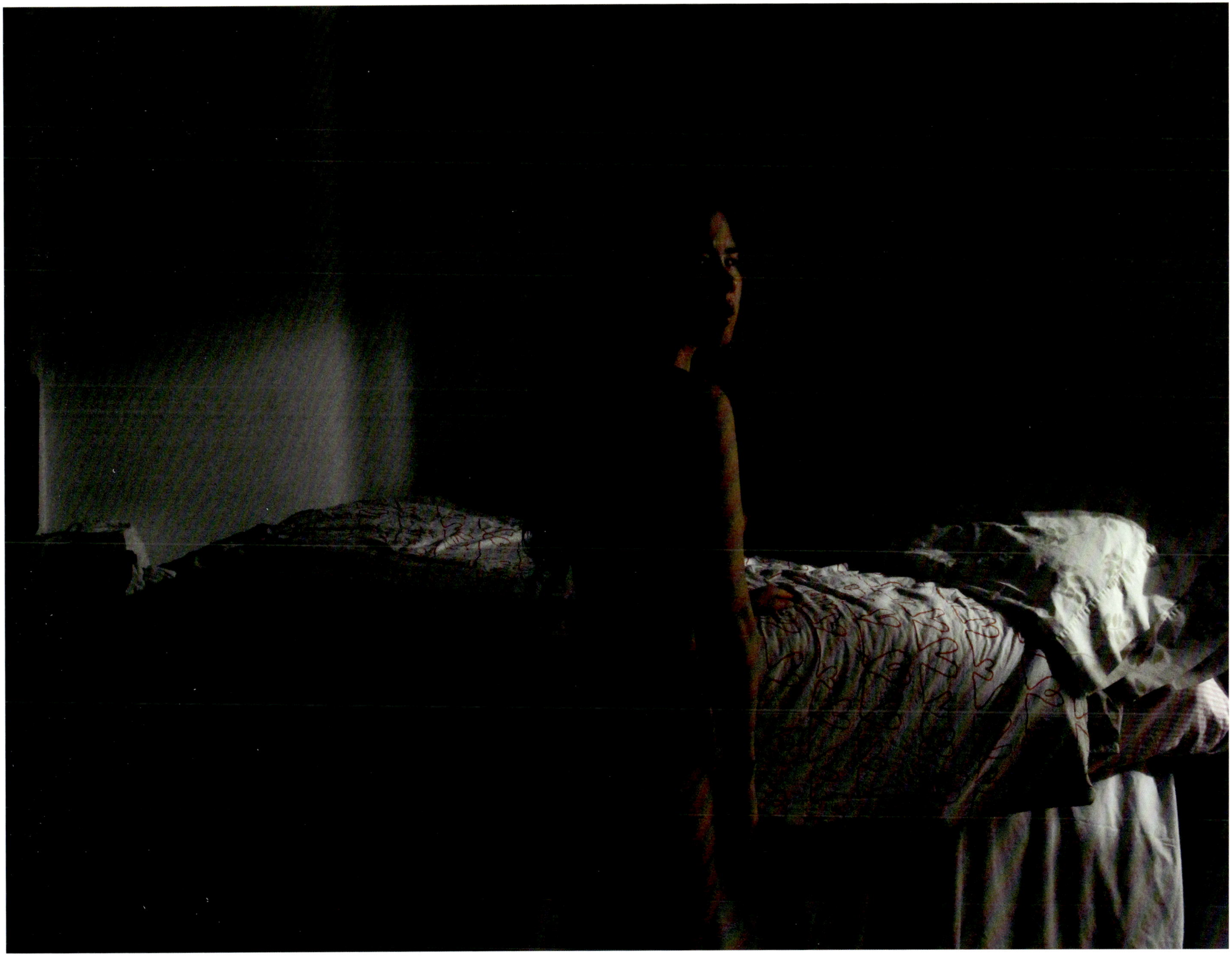

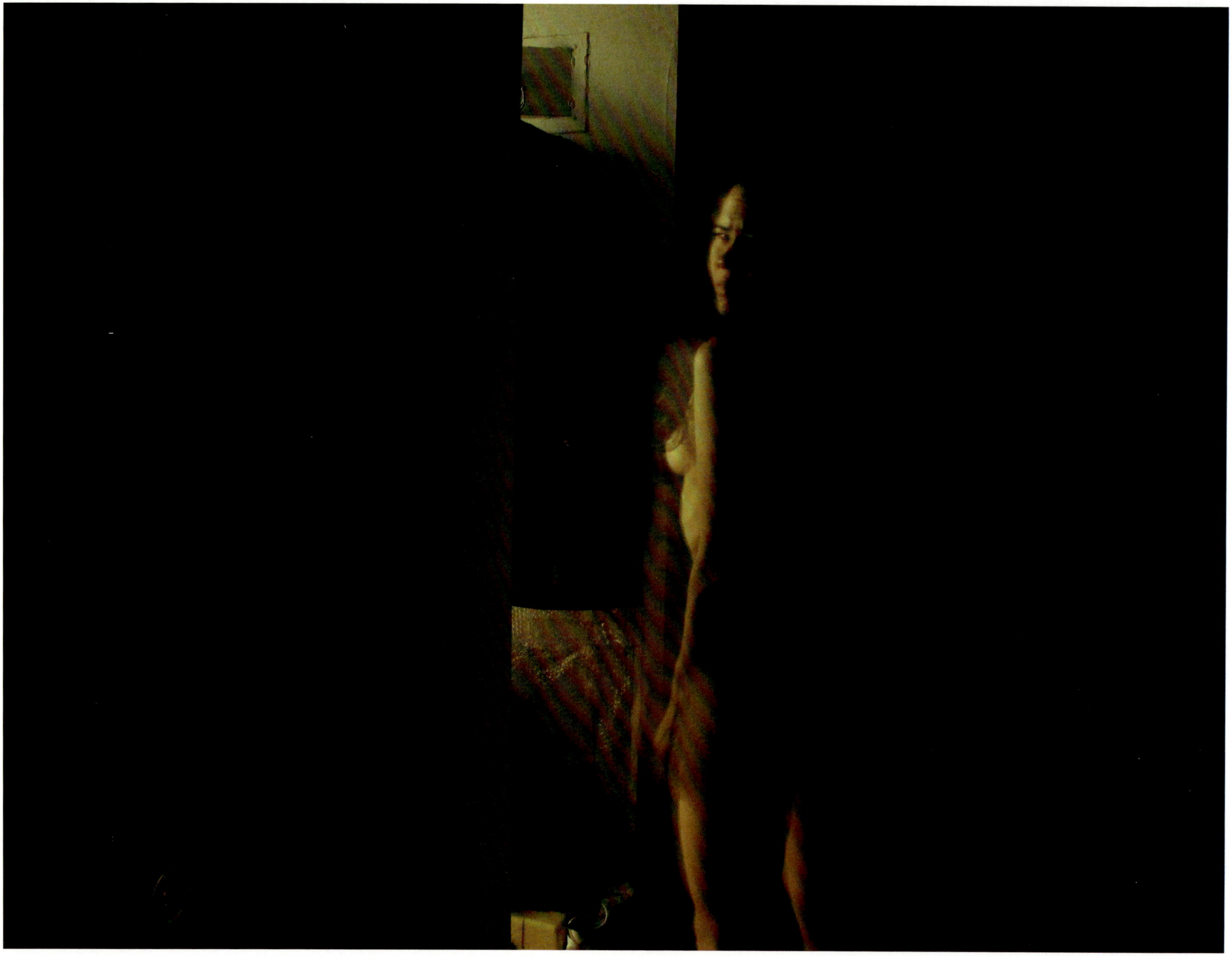

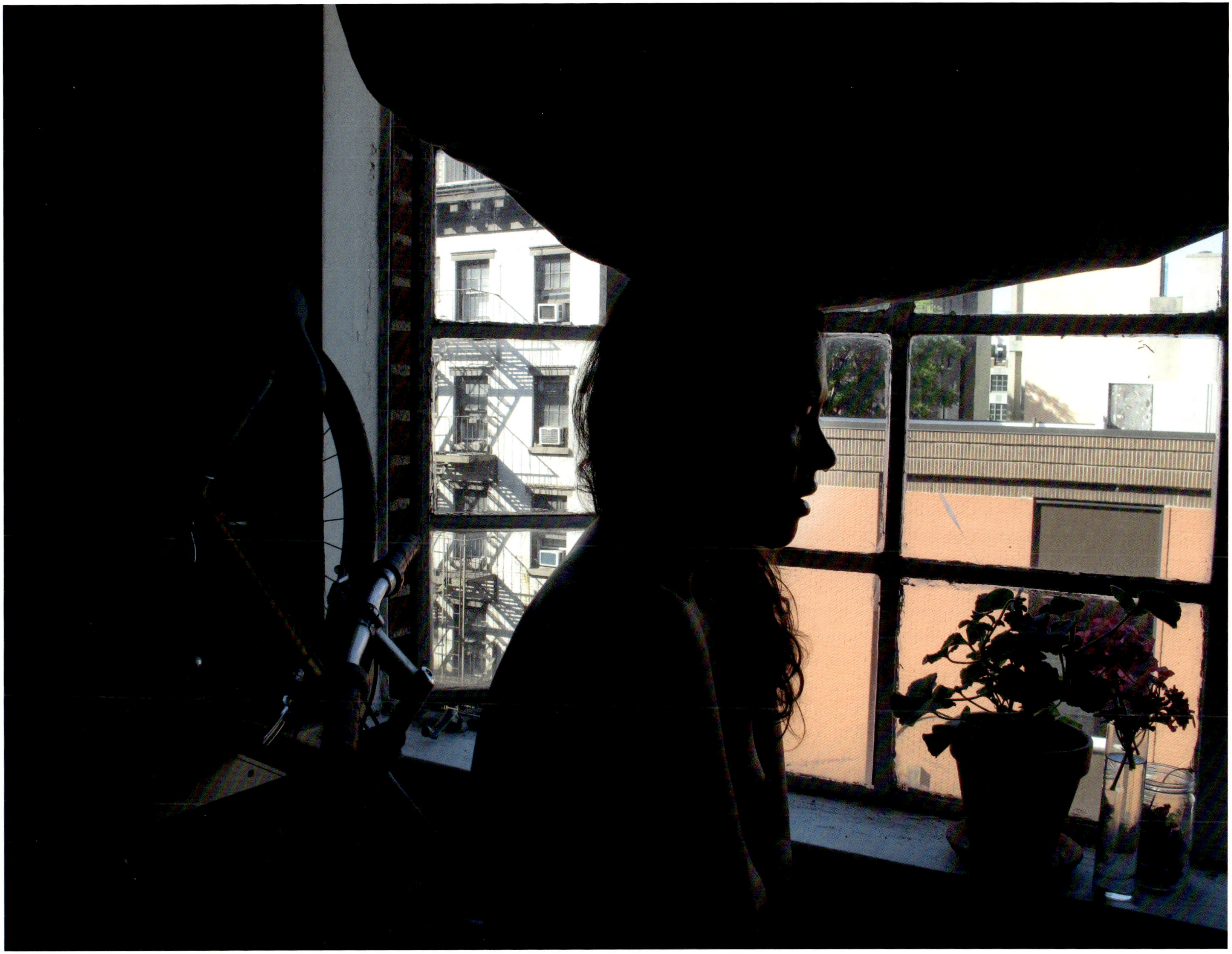

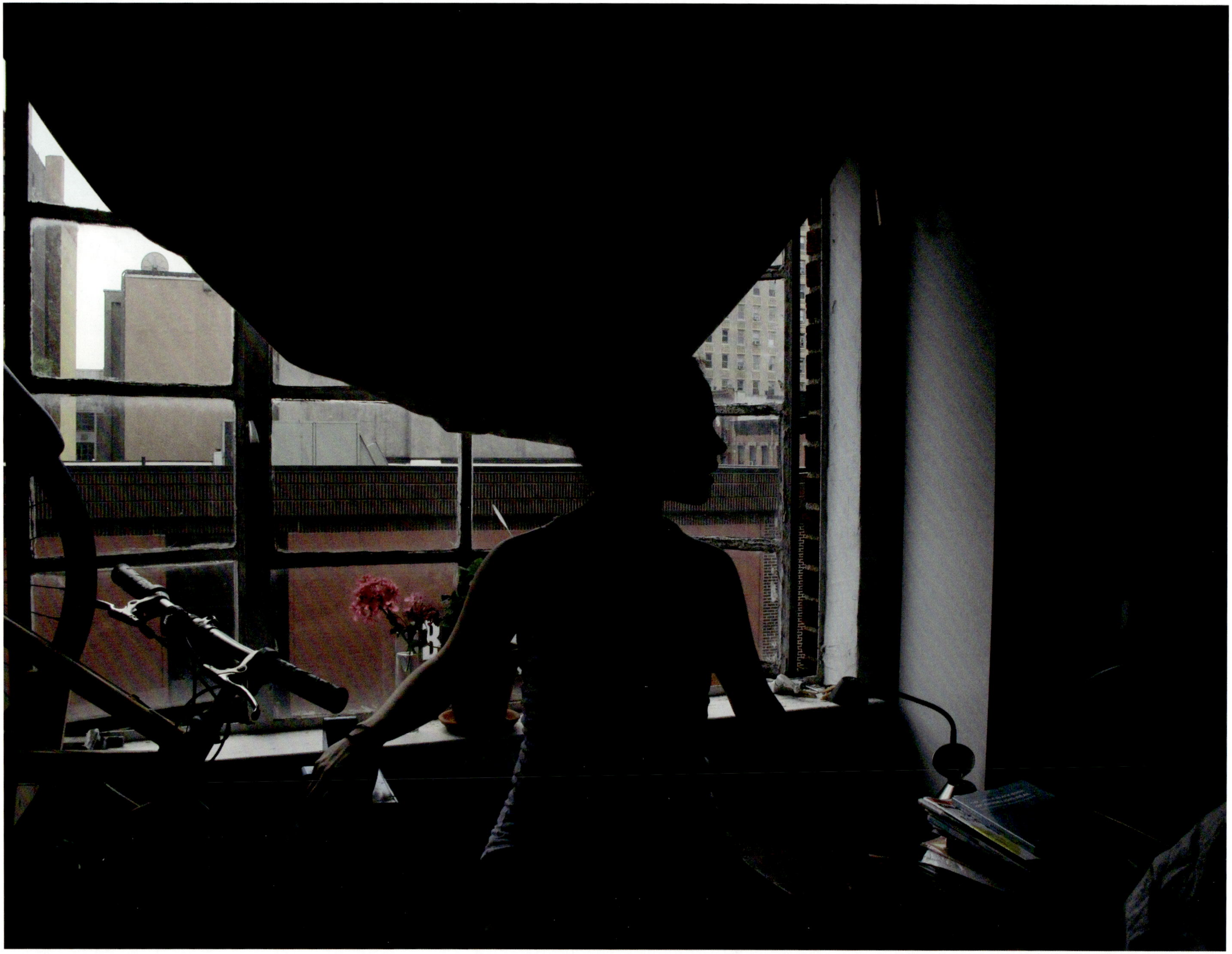

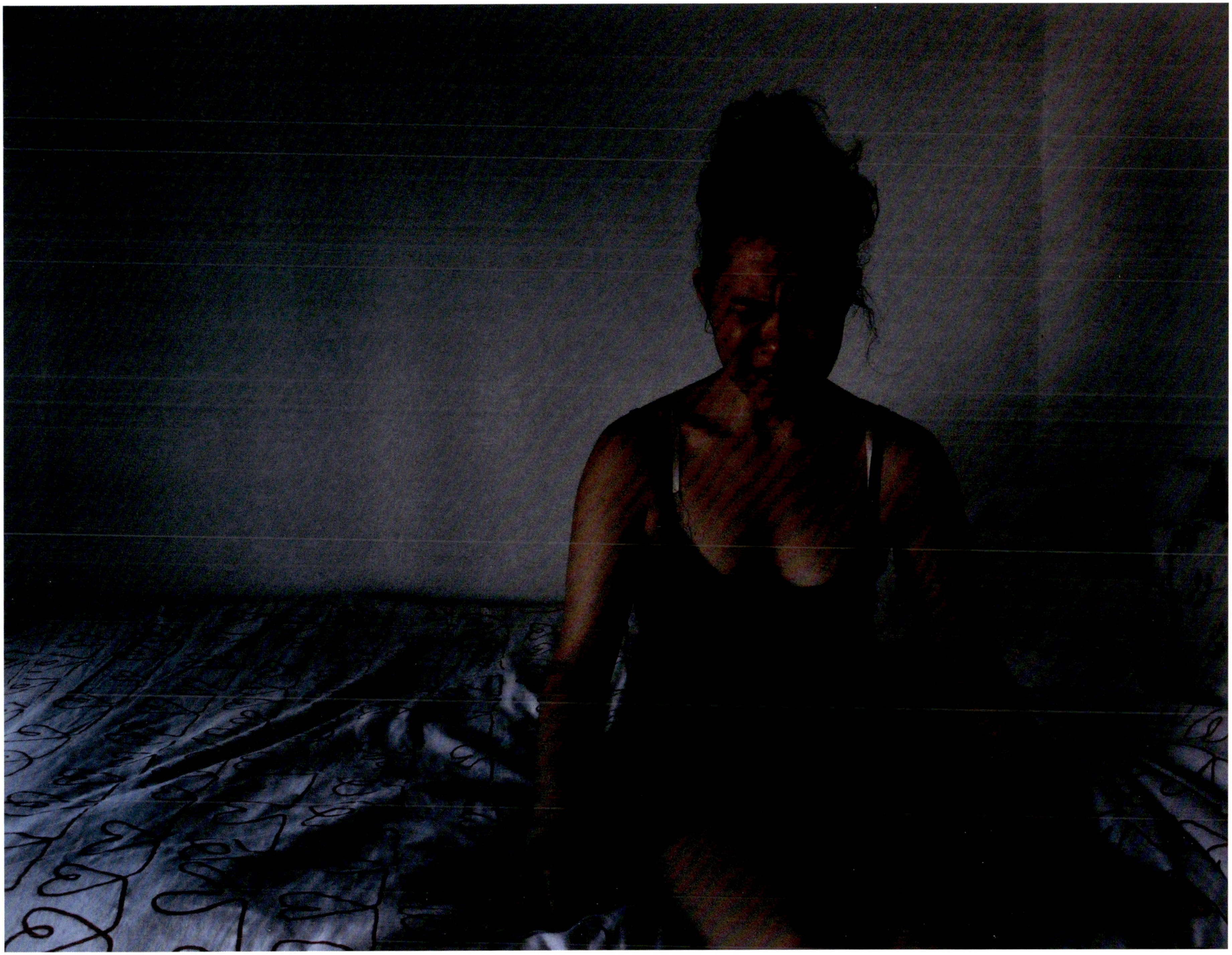

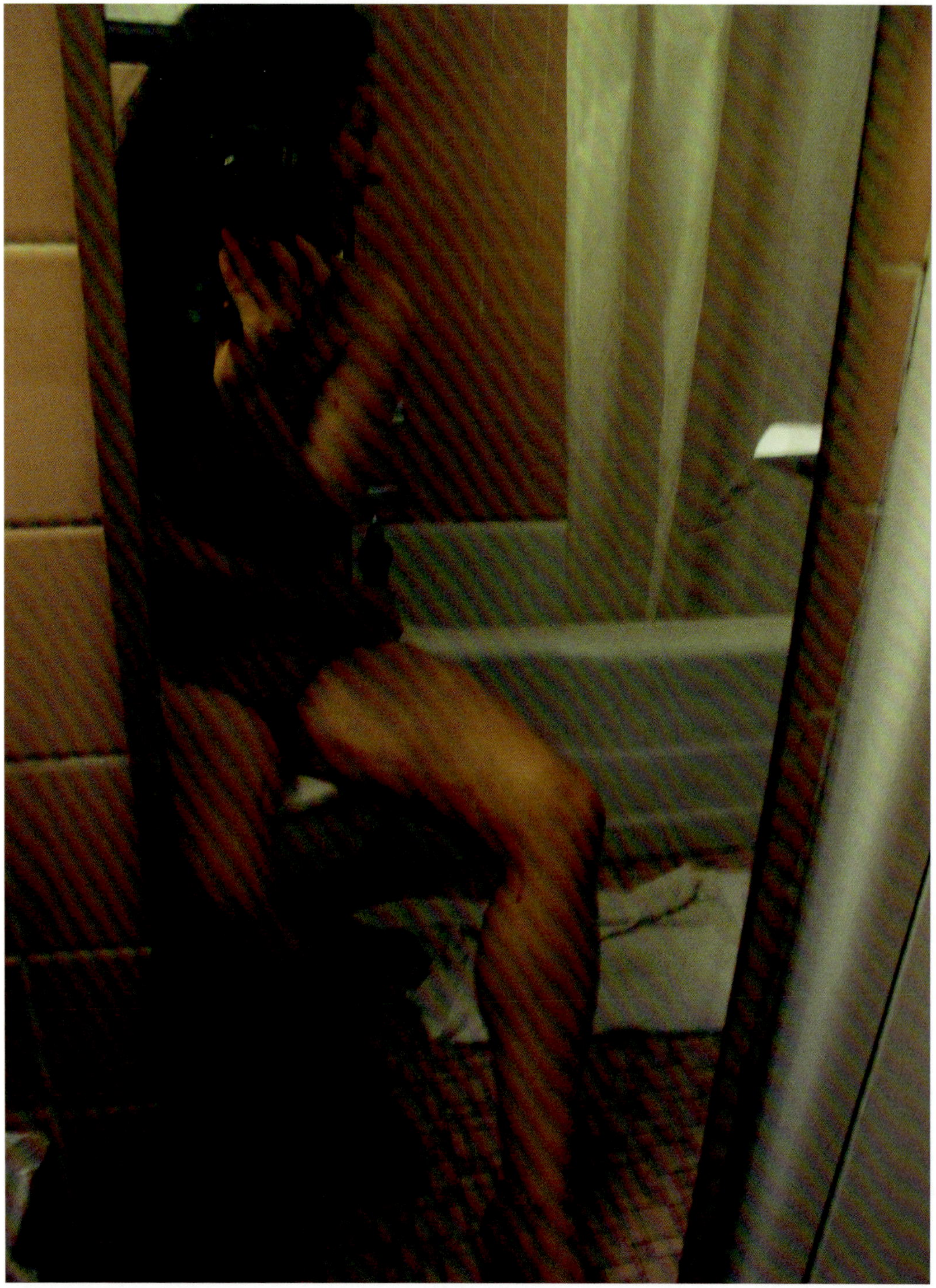

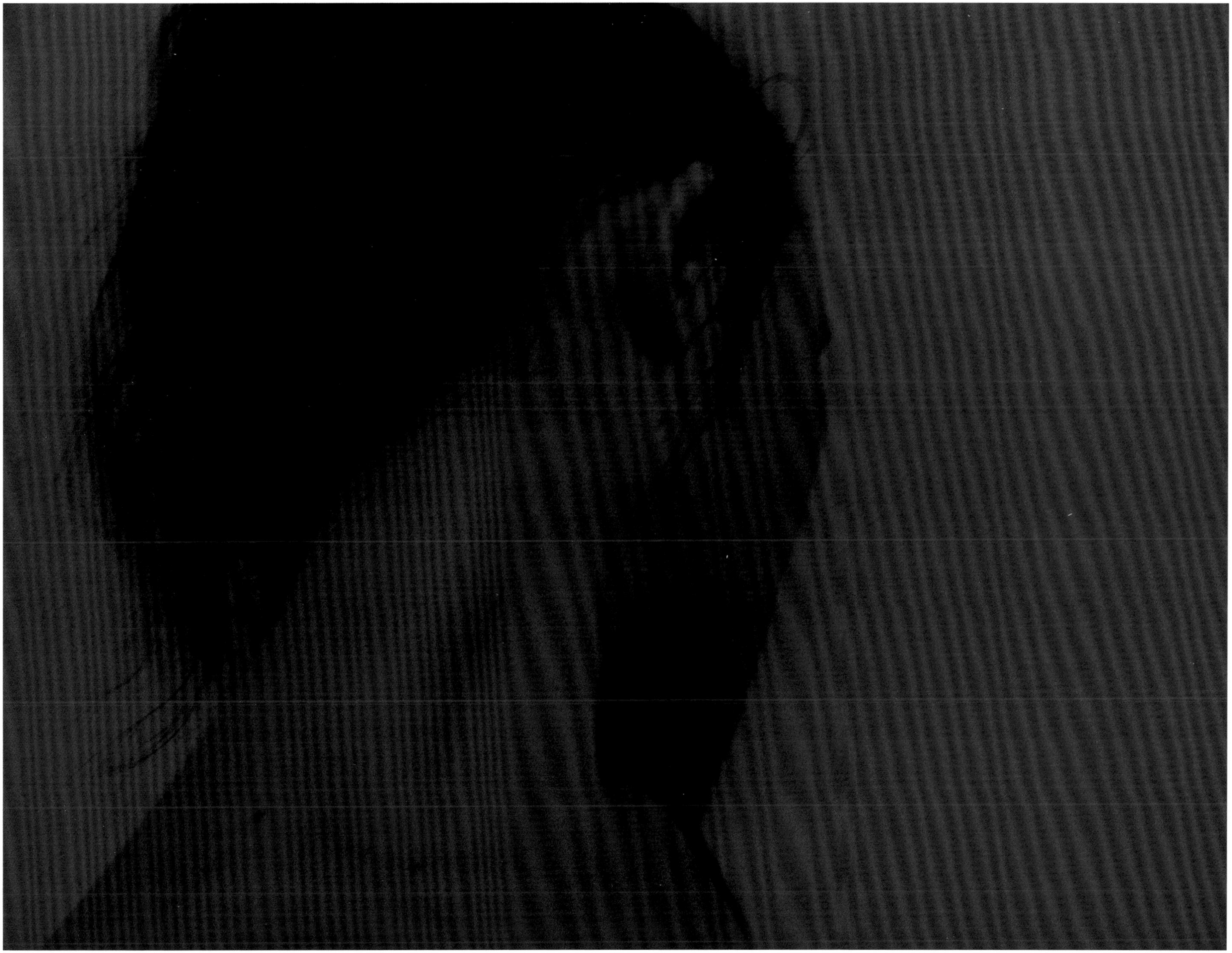

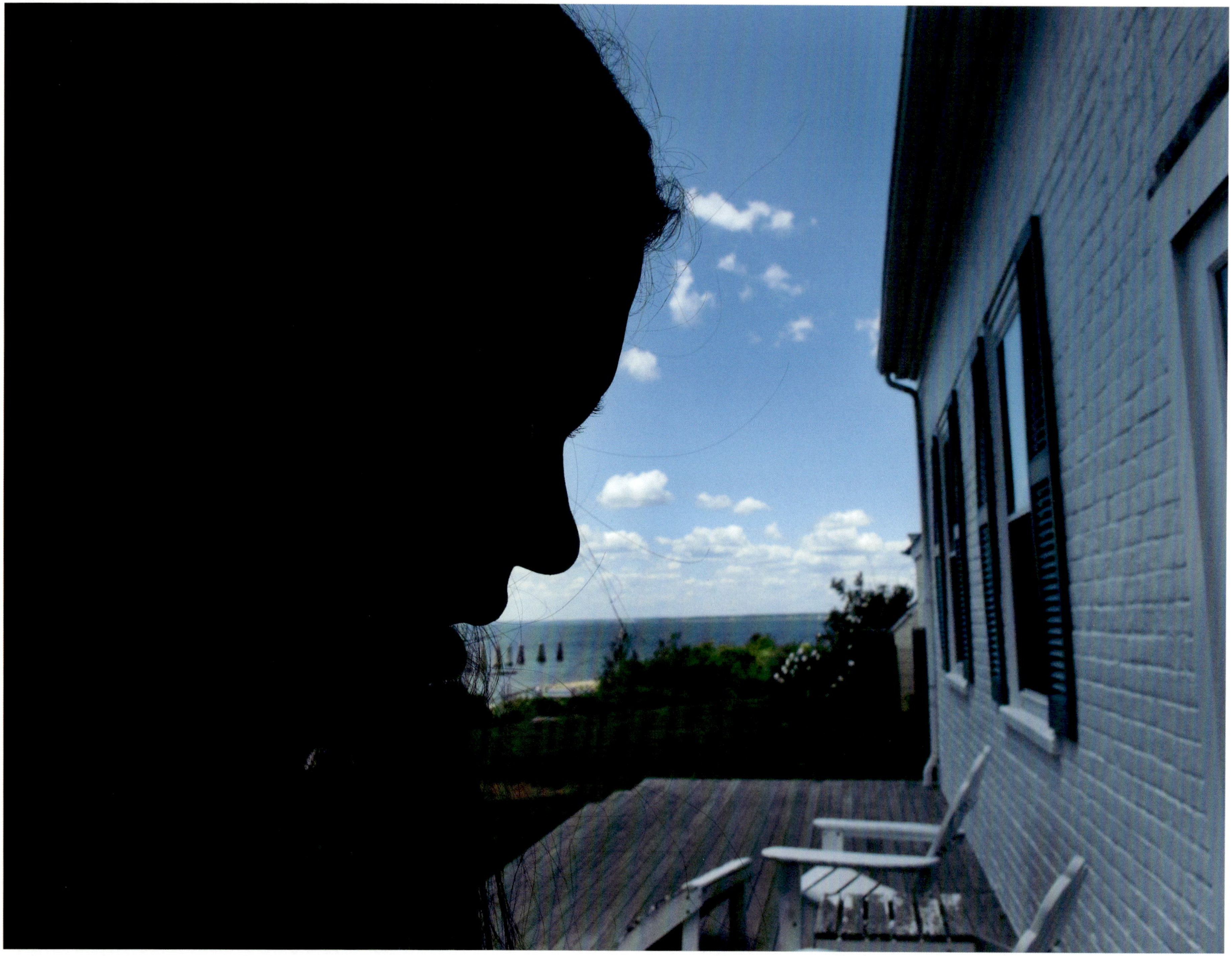

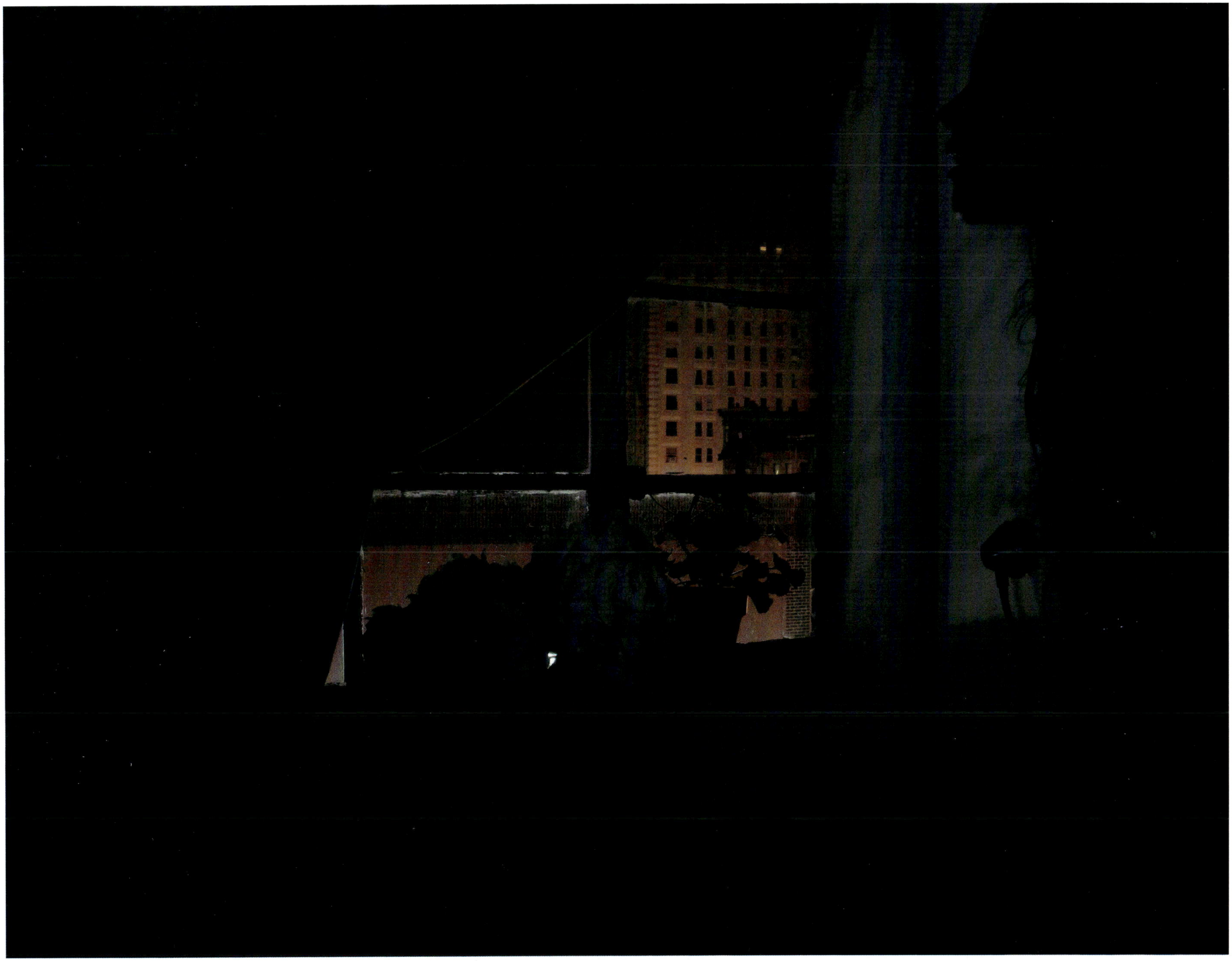

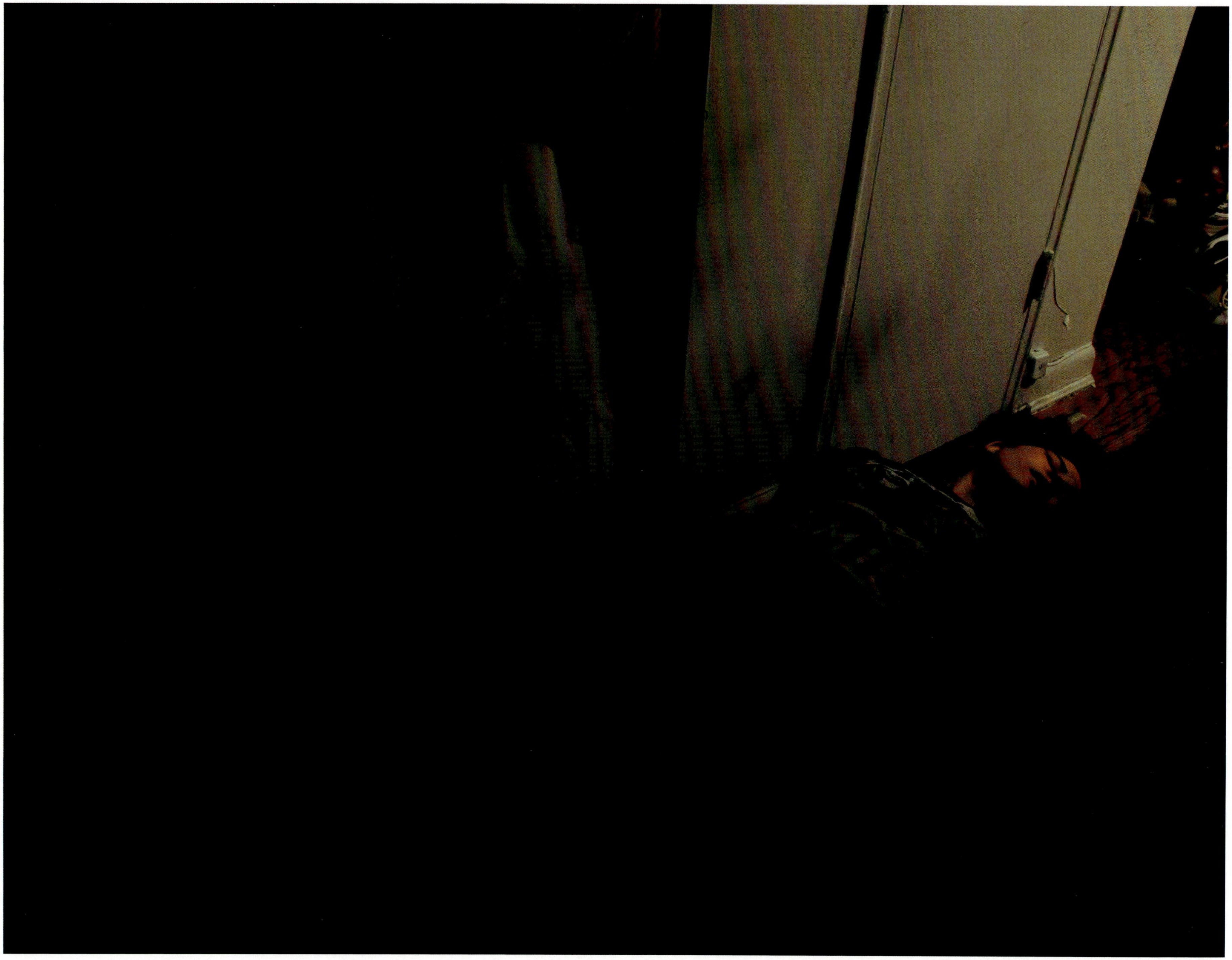

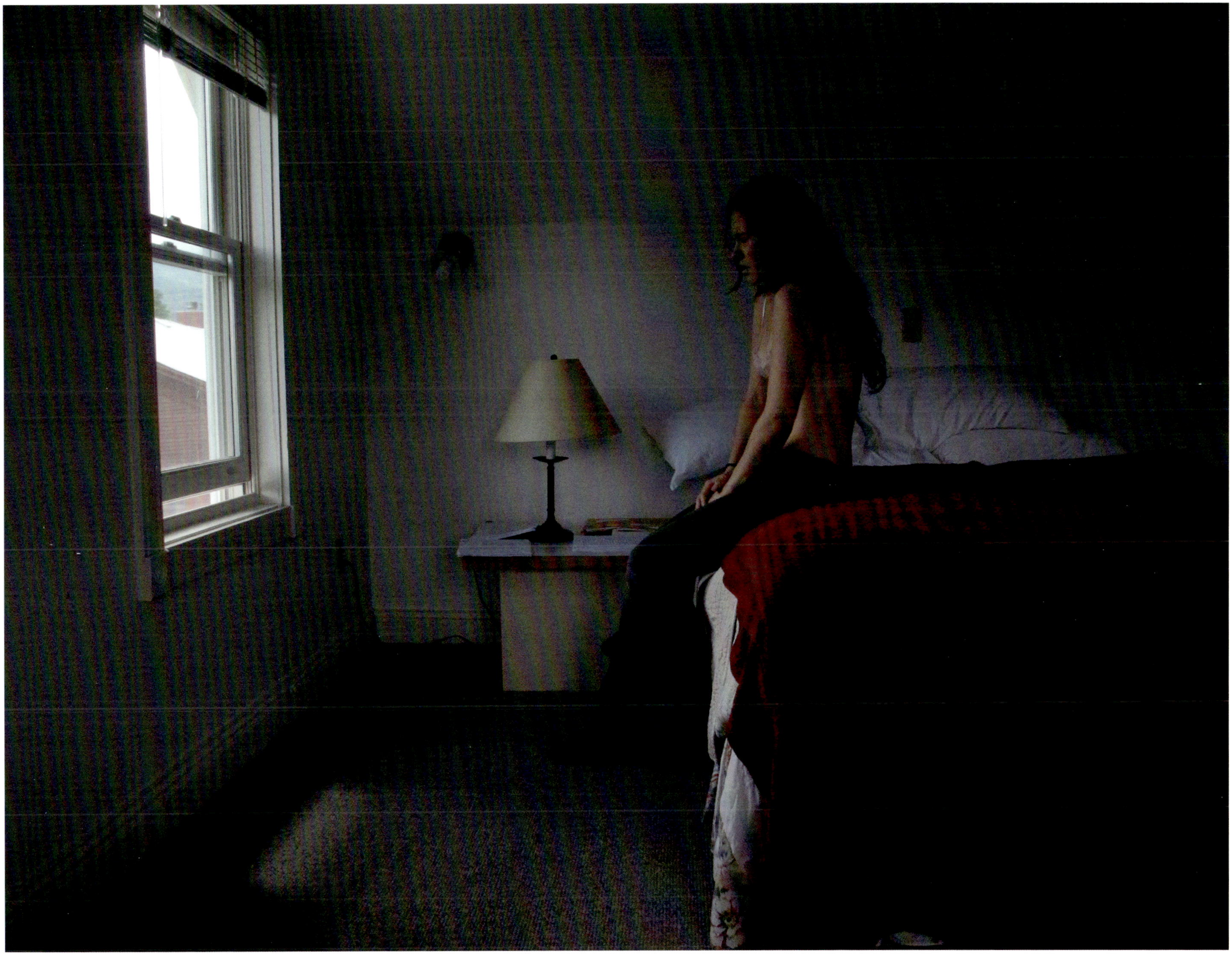

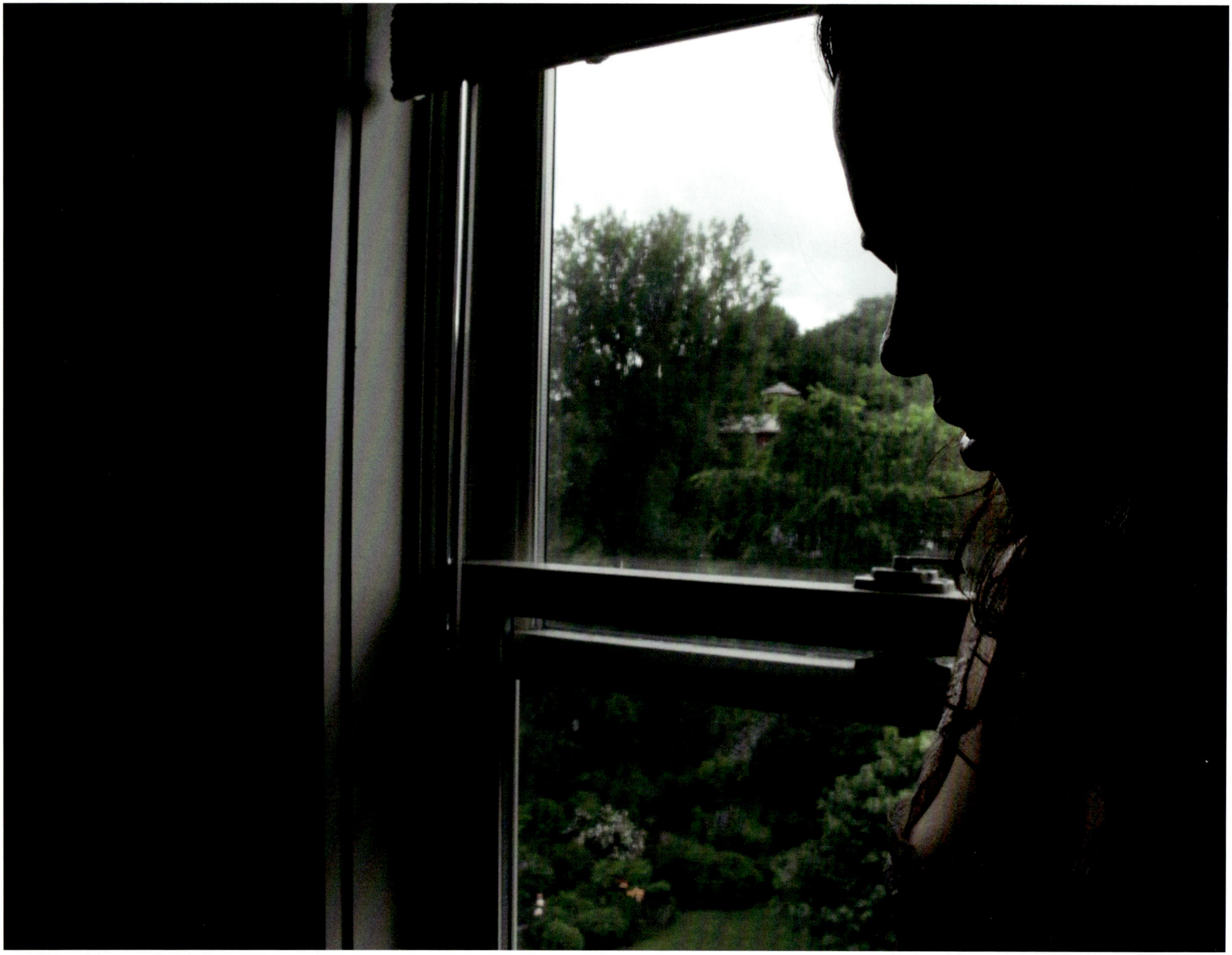

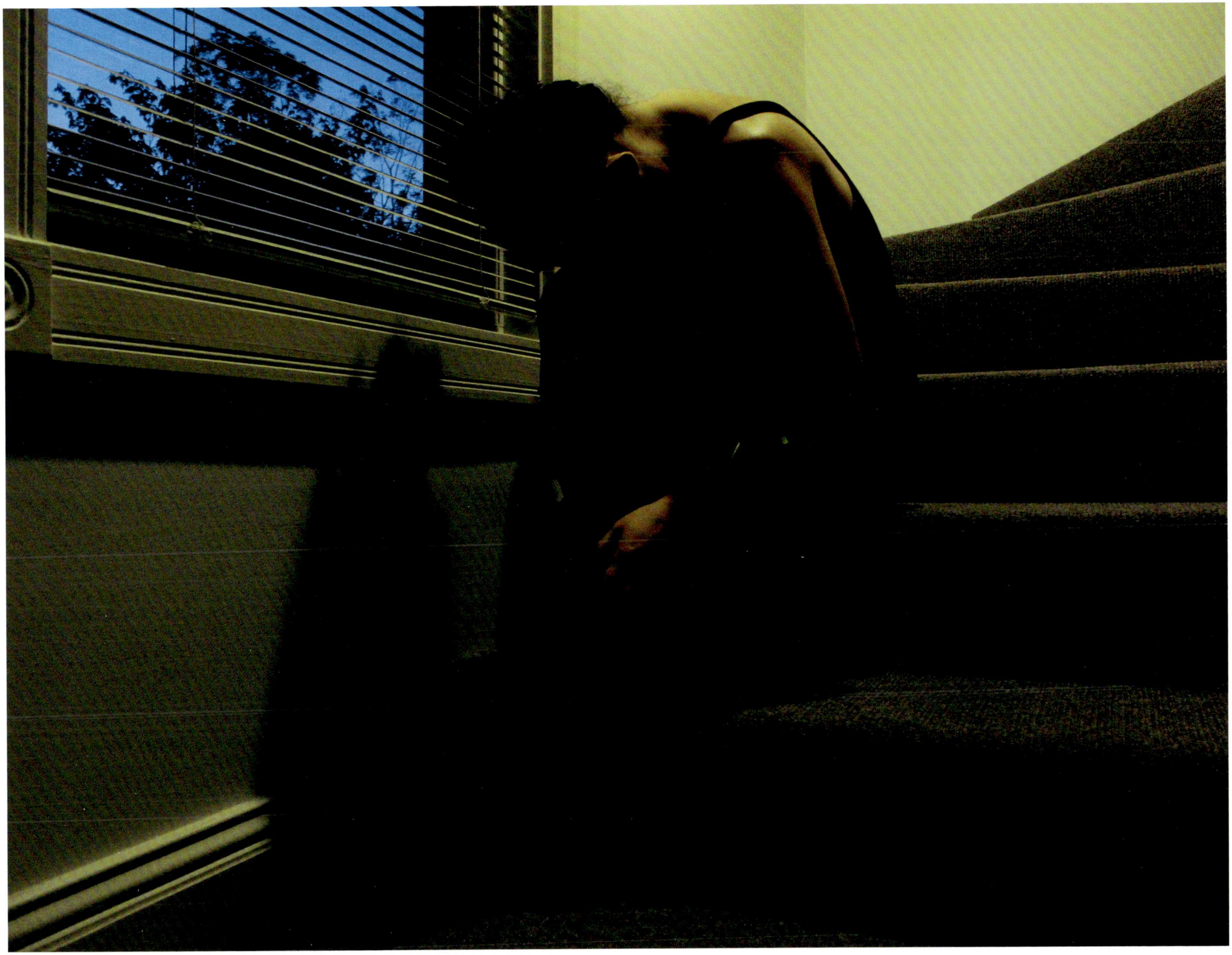

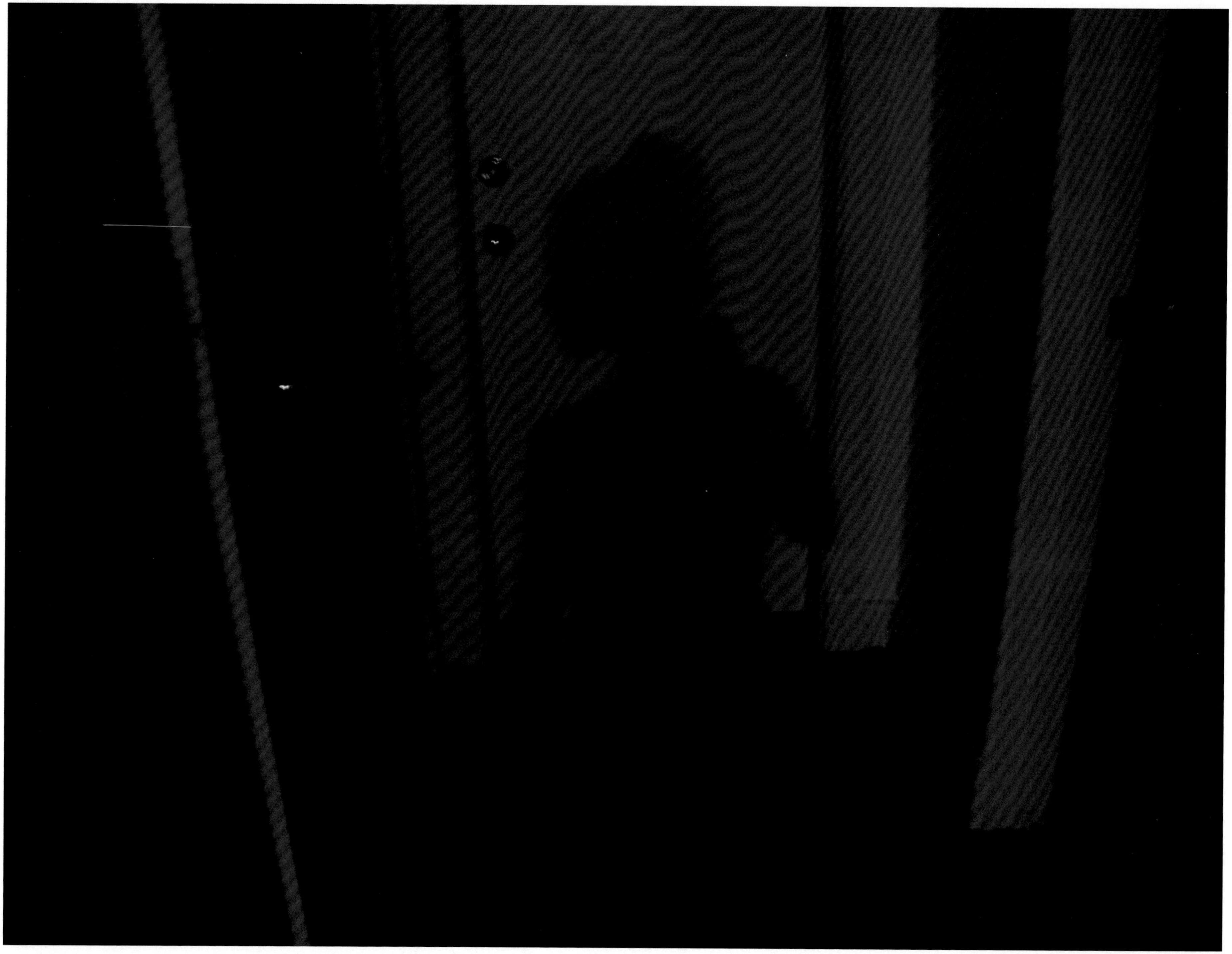

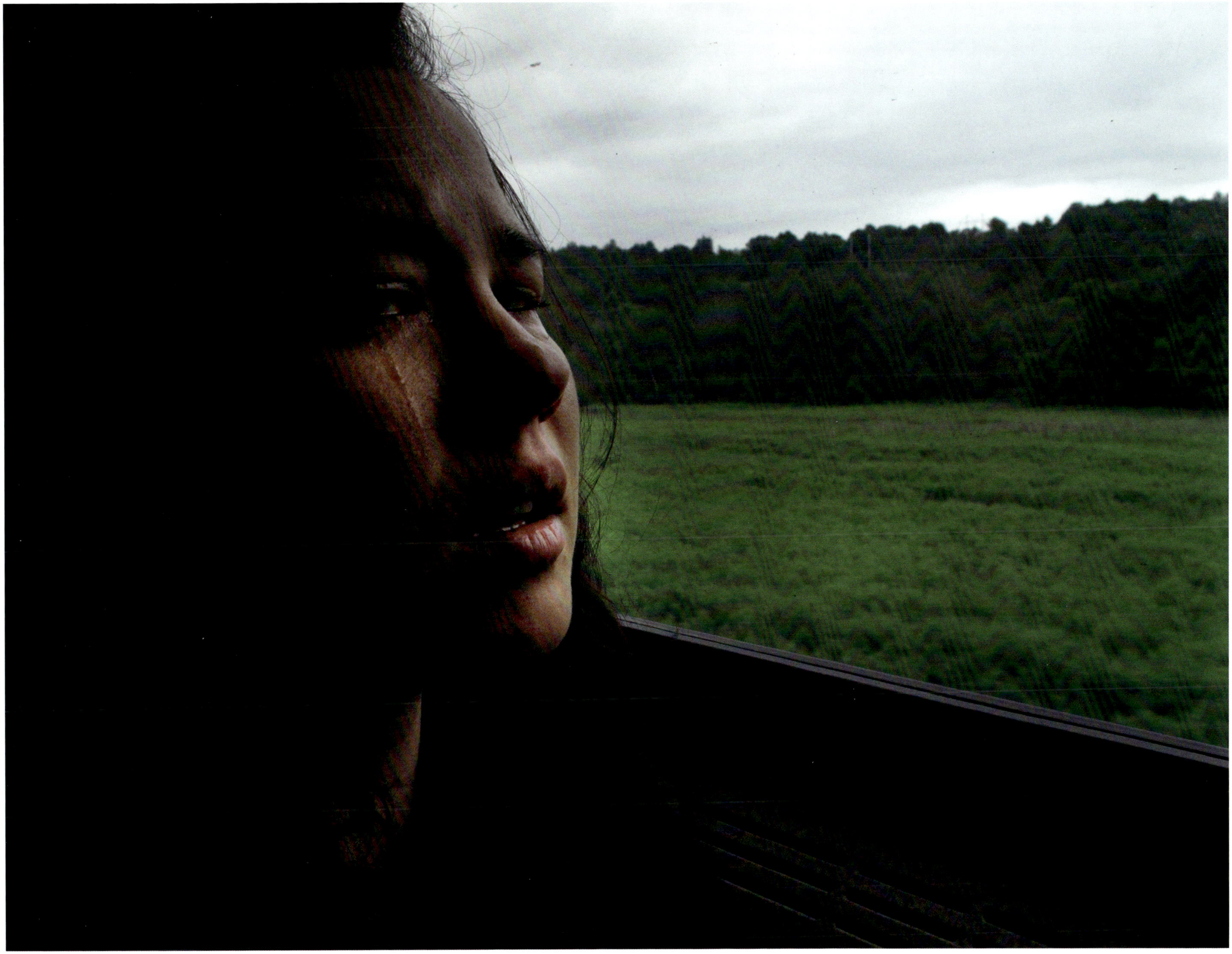

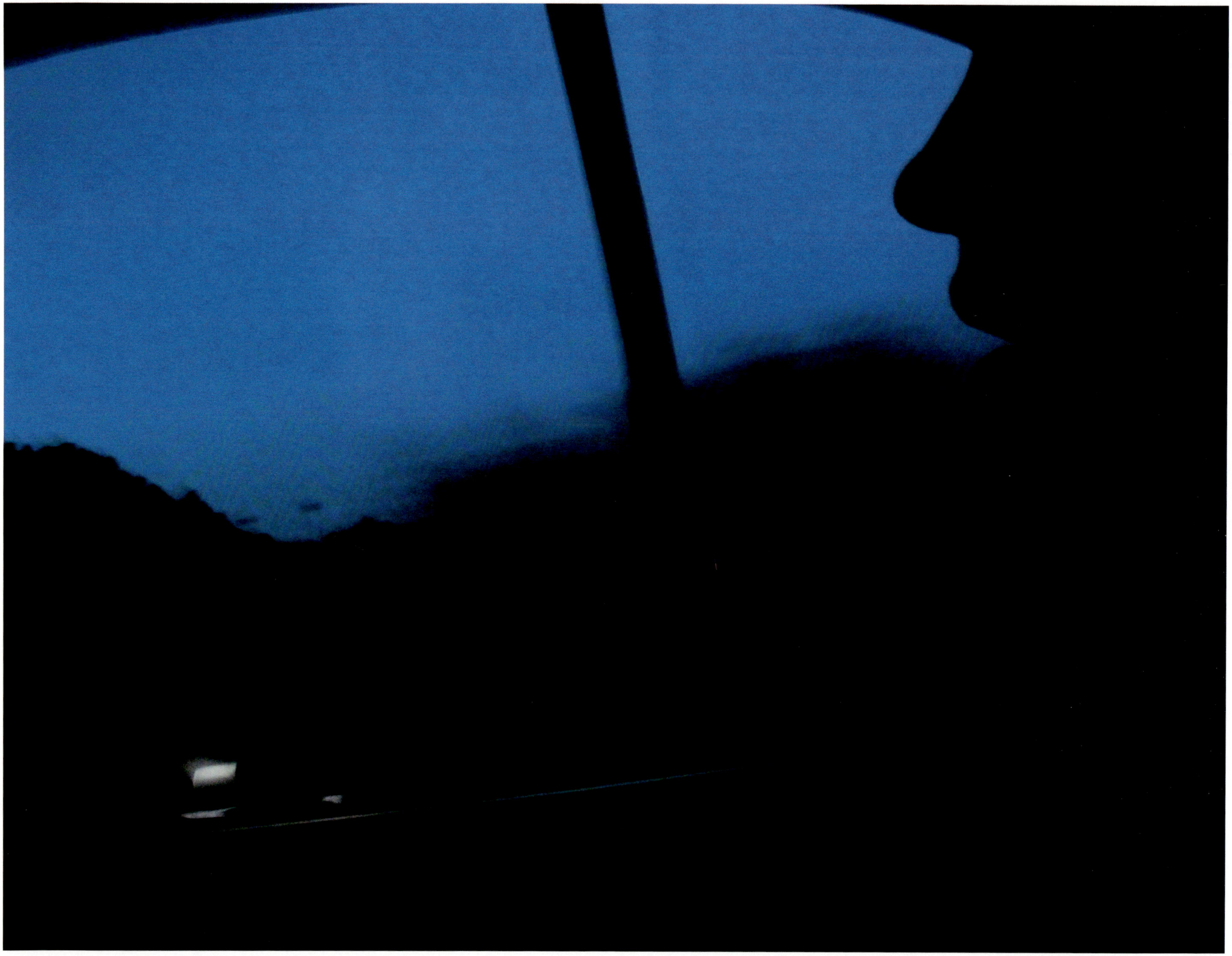

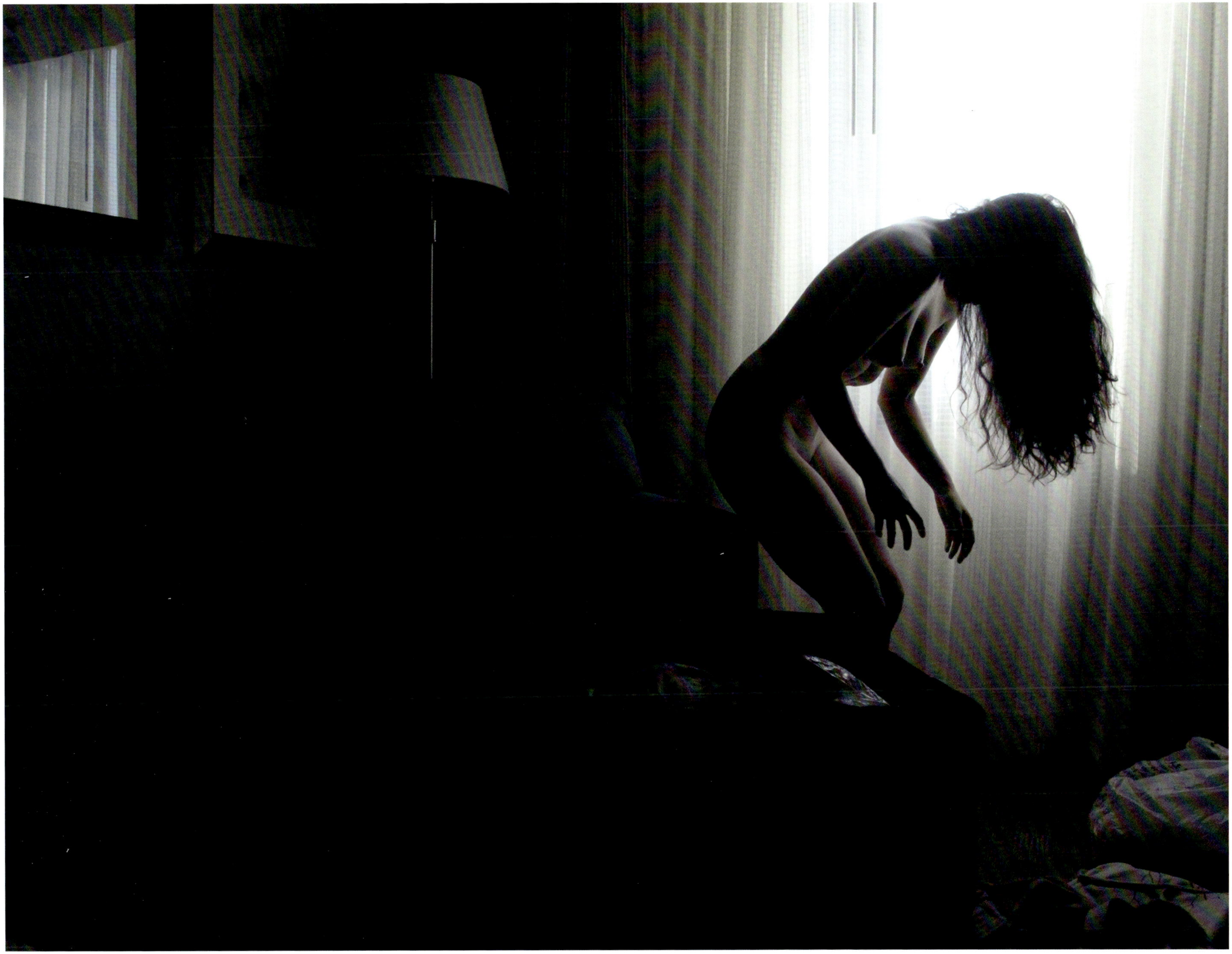

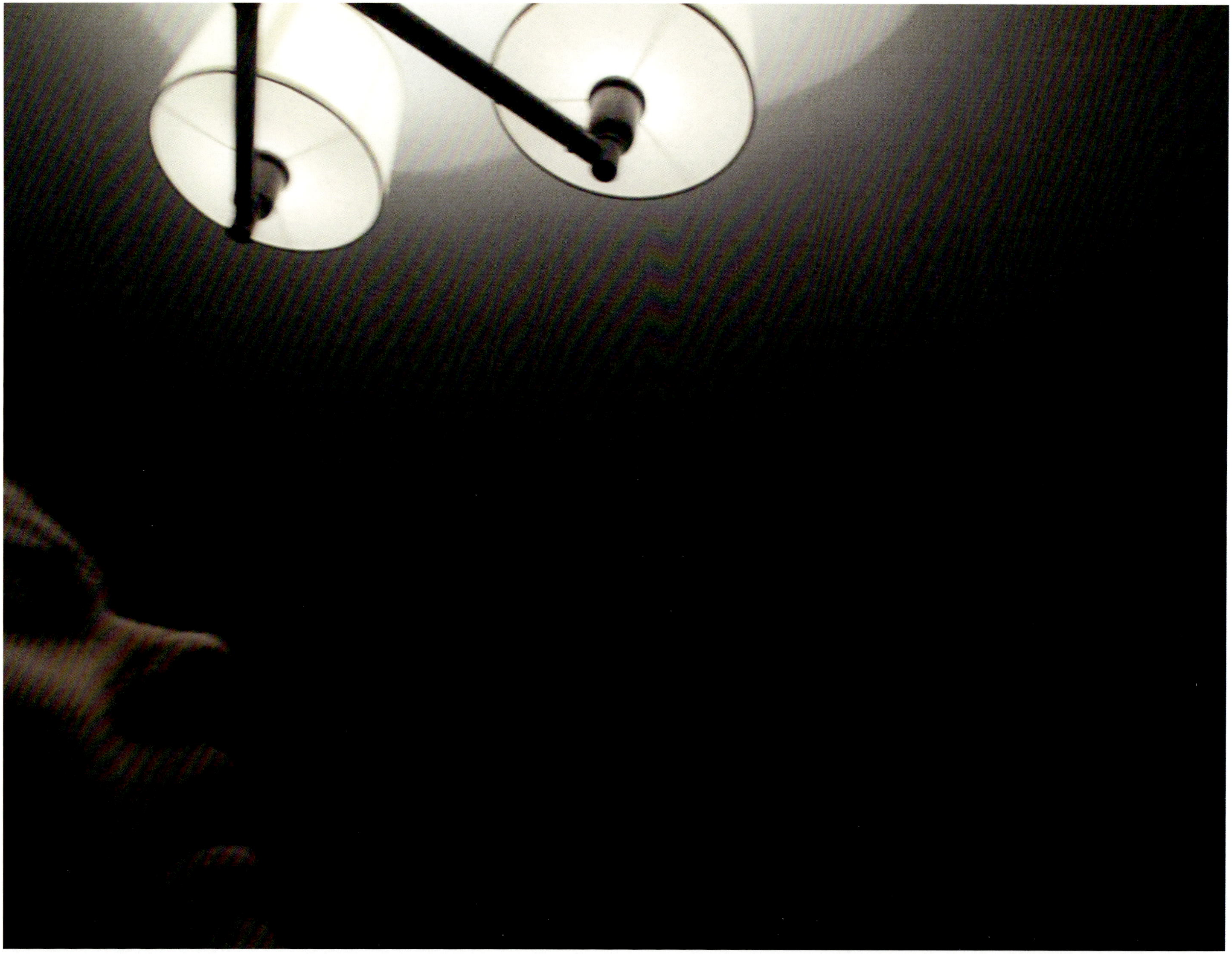

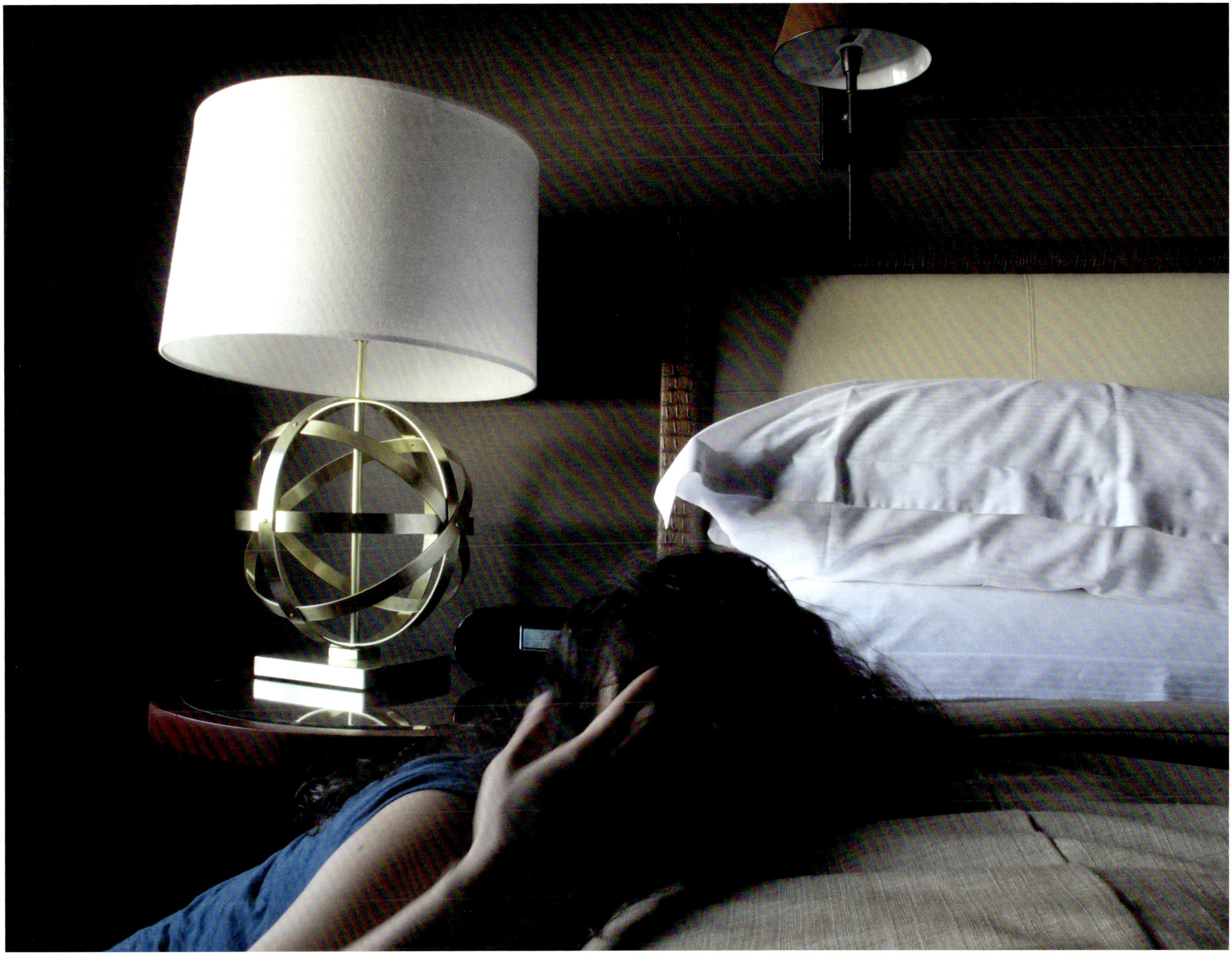

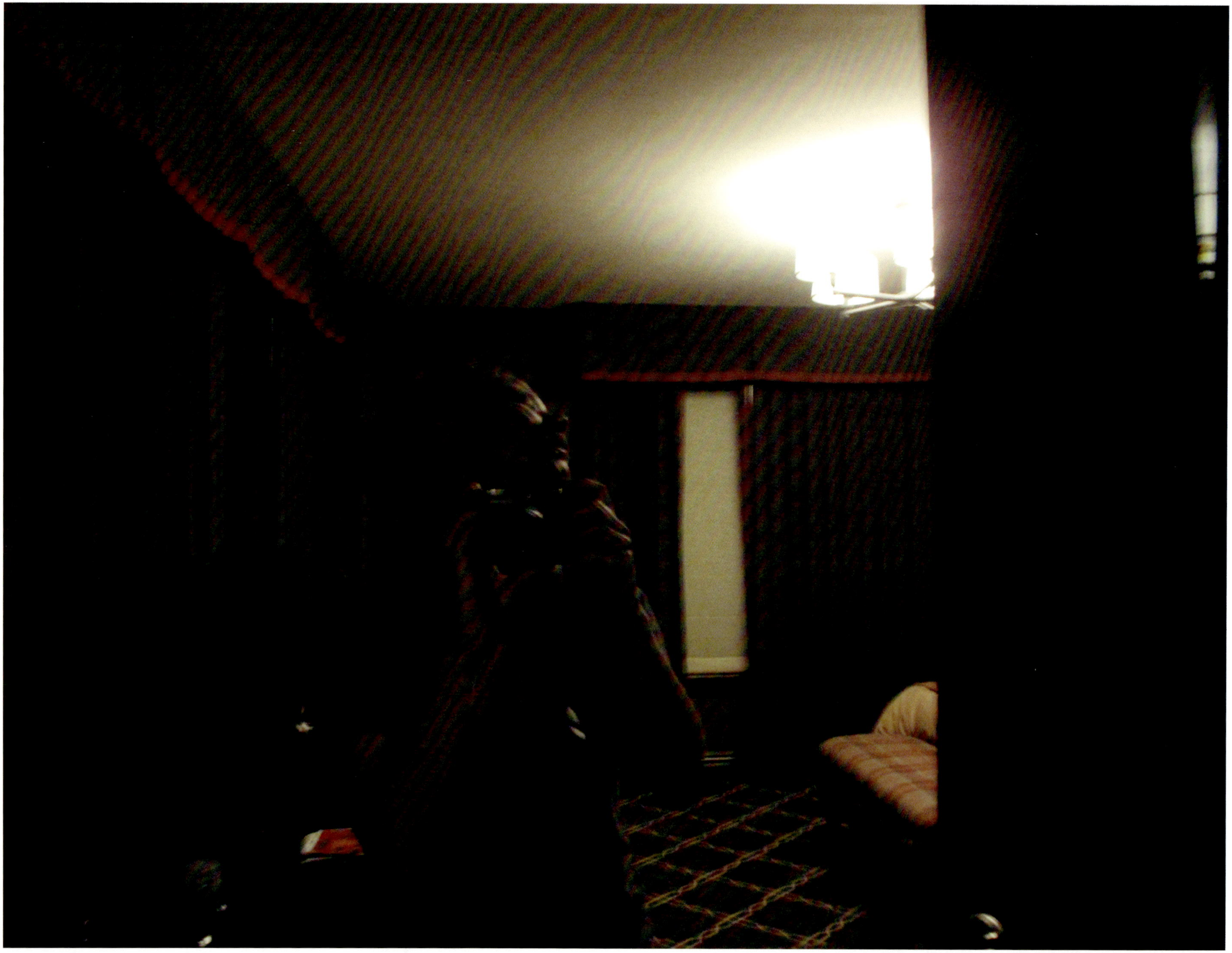

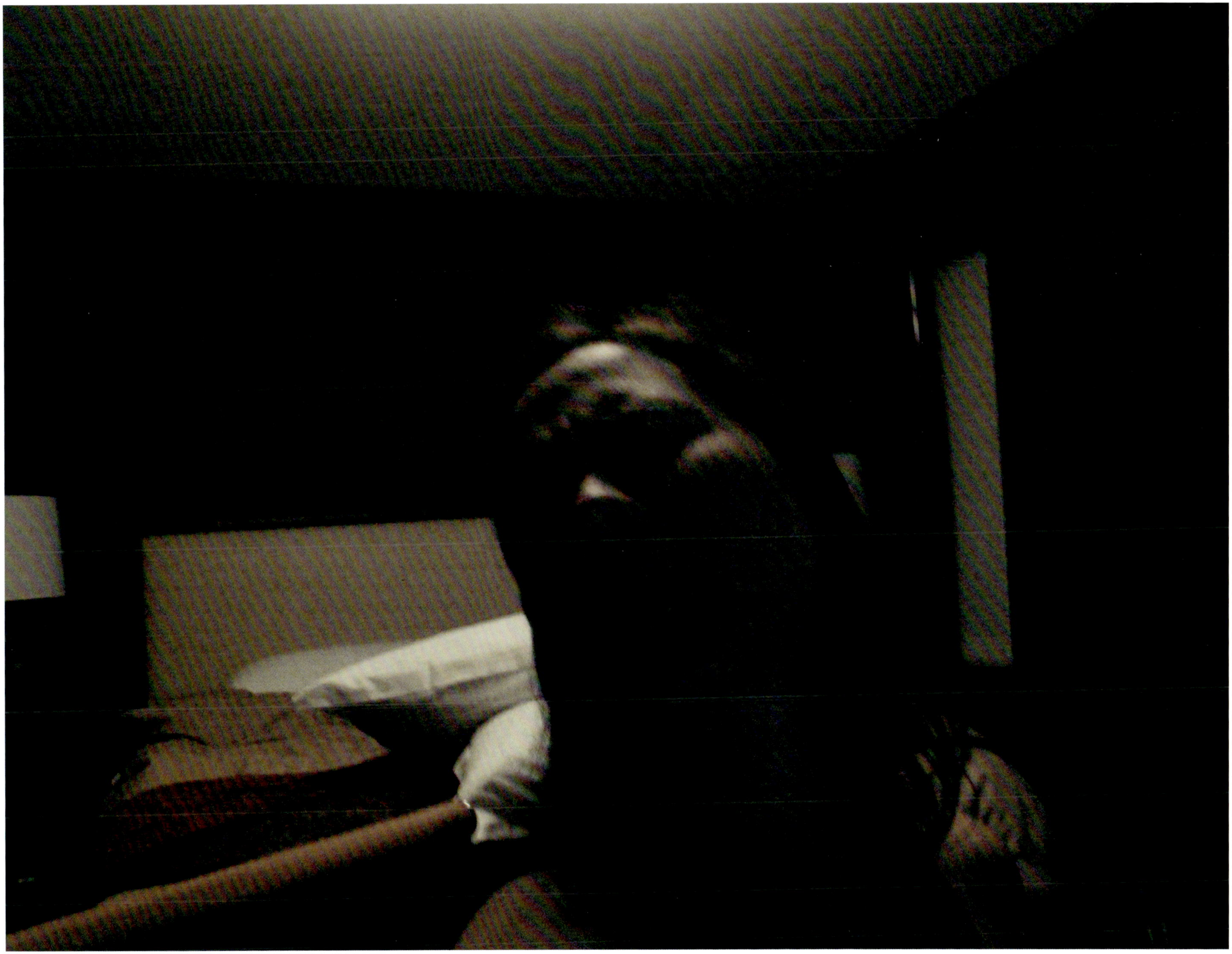

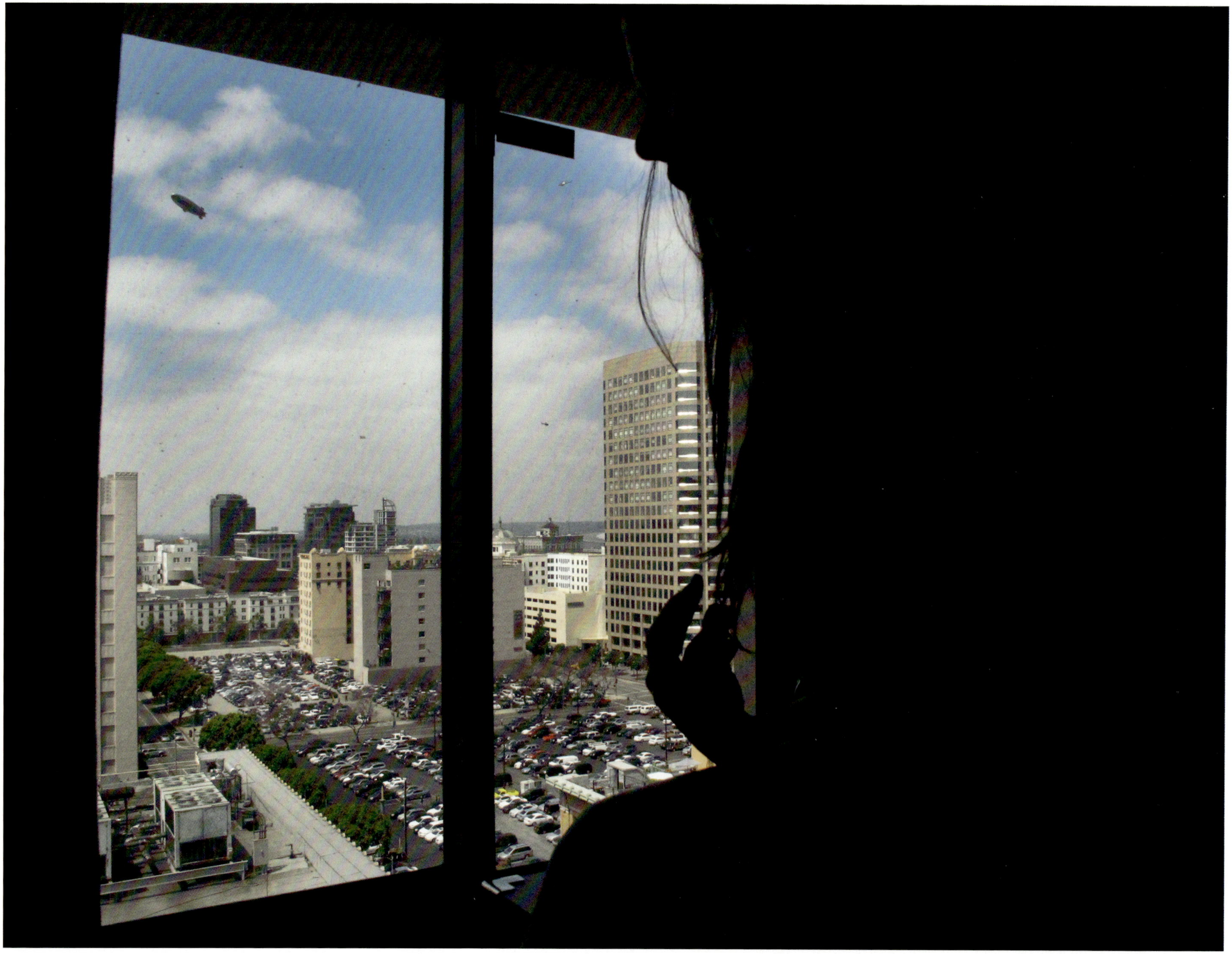

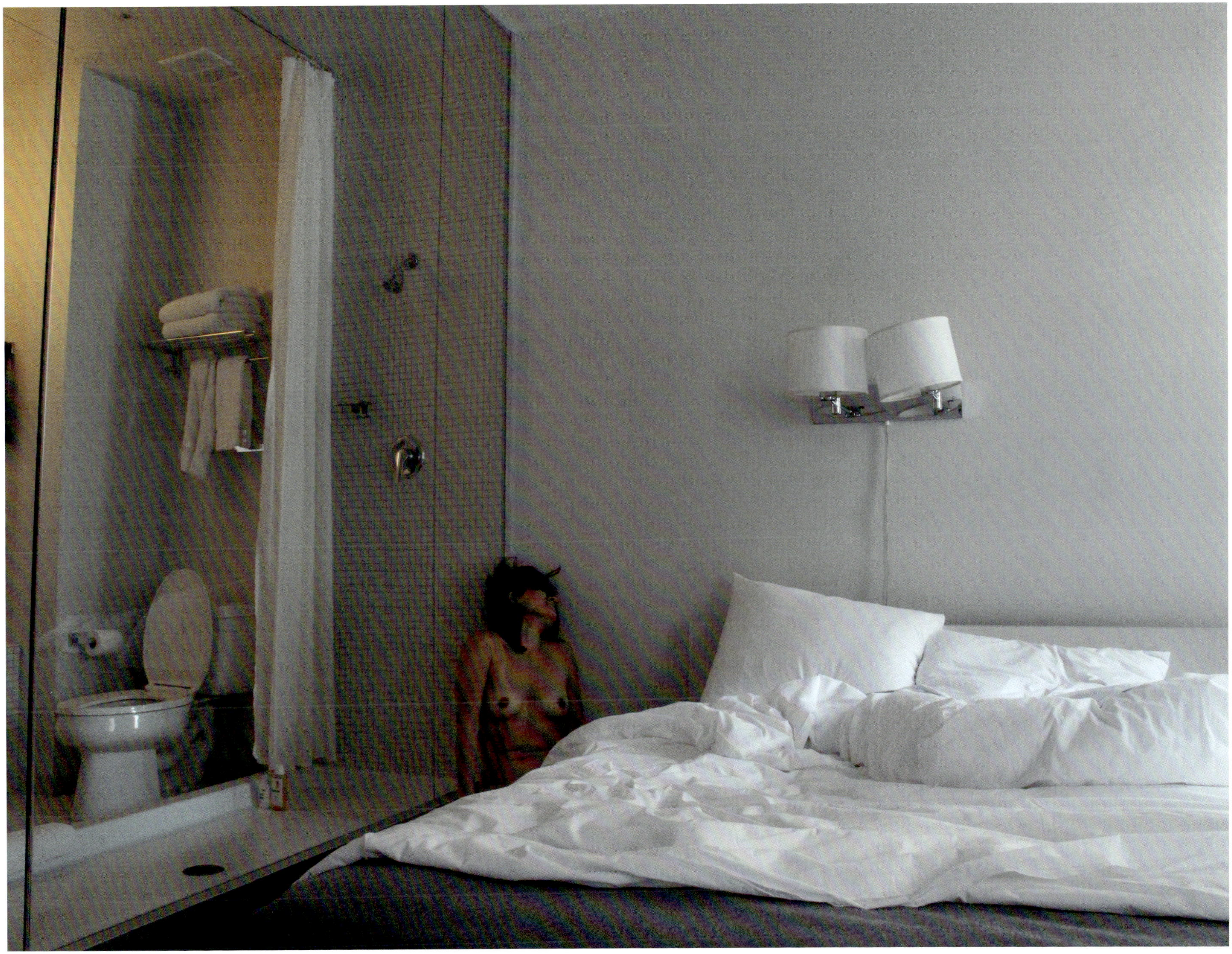

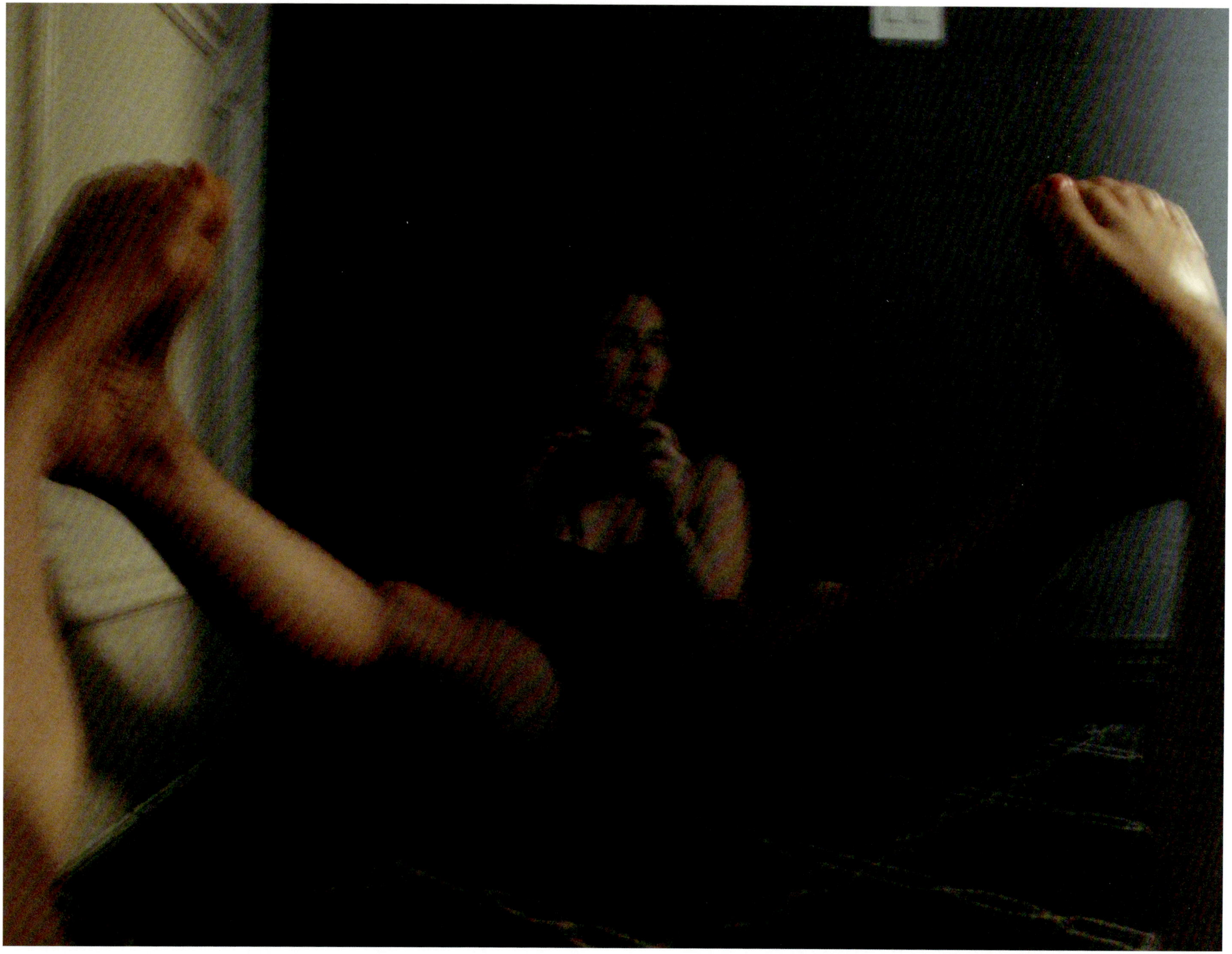

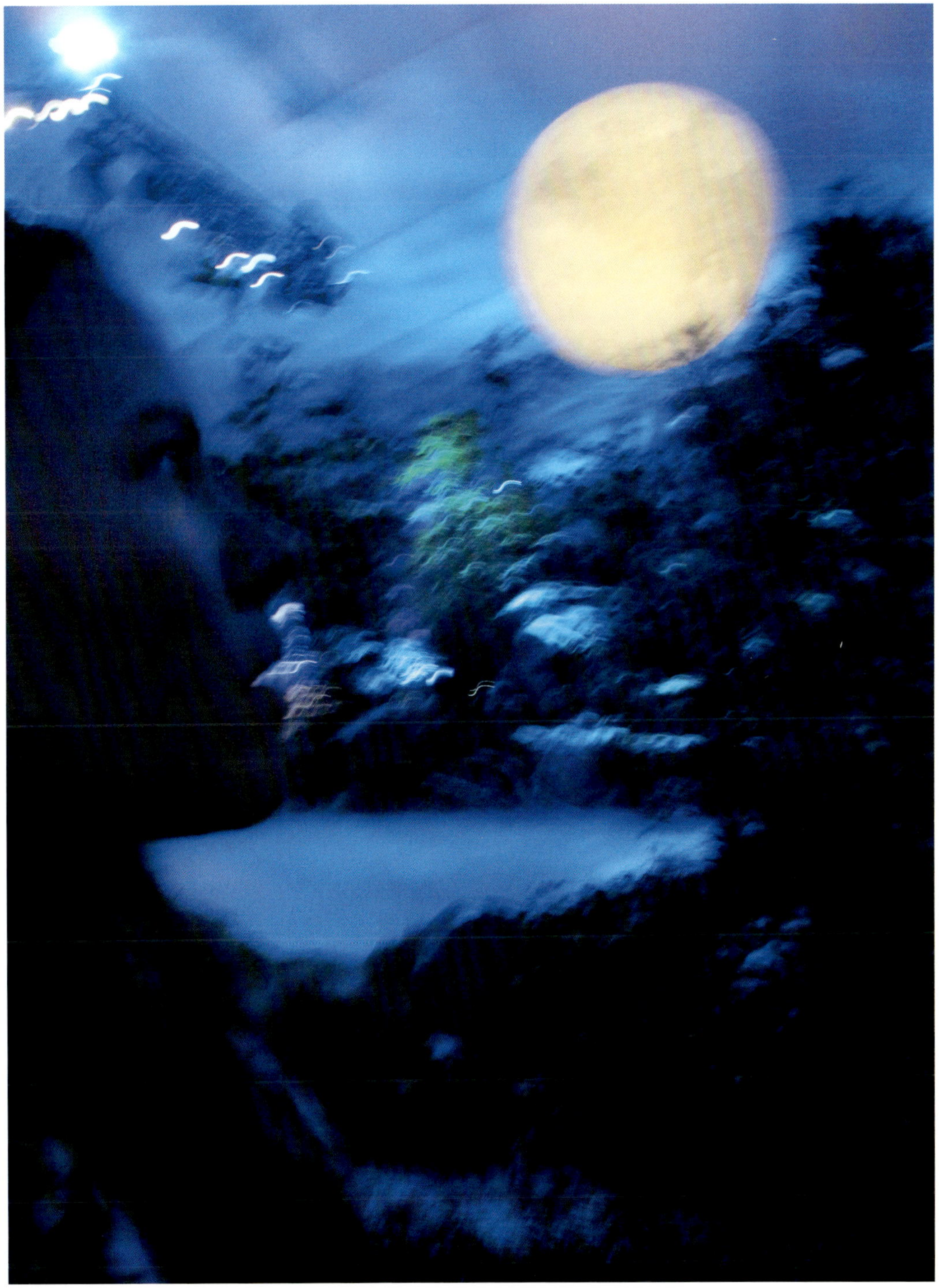

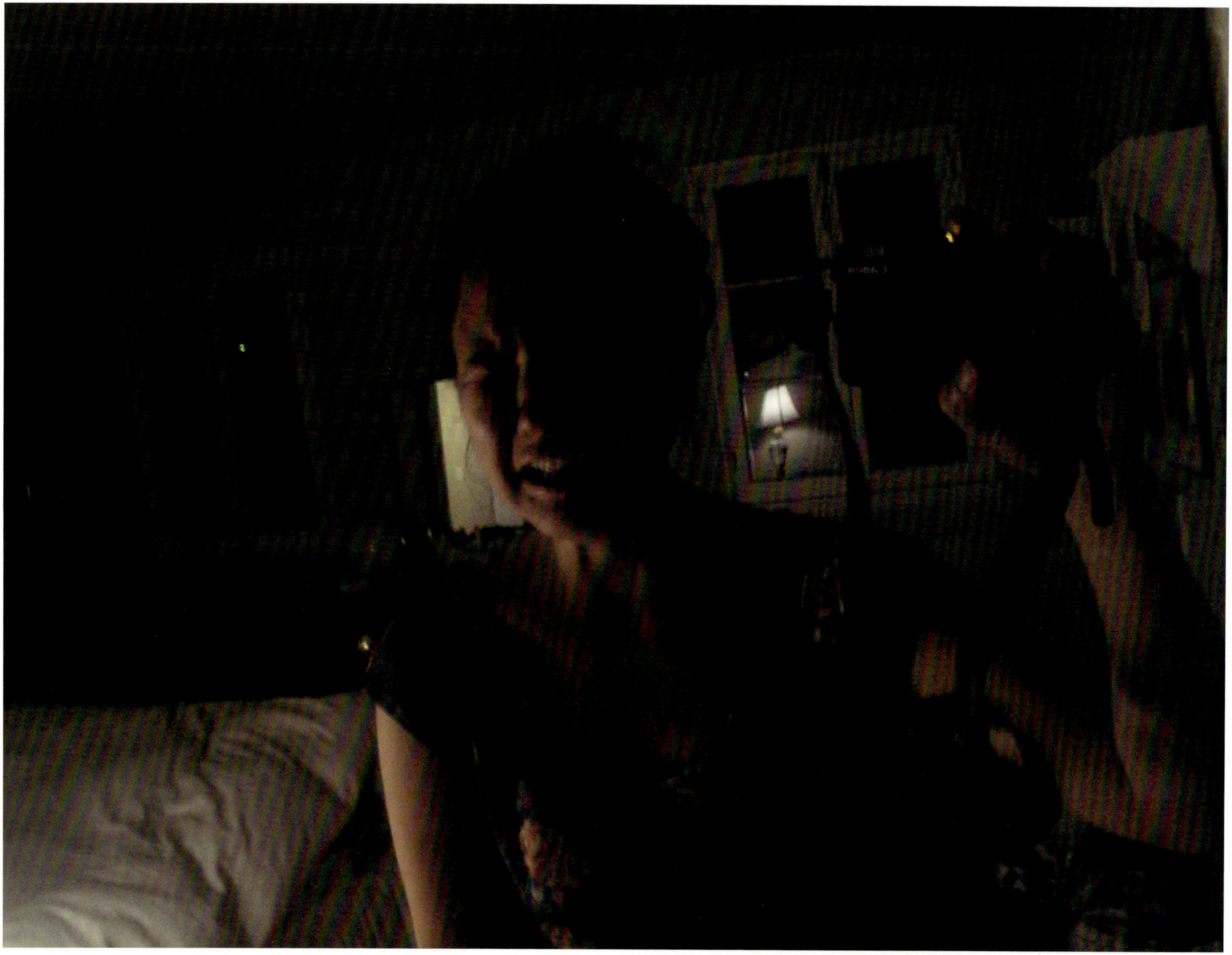

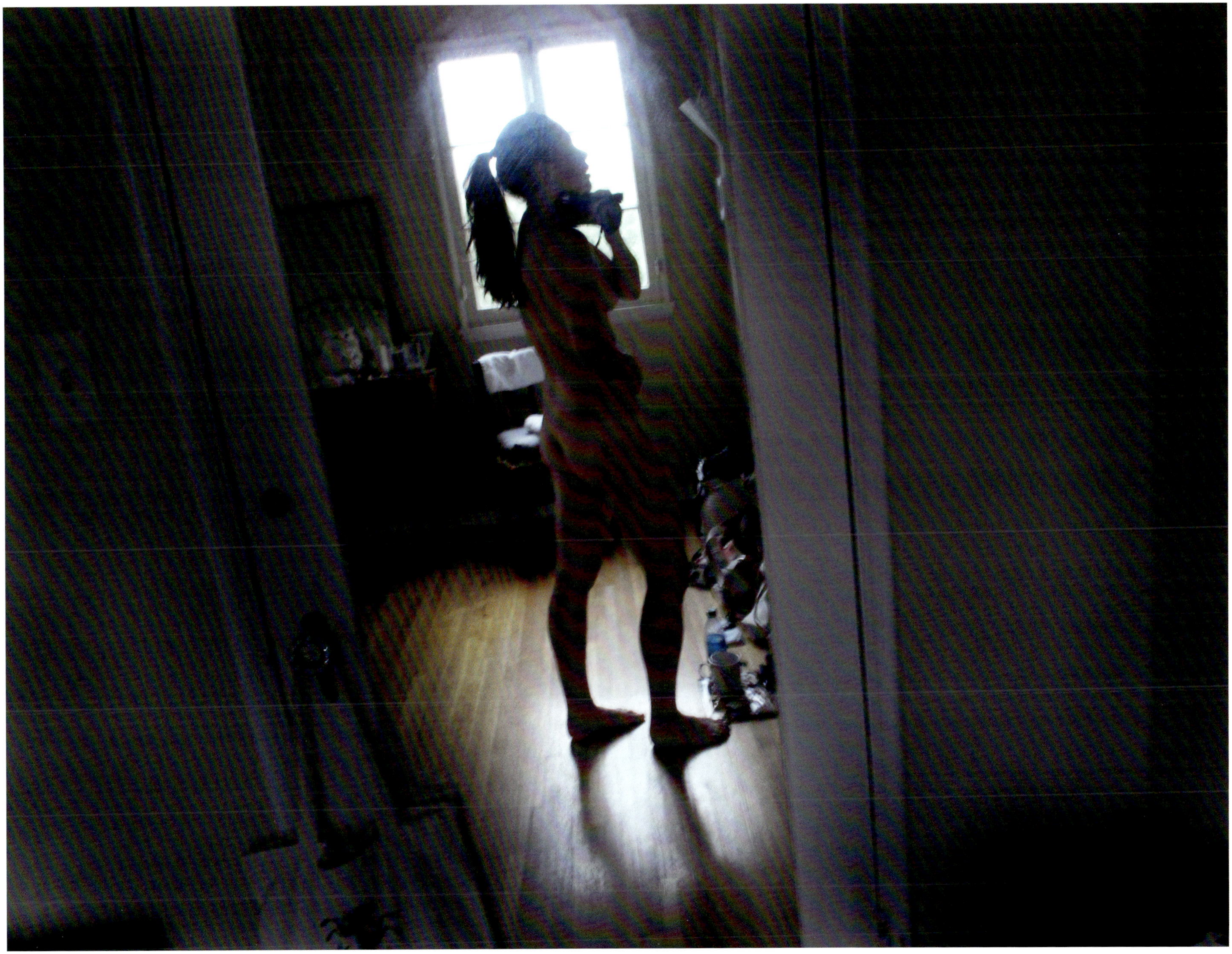

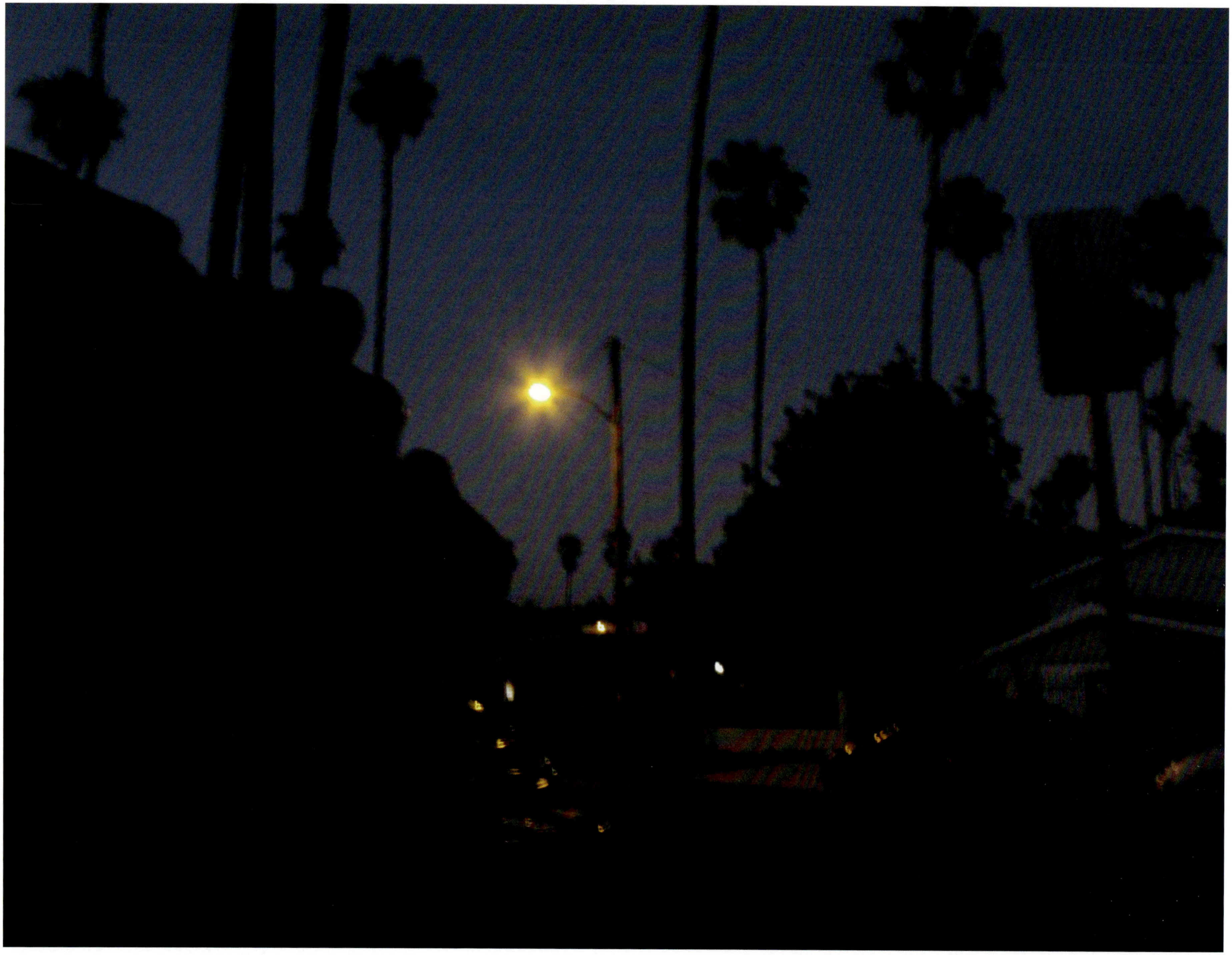

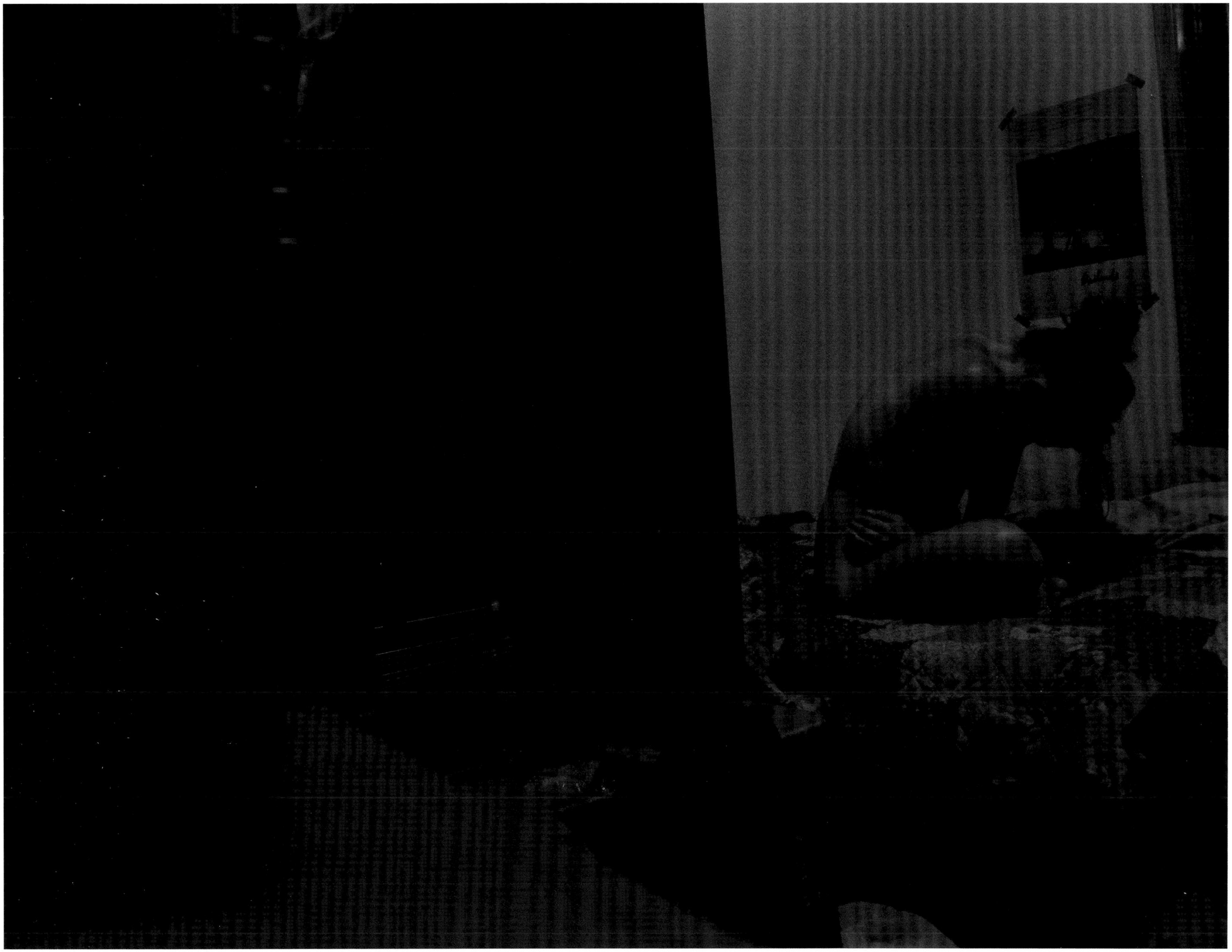

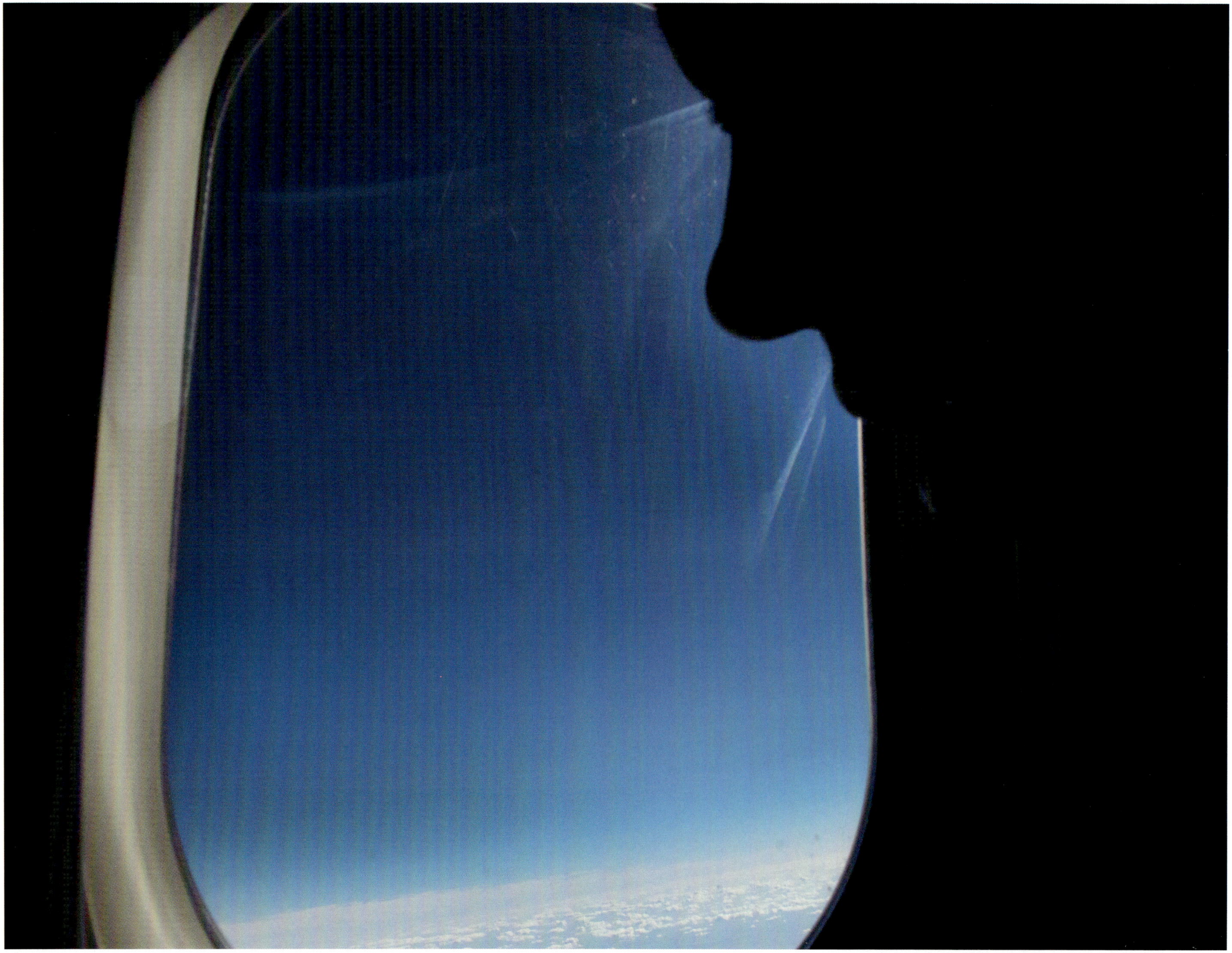

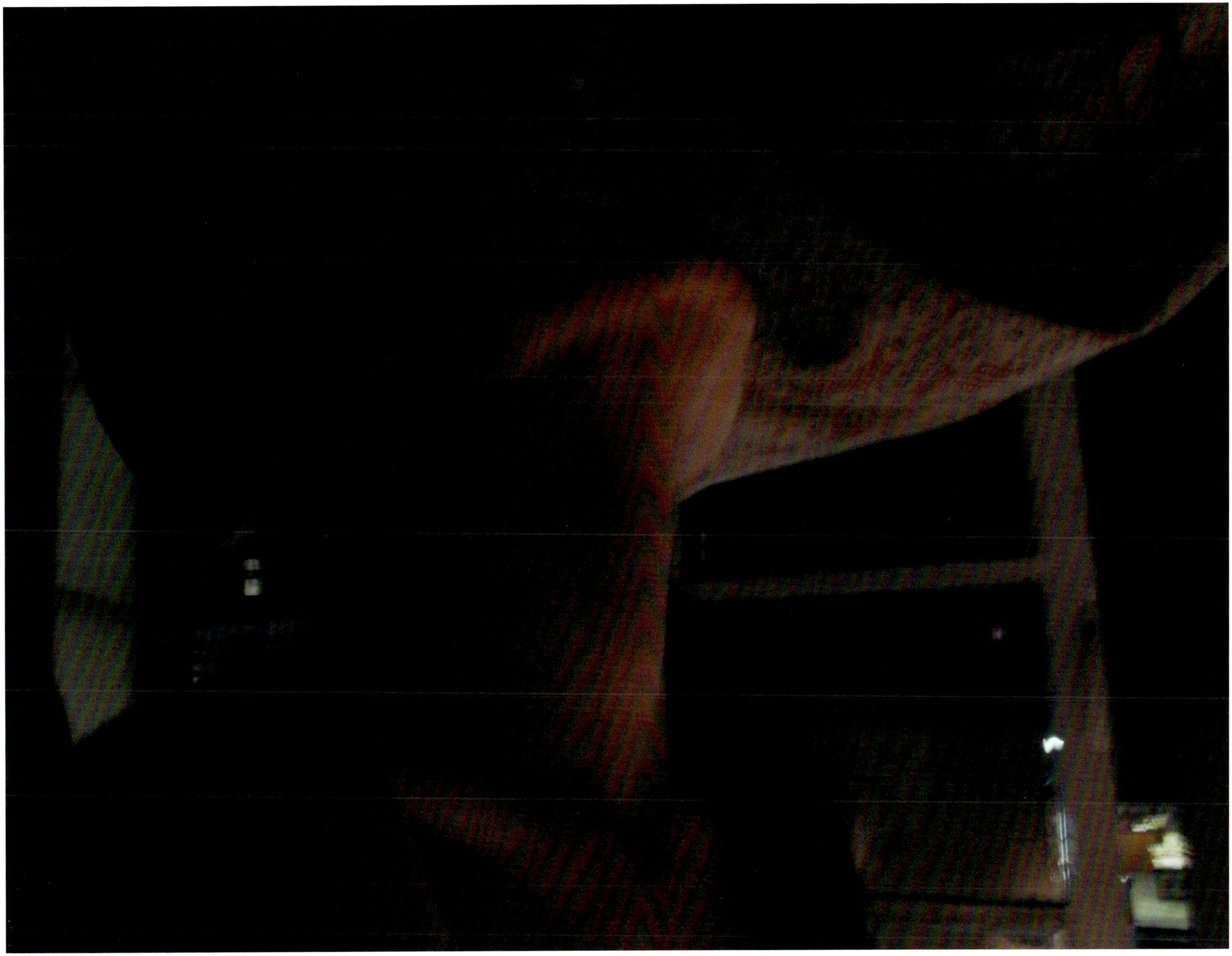

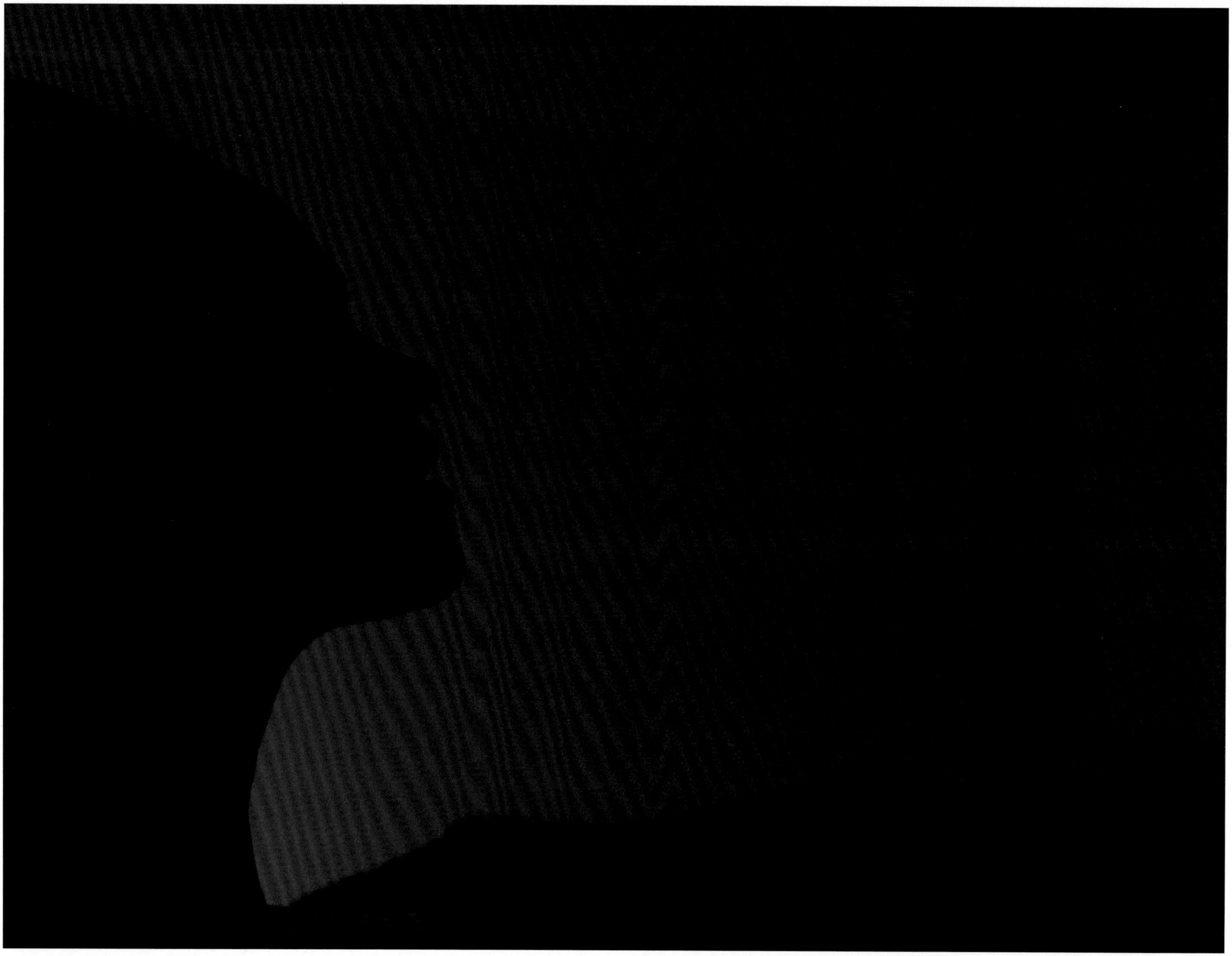

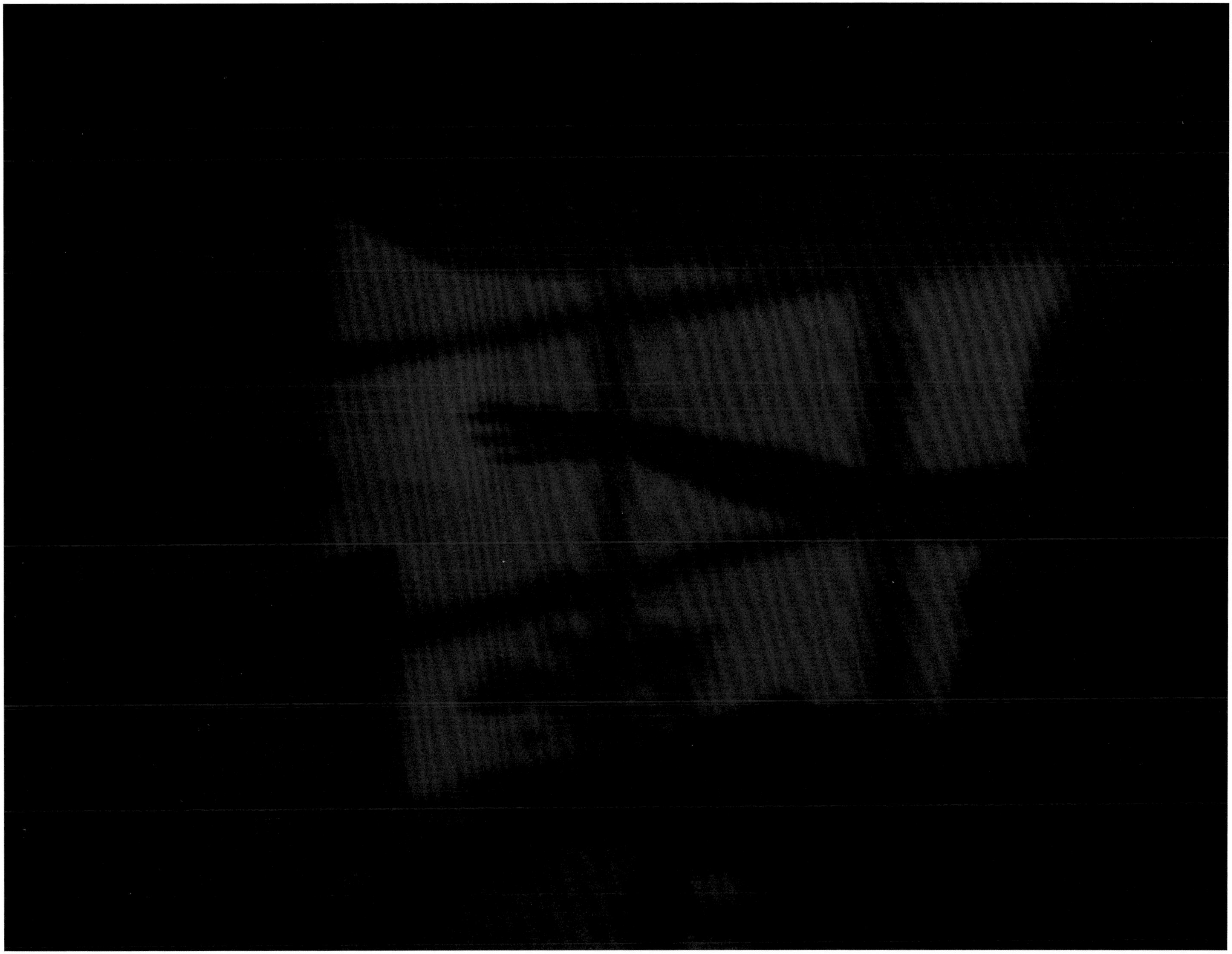

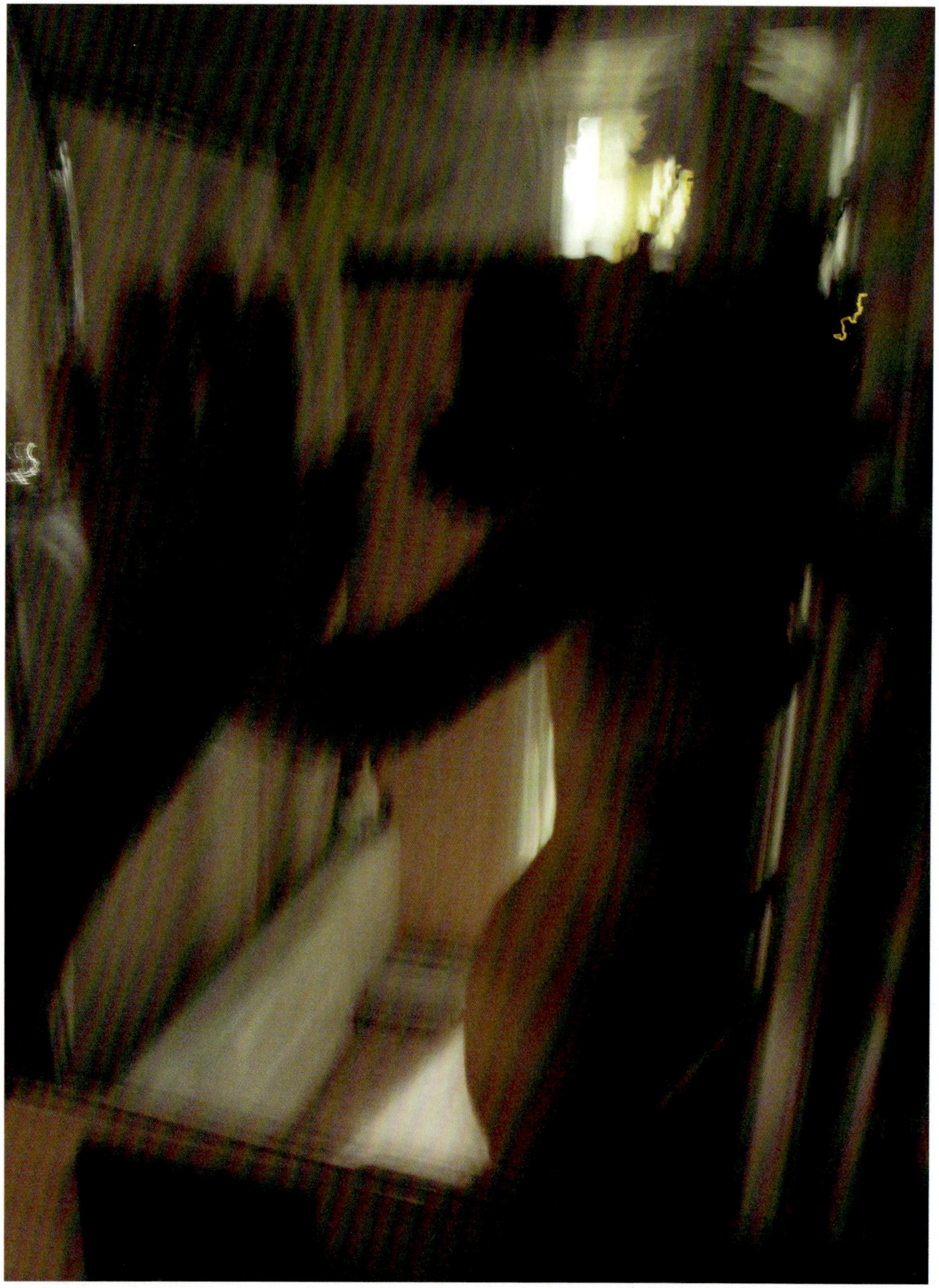

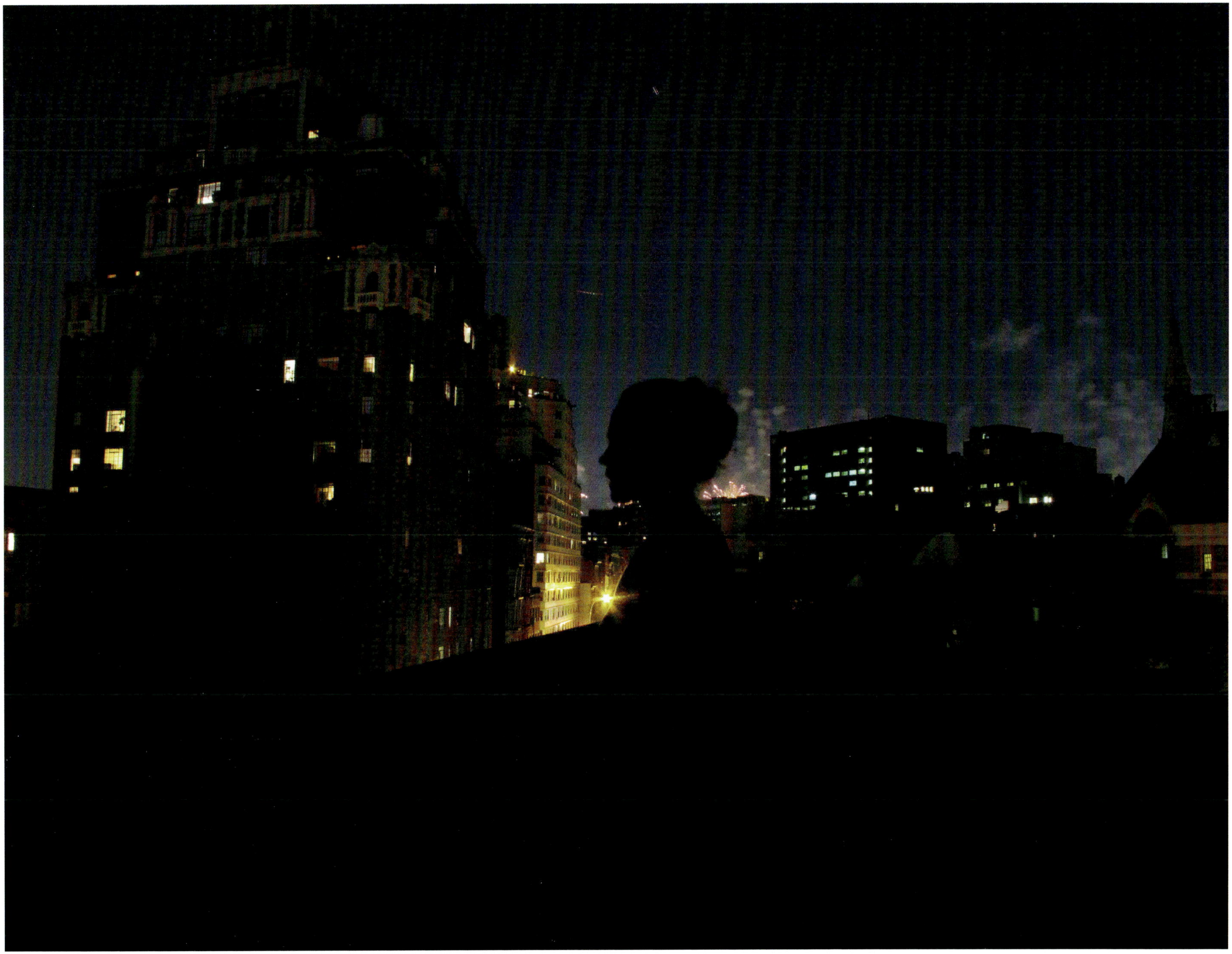

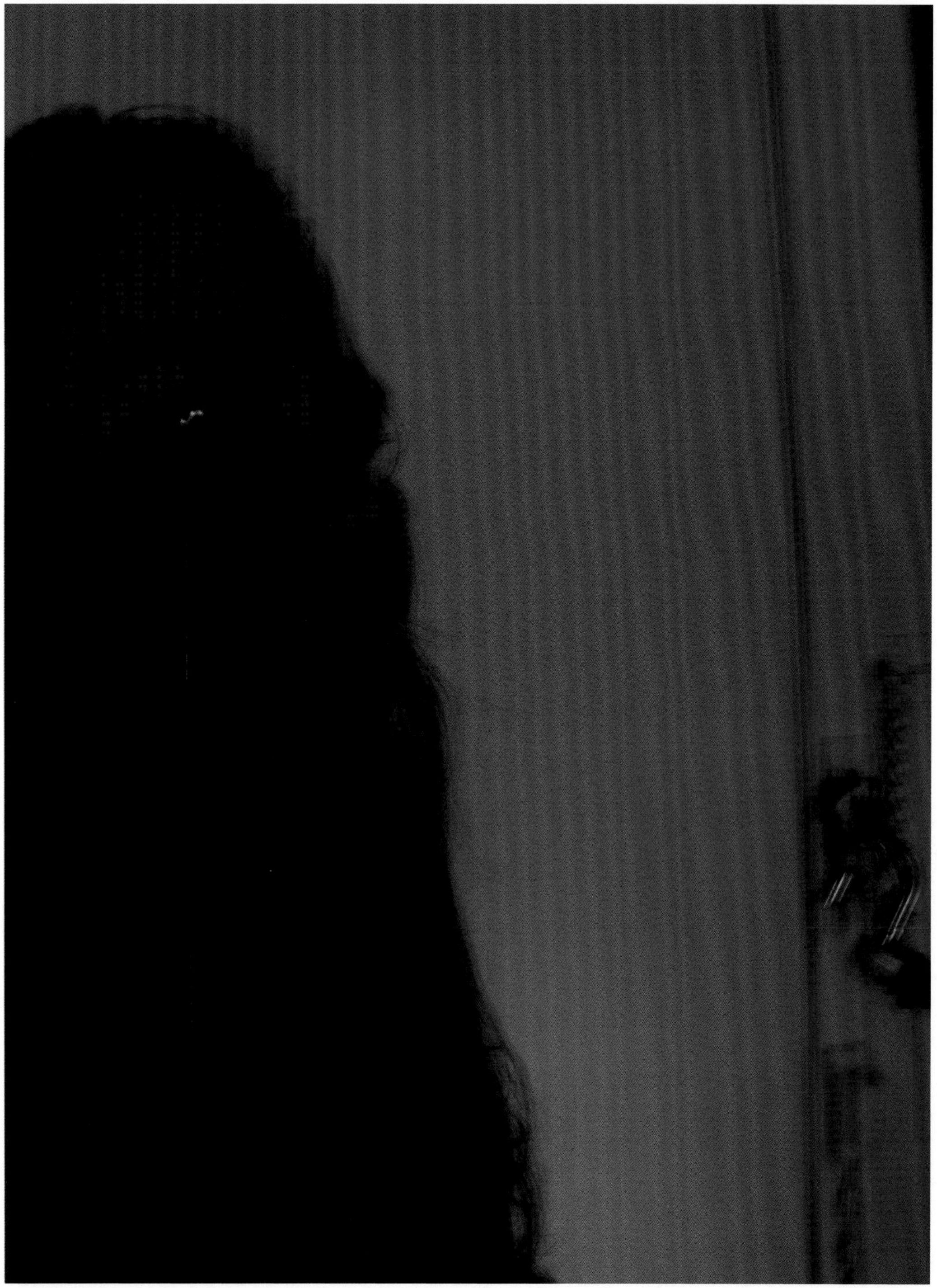

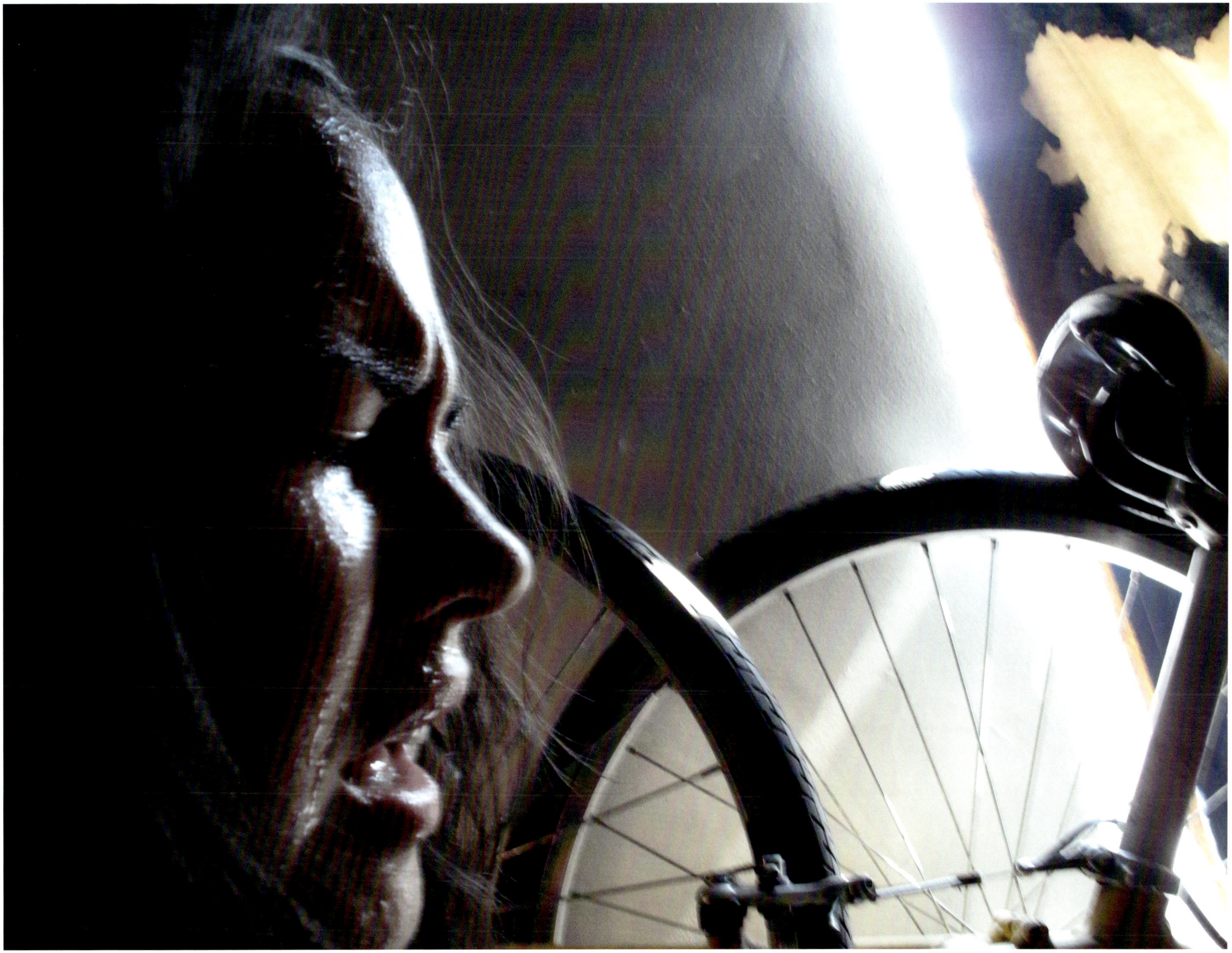

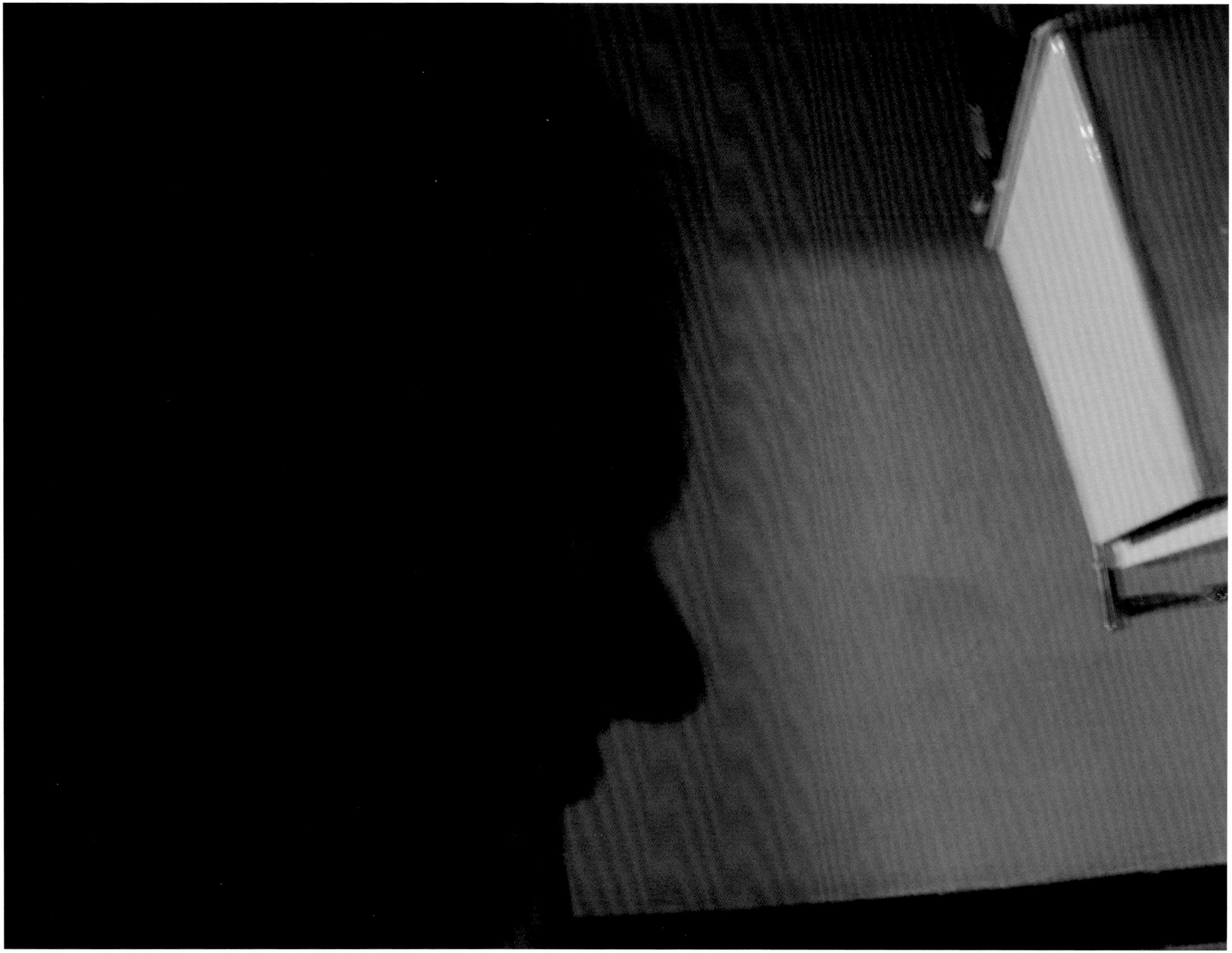

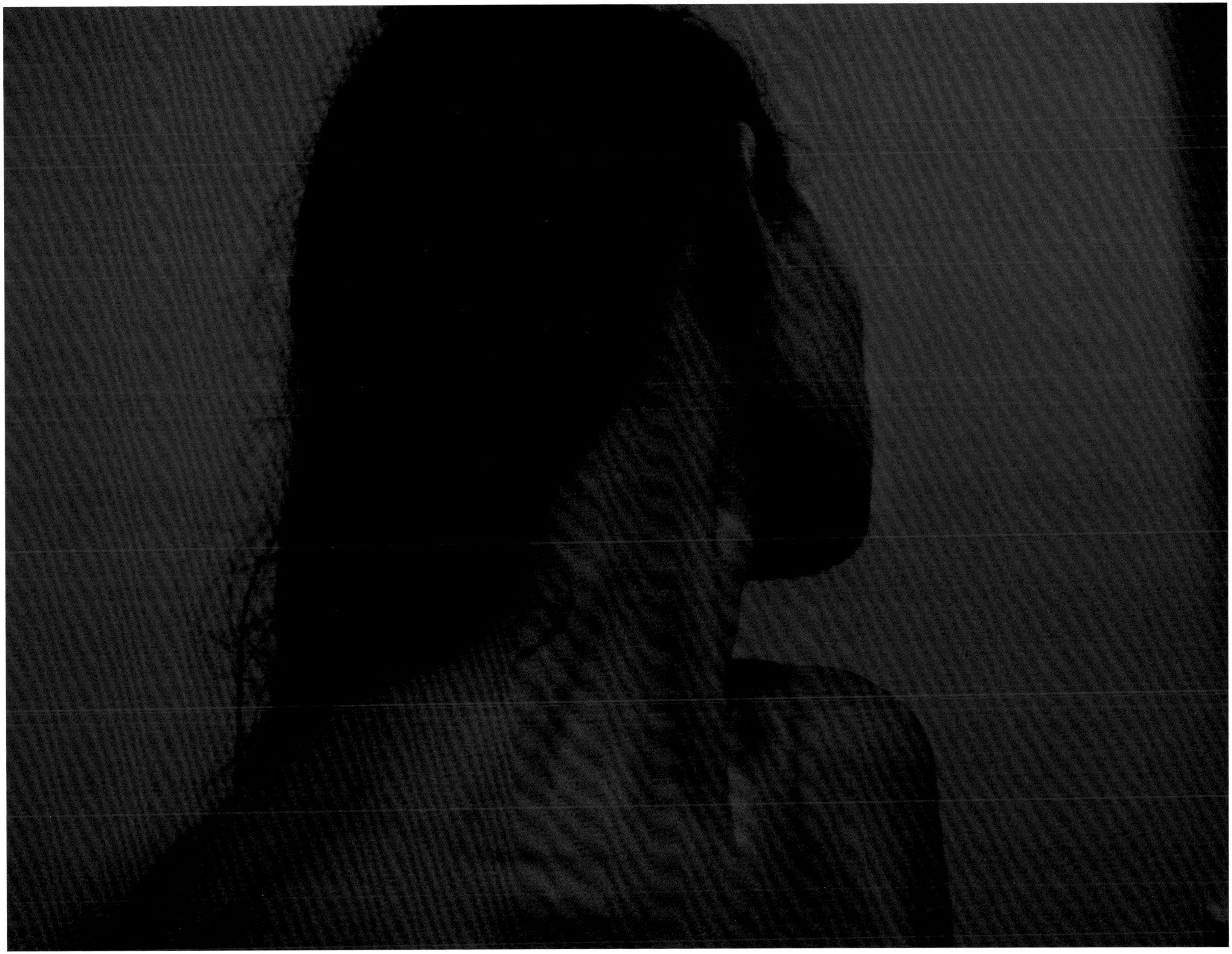

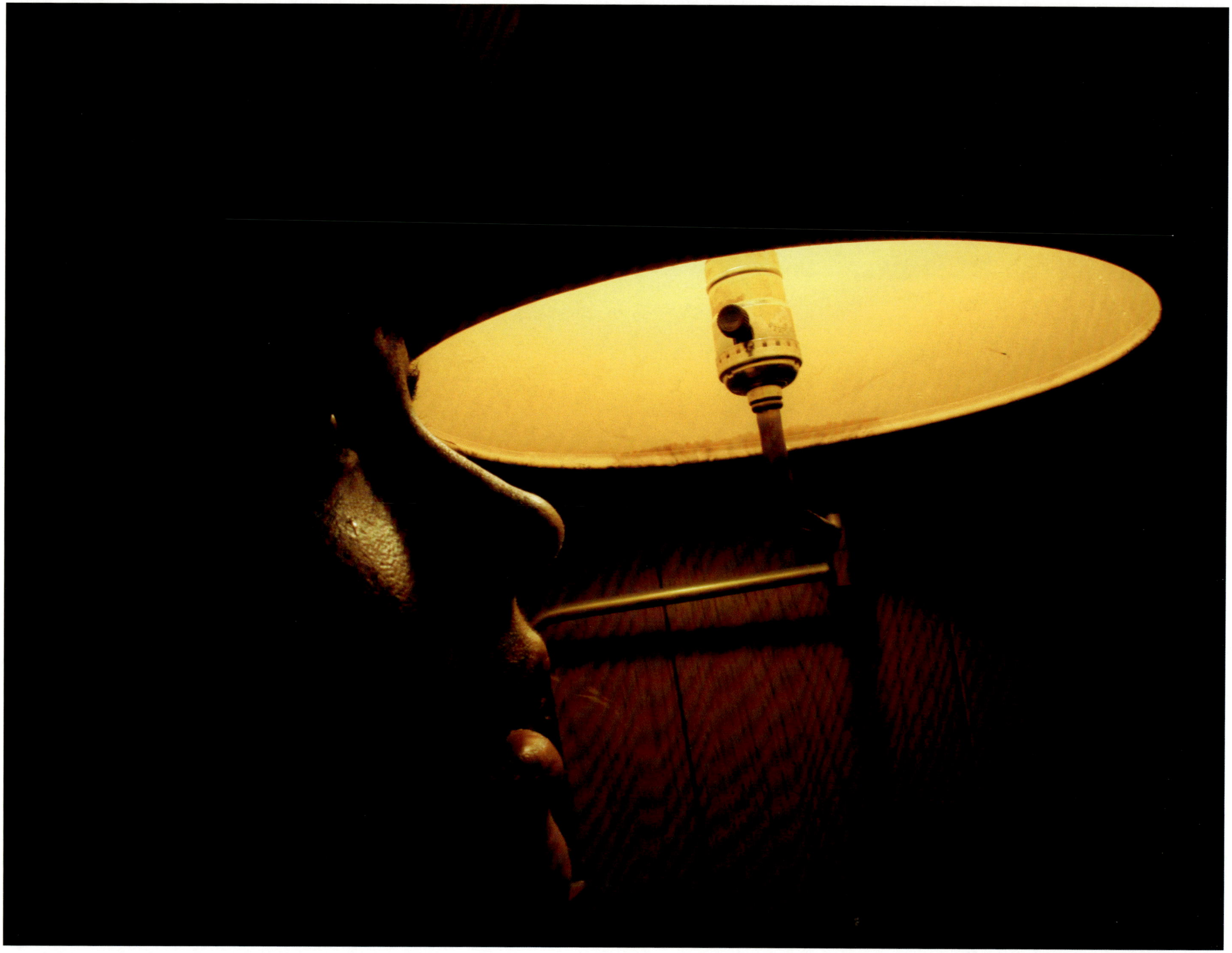

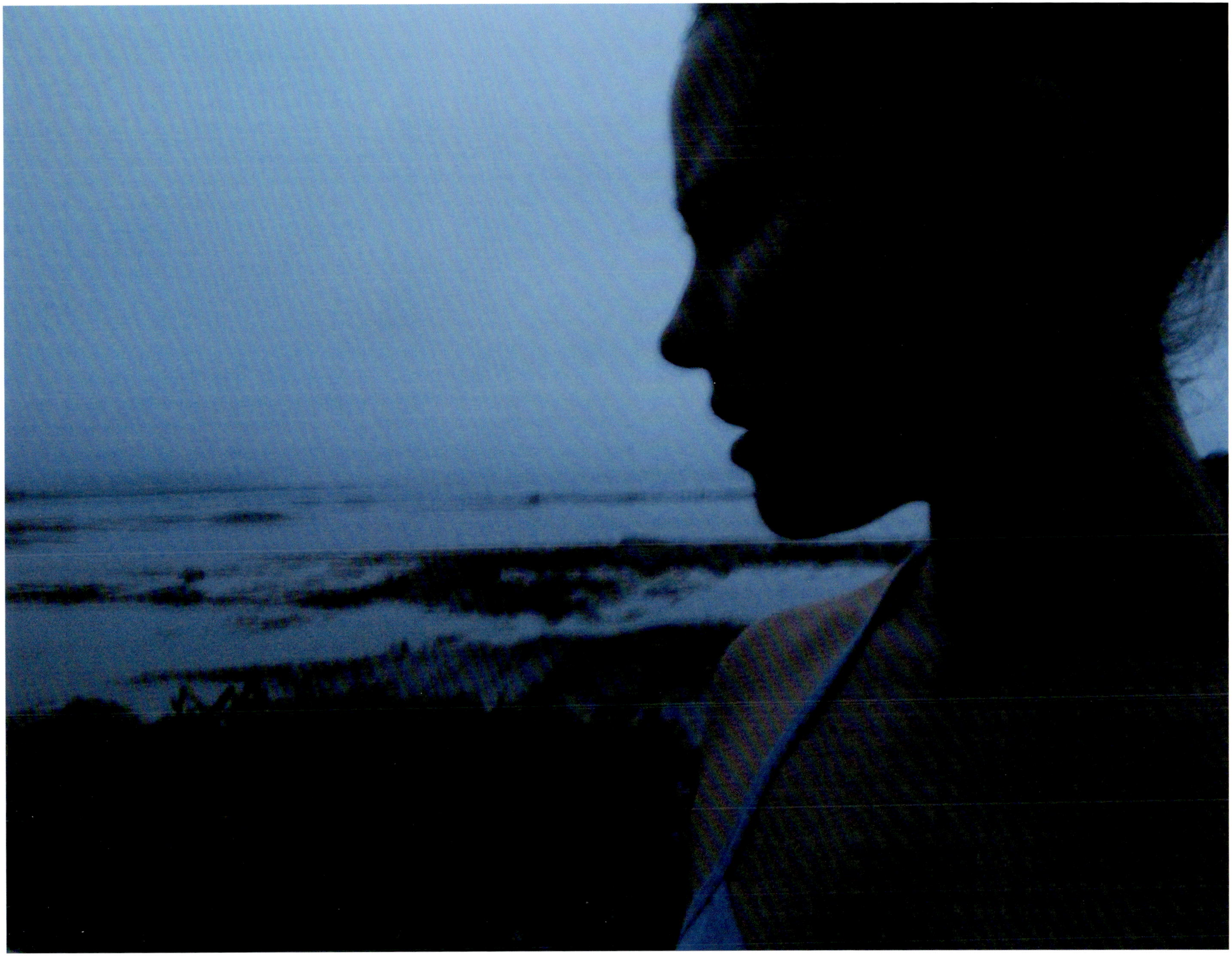

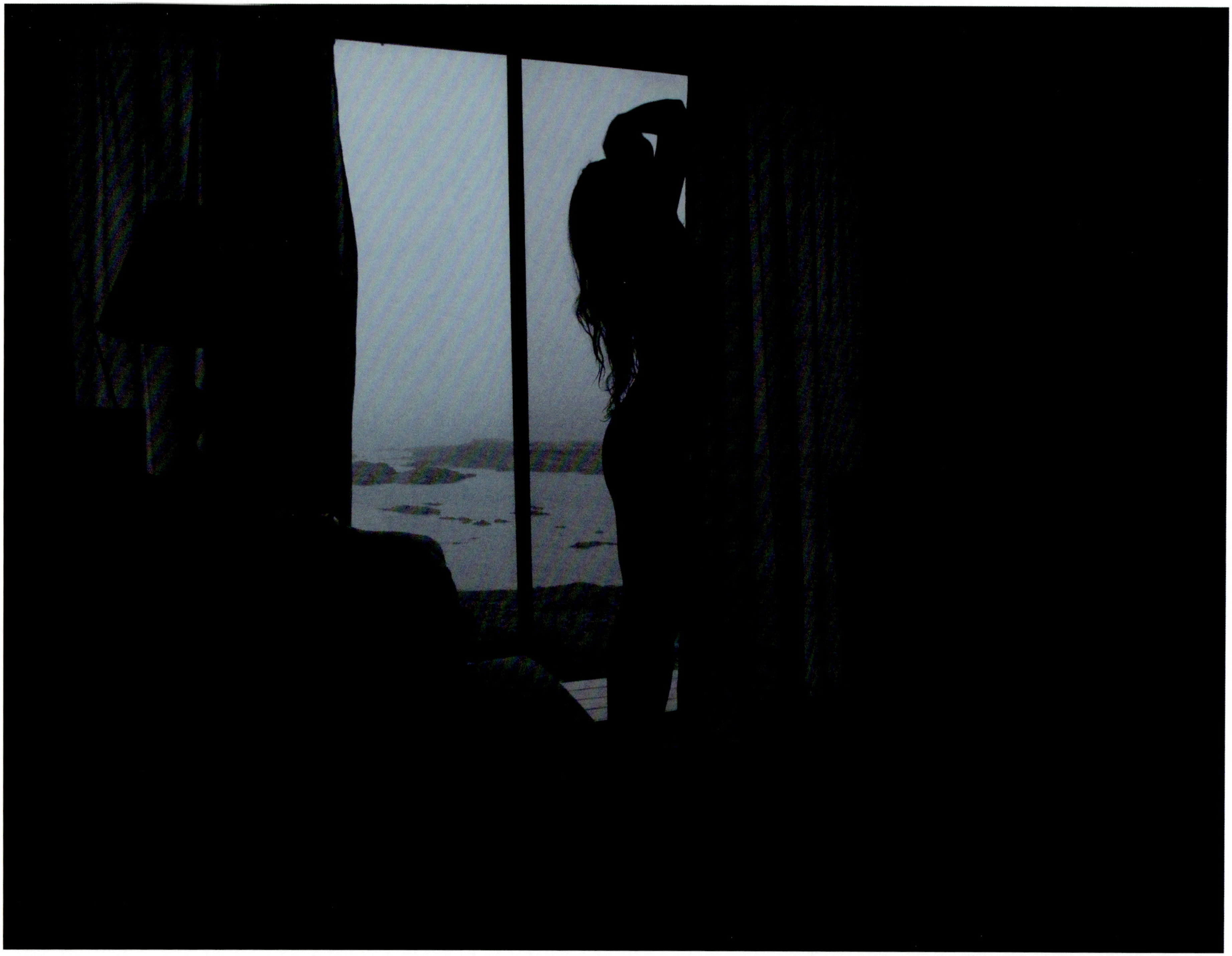

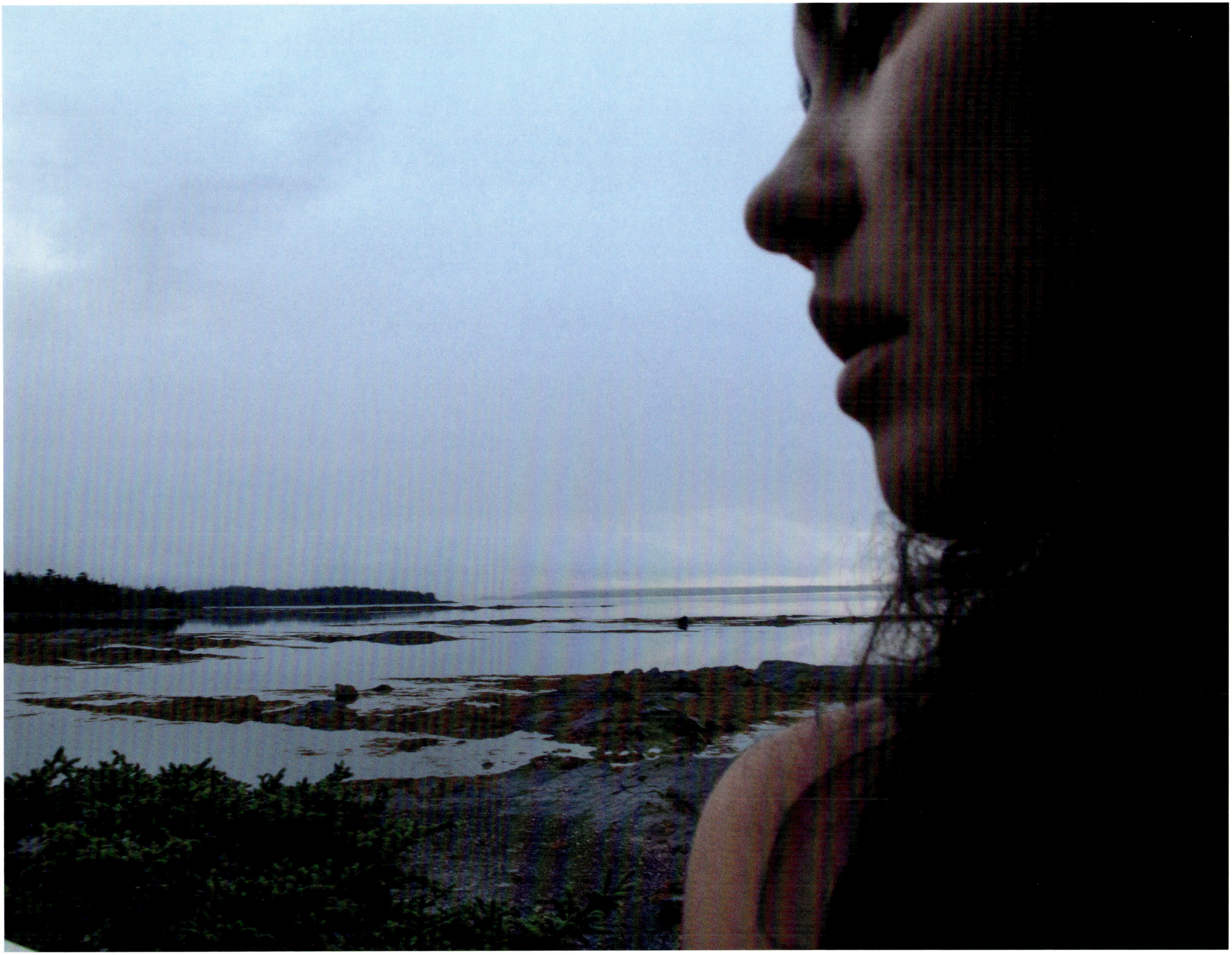

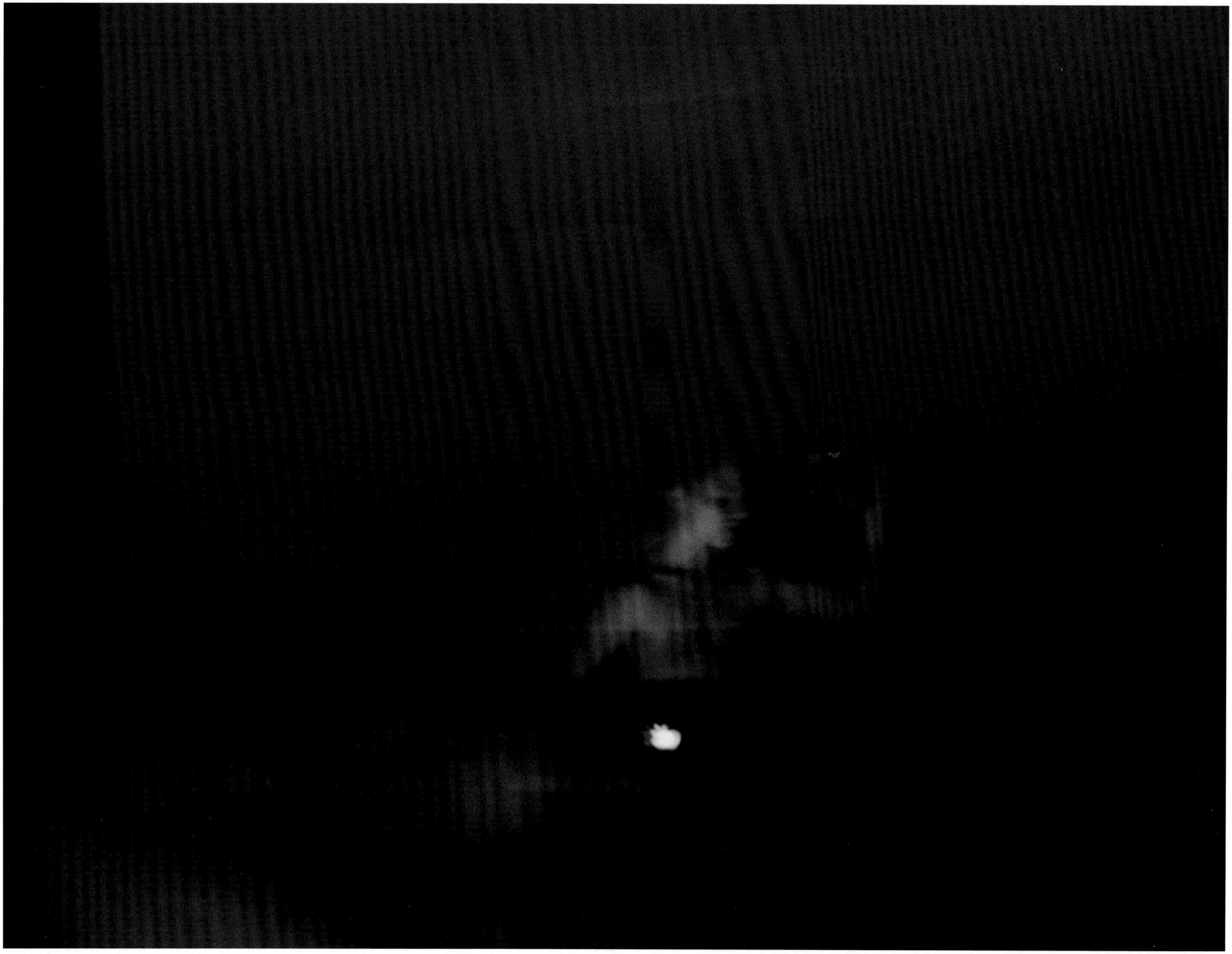

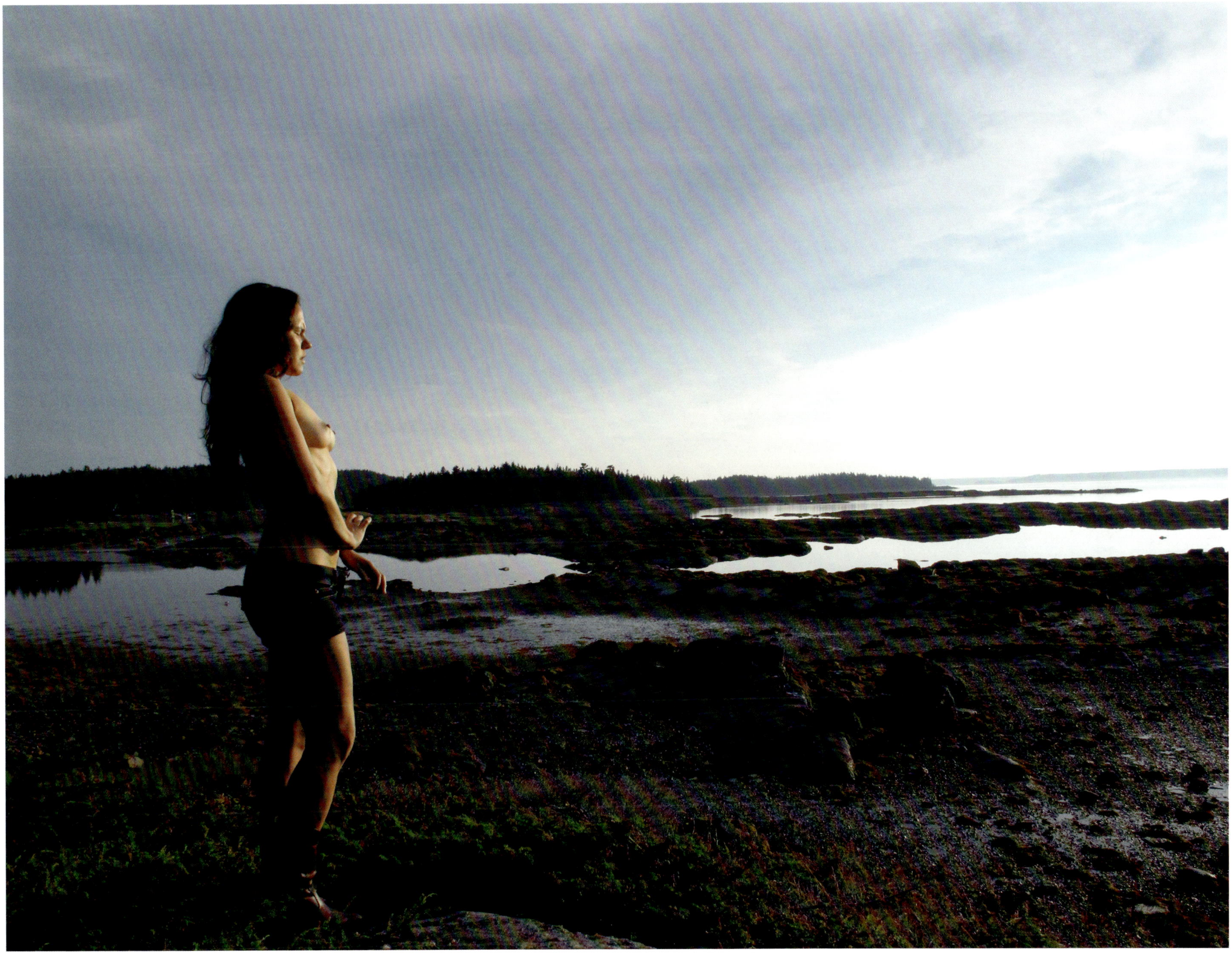

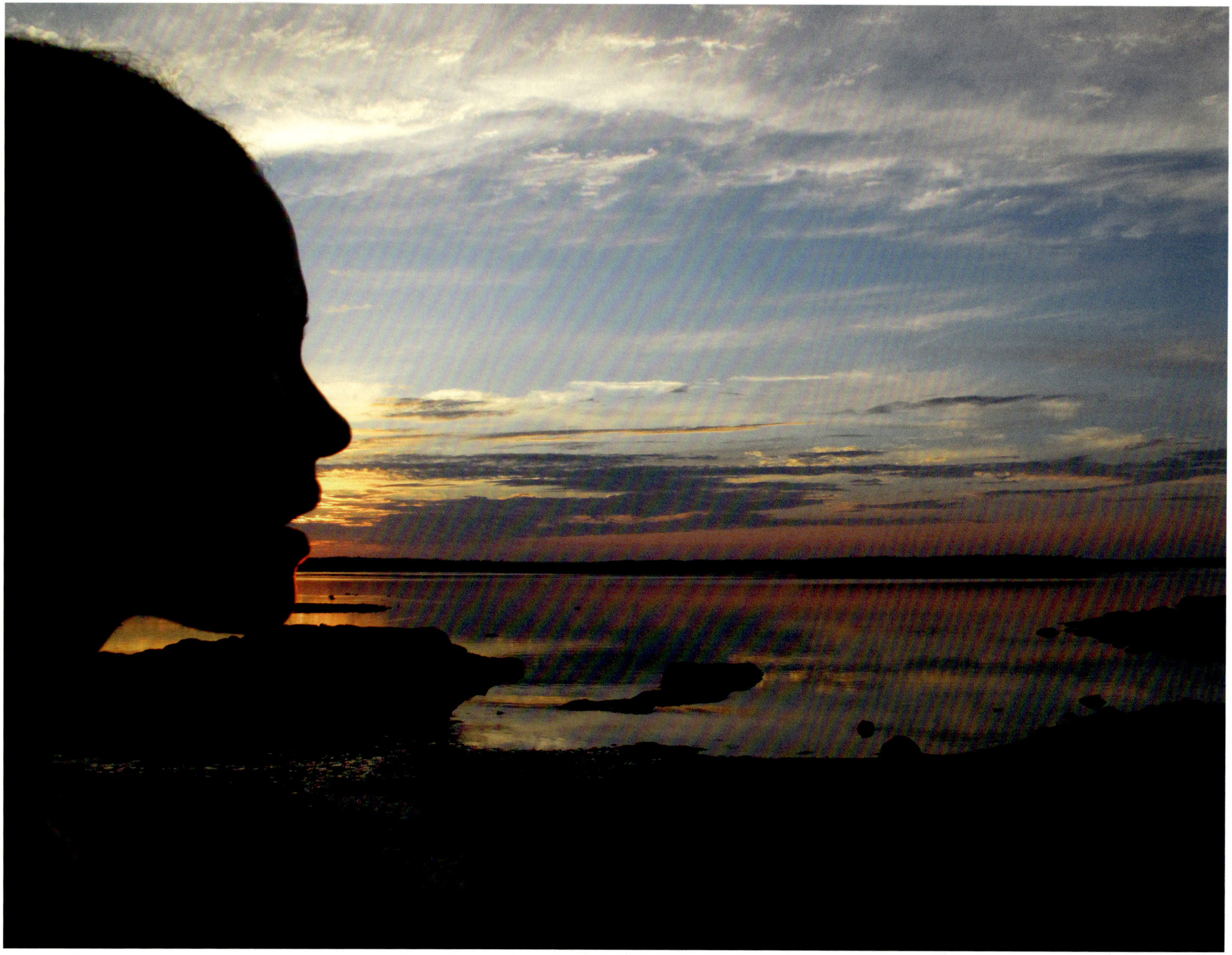

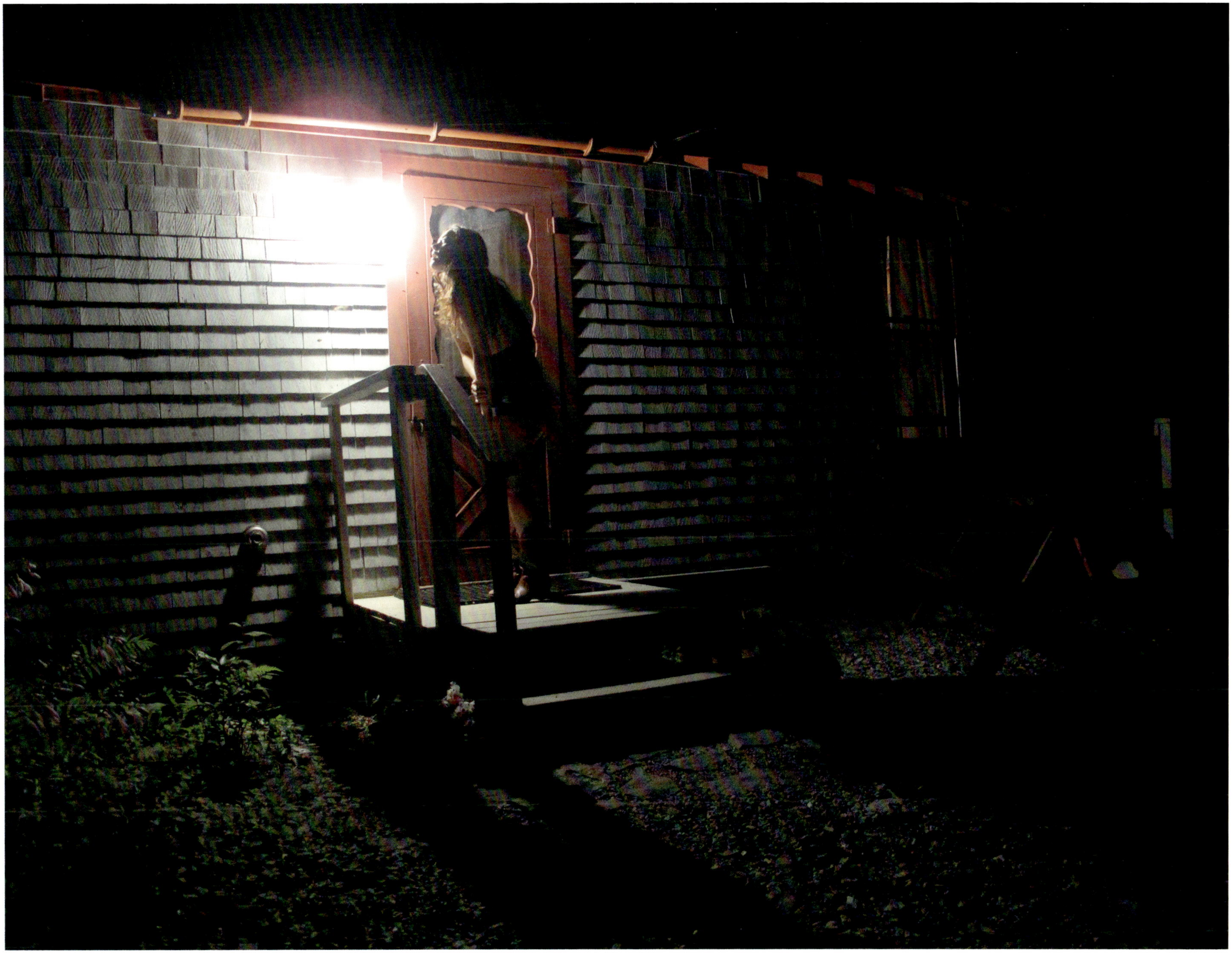

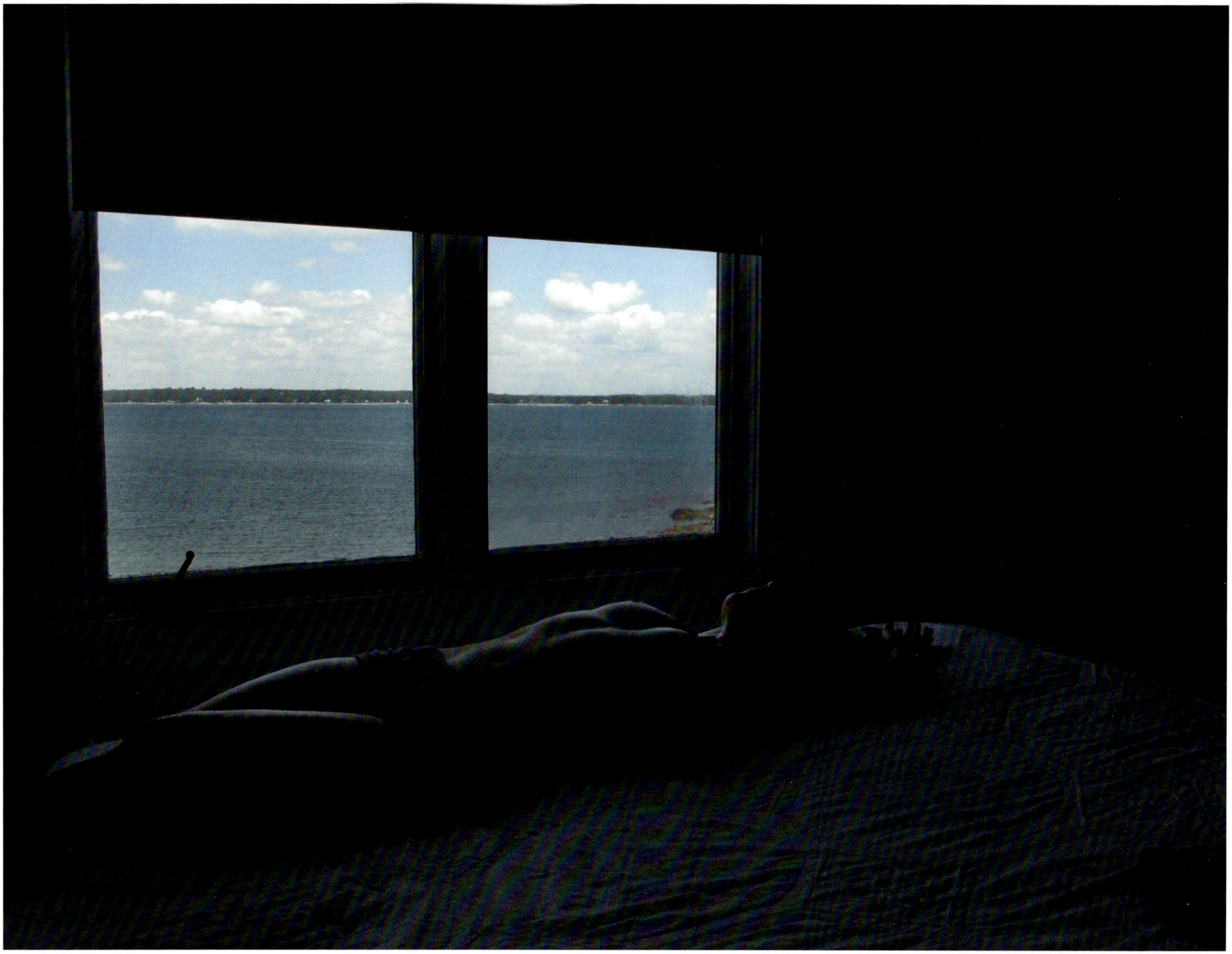

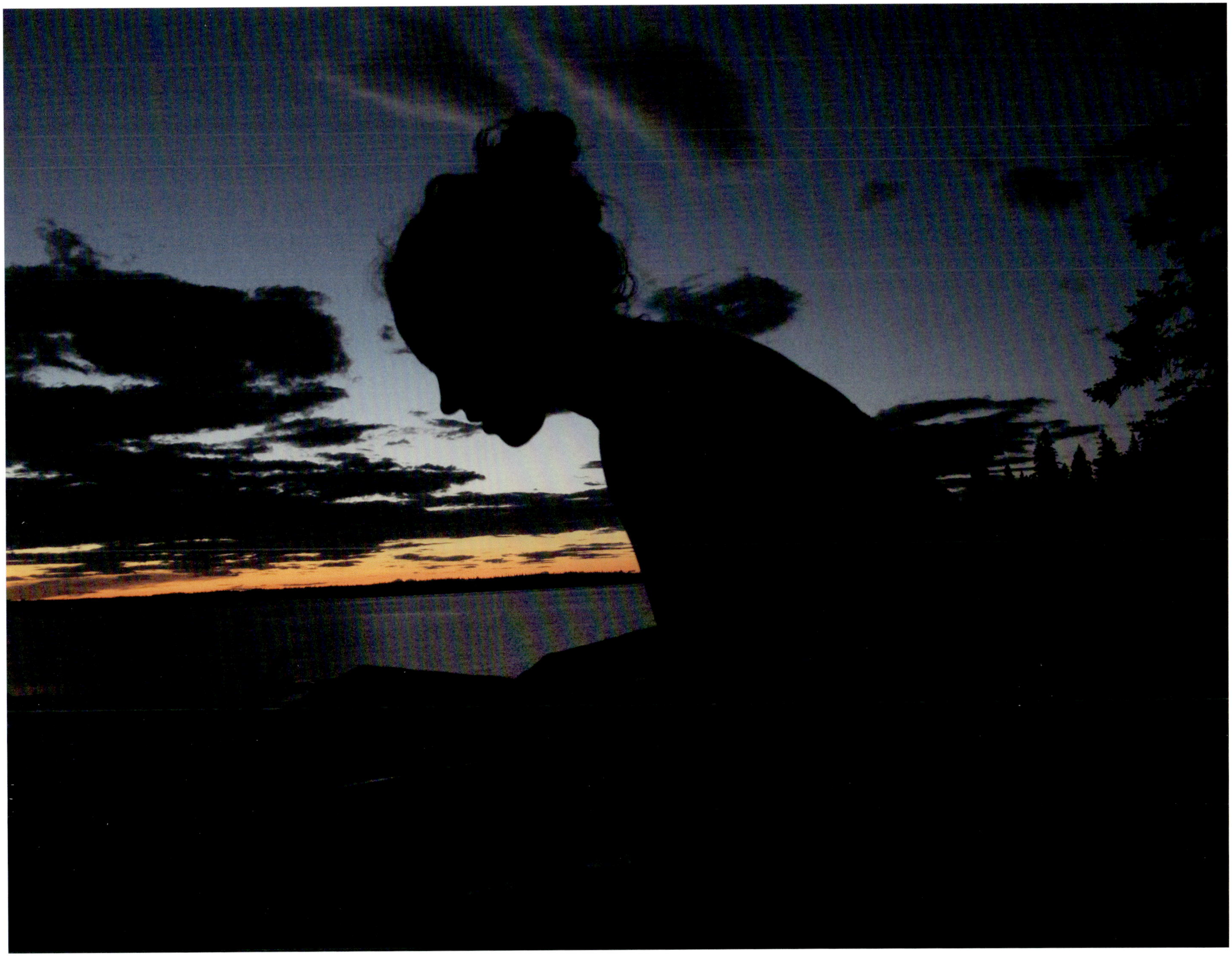

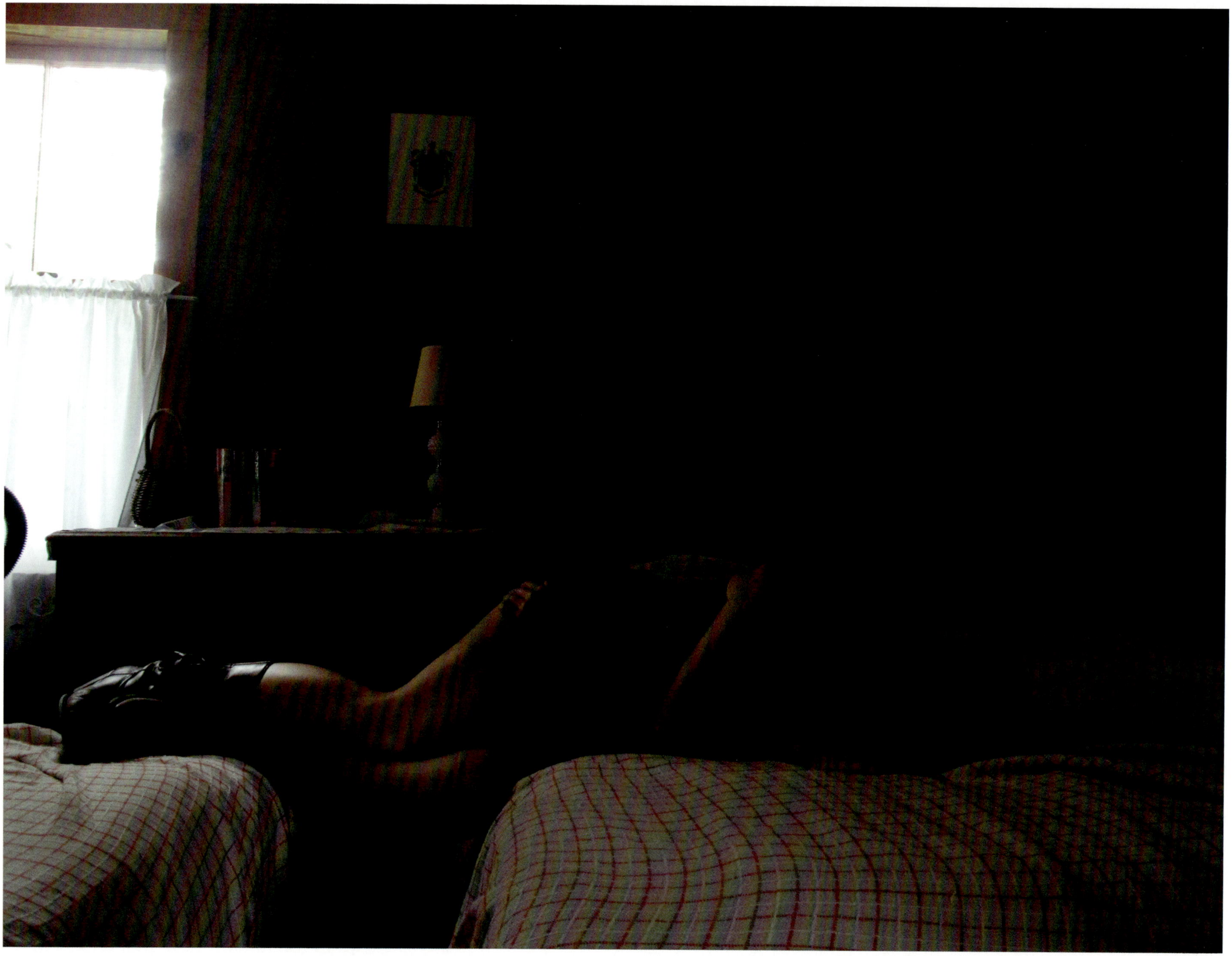

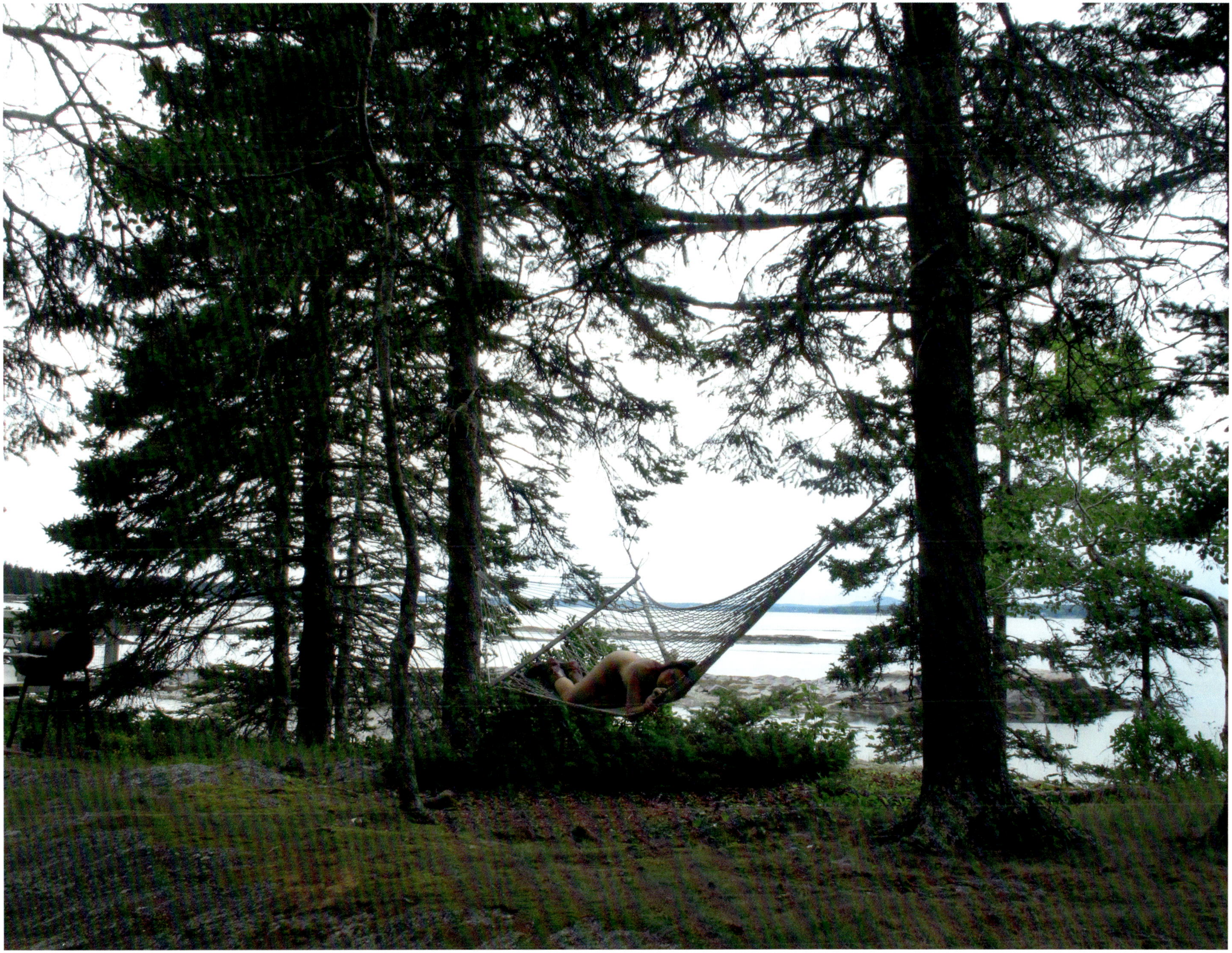

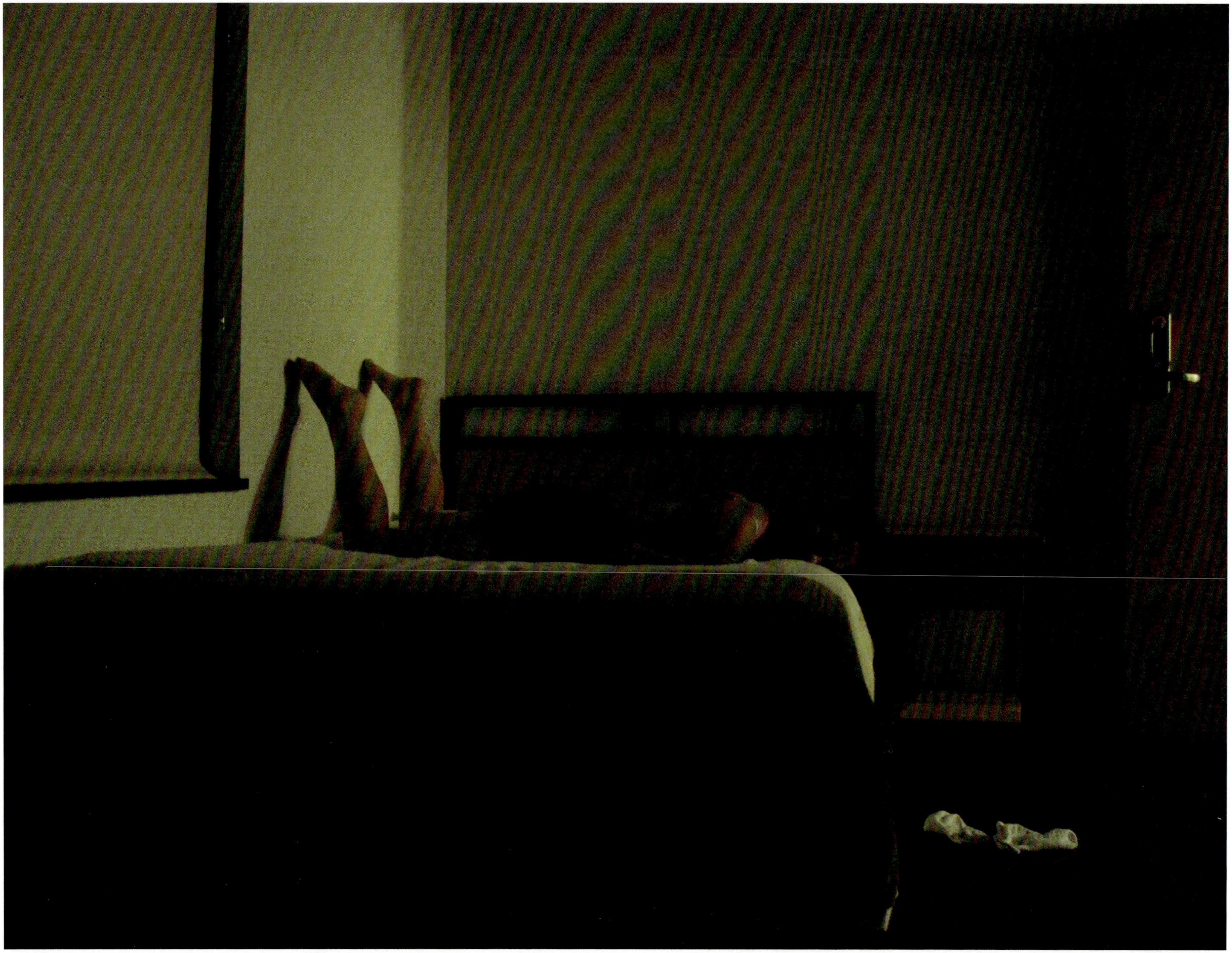

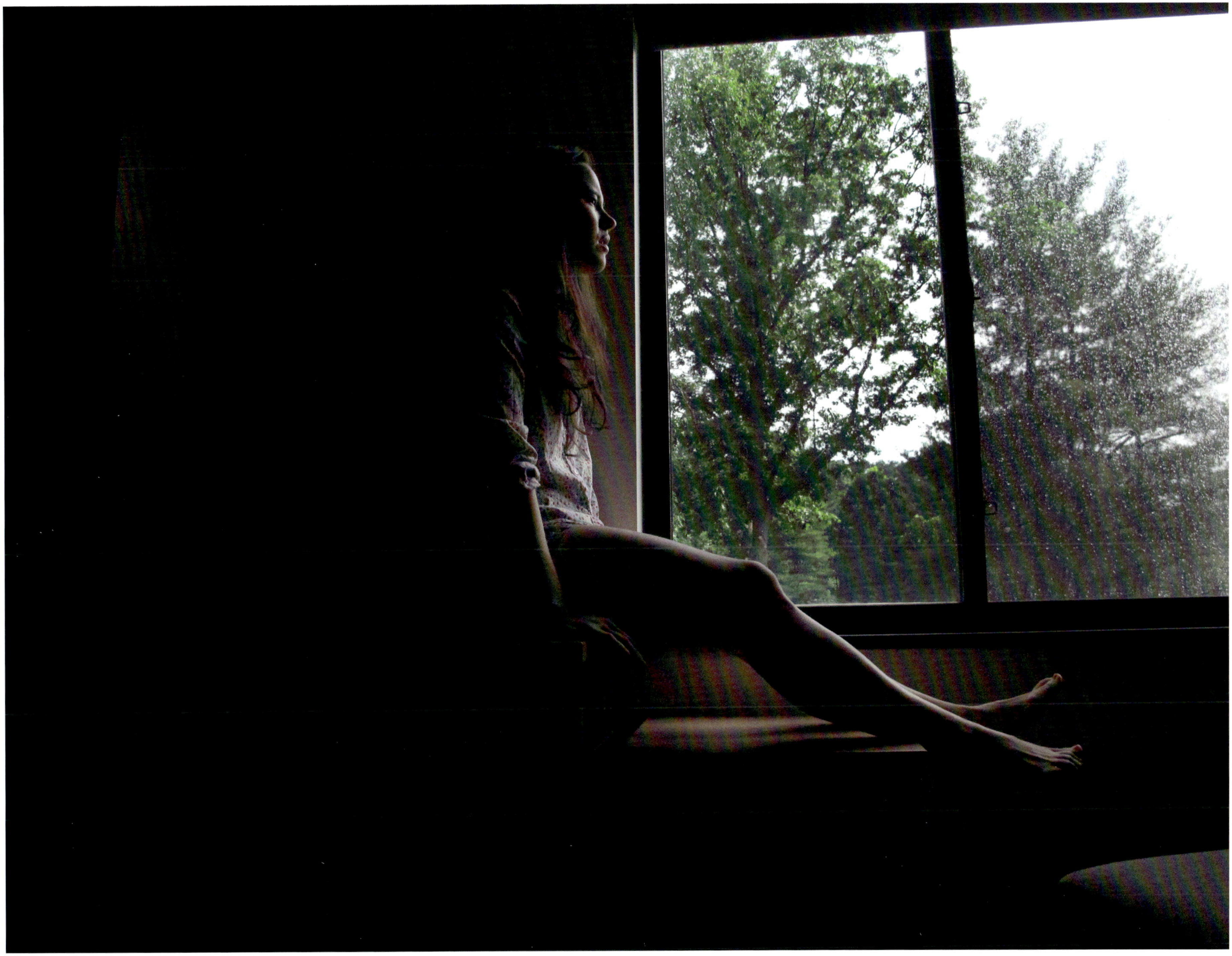

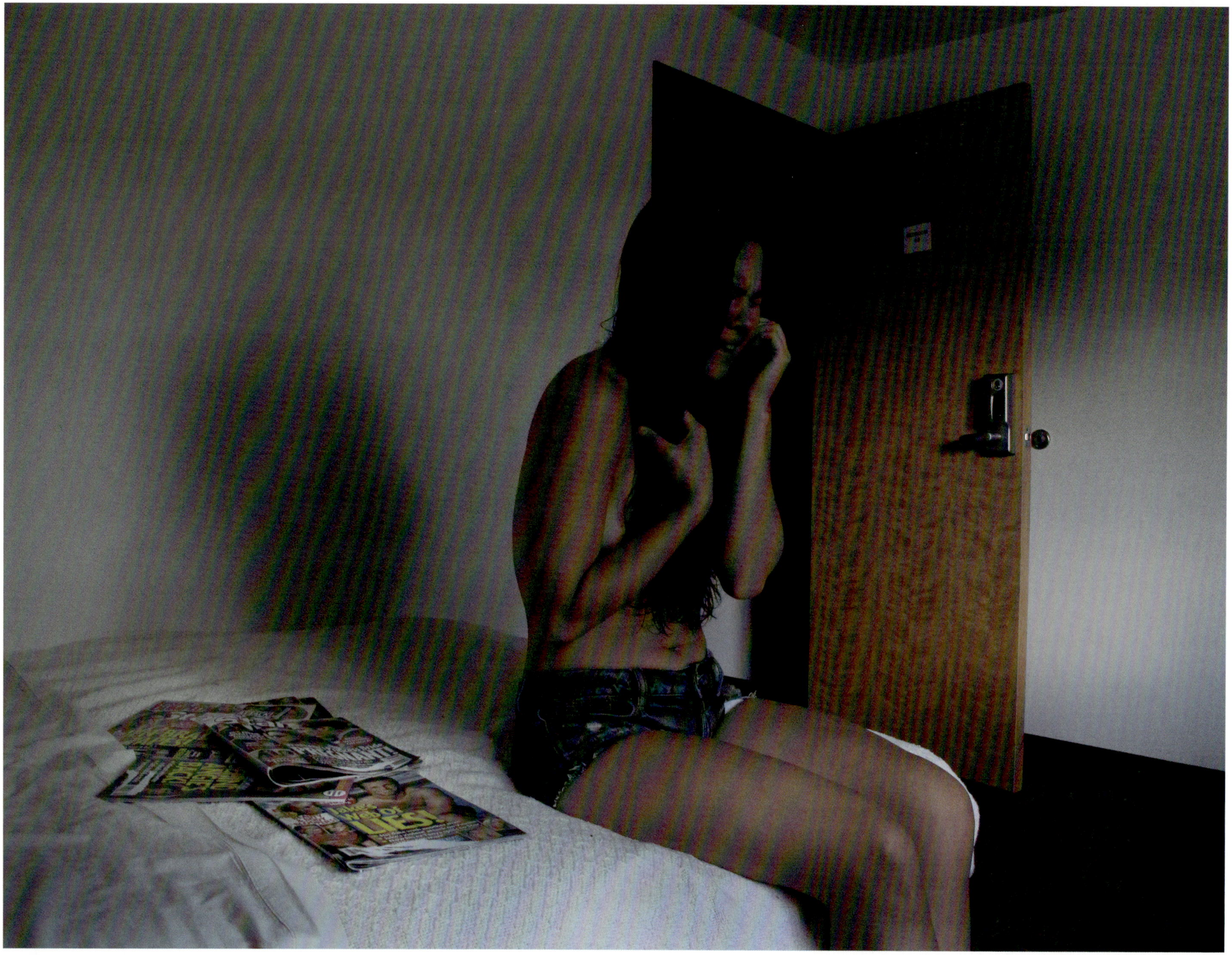
Web of
LIES!

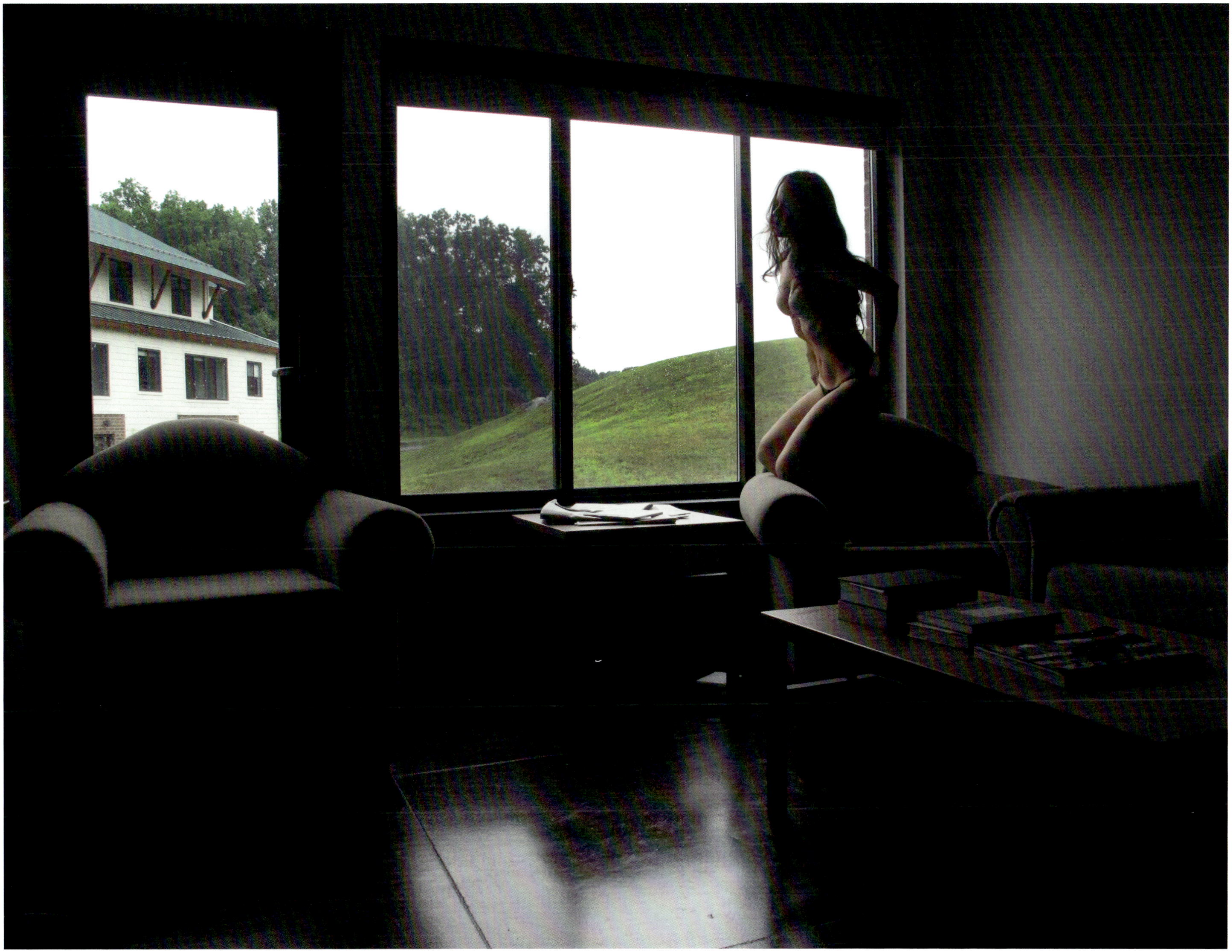

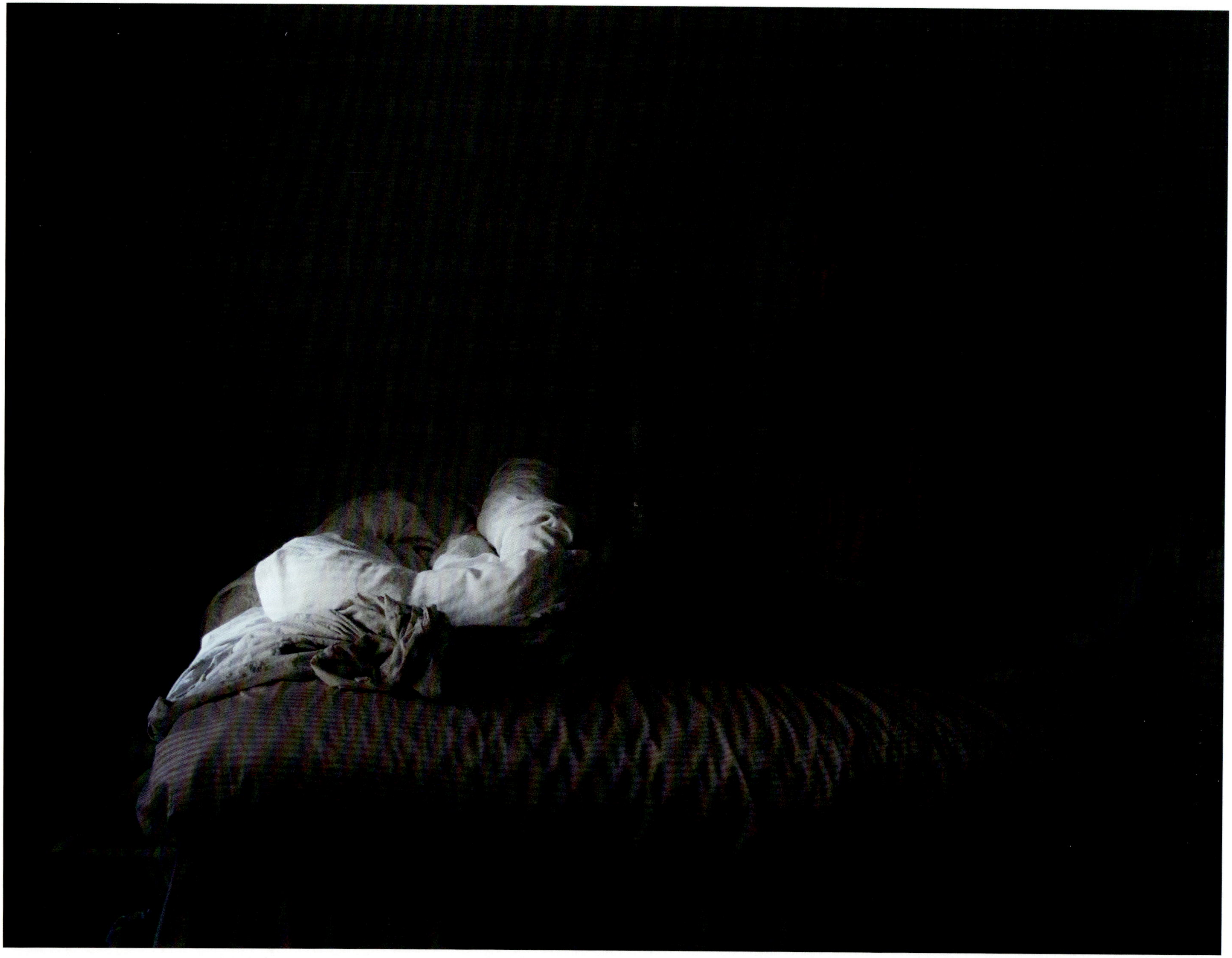

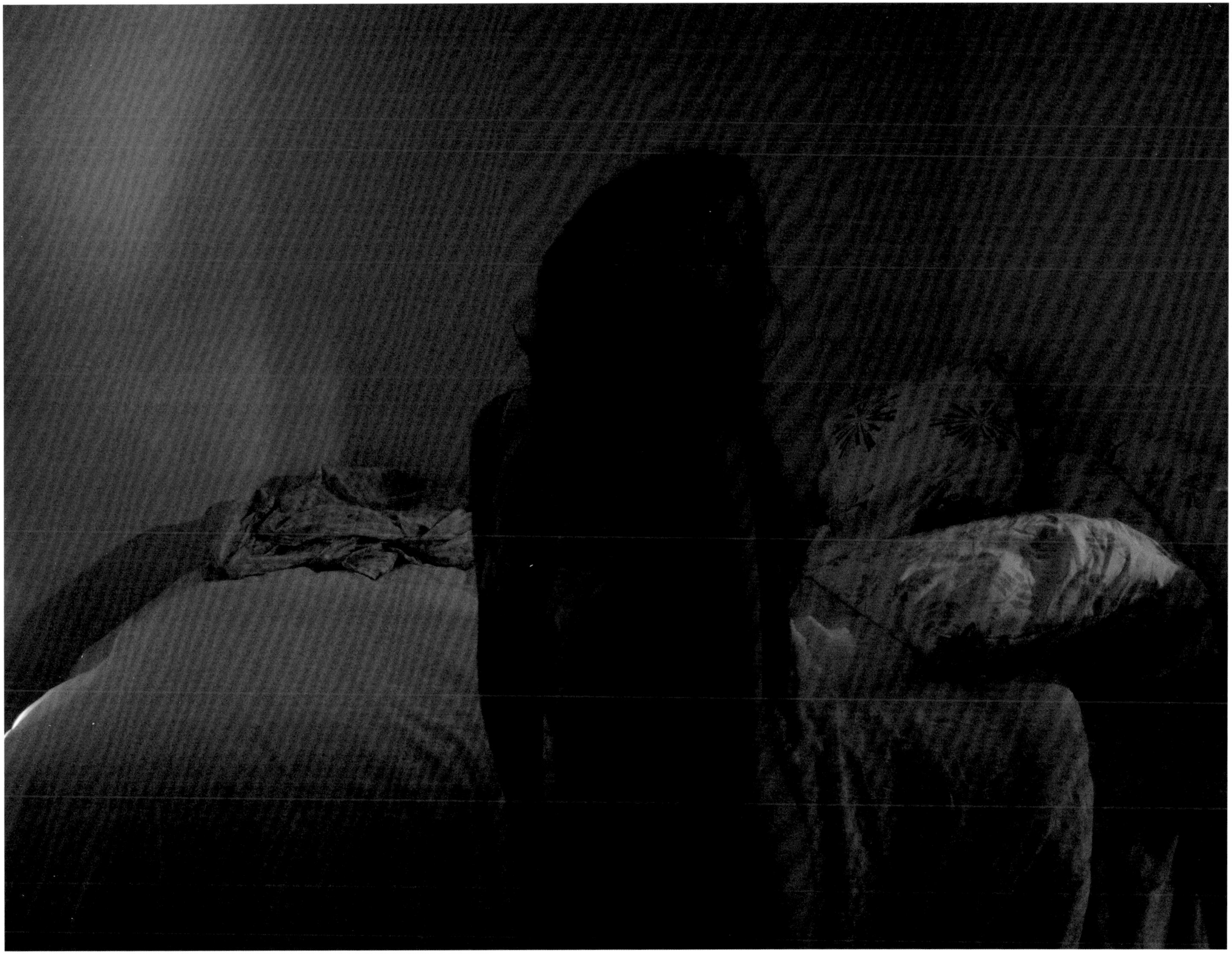

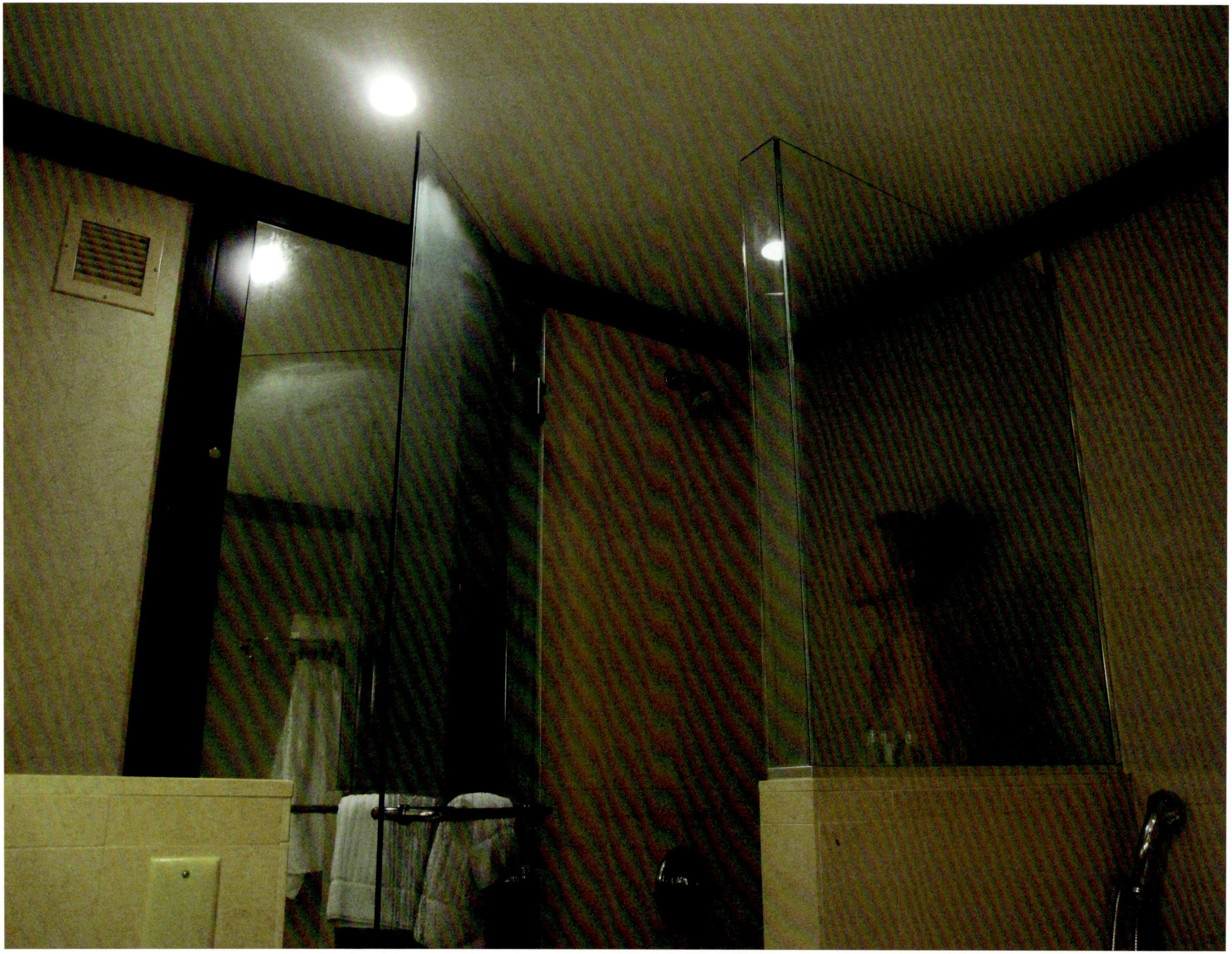

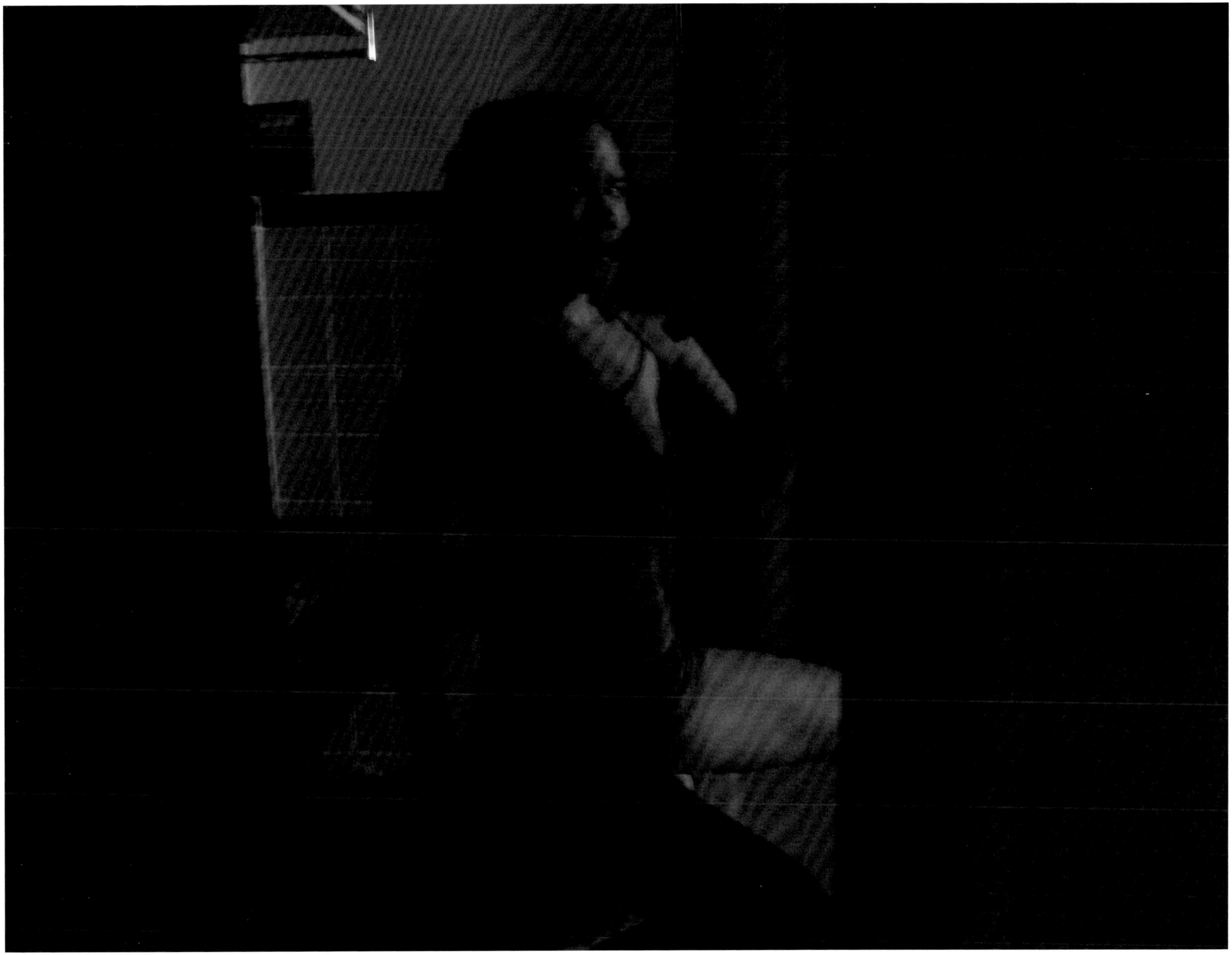

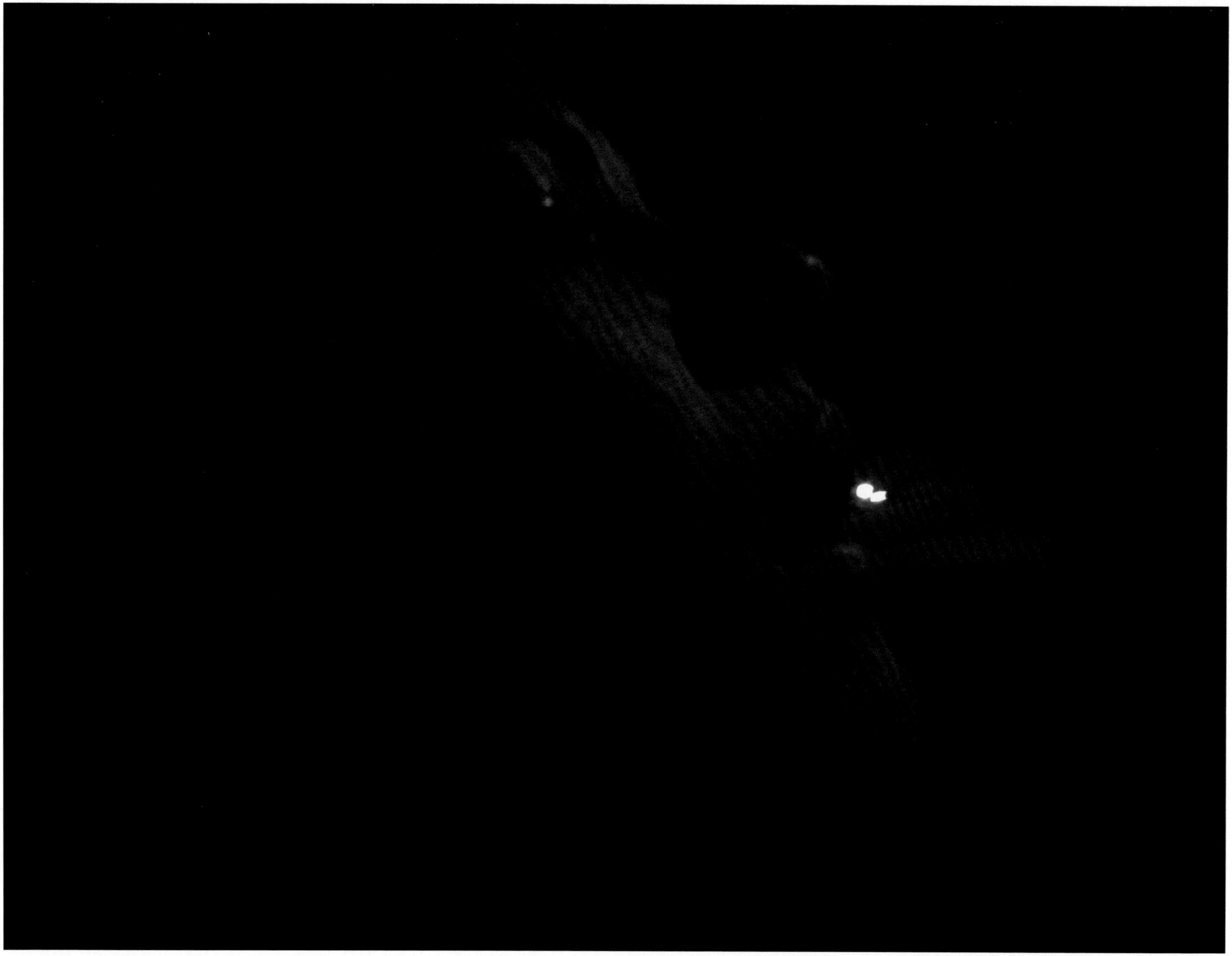

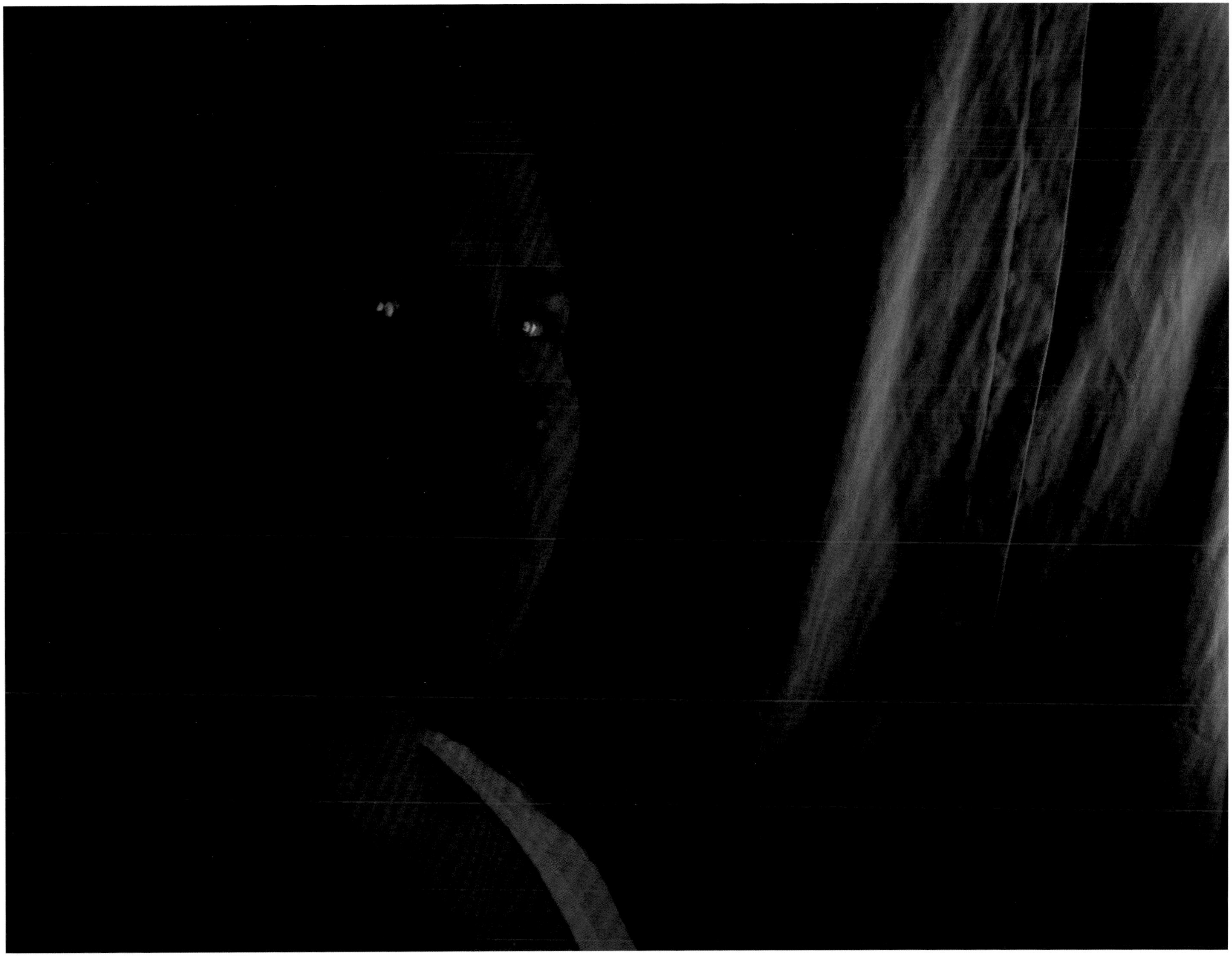

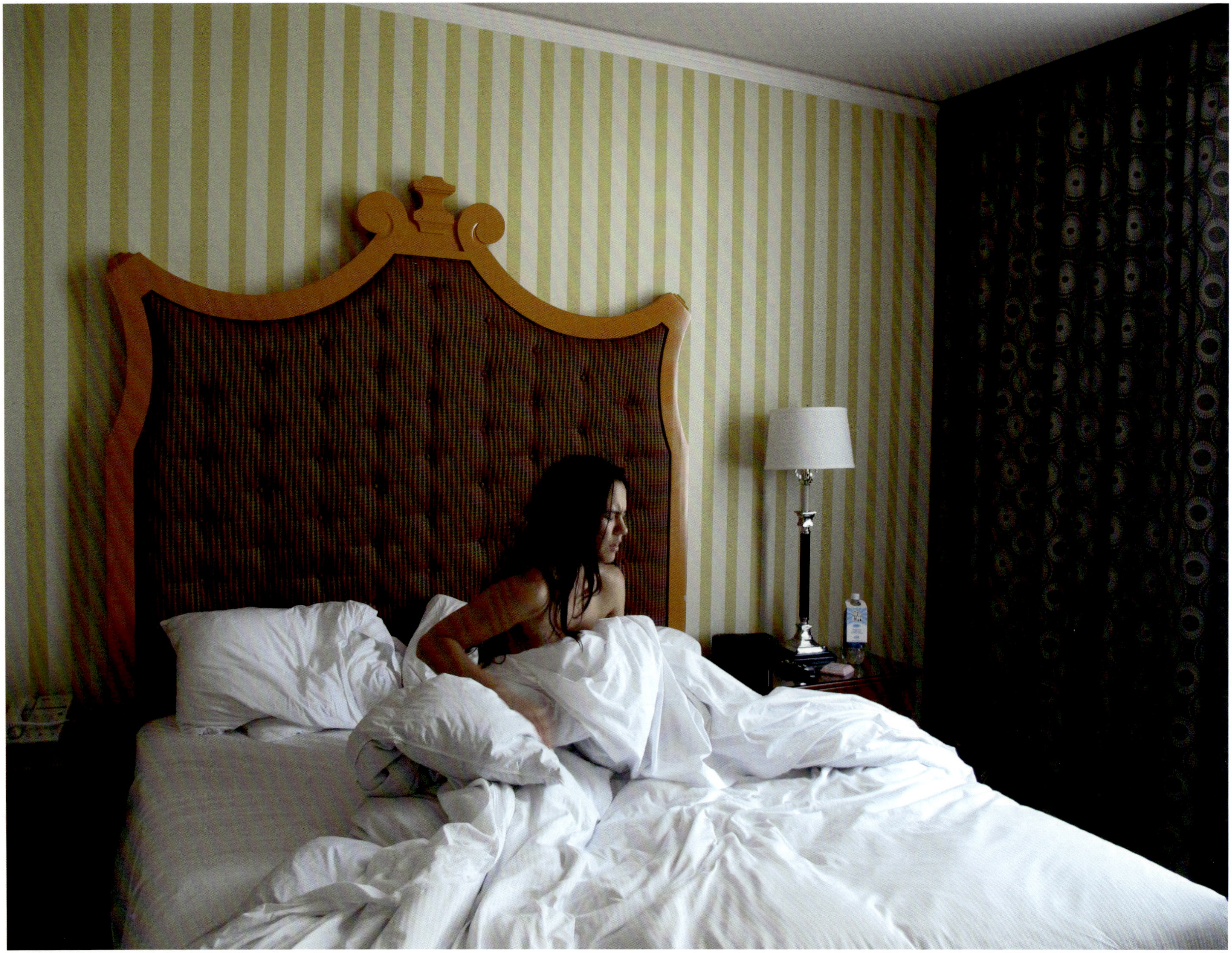

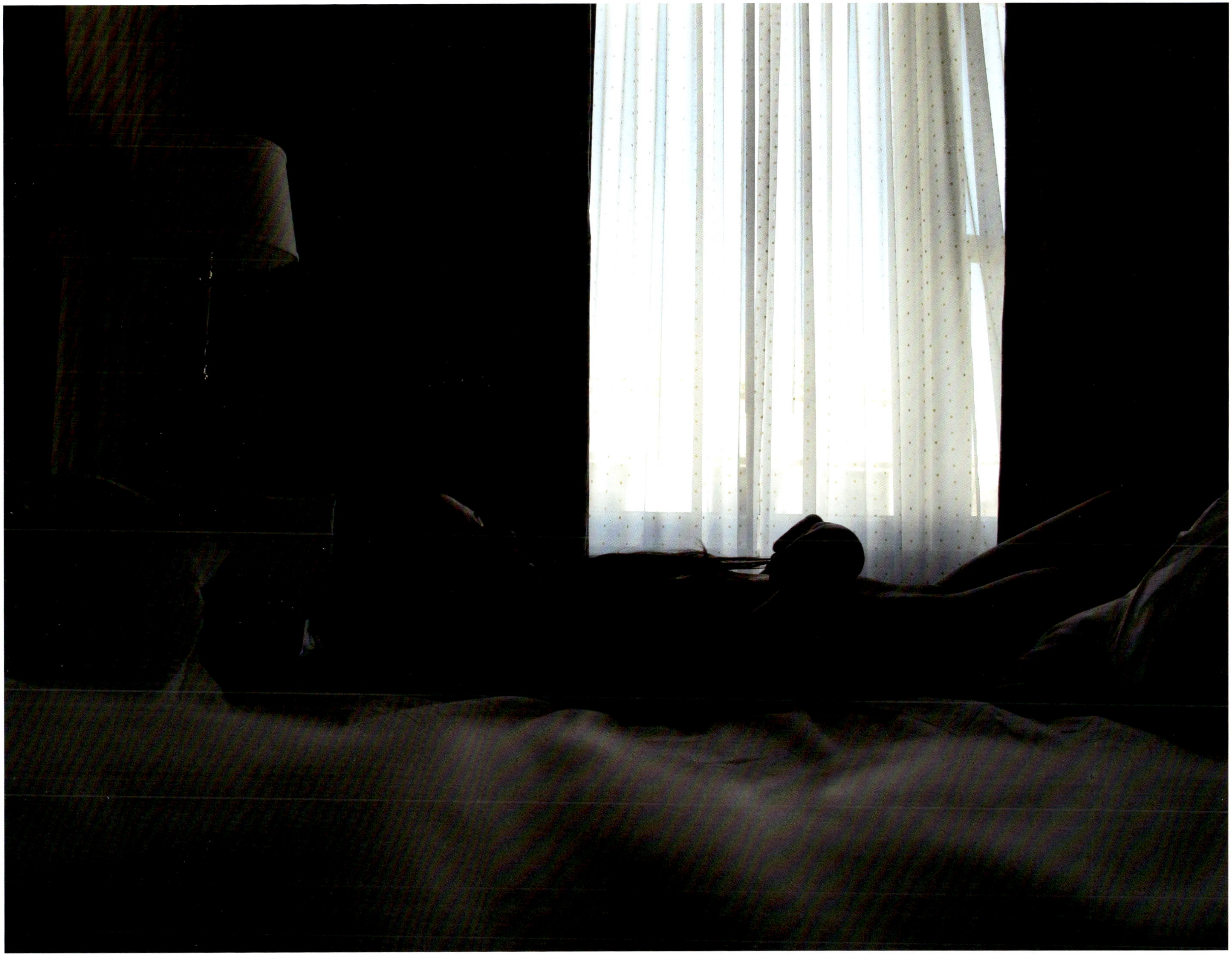

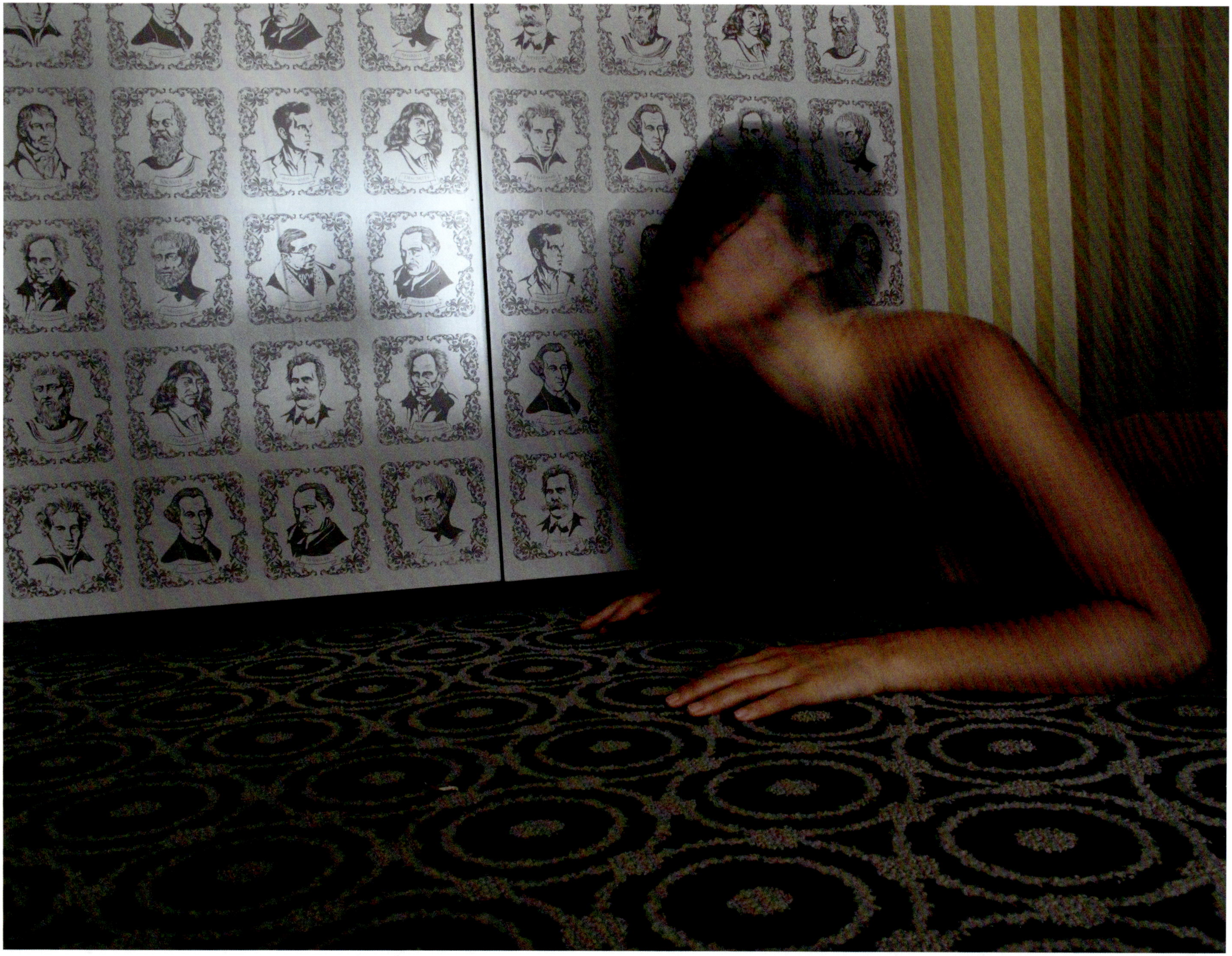

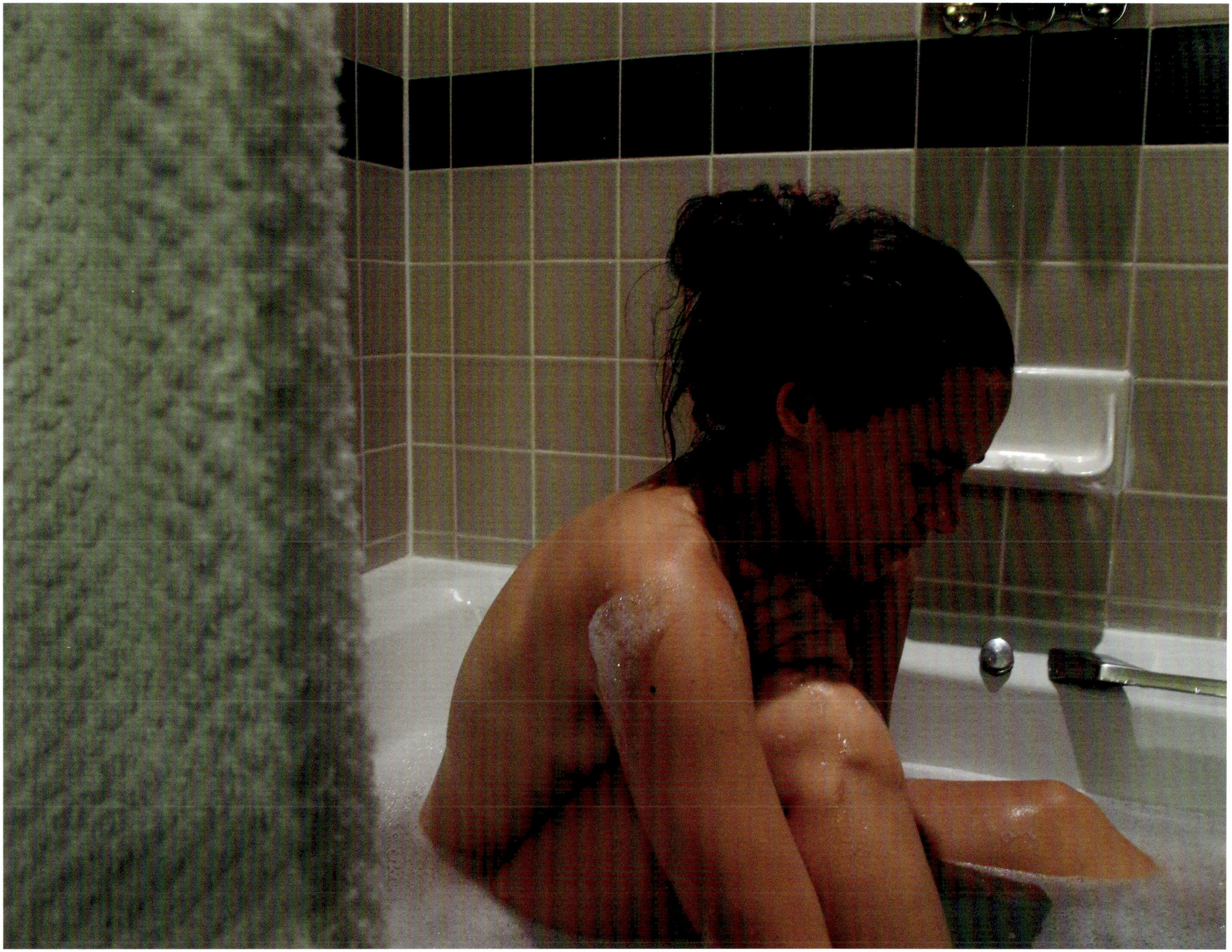

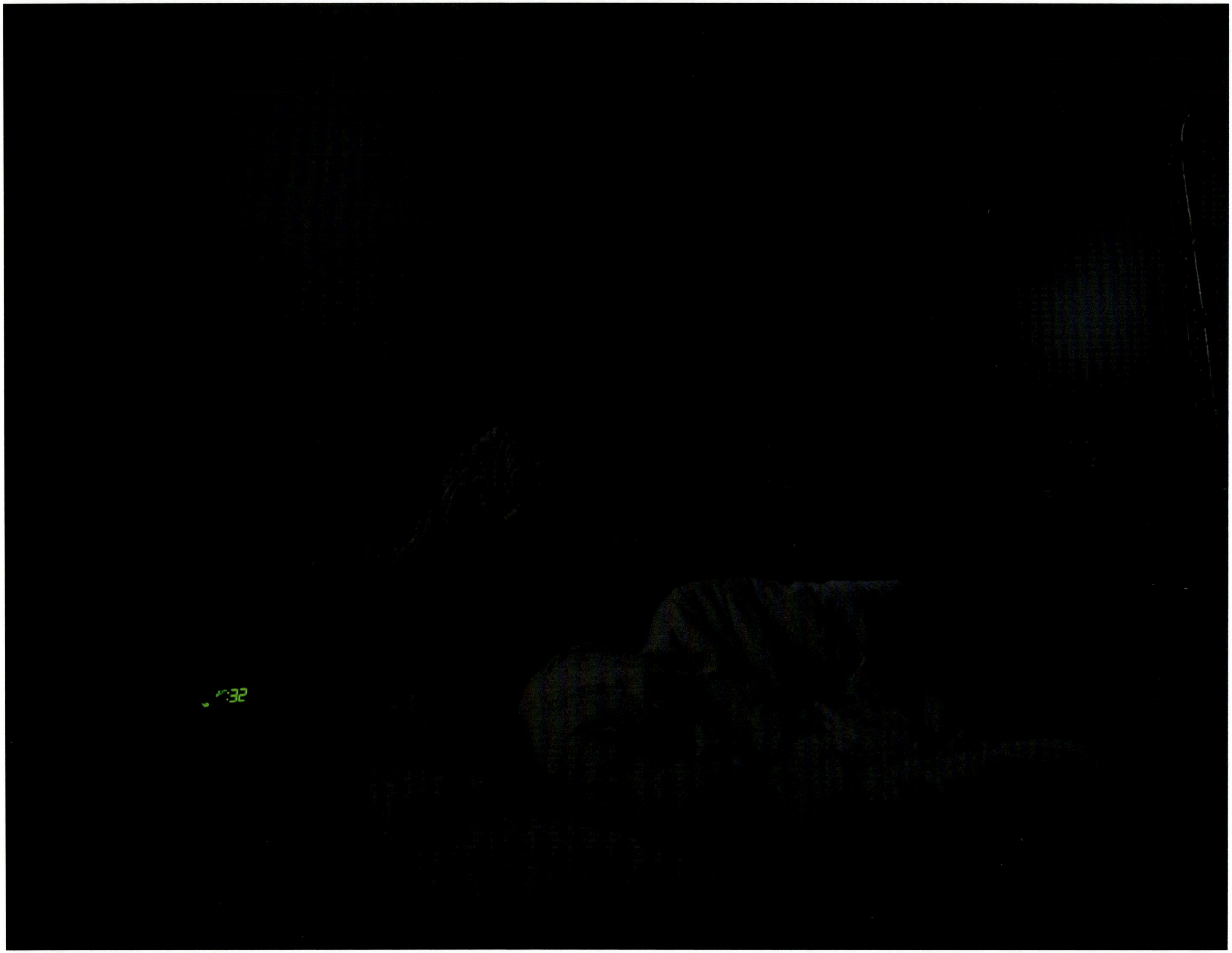

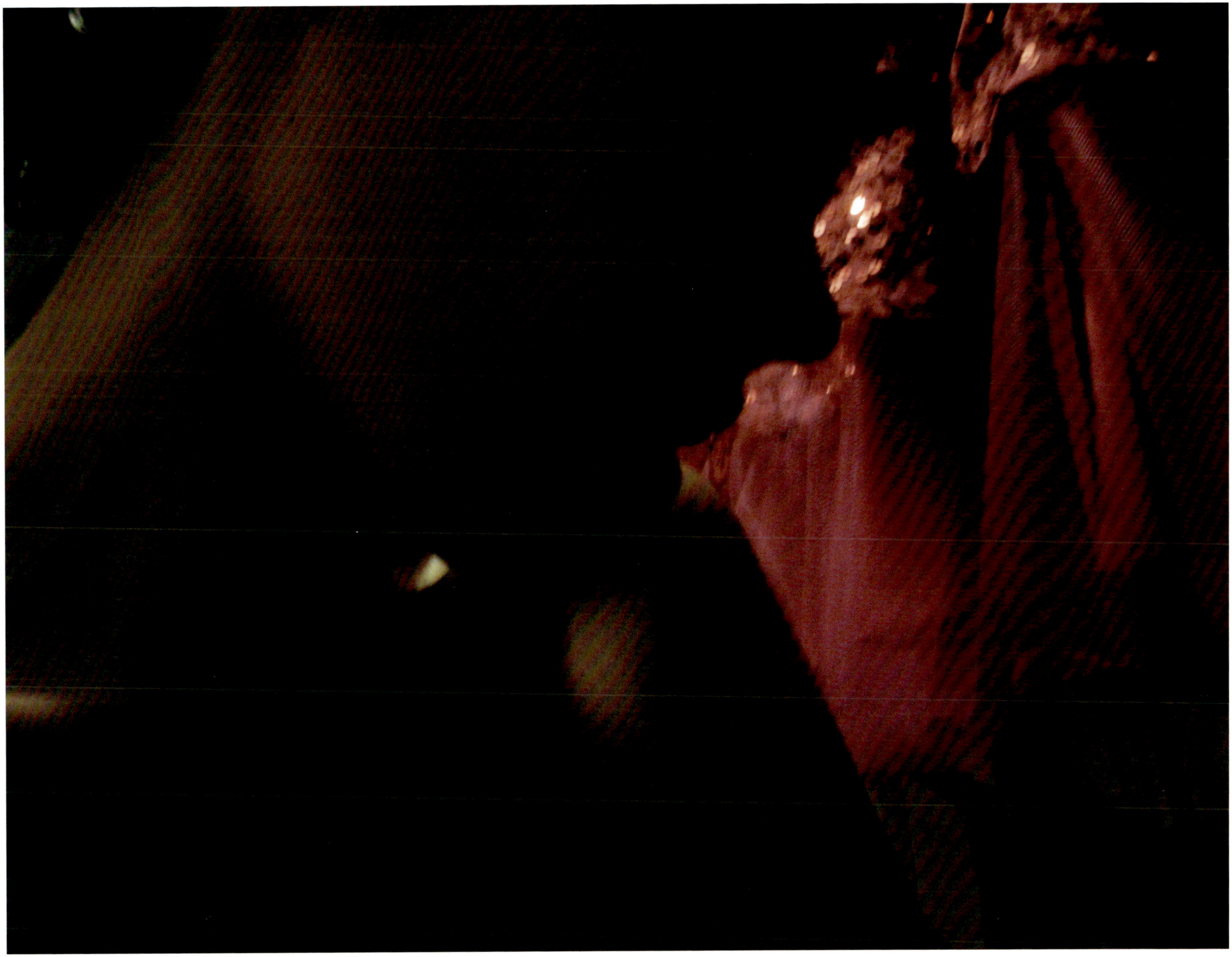

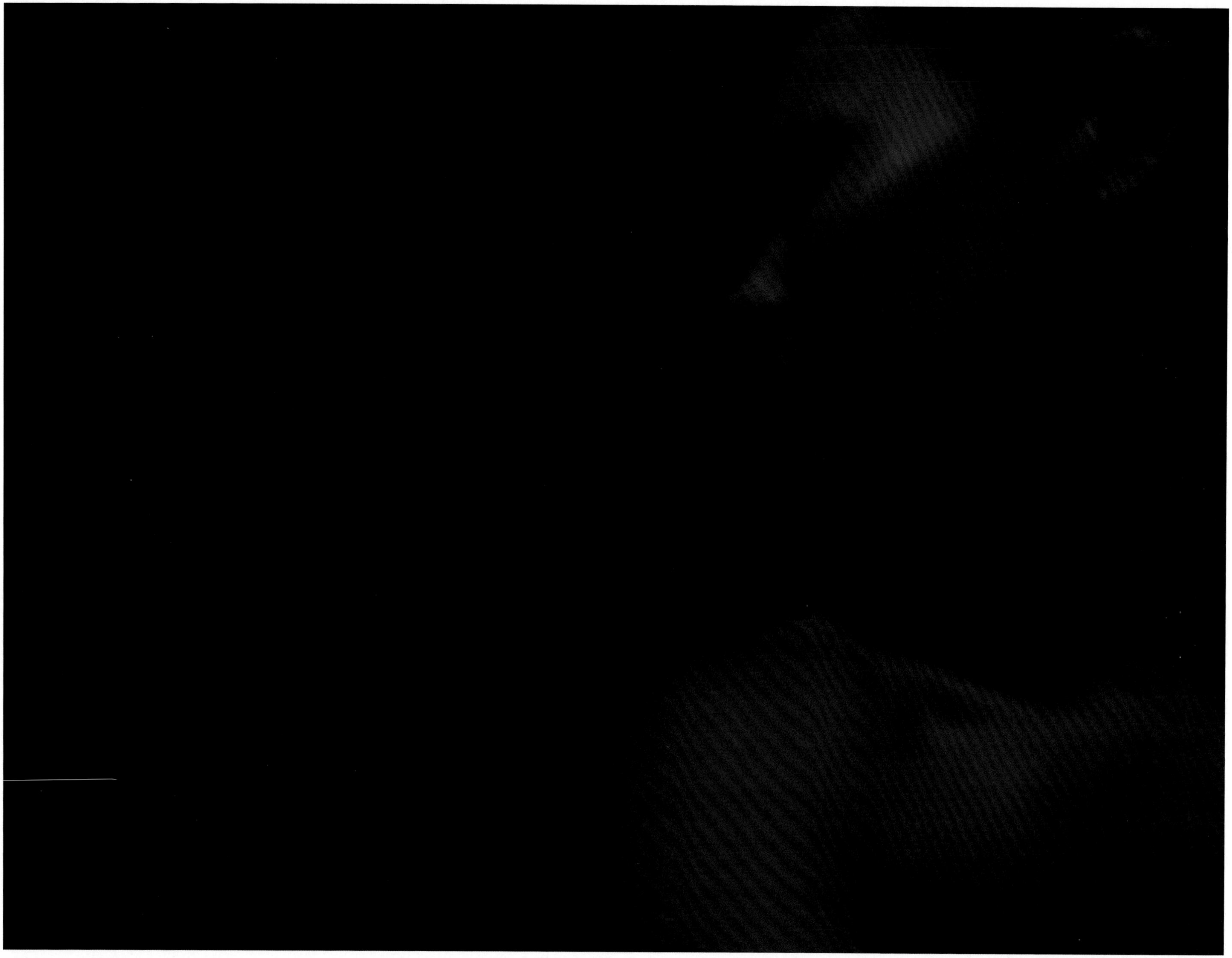

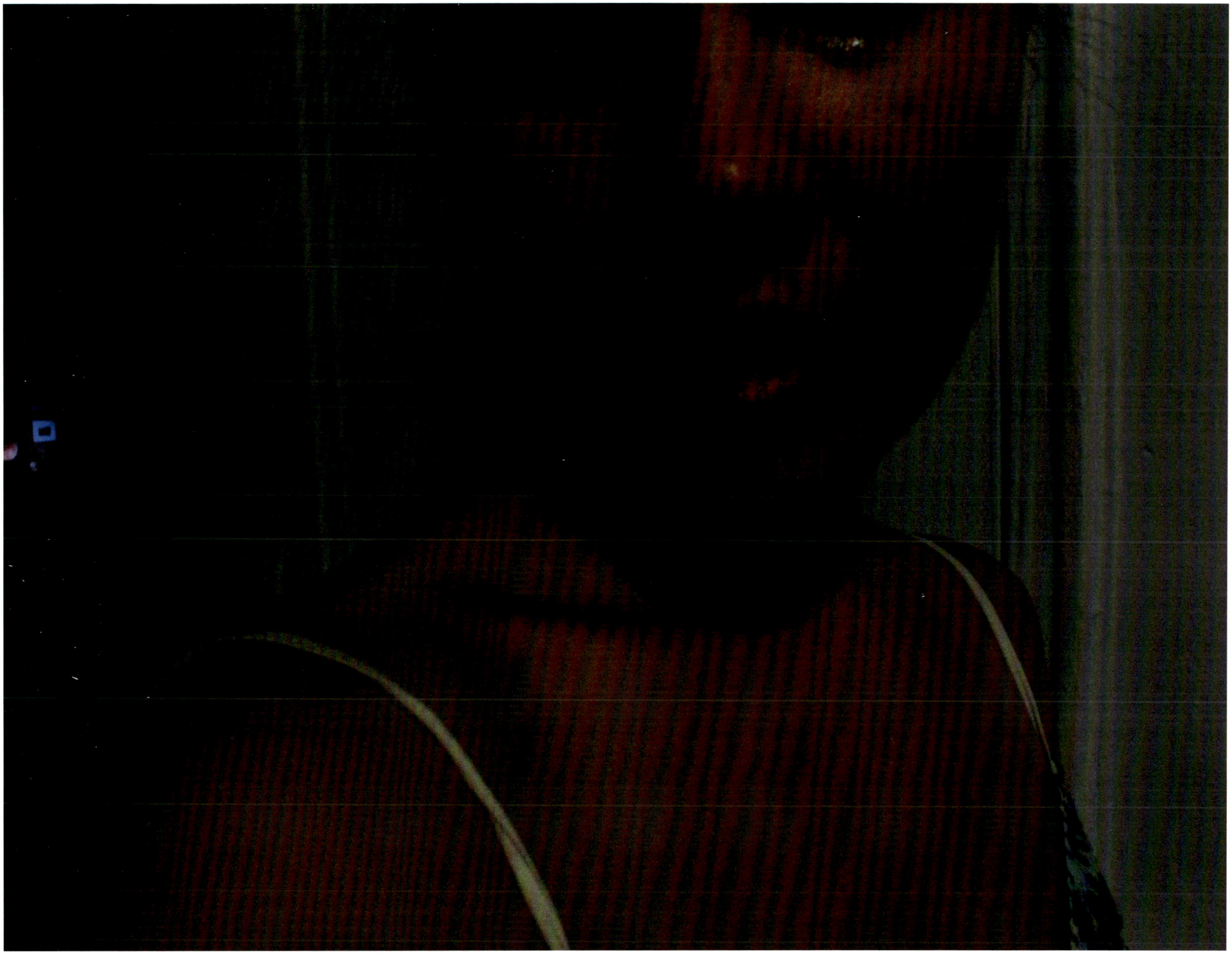

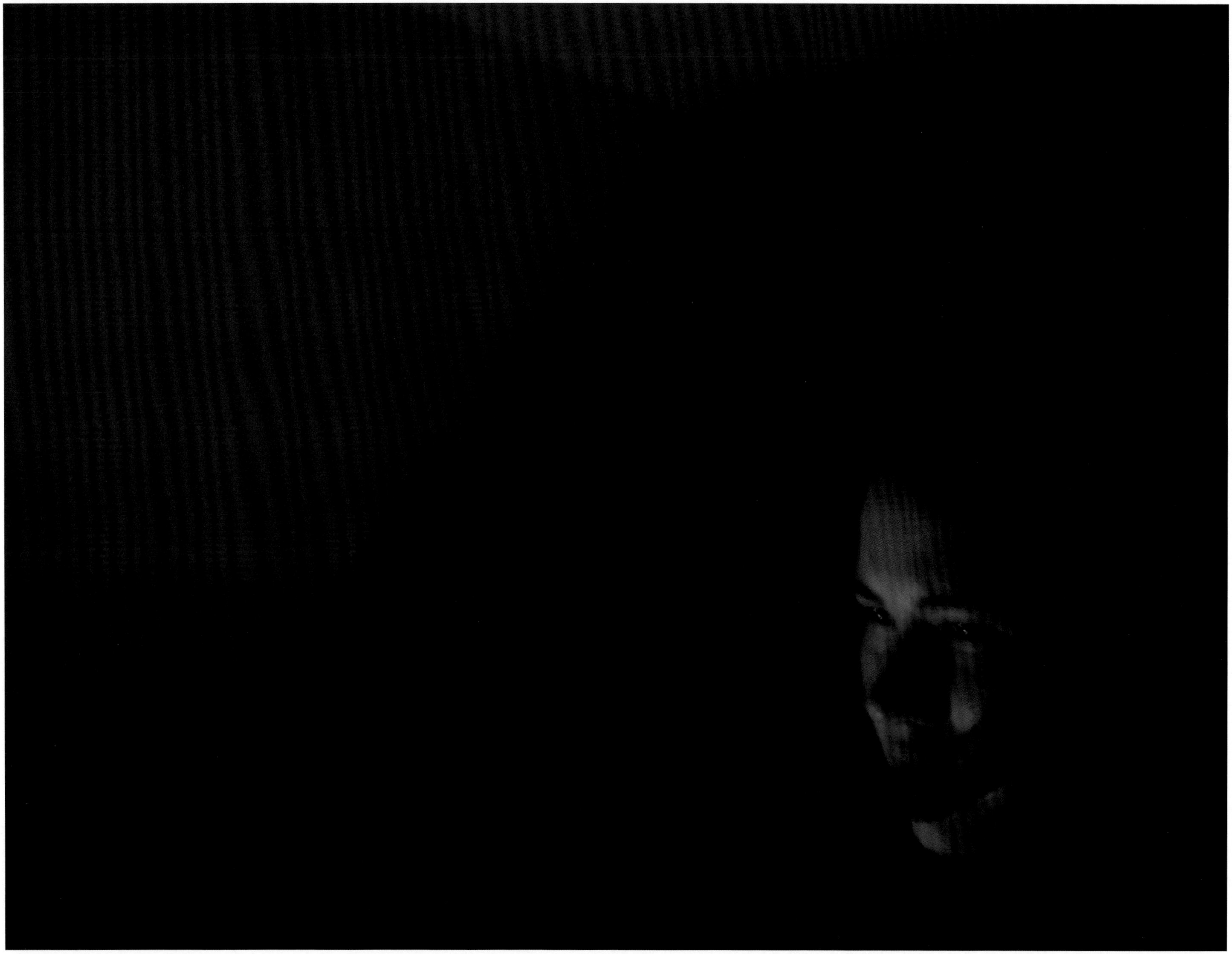

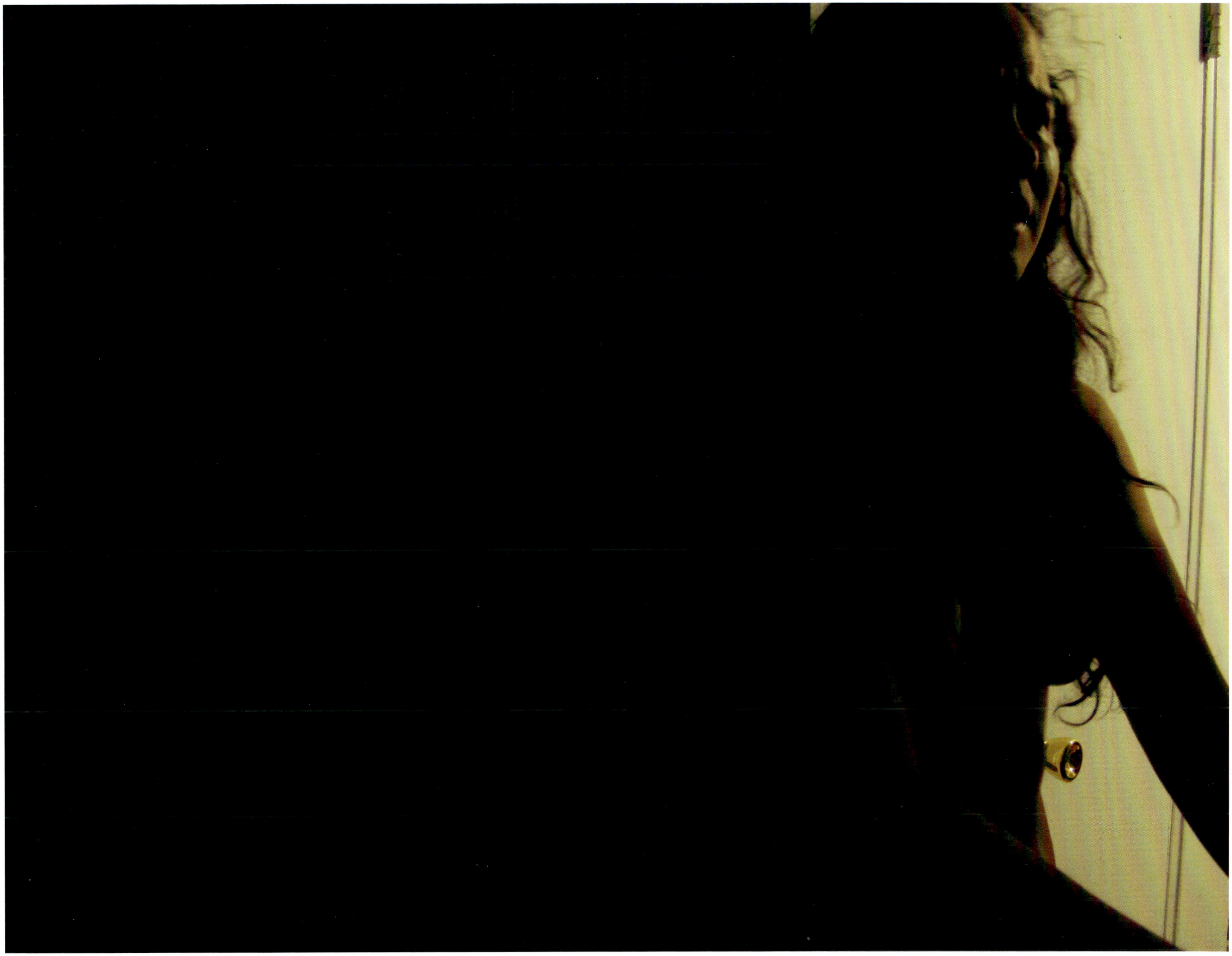

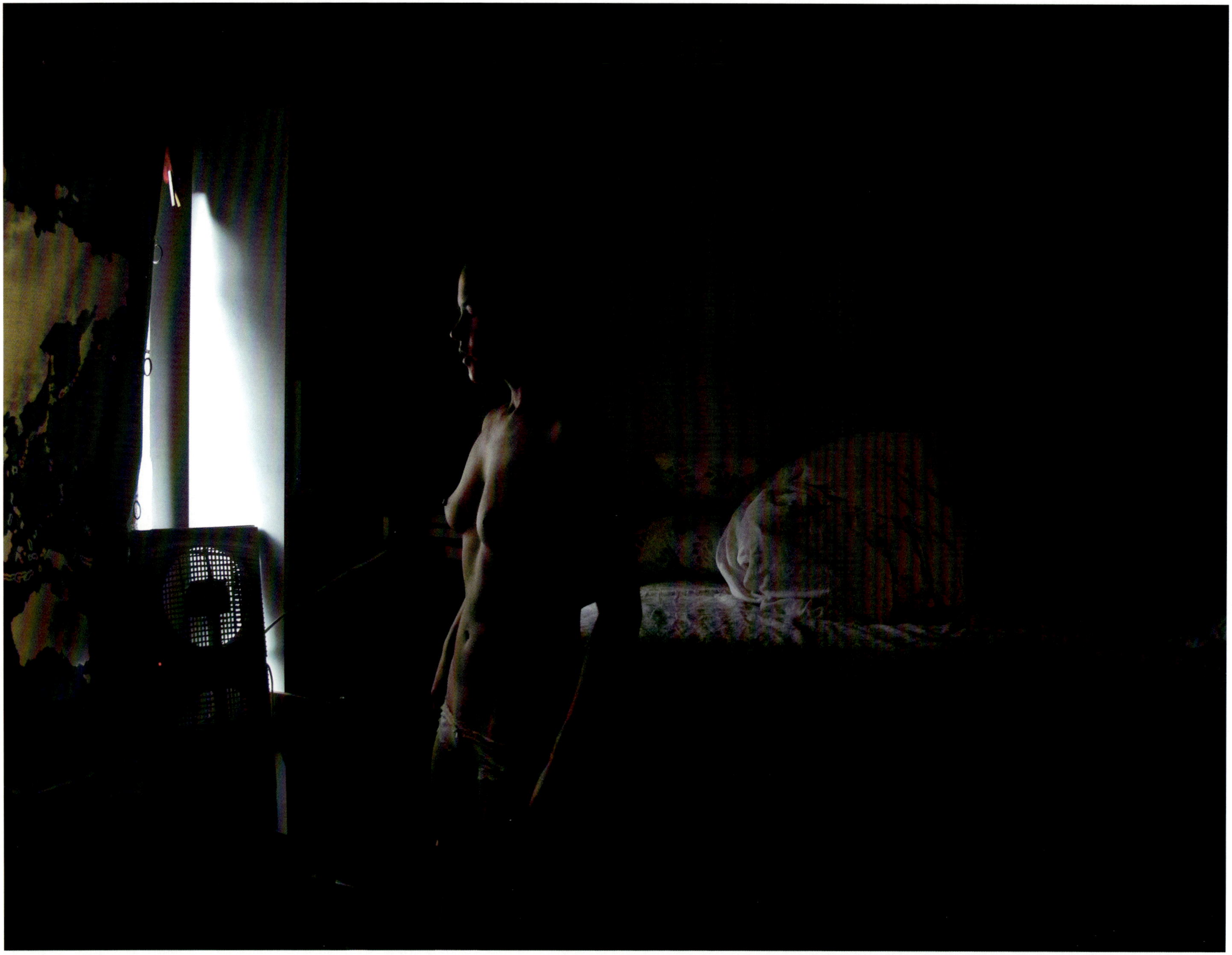

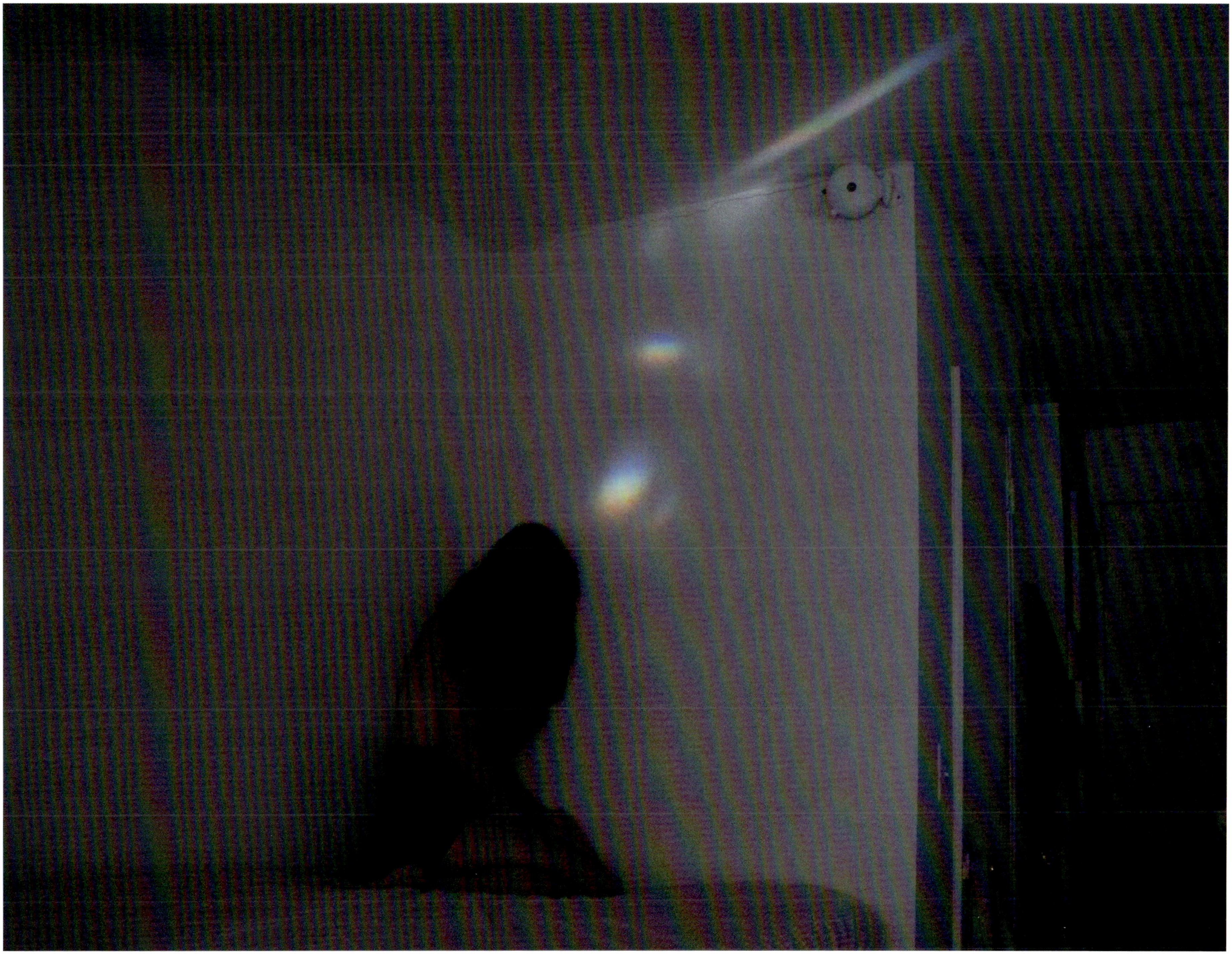

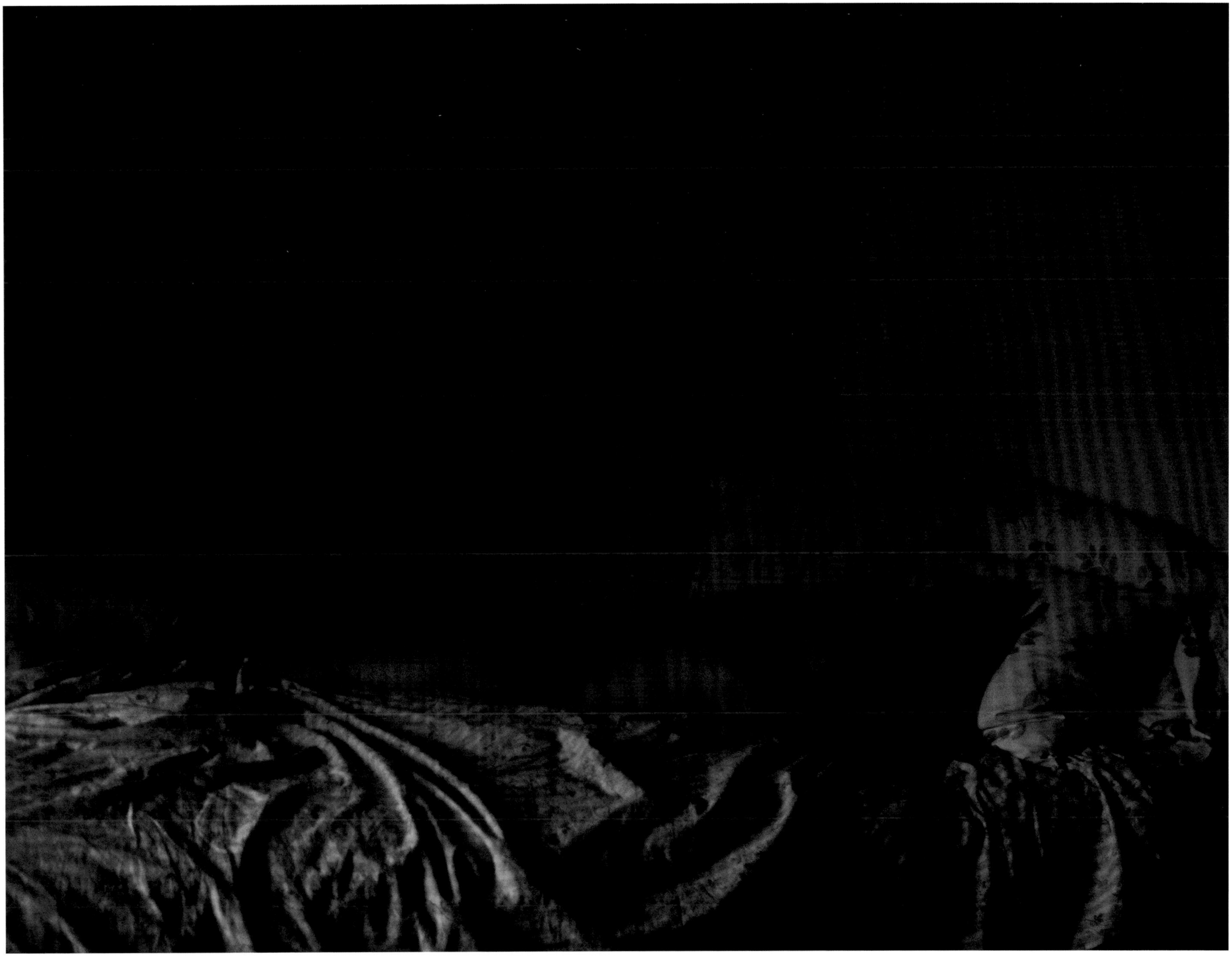

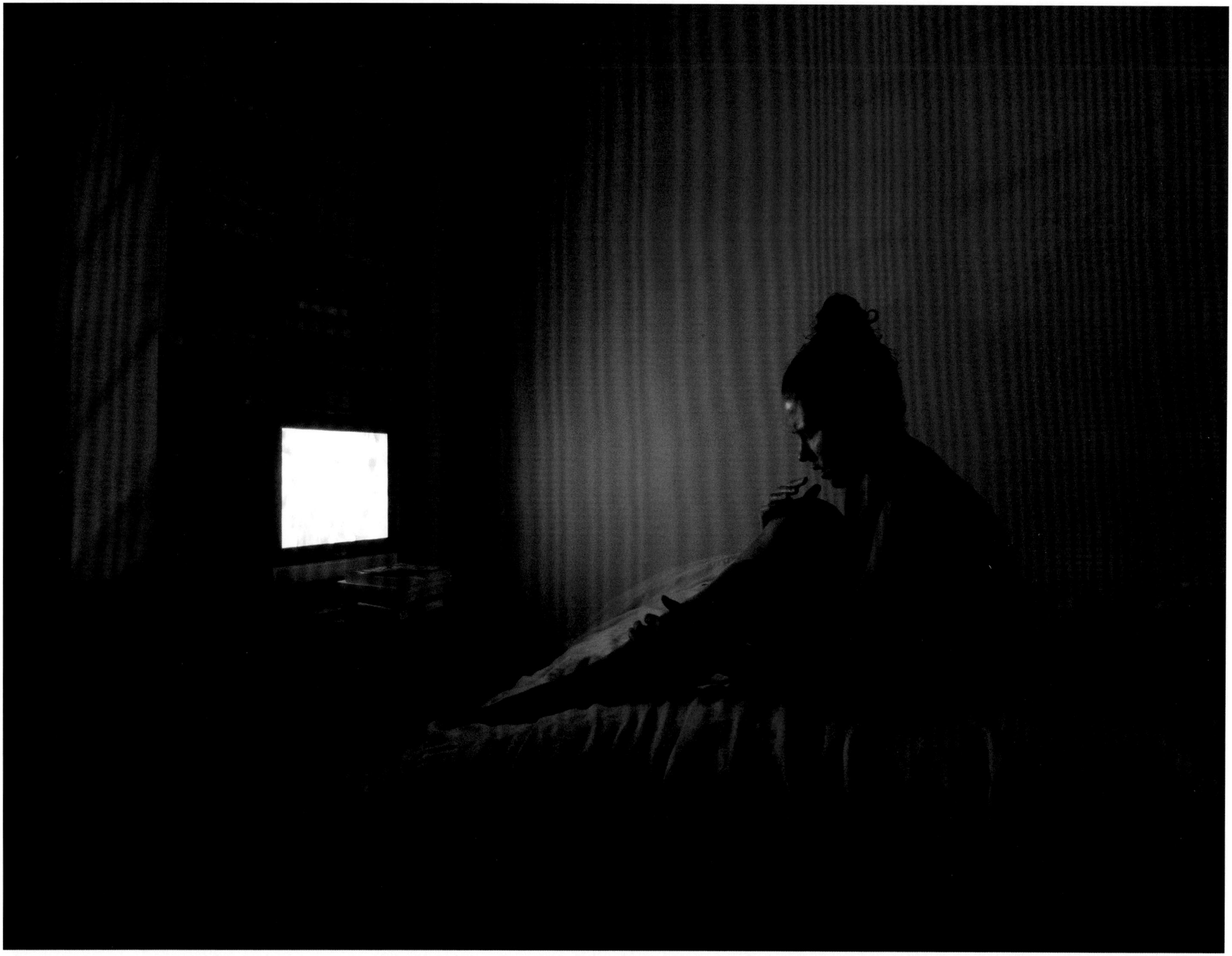

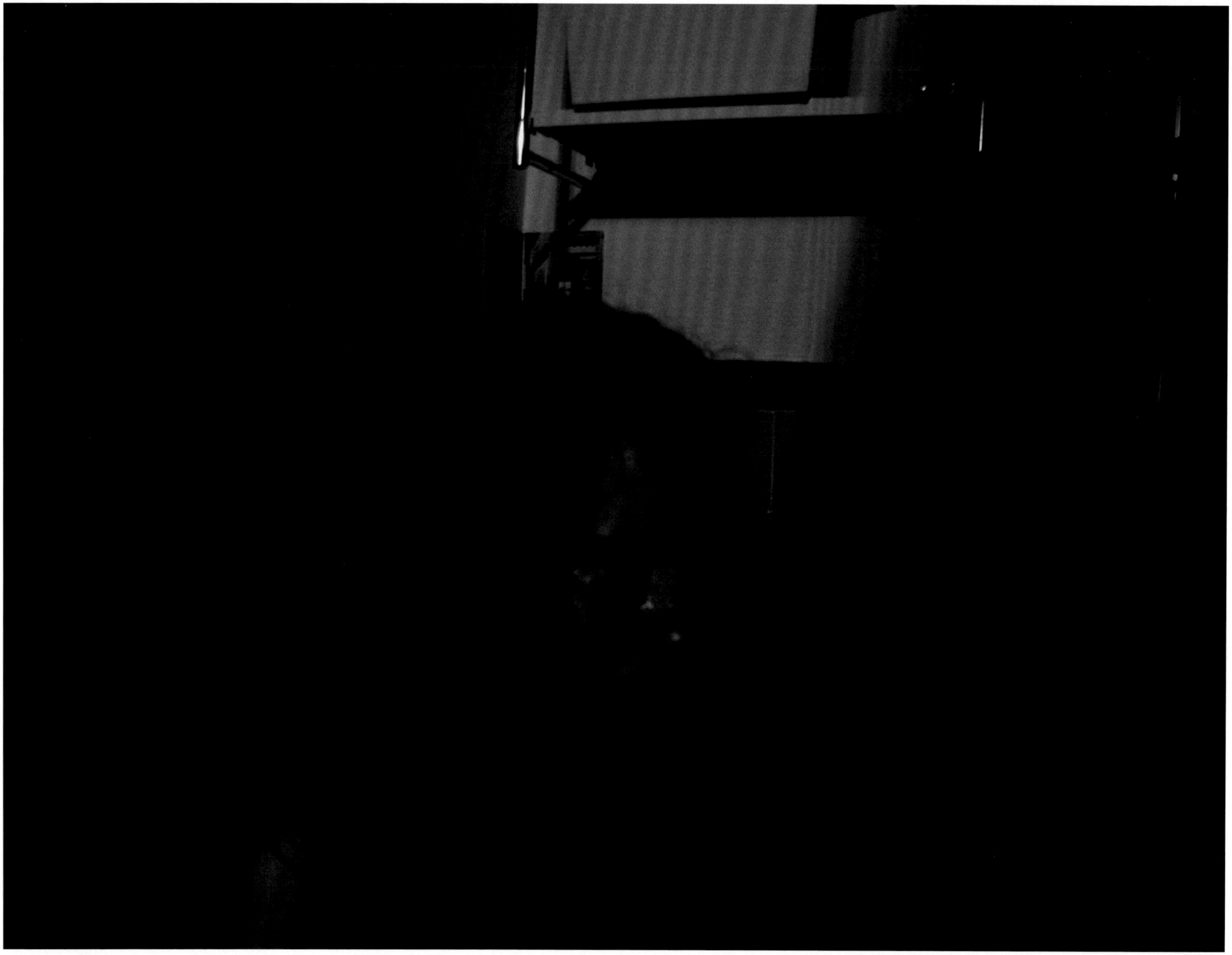

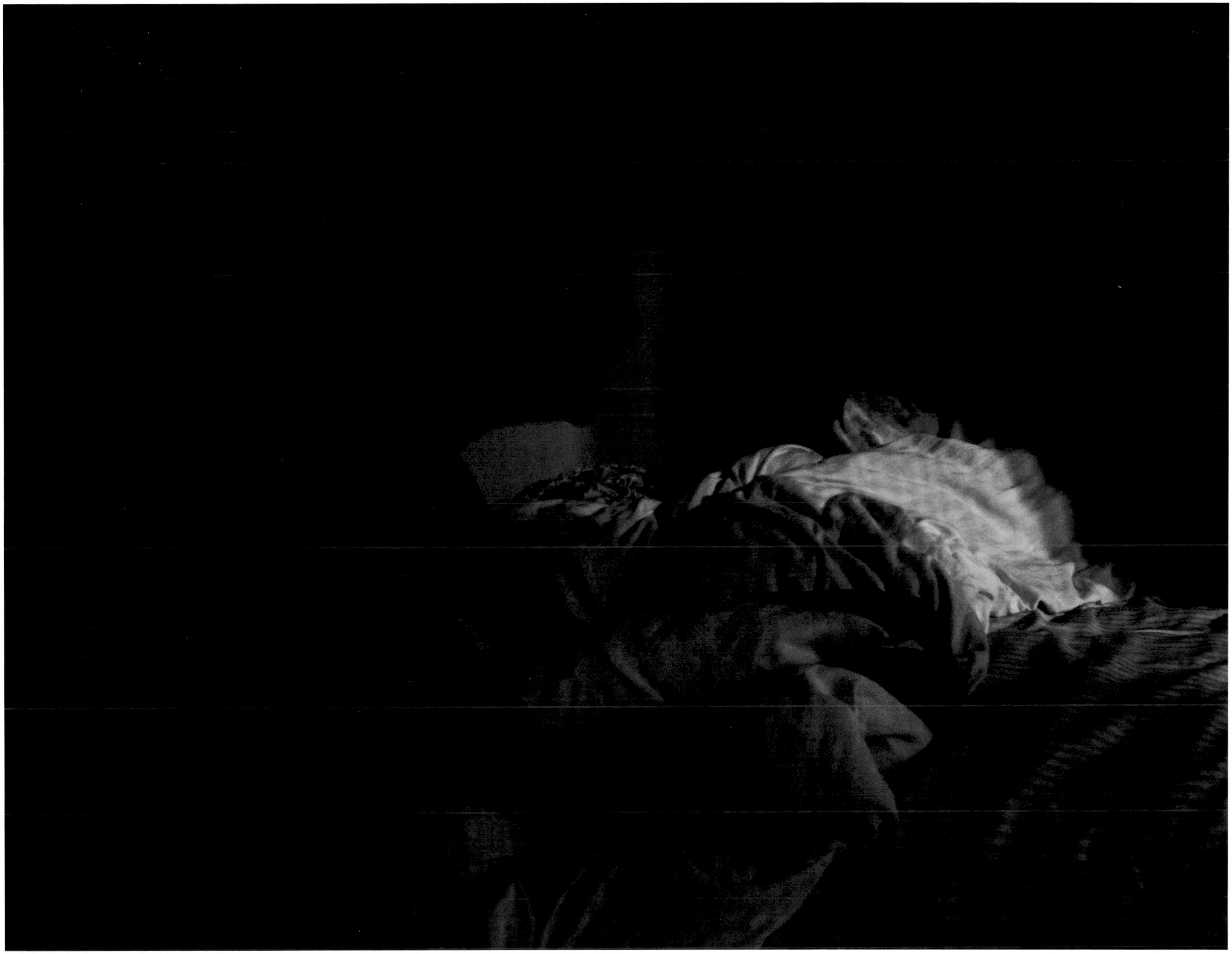

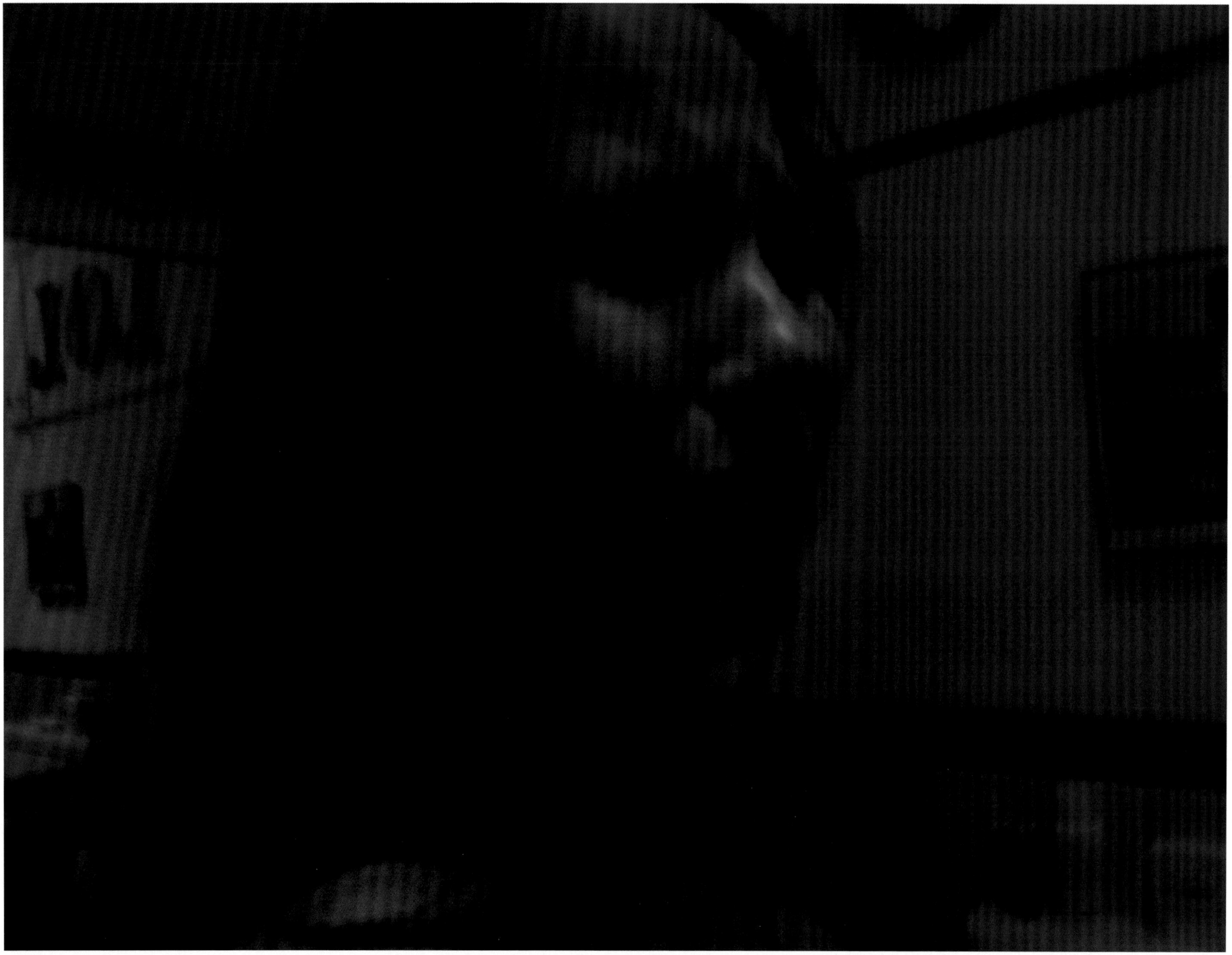

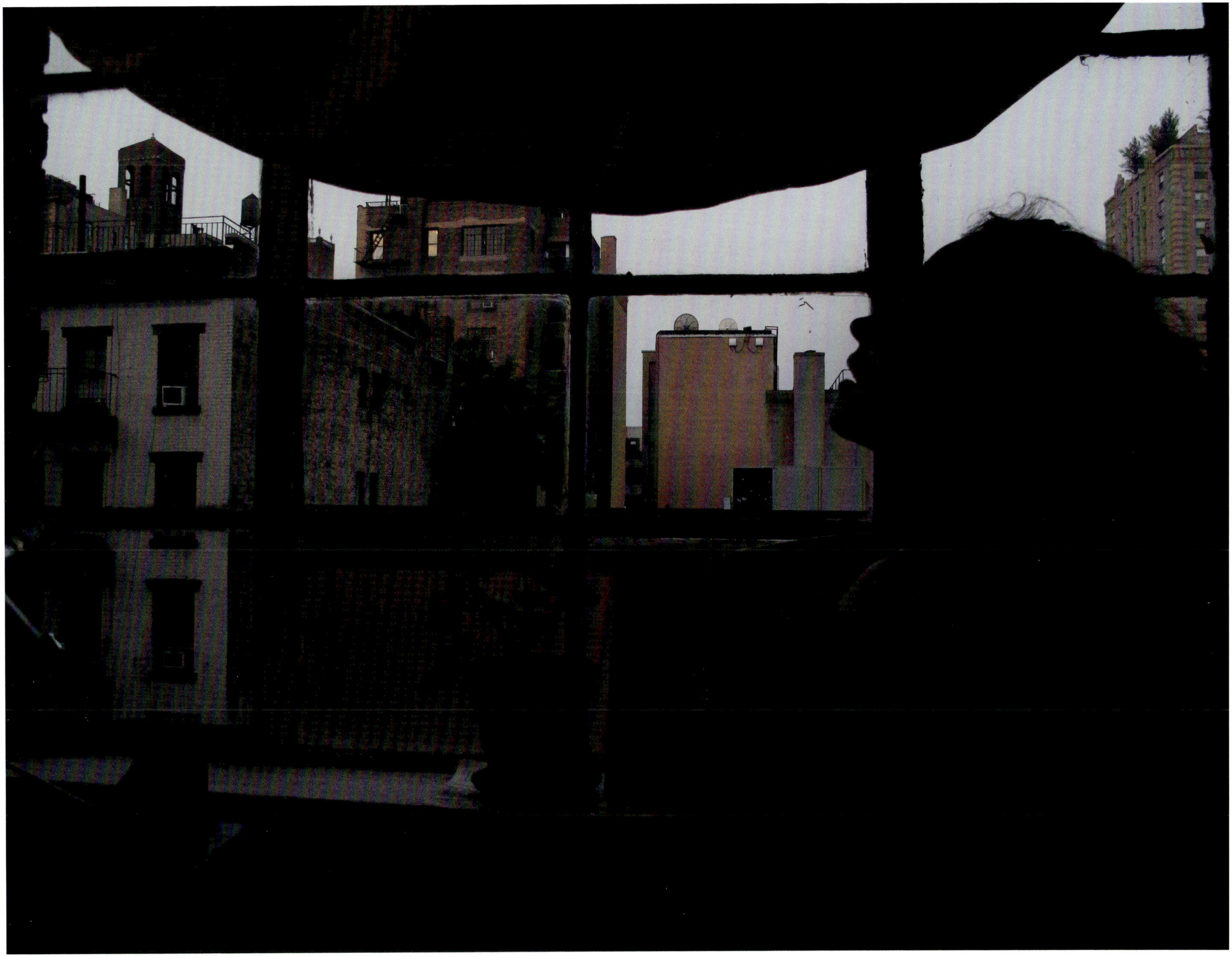

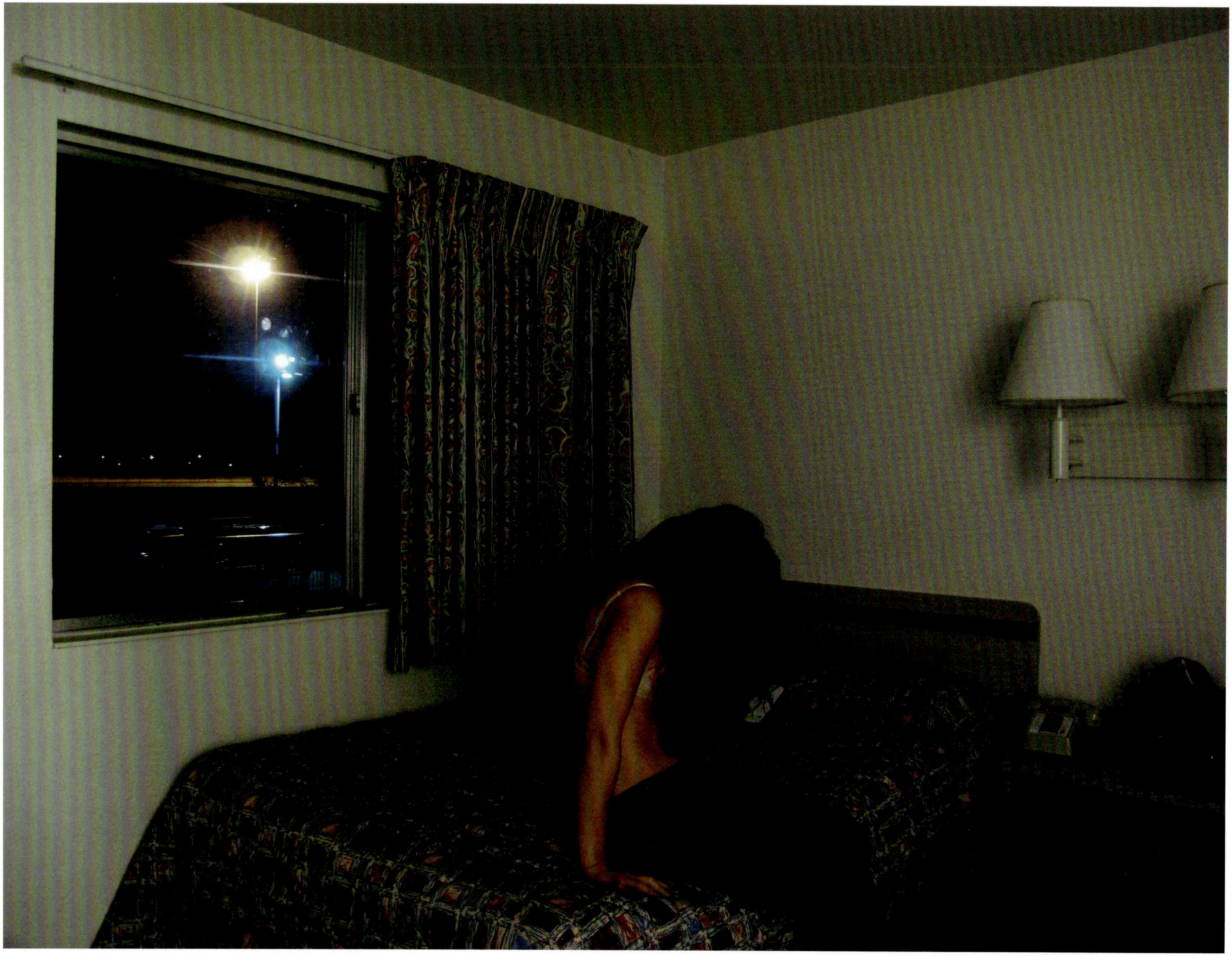

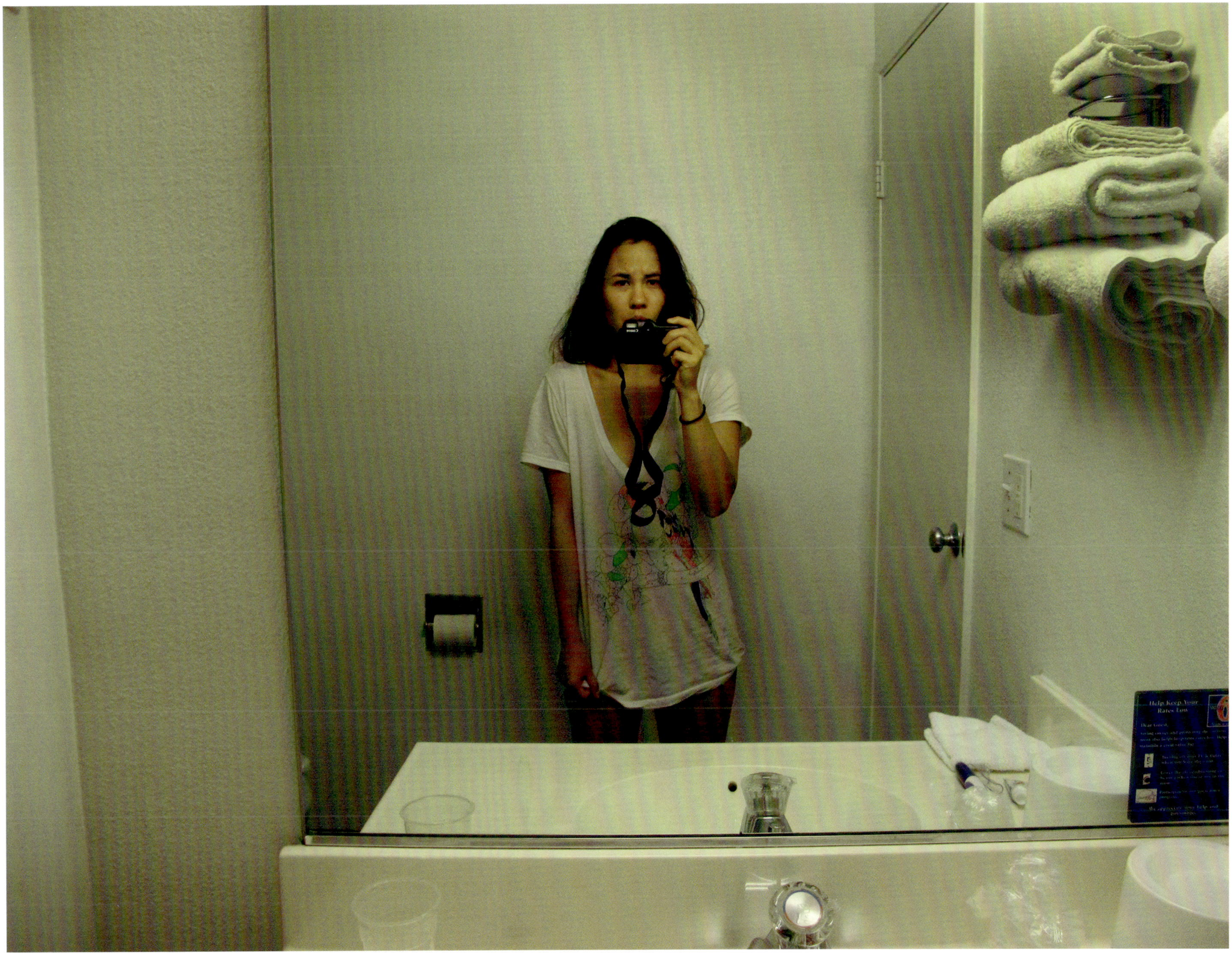
Help Keep Your Rates Low
Dear Guest,

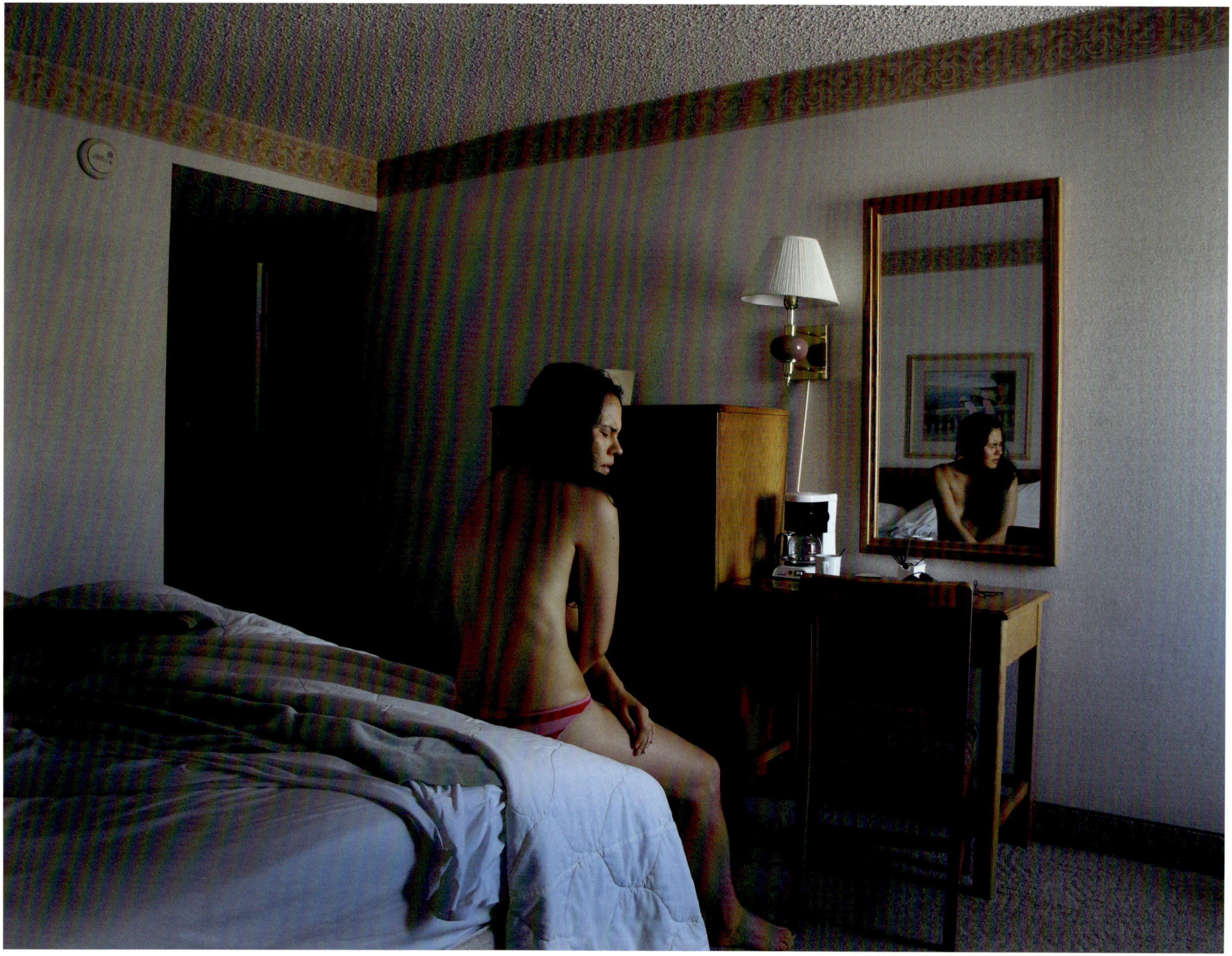

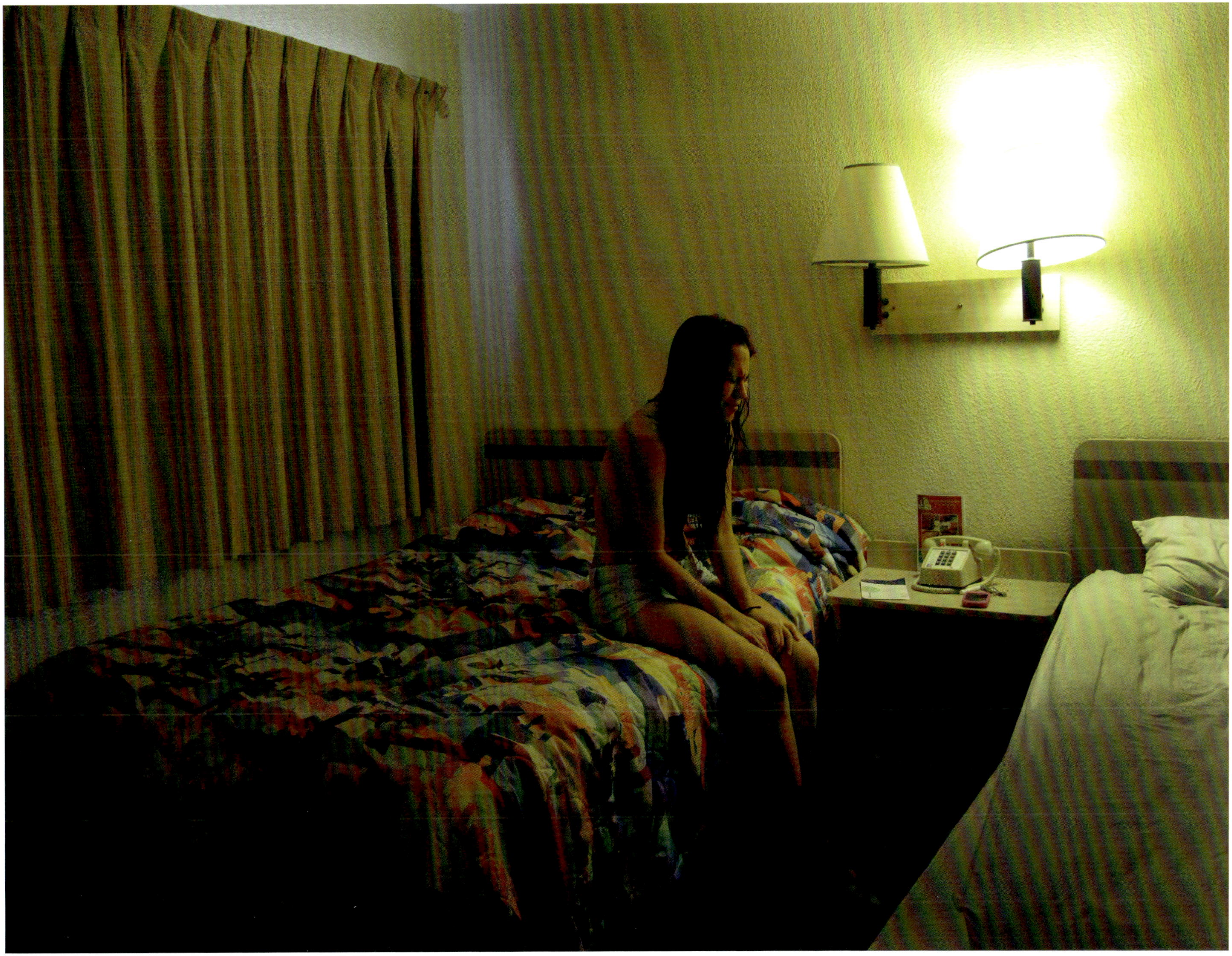

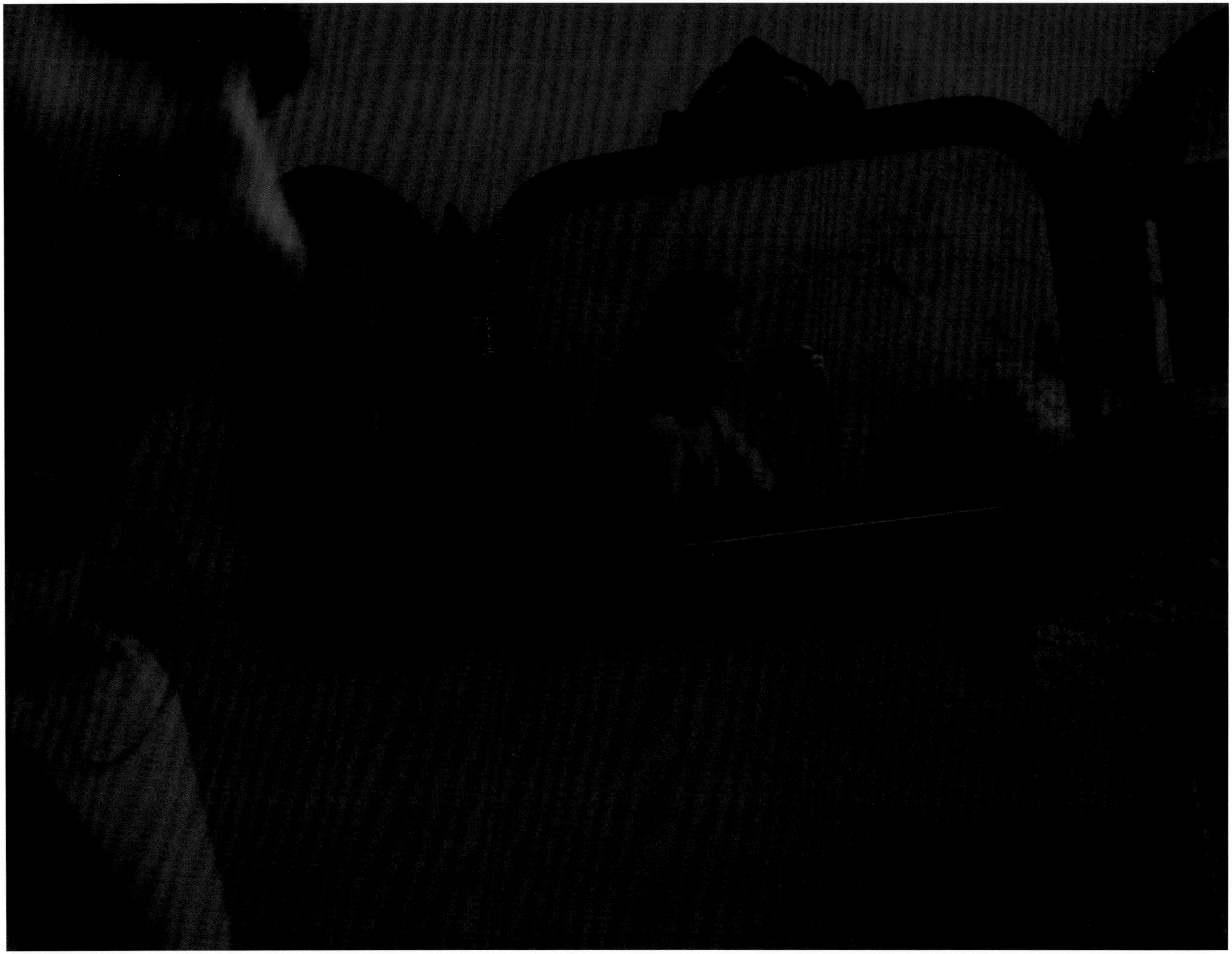

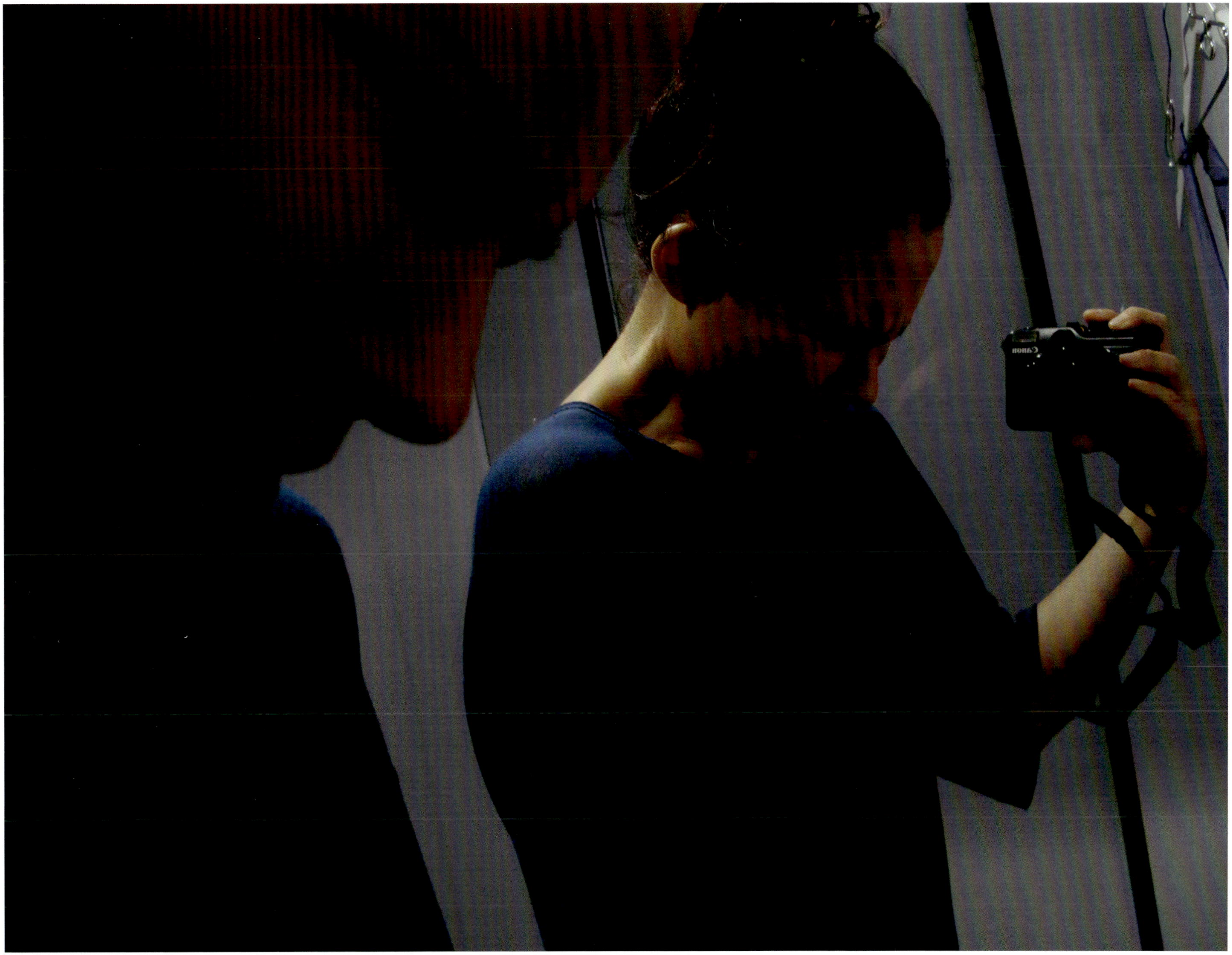

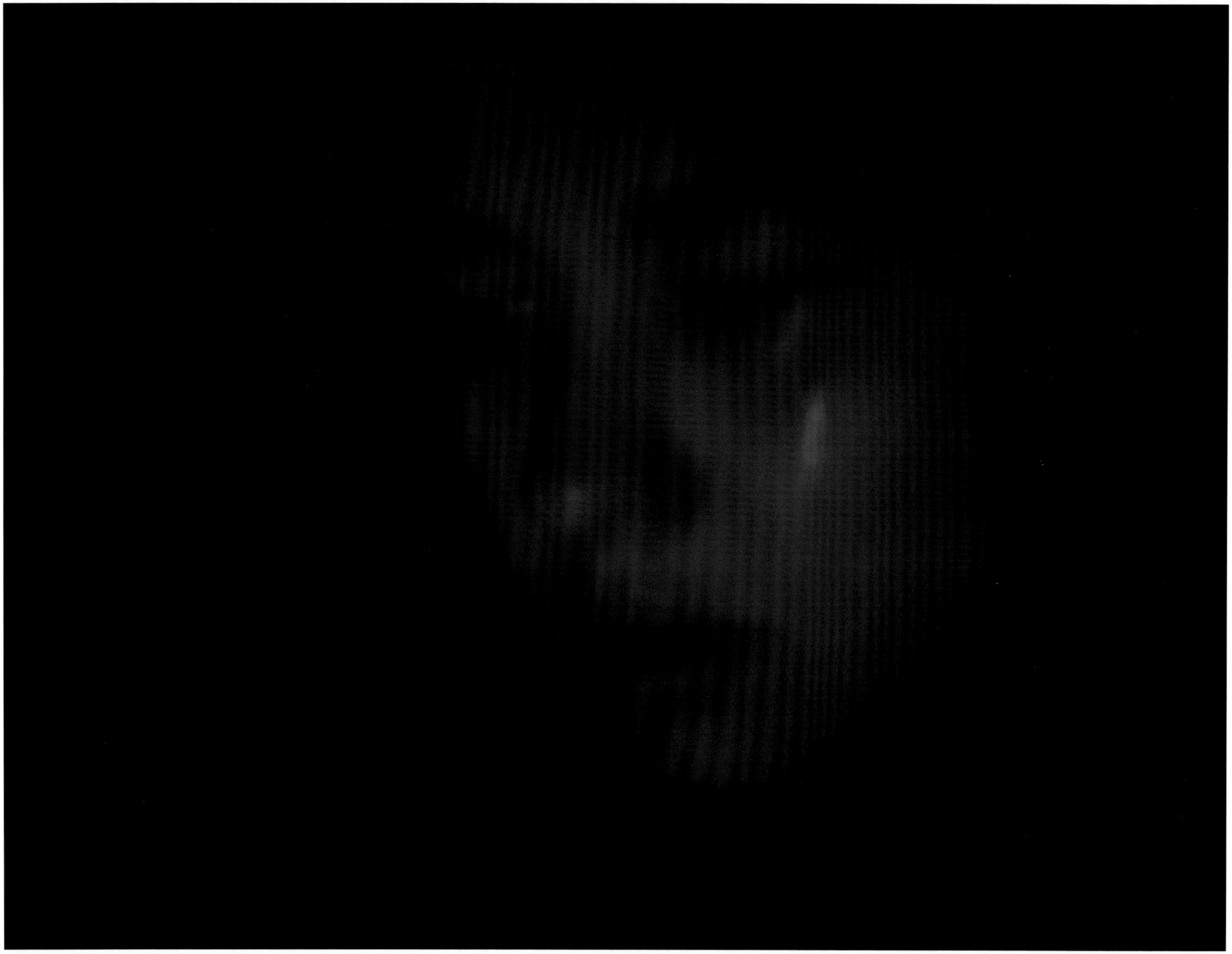

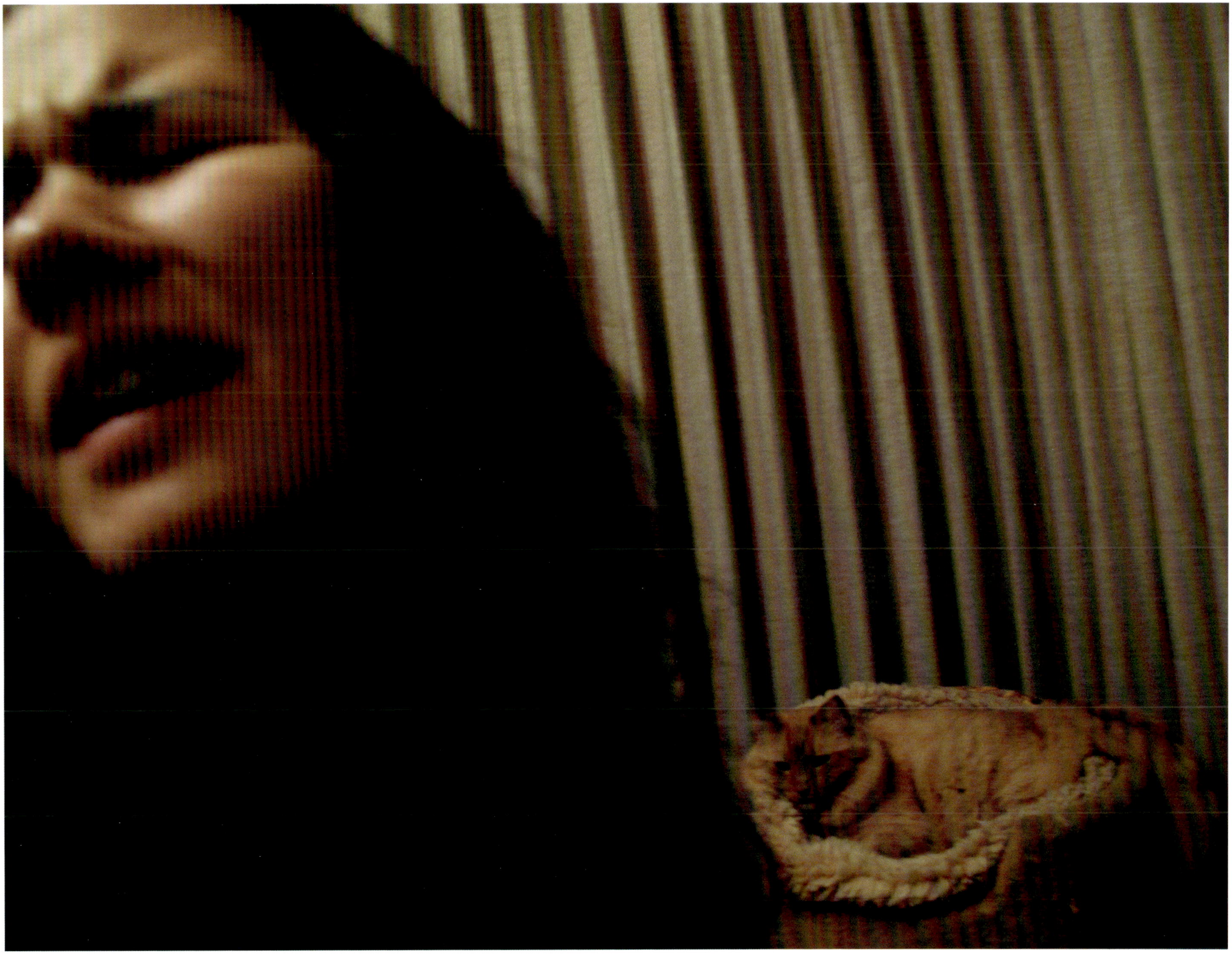

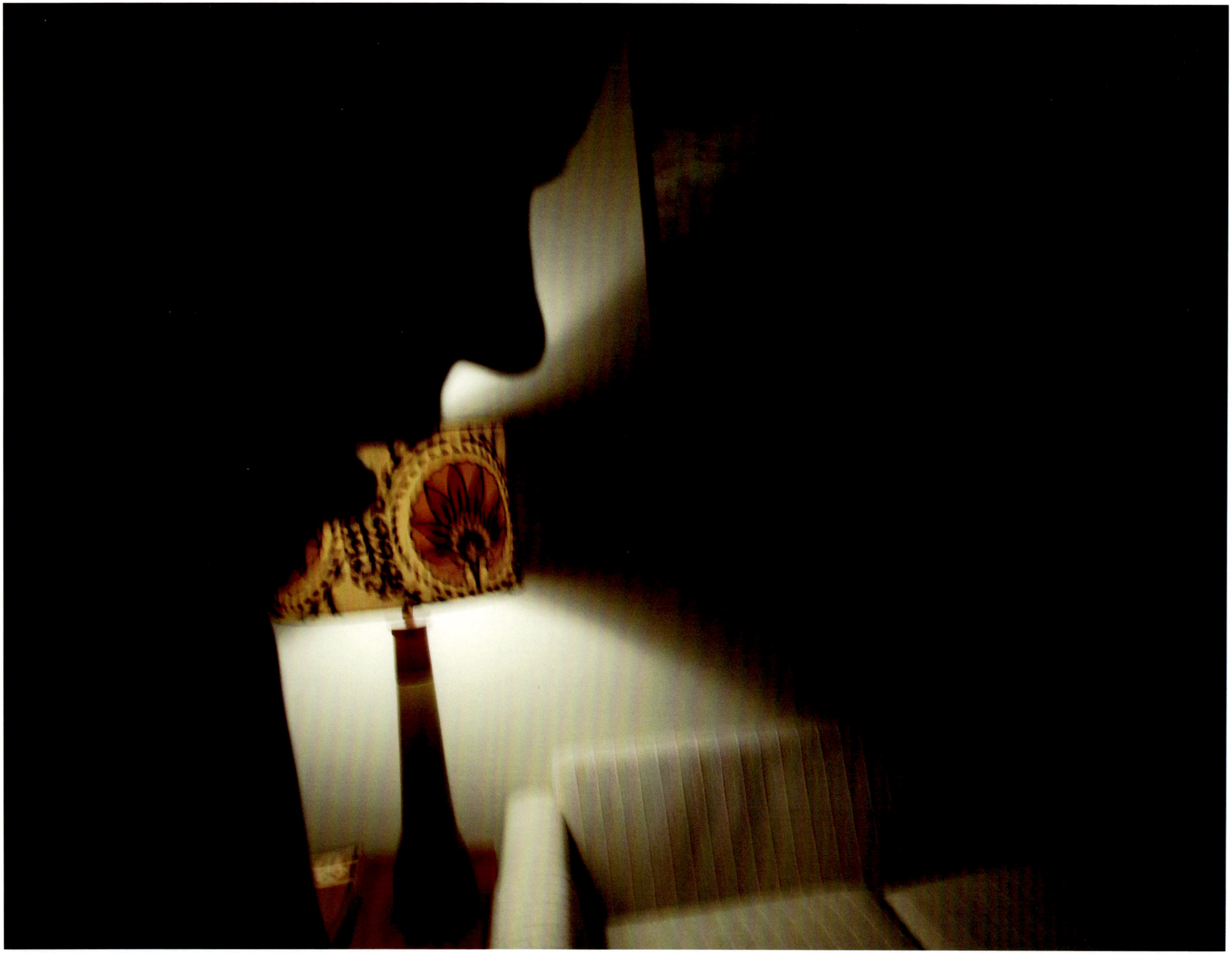

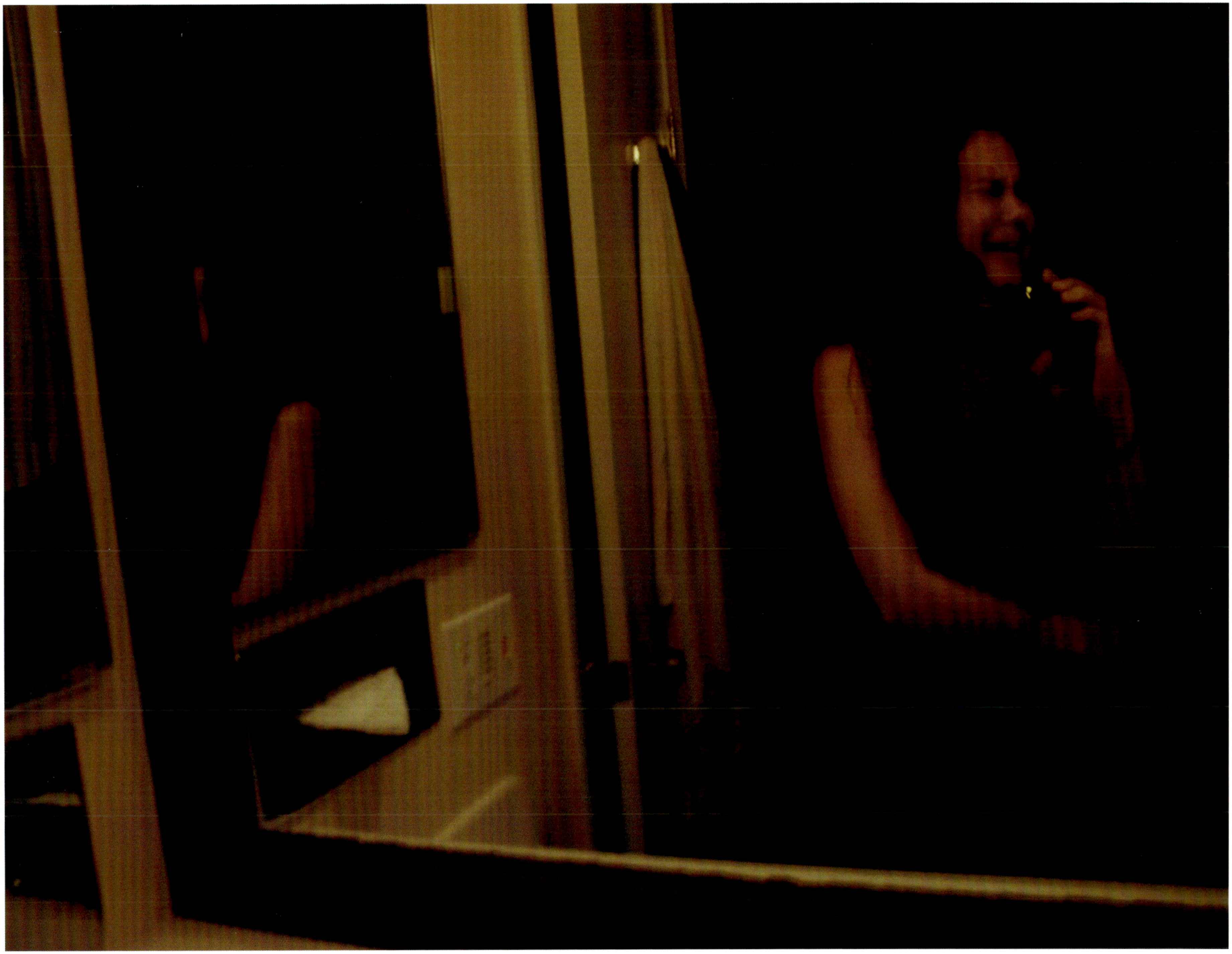

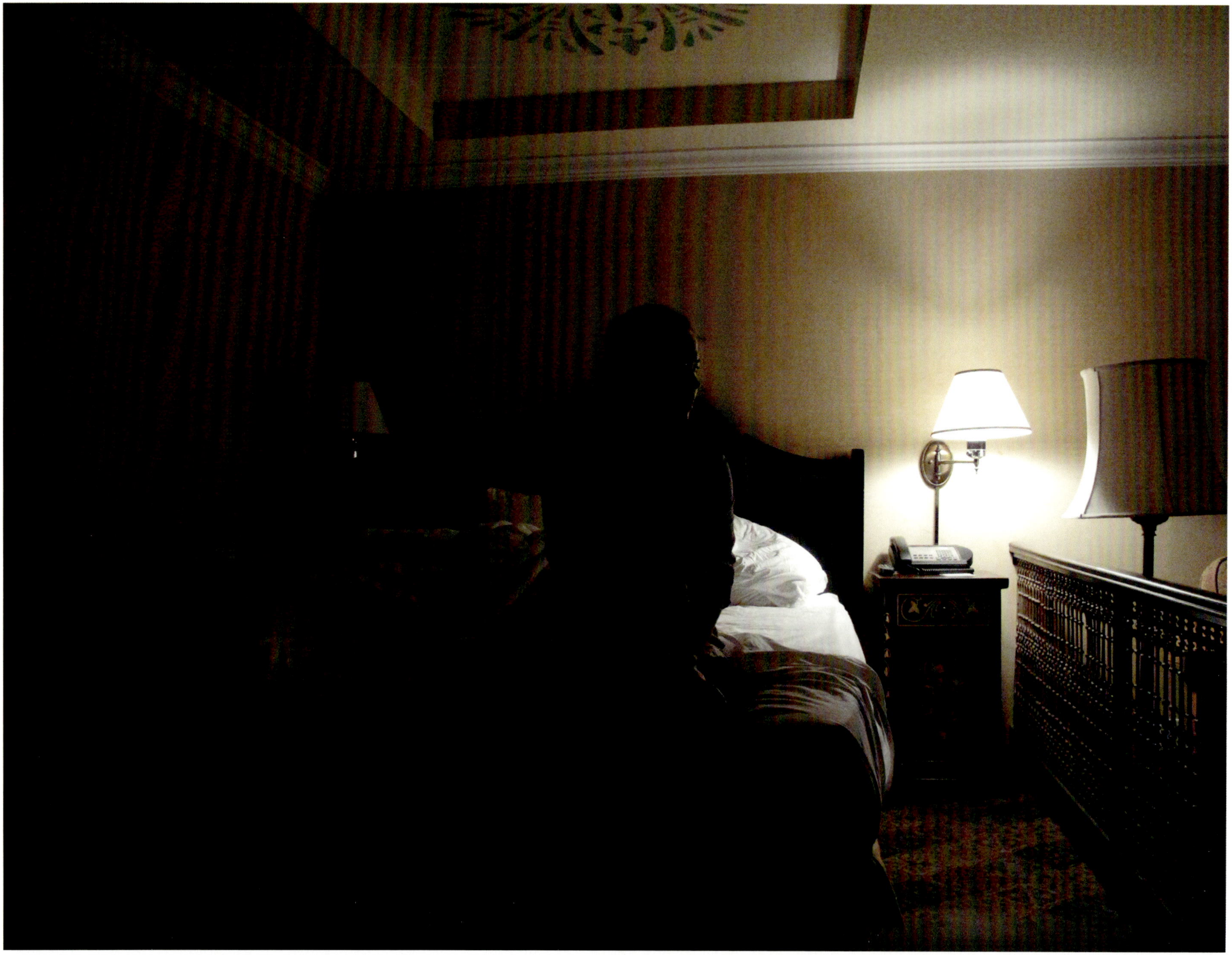

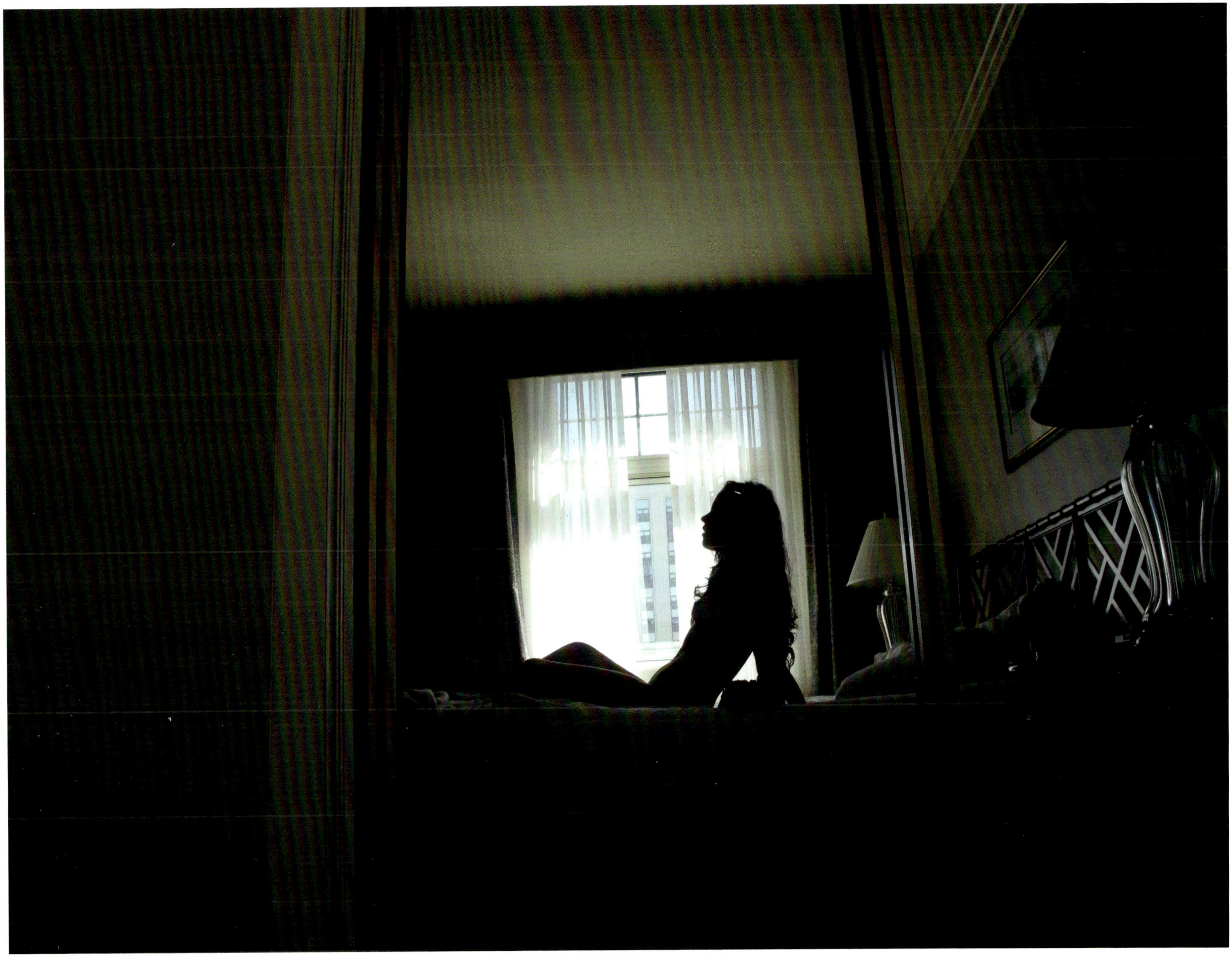

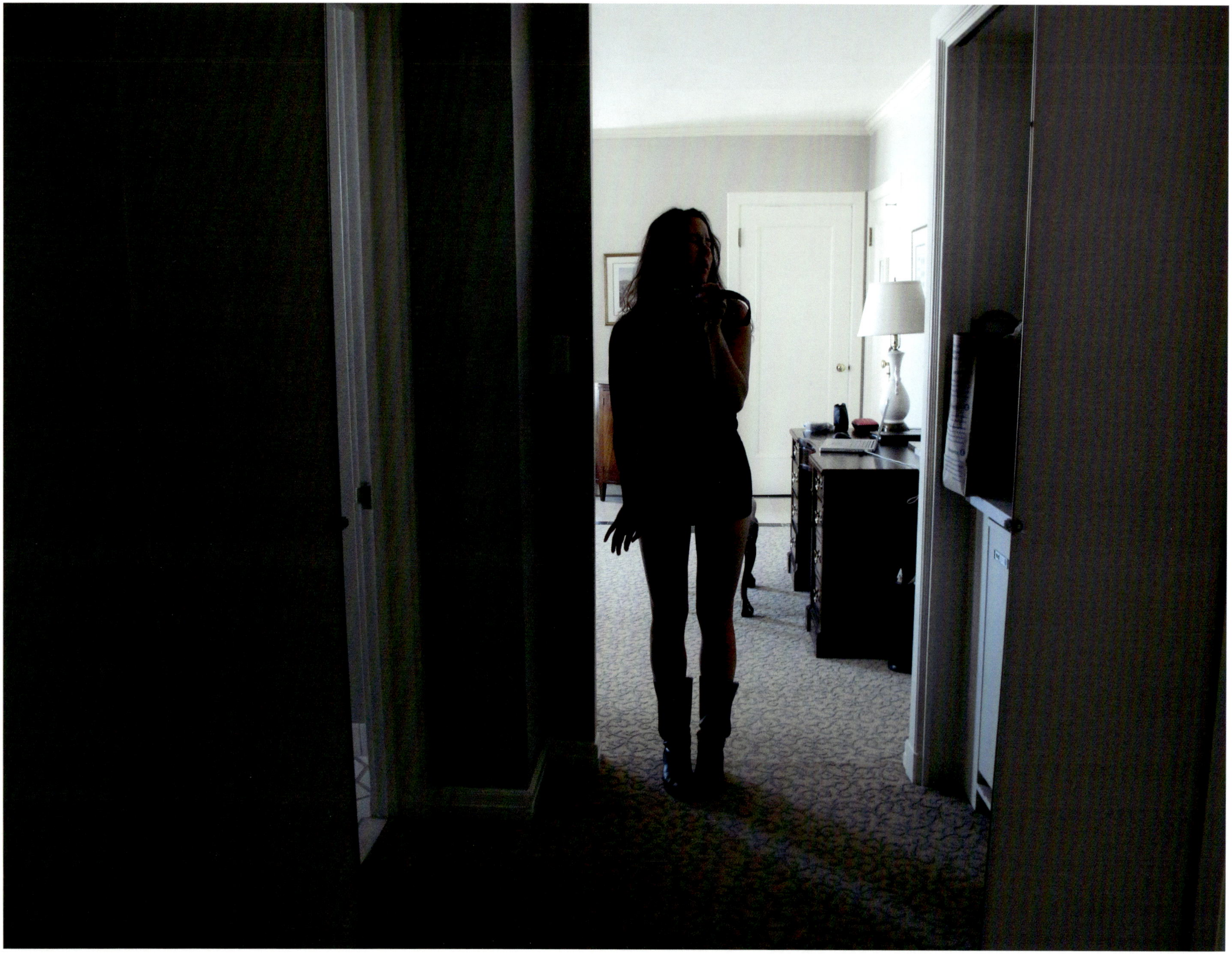

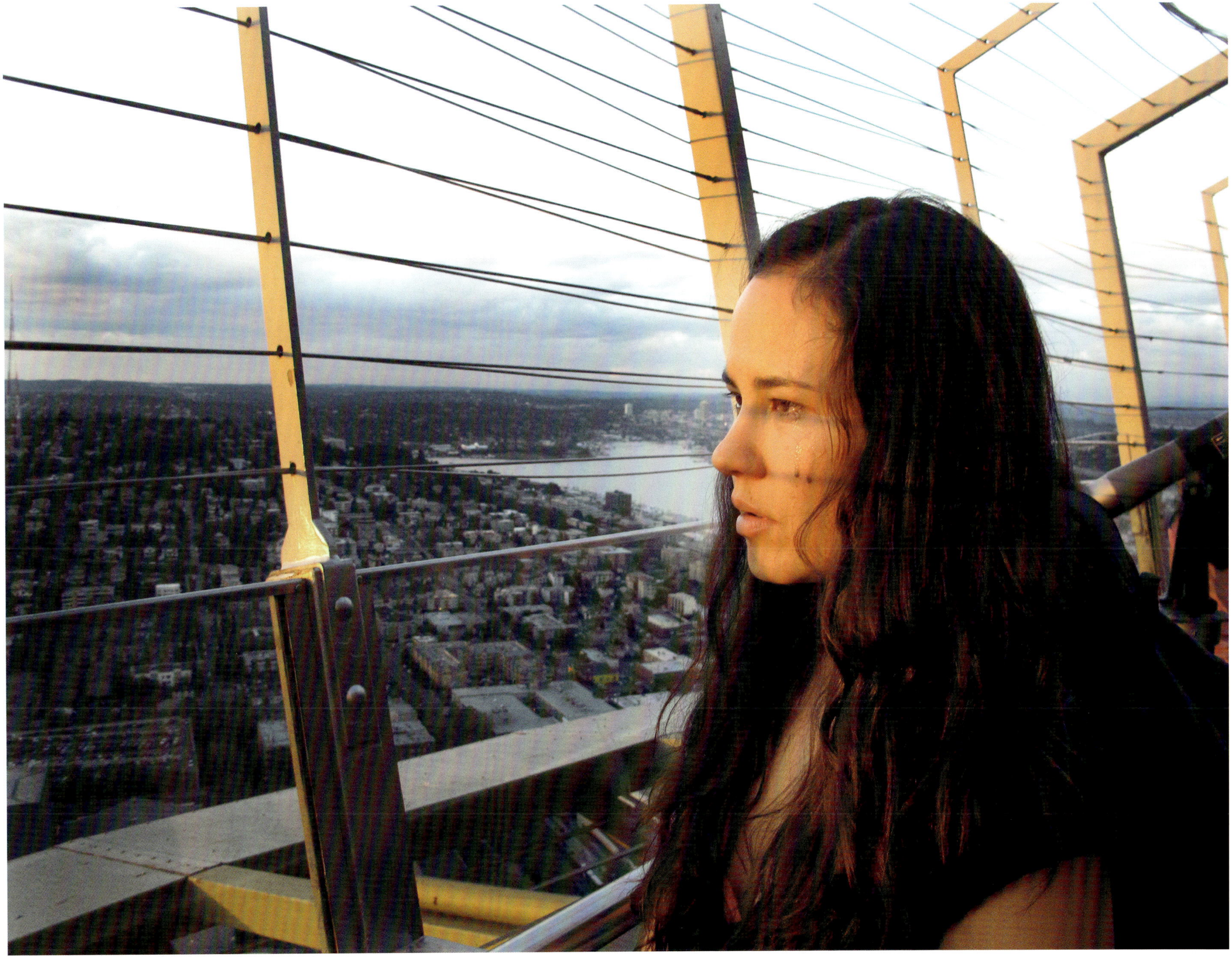

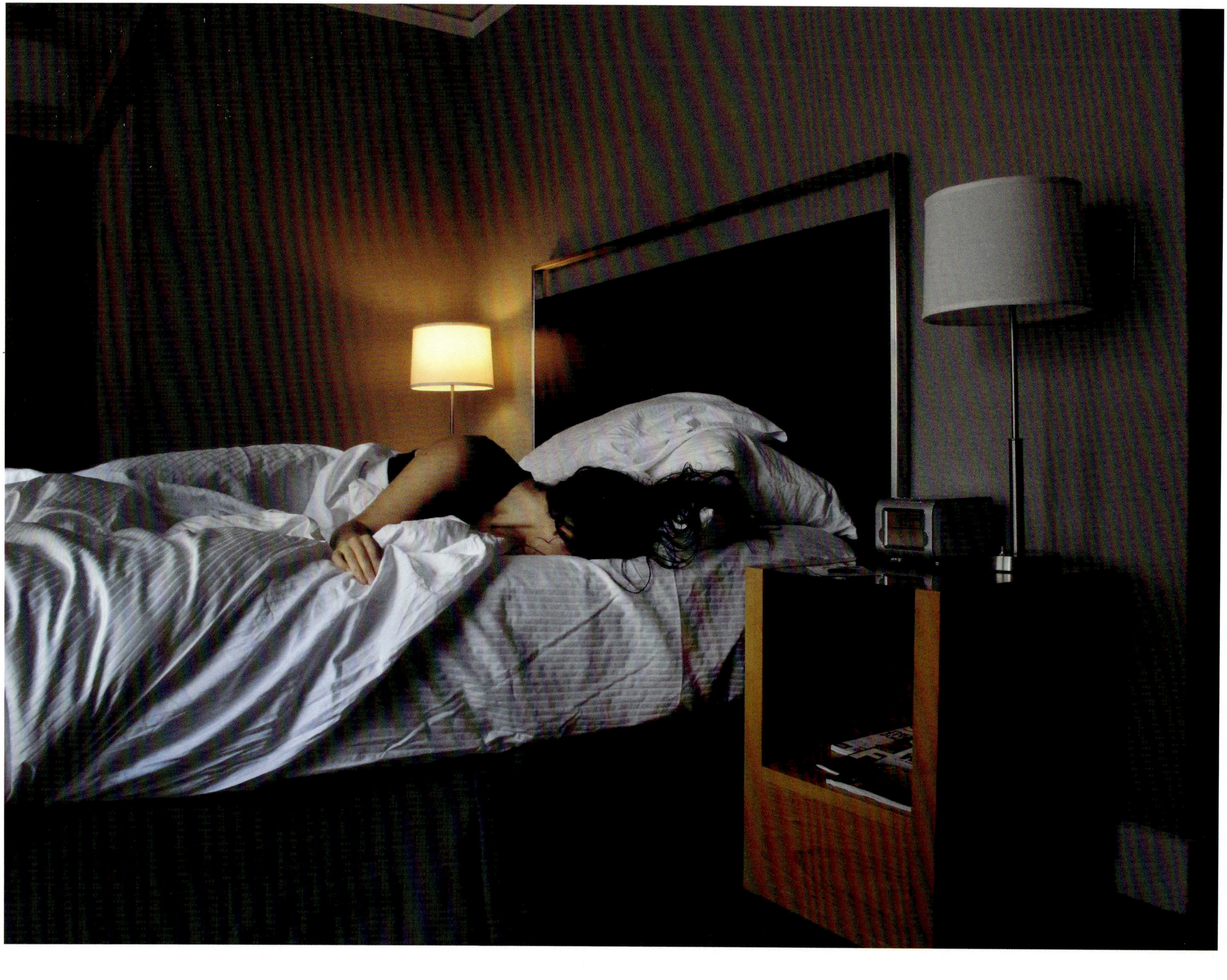

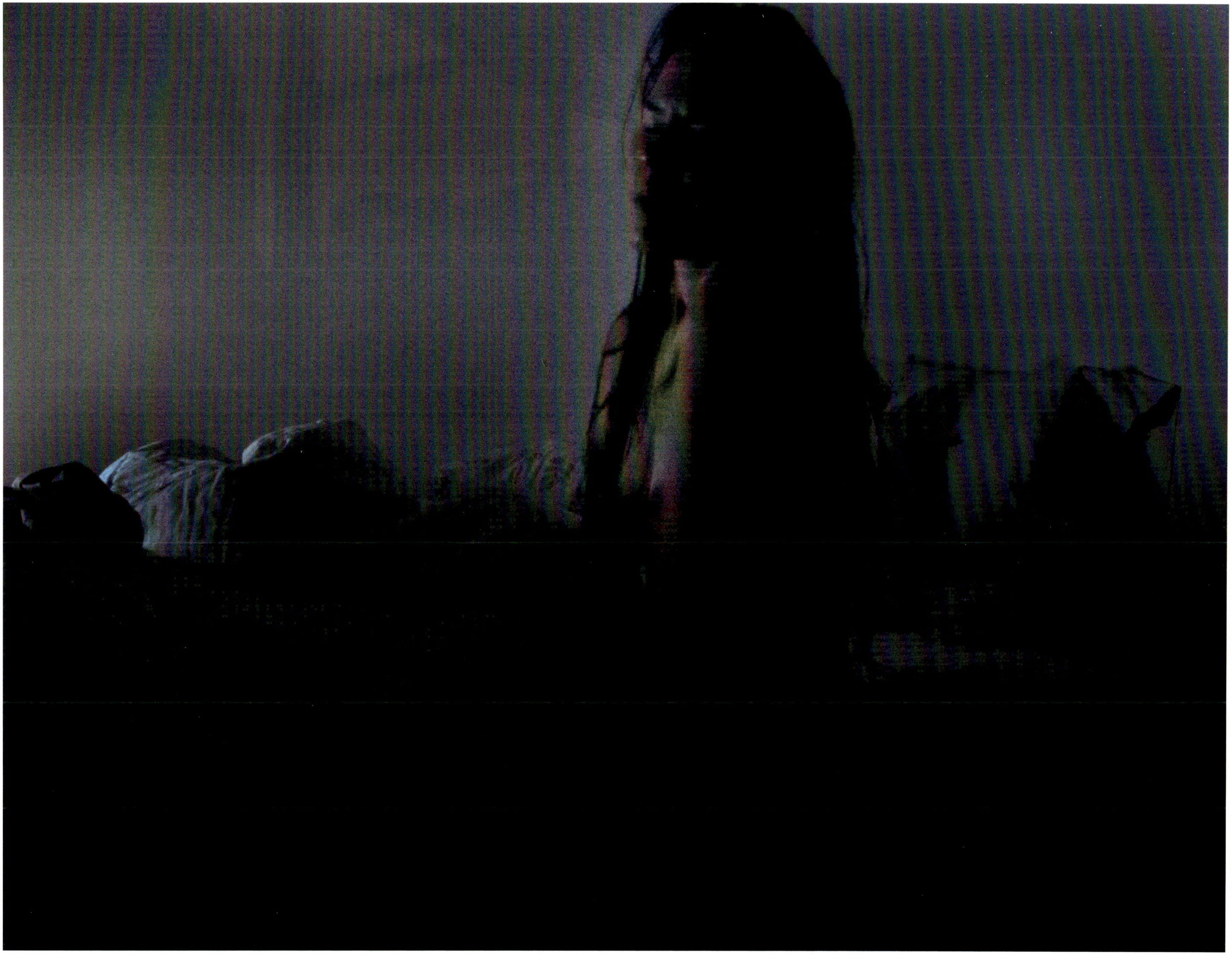

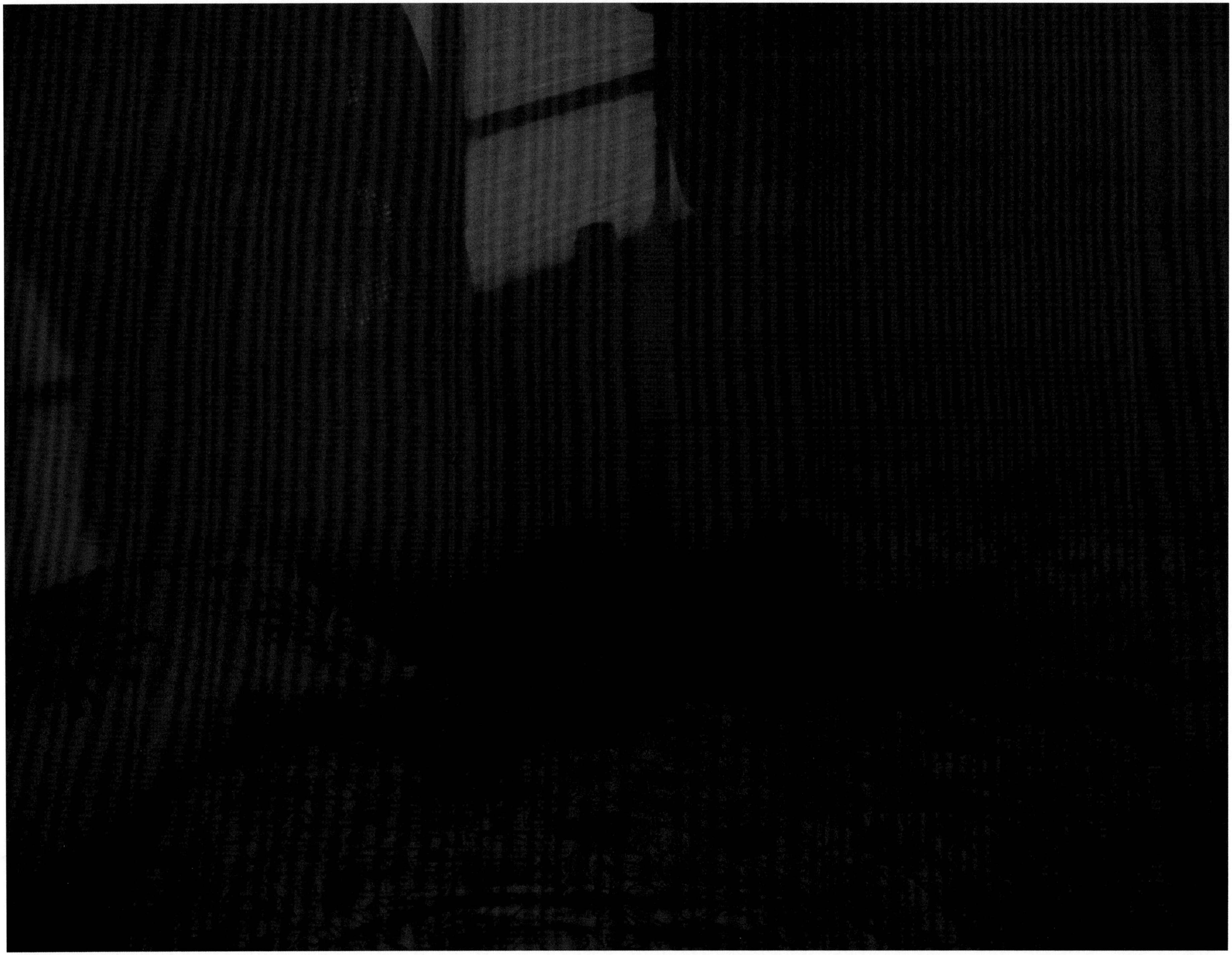

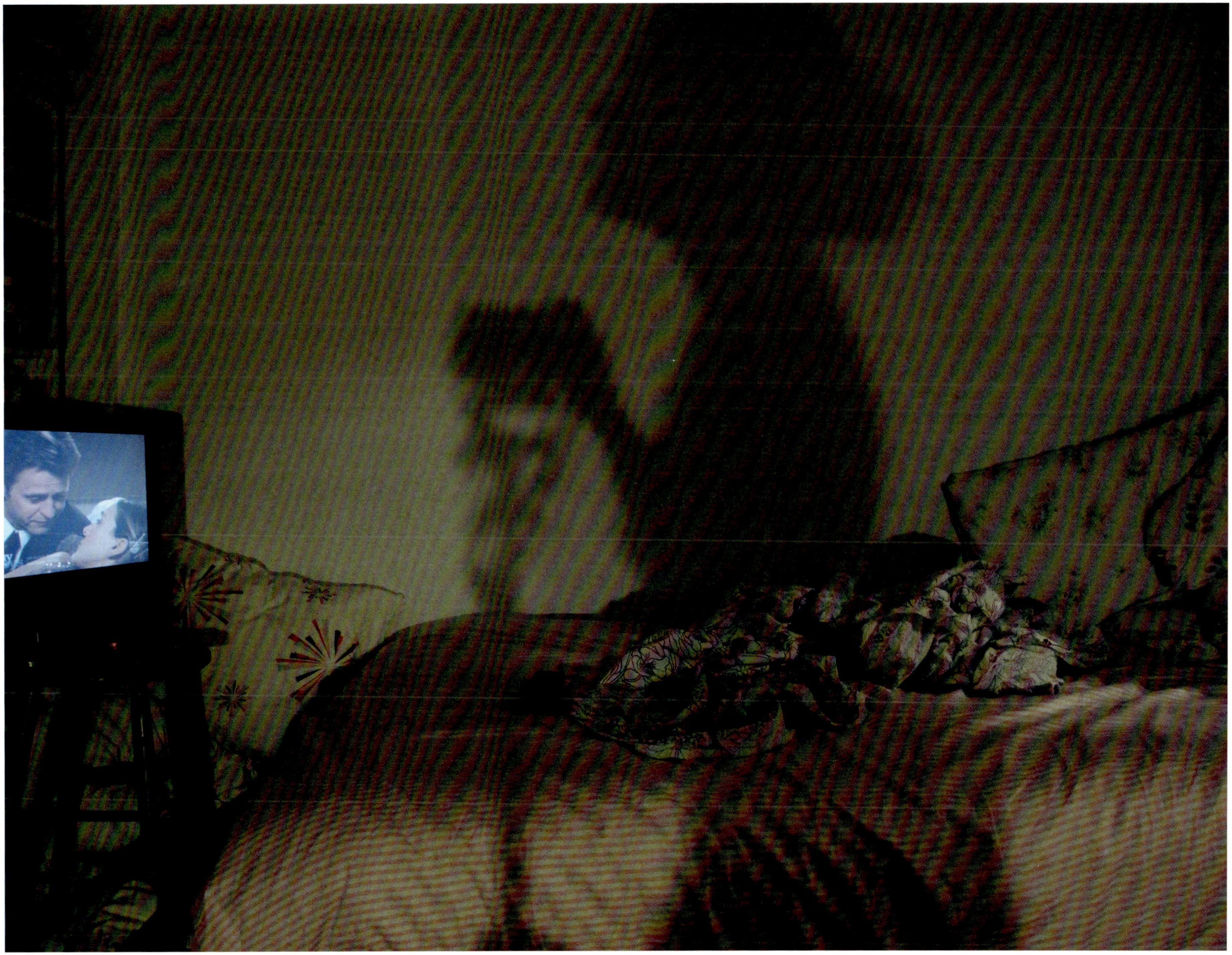

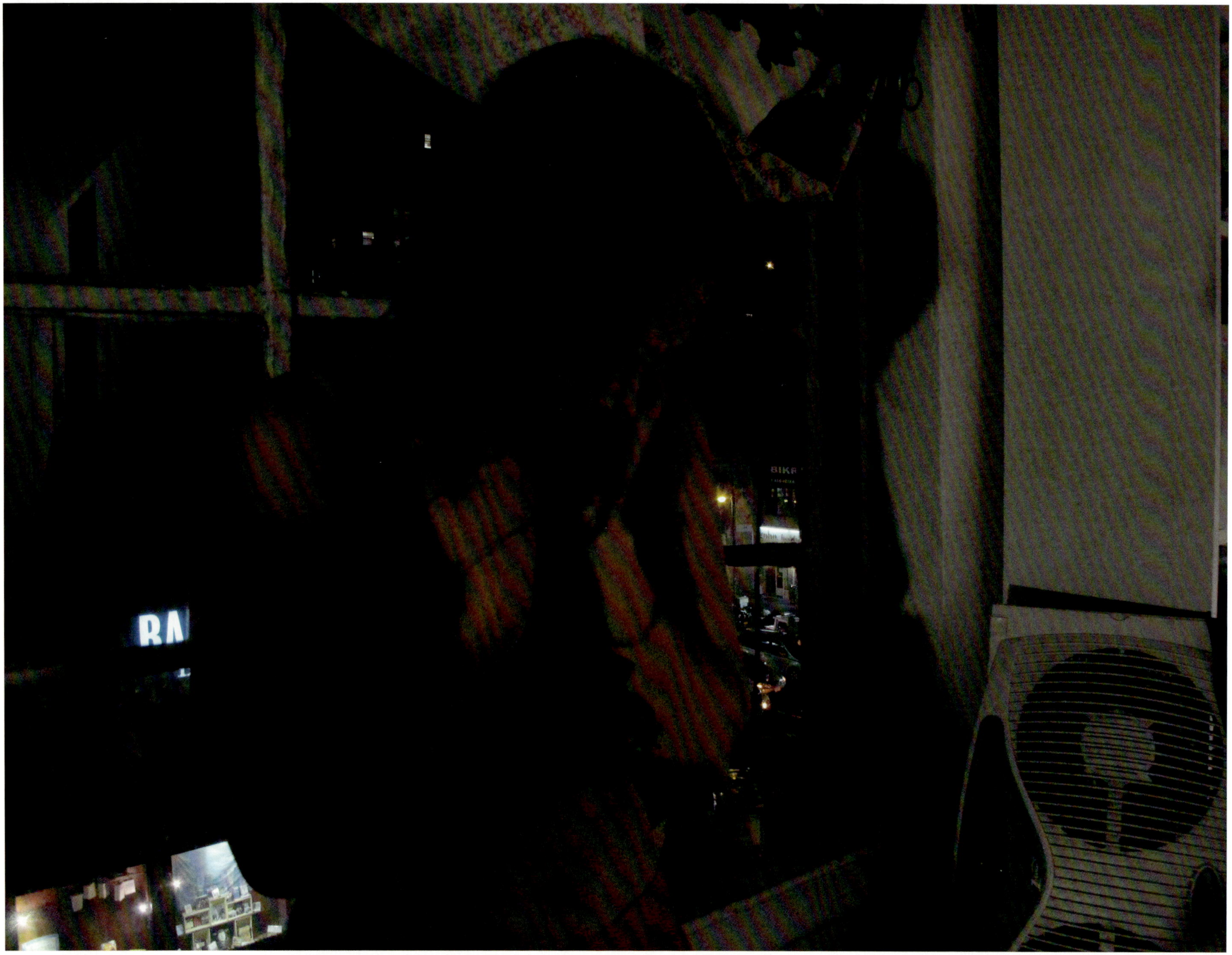

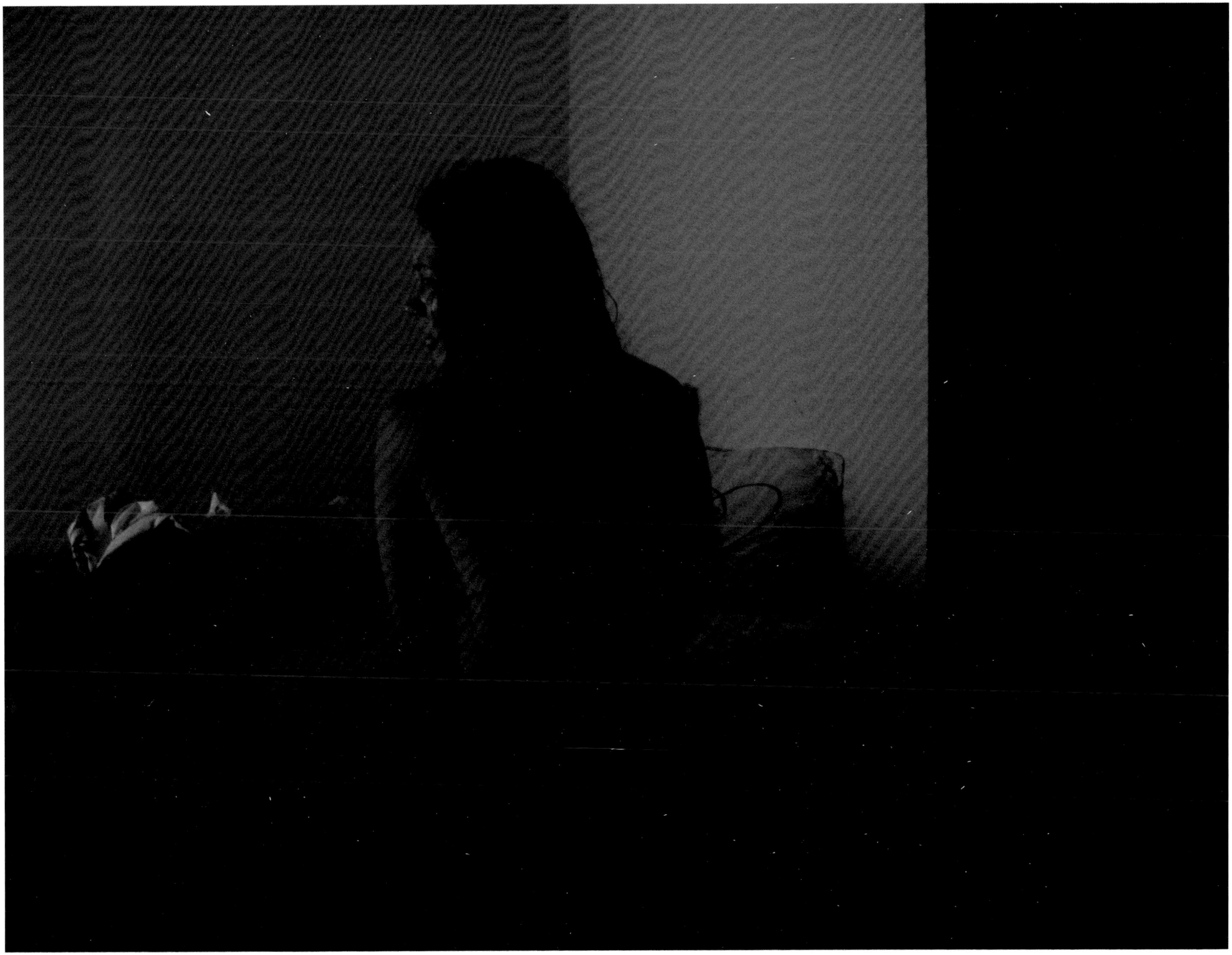

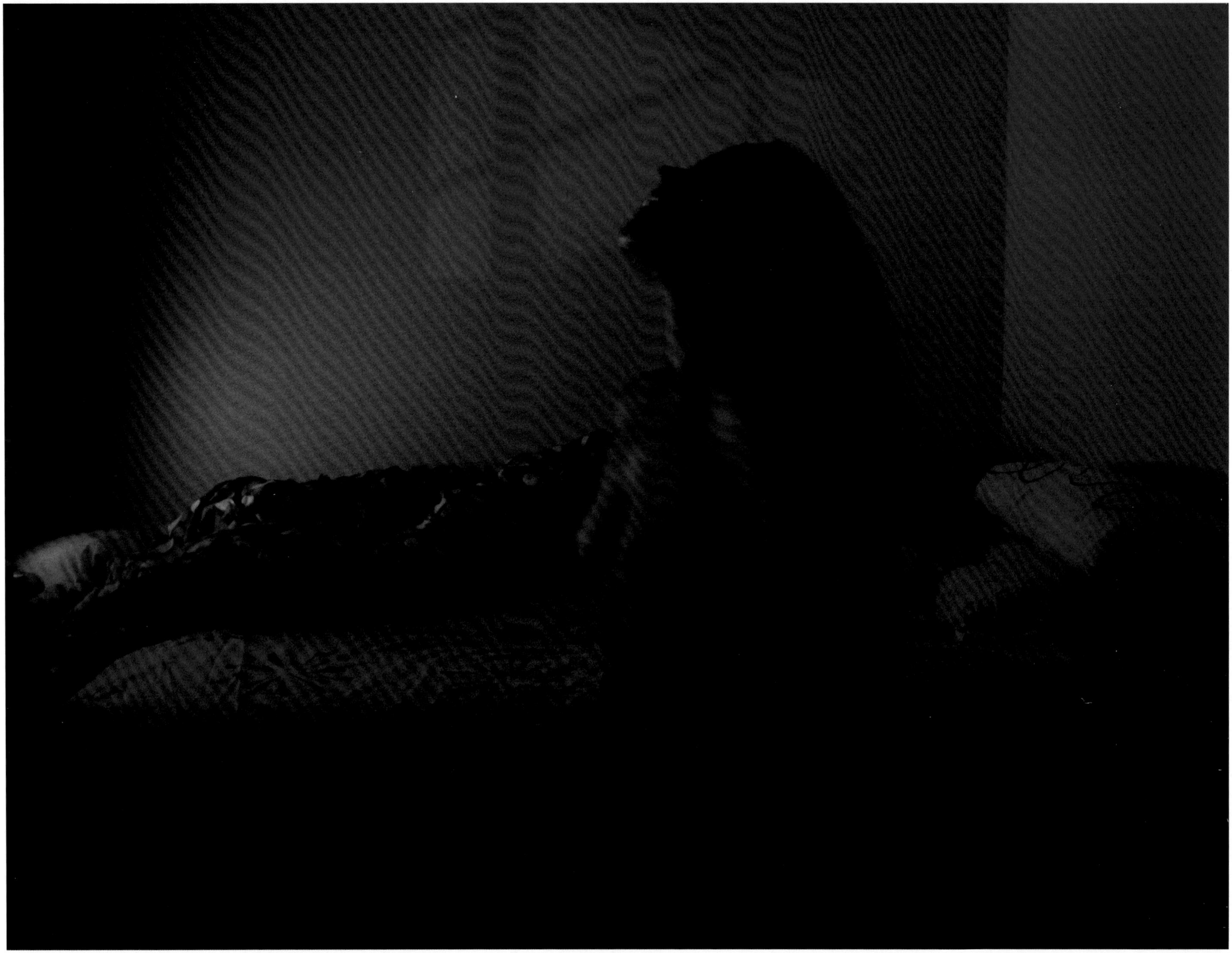

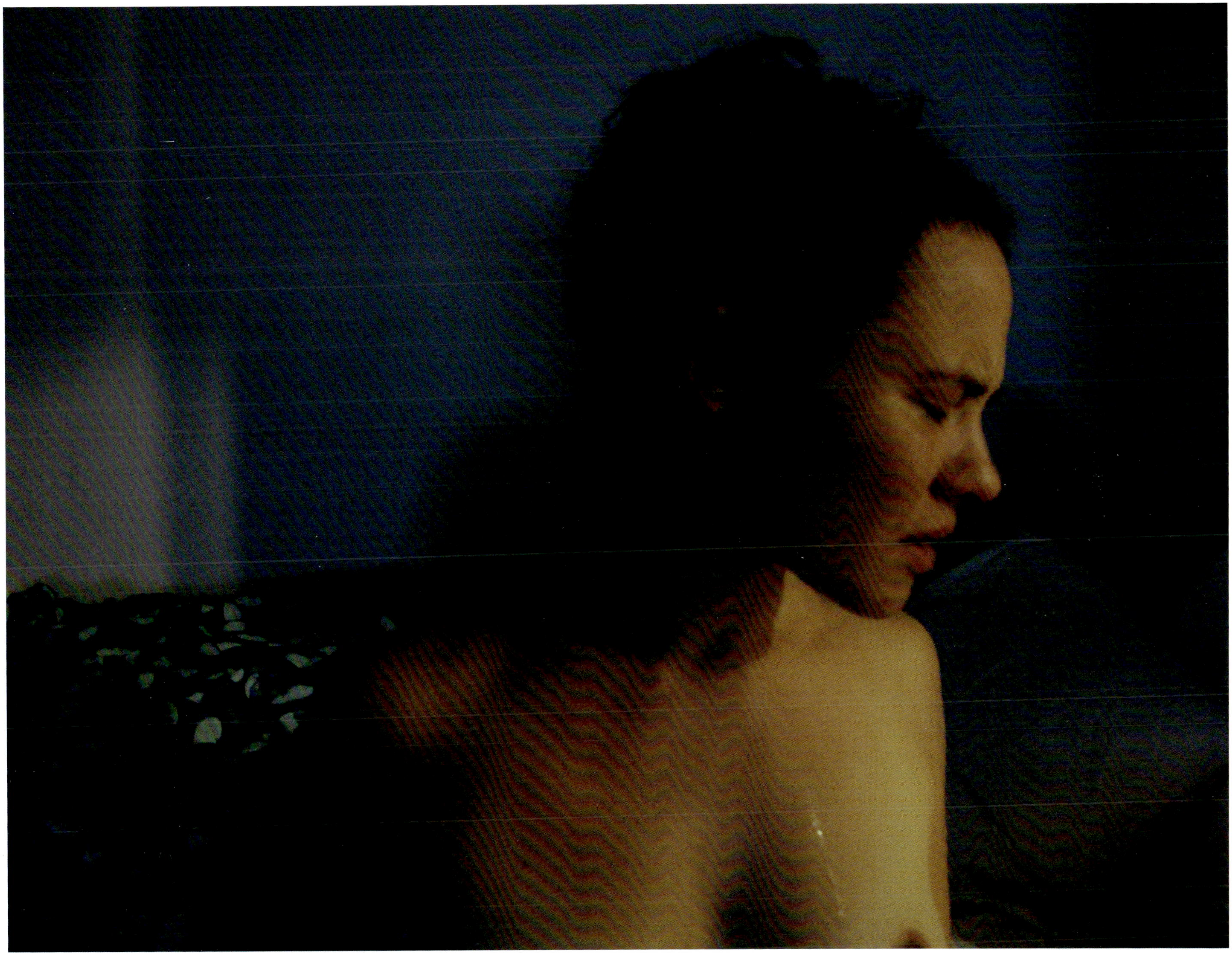

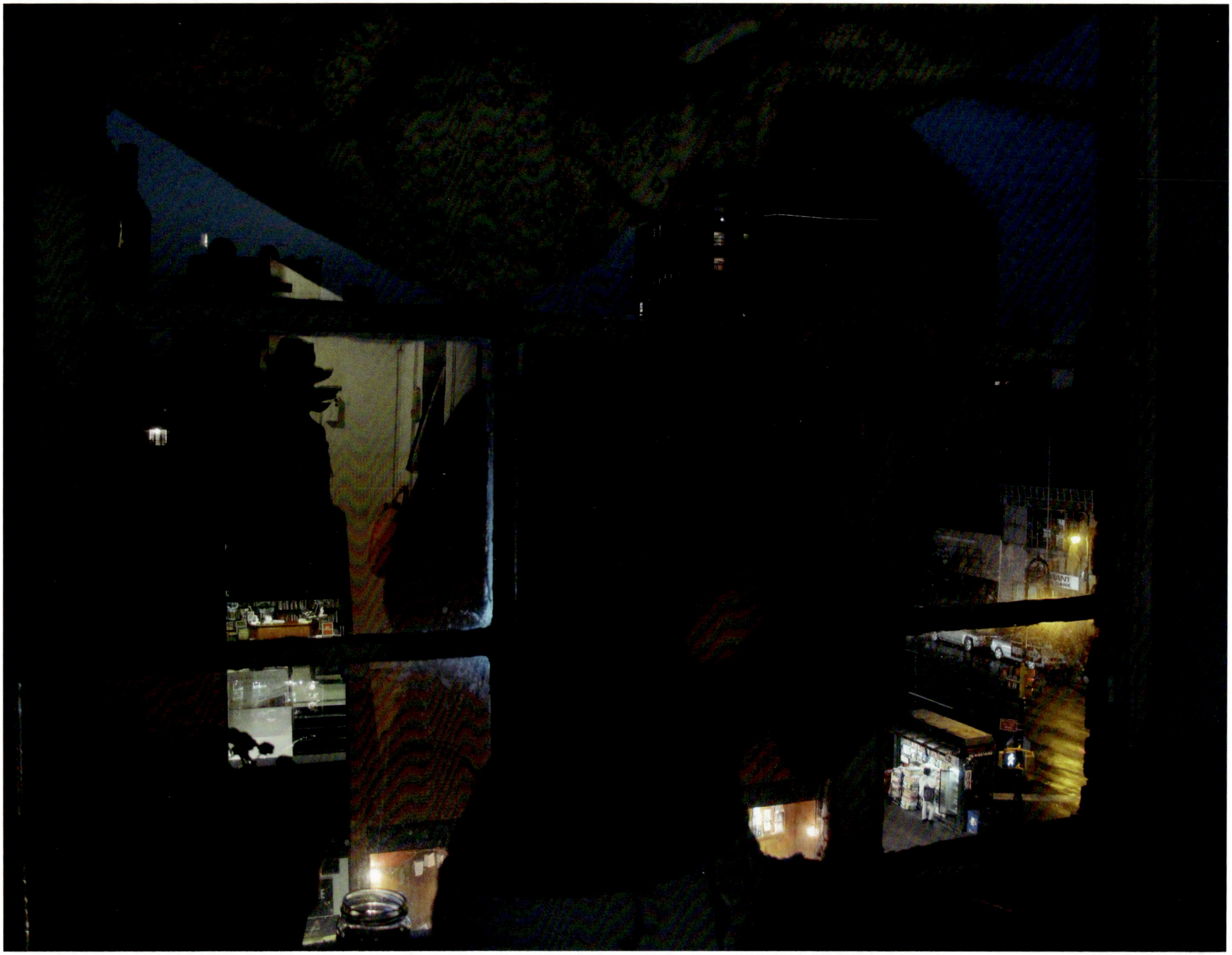

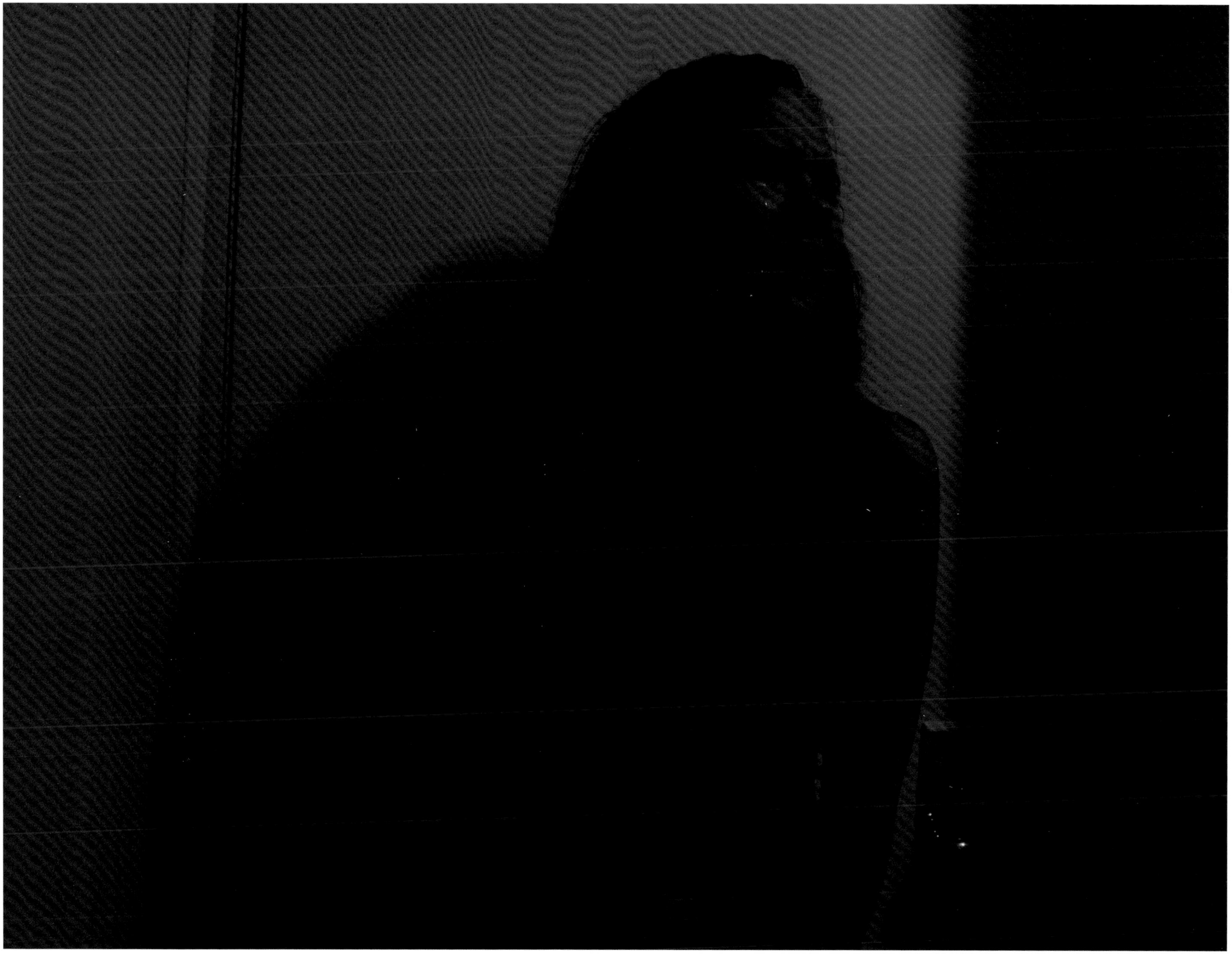

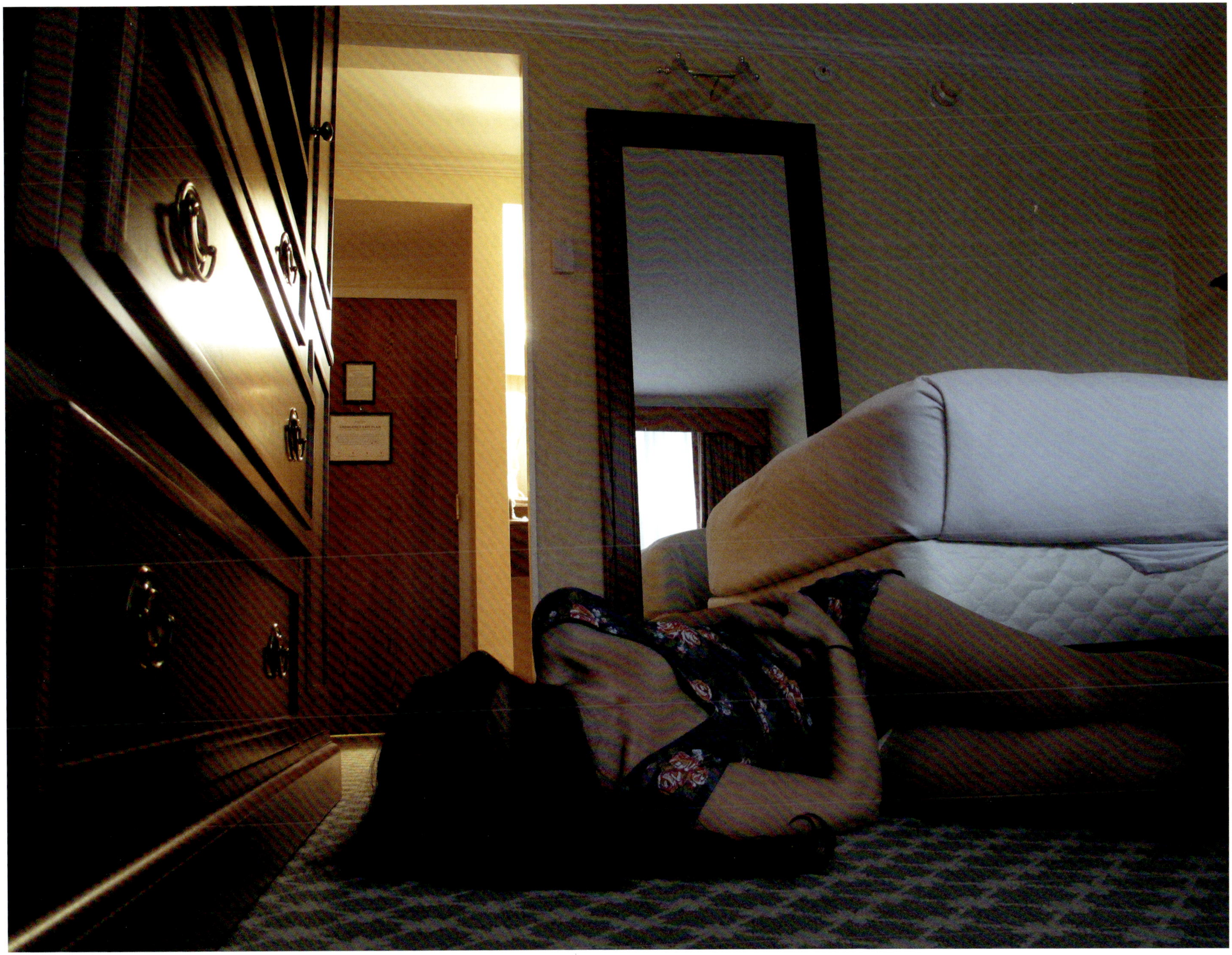

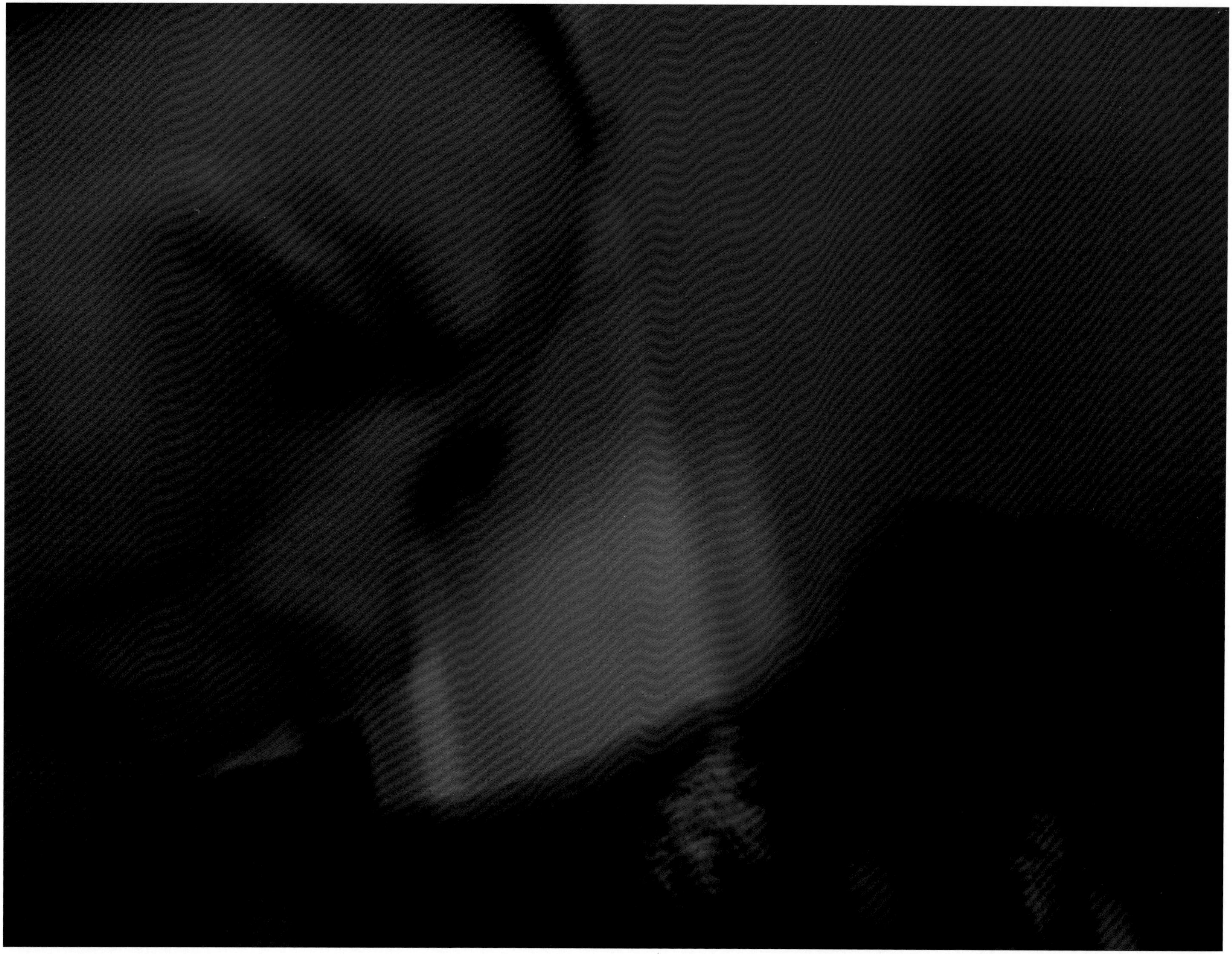

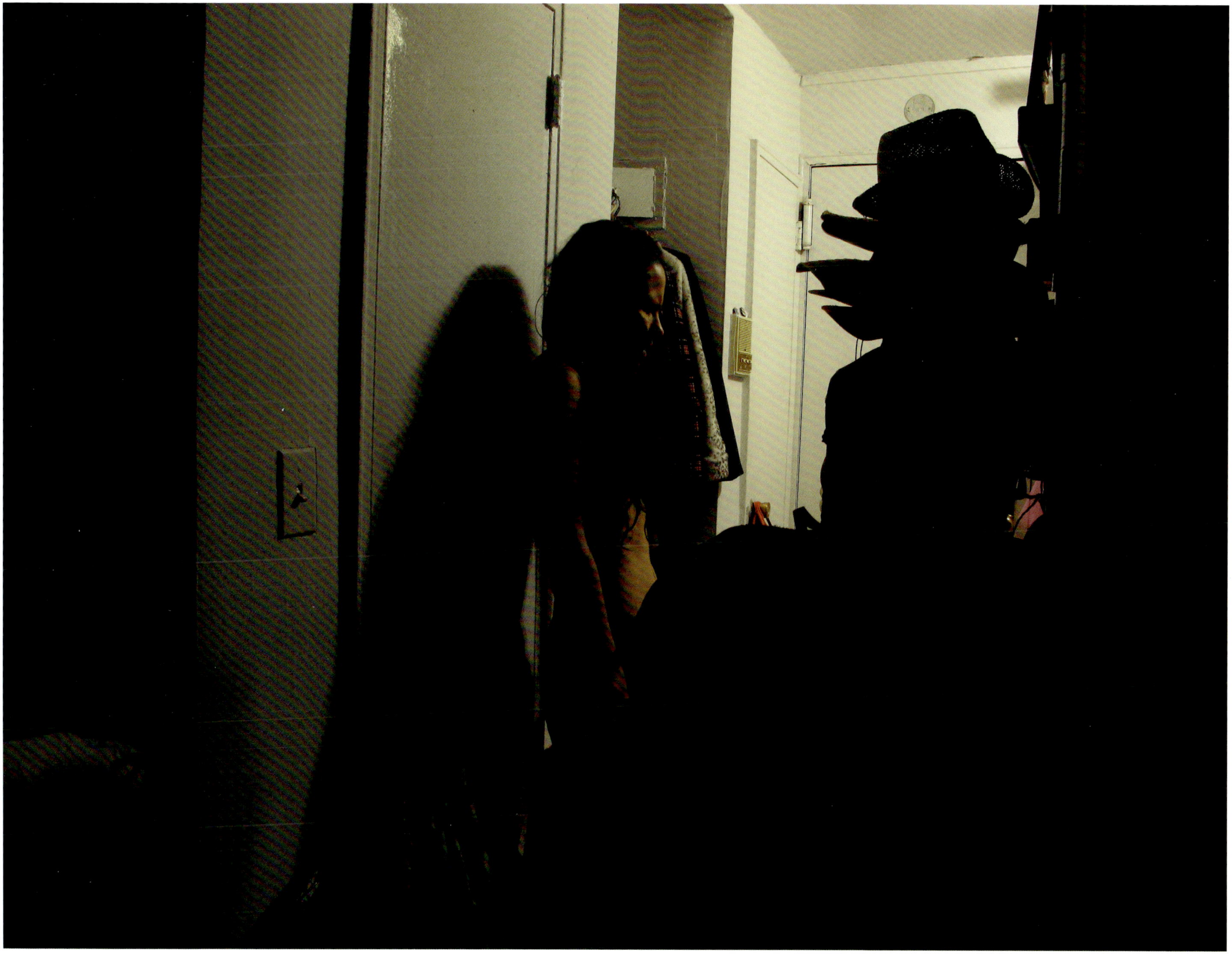

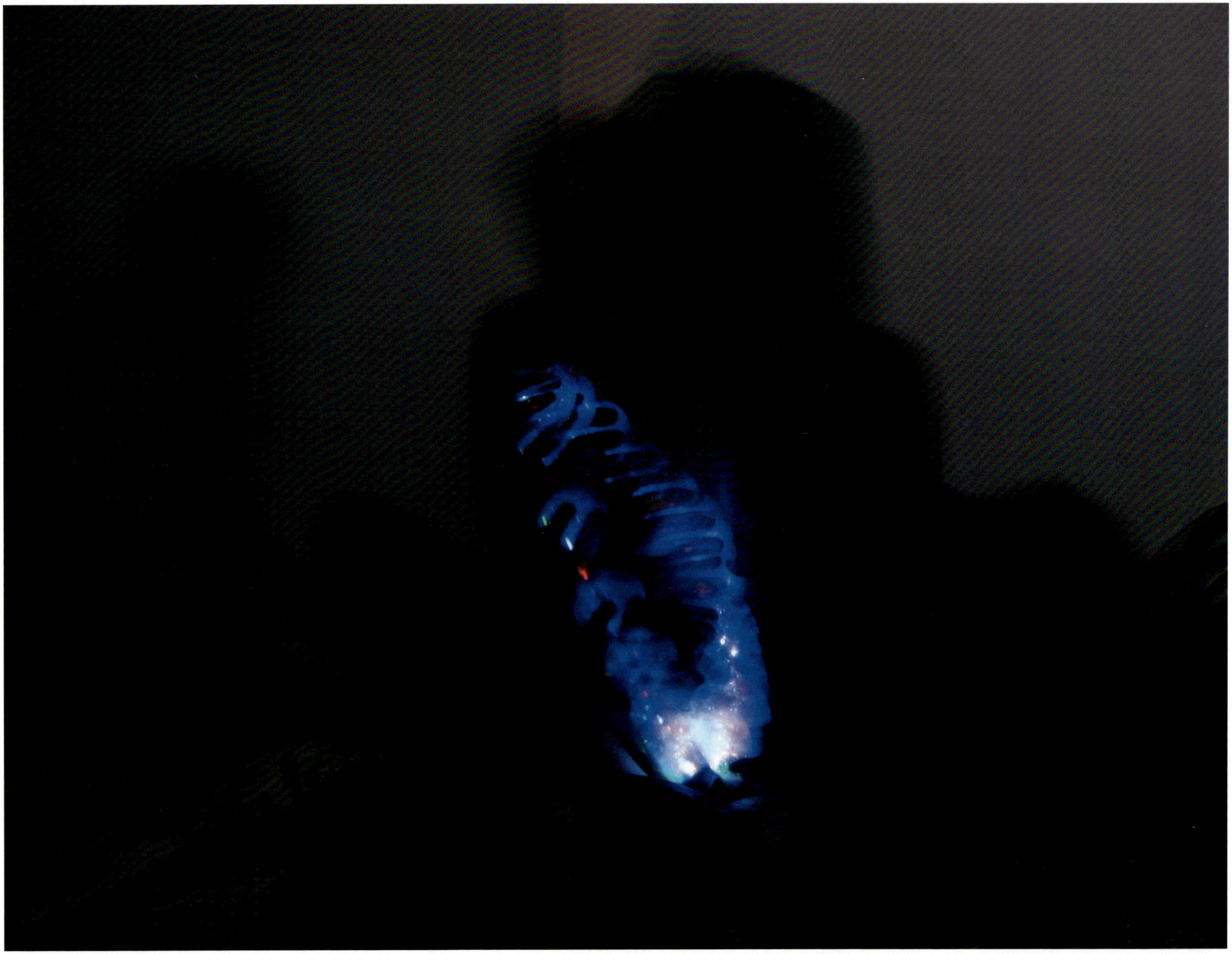

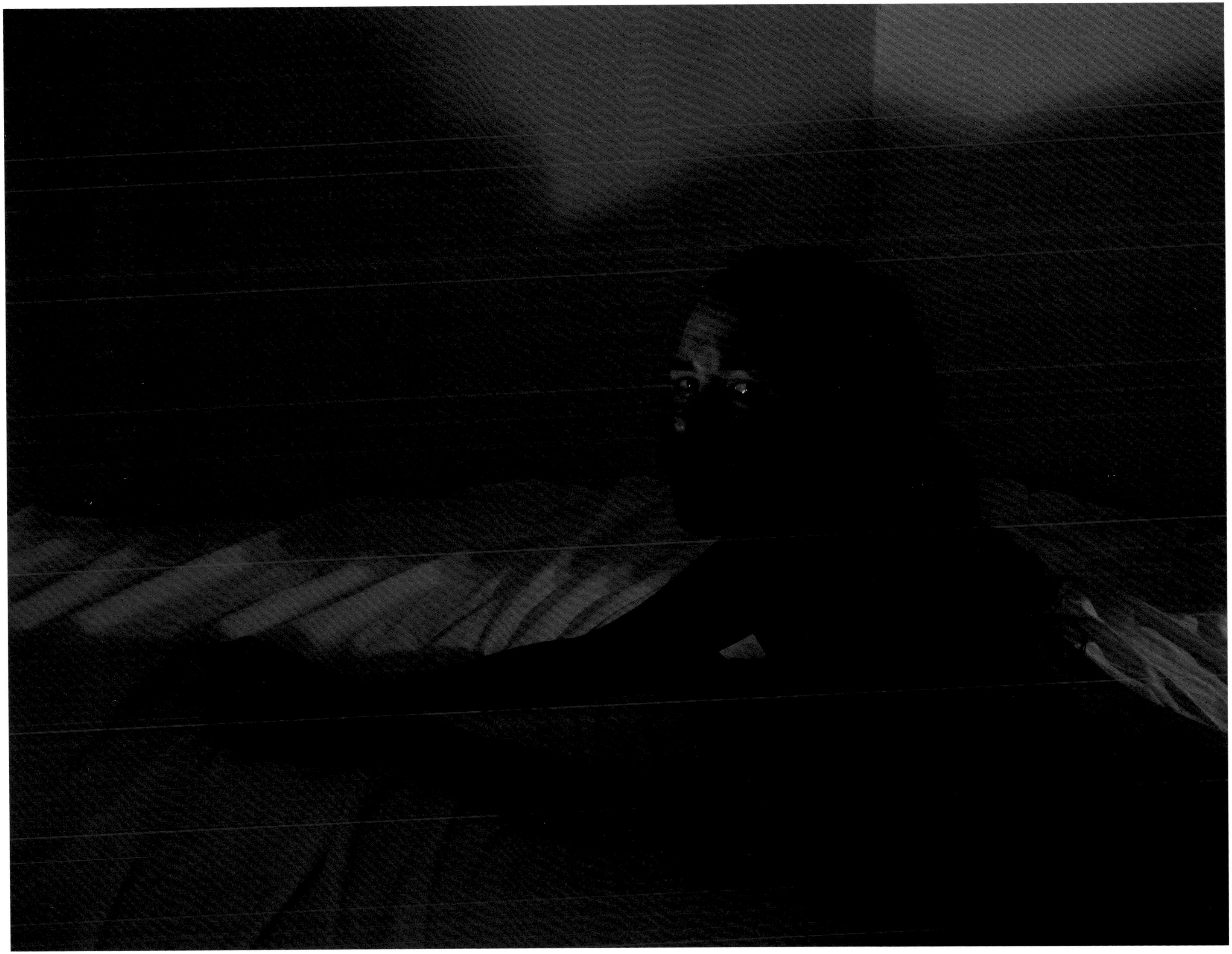

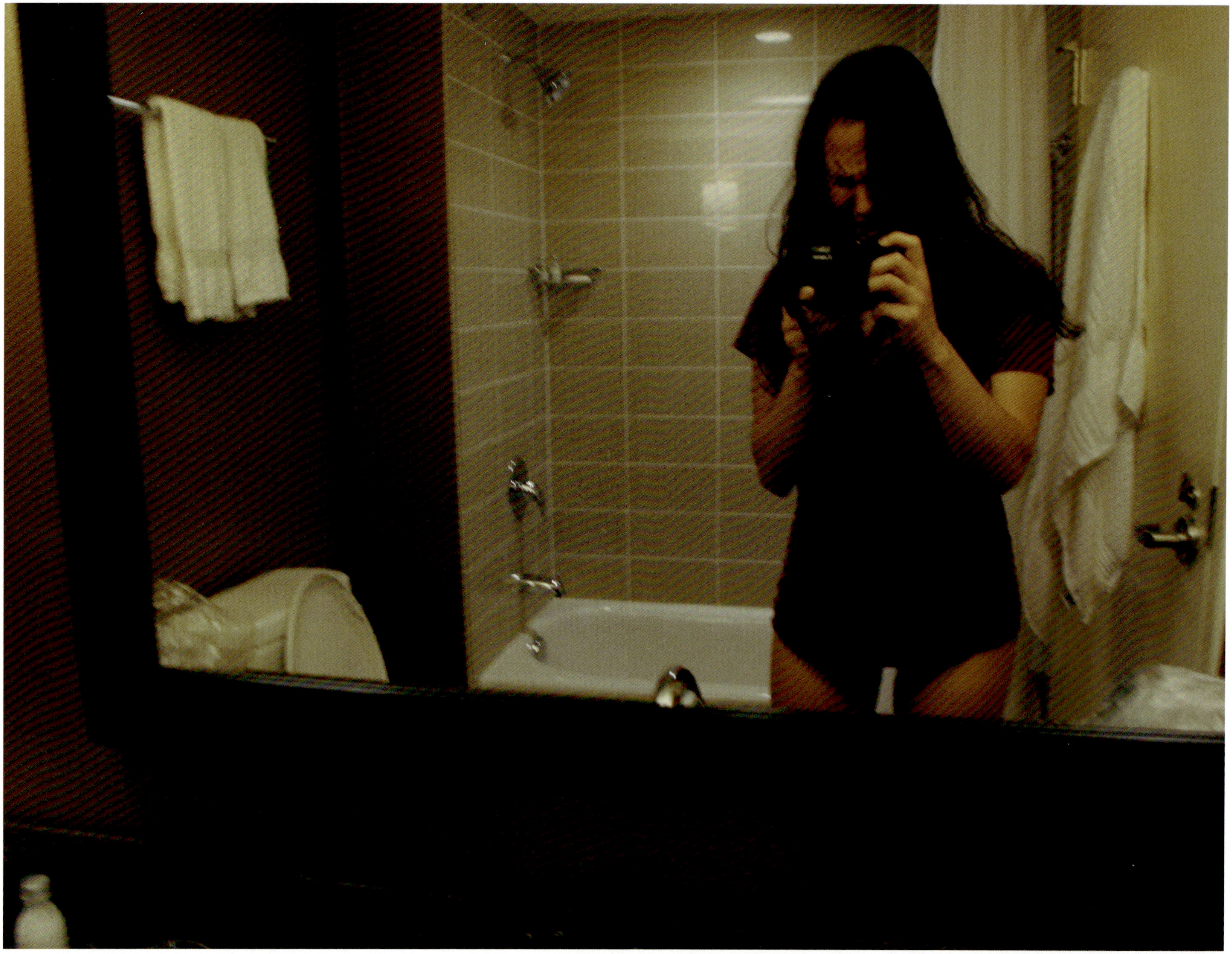

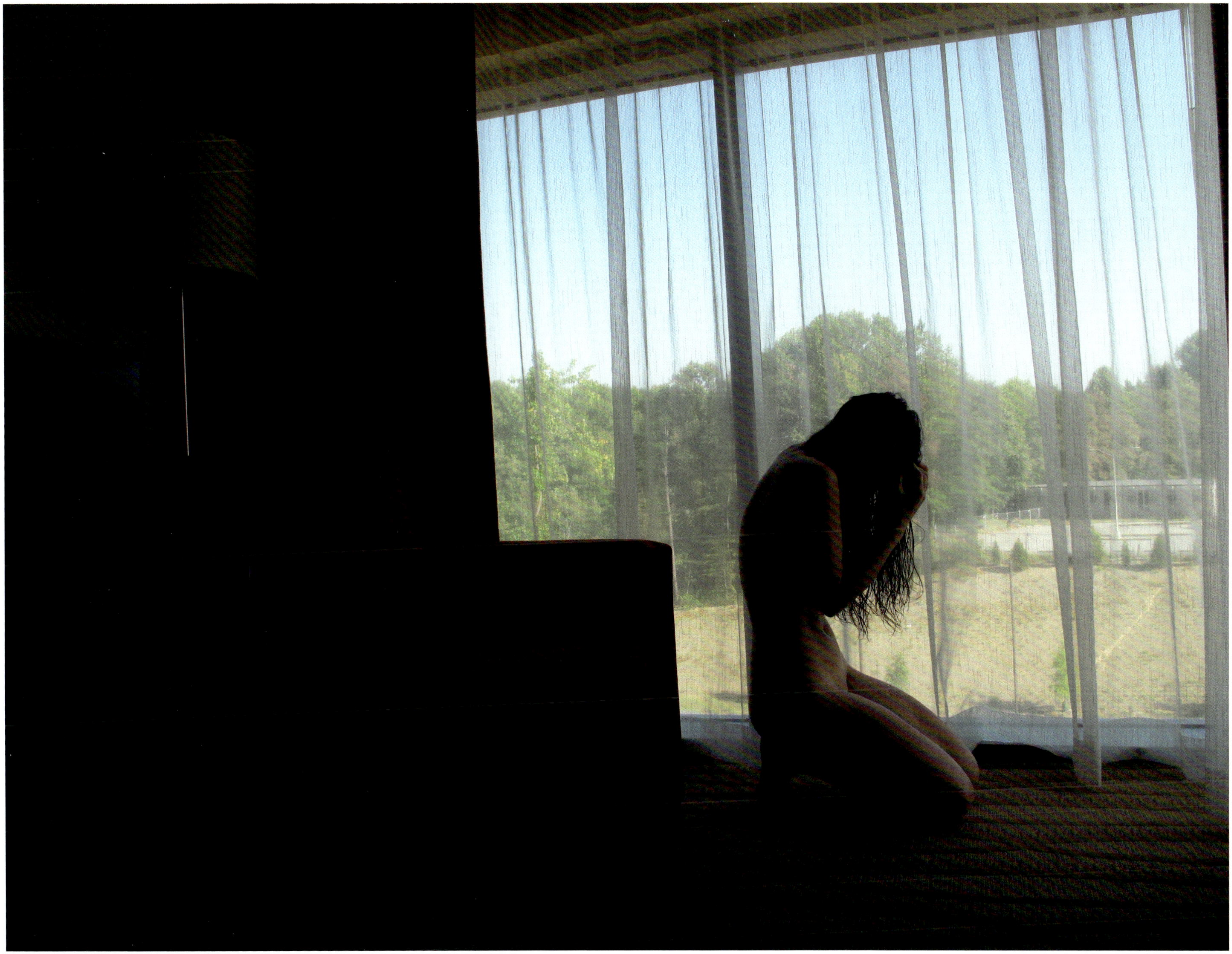

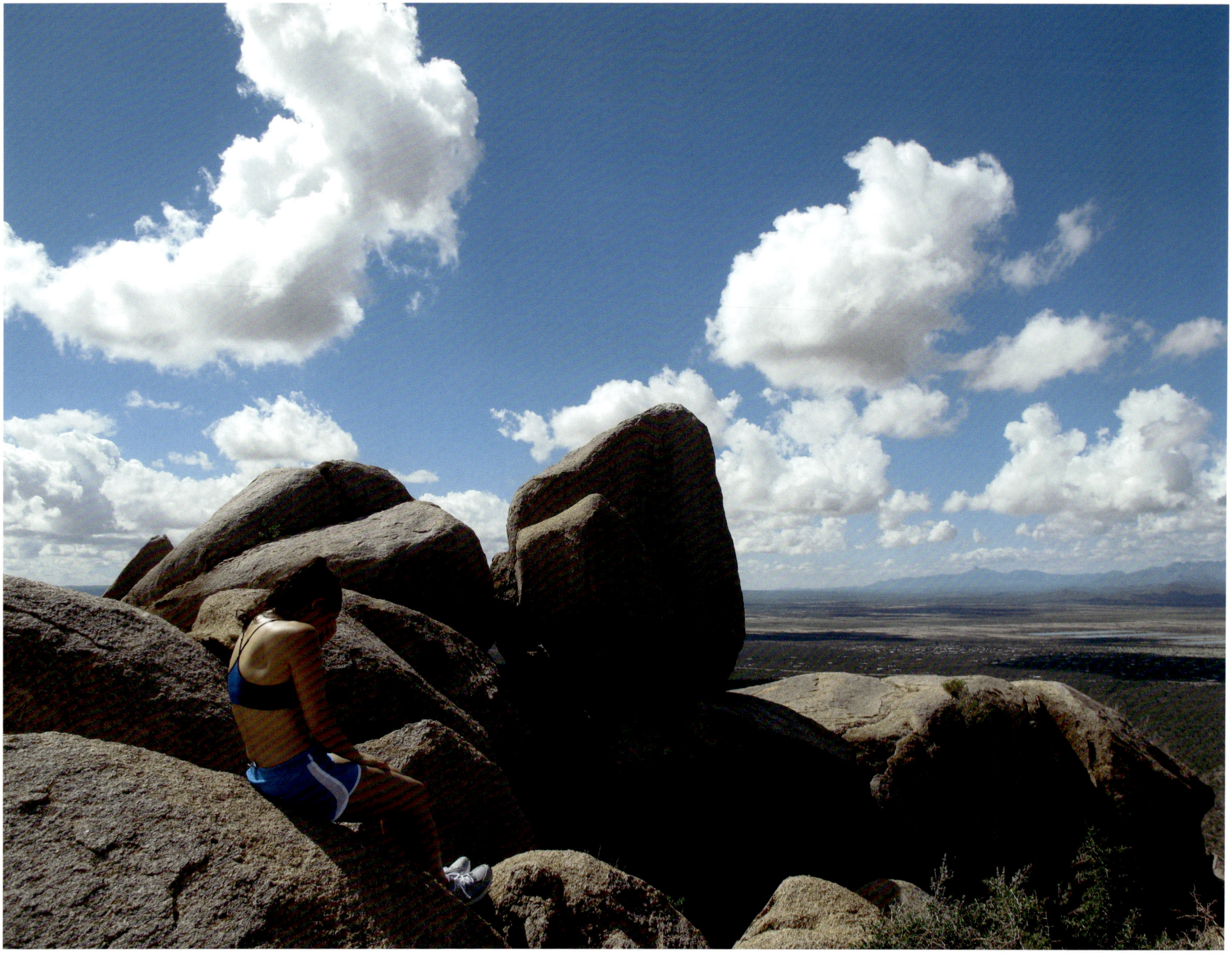

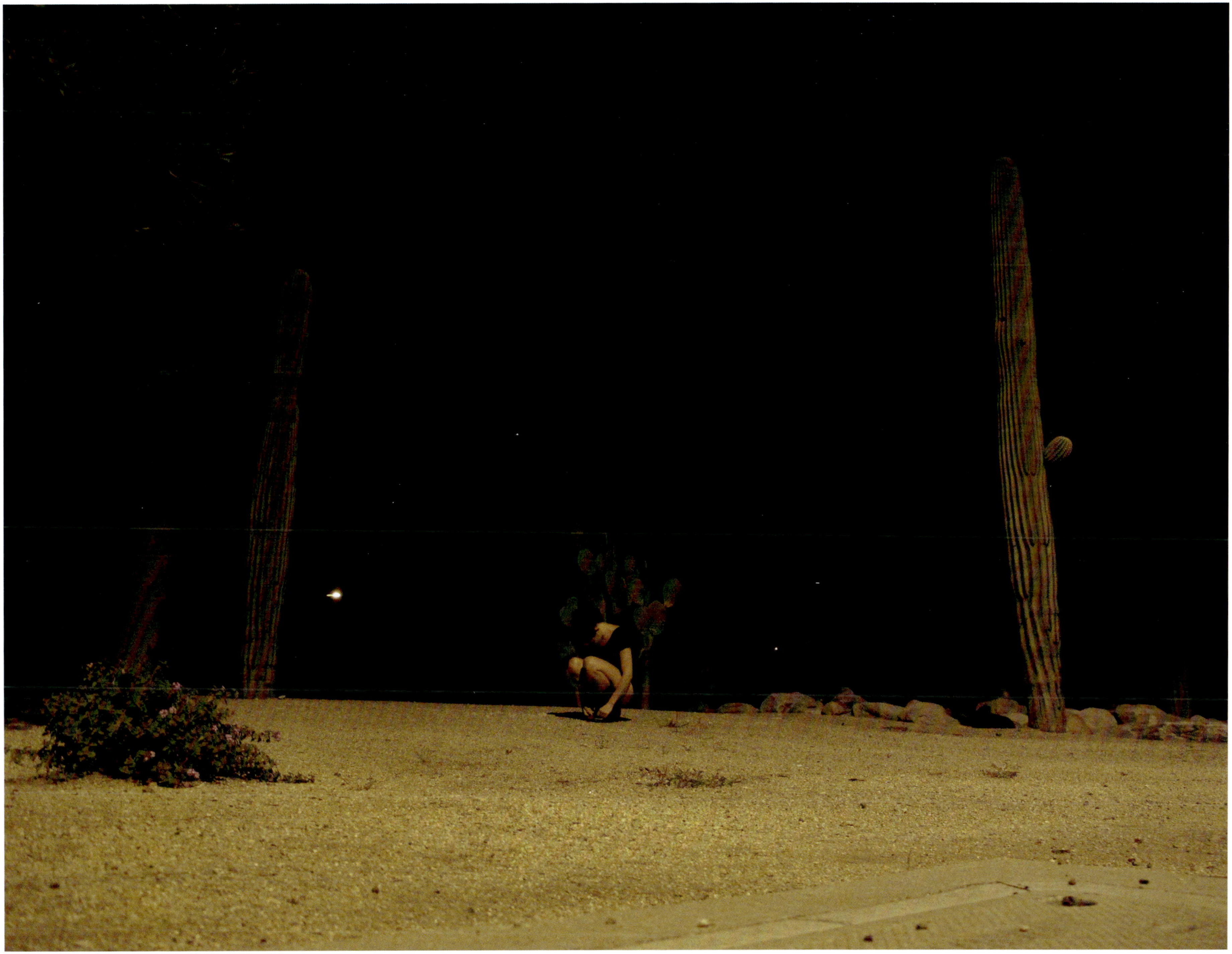

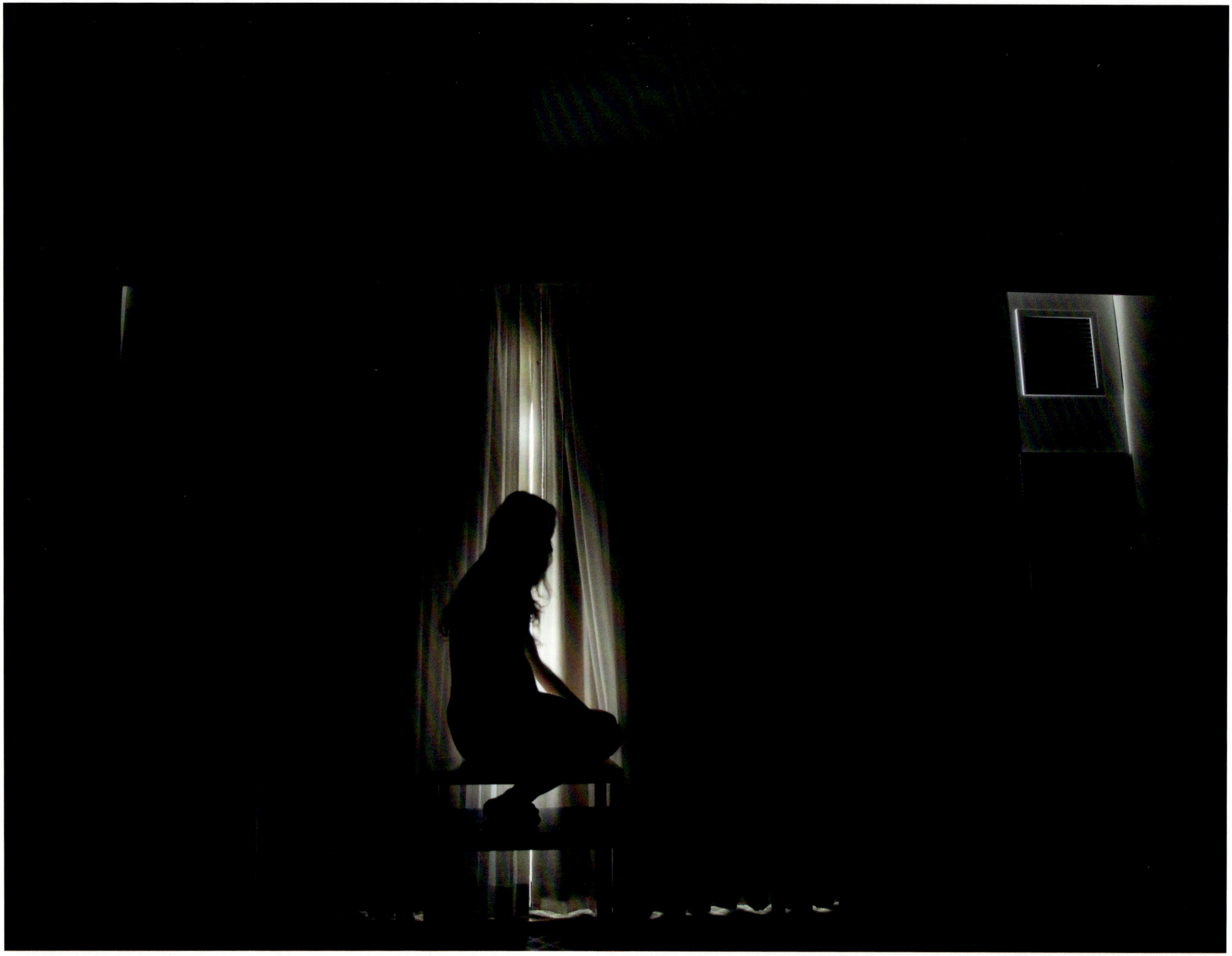

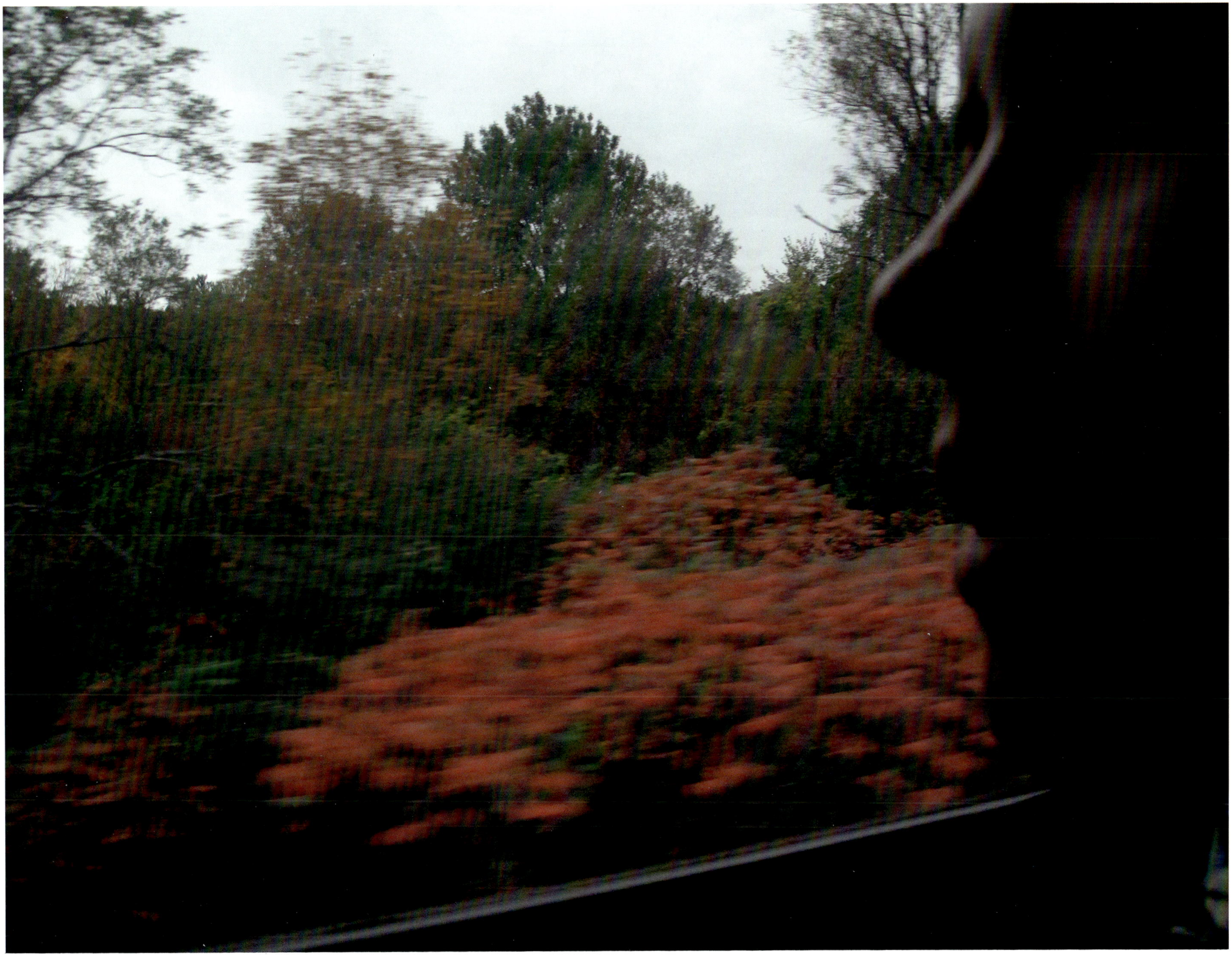

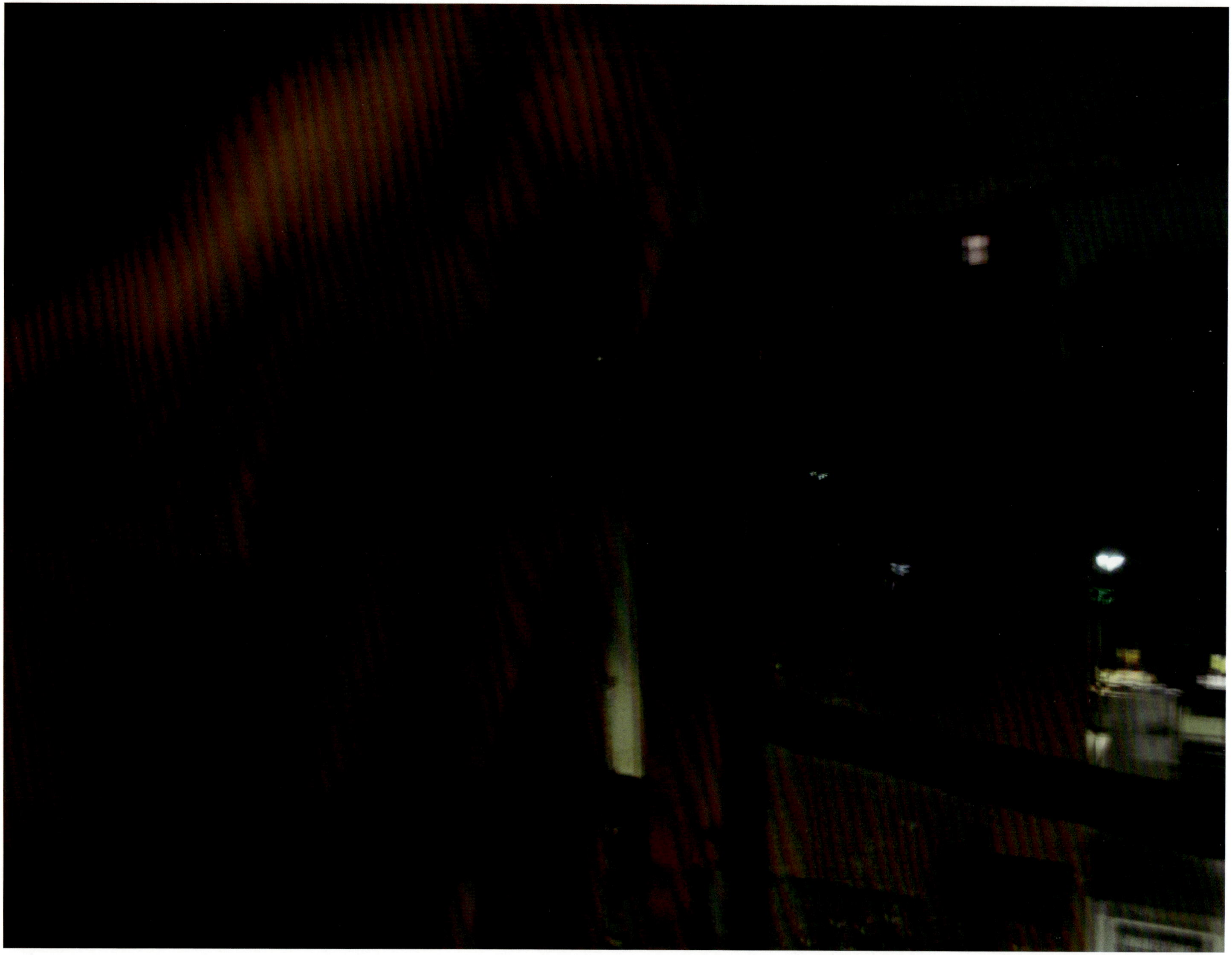

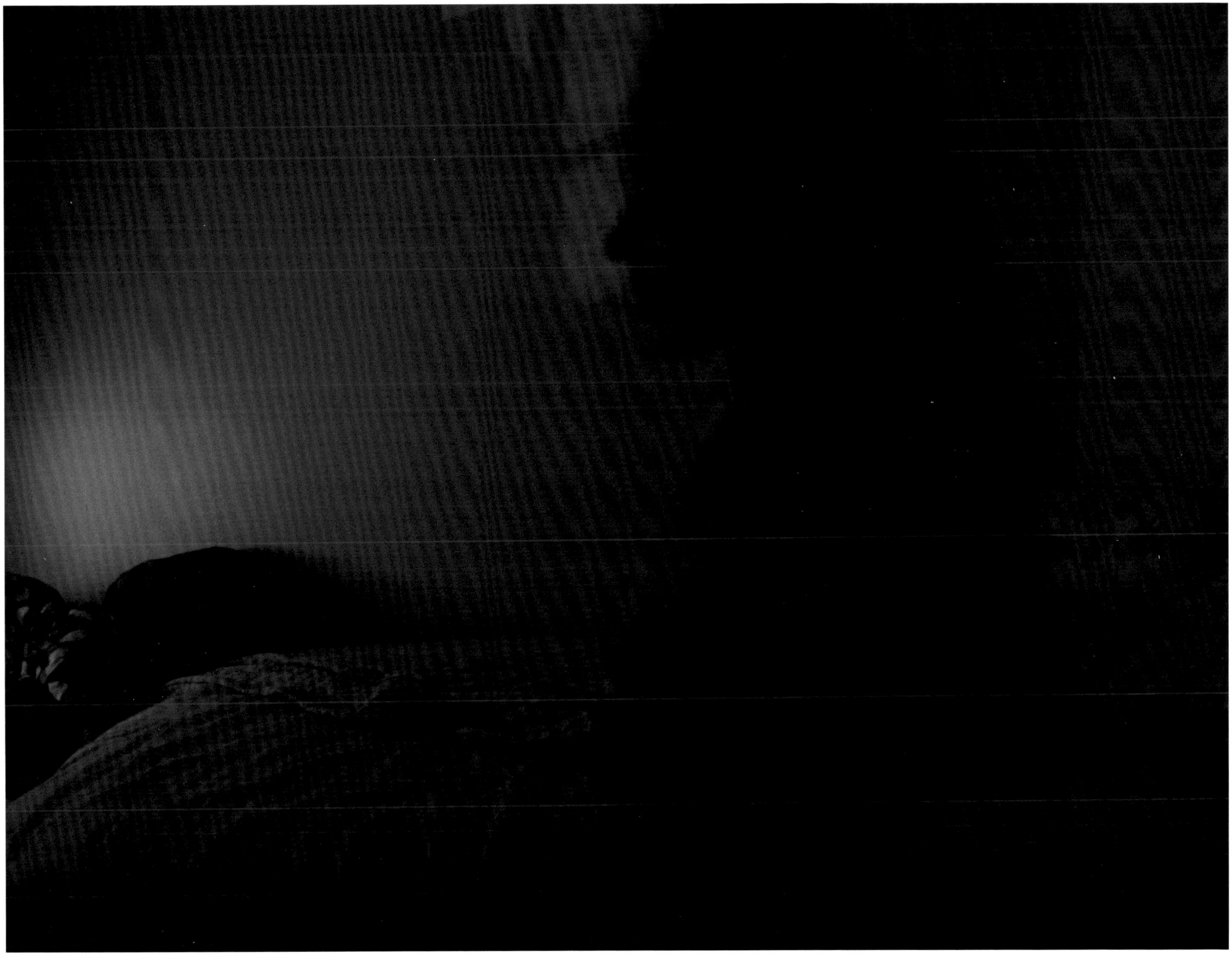

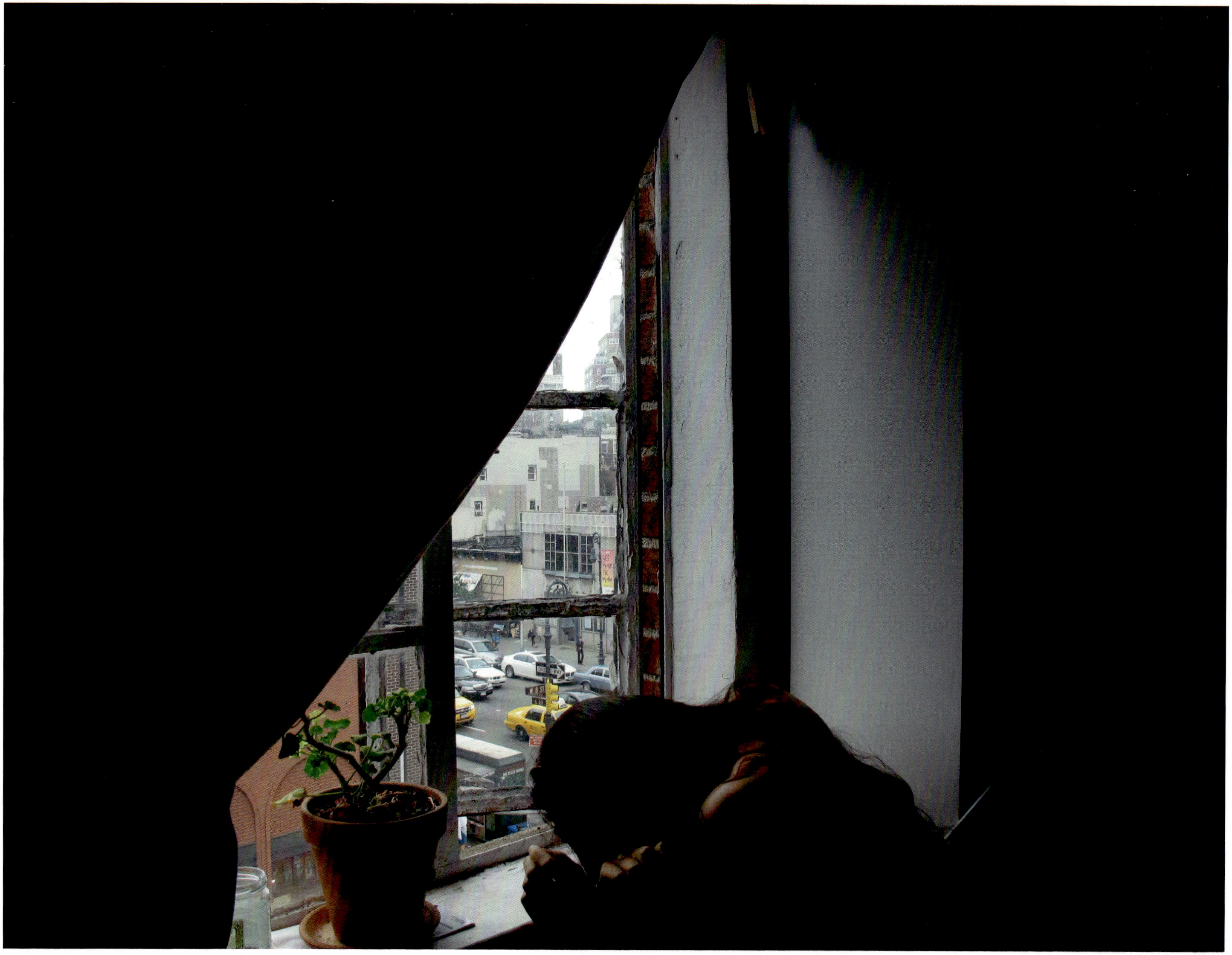

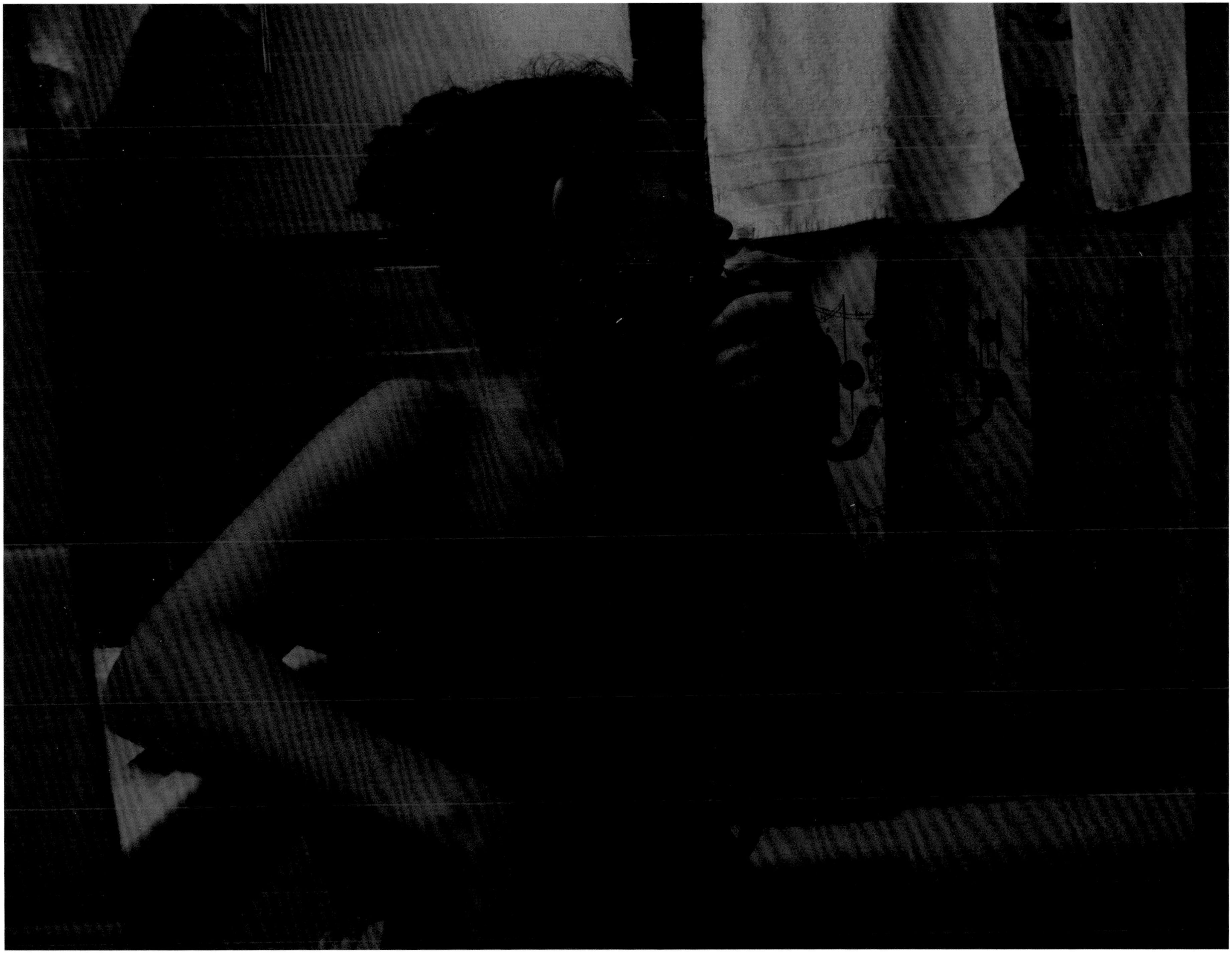

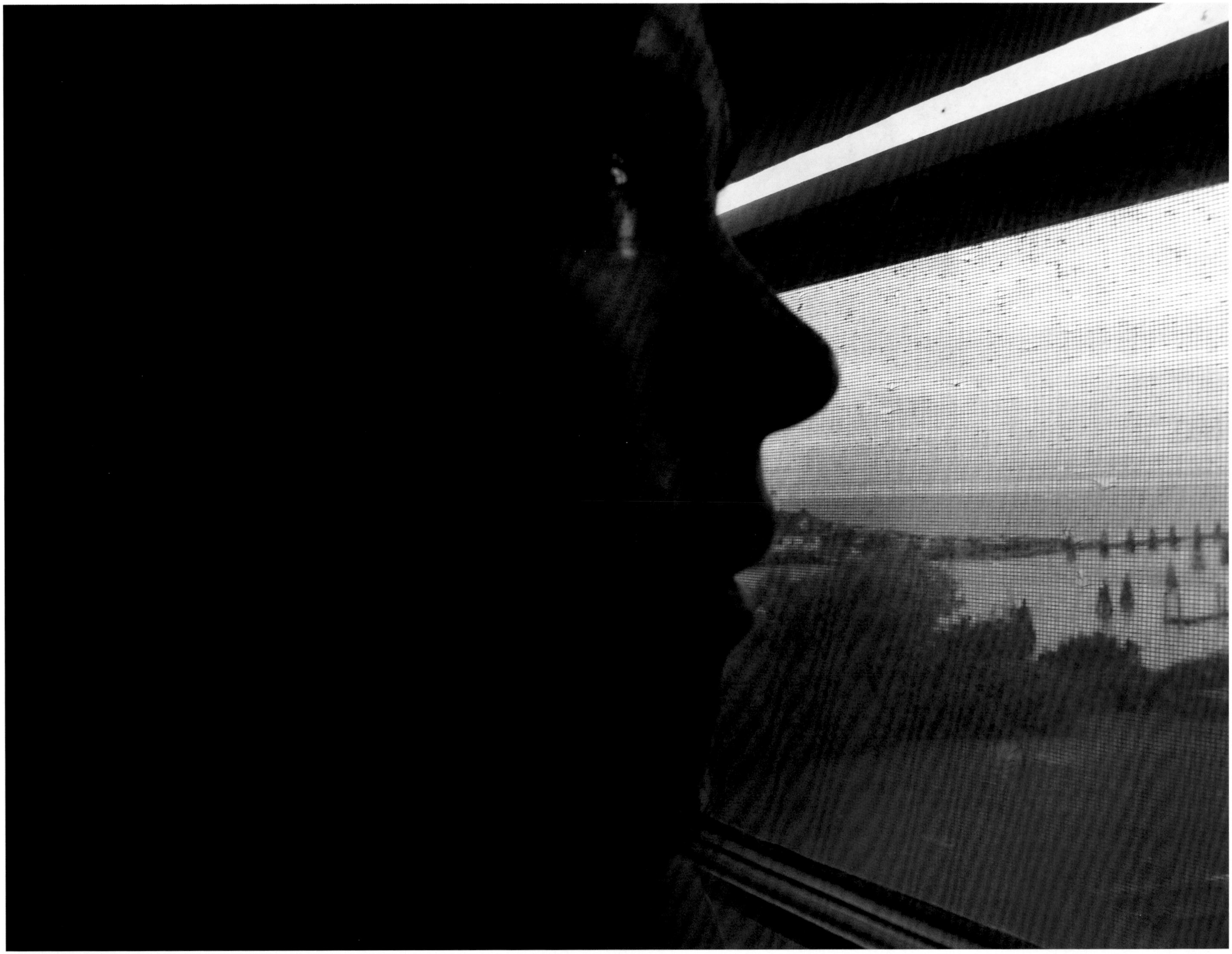

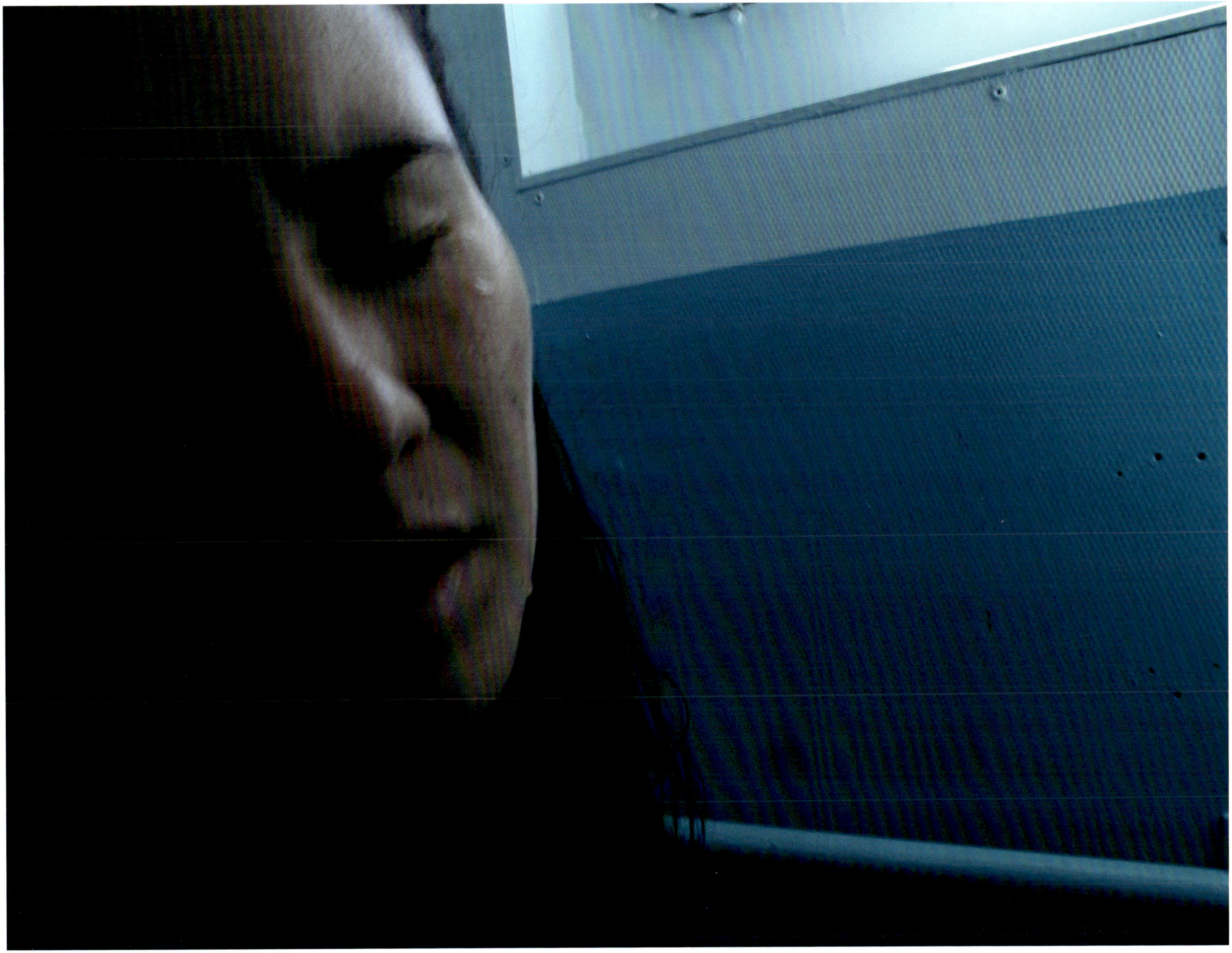

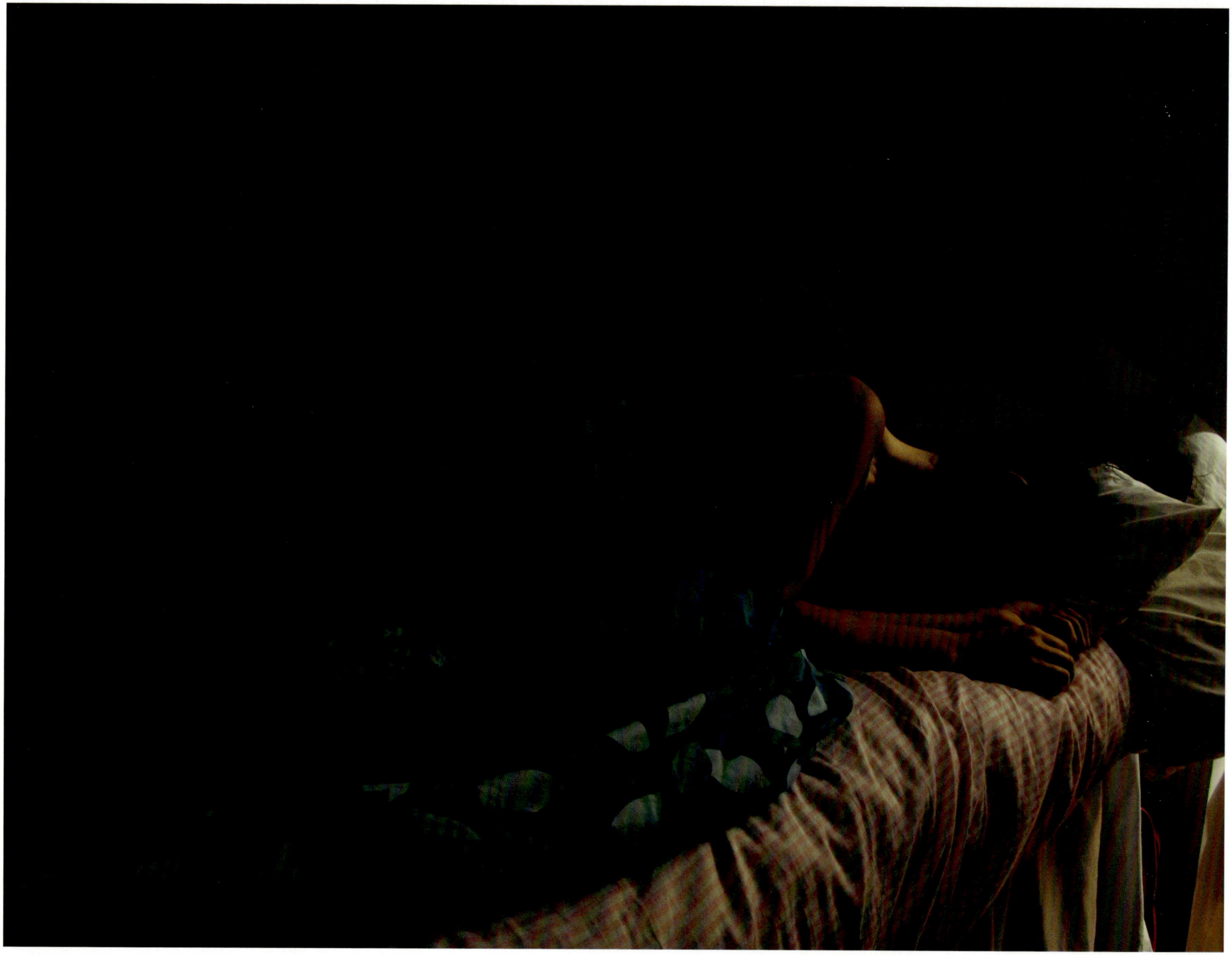

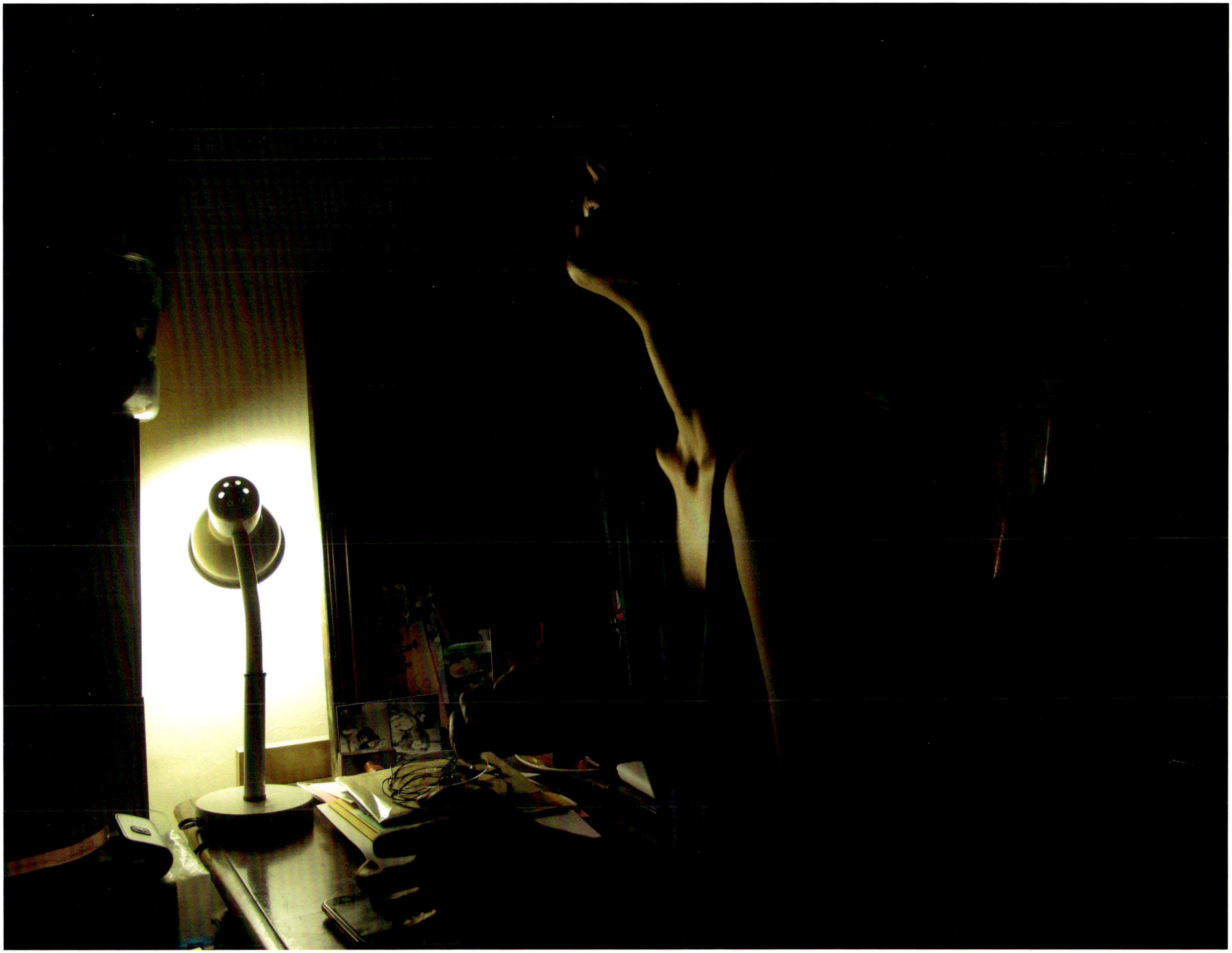

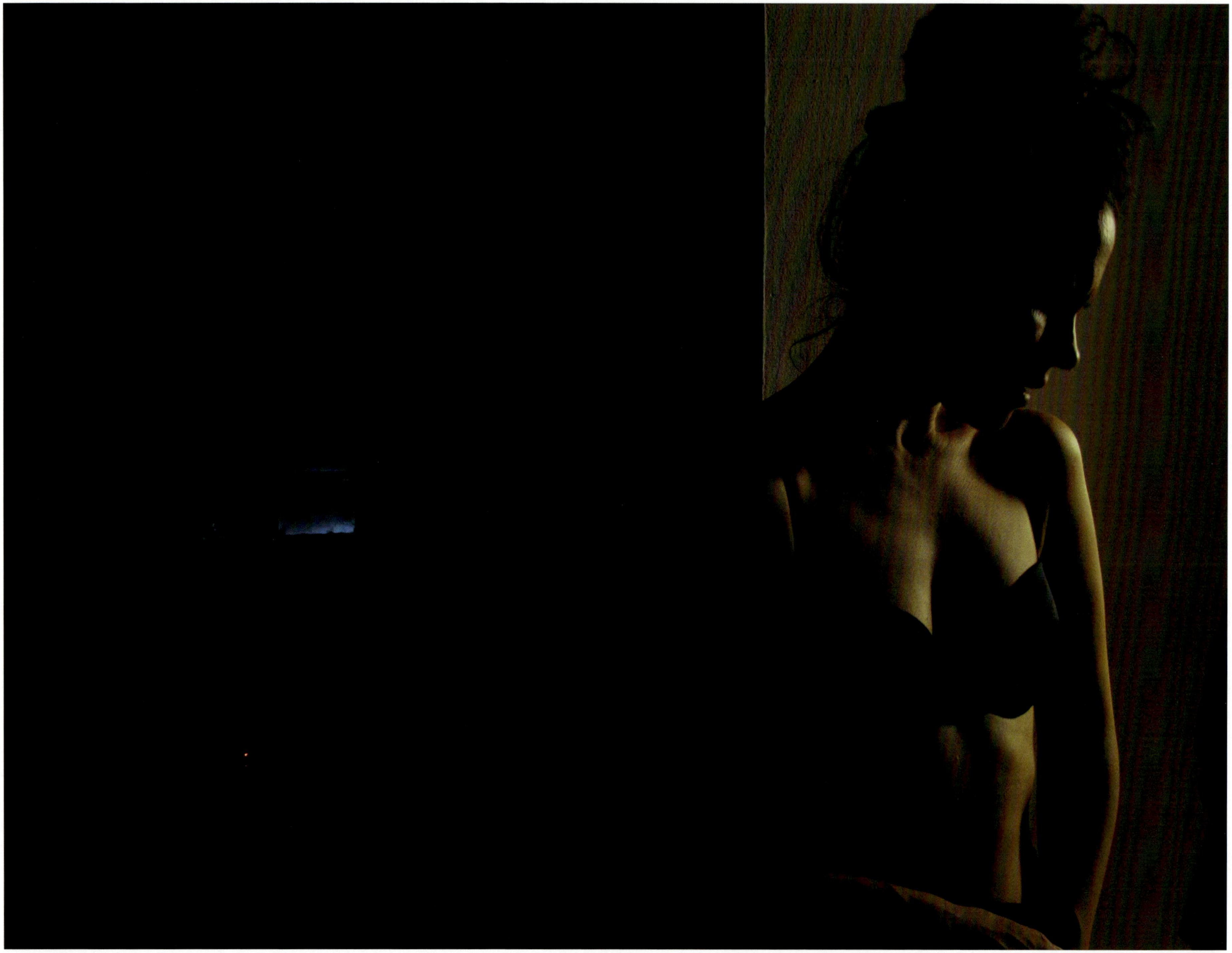

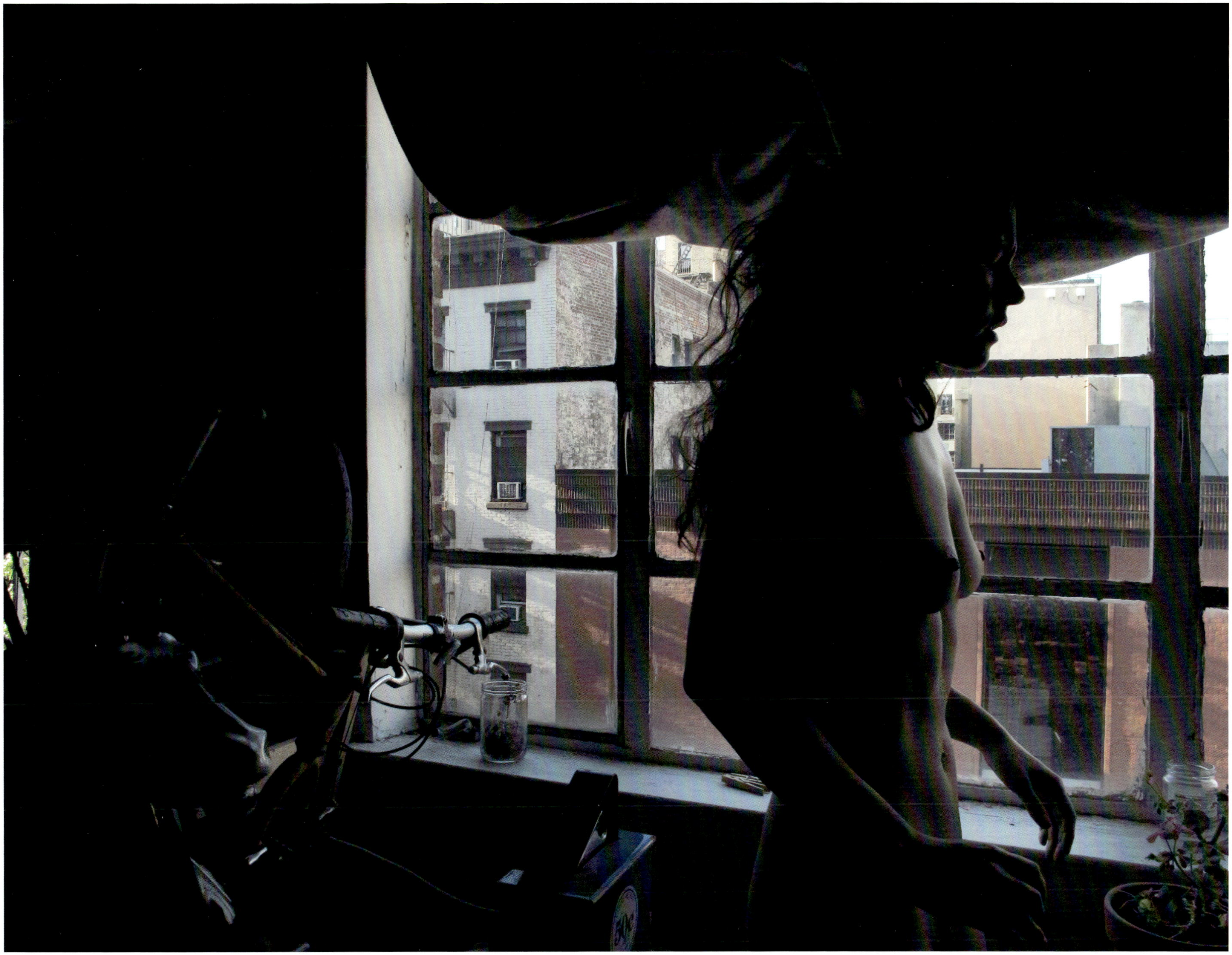

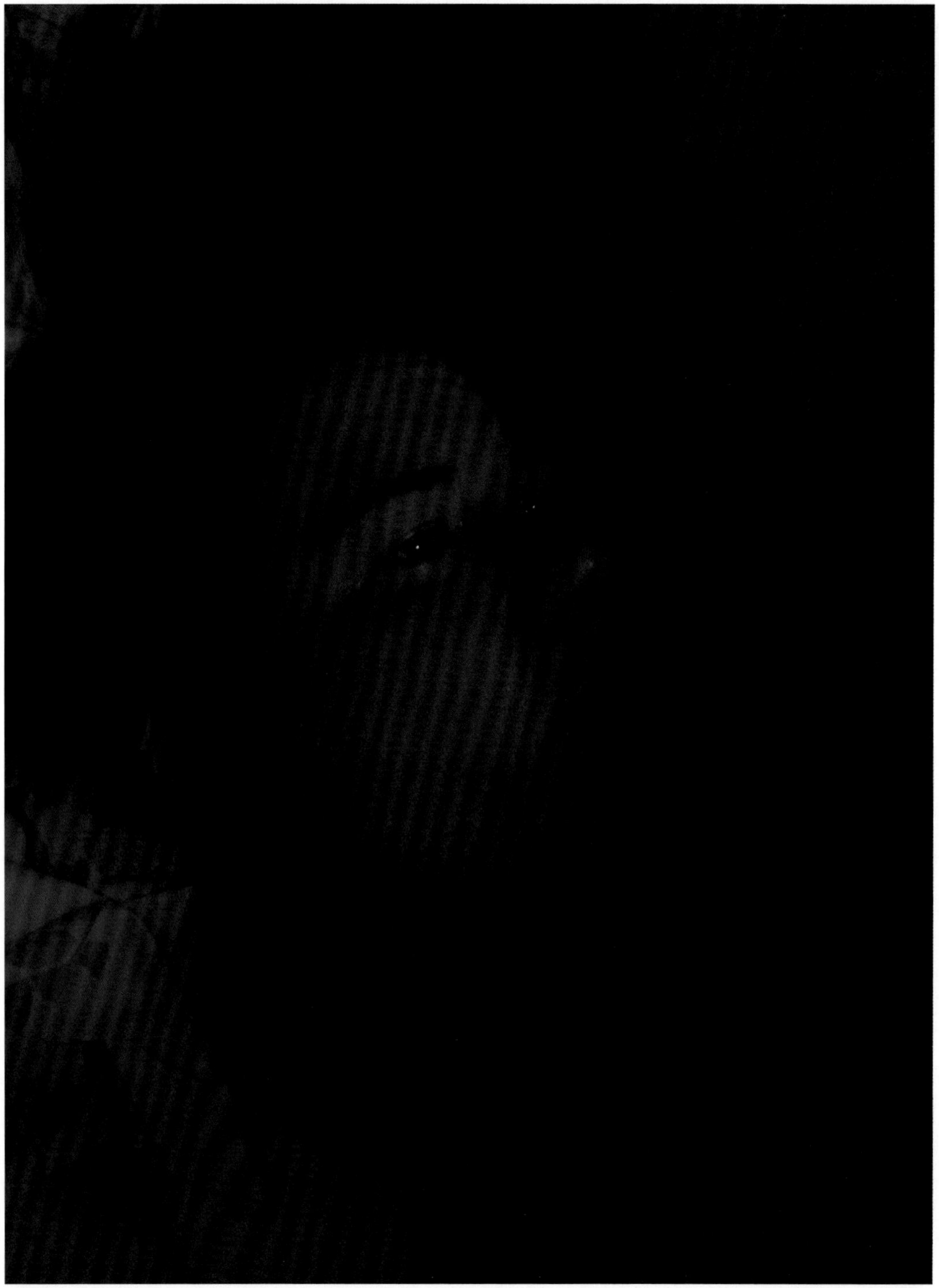

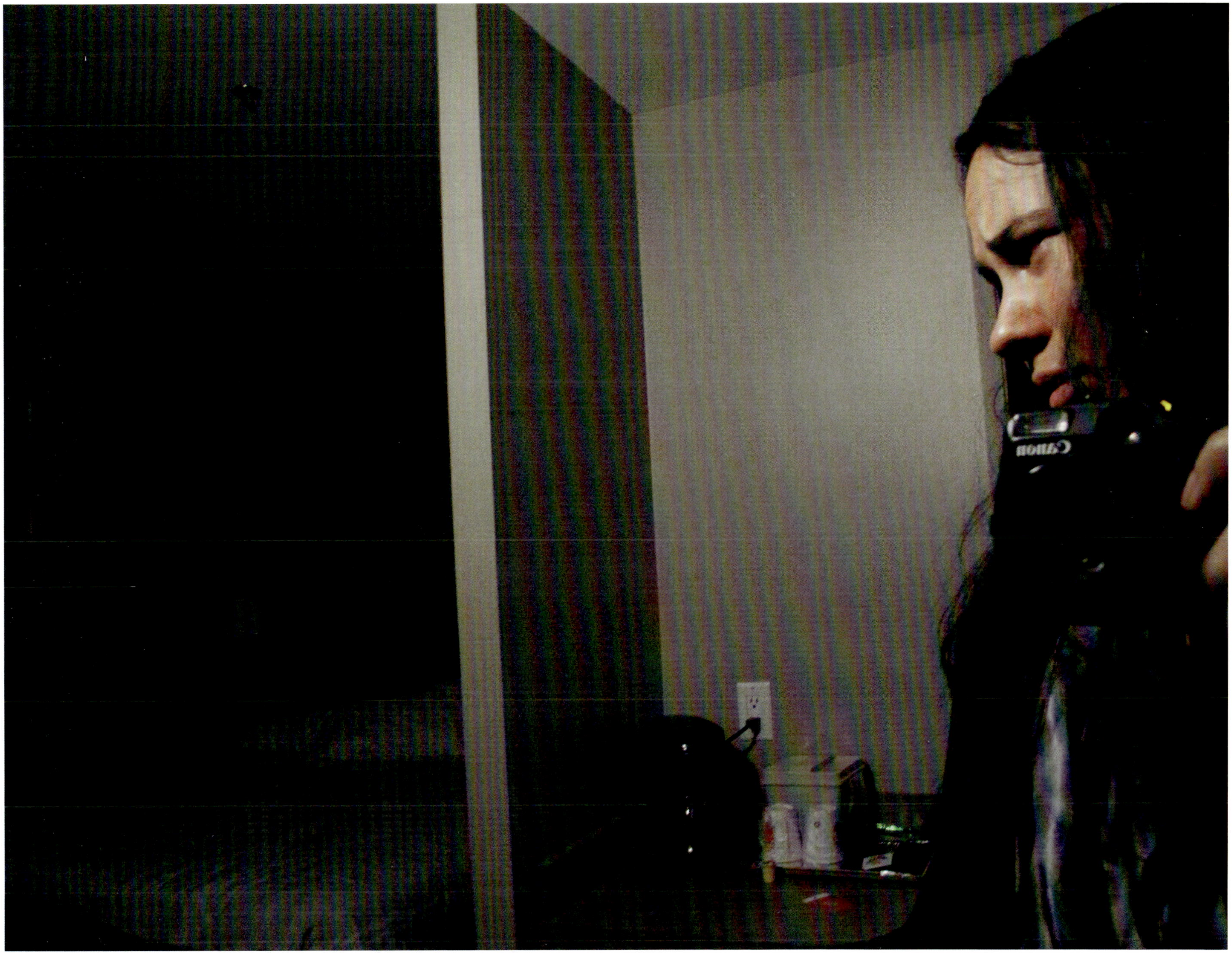
Canon

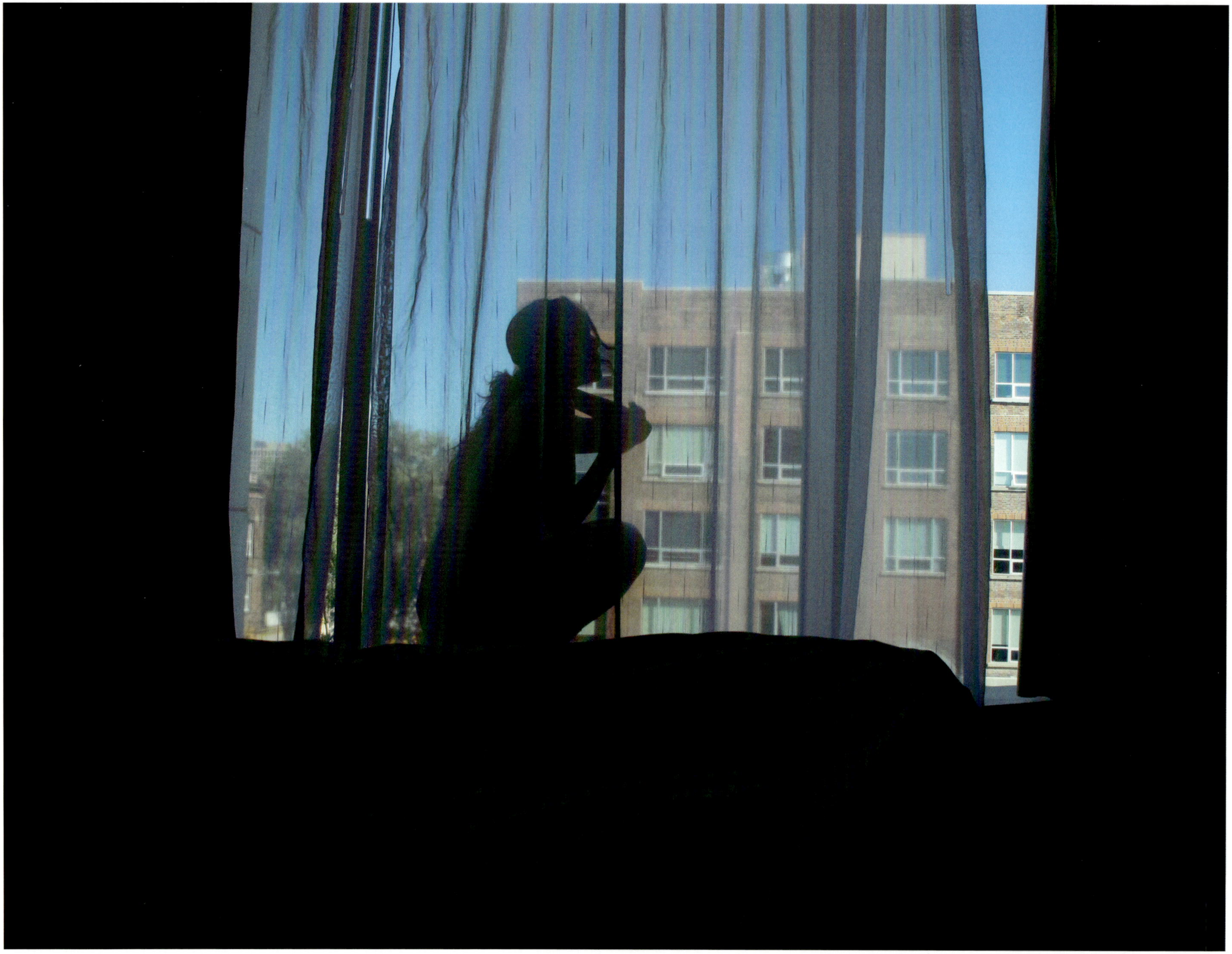

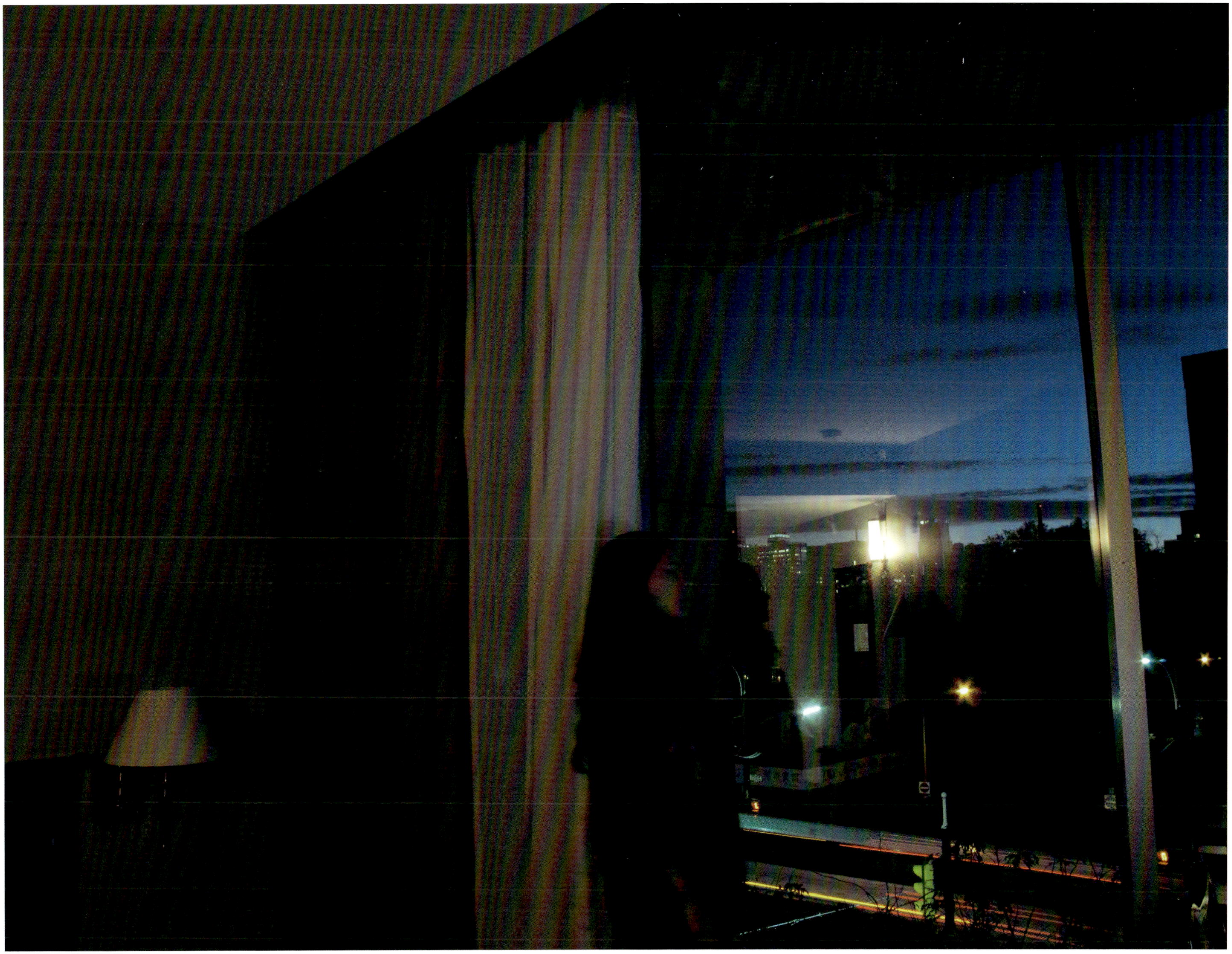

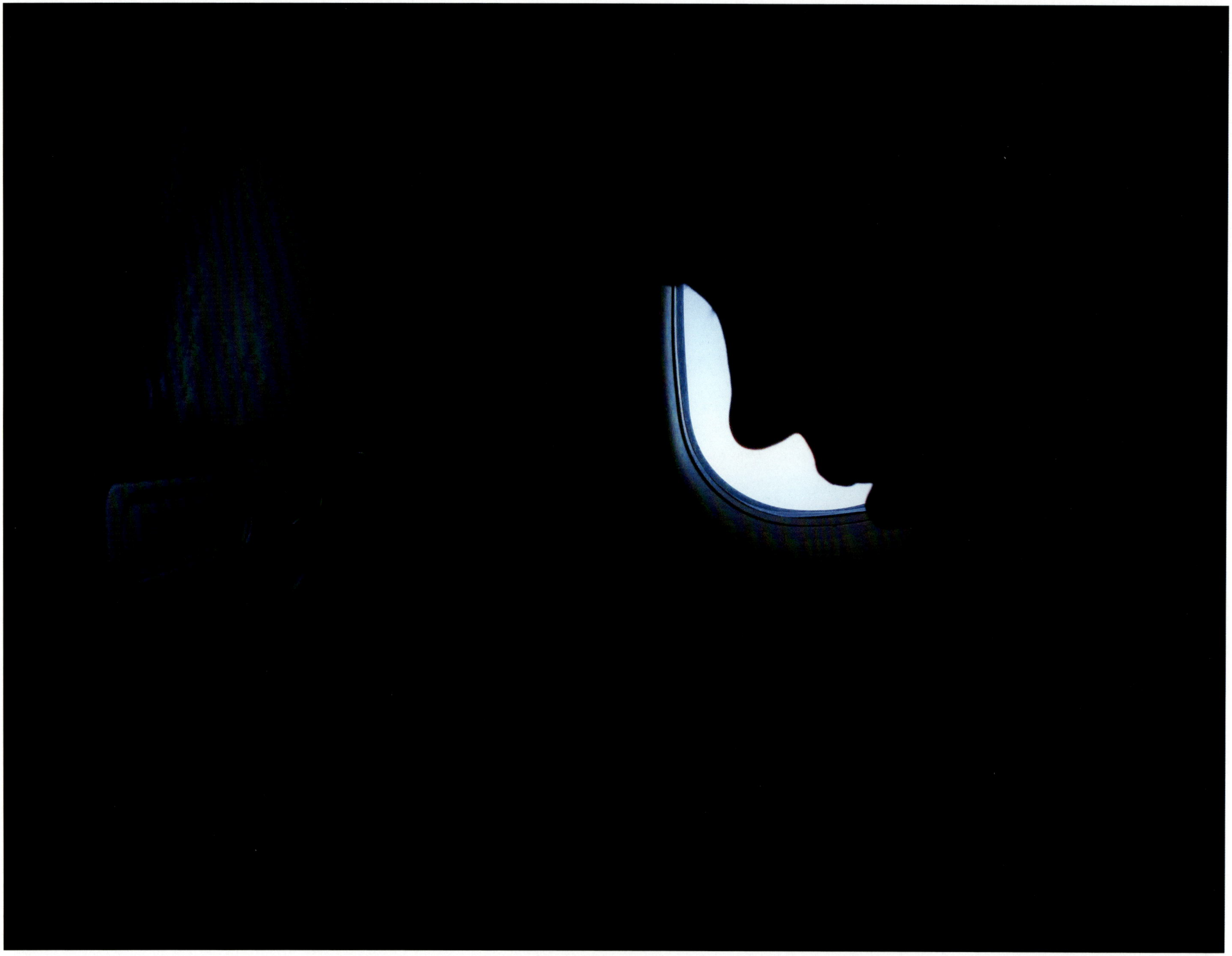

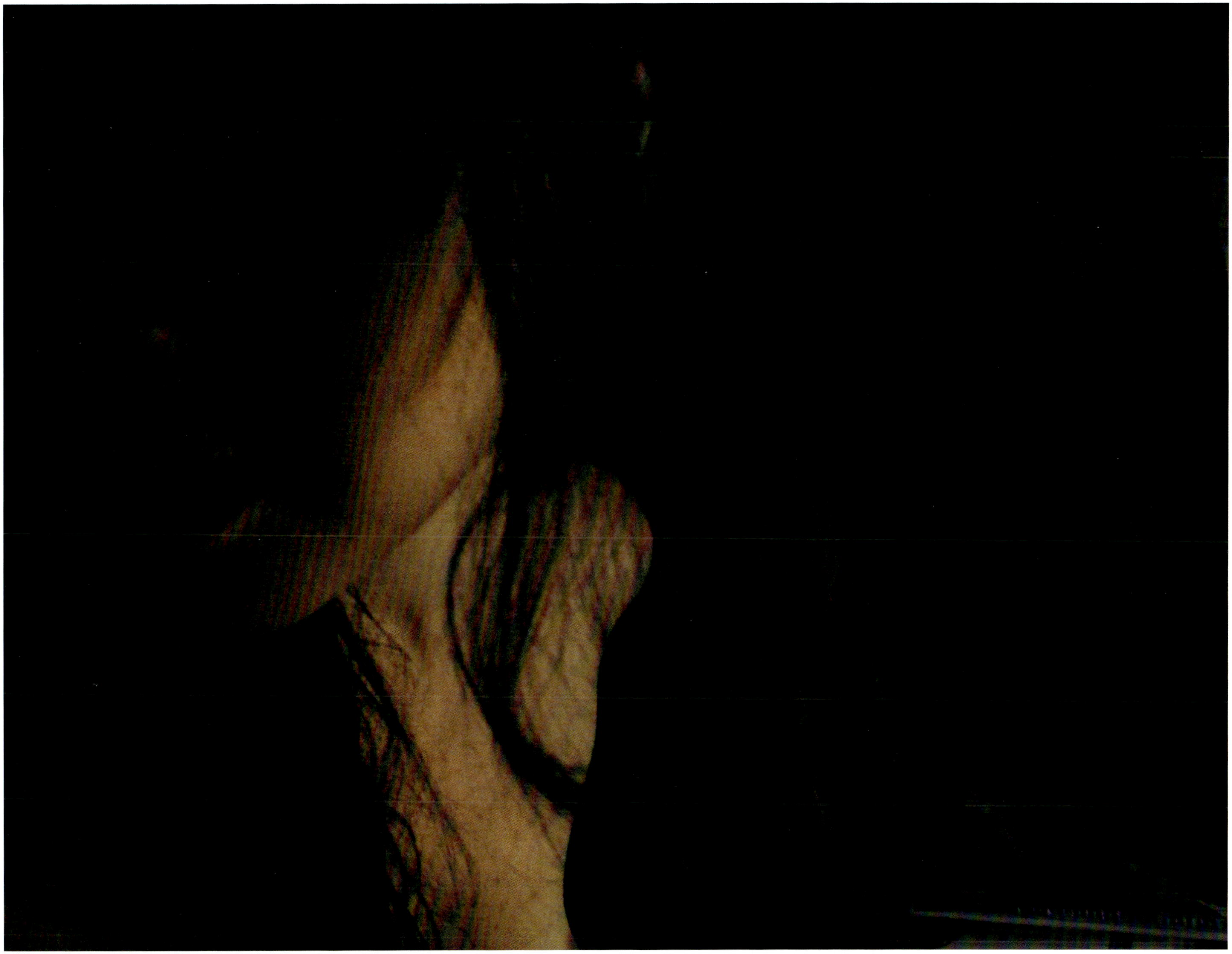

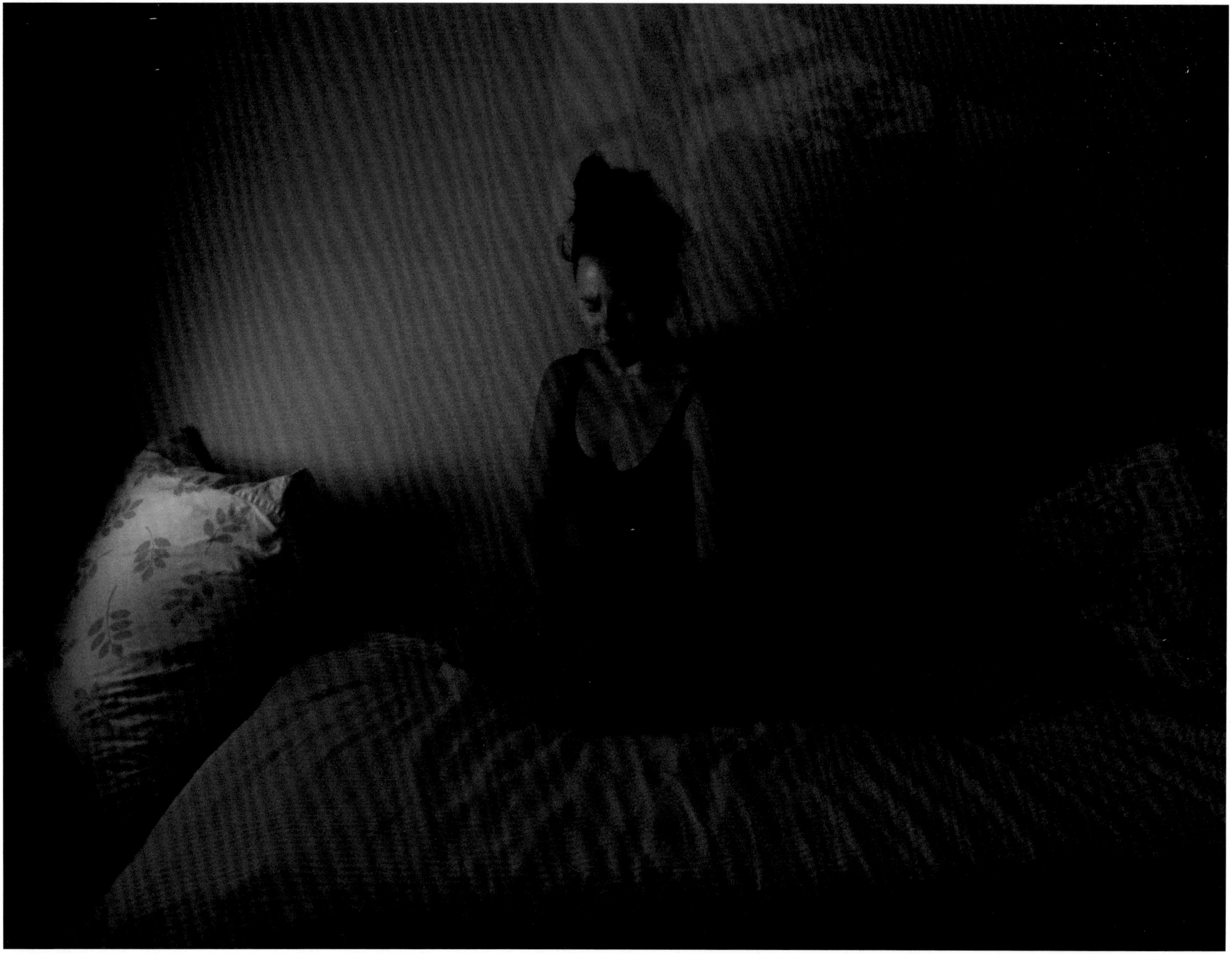

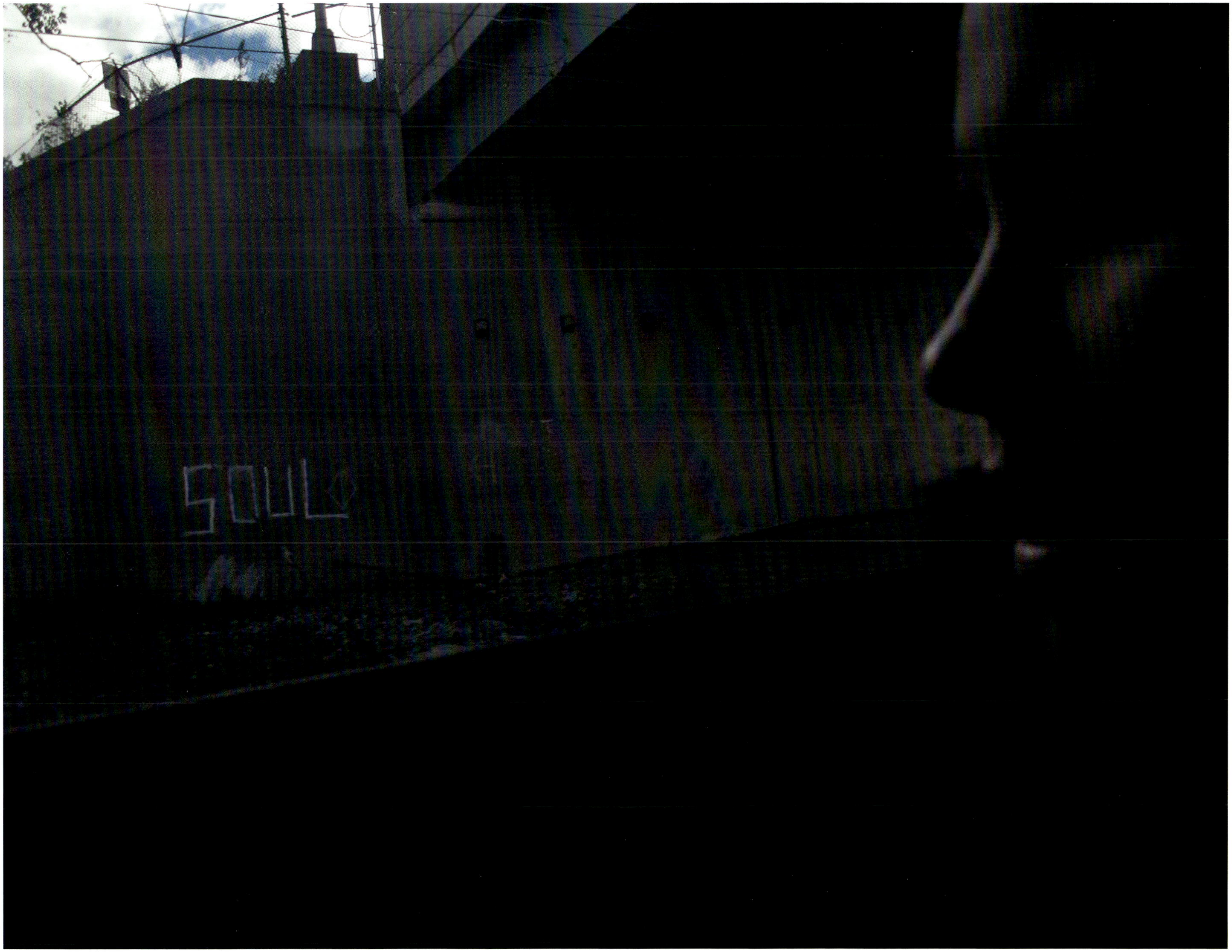
SOUL

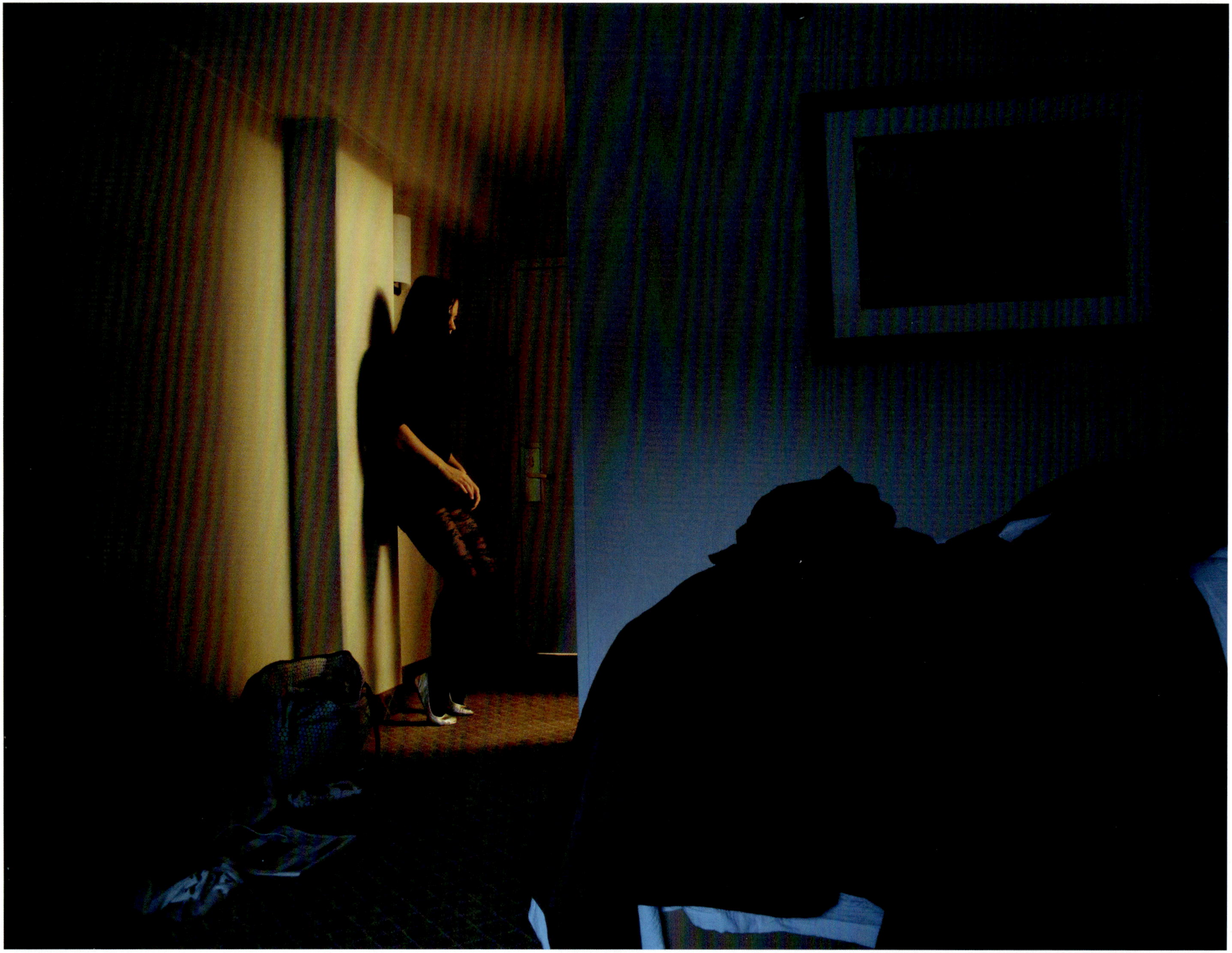

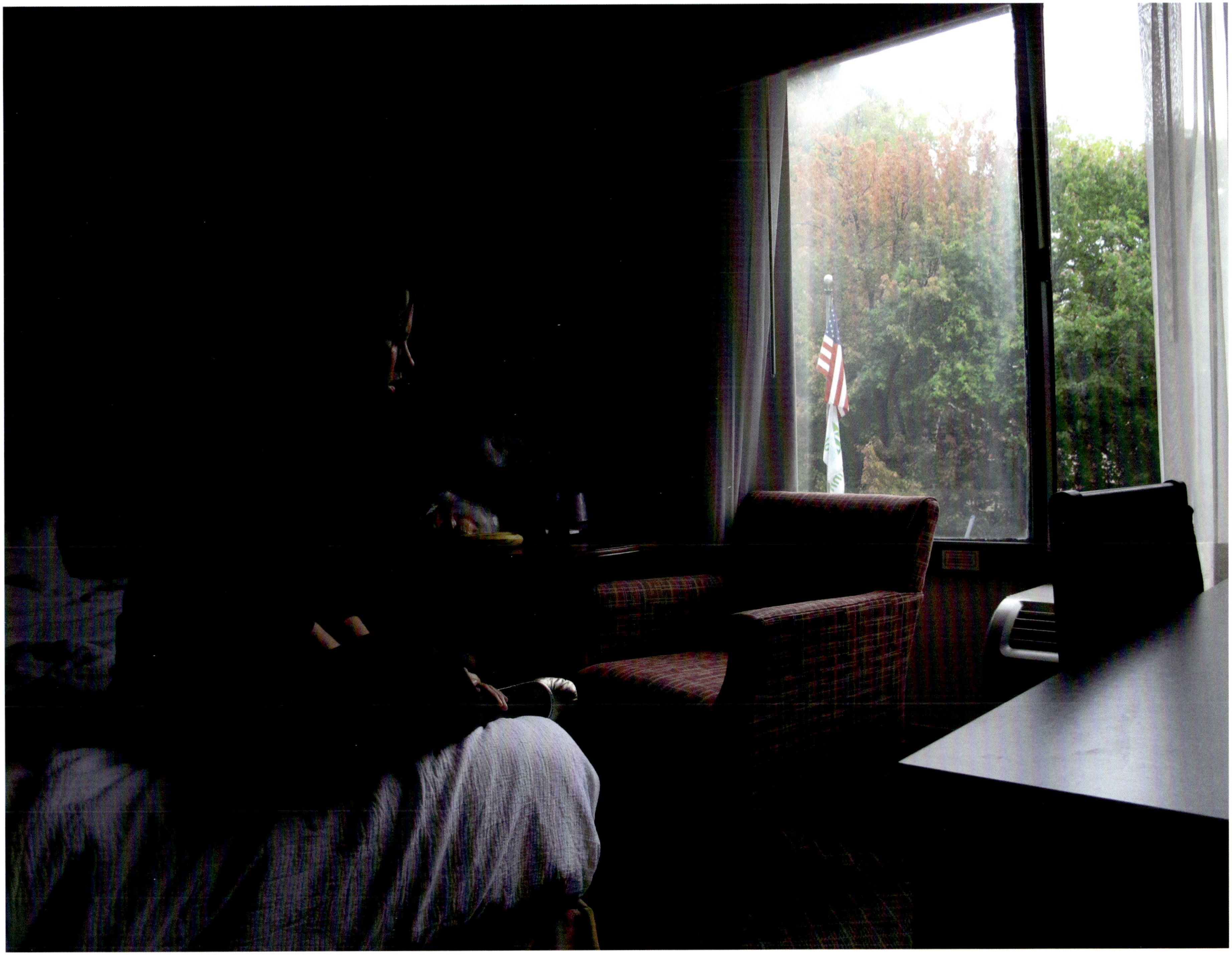

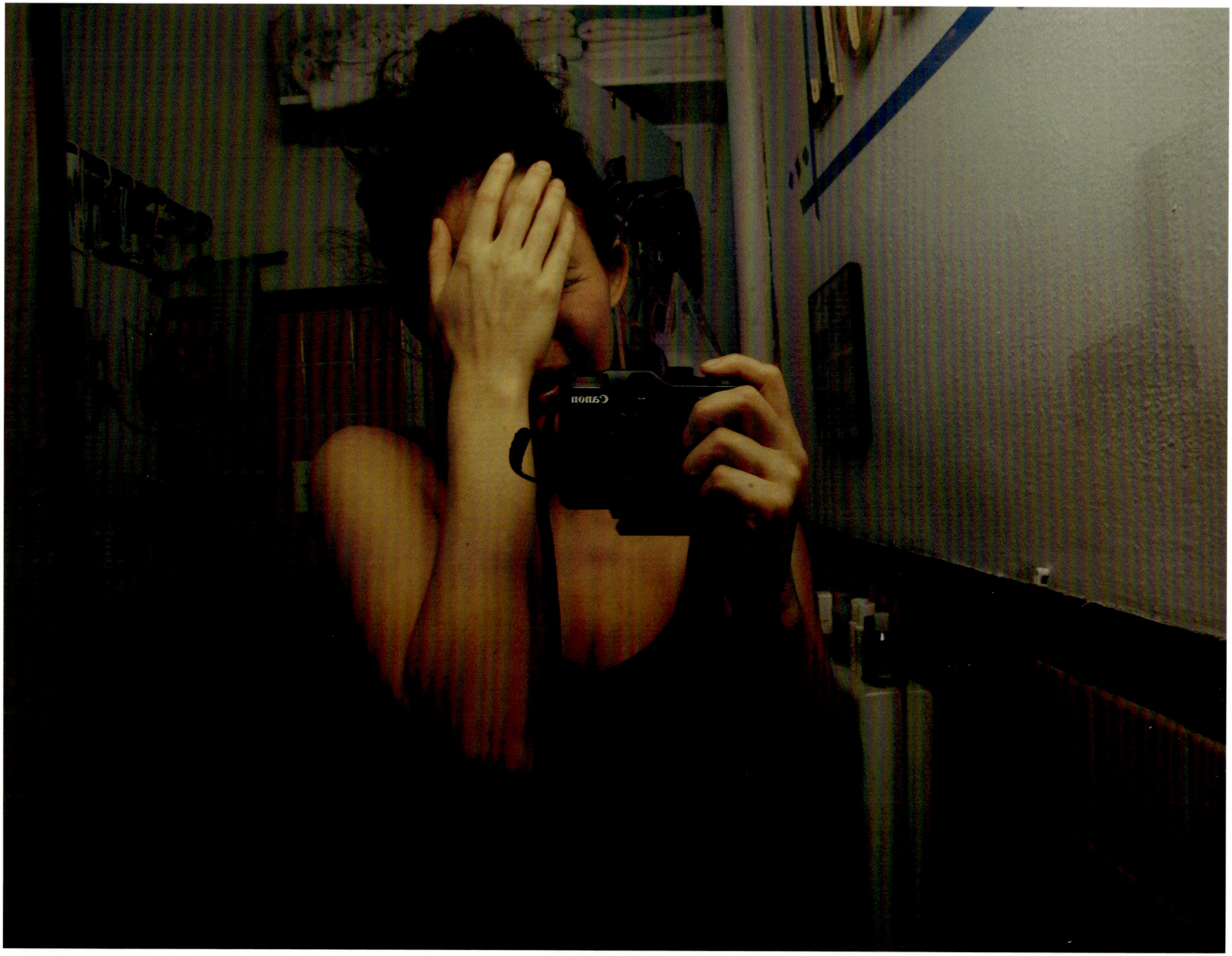
Canon

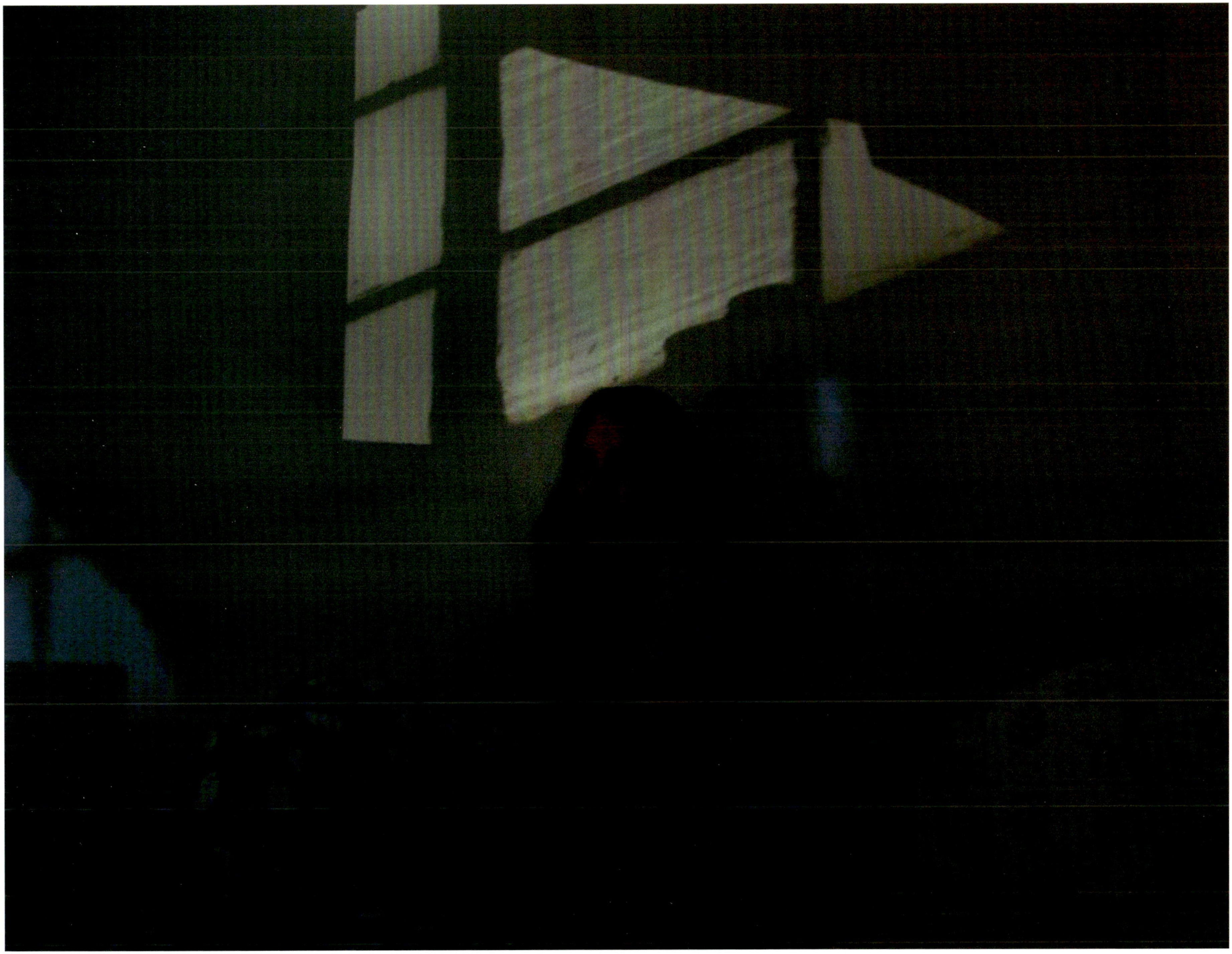

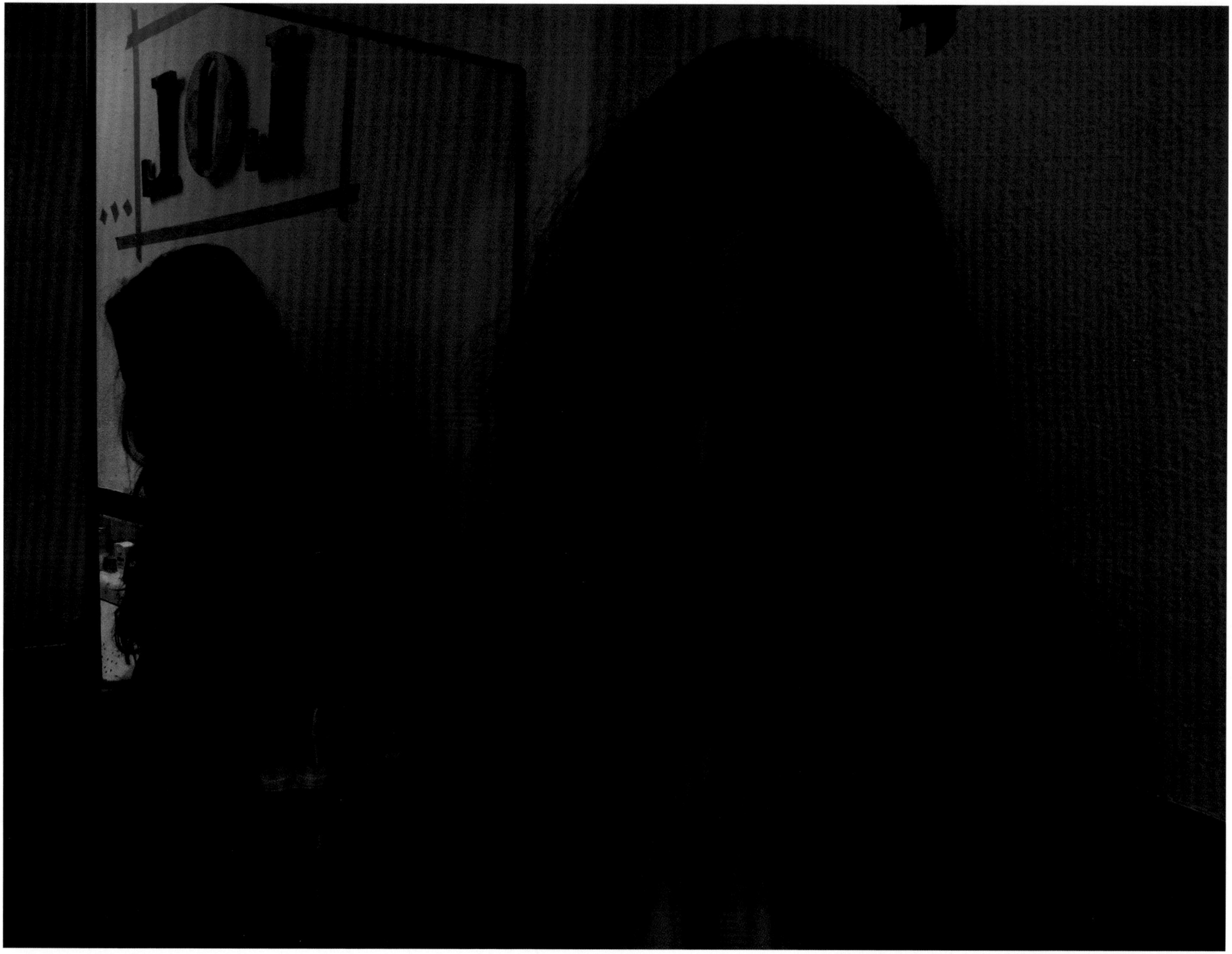
JOJ

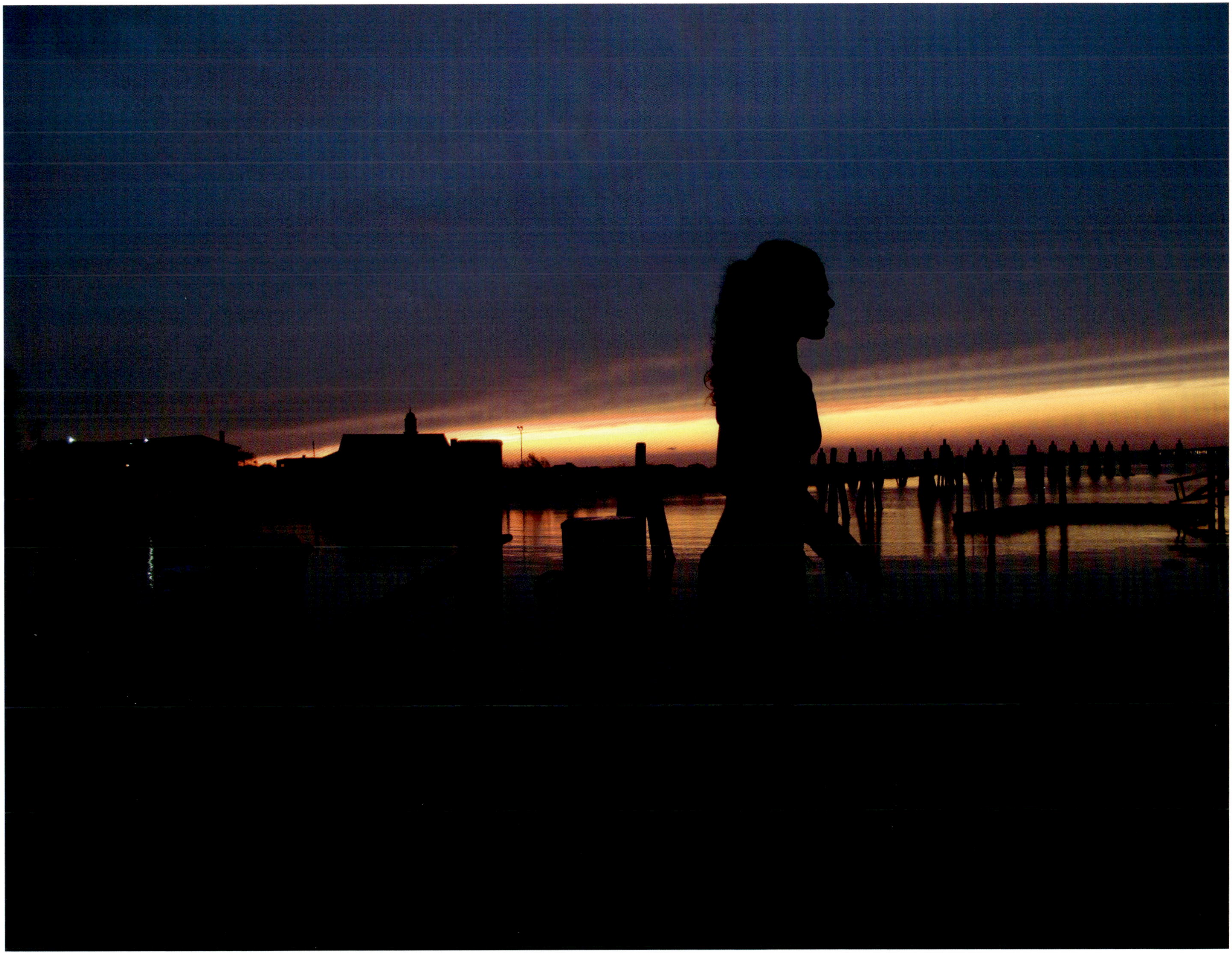

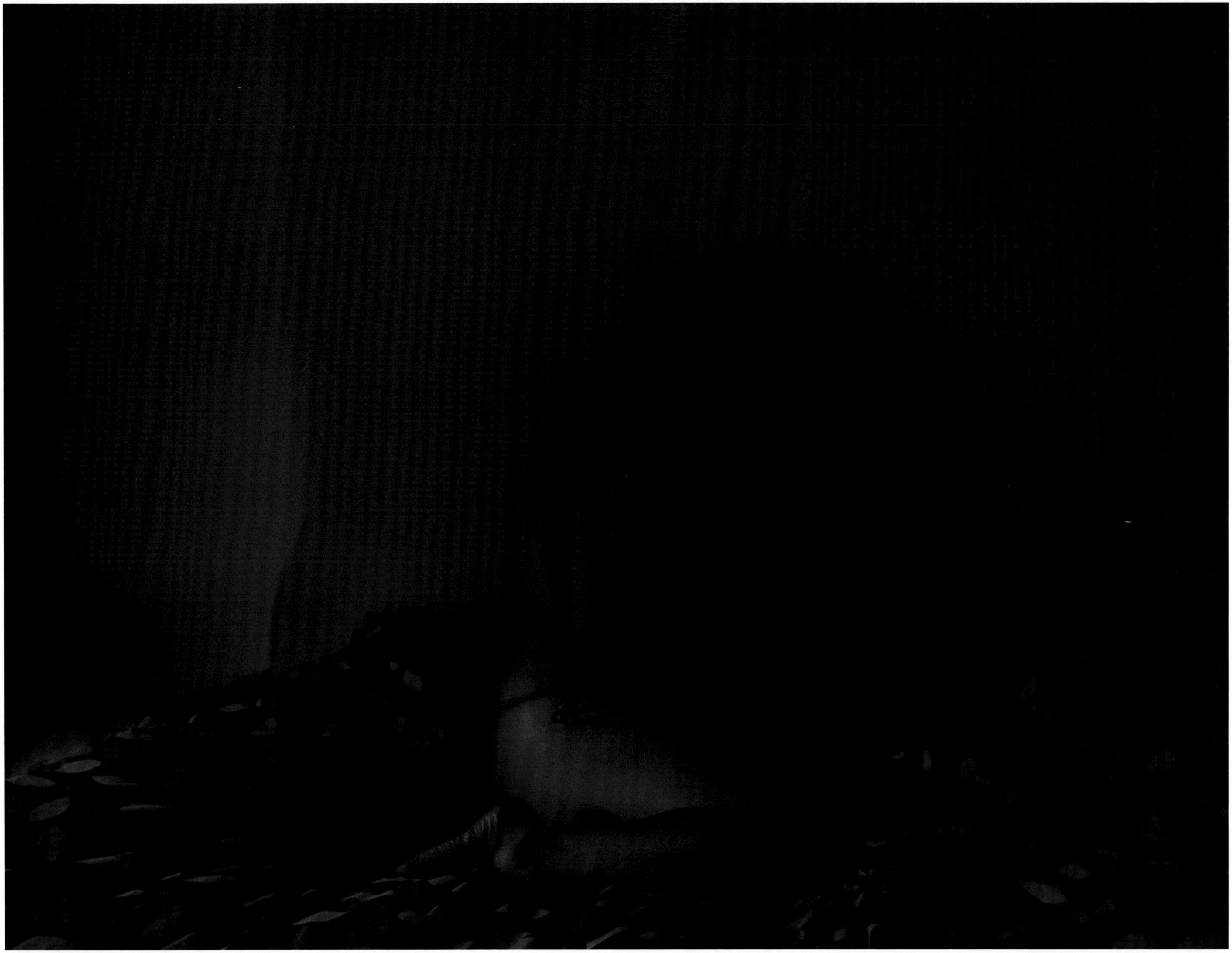

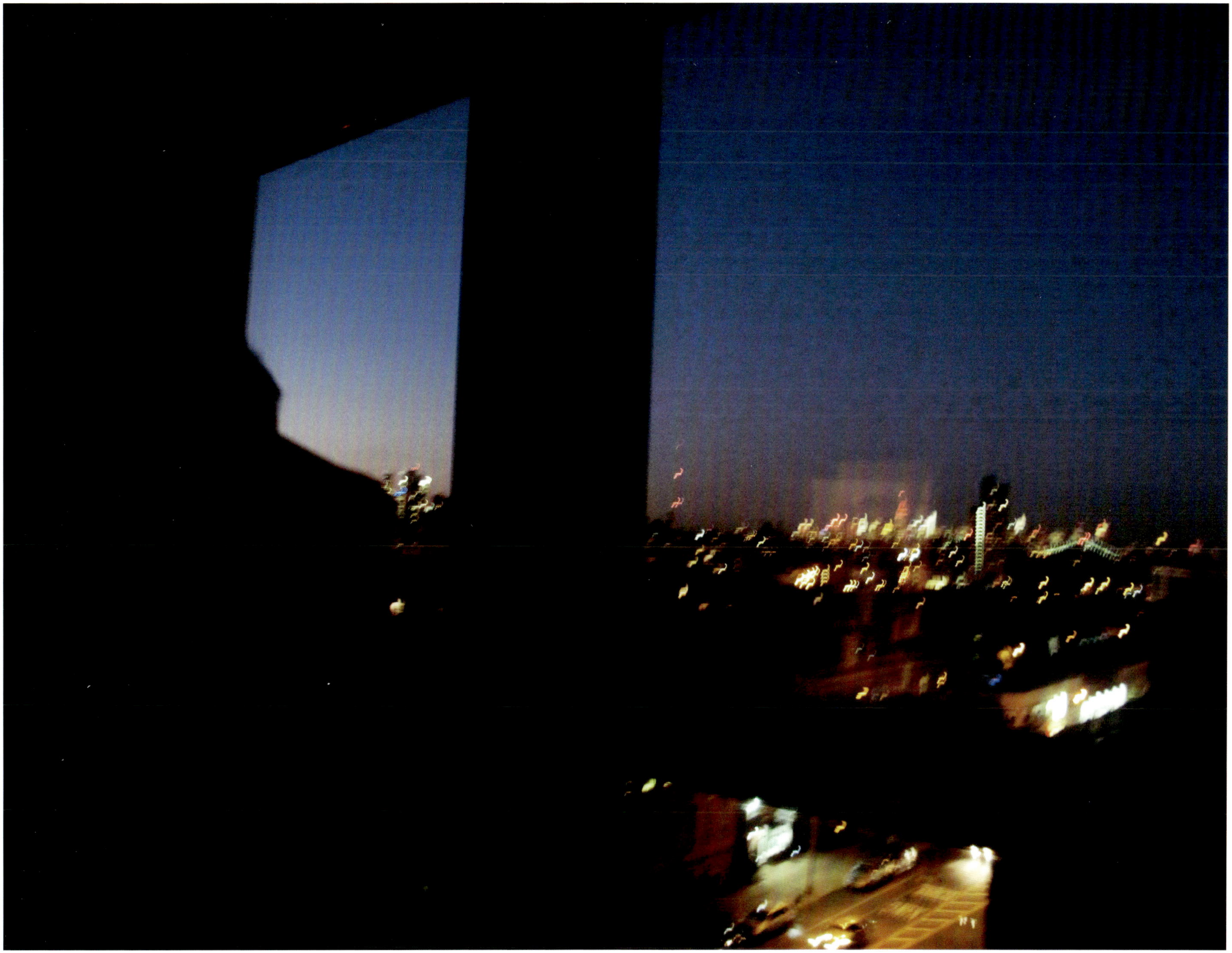

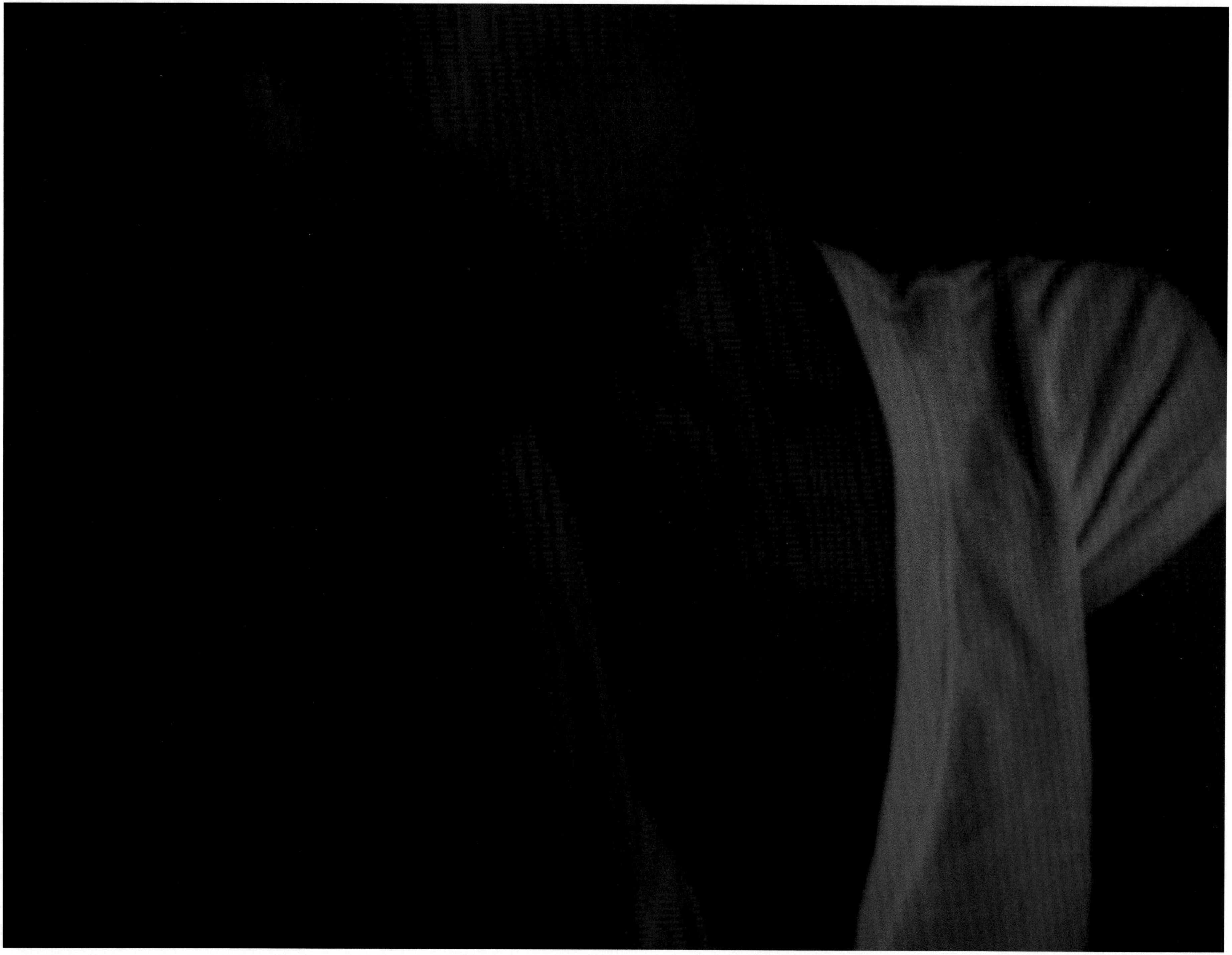

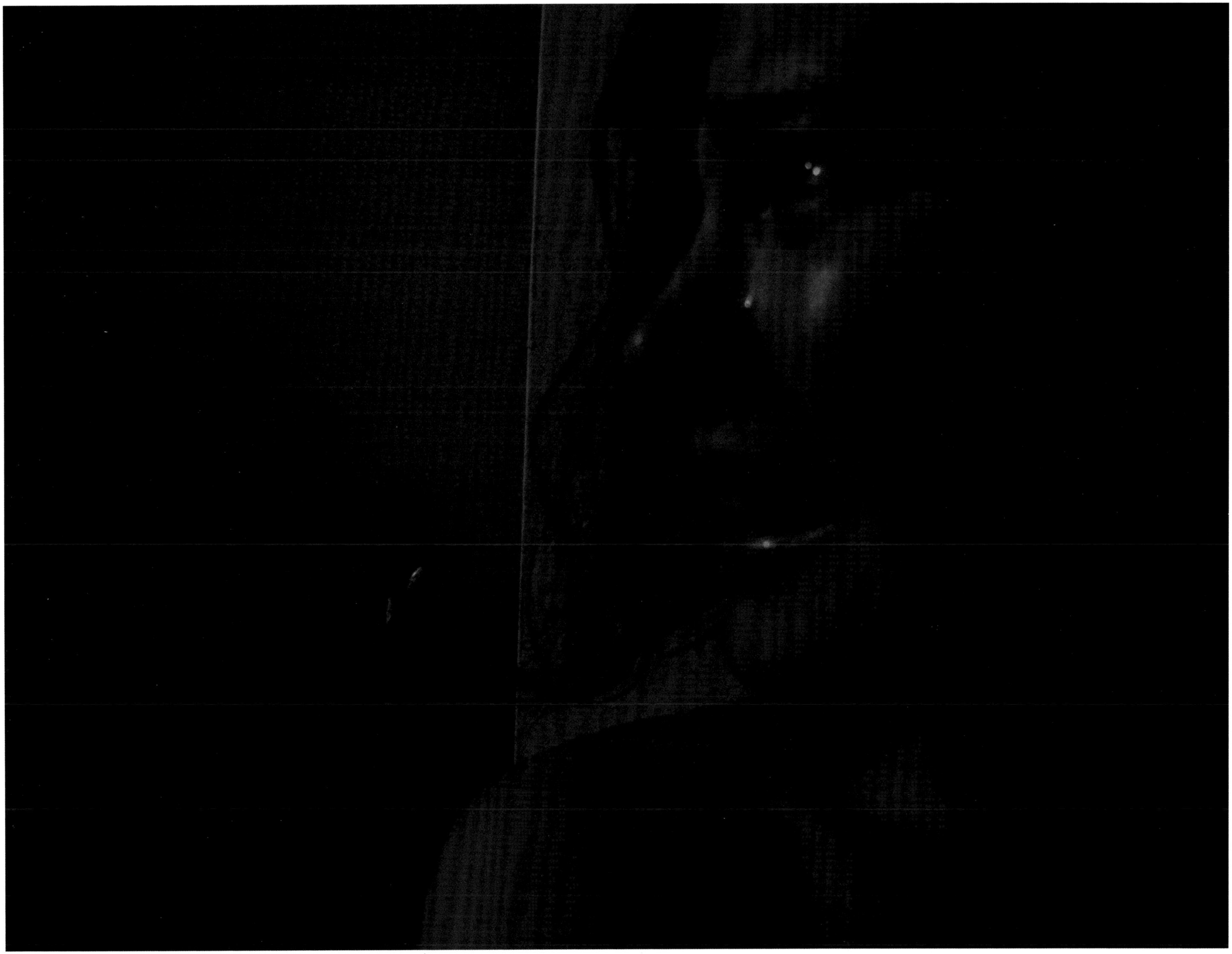

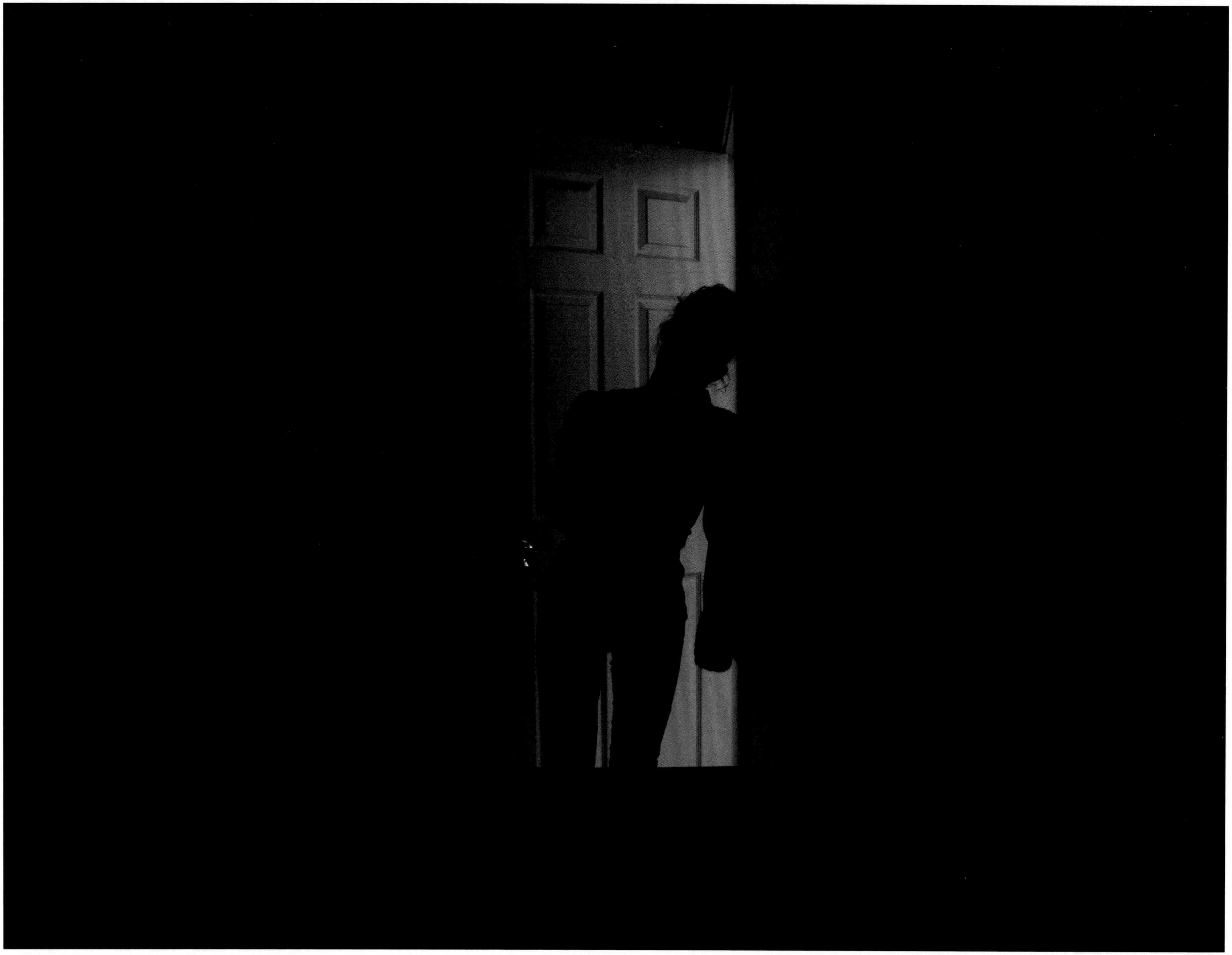

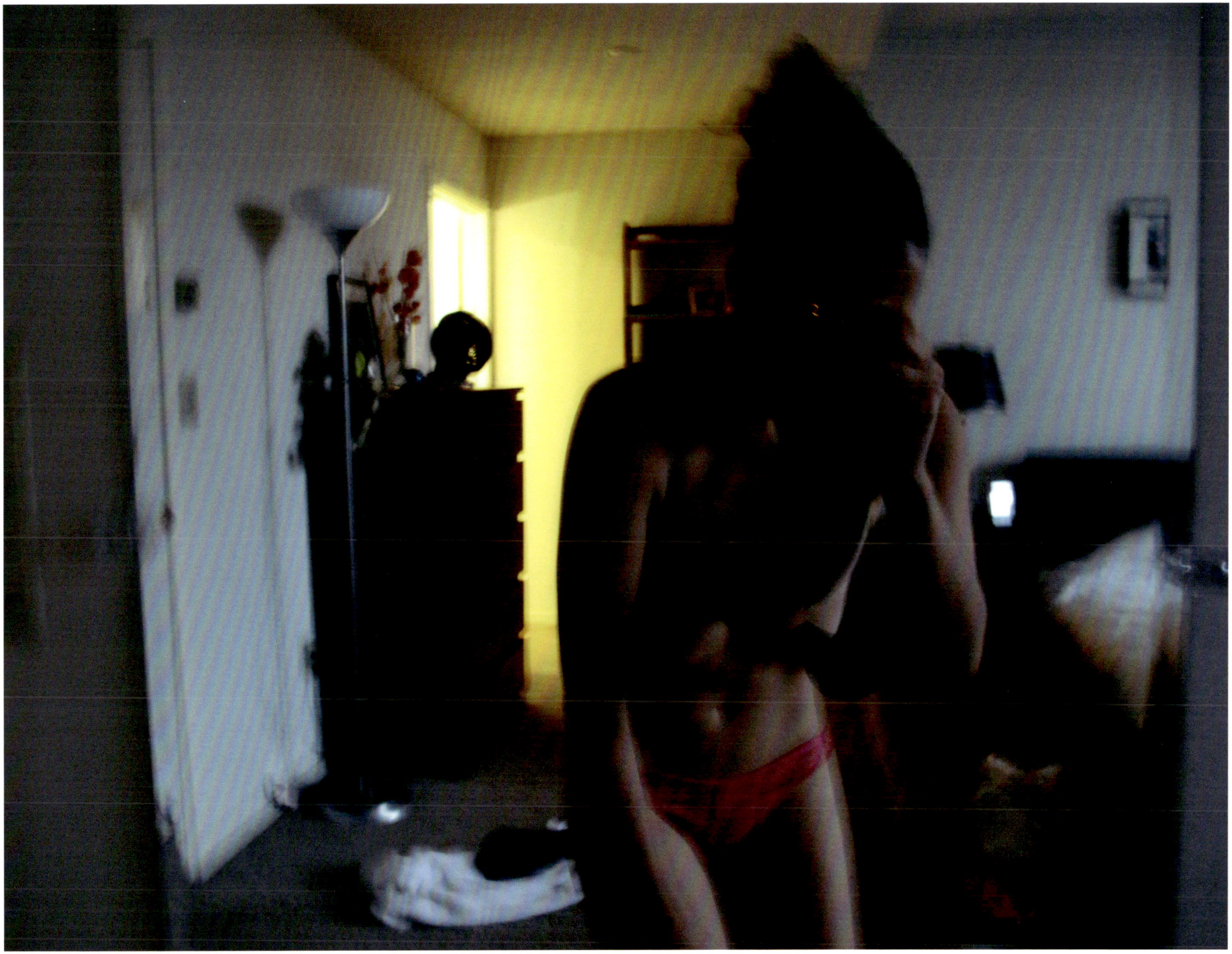

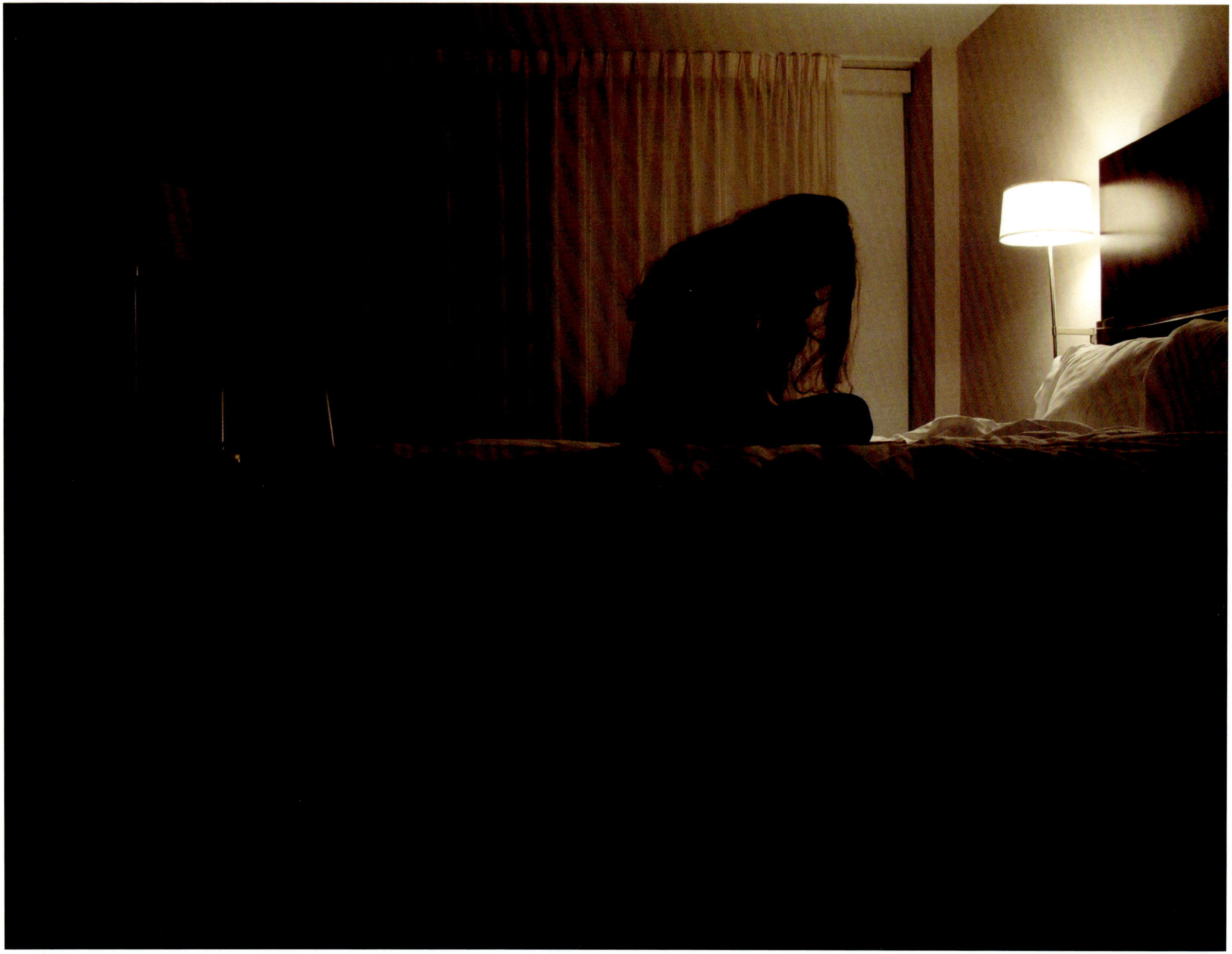

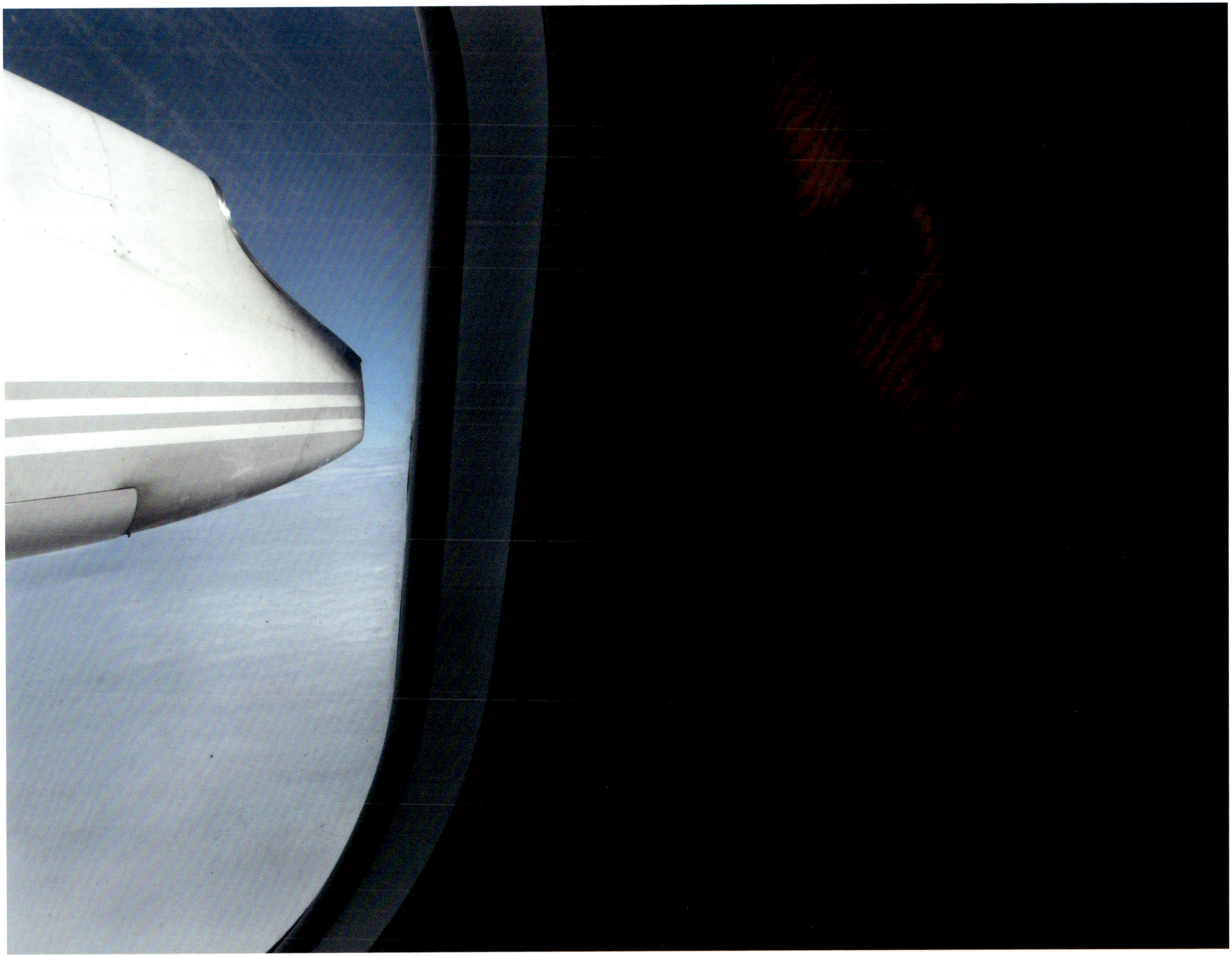

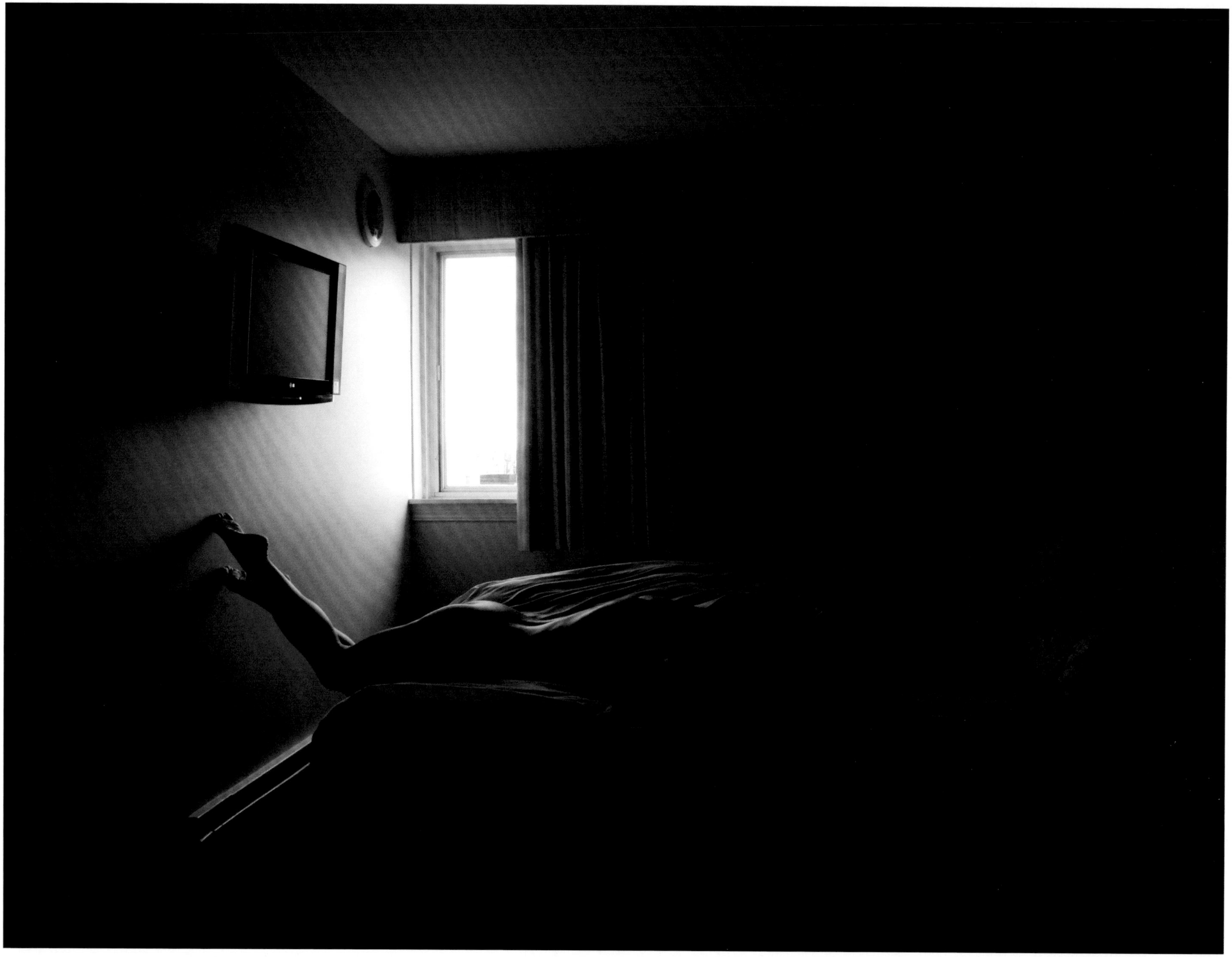

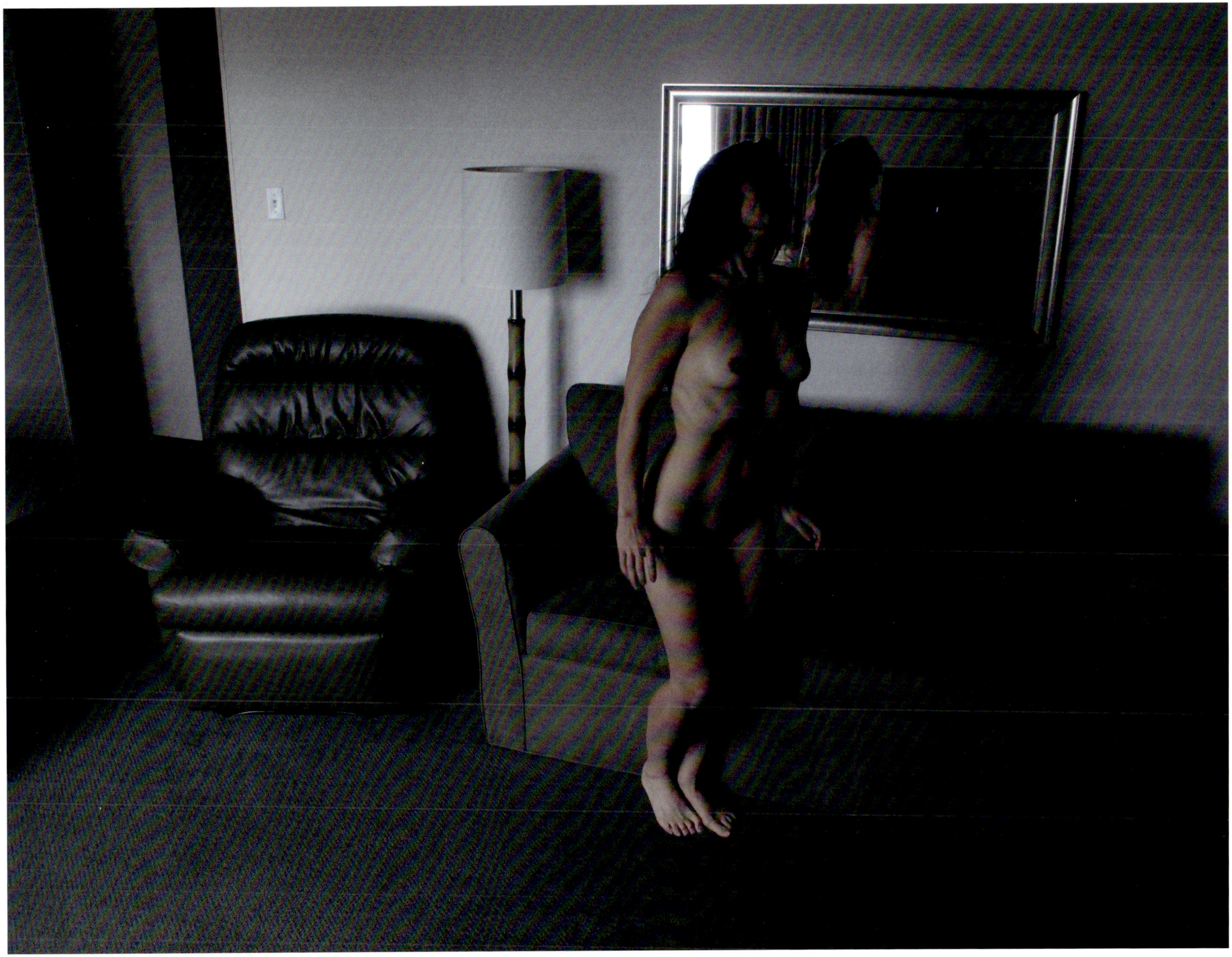

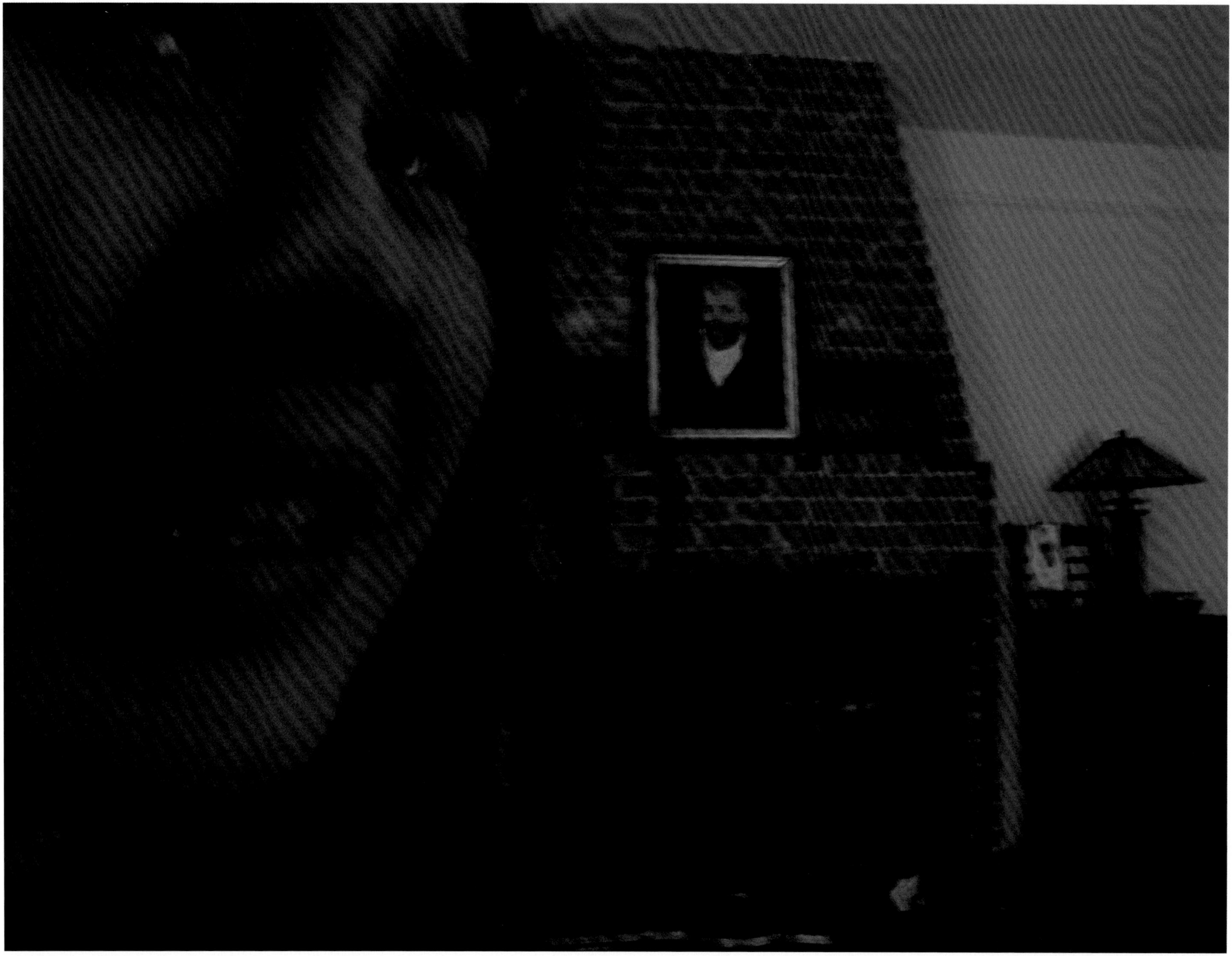

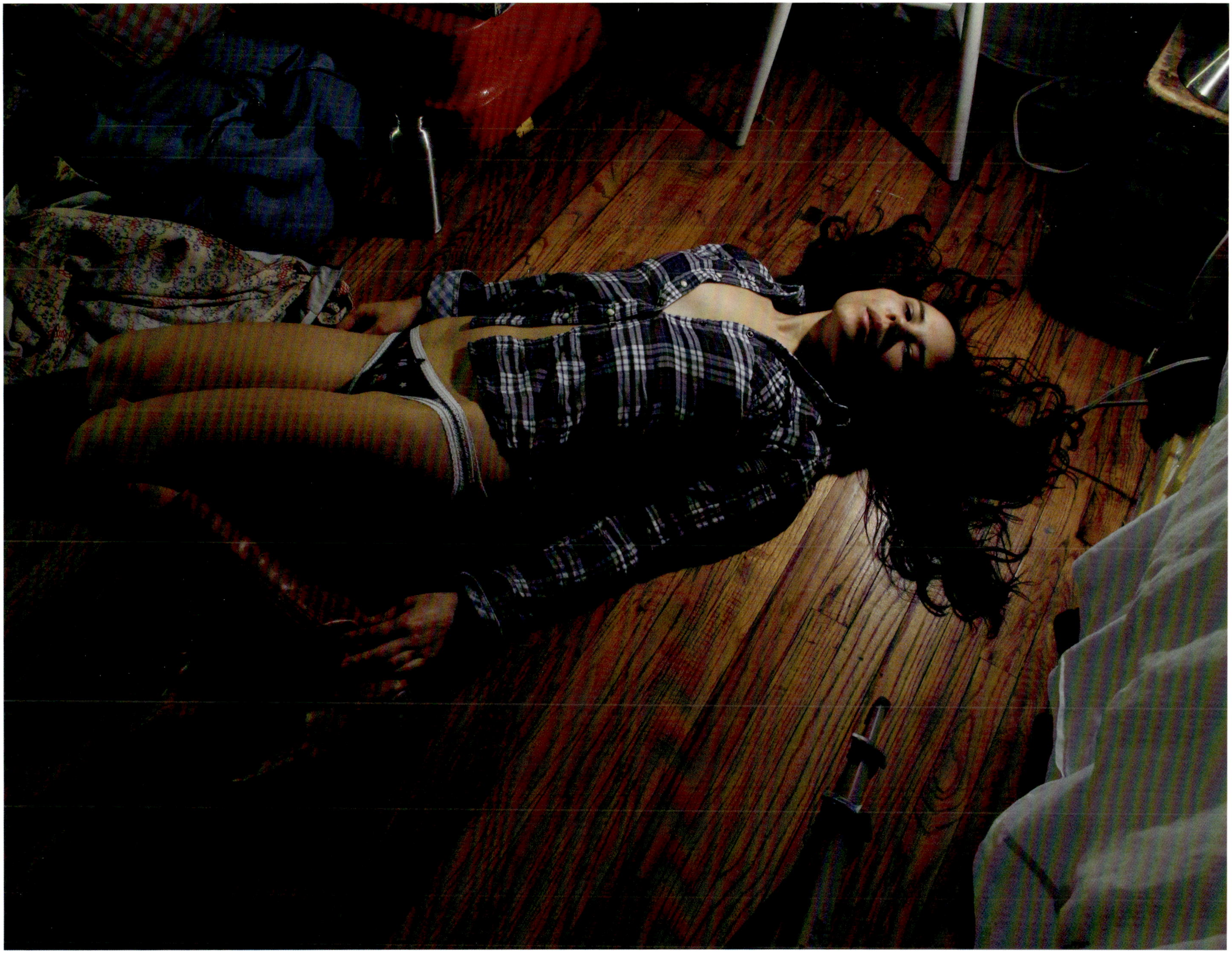

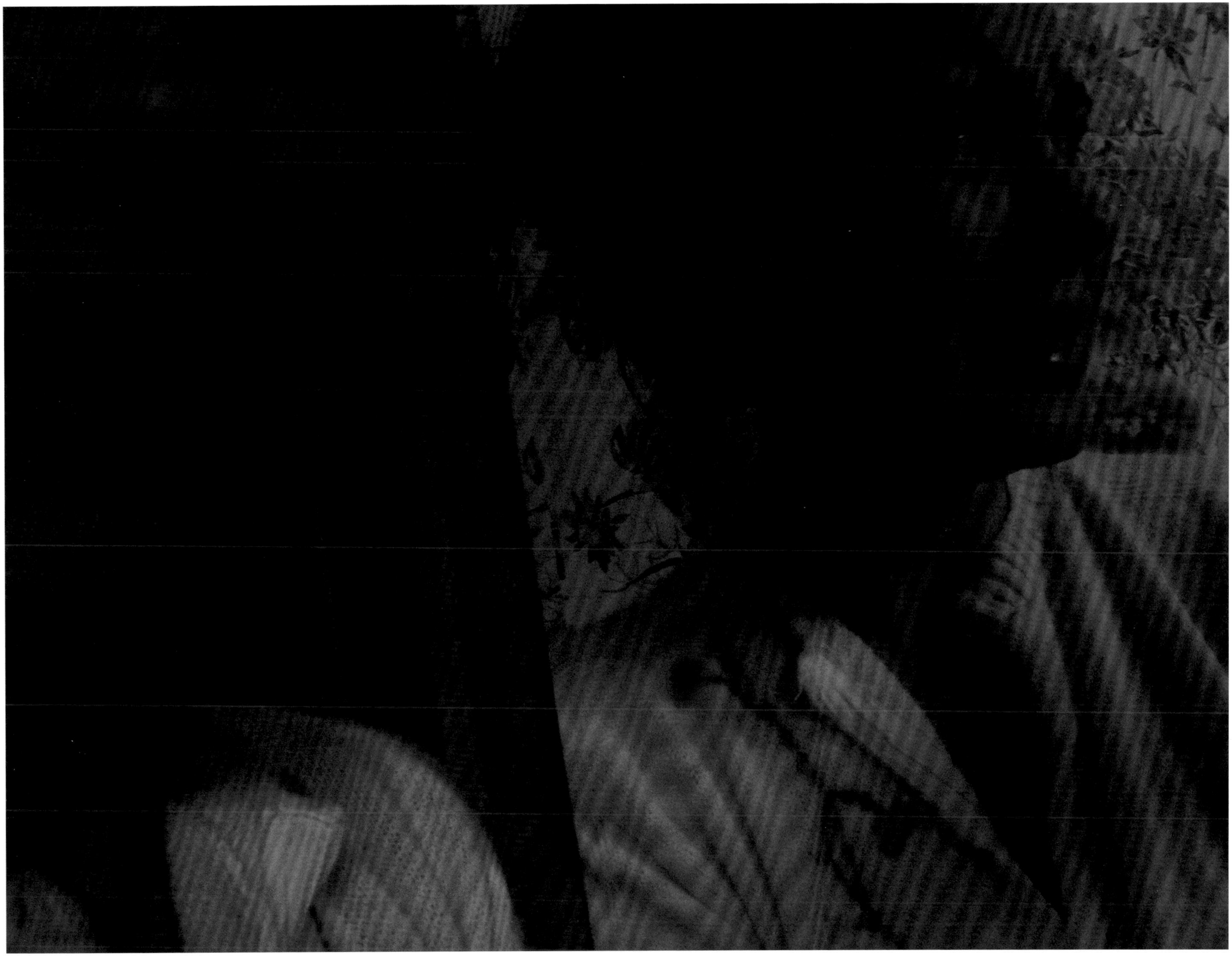

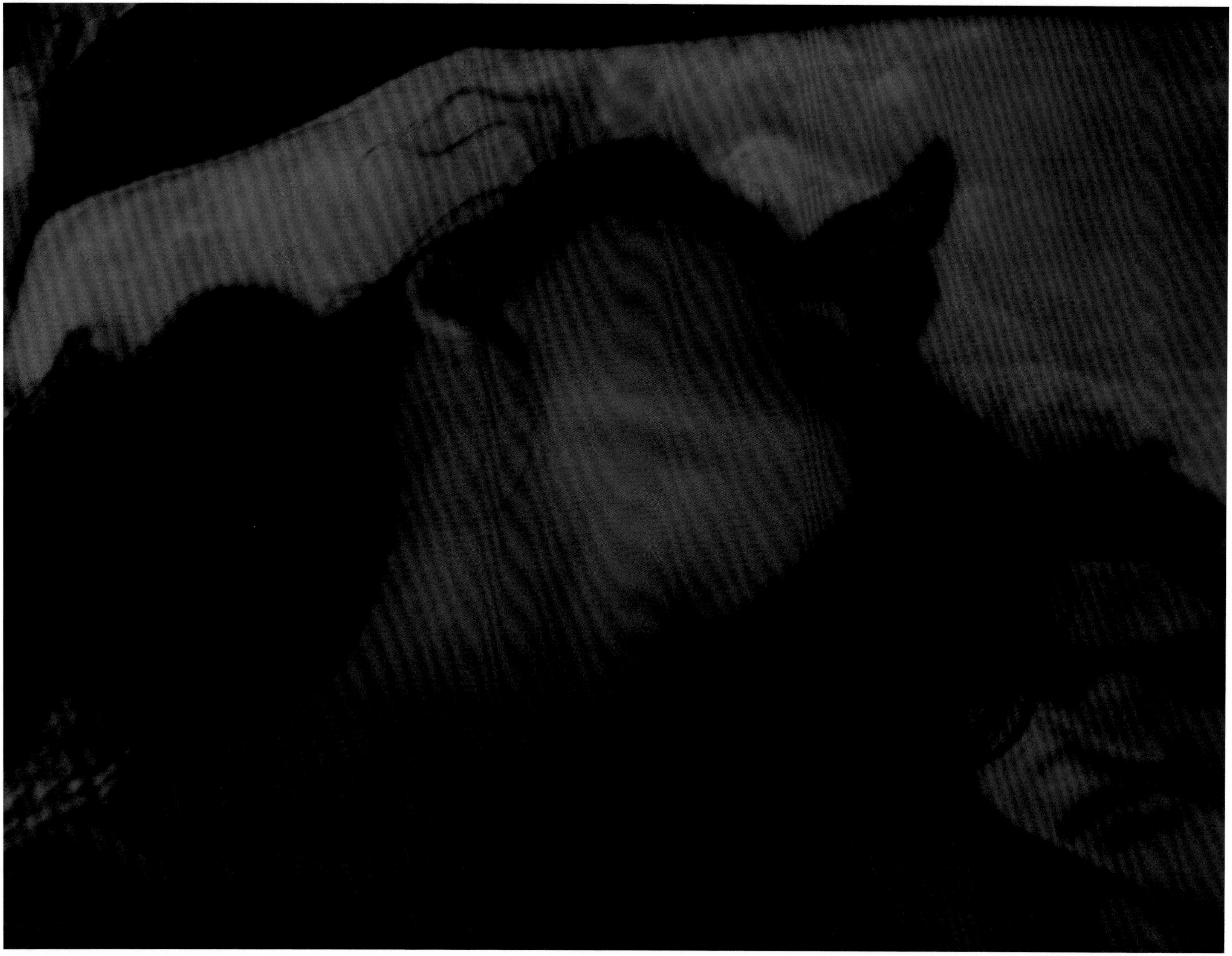

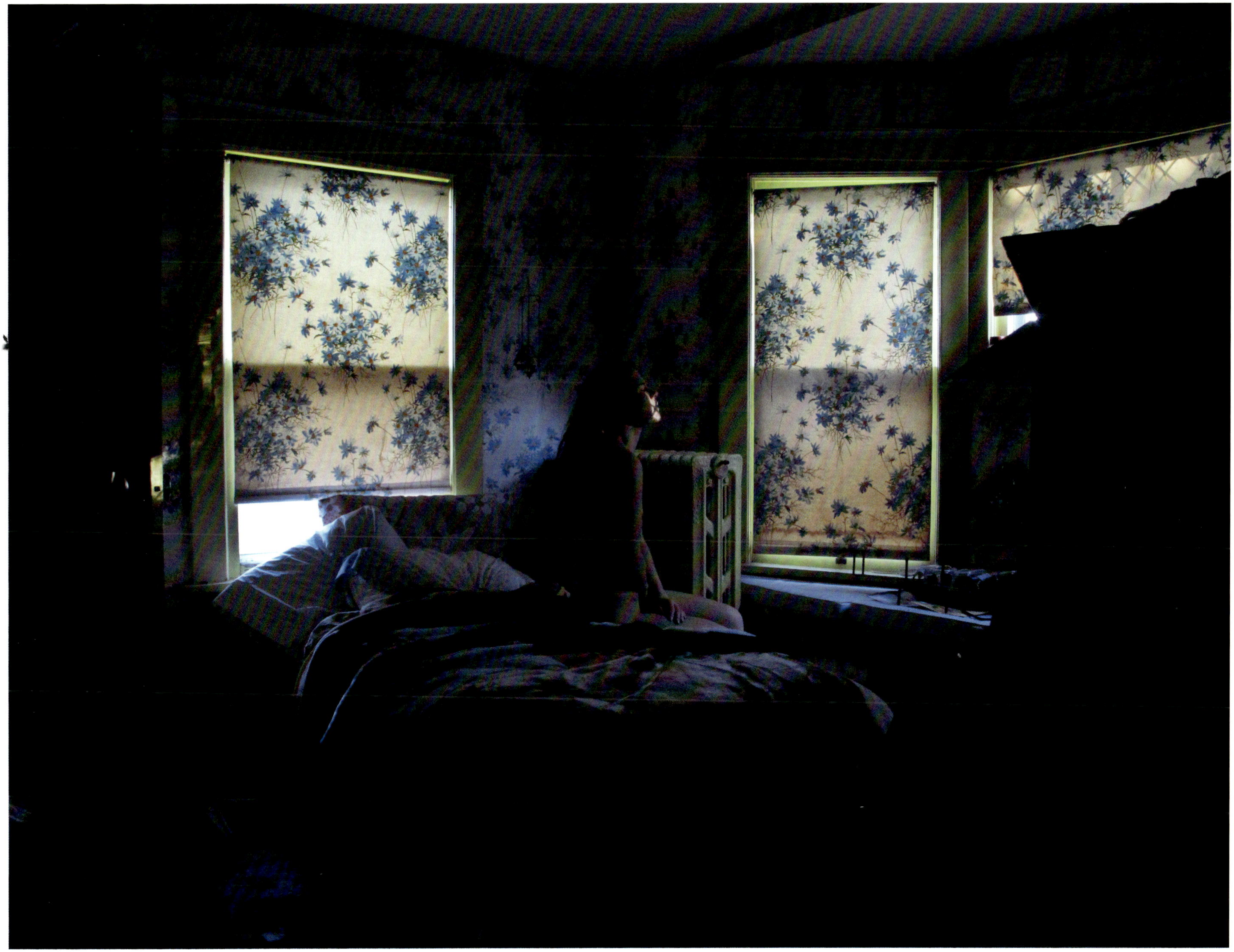

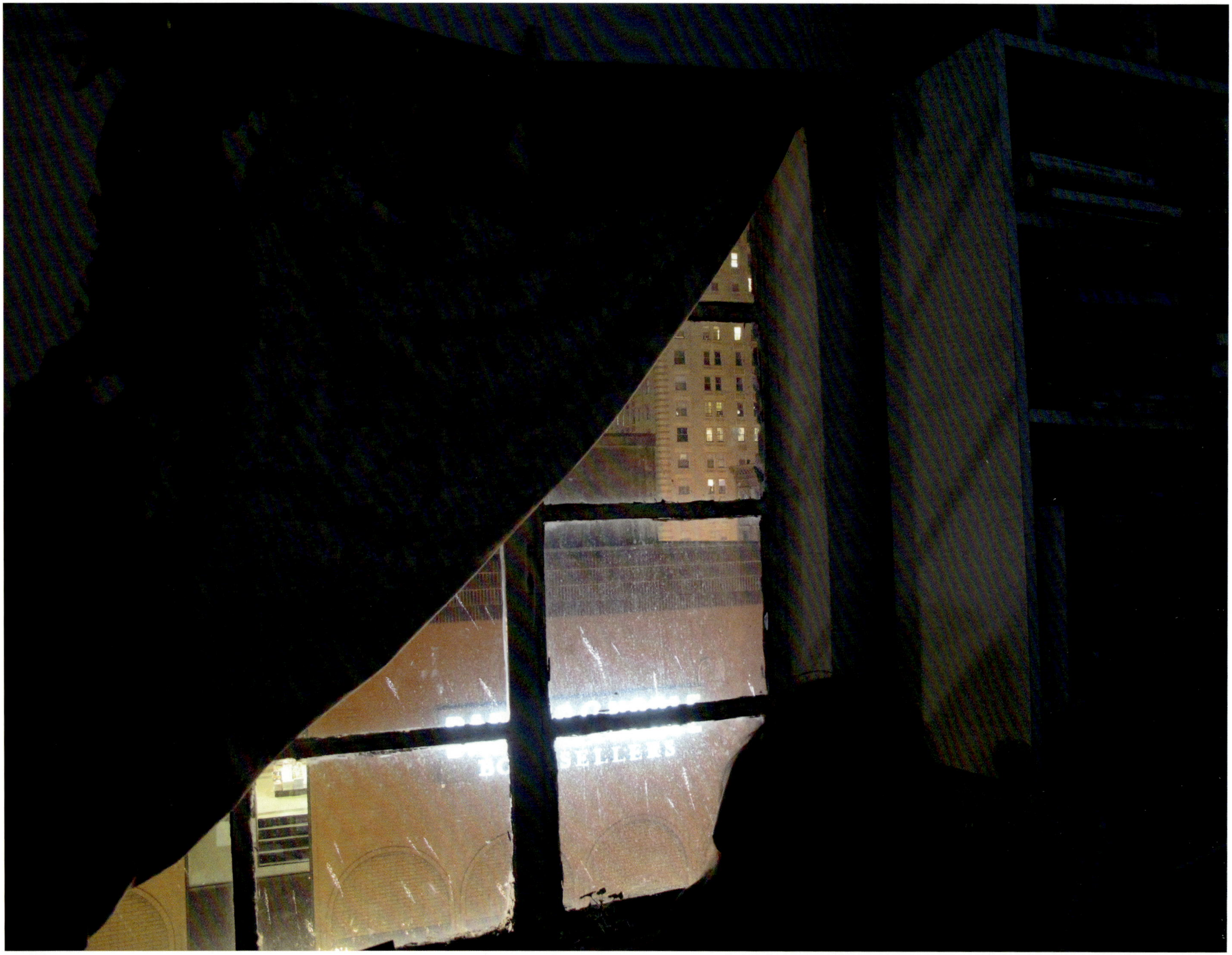

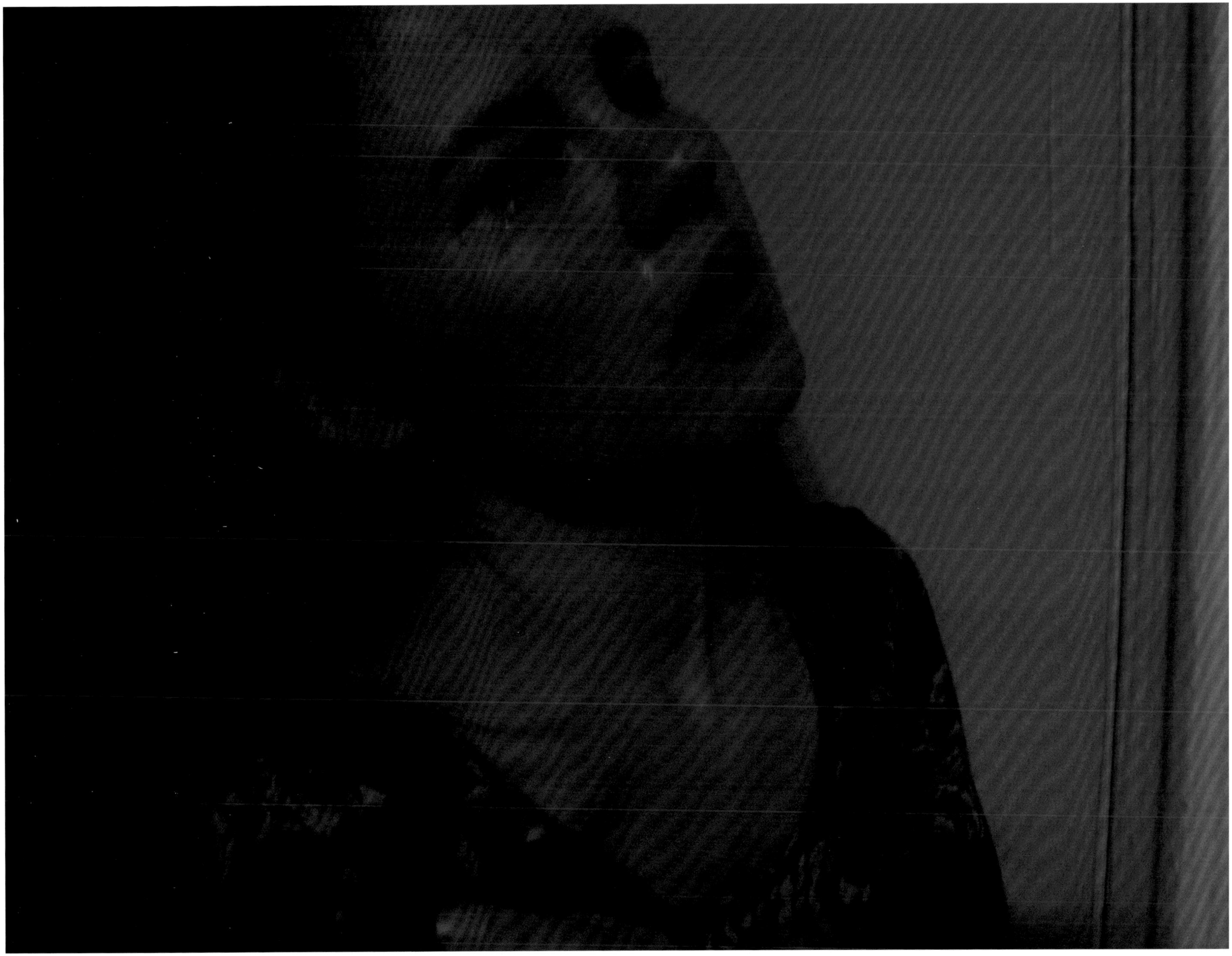

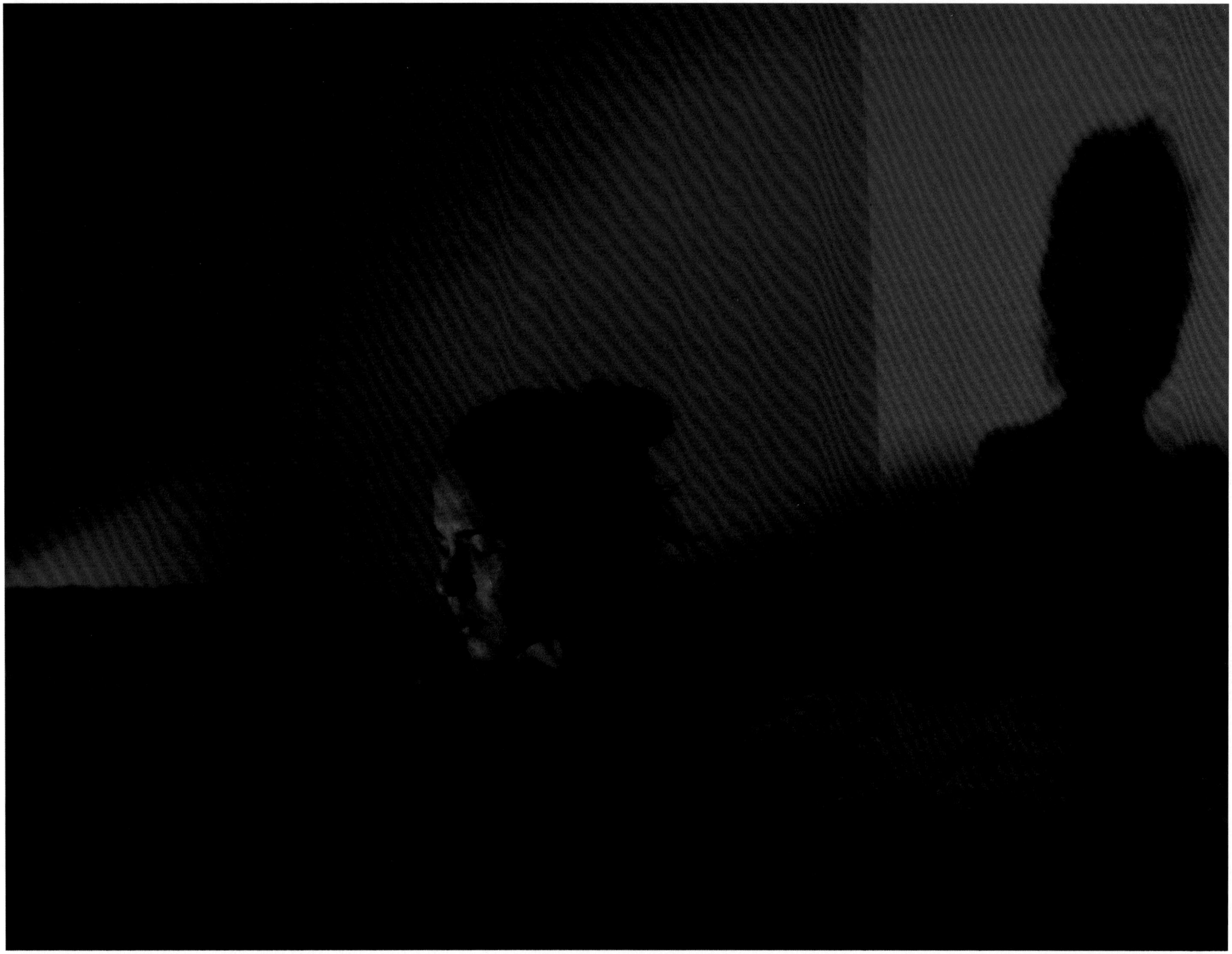

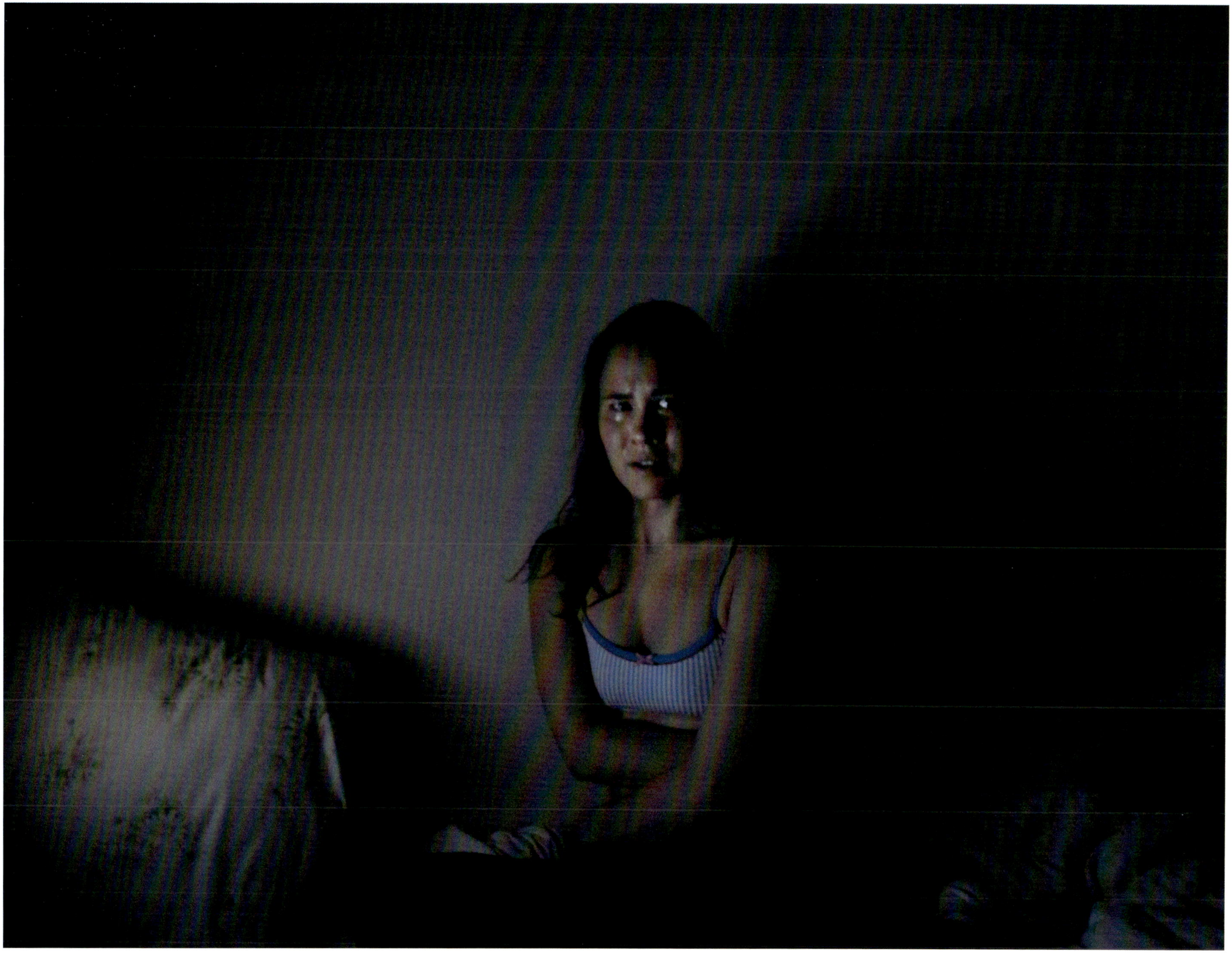

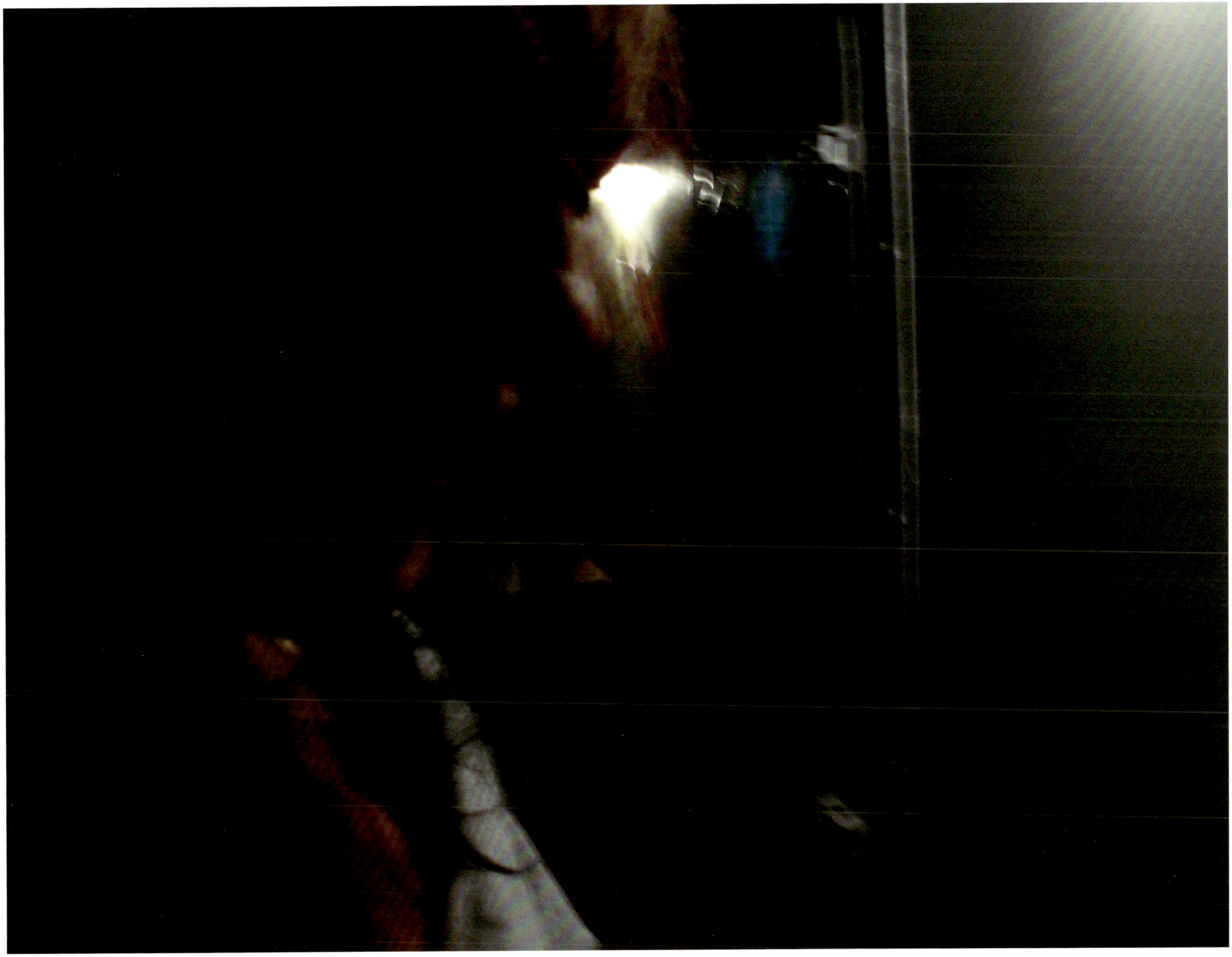

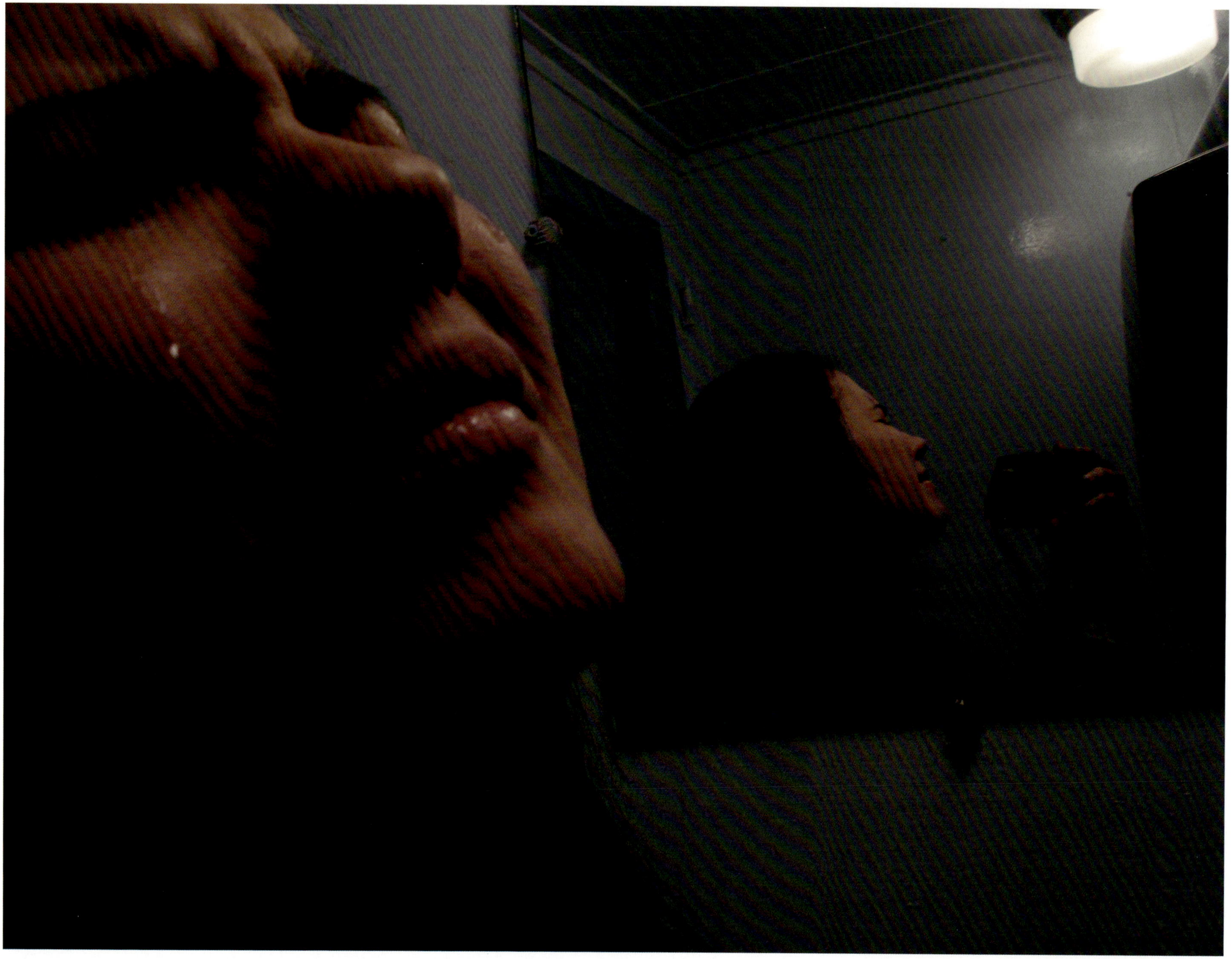

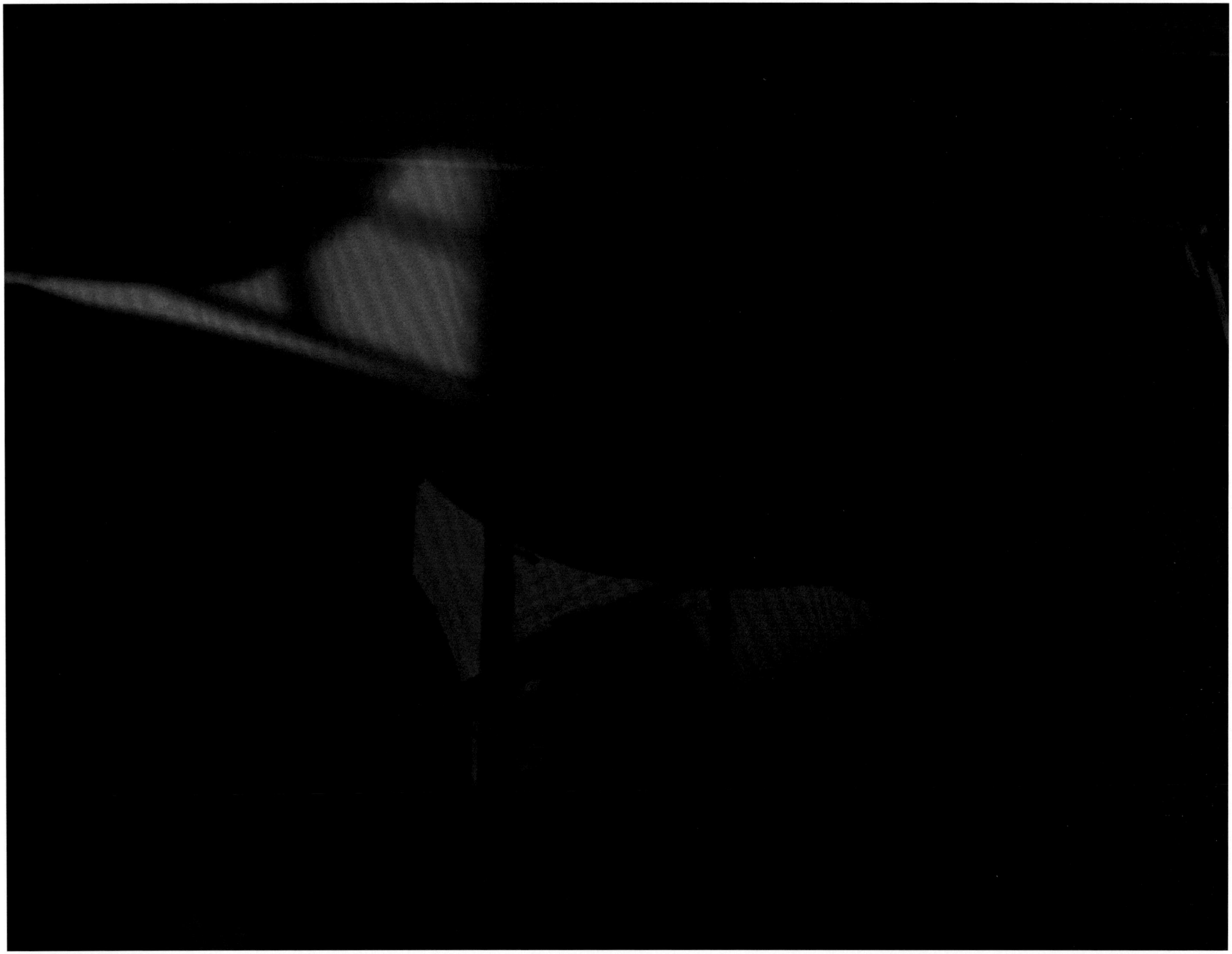

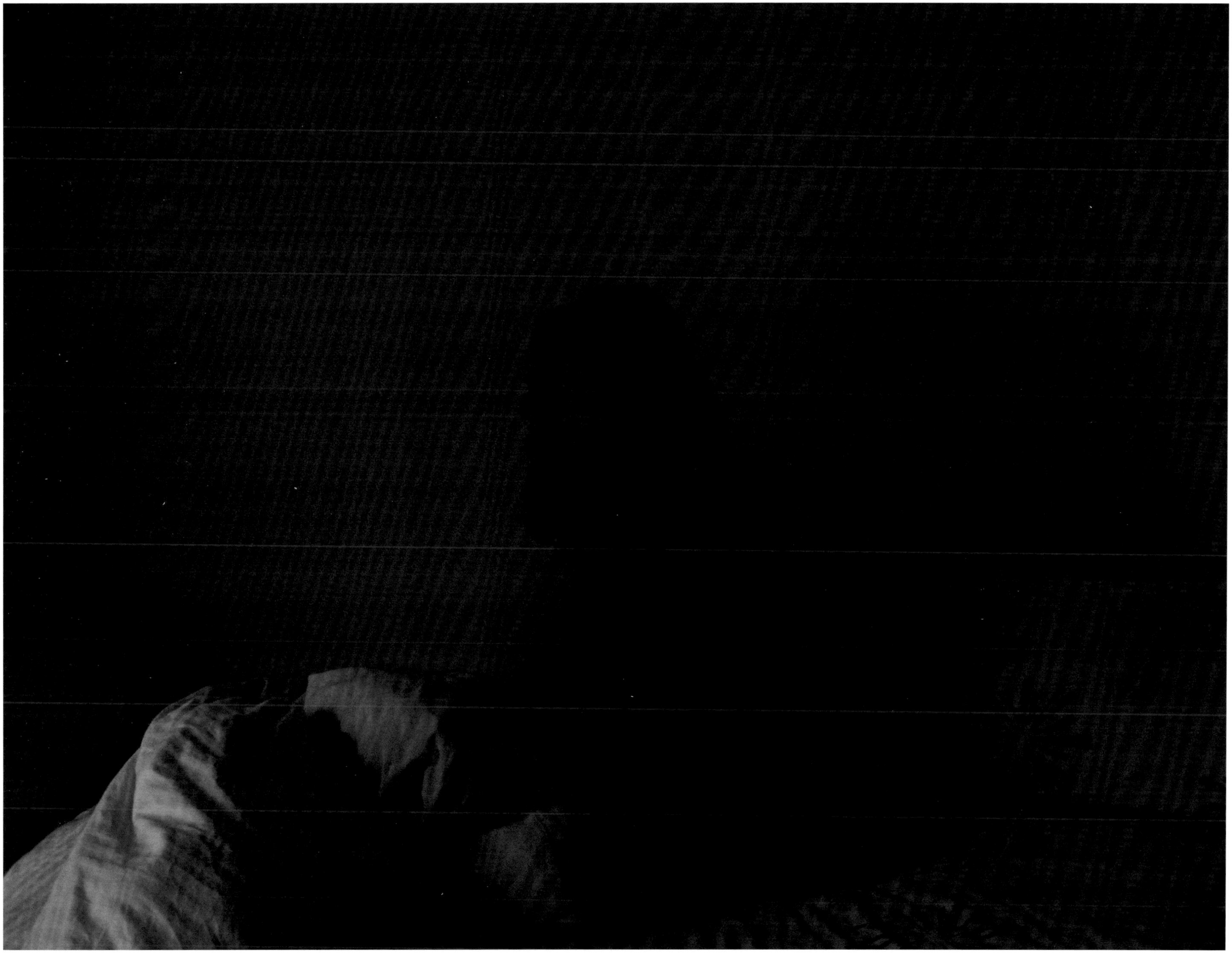

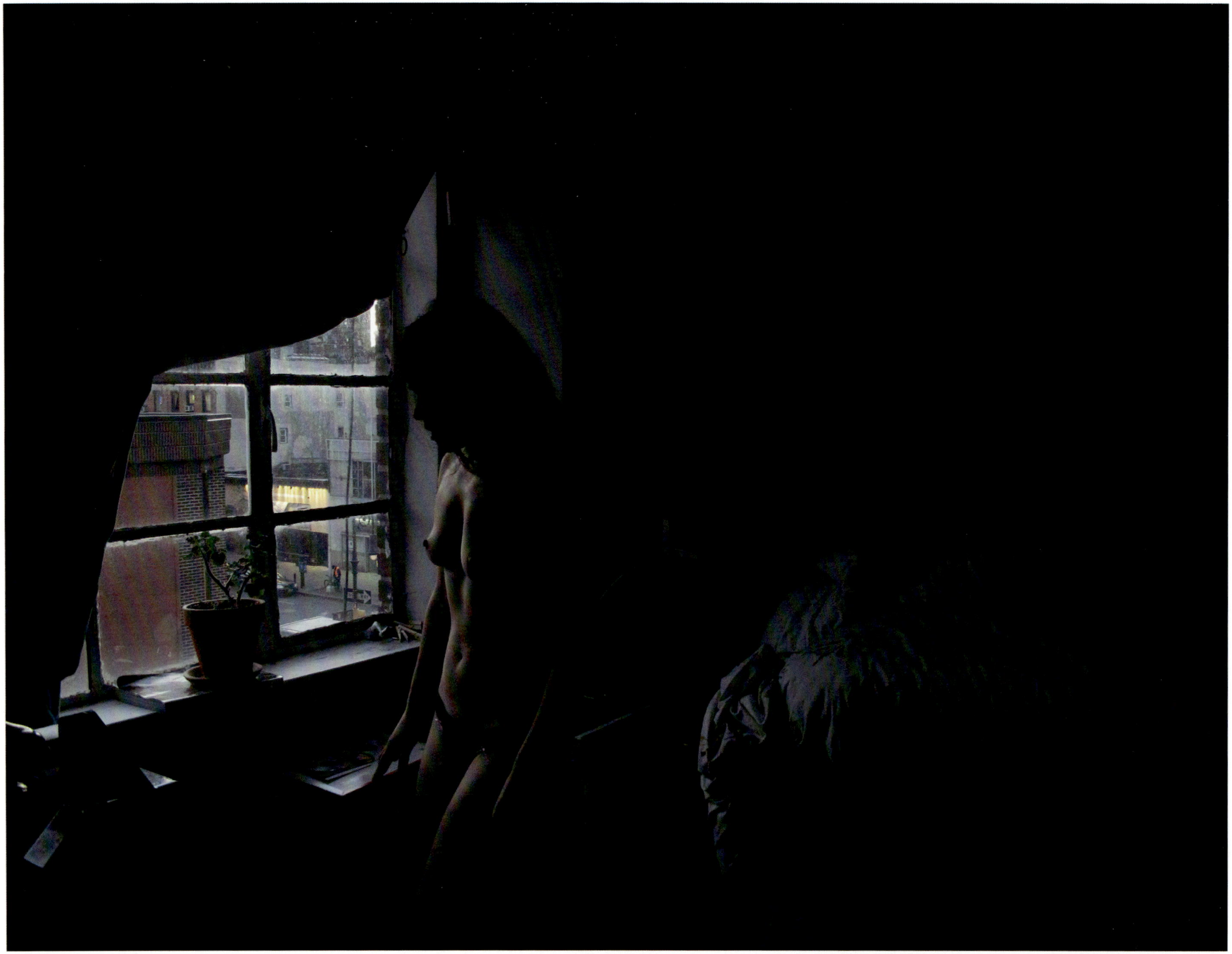

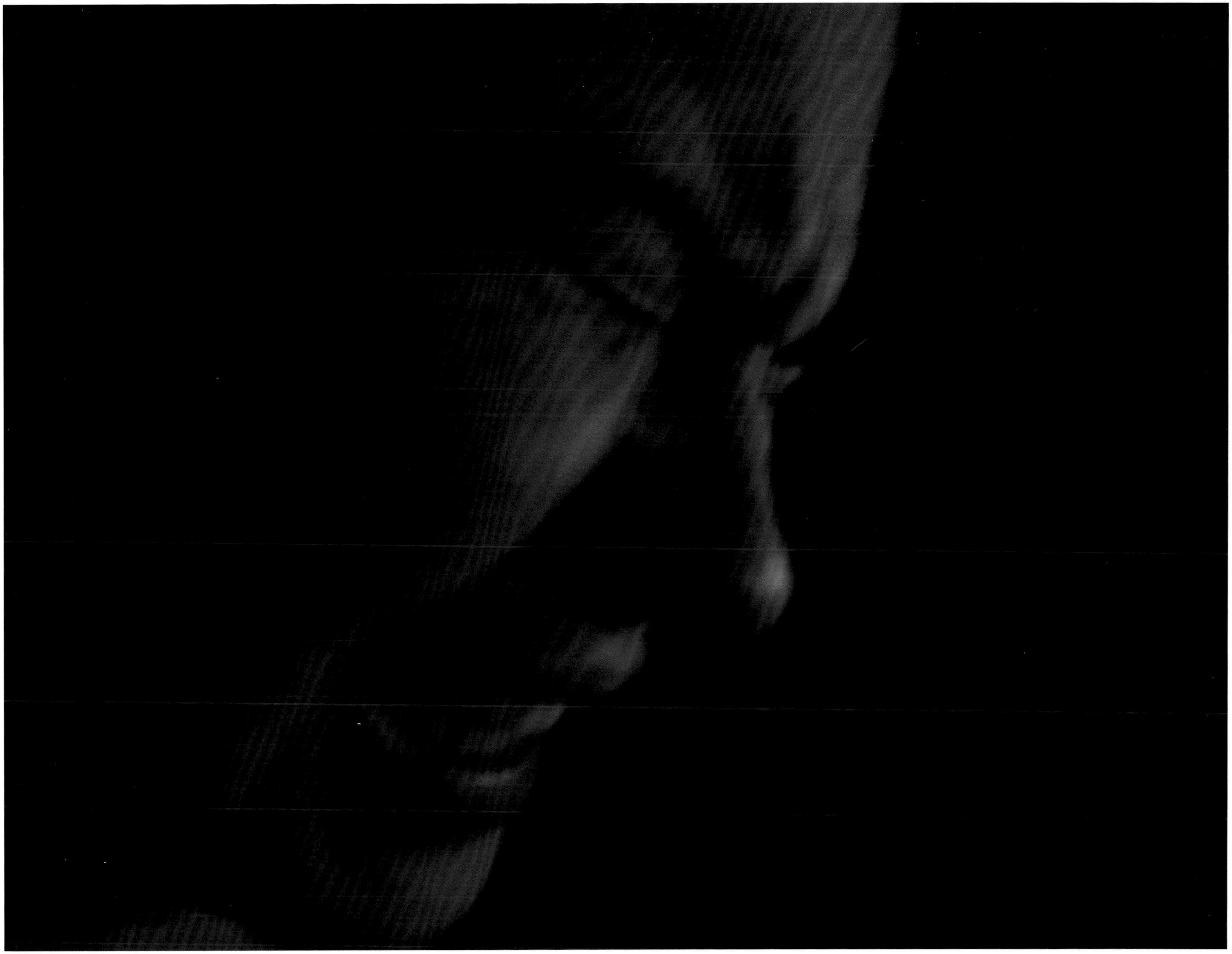

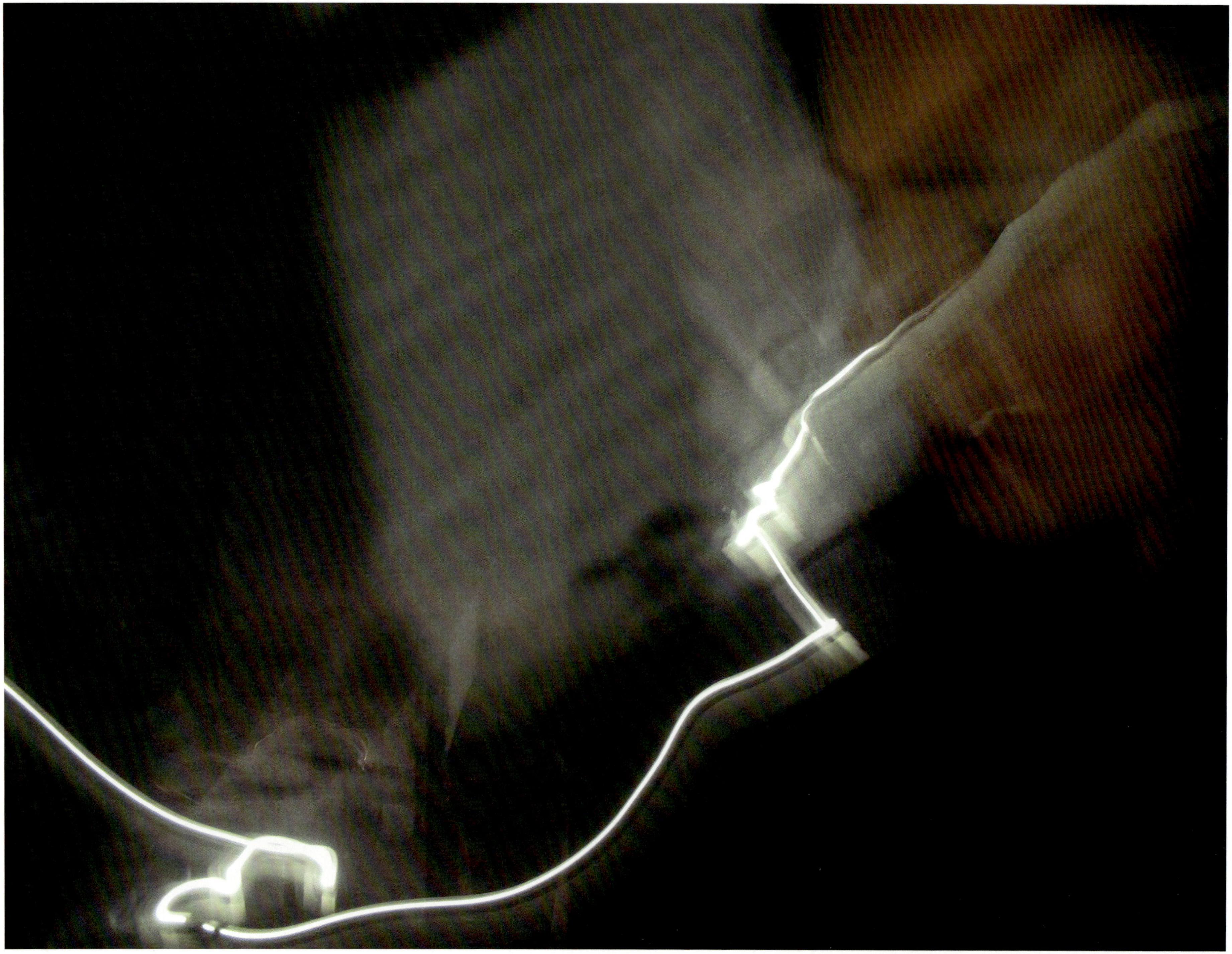

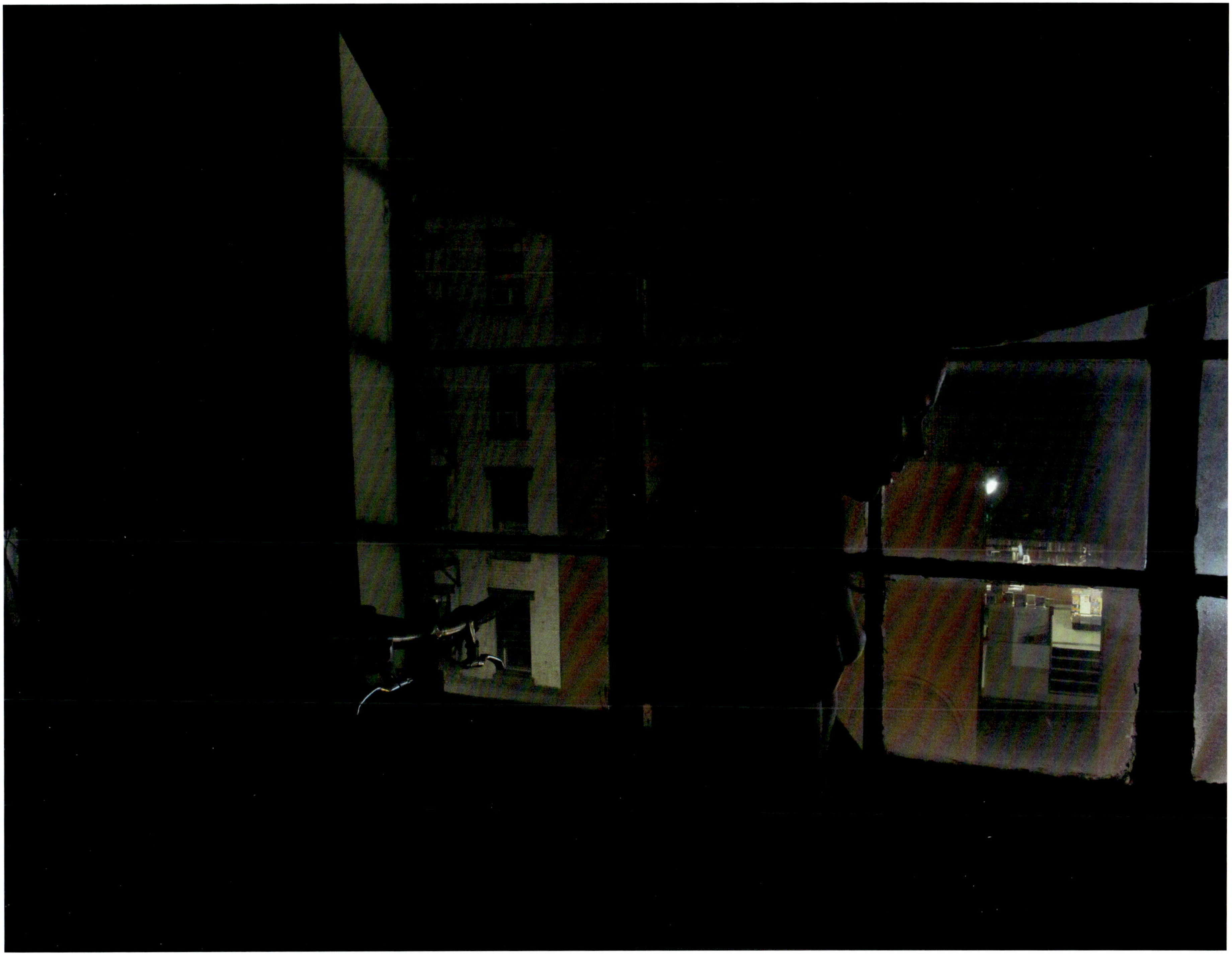

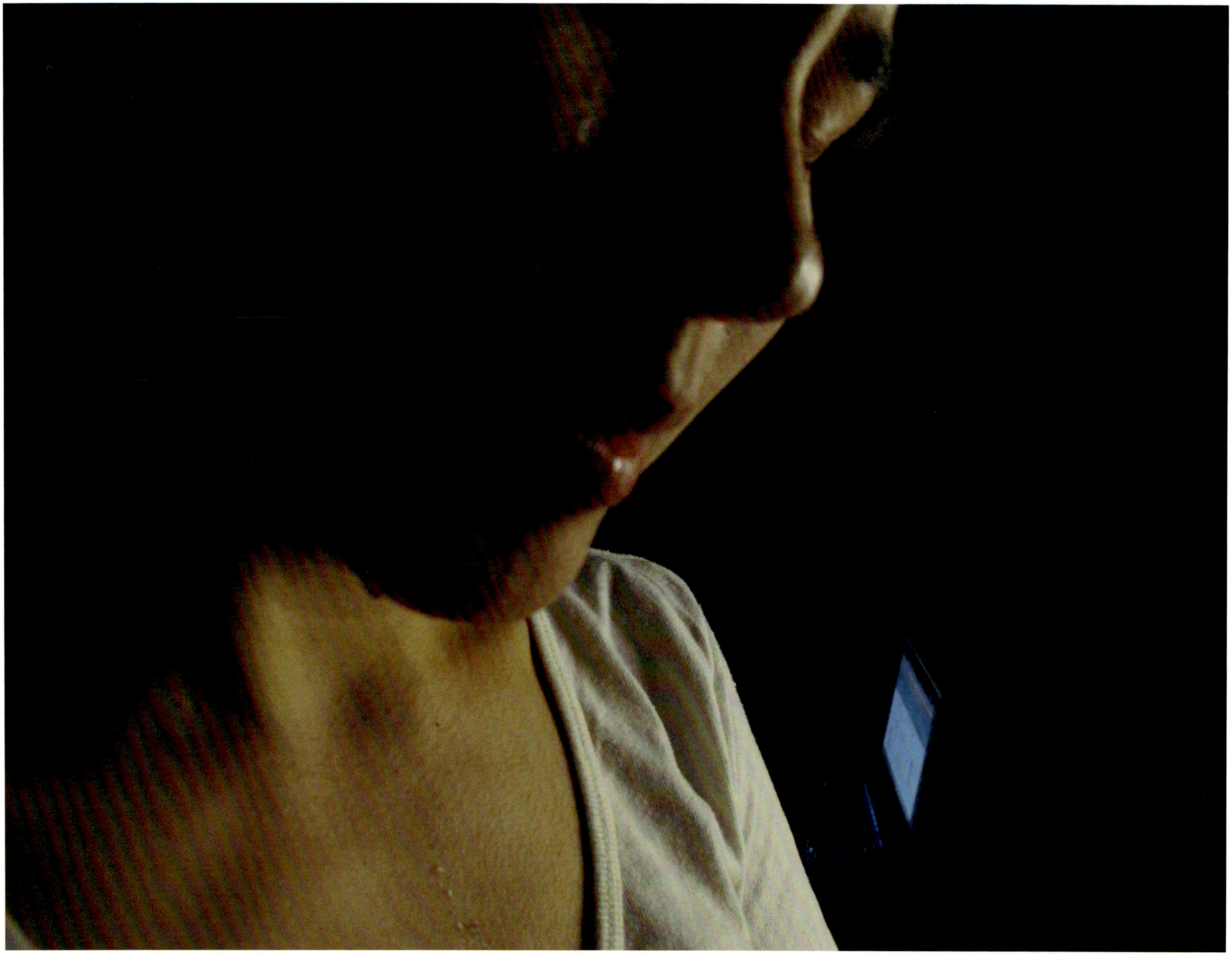

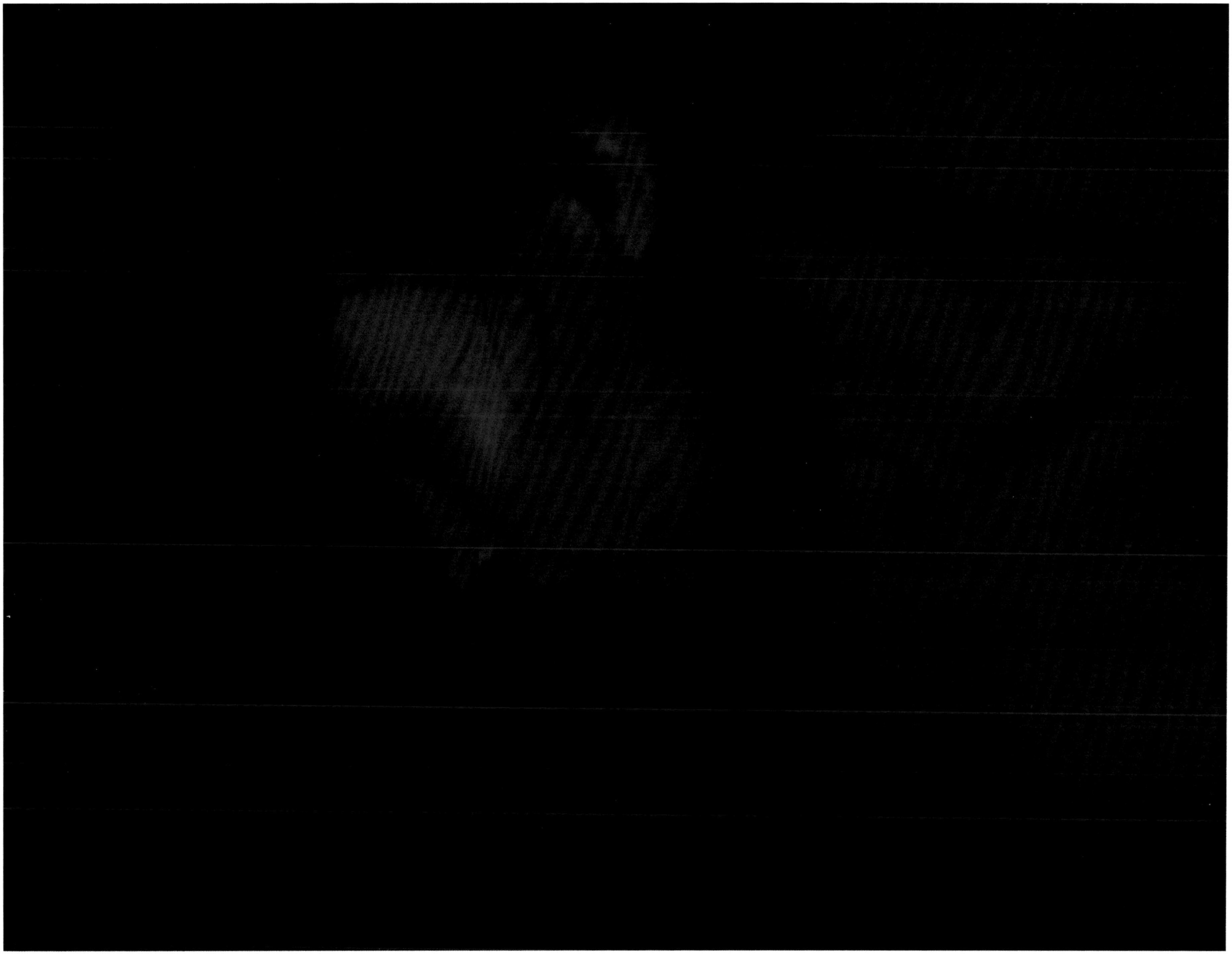

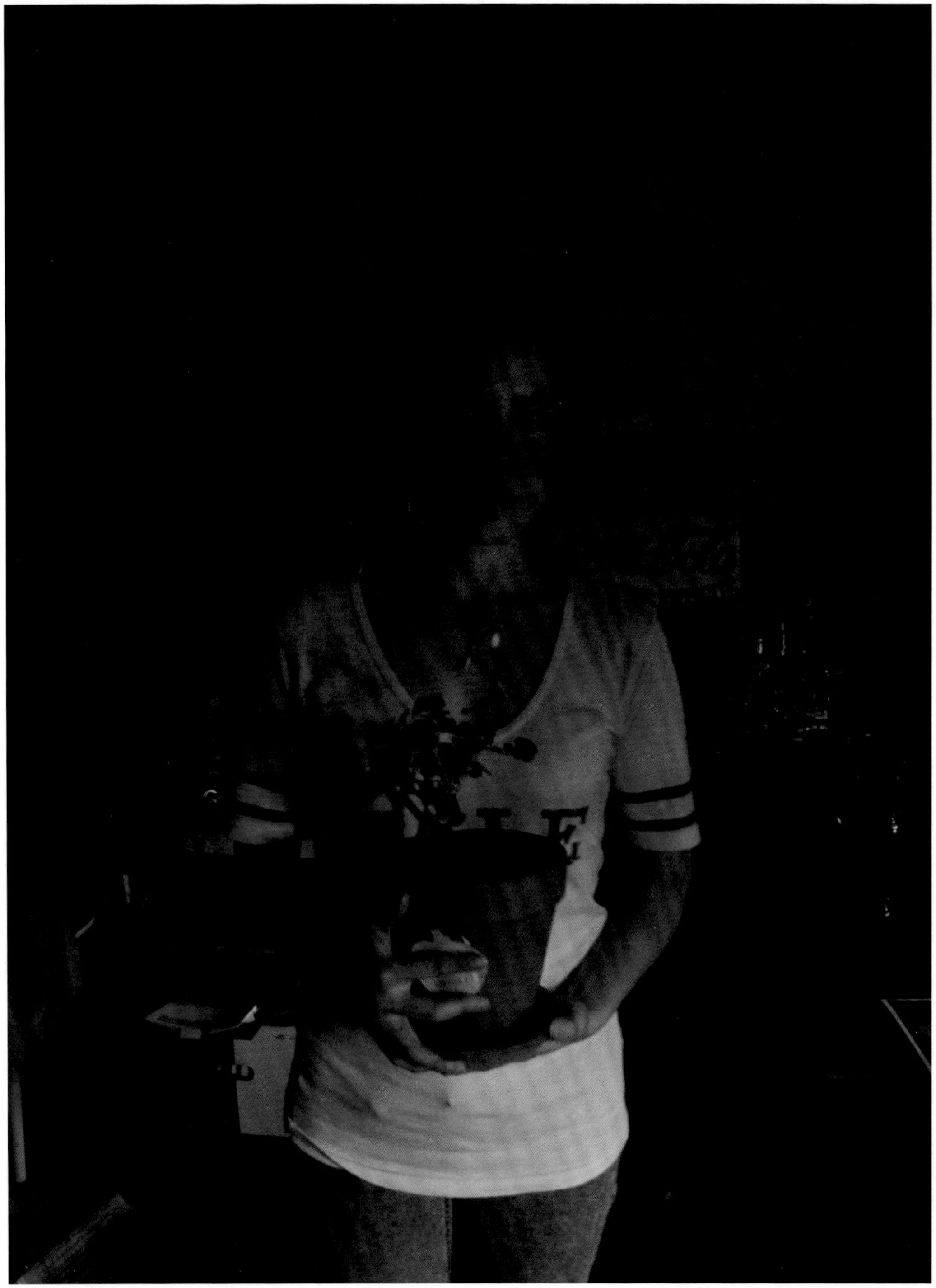

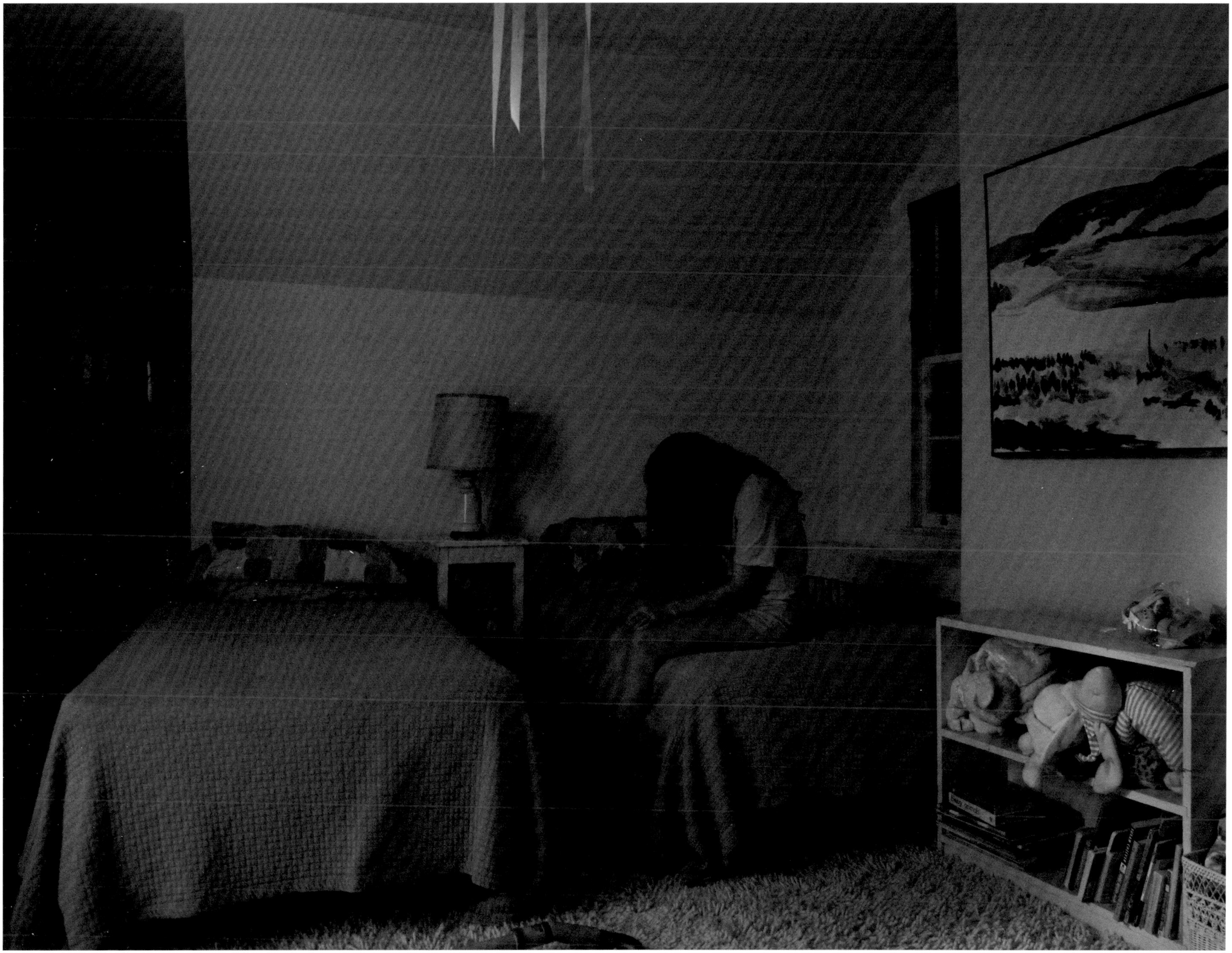

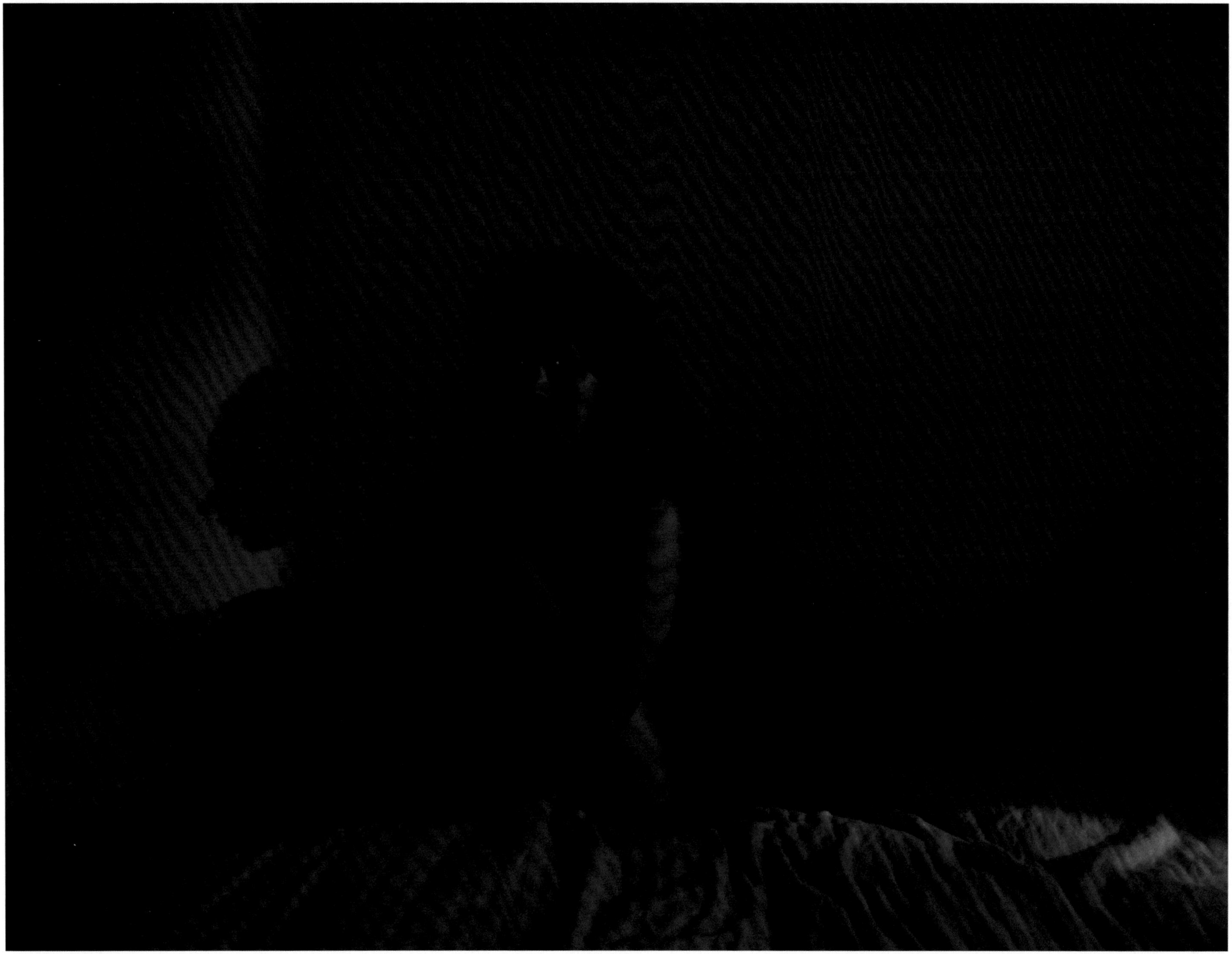

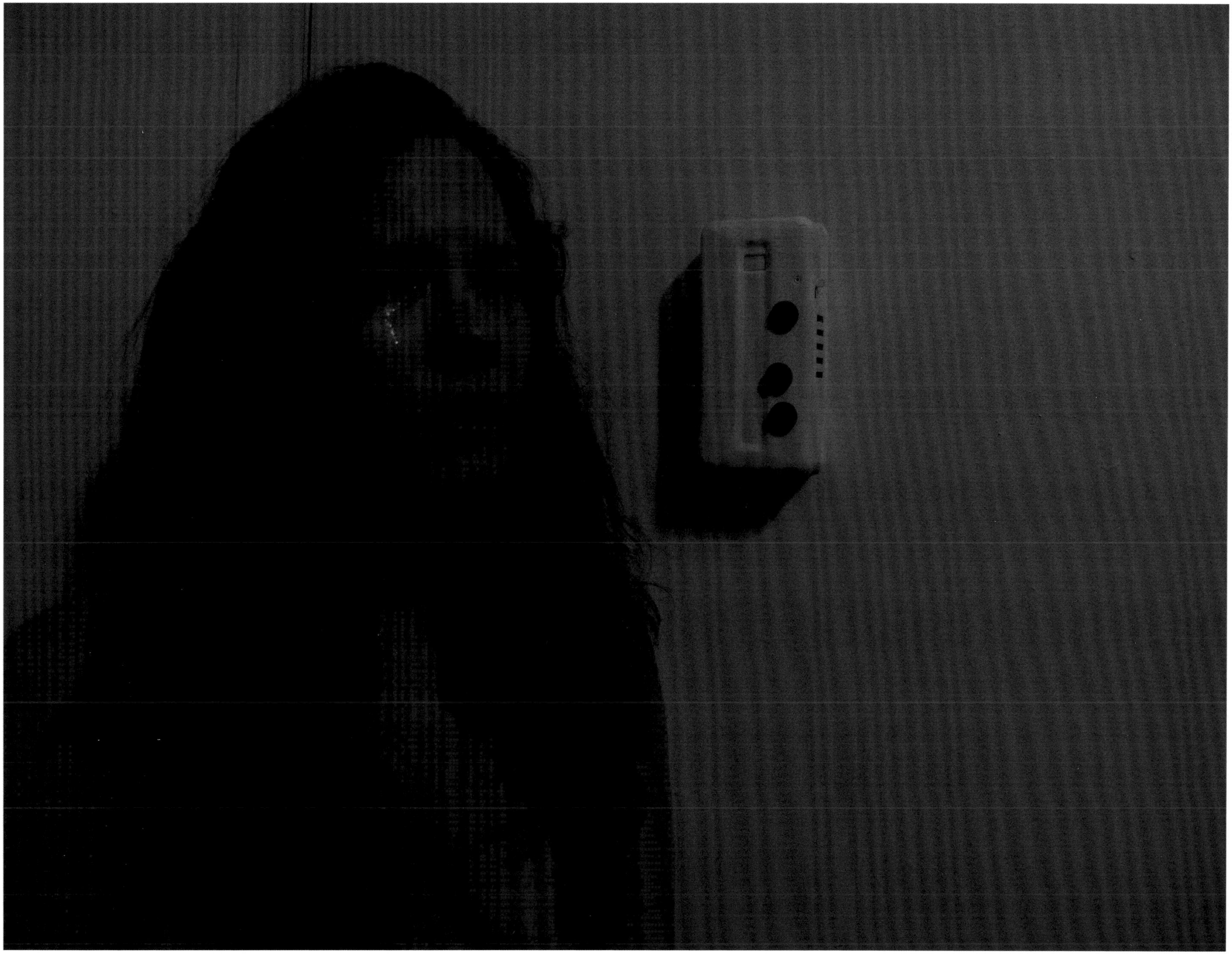

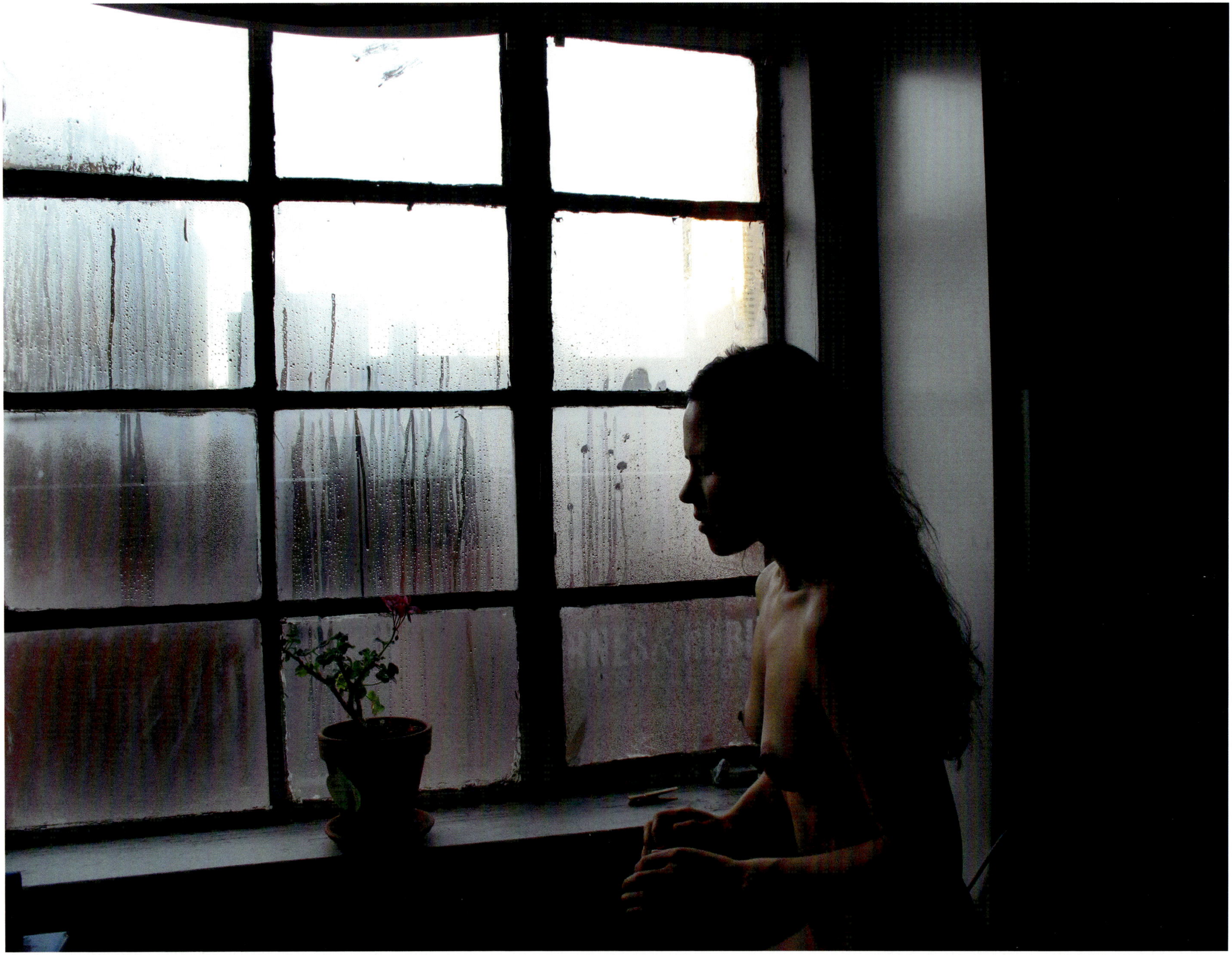

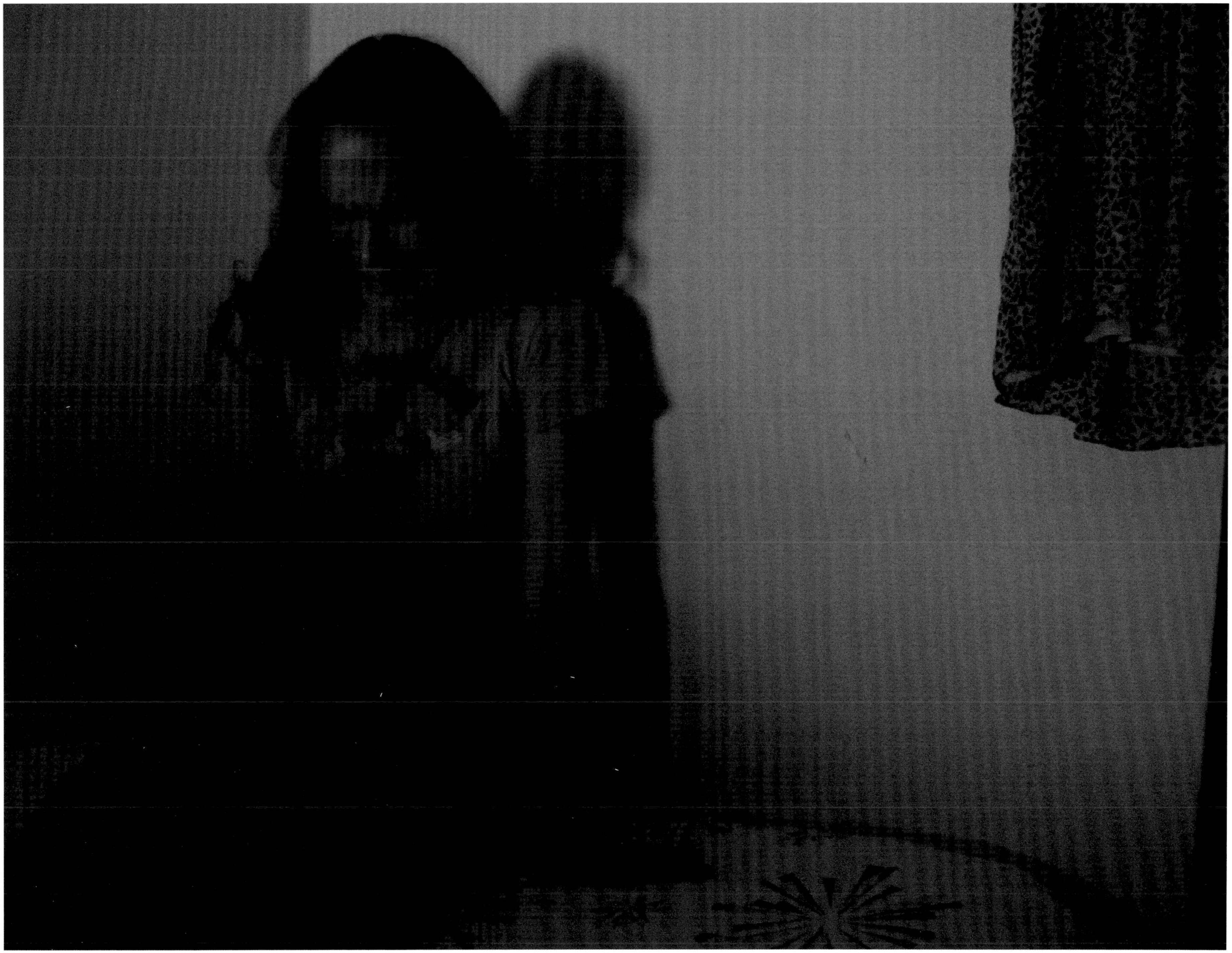

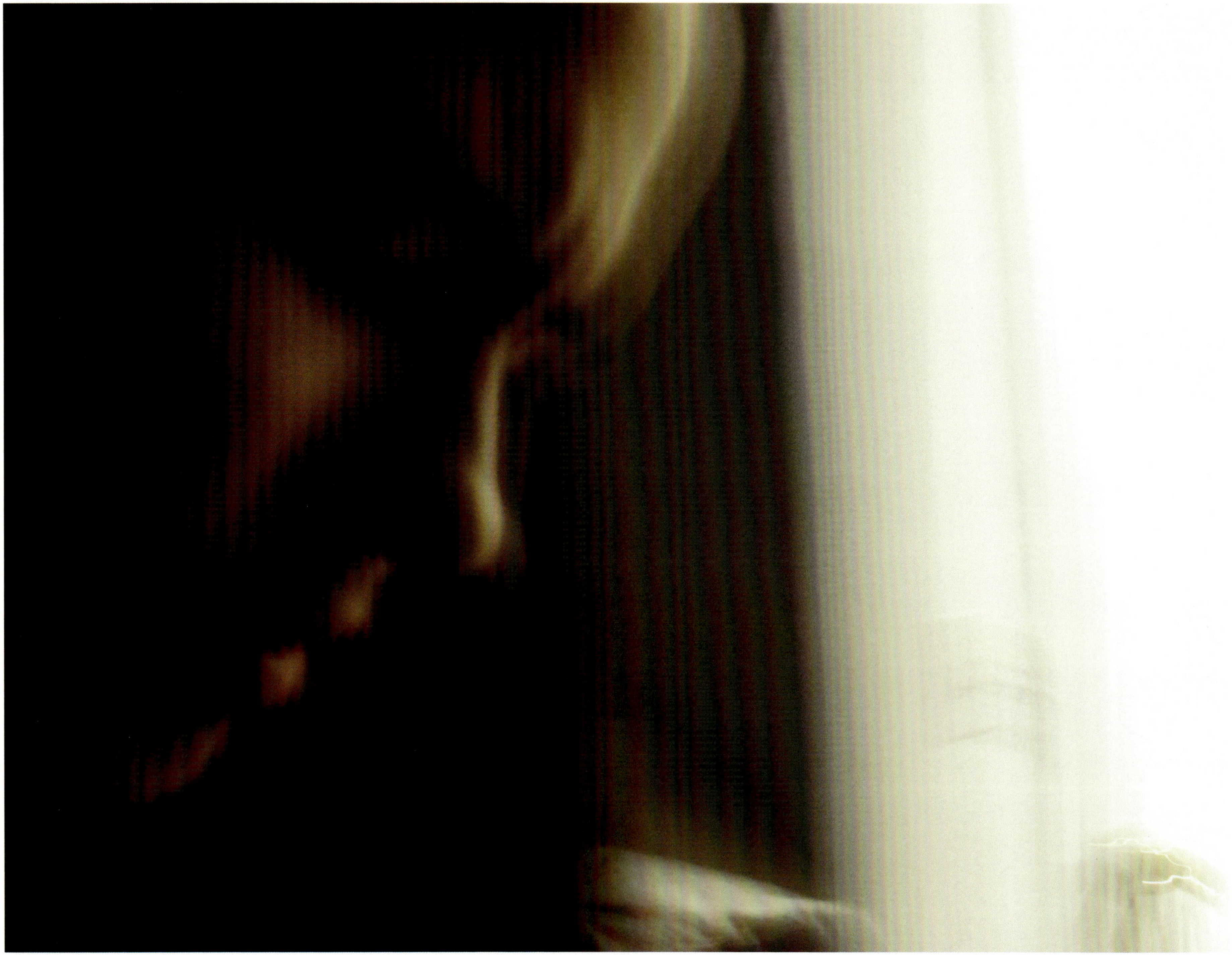

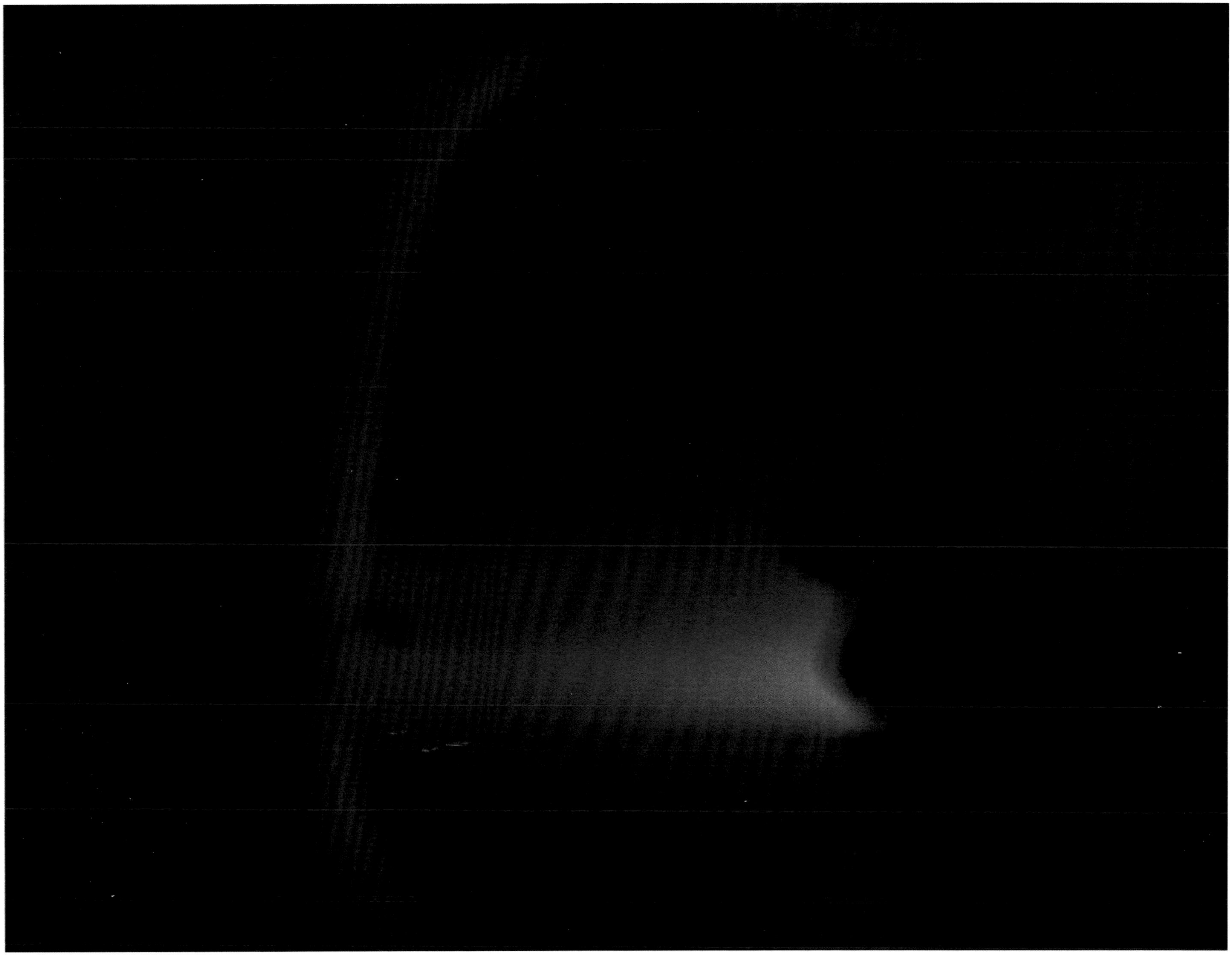

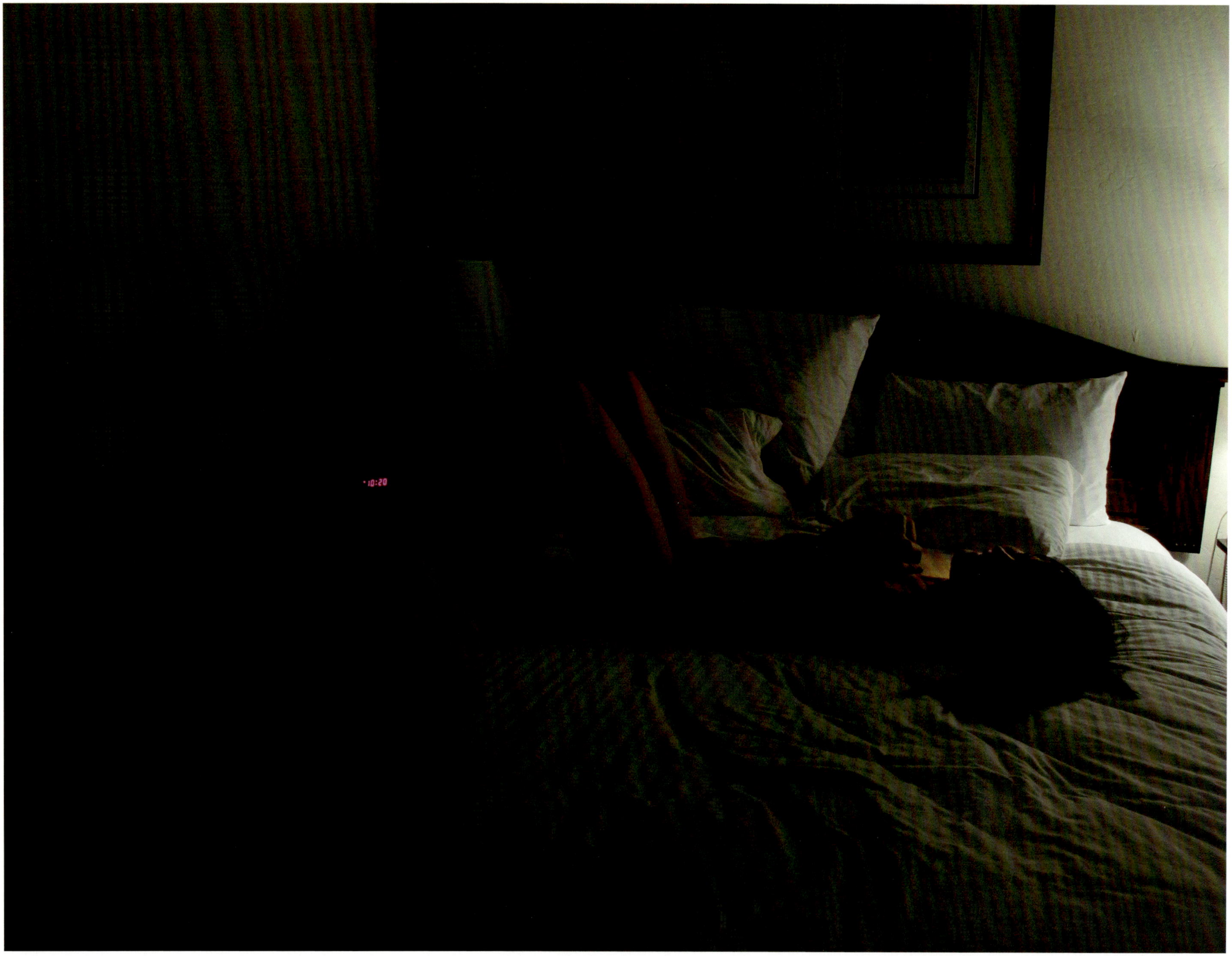

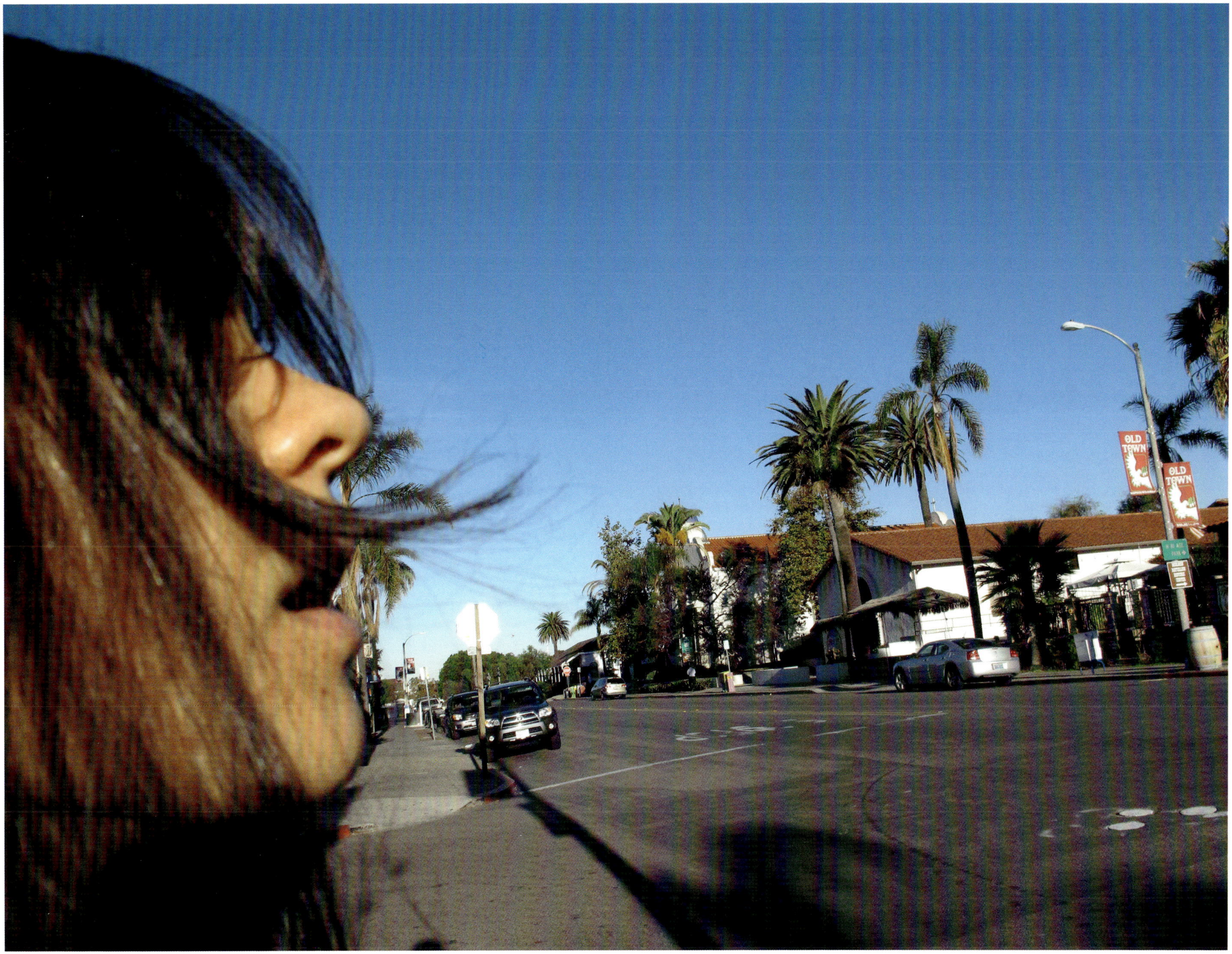
OLD TOWN
OLD TOWN

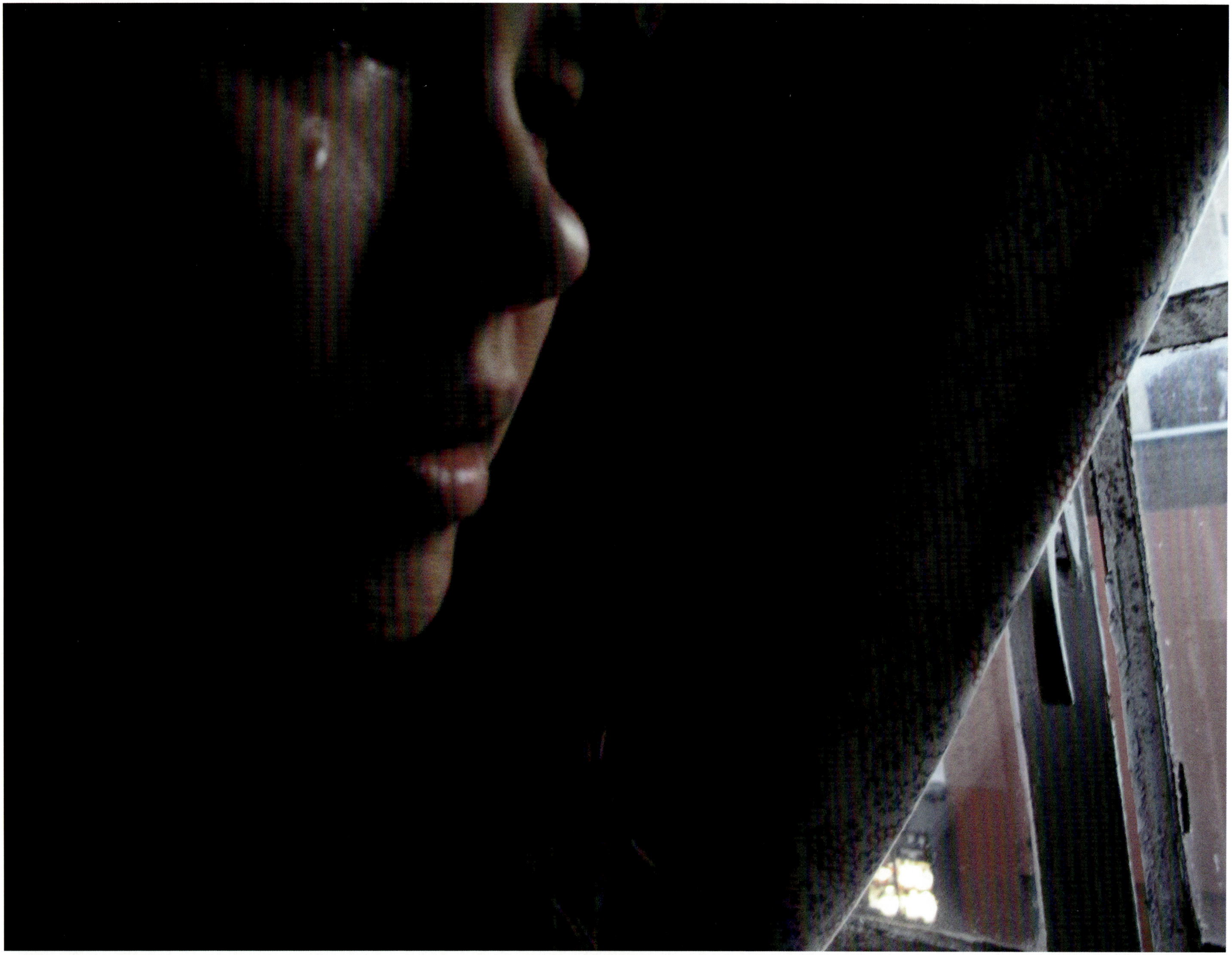

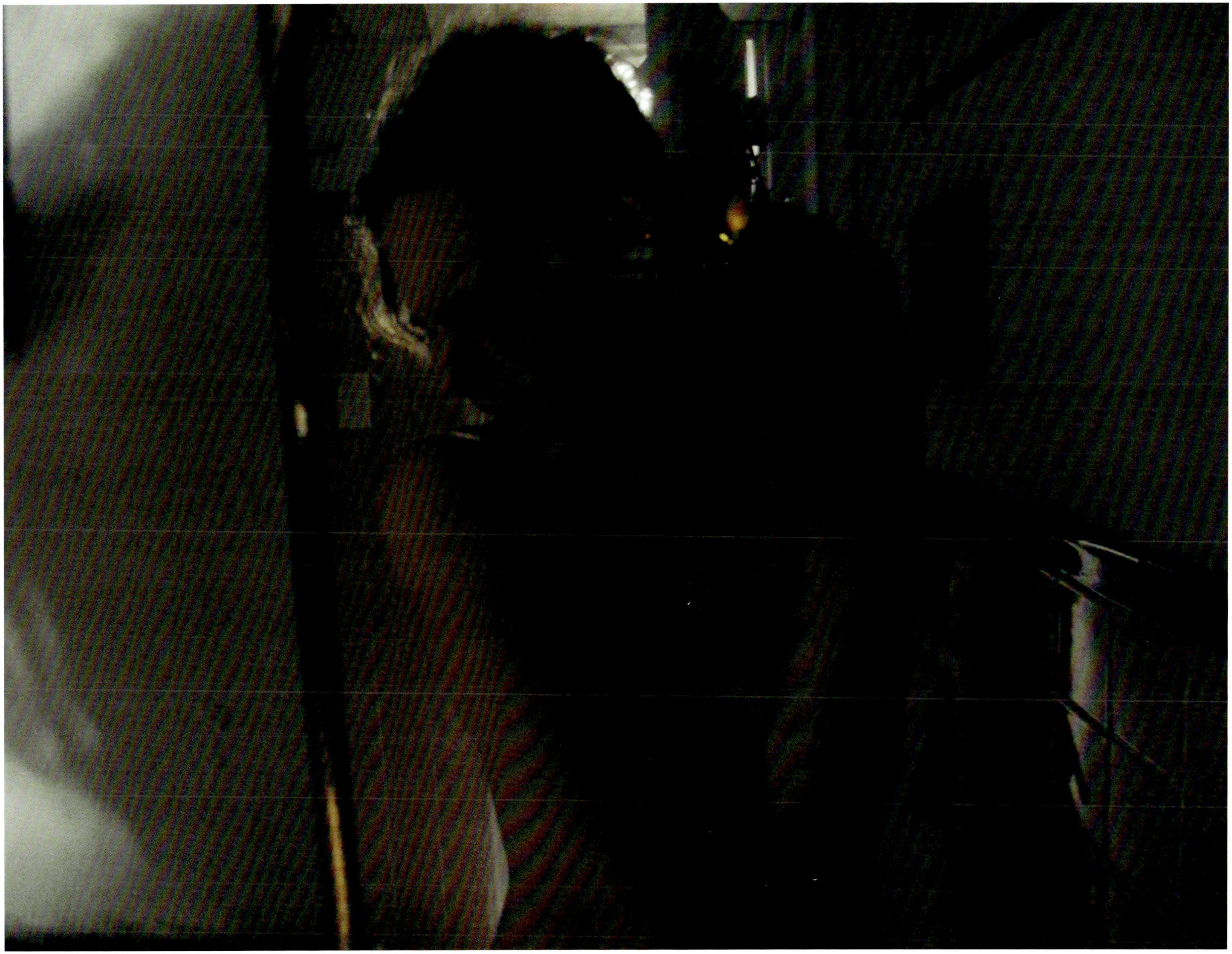

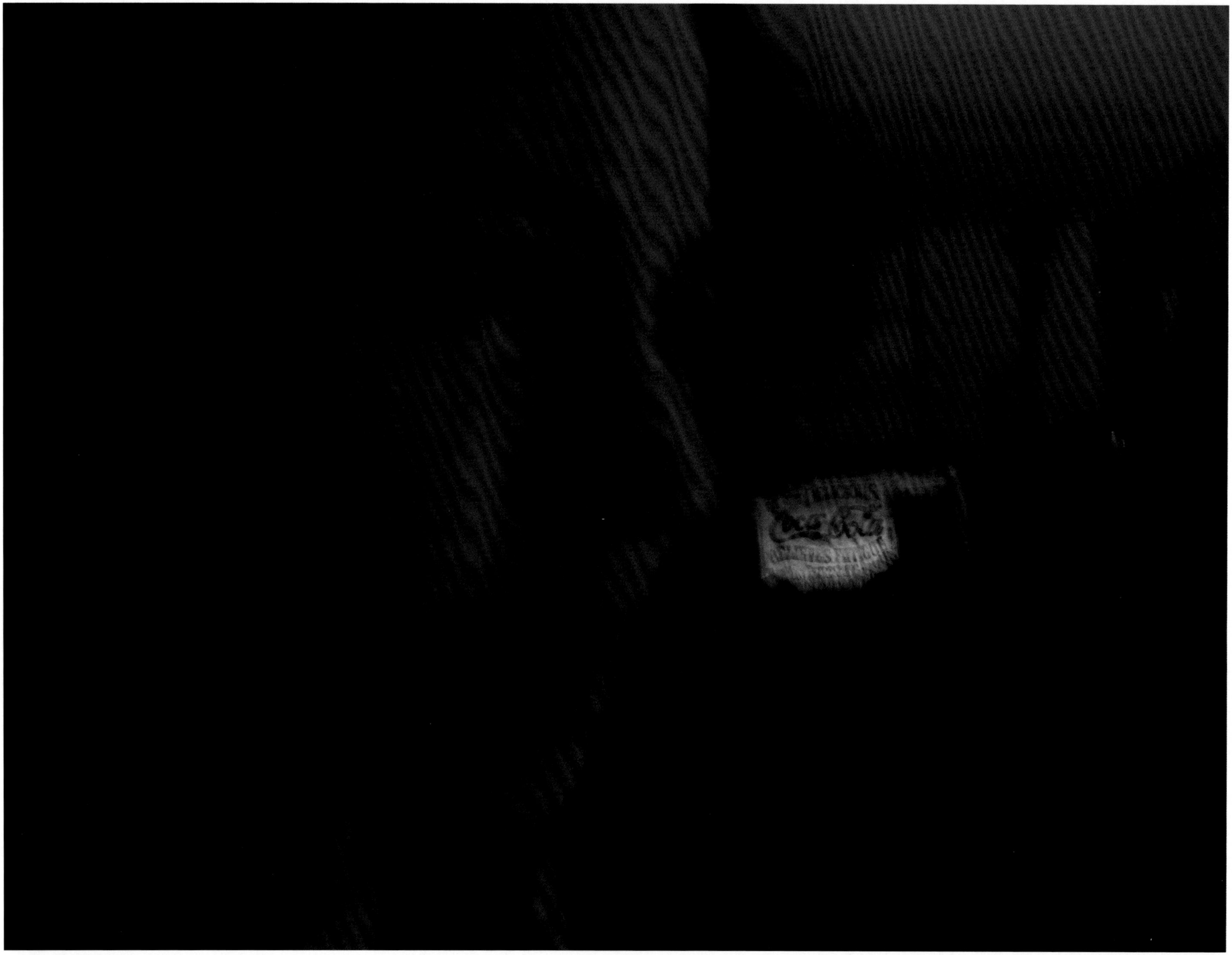

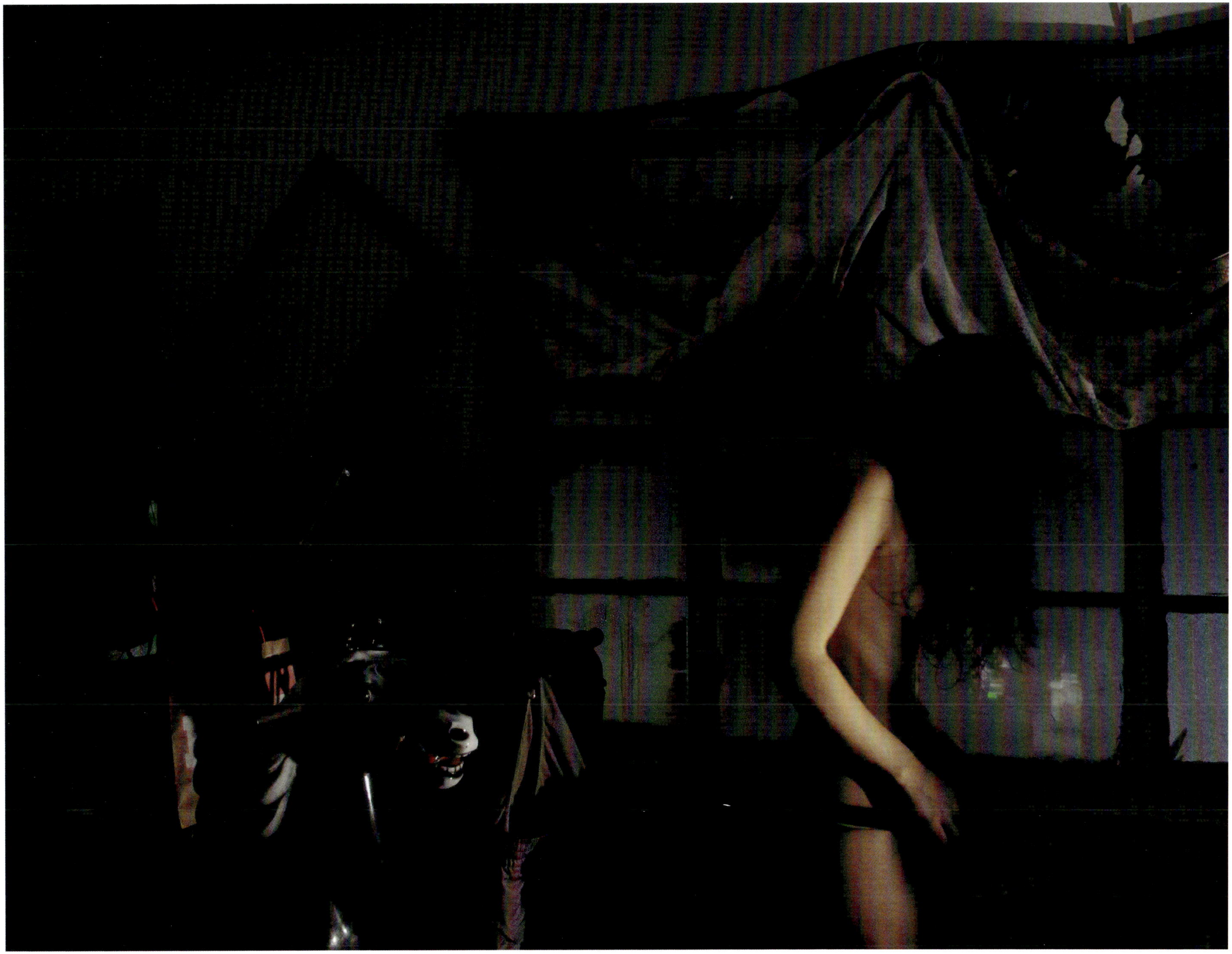

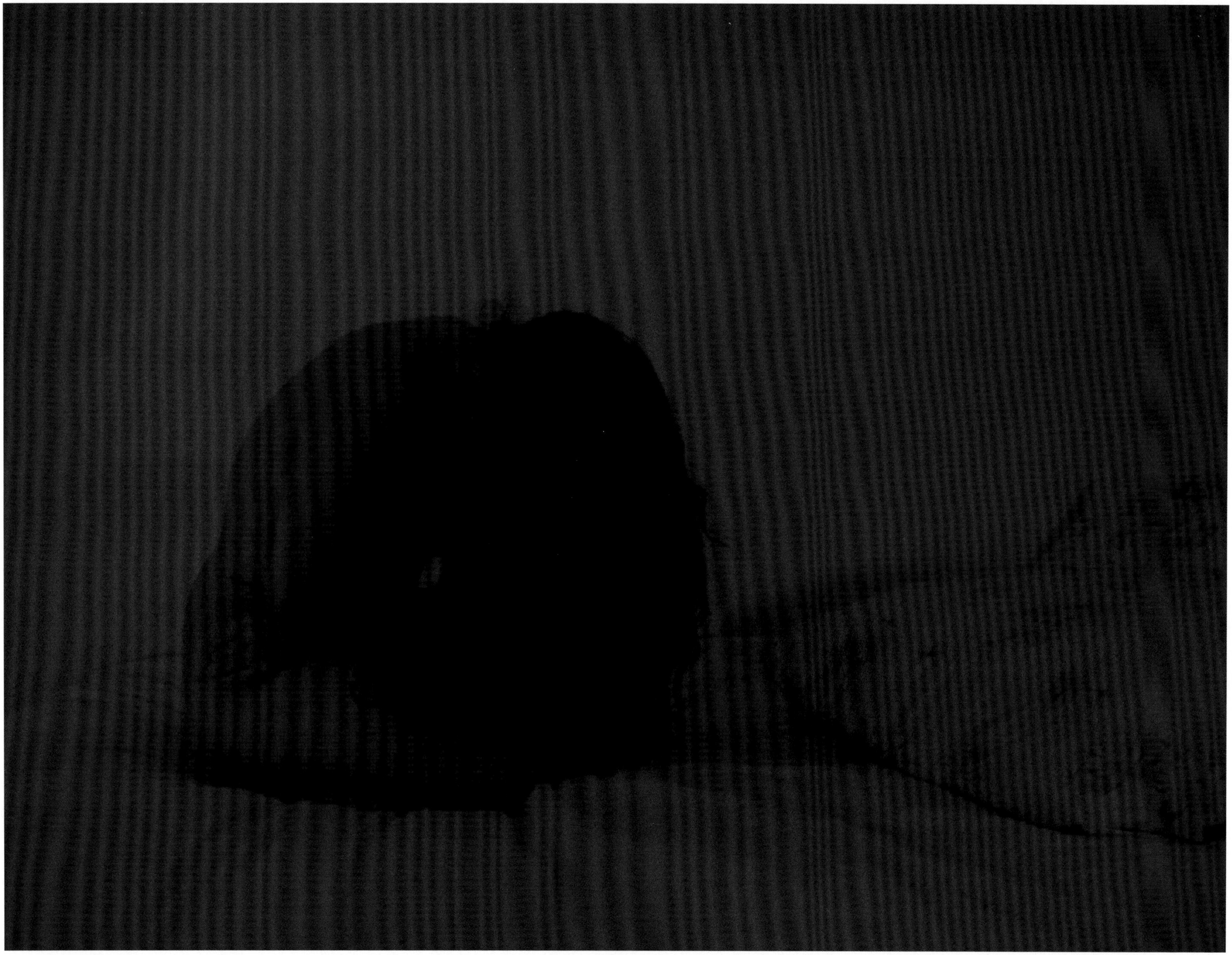

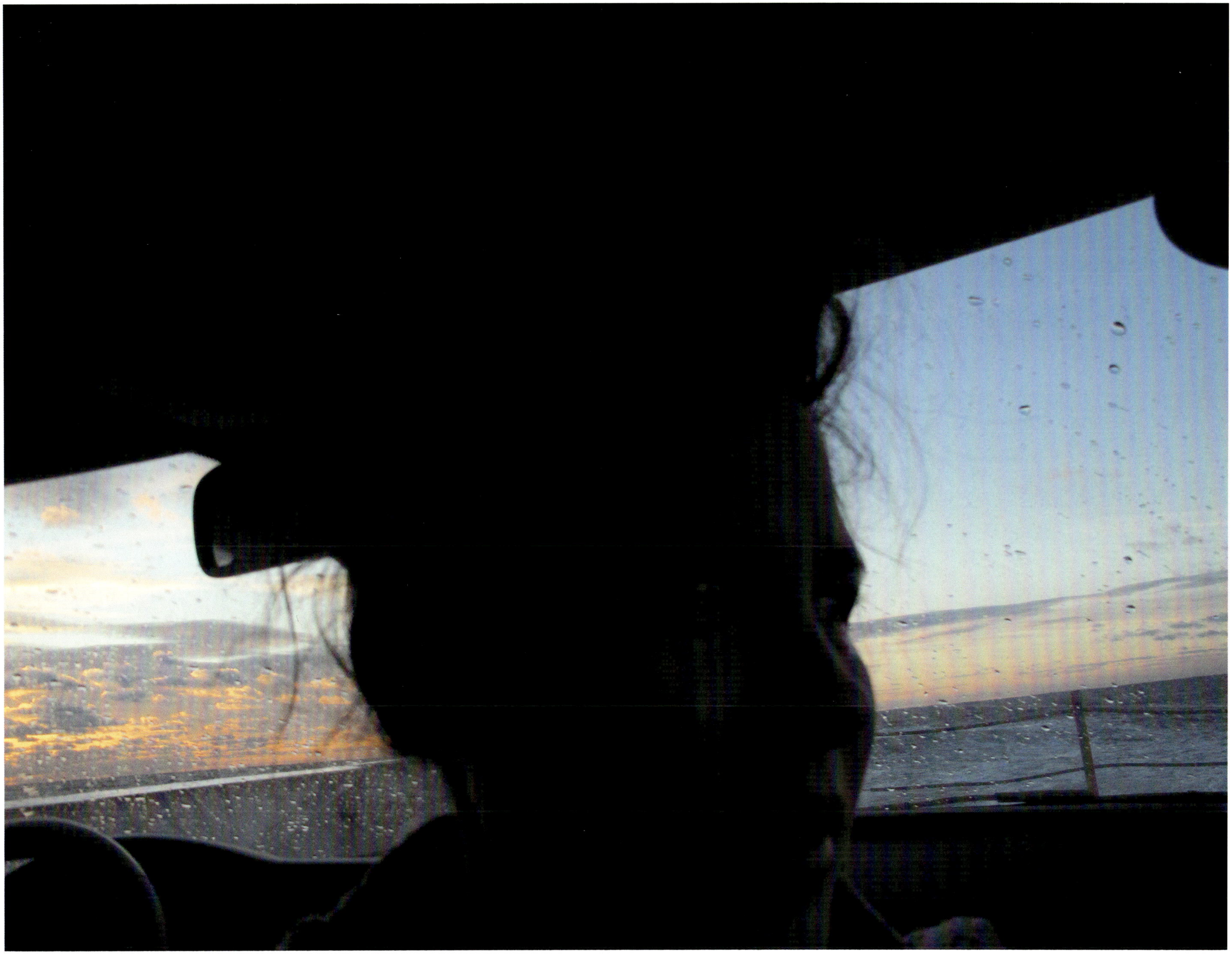

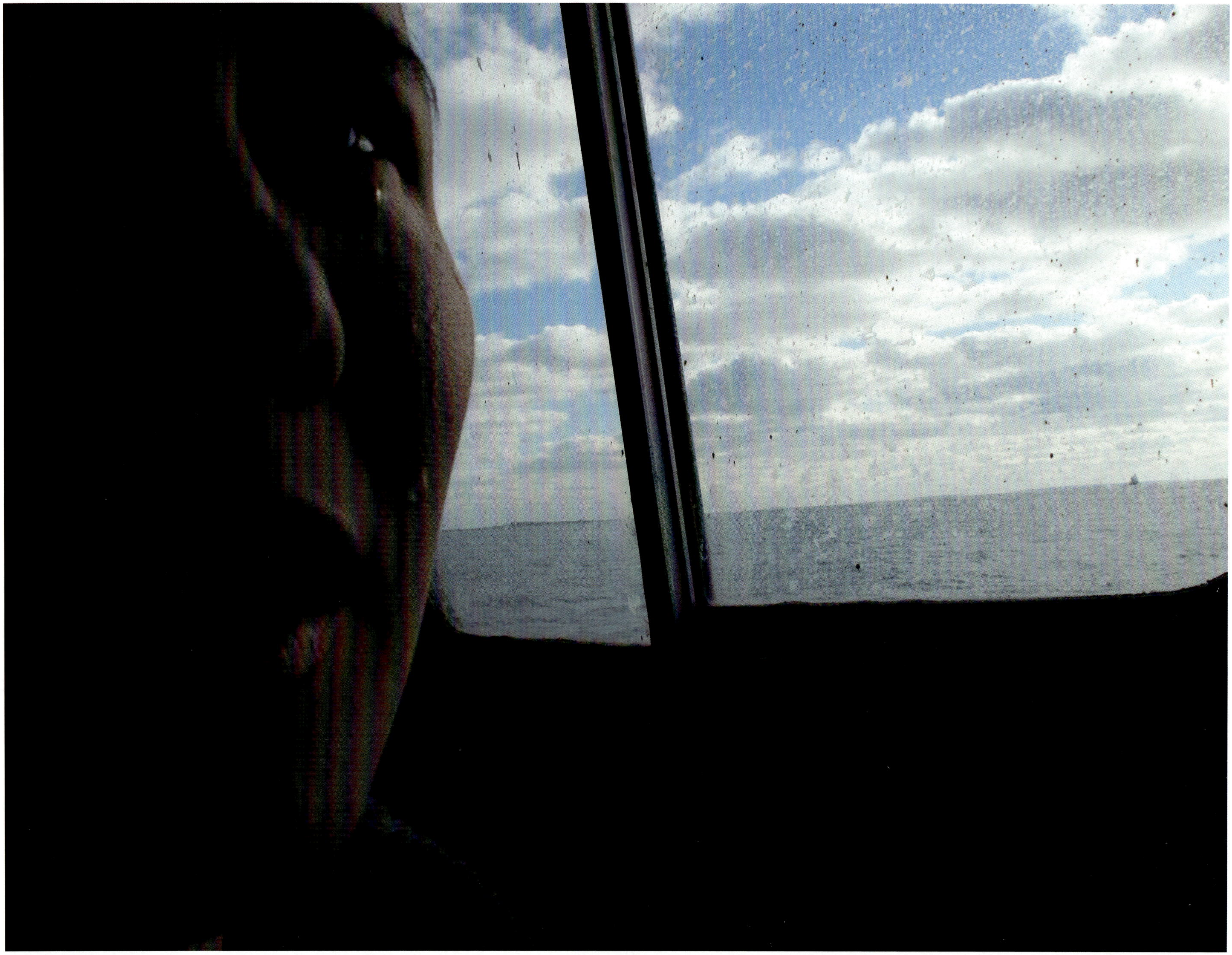

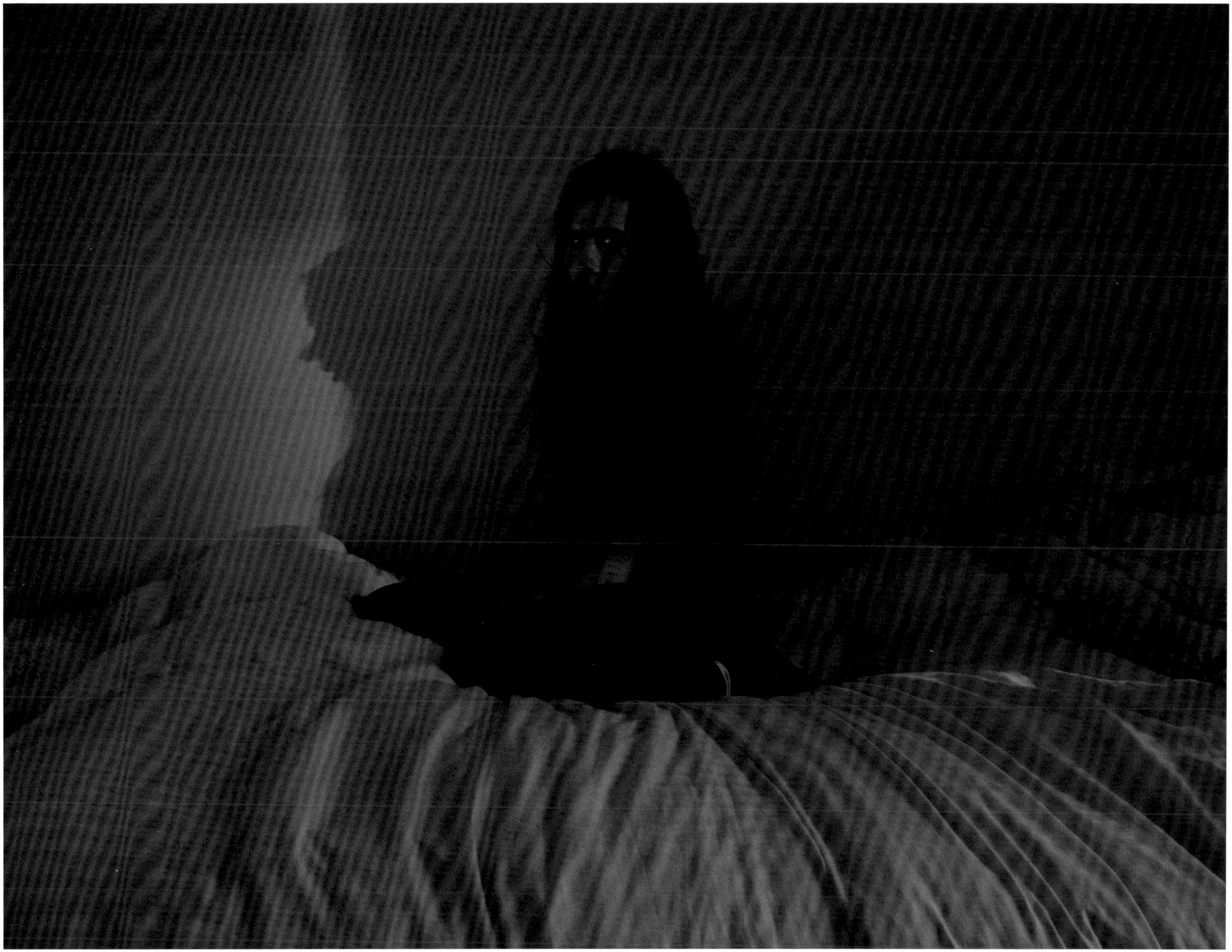

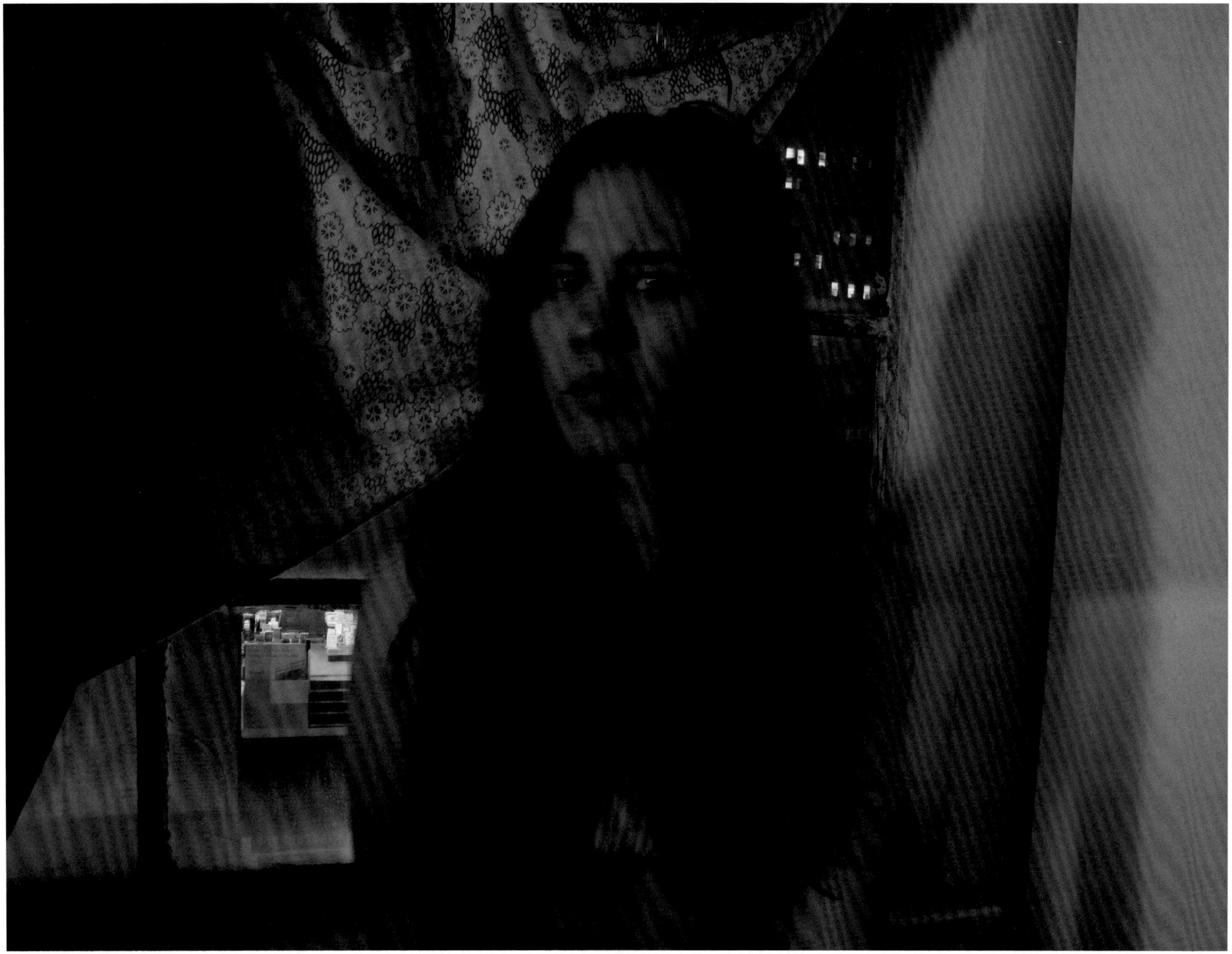

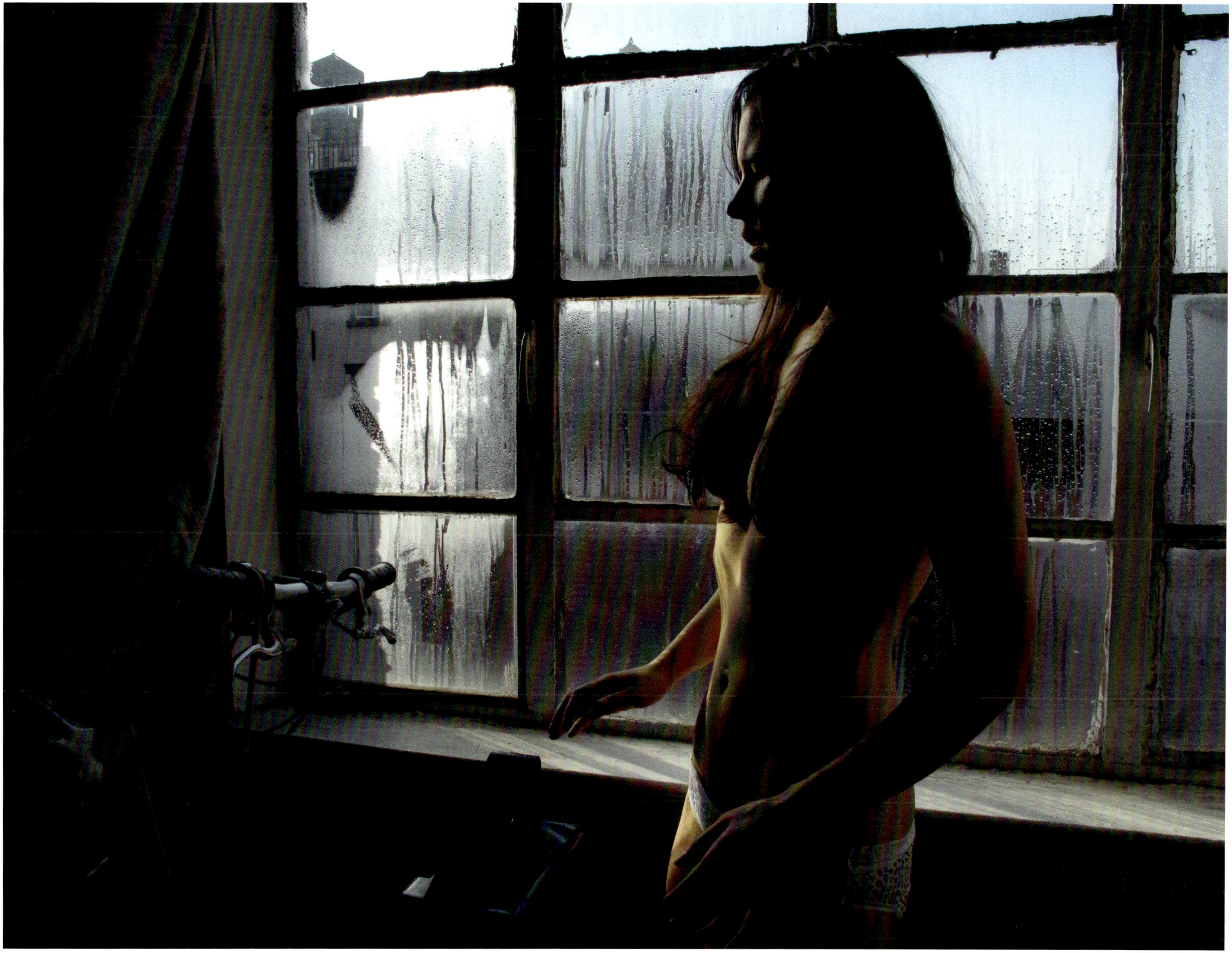

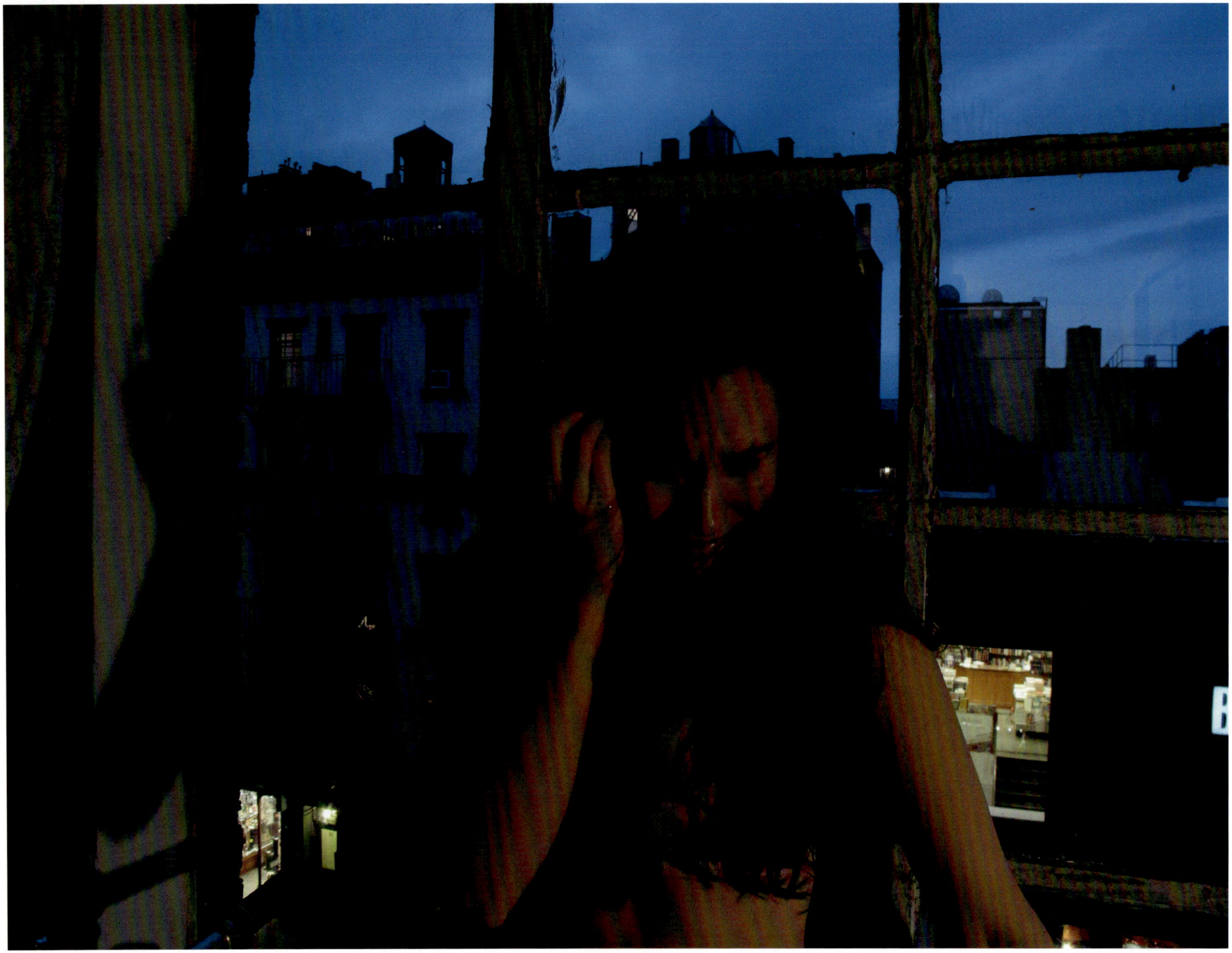

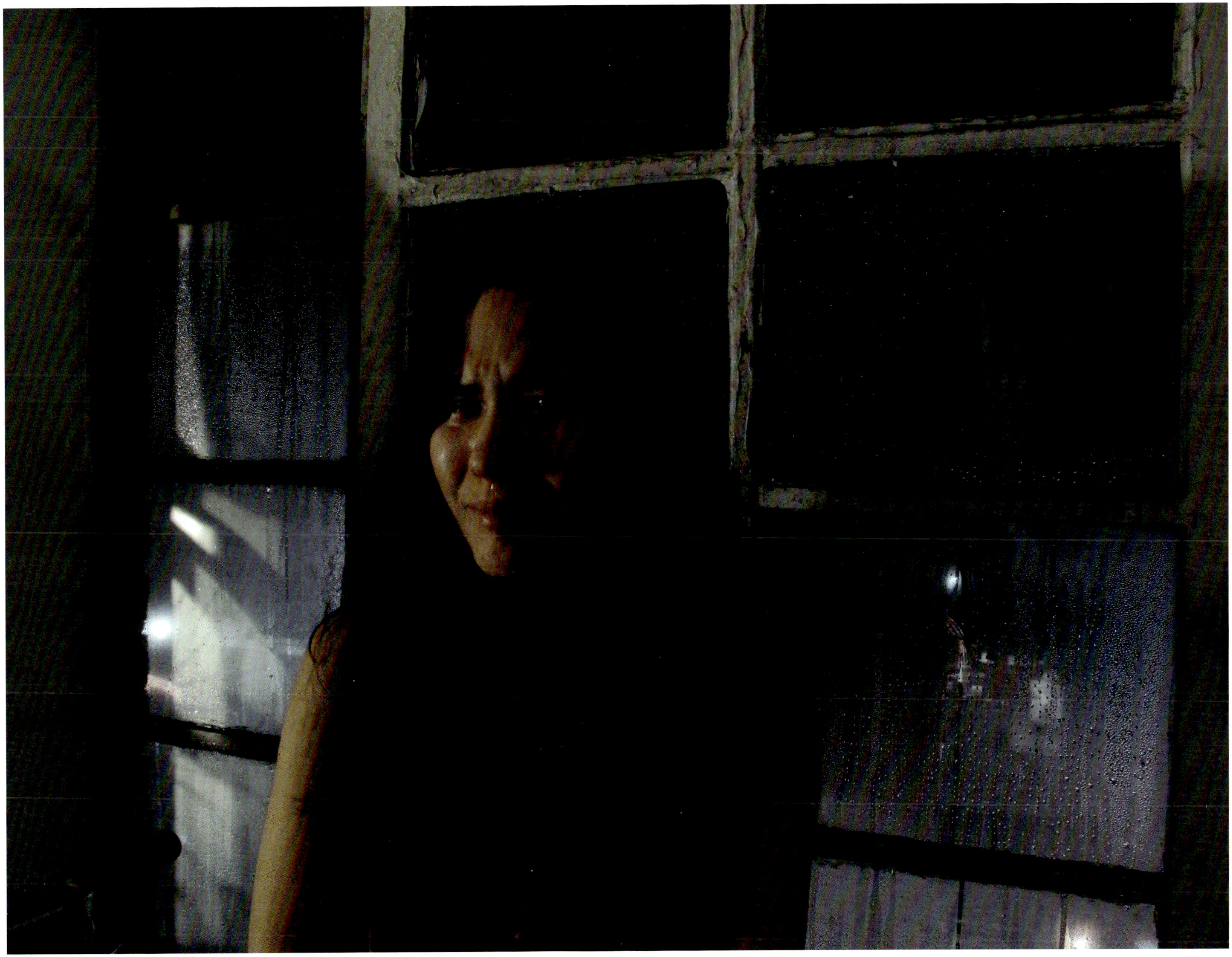

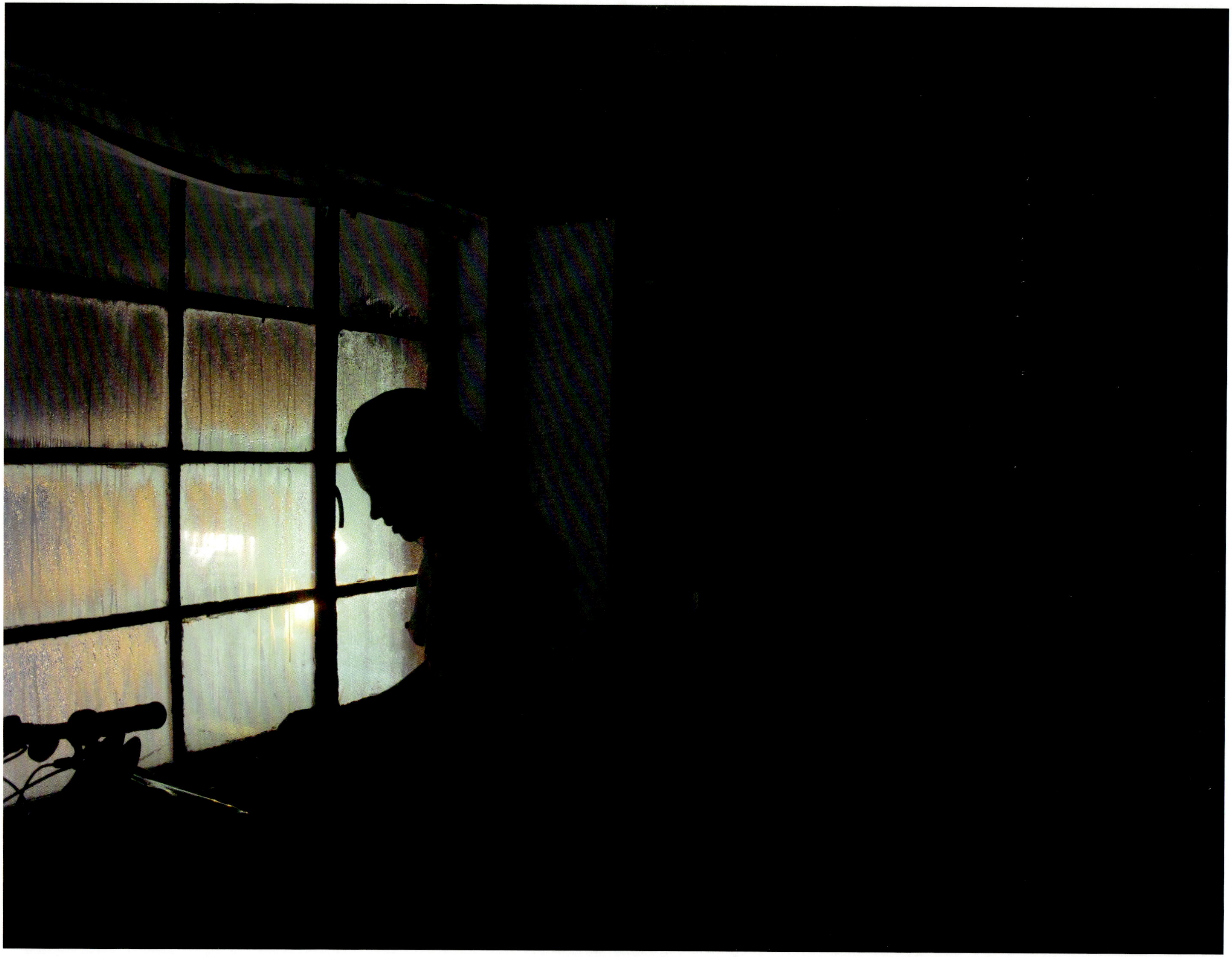

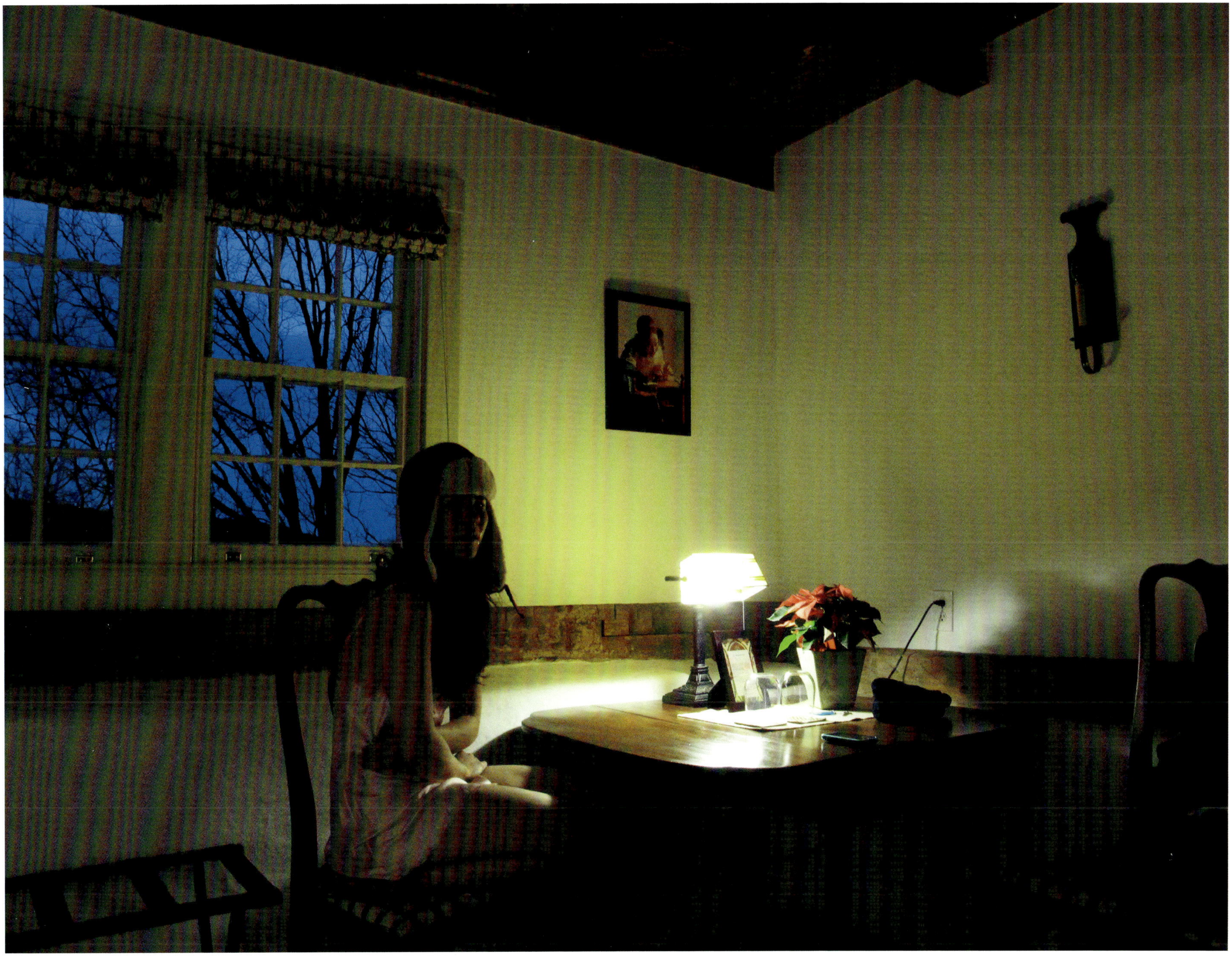

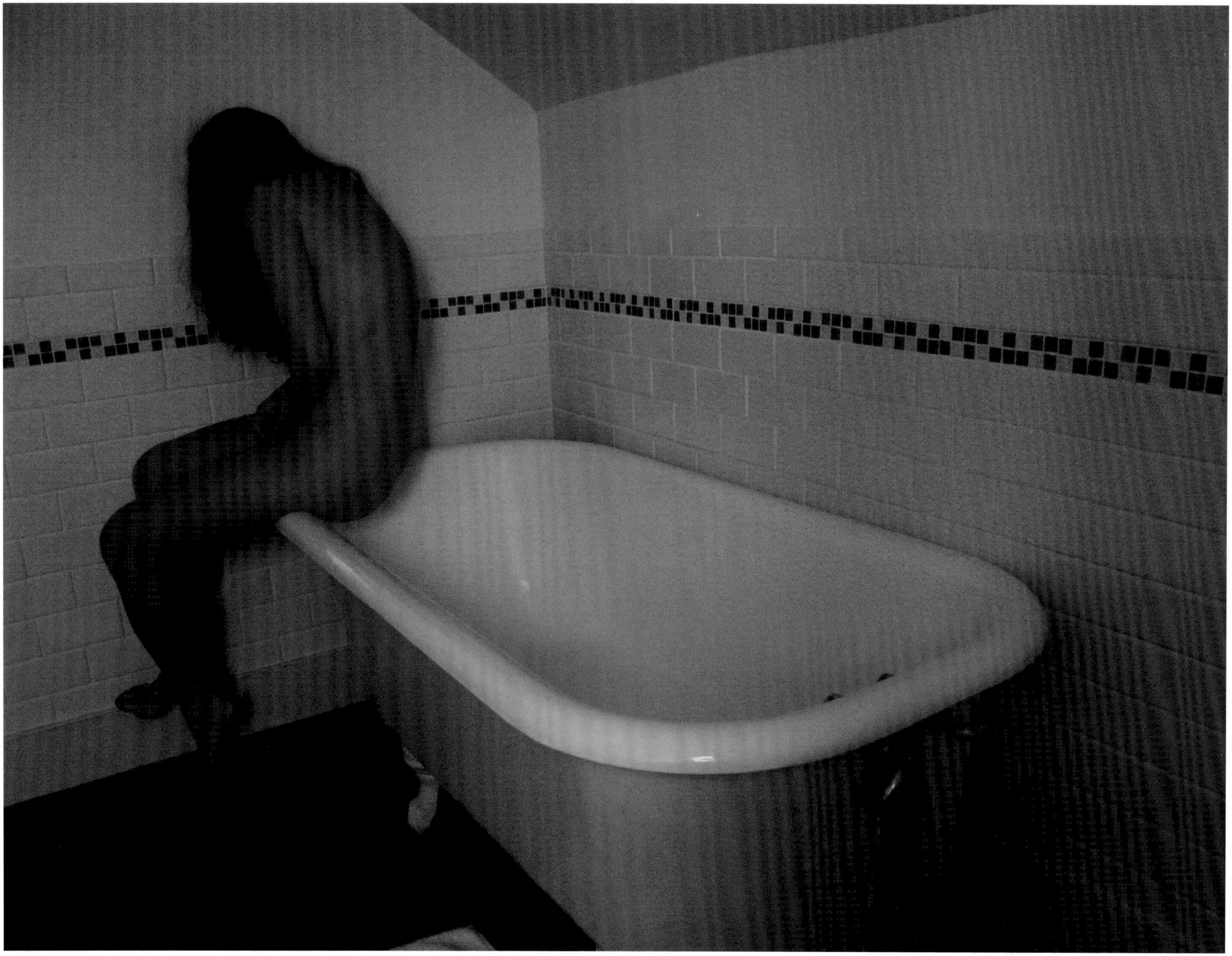

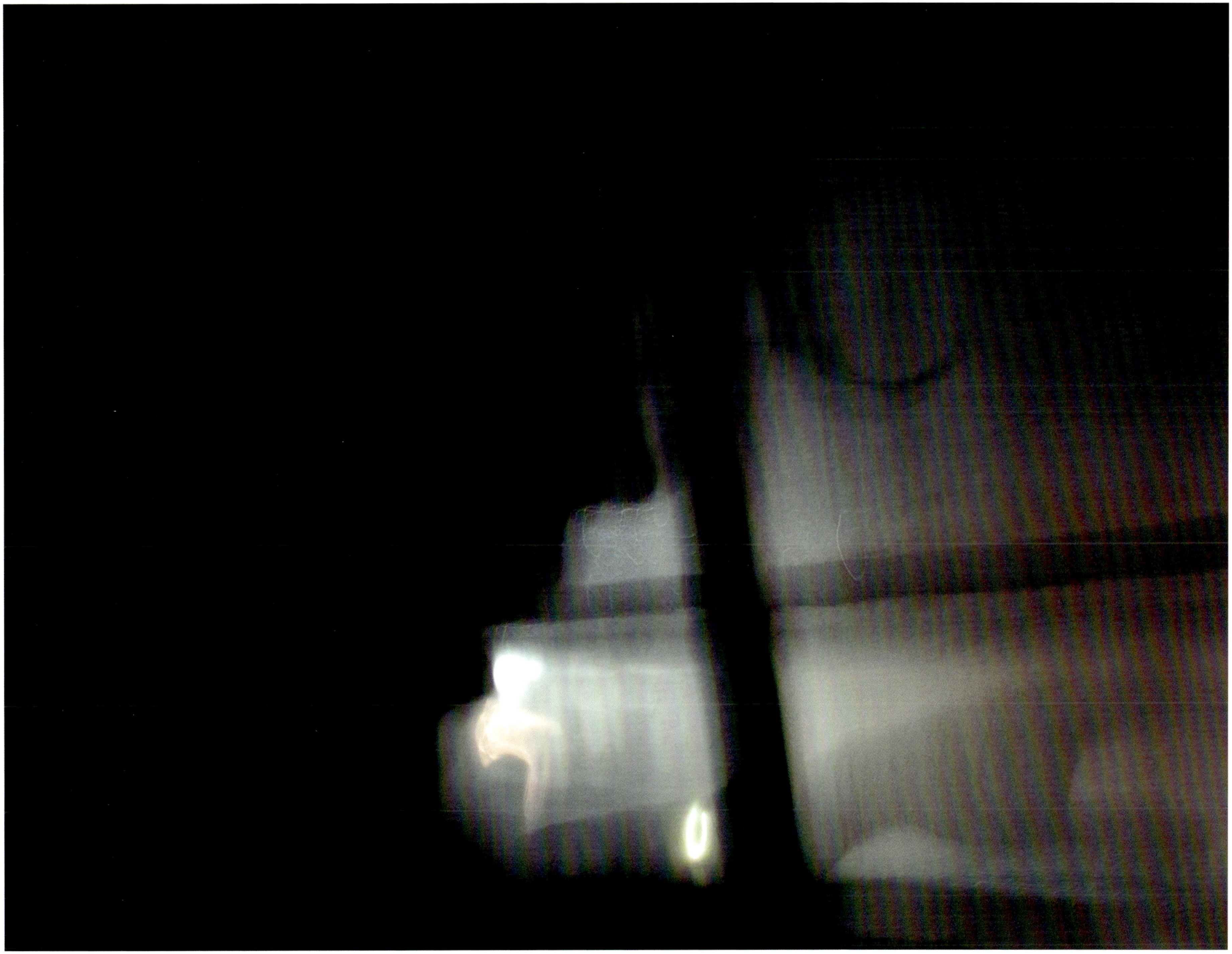

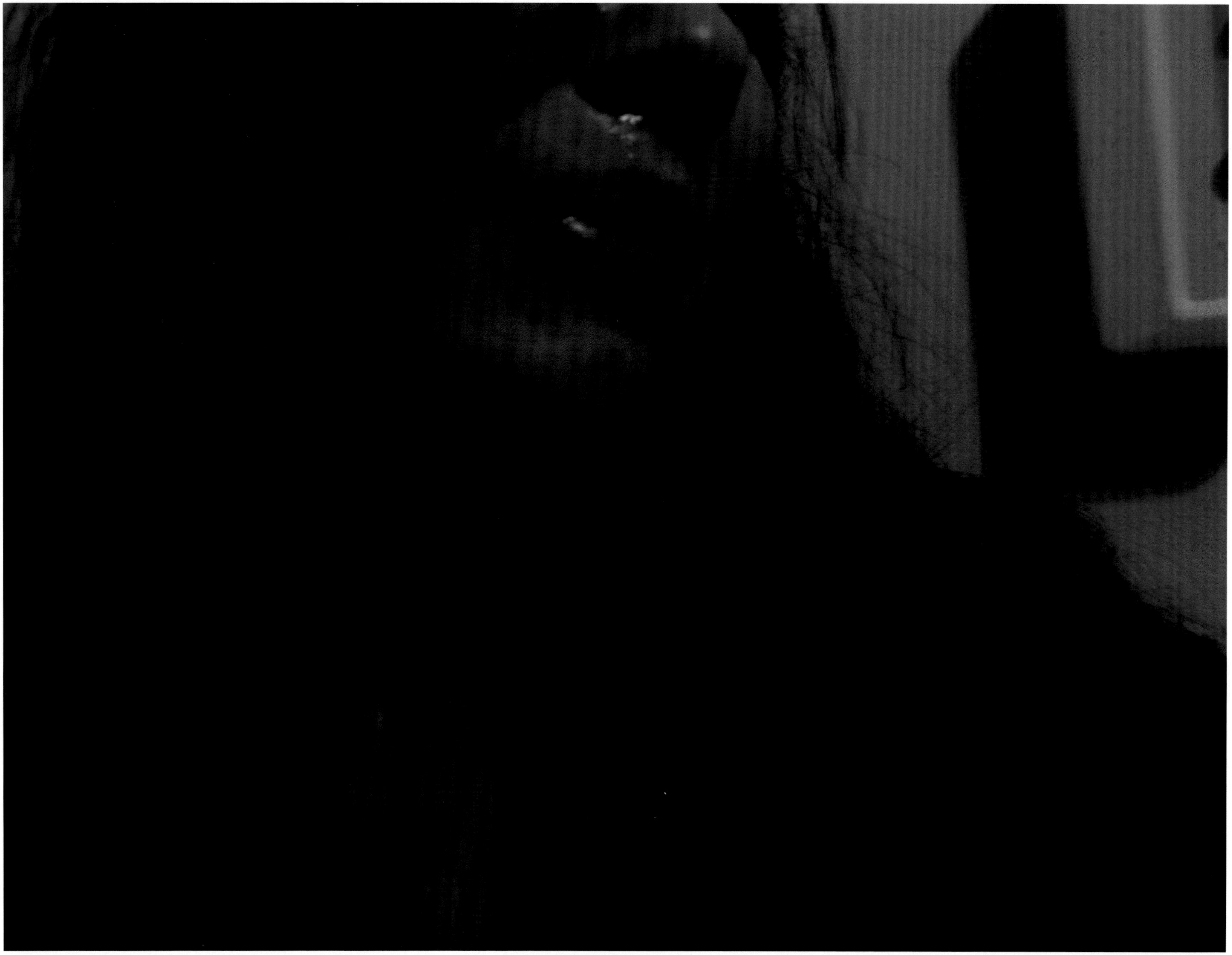

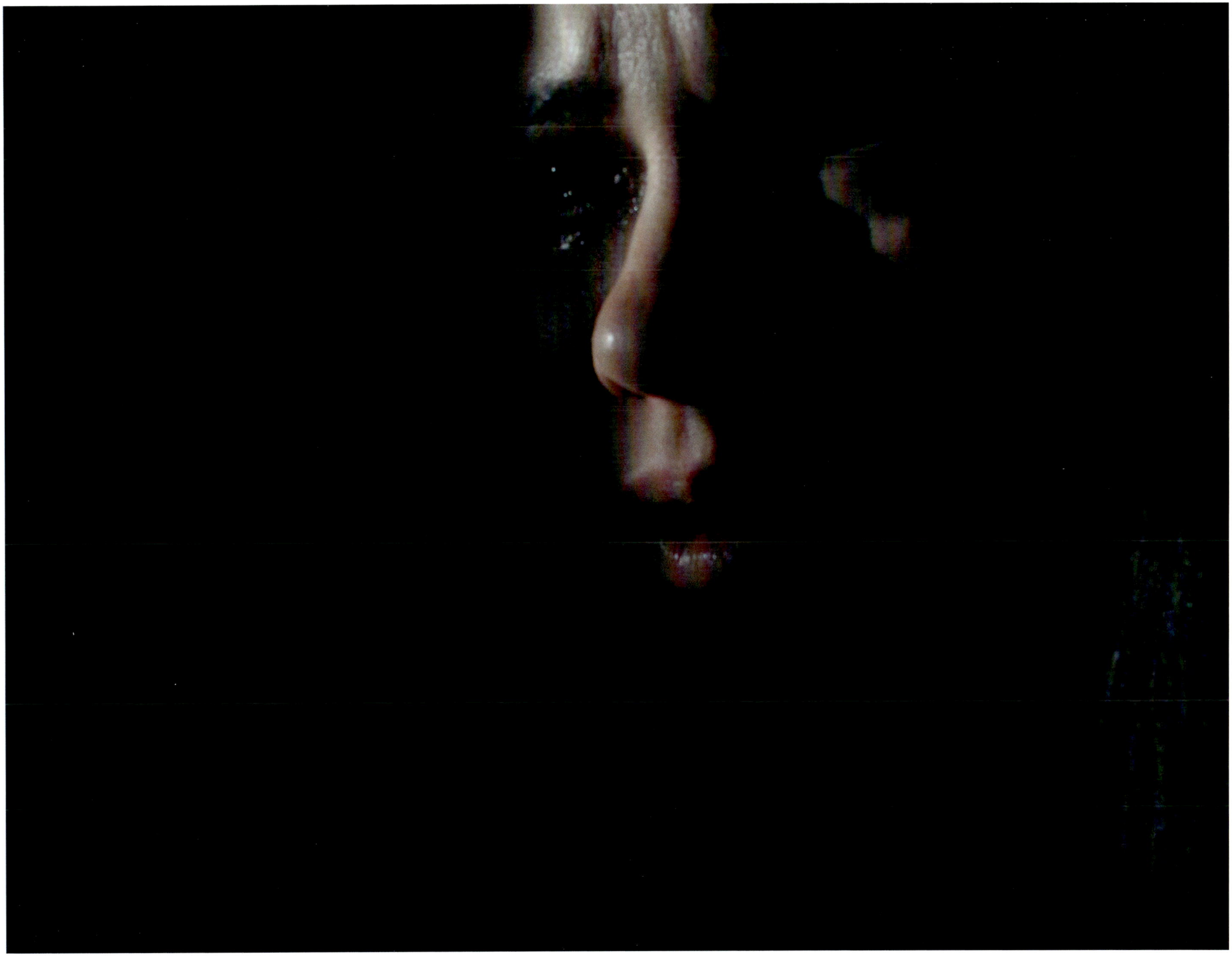

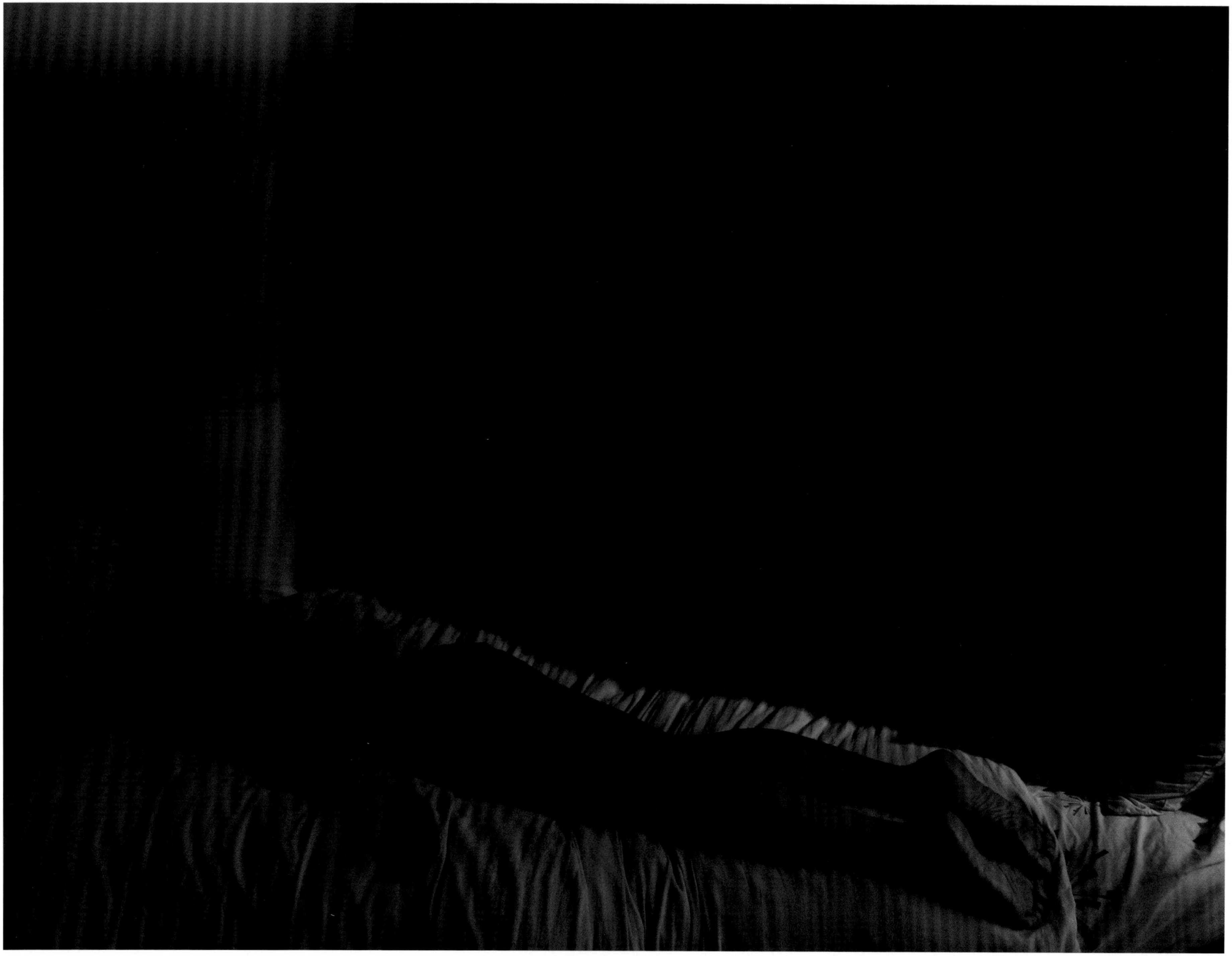

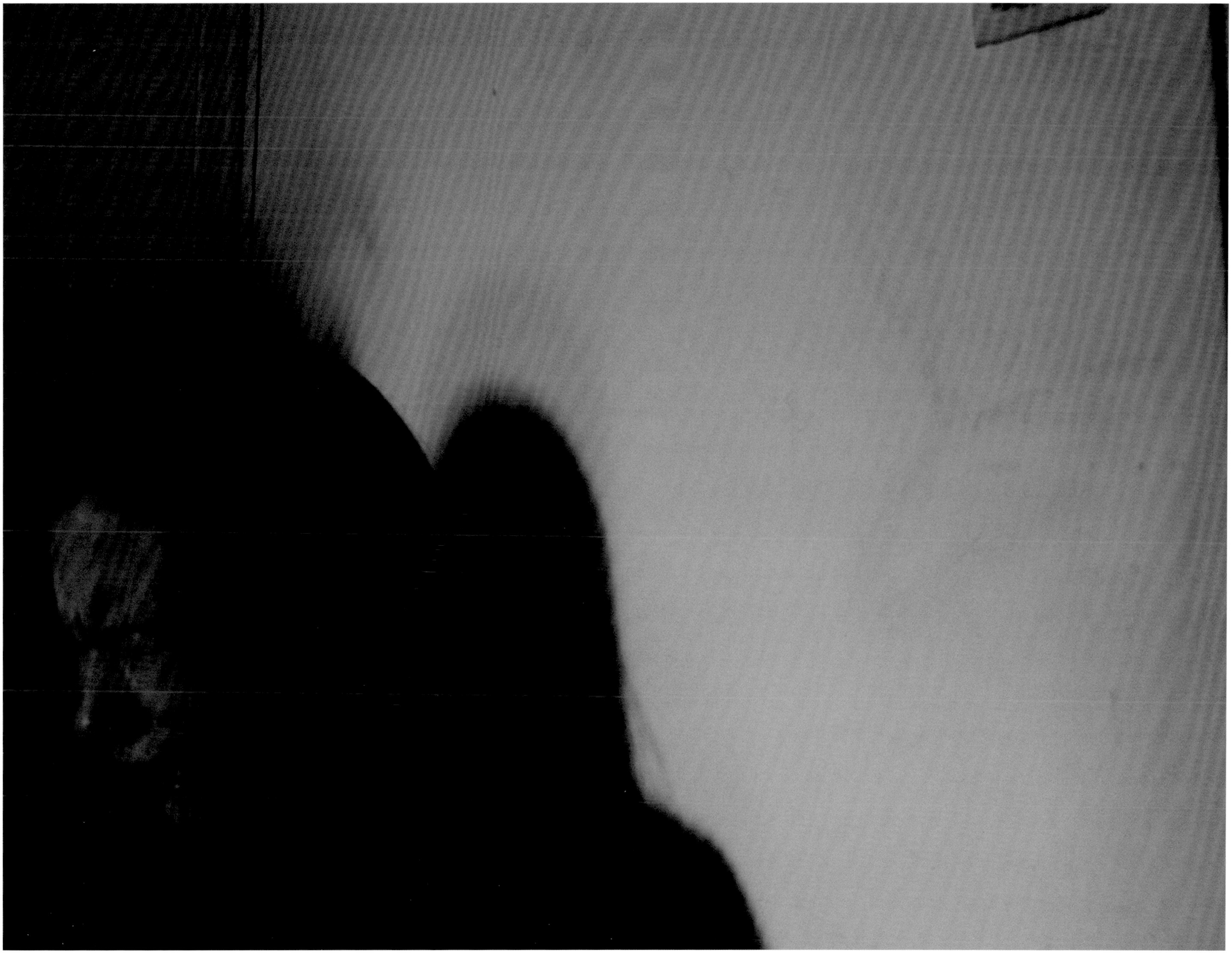

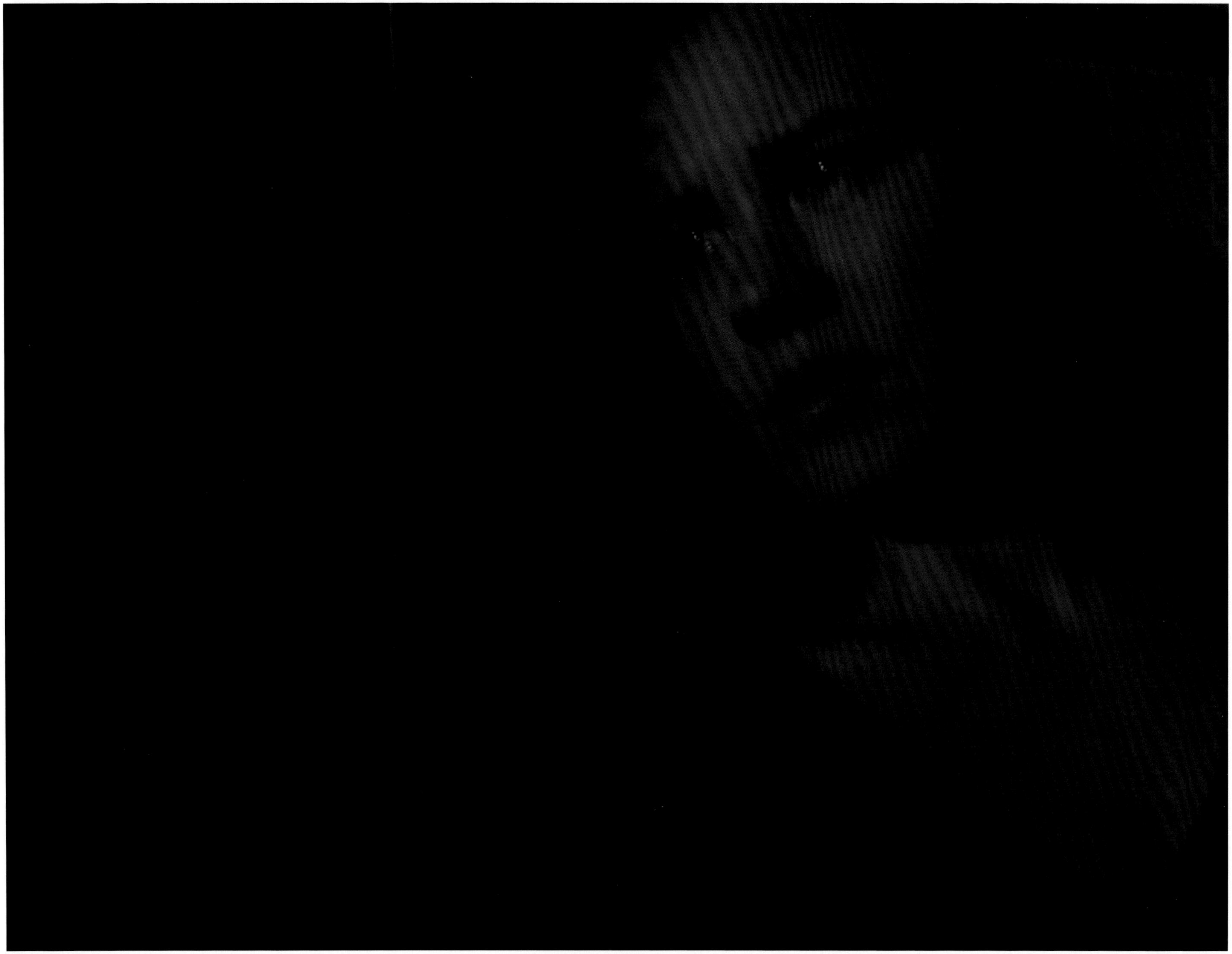

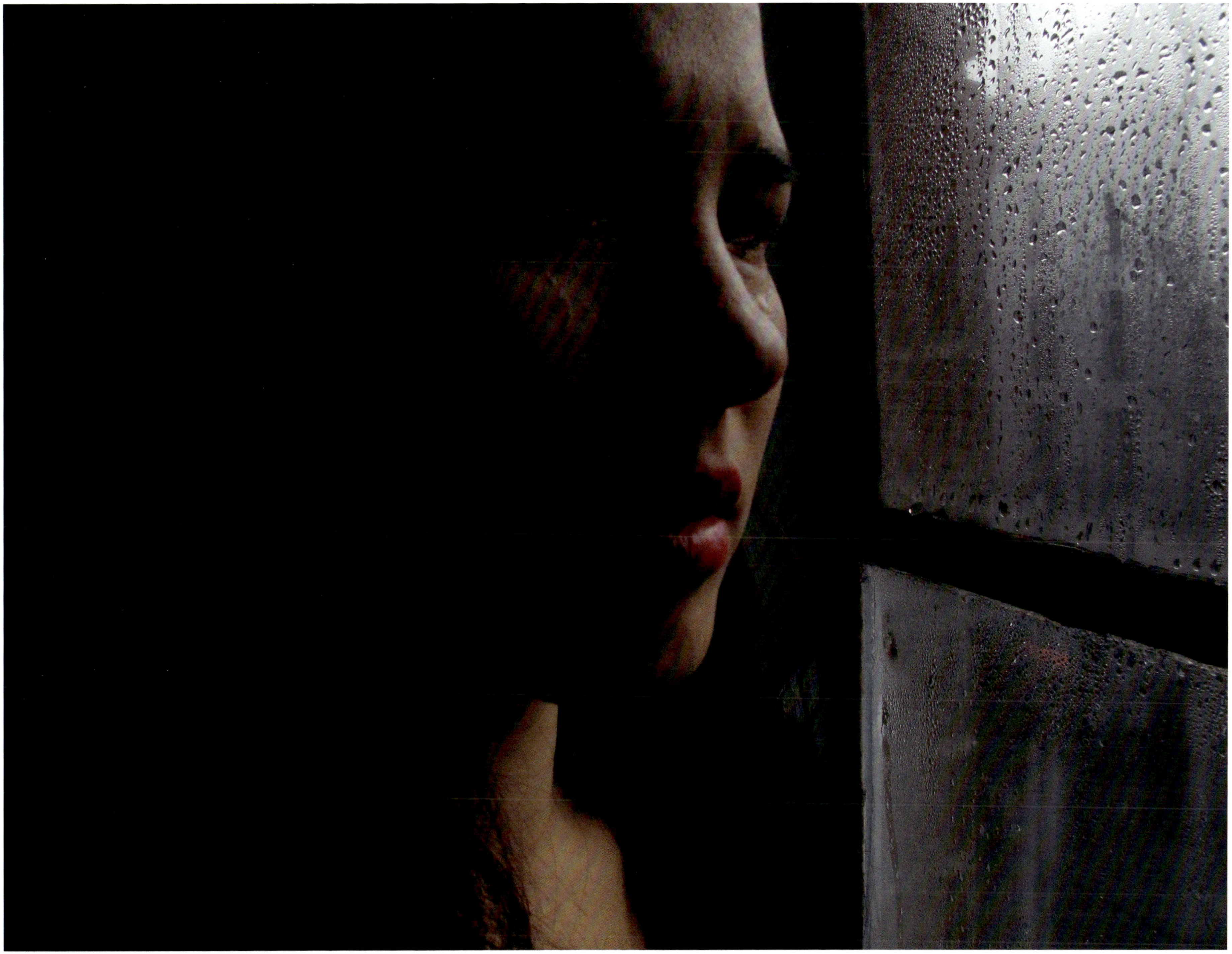

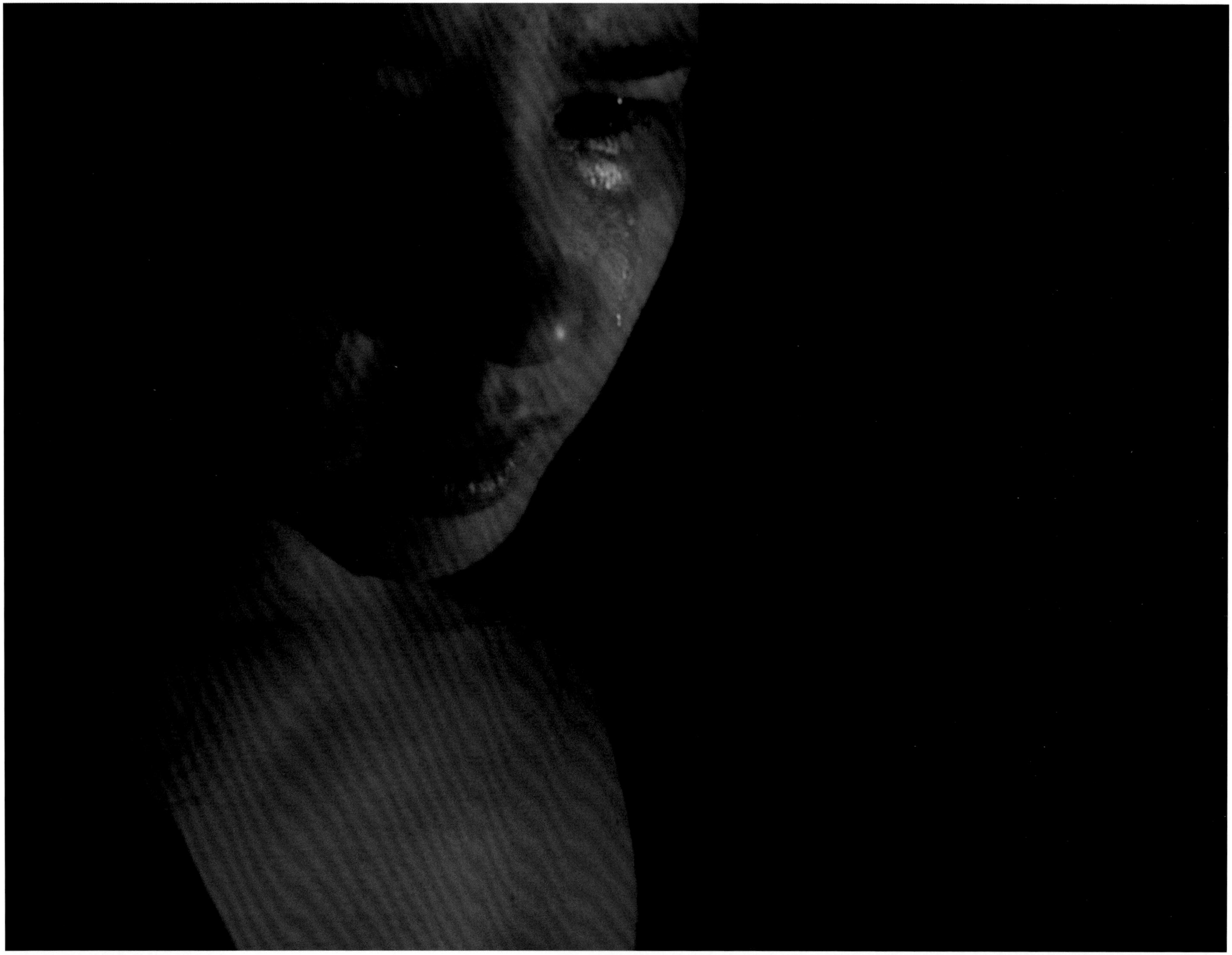

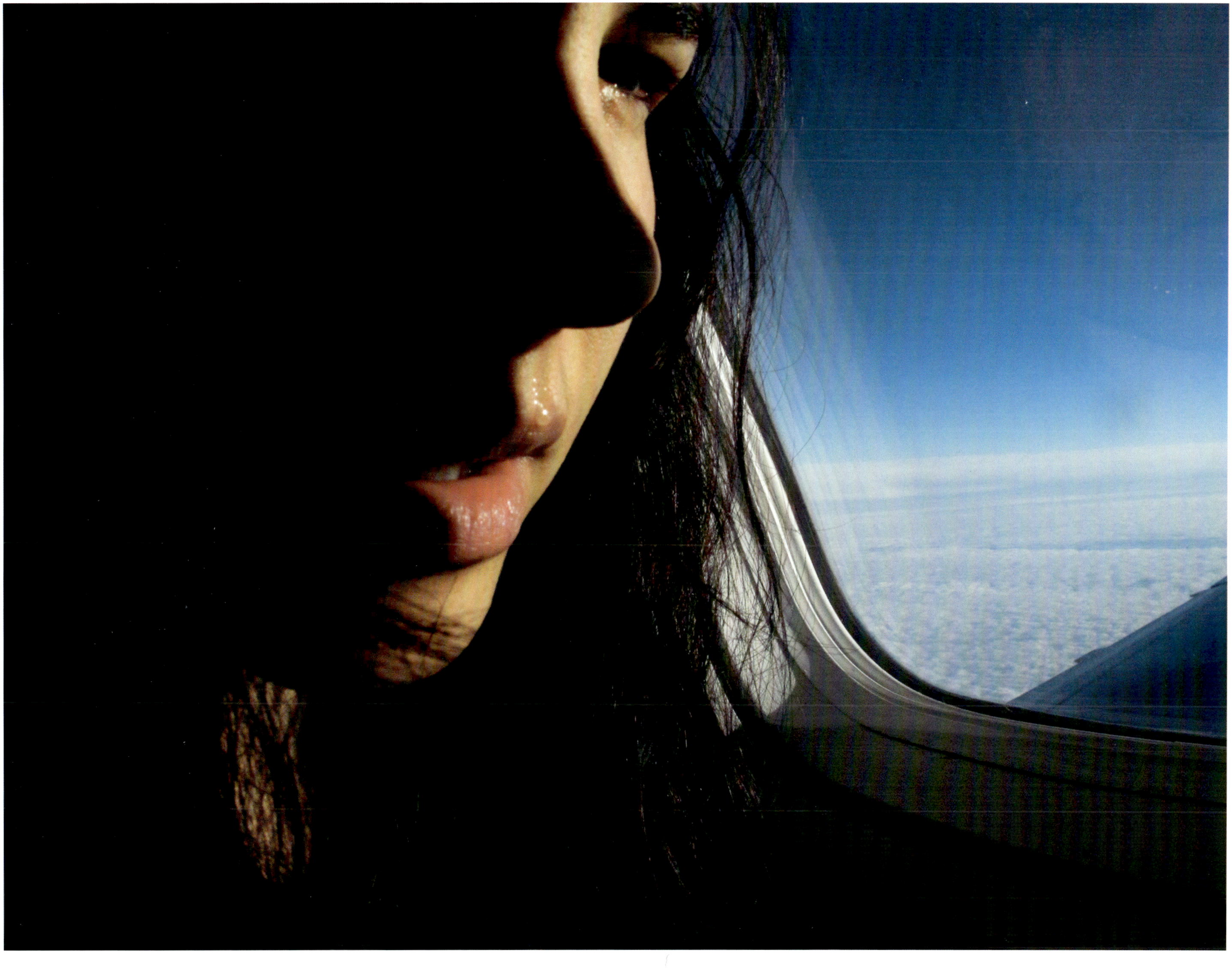

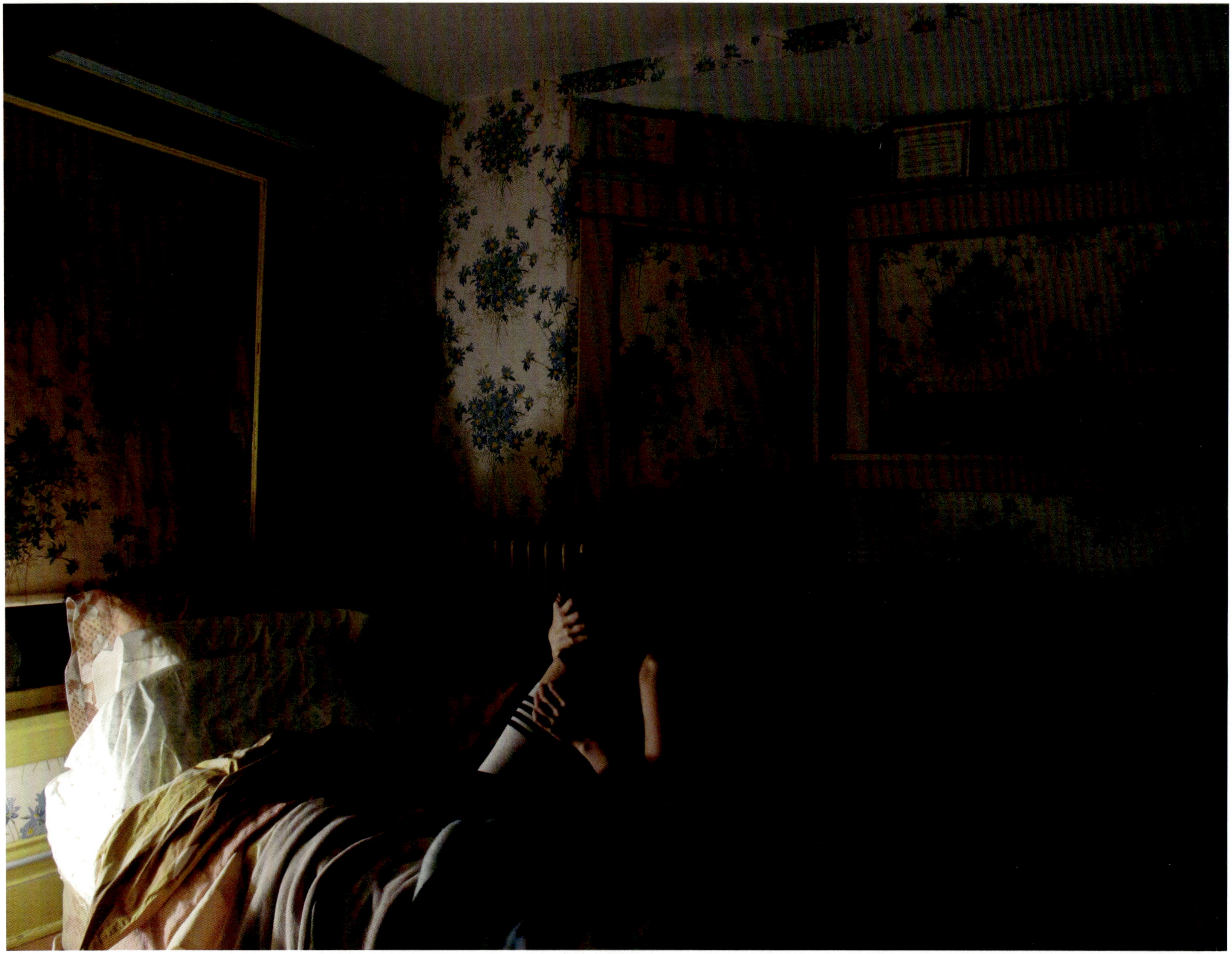

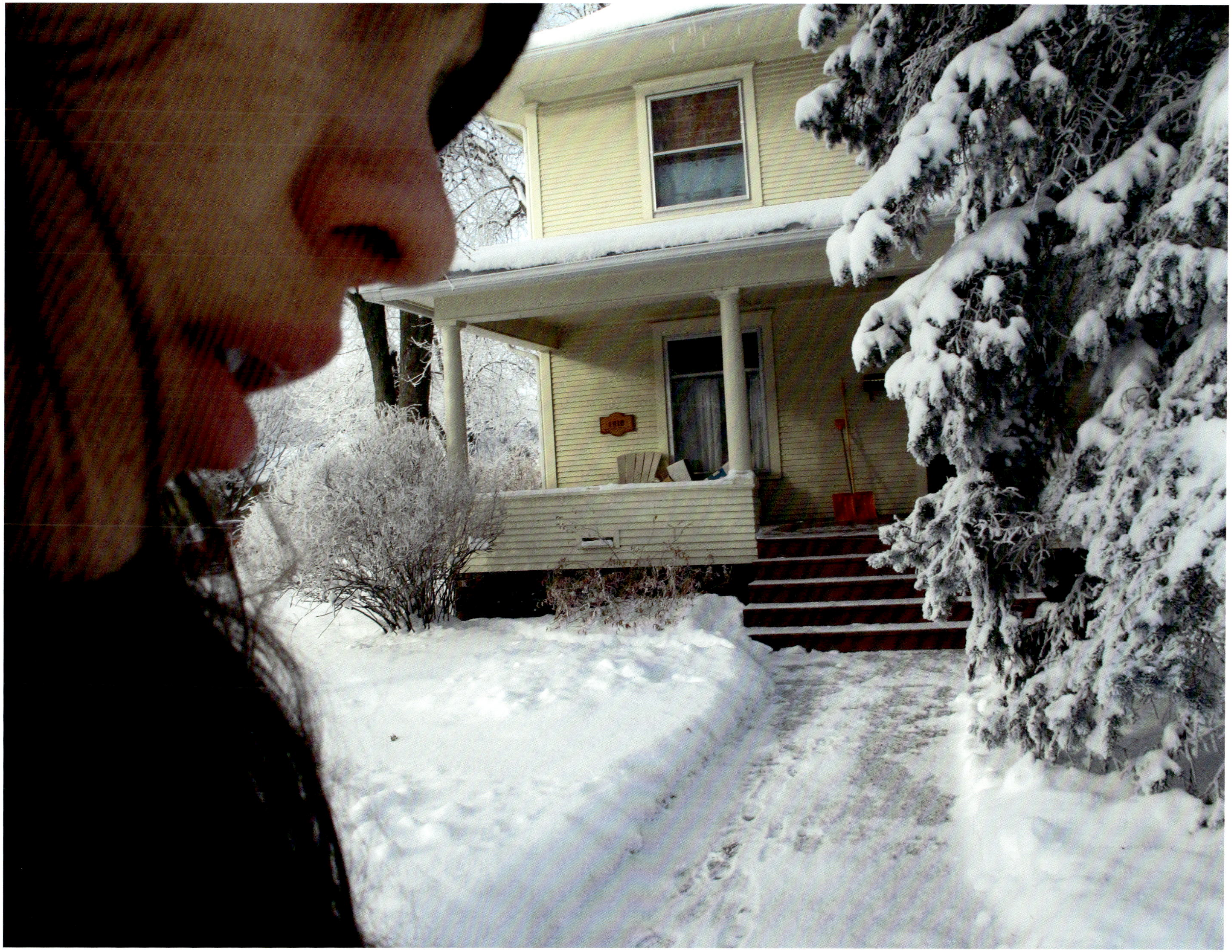

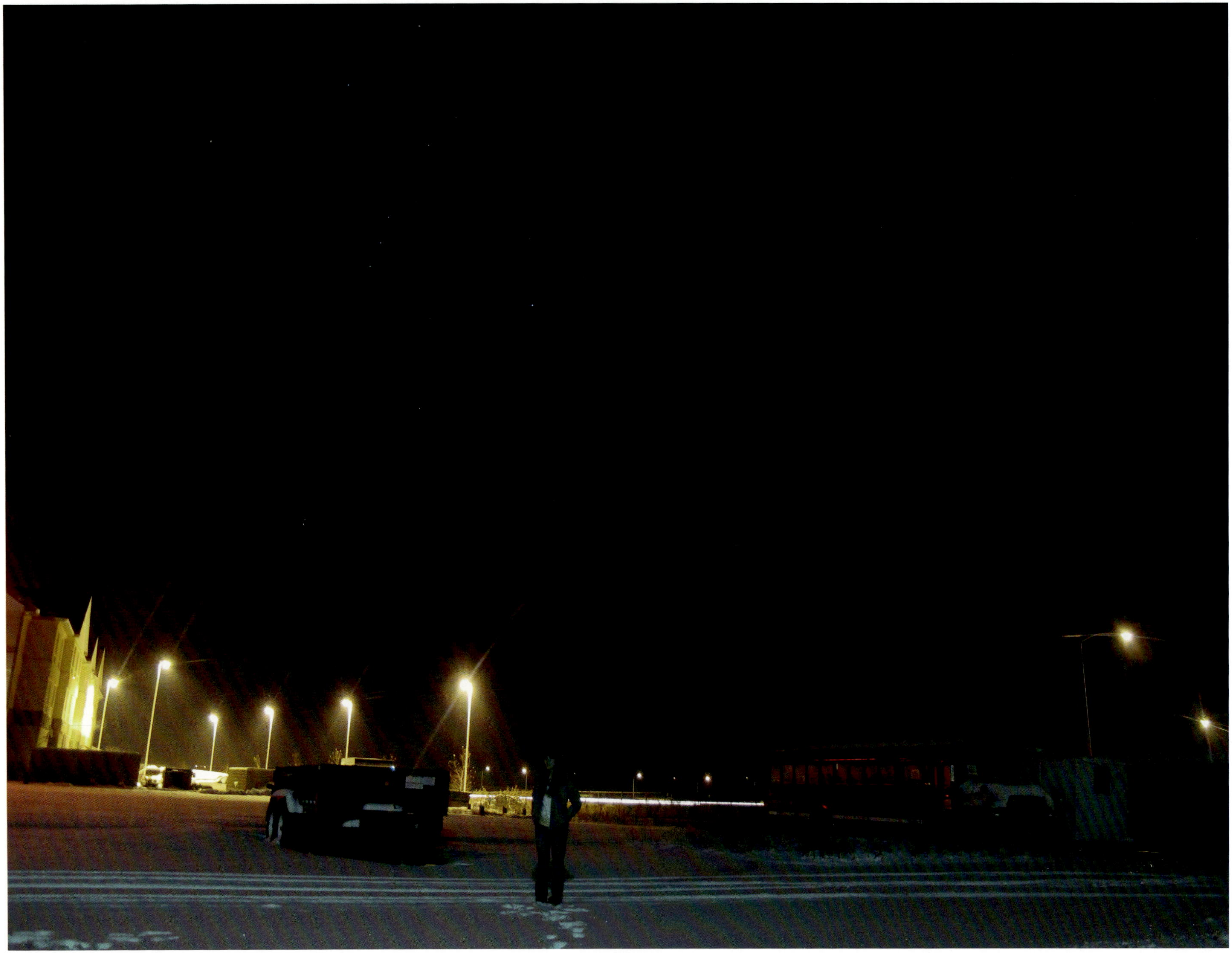

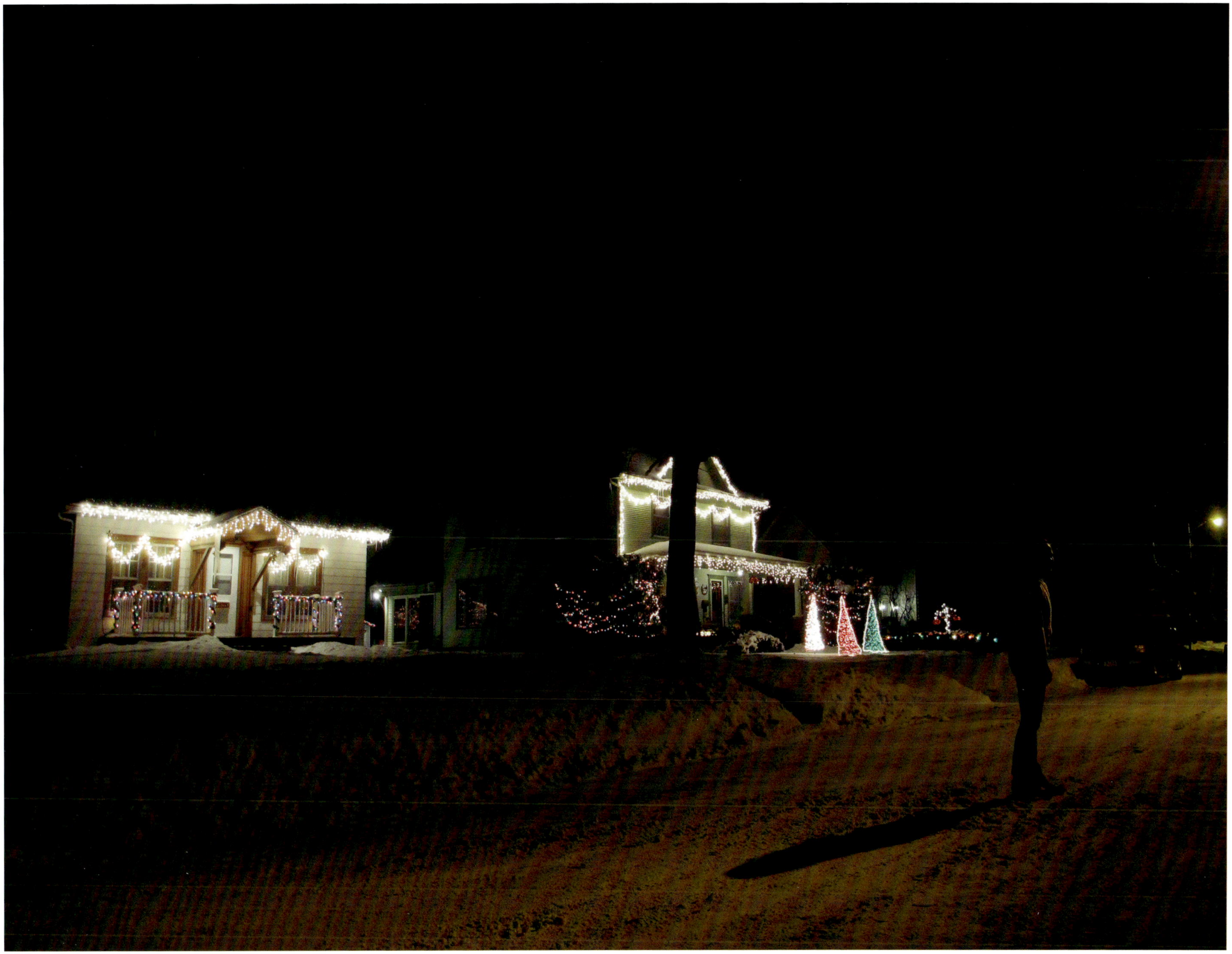

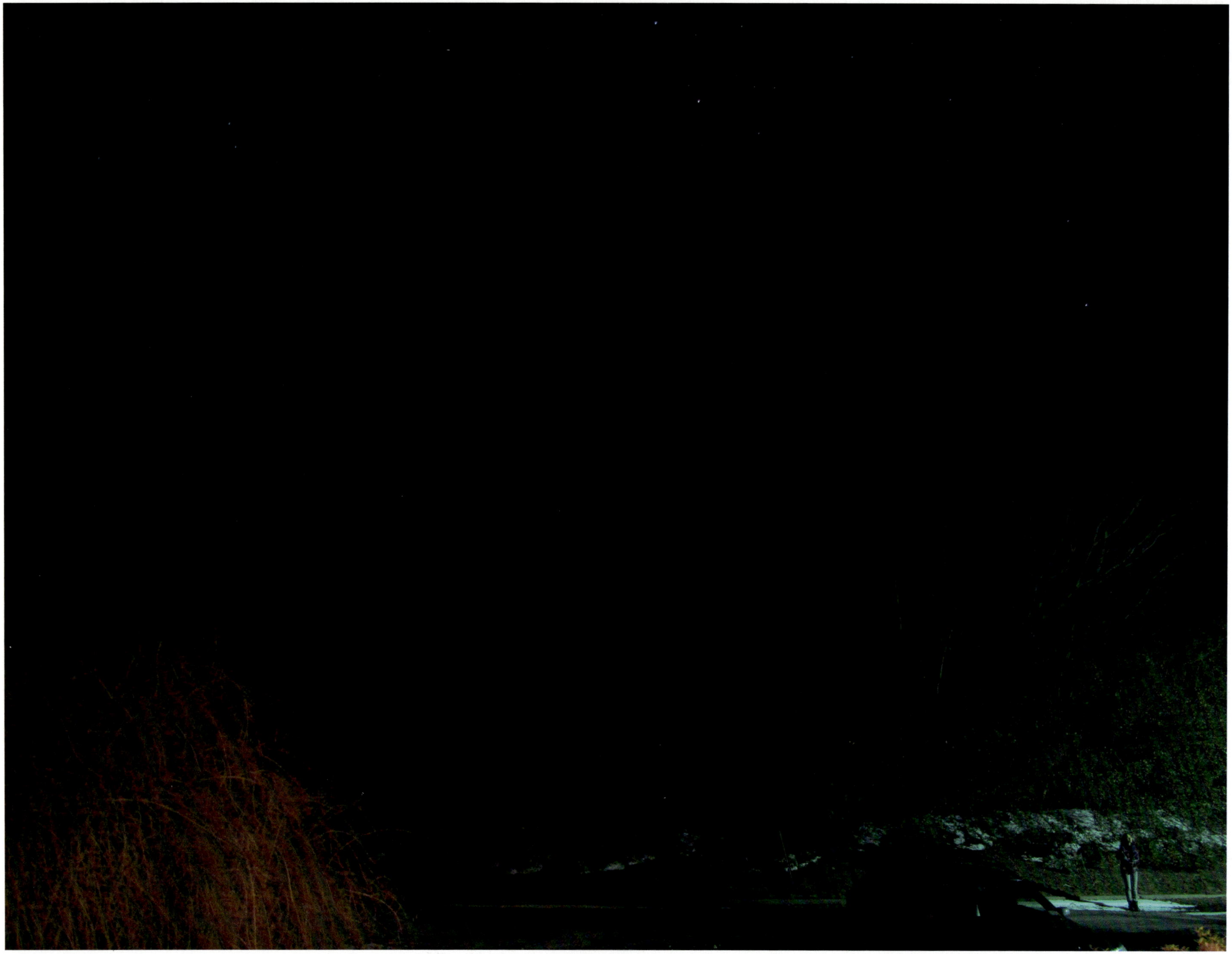

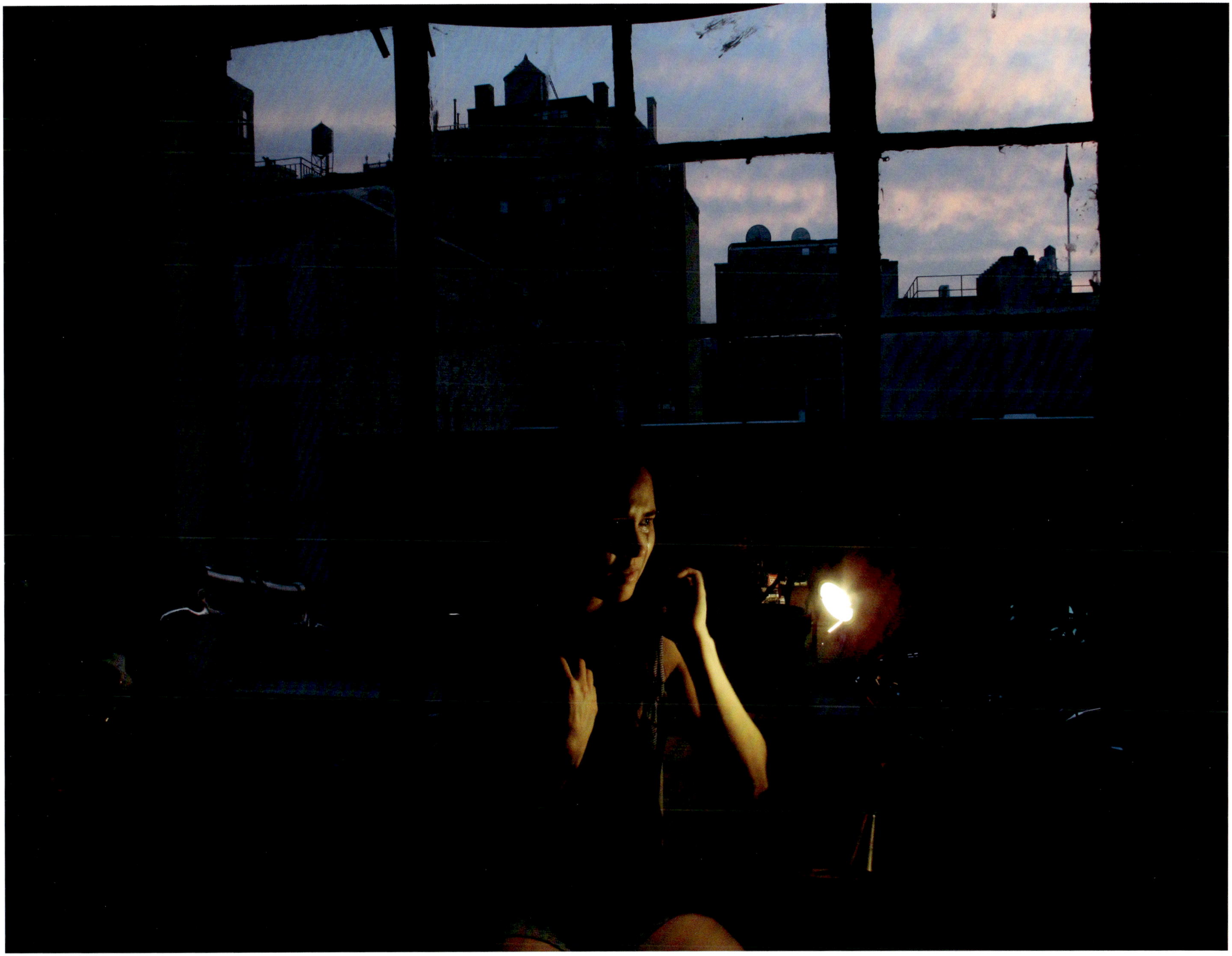

Index

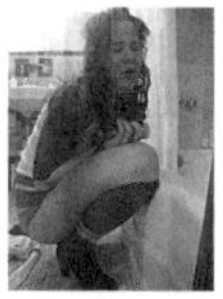
January 1, 2010
New York, NY
Pg. 11

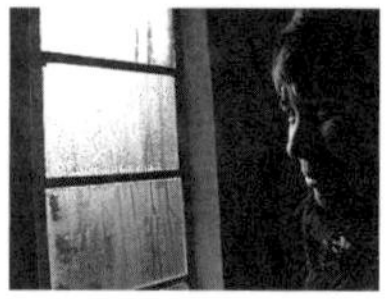
January 2, 2010
New York, NY
Pg. 12

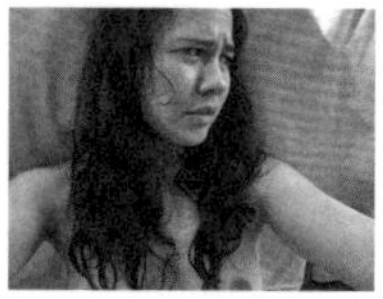
January 3, 2010
New York, NY
Pg. 13

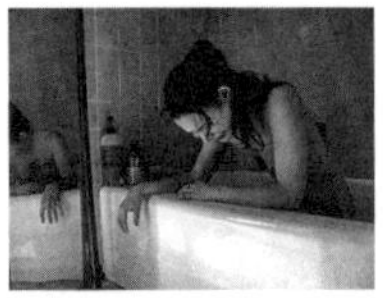
January 4, 2010
New York, NY
Pg. 14

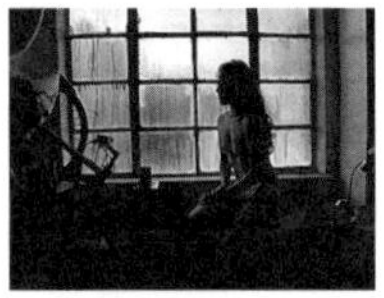
January 5, 2010
New York, NY
Pg. 15

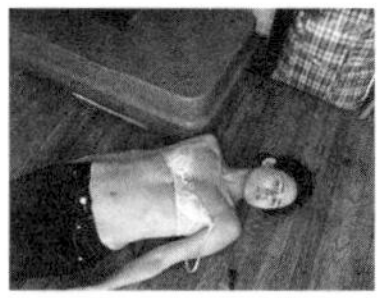
January 6, 2010
New York, NY
Pg. 16

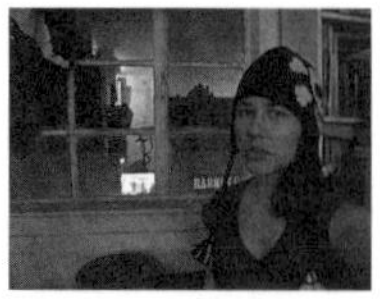
January 7, 2010
New York, NY
Pg. 17

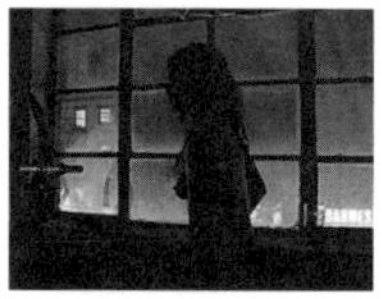
January 8, 2010
New York, NY
Pg. 18

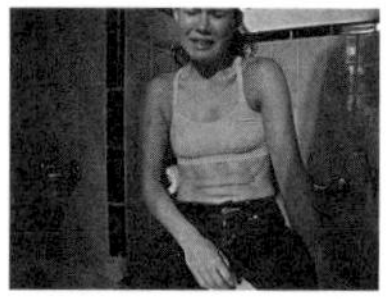
January 9, 2010
New York, NY
Pg. 19

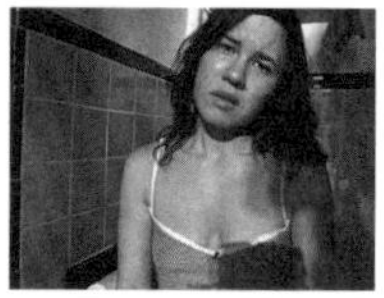
January 10, 2010
New York, NY
Pg. 20

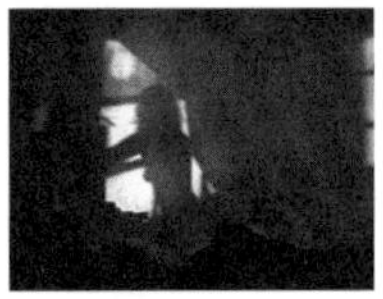
January 11, 2010
New York, NY
Pg. 21

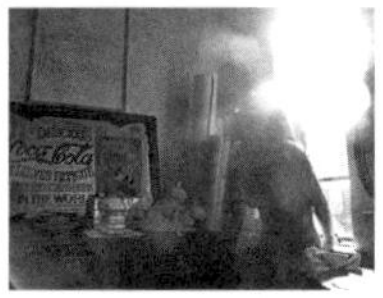
January 12, 2010
New York, NY
Pg. 22

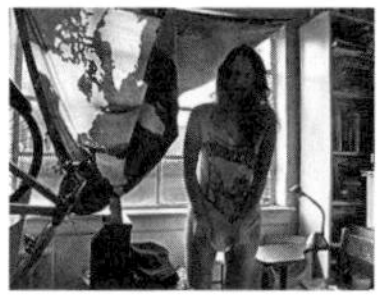
January 13, 2010
New York, NY
Pg. 23

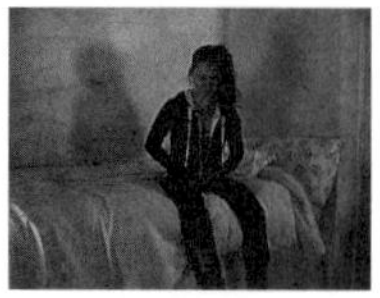
January 14, 2010
New York, NY
Pg. 24

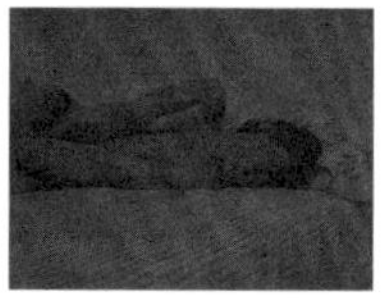
January 15, 2010
New York, NY
Pg. 25

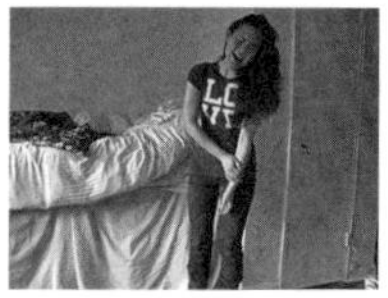
January 16, 2010
New York, NY
Pg. 26

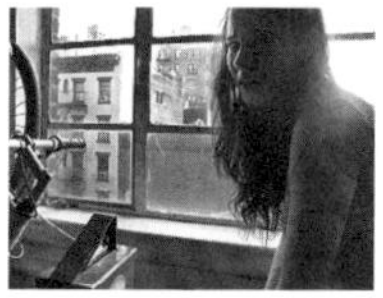
January 17, 2010
New York, NY
Pg. 27

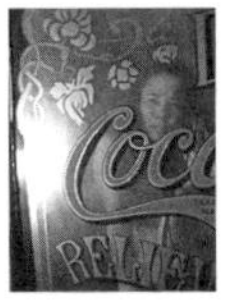
January 18, 2010
New York, NY
Pg. 28

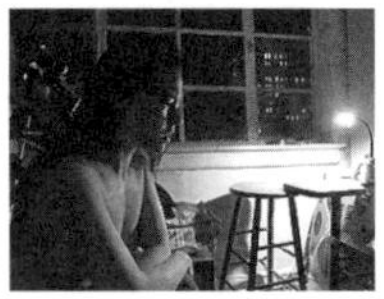
January 19, 2010
New York, NY
Pg. 29

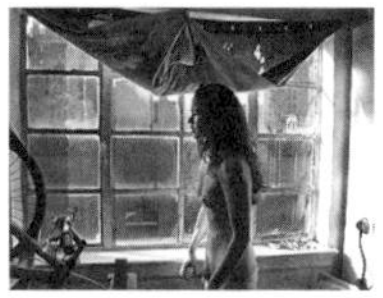
January 20, 2010
New York, NY
Pg. 30

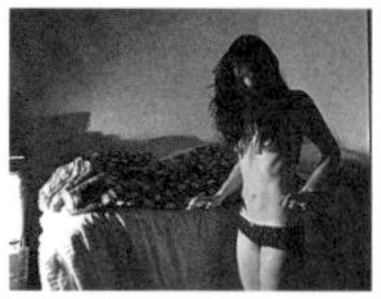
January 21, 2010
New York, NY
Pg. 31

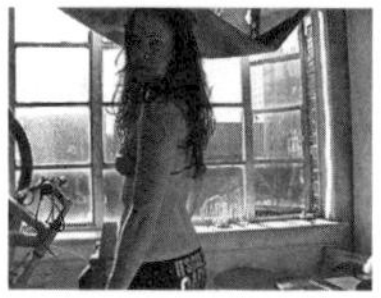
January 22, 2010
New York, NY
Pg. 32

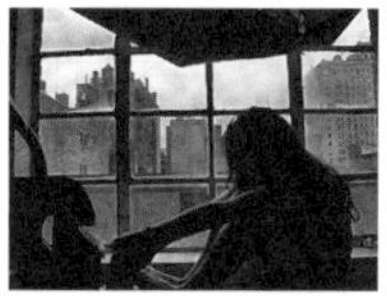
January 23, 2010
New York, NY
Pg. 33

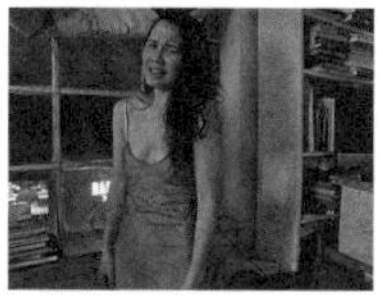
January 24, 2010
New York, NY
Pg. 34

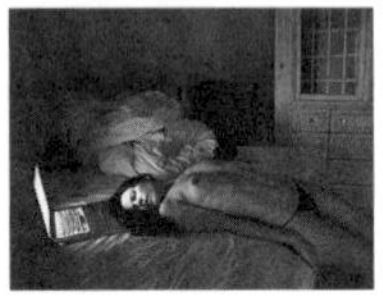
January 25, 2010
London, UK
Pg. 35

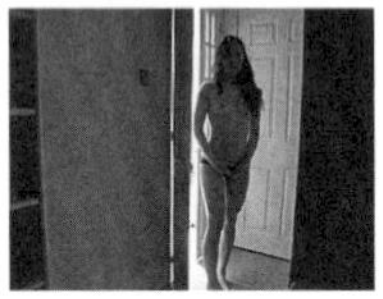
January 26, 2010
London, UK
Pg. 36

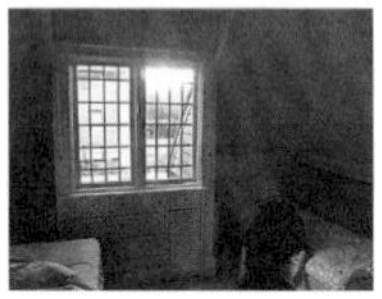
January 27, 2010
London, UK
Pg. 37

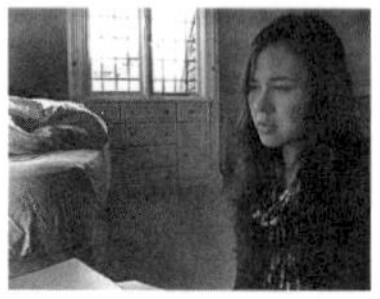
January 28, 2010
London, UK
Pg. 38

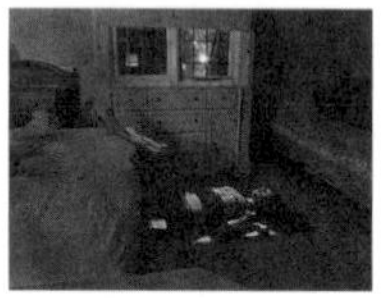
January 29, 2010
London, UK
Pg. 39

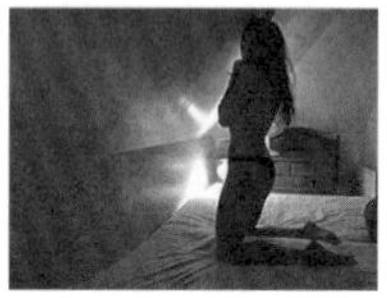
January 30, 2010
London, UK
Pg. 40

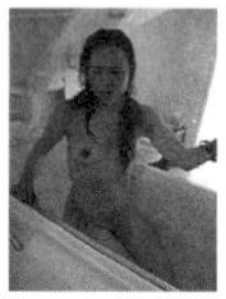
January 31, 2010
London, UK
Pg. 41

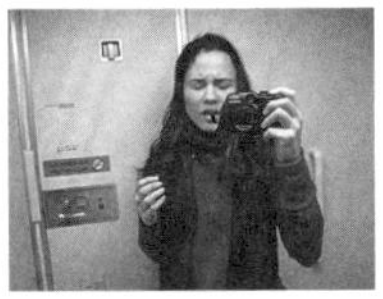

February 1, 2010
Somewhere over the Atlantic Ocean
Pg. 42

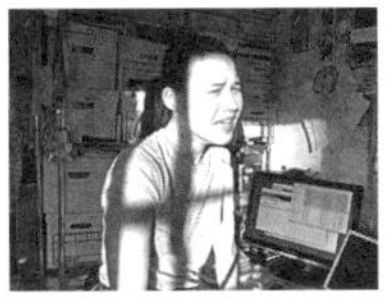

February 2, 2010
New York, NY
Pg. 43

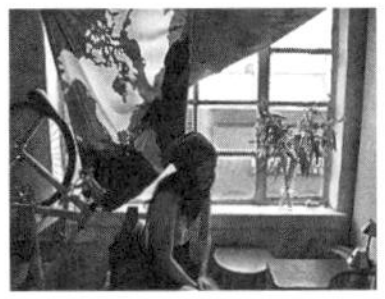

February 3, 2010
New York, NY
Pg. 44

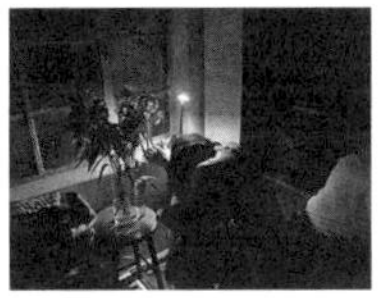

February 4, 2010
New York, NY
Pg. 45

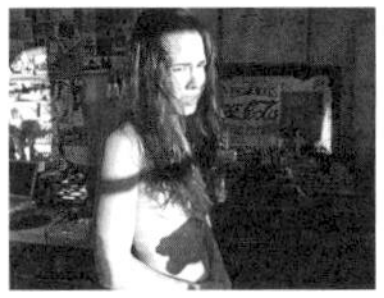

February 5, 2010
New York, NY
Pg. 46

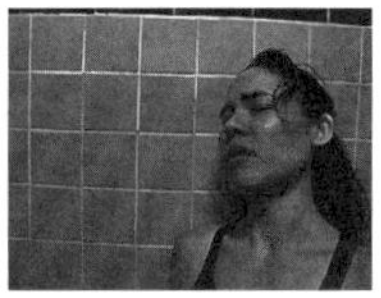

February 6, 2010
New York, NY
Pg. 47

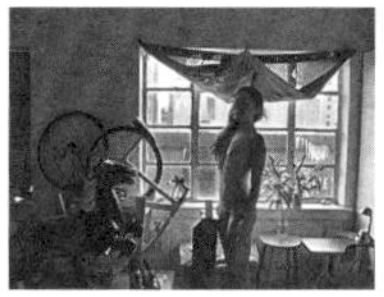

February 7, 2010
New York, NY
Pg. 48

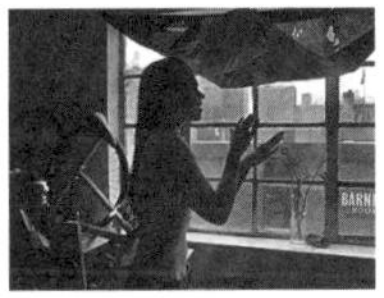

February 8, 2010
New York, NY
Pg. 49

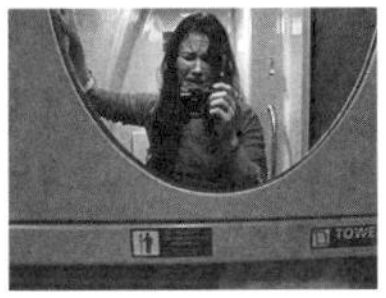

February 9, 2010
On Amtrak, near New London, CT
Pg. 50

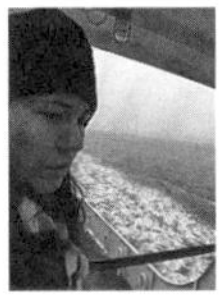

February 10, 2010
Off the coast of Fishers Island, NY
Pg. 51

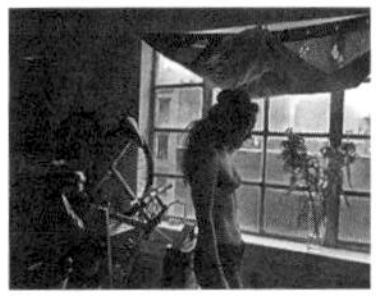

February 11, 2010
New York, NY
Pg. 52

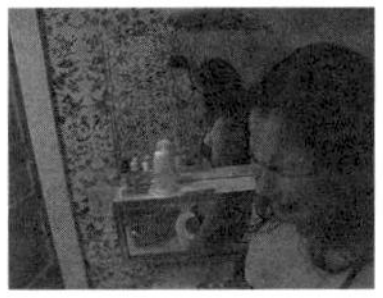

February 12, 2010
Sewanee, TN
Pg. 53

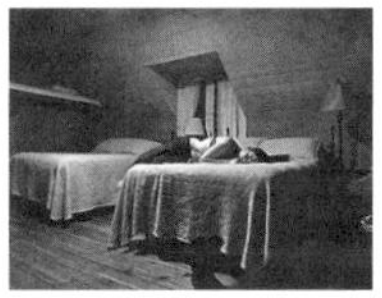

February 13, 2010
Sewanee, TN
Pg. 54

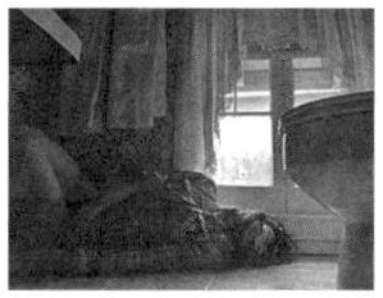

February 14, 2010
Sewanee, TN
Pg. 55

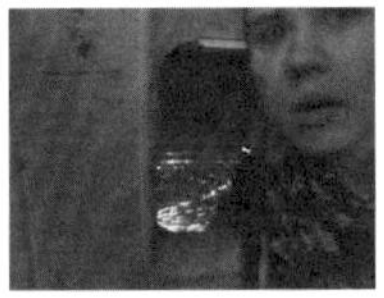

February 15, 2010
Somewhere over New York State
Pg. 56

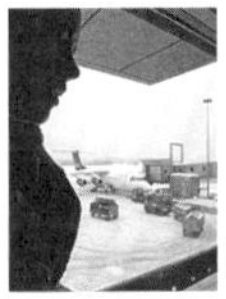

February 16, 2010
Helsinki, Finland
Pg. 57

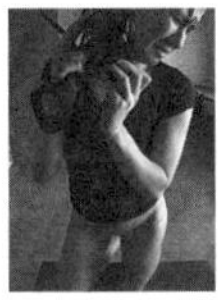

February 17, 2010
Tallinn, Estonia
Pg. 58

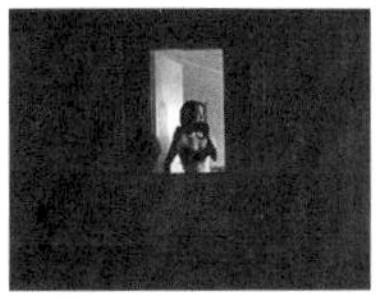

February 18, 2010
Tallinn, Estonia
Pg. 59

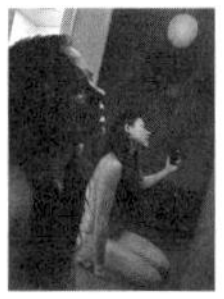

February 19, 2010
Tallinn, Estonia
Pg. 60

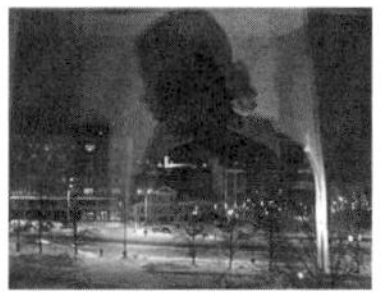

February 20, 2010
Tallinn, Estonia
Pg. 61

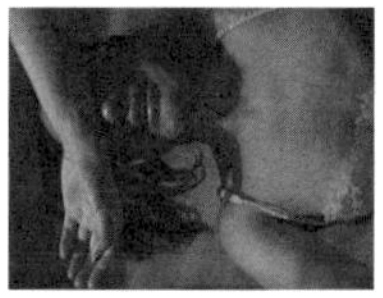

February 21, 2010
Tallinn, Estonia
Pg. 62

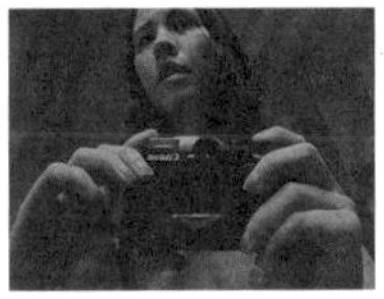

February 22, 2010
Tallinn, Estonia
Pg. 63

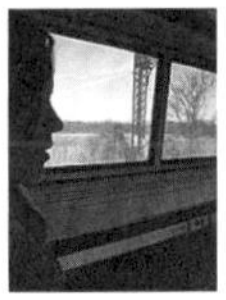

February 23, 2010
On Amtrak, somewhere in Connecticut
Pg. 64

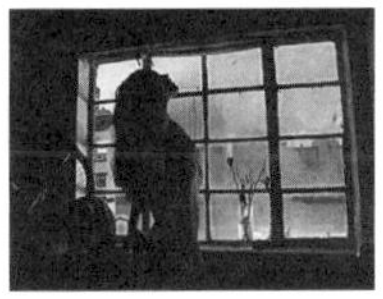

February 24, 2010
New York, NY
Pg. 65

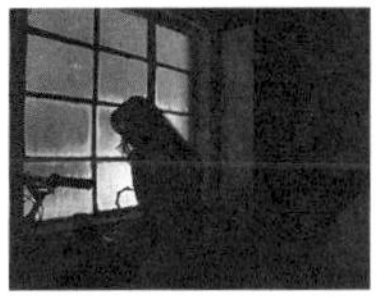

February 25, 2010
New York, NY
Pg. 66

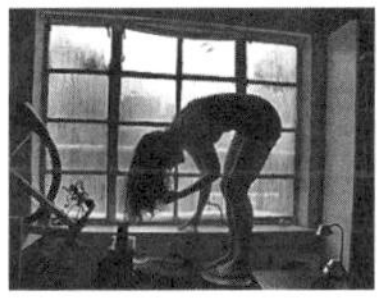

February 26, 2010
New York, NY
Pg. 67

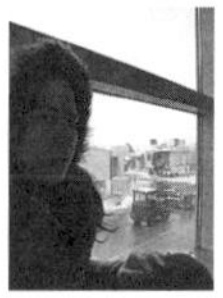

February 27, 2010
O'Hare Airport, Chicago, IL
Pg. 68

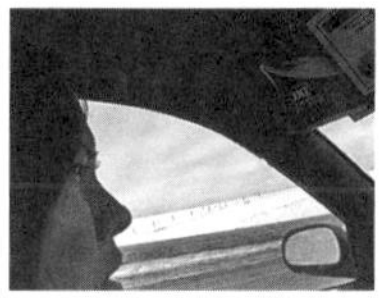

February 28, 2010
Somewhere on I-35 in Iowa
Pg. 69

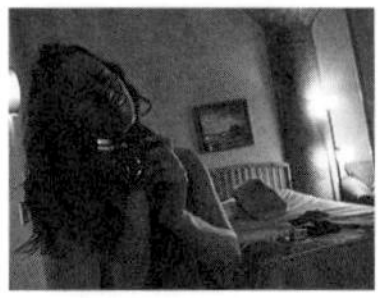

March 1, 2010
Milwaukee, WI
Pg. 70

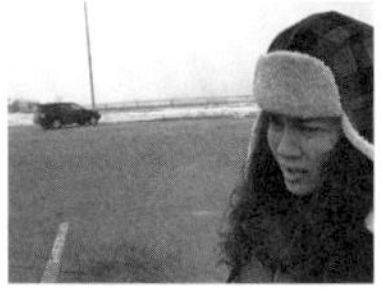

March 2, 2010
Somewhere off a highway in Wisconsin
Pg. 71

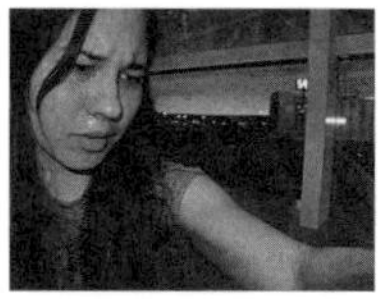

March 3, 2010
O'Hare Airport, Chicago, IL
Pg. 72

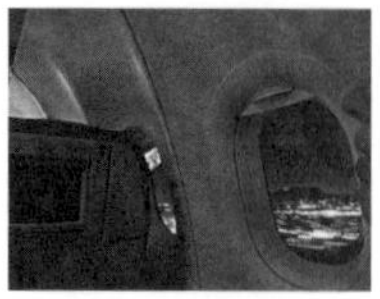

March 4, 2010
Above Los Angeles, CA
Pg. 73

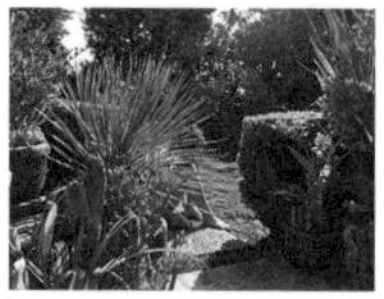

March 5, 2010
Los Angeles, CA
Pg. 74

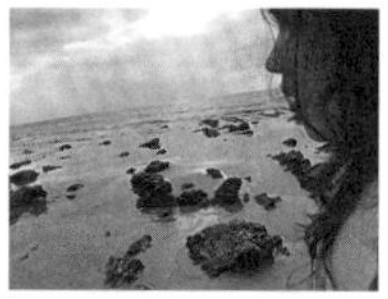

March 6, 2010
Pacific Ocean, Los Angeles, CA
Pg. 75

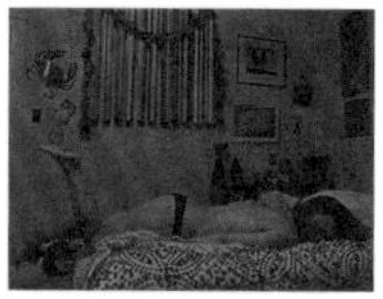

March 7, 2010
Los Angeles, CA
Pg. 76

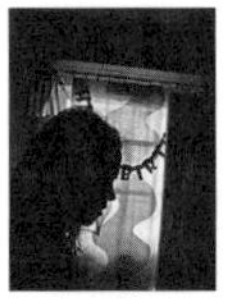

March 8, 2010
Los Angeles, CA
Pg. 77

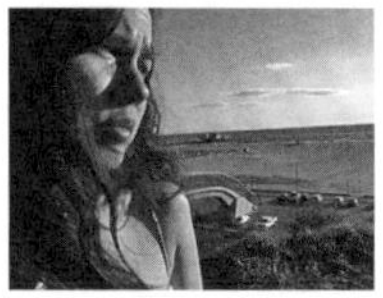

March 9, 2010
Santa Monica, CA
Pg. 78

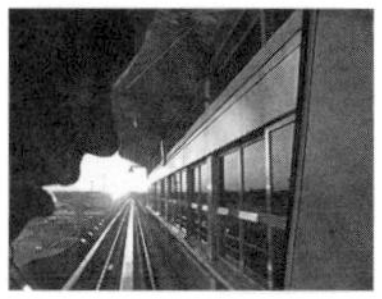

March 10, 2010
JFK Airport, New York, NY
Pg. 79

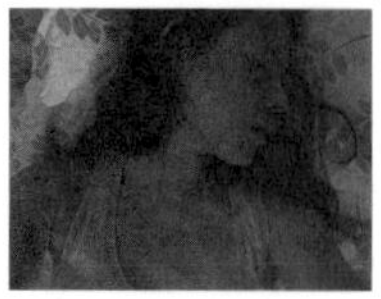

March 11, 2010
New York, NY
Pg. 80

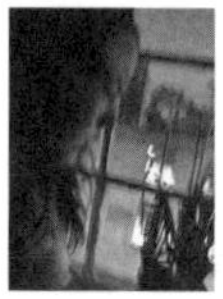

March 12, 2010
New York, NY
Pg. 81

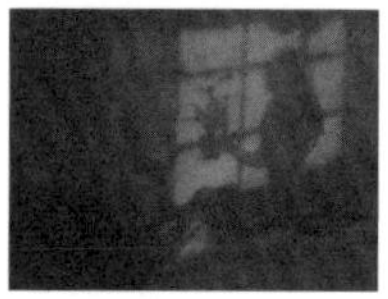

March 13, 2010
New York, NY
Pg. 82

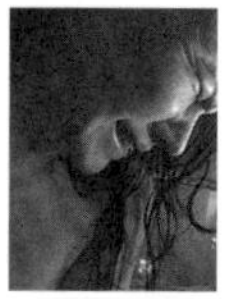

March 14, 2010
New York, NY
Pg. 83

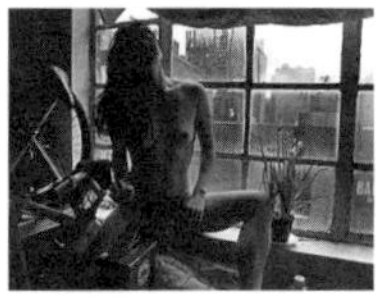

March 15, 2010
New York, NY
Pg. 84

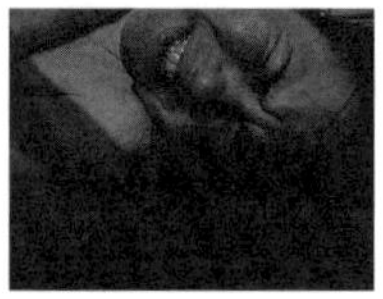

March 16, 2010
New York, NY
Pg. 85

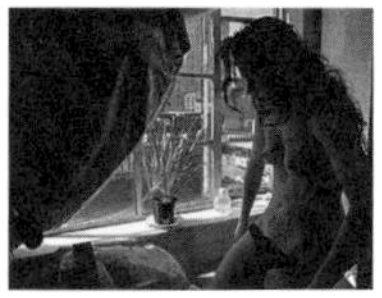

March 17, 2010
New York, NY
Pg. 86

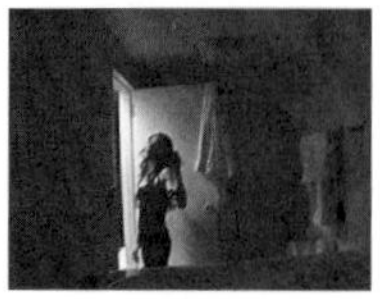

March 18, 2010
New York, NY
Pg. 87

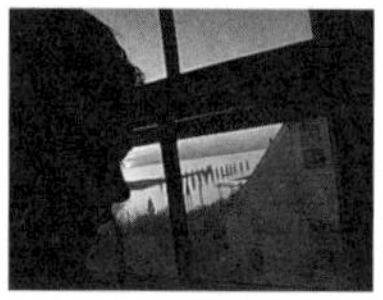

March 19, 2010
Fishers Island, NY
Pg. 88

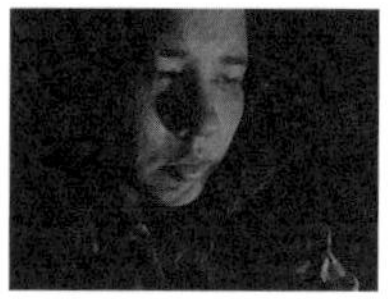

March 20, 2010
New York, NY
Pg. 89

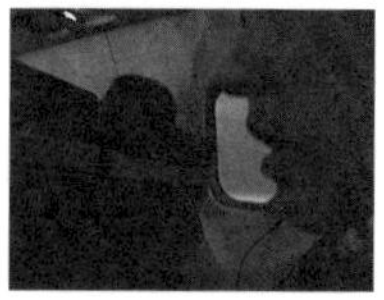

March 21, 2010
Somewhere over Ohio
Pg. 90

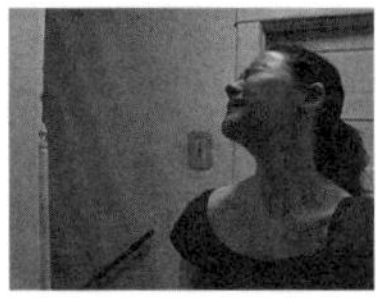

March 22, 2010
Ames, IA
Pg. 91

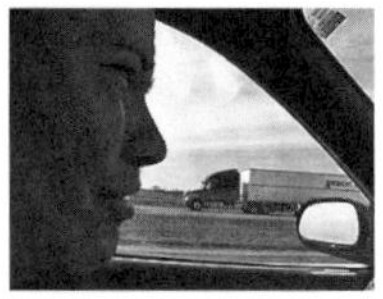

March 23, 2010
Somewhere on I-35 near the IA/MN border
Pg. 92

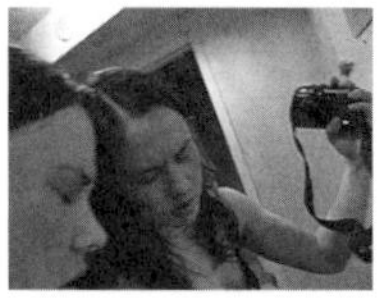

March 24, 2010
Minneapolis, MN
Pg. 93

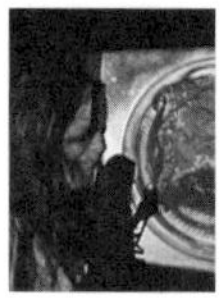

March 25, 2010
Walker Art Center, Minneapolis, MN
Pg. 94

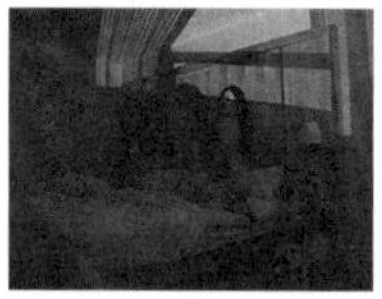

March 26, 2010
Minneapolis, MN
Pg. 95

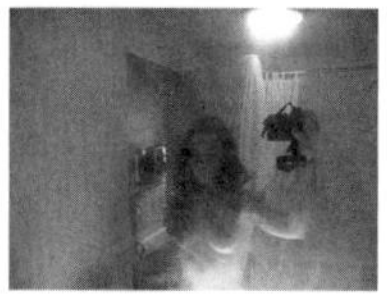

March 27, 2010
Somewhere outside Minneapolis, MN
Pg. 96

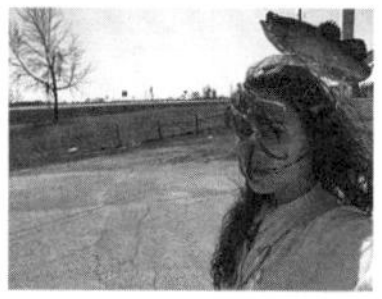

March 28, 2010
Gas station somewhere on I-35 outside Minneapolis, MN
Pg. 97

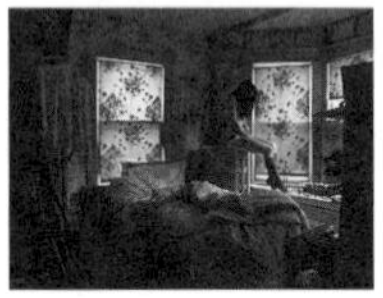

March 29, 2010
Ames, IA
Pg. 98

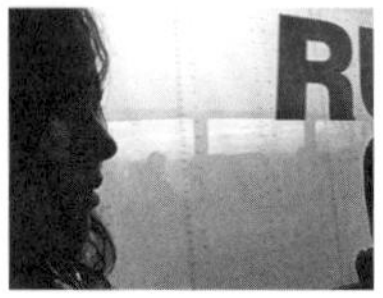

March 30, 2010
Somewhere in New Jersey
Pg. 99

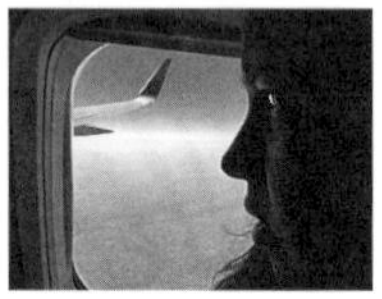

March 31, 2010
Somewhere in the air between New York and Texas
Pg. 100

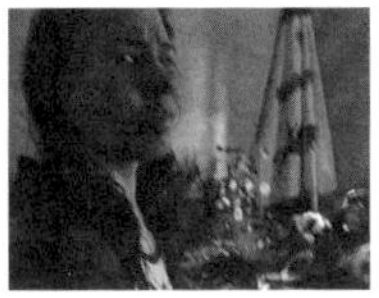
April 1, 2010
Houston, TX
Pg. 101

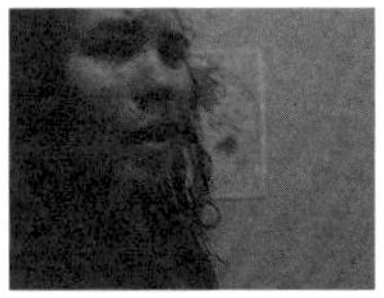
April 2, 2010
Houston, TX
Pg. 102

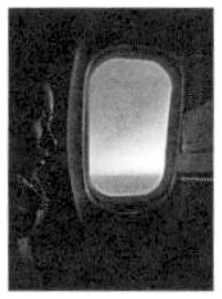
April 3, 2010
Somewhere above Texas
Pg. 103

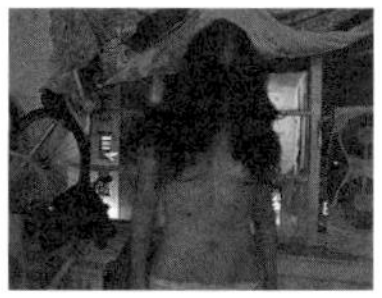
April 4, 2010
New York, NY
Pg. 104

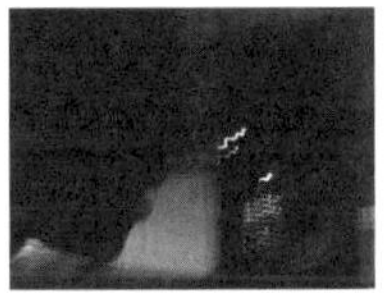
April 5, 2010
New York, NY
Pg. 105

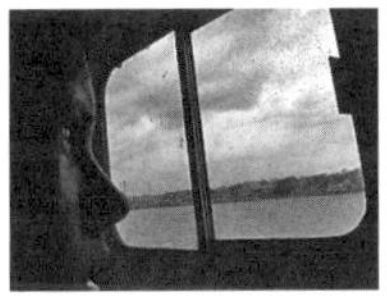
April 6, 2010
Off the coast of
New London, CT
Pg. 106

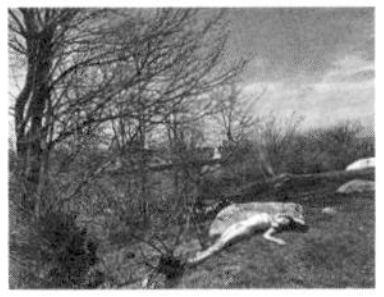
April 7, 2010
Fishers Island, NY
Pg. 107

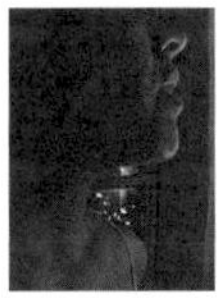
April 8, 2010
New York, NY
Pg. 108

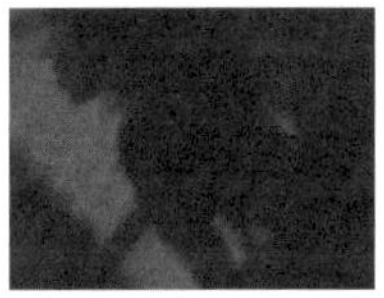
April 9, 2010
New York, NY
Pg. 109

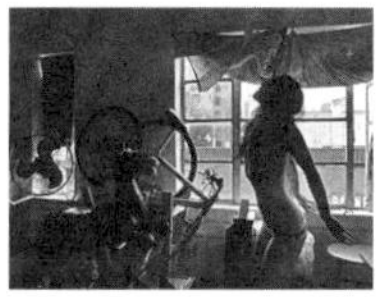
April 10, 2010
New York, NY
Pg. 110

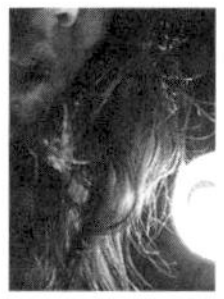
April 11, 2010
New York, NY
Pg. 111

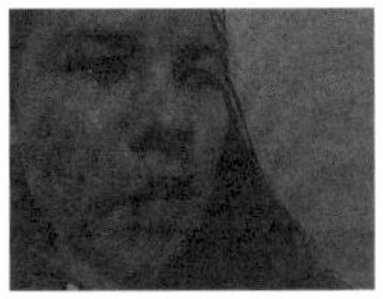
April 12, 2010
New York, NY
Pg. 112

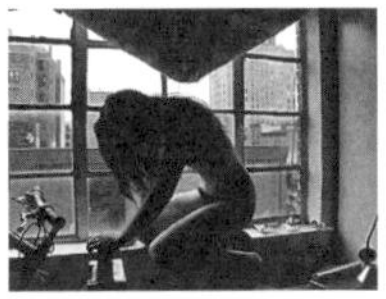
April 13, 2010
New York, NY
Pg. 113

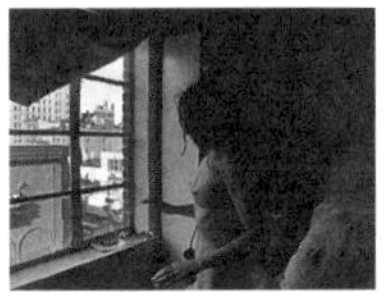
April 14, 2010
New York, NY
Pg. 114

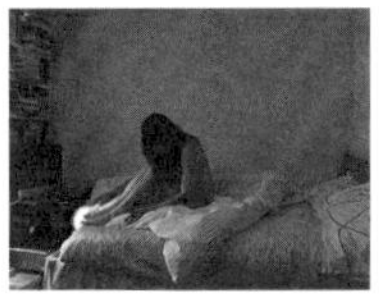
April 15, 2010
New York, NY
Pg. 115

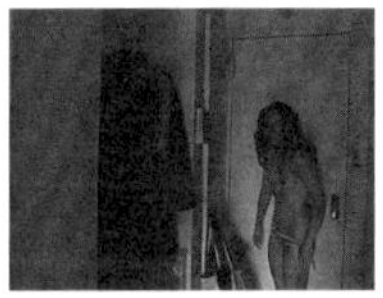
April 16, 2010
New York, NY
Pg. 116

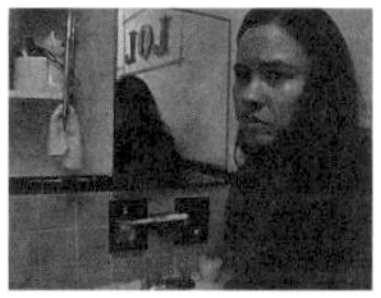
April 17, 2010
New York, NY
Pg. 117

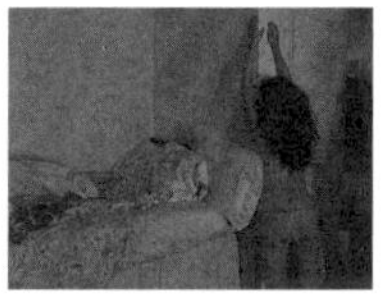
April 18, 2010
New York, NY
Pg. 118

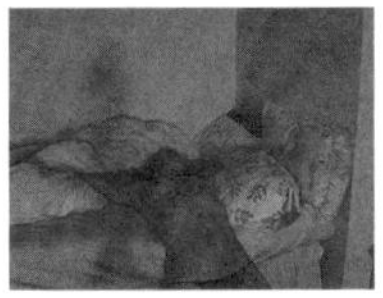
April 19, 2010
New York, NY
Pg. 119

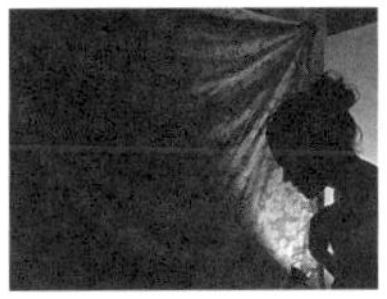
April 20, 2010
New York, NY
Pg. 120

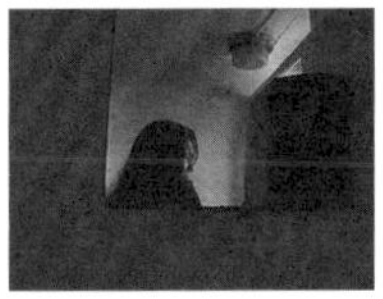
April 21, 2010
Fishers Island, NY
Pg. 121

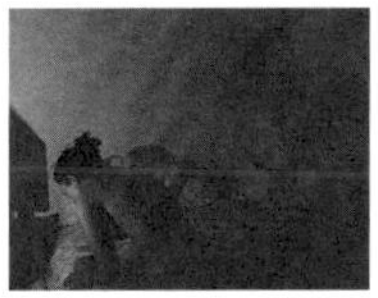
April 22, 2010
New York, NY
Pg. 122

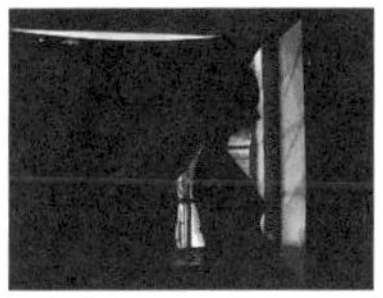
April 23, 2010
New York, NY
Pg. 123

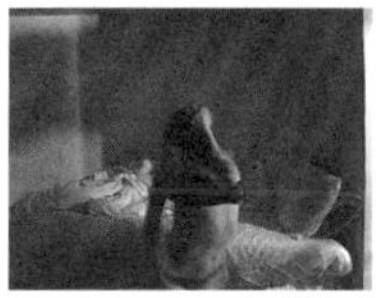
April 24, 2010
New York, NY
Pg. 124

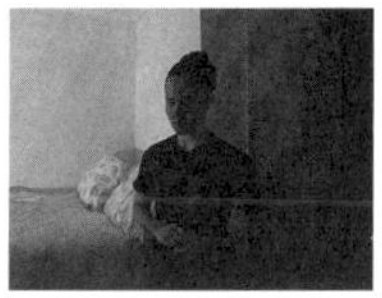
April 25, 2010
New York, NY
Pg. 125

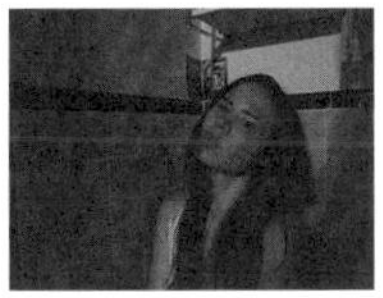
April 26, 2010
New York, NY
Pg. 126

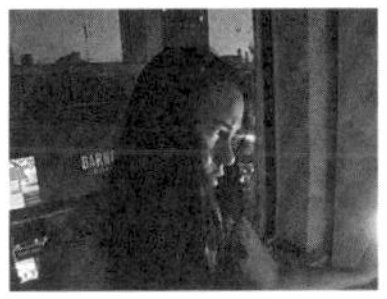
April 27, 2010
New York, NY
Pg. 127

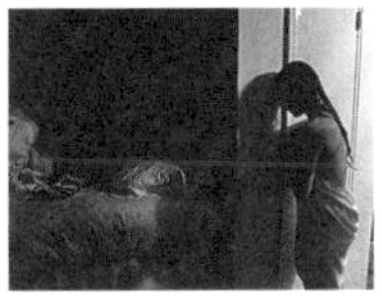
April 28, 2010
New York, NY
Pg. 128

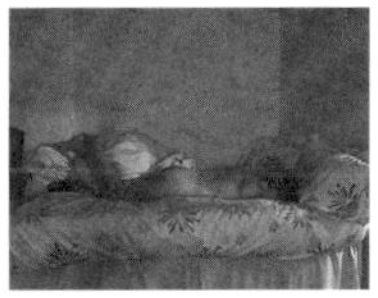
April 29, 2010
New York, NY
Pg. 129

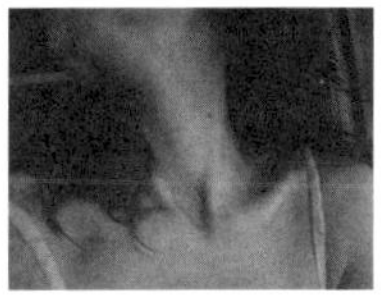
April 30, 2010
New York, NY
Pg. 130

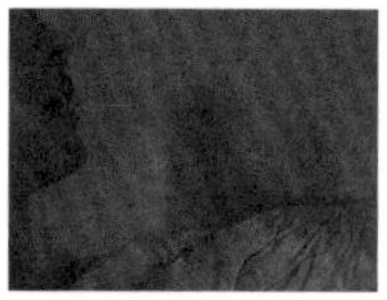
May 1, 2010
New York, NY
Pg. 131

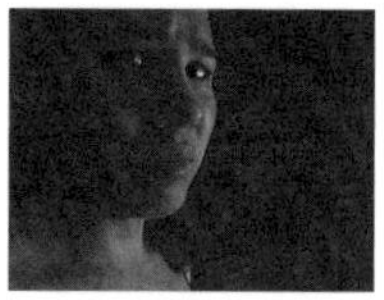
May 2, 2010
New York, NY
Pg. 132

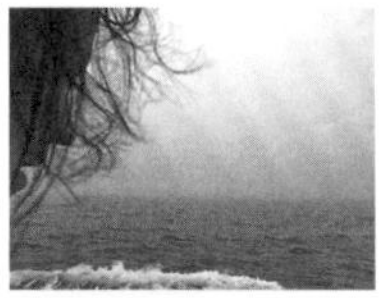
May 3, 2010
Off the coast of
New London, CT
Pg. 133

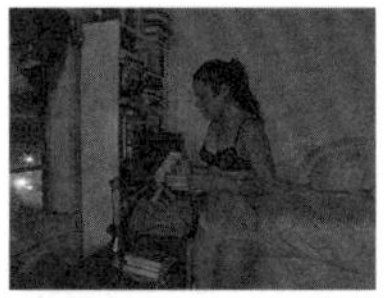
May 4, 2010
New York, NY
Pg. 134

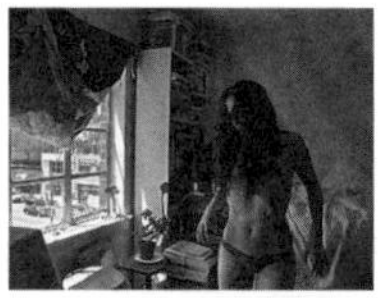
May 5, 2010
New York, NY
Pg. 135

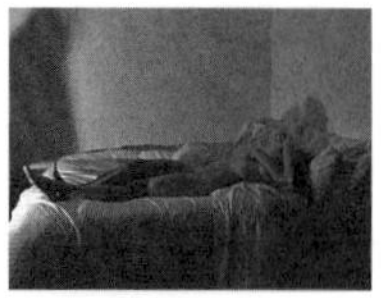
May 6, 2010
New York, NY
Pg. 136

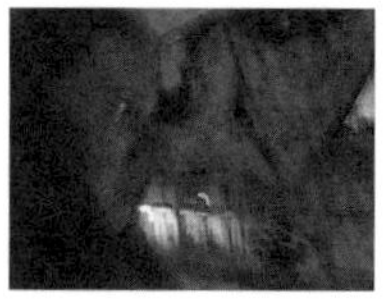
May 7, 2010
New York, NY
Pg. 137

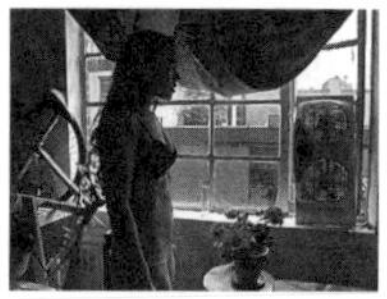
May 8, 2010
New York, NY
Pg. 138

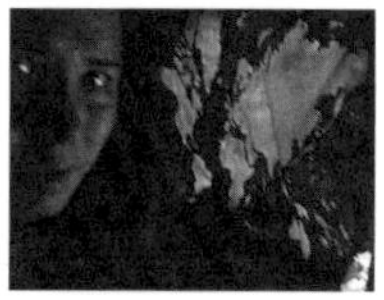
May 9, 2010
New York, NY
Pg. 139

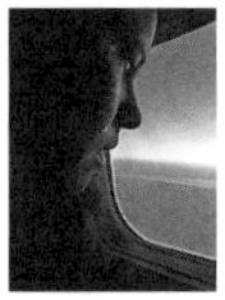
May 10, 2010
Above New York State
Pg. 140

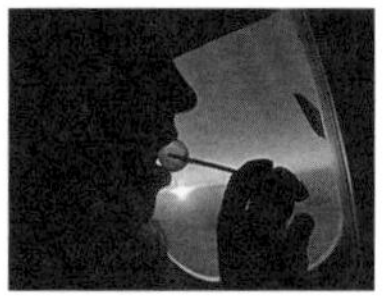
May 11, 2010
Above Copenhagen, Denmark
Pg. 141

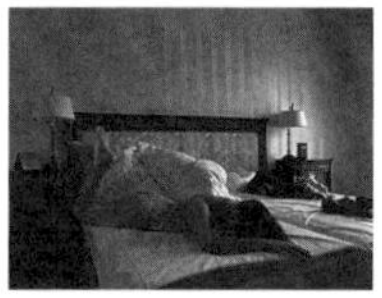
May 12, 2010
Copenhagen, Denmark
Pg. 142

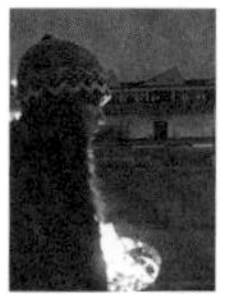
May 13, 2010
Copenhagen, Denmark
Pg. 143

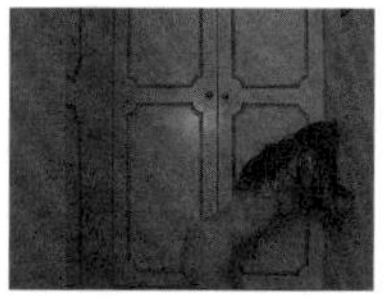
May 14, 2010
Copenhagen, Denmark
Pg. 144

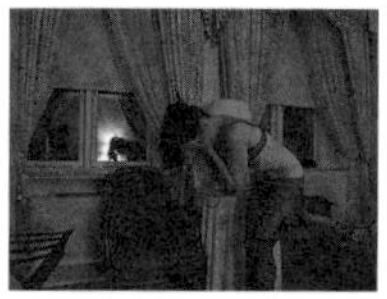
May 15, 2010
Copenhagen, Denmark
Pg. 145

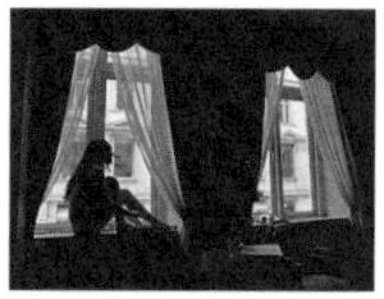
May 16, 2010
Copenhagen, Denmark
Pg. 146

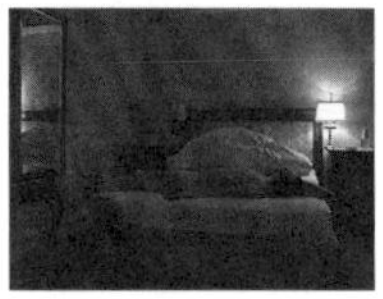
May 17, 2010
Copenhagen, Denmark
Pg. 147

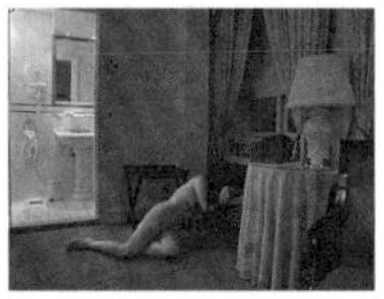
May 18, 2010
Copenhagen, Denmark
Pg. 148

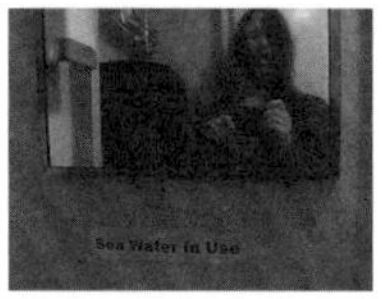
May 19, 2010
Off the coast of
New London, CT
Pg. 149

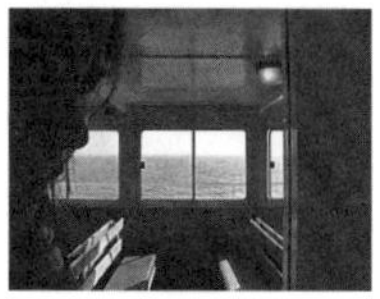
May 20, 2010
Off the coast of
Fishers Island, NY
Pg. 150

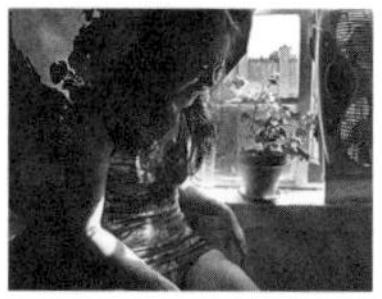
May 21, 2010
New York, NY
Pg. 151

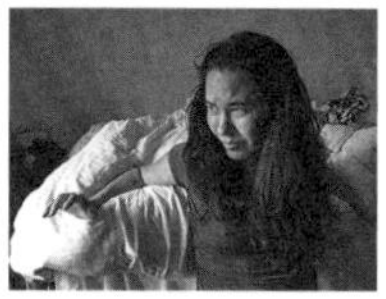
May 22, 2010
New York, NY
Pg. 152

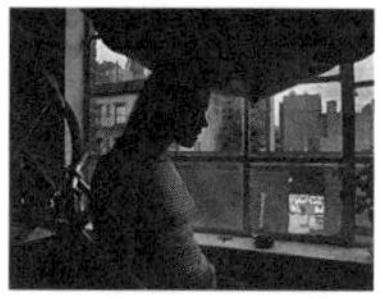
May 23, 2010
New York, NY
Pg. 153

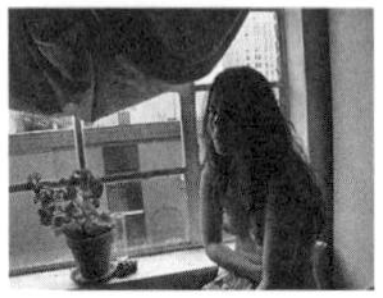
May 24, 2010
New York, NY
Pg. 154

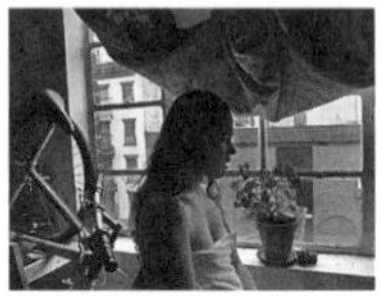
May 25, 2010
New York, NY
Pg. 155

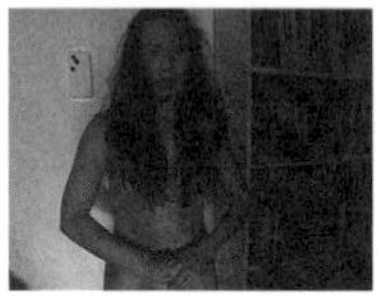
May 26, 2010
New York, NY
Pg. 156

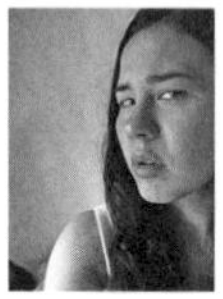
May 27, 2010
New York, NY
Pg. 157

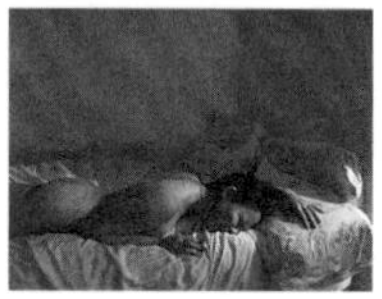
May 28, 2010
New York, NY
Pg. 158

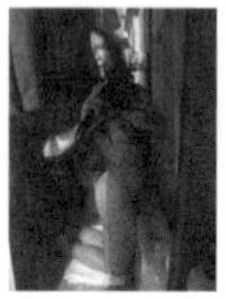
May 29, 2010
New York, NY
Pg. 159

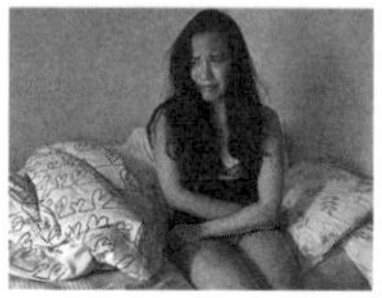
May 30, 2010
New York, NY
Pg. 160

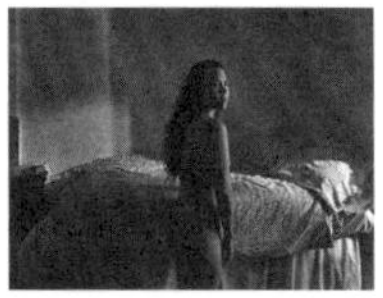
May 31, 2010
New York, NY
Pg. 161

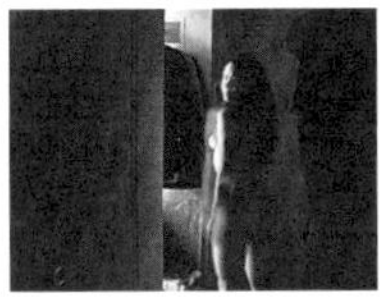

June 1, 2010
New York, NY
Pg. 162

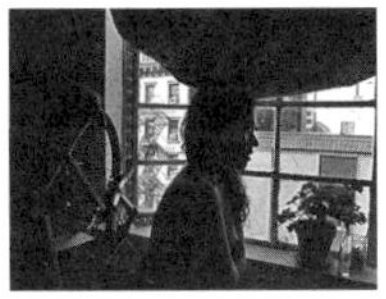

June 2, 2010
New York, NY
Pg. 163

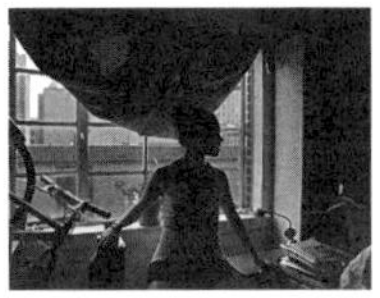

June 3, 2010
New York, NY
Pg. 164

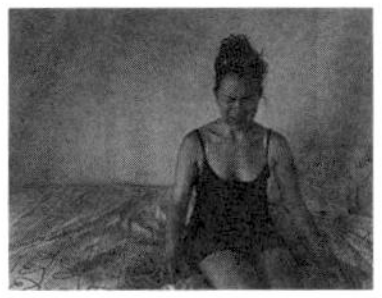

June 4, 2010
New York, NY
Pg. 165

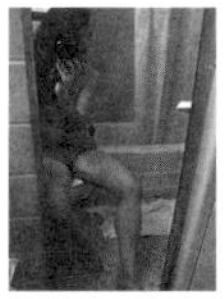

June 5, 2010
New York, NY
Pg. 166

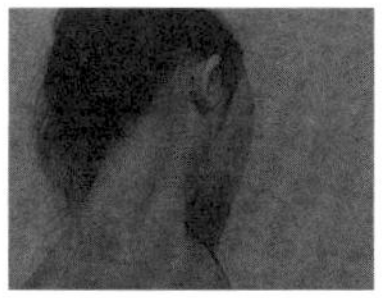

June 6, 2010
New York, NY
Pg. 167

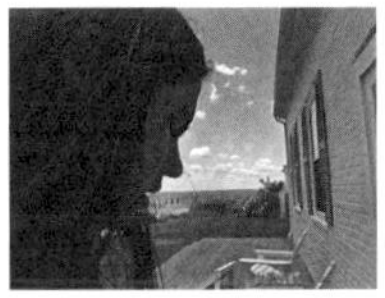

June 7, 2010
Fishers Island, NY
Pg. 168

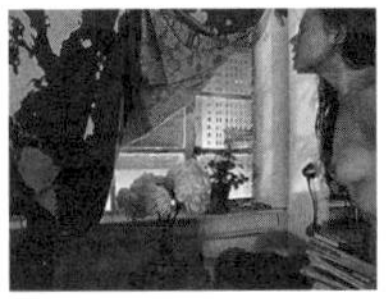

June 8, 2010
New York, NY
Pg. 169

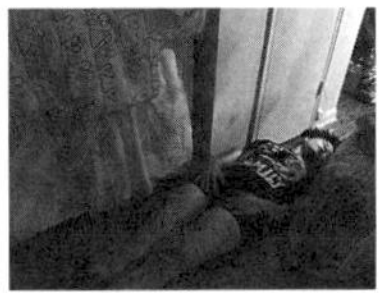

June 9, 2010
New York, NY
Pg. 170

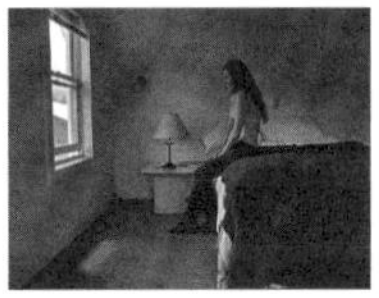

June 10, 2010
Johnson, VT
Pg. 171

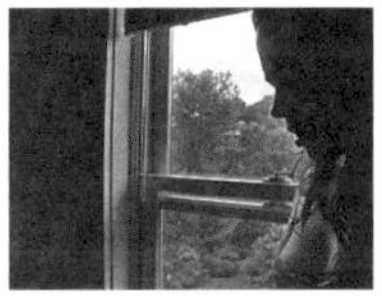

June 11, 2010
Johnson, VT
Pg. 172

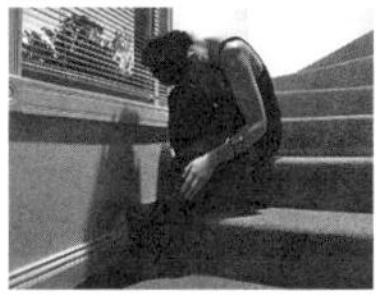

June 12, 2010
Johnson, VT
Pg. 173

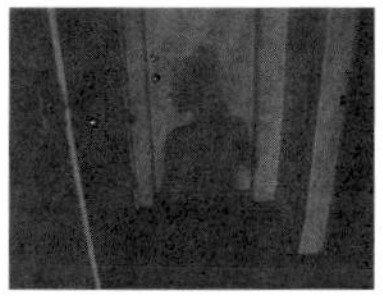

June 13, 2010
Johnson, VT
Pg. 174

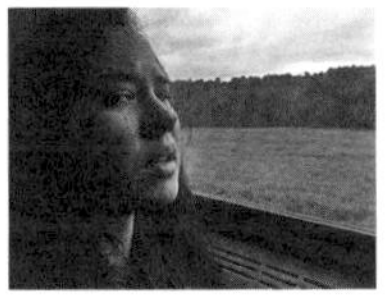

June 14, 2010
On Amtrak,
somewhere in Vermont
Pg. 175

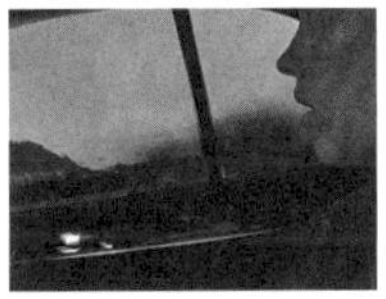

June 15, 2010
San Francisco, CA
Pg. 176

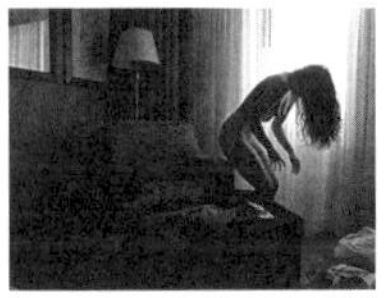

June 16, 2010
Marin County, CA
Pg. 177

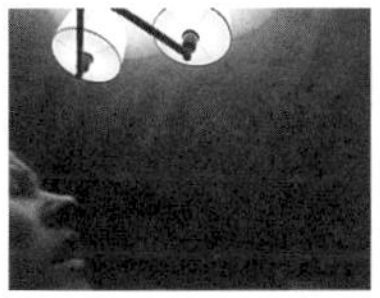

June 17, 2010
Los Angeles, CA
Pg. 178

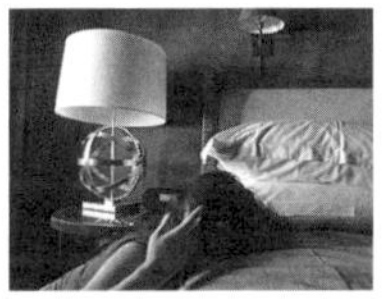

June 18, 2010
Los Angeles, CA
Pg. 179

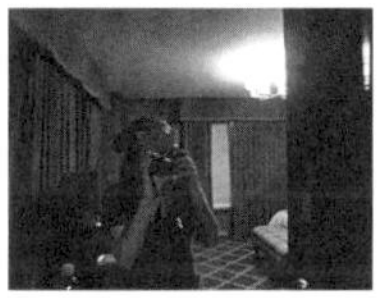

June 19, 2010
Los Angeles, CA
Pg. 180

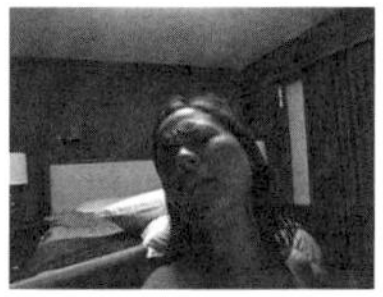

June 20, 2010
Los Angeles, CA
Pg. 181

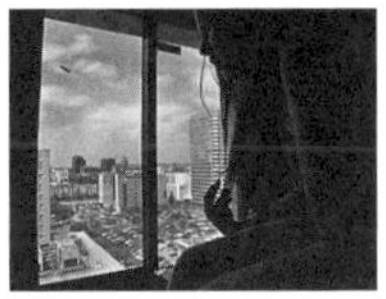

June 21, 2010
Los Angeles, CA
Pg. 182

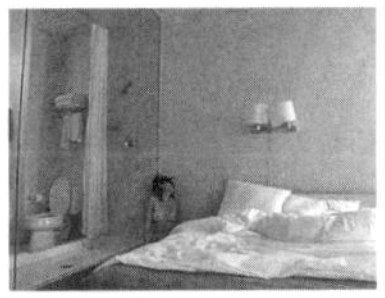

June 22, 2010
Los Angeles, CA
Pg. 183

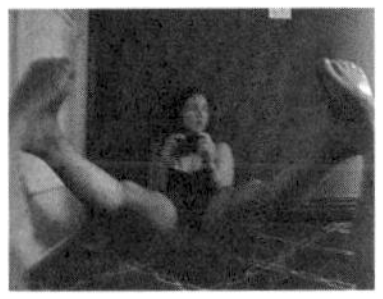

June 23, 2010
Los Angeles, CA
Pg. 184

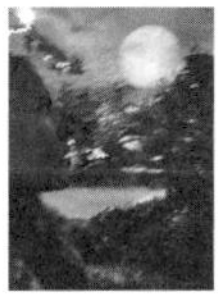

June 24, 2010
Los Angeles, CA
Pg. 185

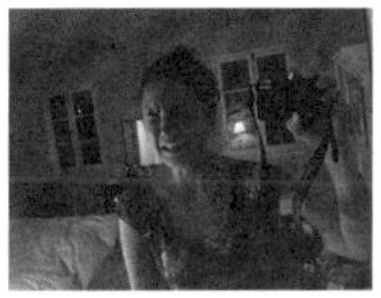

June 25, 2010
Los Angeles, CA
Pg. 186

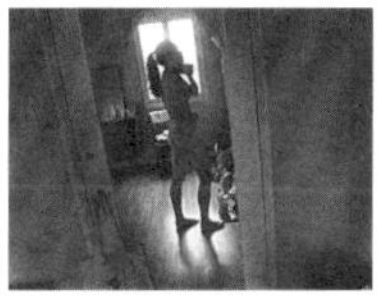

June 26, 2010
Los Angeles, CA
Pg. 187

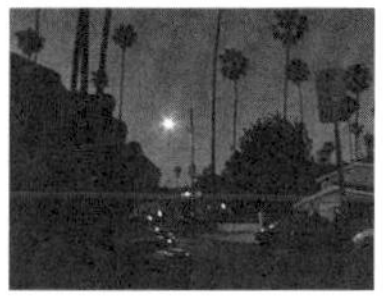

June 27, 2010
Los Angeles, CA
Pg. 188

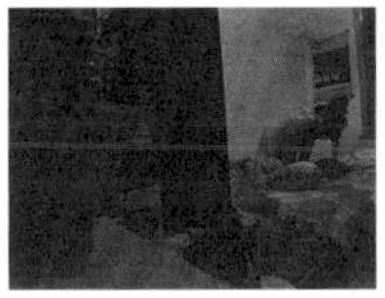

June 28, 2010
Chicago, IL
Pg. 189

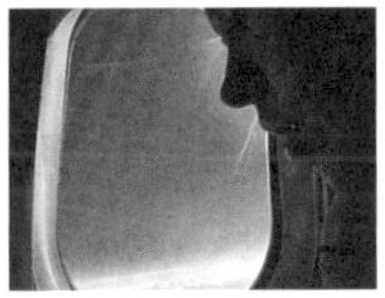

June 29, 2010
Somewhere
above Chicago, IL
Pg. 190

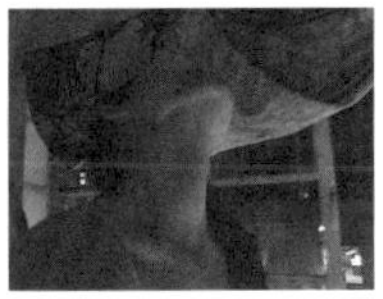

June 30, 2010
New York, NY
Pg. 191

July 1, 2010
New York, NY
Pg. 192

July 2, 2010
New York, NY
Pg. 193

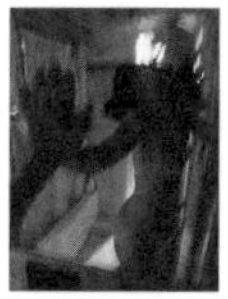
July 3, 2010
New York, NY
Pg. 194

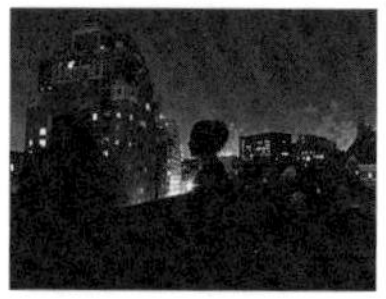
July 4, 2010
New York, NY
Pg. 195

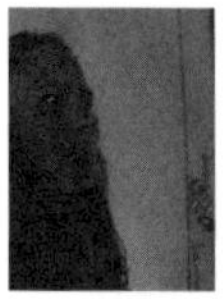
July 5, 2010
New York, NY
Pg. 196

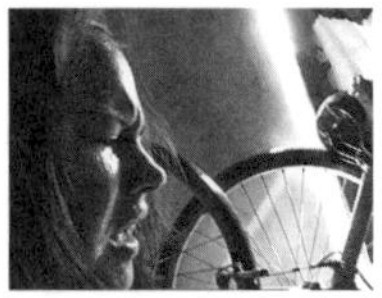
July 6, 2010
New York, NY
Pg. 197

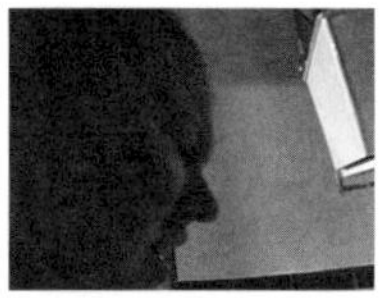
July 7, 2010
New York, NY
Pg. 198

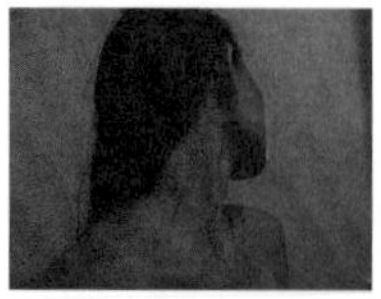
July 8, 2010
New York, NY
Pg. 199

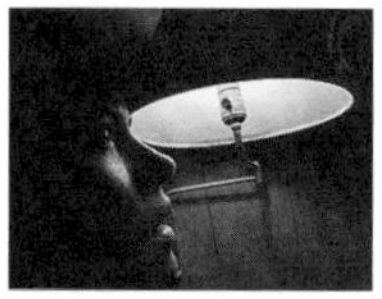
July 9, 2010
Bar Harbor, ME
Pg. 200

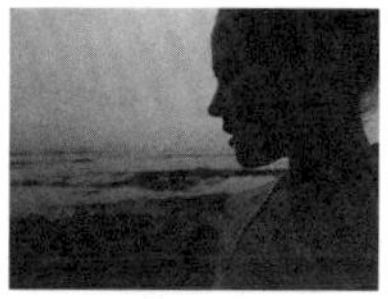
July 10, 2010
Bar Harbor, ME
Pg. 201

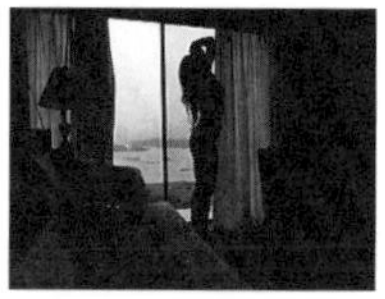
July 11, 2010
Bar Harbor, ME
Pg. 202

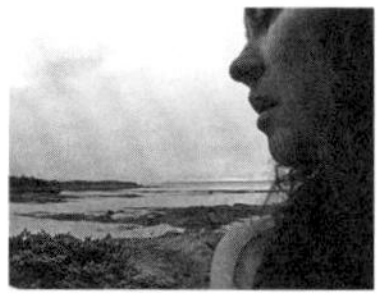
July 12, 2010
Bar Harbor, ME
Pg. 203

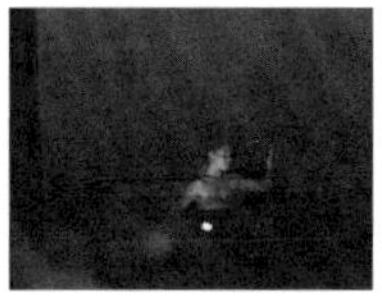
July 13, 2010
Bar Harbor, ME
Pg. 204

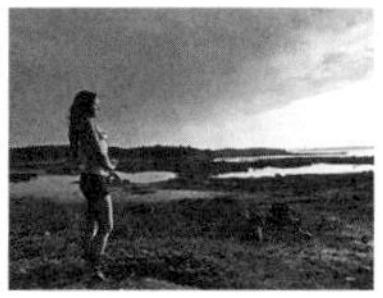
July 14, 2010
Bar Harbor, ME
Pg. 205

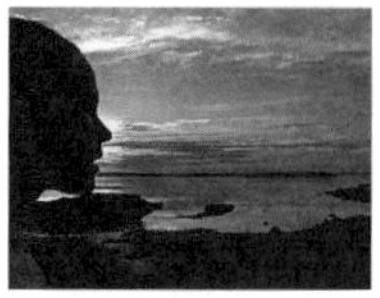
July 15, 2010
Bar Harbor, ME
Pg. 206

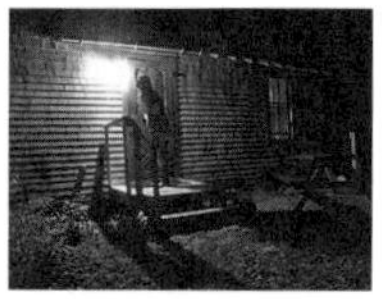
July 16, 2010
Bar Harbor, ME
Pg. 207

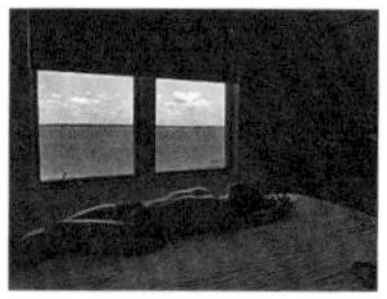
July 17, 2010
Bar Harbor, ME
Pg. 208

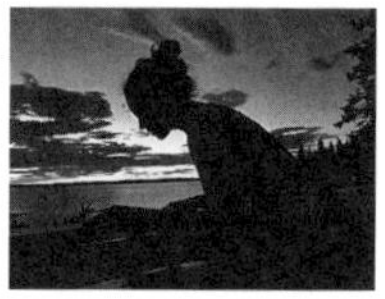
July 18, 2010
Bar Harbor, ME
Pg. 209

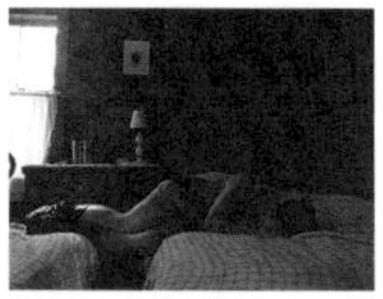
July 19, 2010
Bar Harbor, ME
Pg. 210

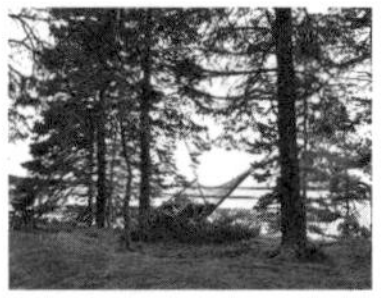
July 20, 2010
Bar Harbor, ME
Pg. 211

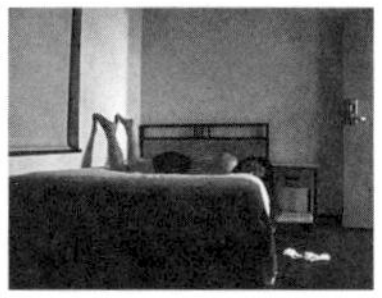
July 21, 2010
Saratoga Springs, NY
Pg. 212

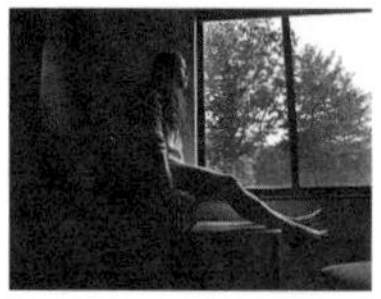
July 22, 2010
Saratoga Springs, NY
Pg. 213

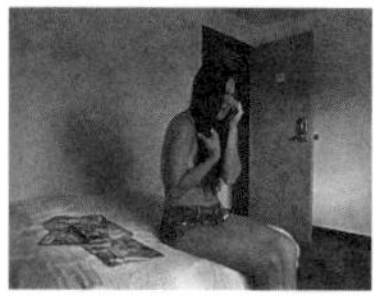
July 23, 2010
Saratoga Springs, NY
Pg. 214

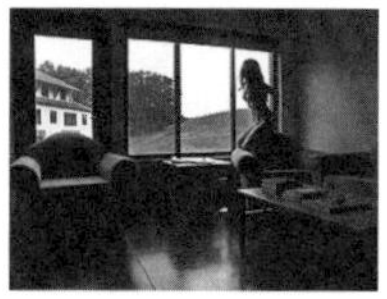
July 24, 2010
Saratoga Springs, NY
Pg. 215

July 25, 2010
New York, NY
Pg. 216

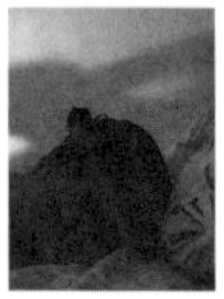
July 26, 2010
New York, NY
Pg. 217

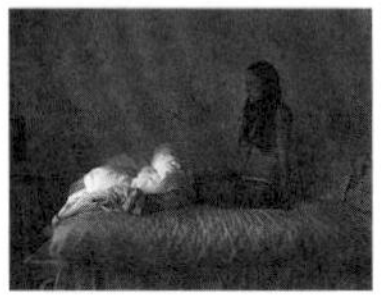
July 27, 2010
New York, NY
Pg. 218

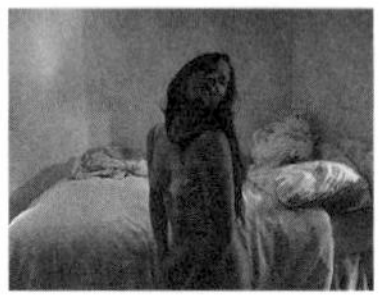
July 28, 2010
New York, NY
Pg. 219

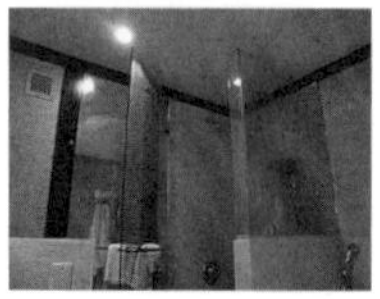
July 29, 2010
Philadelphia, PA
Pg. 220

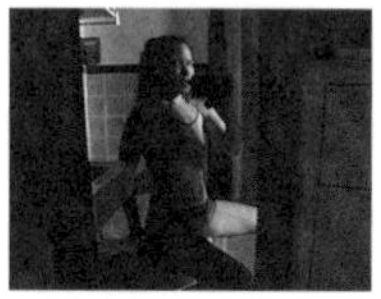
July 30, 2010
New York, NY
Pg. 221

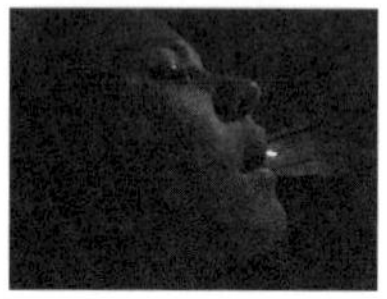
July 31, 2010
Somewhere over Wyoming
Pg. 222

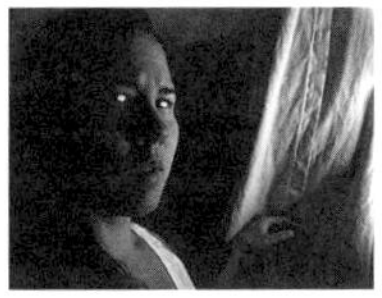
August 1, 2010
Portland, OR
Pg. 223

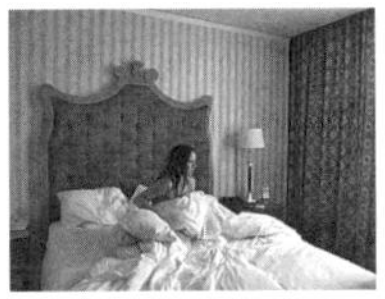
August 2, 2010
Portland, OR
Pg. 224

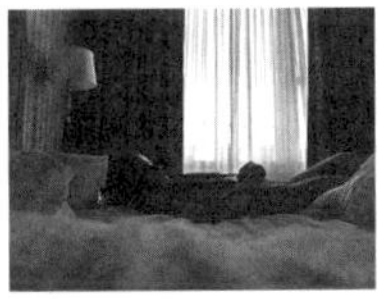
August 3, 2010
Portland, OR
Pg. 225

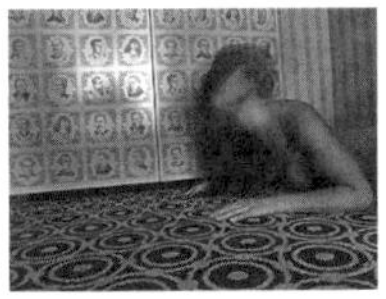
August 4, 2010
Portland, OR
Pg. 226

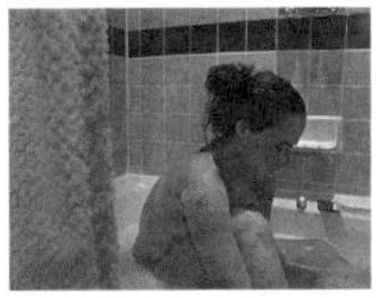
August 5, 2010
Seattle, WA
Pg. 227

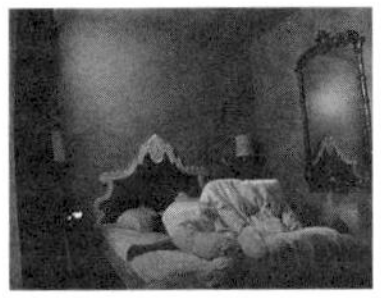
August 6, 2010
Seattle, WA
Pg. 228

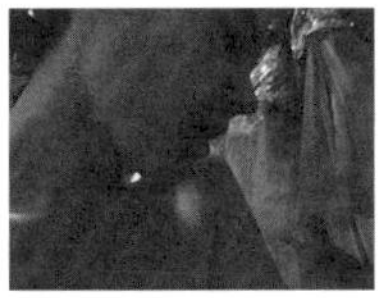
August 7, 2010
New York, NY
Pg. 229

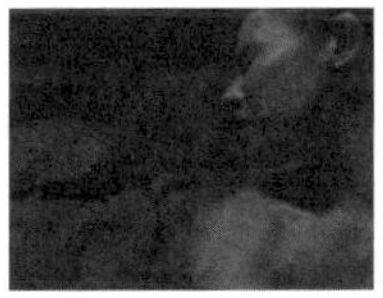
August 8, 2010
New York, NY
Pg. 230

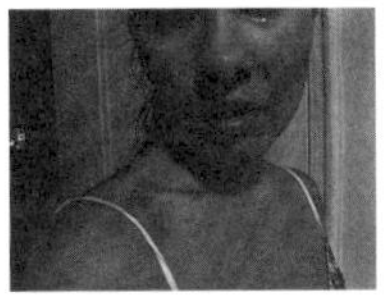
August 9, 2010
New York, NY
Pg. 231

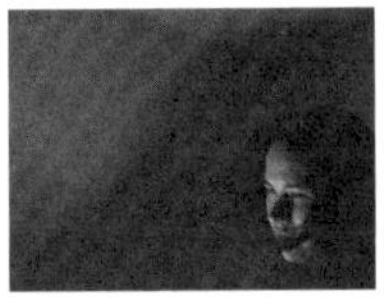
August 10, 2010
New York, NY
Pg. 232

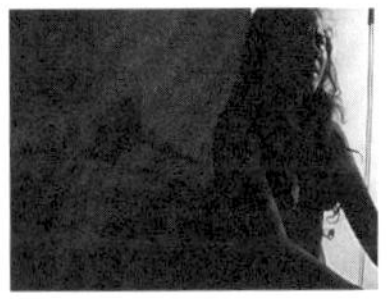
August 11, 2010
New York, NY
Pg. 233

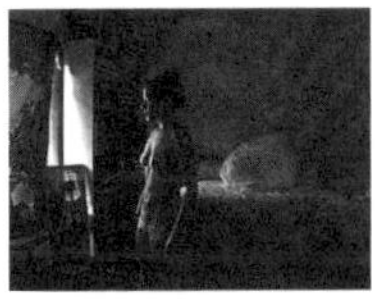
August 12, 2010
New York, NY
Pg. 234

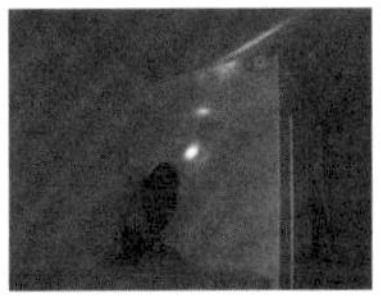
August 13, 2010
New York, NY
Pg. 235

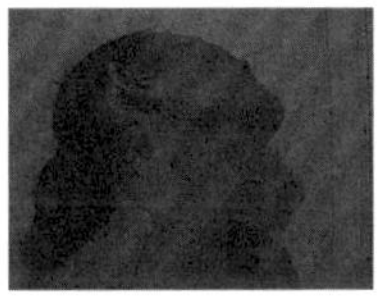
August 14, 2010
New York, NY
Pg. 236

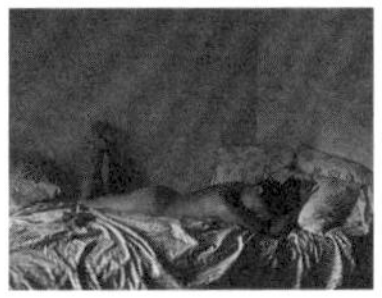
August 15, 2010
New York, NY
Pg. 237

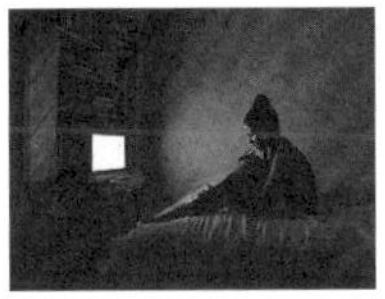
August 16, 2010
New York, NY
Pg. 238

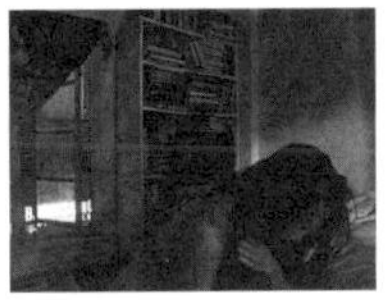
August 17, 2010
New York, NY
Pg. 239

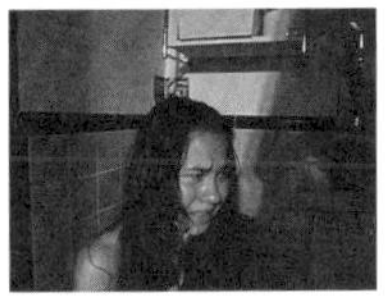
August 18, 2010
New York, NY
Pg. 240

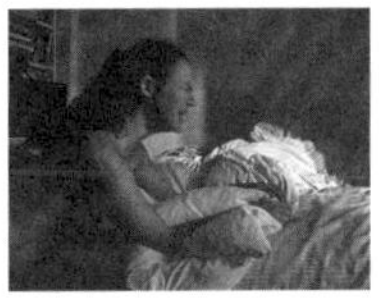
August 19, 2010
New York, NY
Pg. 241

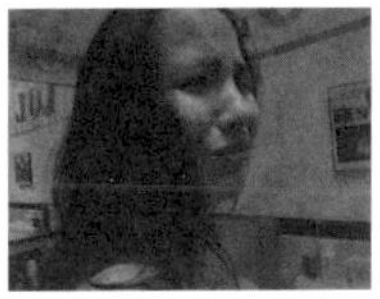
August 20, 2010
New York, NY
Pg. 242

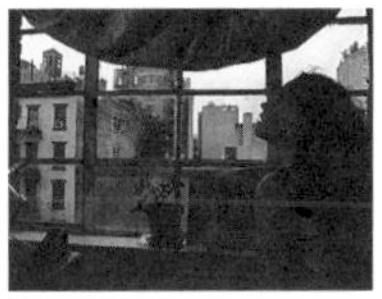
August 21, 2010
New York, NY
Pg. 243

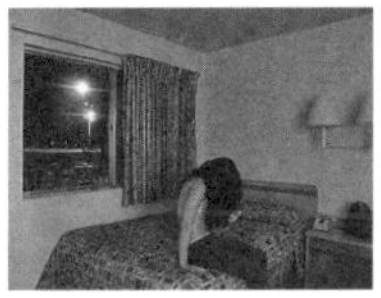
August 22, 2010
Motel outside
Laramie, WY
Pg. 244

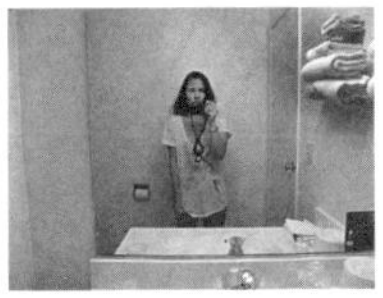
August 23, 2010
Motel outside
Laramie, WY
Pg. 245

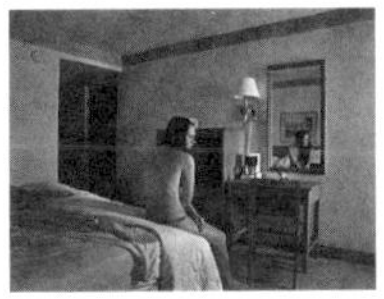
August 24, 2010
Elko, NV
Pg. 246

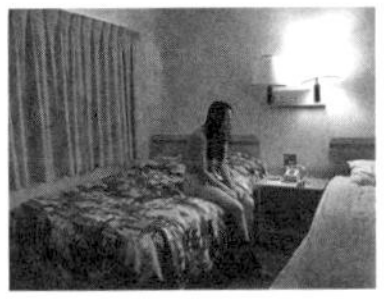
August 25, 2010
Motel somewhere
near the NV/CA border
Pg. 247

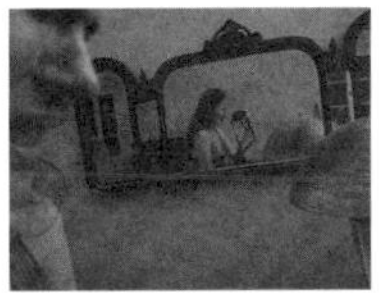
August 26, 2010
Los Angeles, CA
Pg. 248

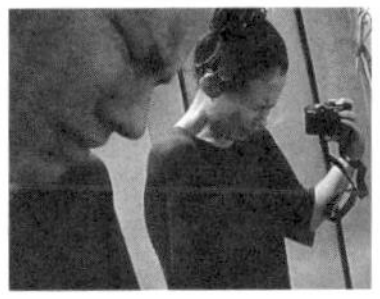
August 27, 2010
Los Angeles, CA
Pg. 249

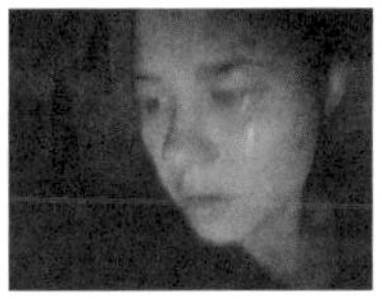
August 28, 2010
Berkeley, CA
Pg. 250

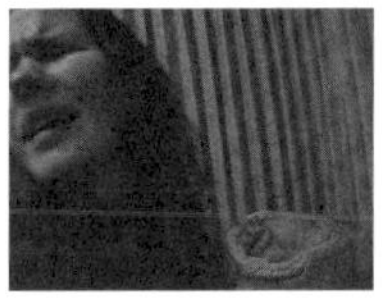
August 29, 2010
Berkeley, CA
Pg. 251

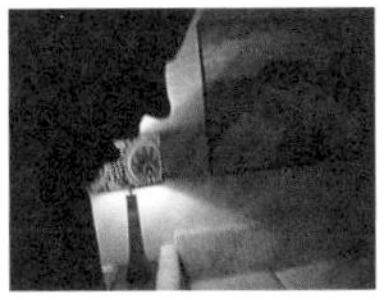
August 30, 2010
Berkeley, CA
Pg. 252

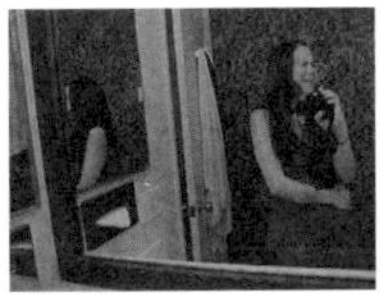
August 31, 2010
West Hollywood, CA
Pg. 253

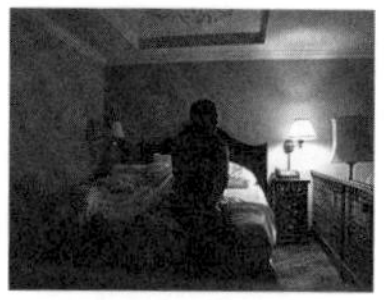
September 1, 2010
West Hollywood, CA
Pg. 254

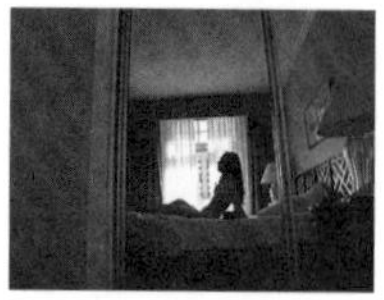
September 2, 2010
San Francisco, CA
Pg. 255

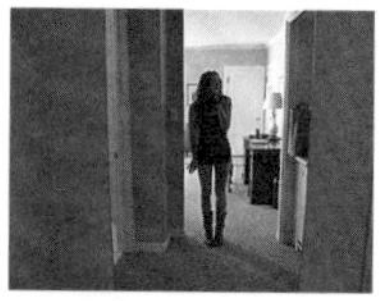
September 3, 2010
San Francisco, CA
Pg. 256

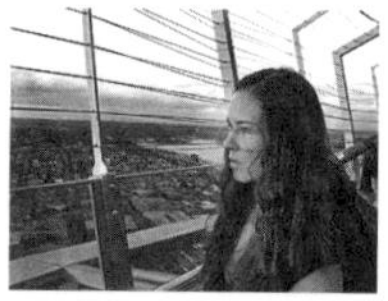
September 4, 2010
Top of the Space Needle,
Seattle, WA
Pg. 257

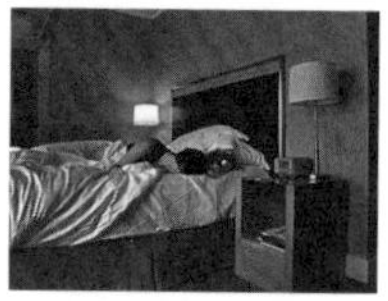
September 5, 2010
Seattle, WA
Pg. 258

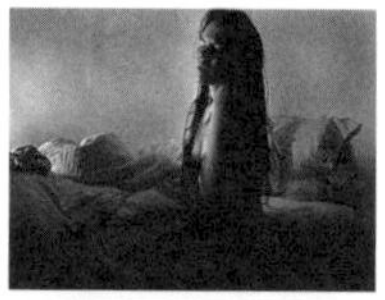
September 6, 2010
New York, NY
Pg. 259

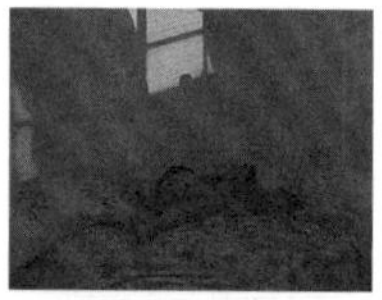
September 7, 2010
New York, NY
Pg. 260

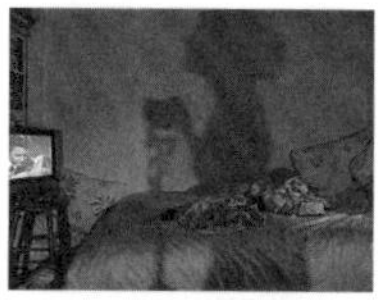
September 8, 2010
New York, NY
Pg. 261

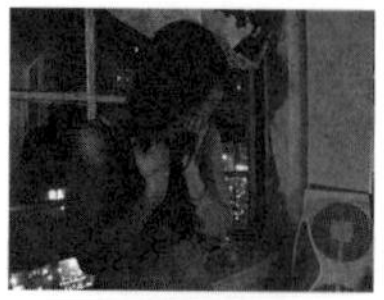
September 9, 2010
New York, NY
Pg. 262

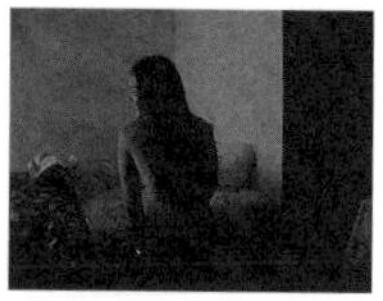
September 10, 2010
New York, NY
Pg. 263

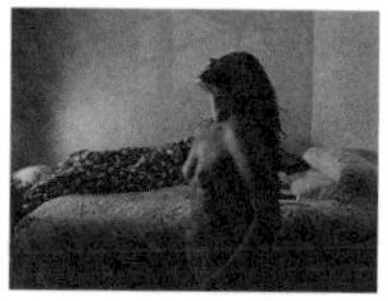
September 11, 2010
New York, NY
Pg. 264

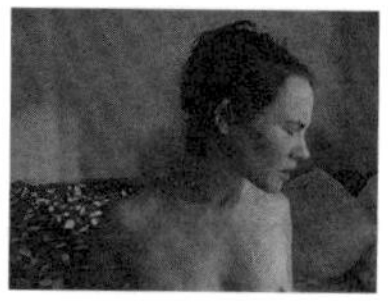
September 12, 2010
New York, NY
Pg. 265

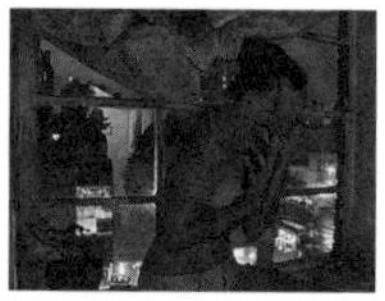
September 13, 2010
New York, NY
Pg. 266

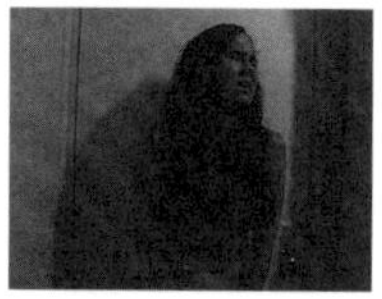
September 14, 2010
New York, NY
Pg. 267

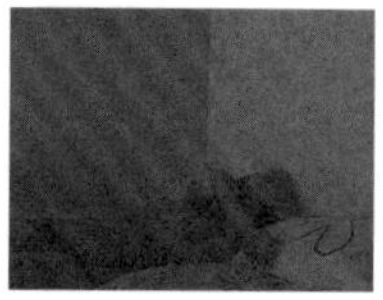
September 15, 2010
New York, NY
Pg. 268

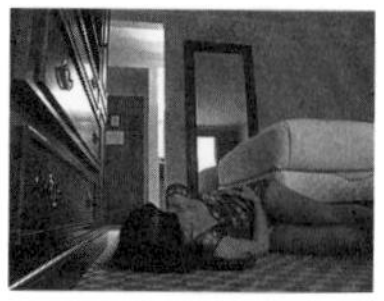
September 16, 2010
Bryn Mawr, PA
Pg. 269

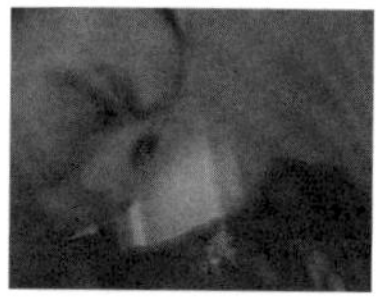
September 17, 2010
New York, NY
Pg. 270

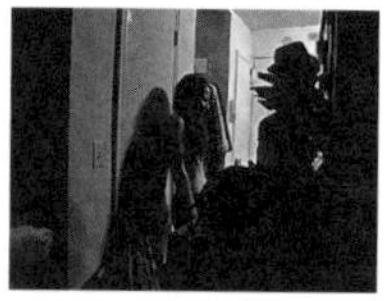
September 18, 2010
New York, NY
Pg. 271

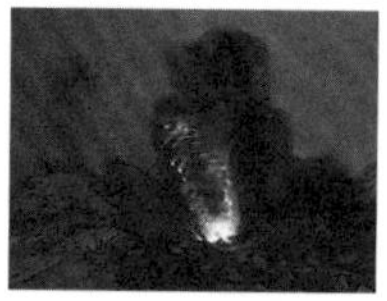
September 19, 2010
New York, NY
Pg. 272

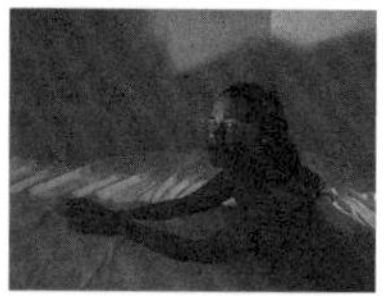
September 20, 2010
New York, NY
Pg. 273

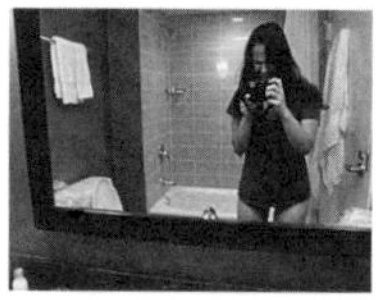
September 21, 2010
Fairfax, VA
Pg. 274

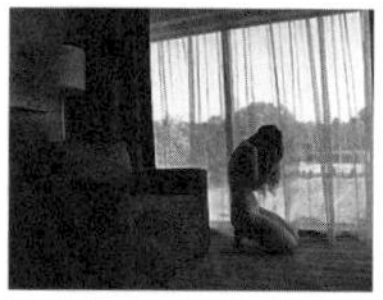
September 22, 2010
Fairfax, VA
Pg. 275

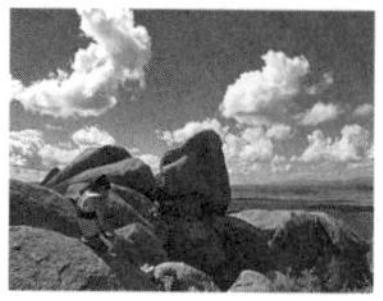
September 23, 2010
Tucson, AZ
Pg. 276

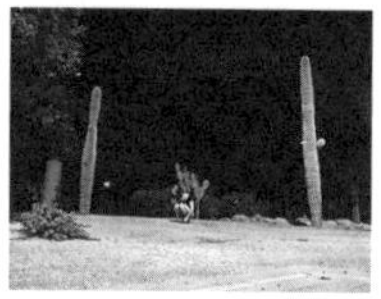
September 24, 2010
Tucson, AZ
Pg. 277

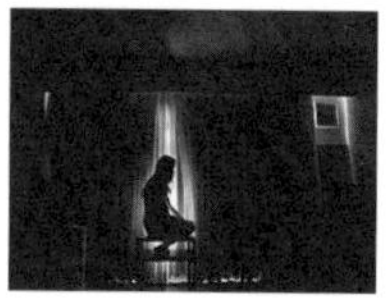
September 25, 2010
Burlington, VT
Pg. 278

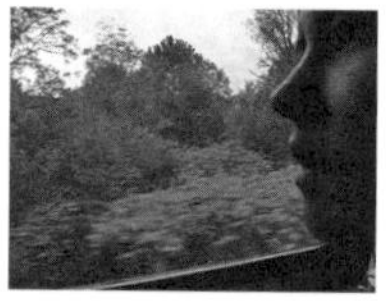
September 26, 2010
On Amtrak, somewhere
outside Burlington, VT
Pg. 279

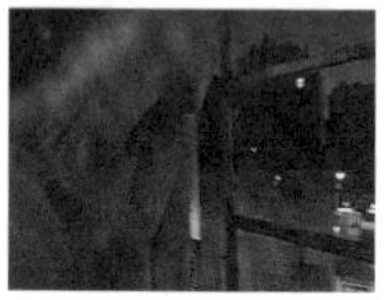
September 27, 2010
New York, NY
Pg. 280

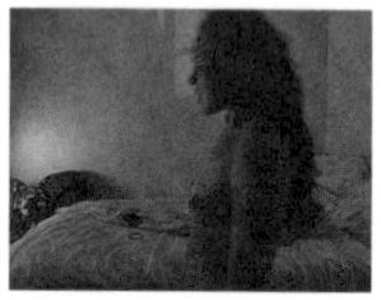
September 28, 2010
New York, NY
Pg. 281

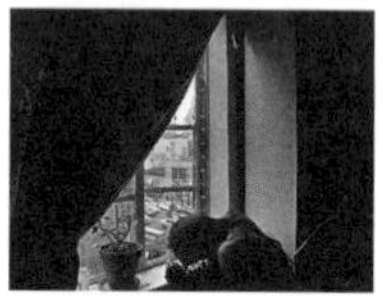
September 29, 2010
New York, NY
Pg. 282

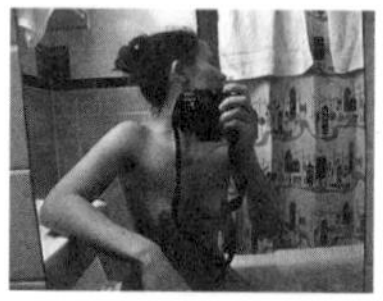
September 30, 2010
New York, NY
Pg. 283

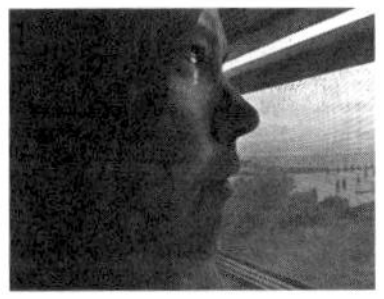

October 1, 2010
Fishers Island, NY
Pg. 284

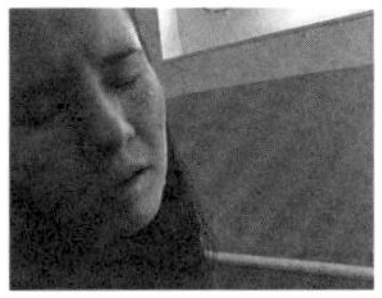

October 2, 2010
Off the coast of
Fishers Island, NY
Pg. 285

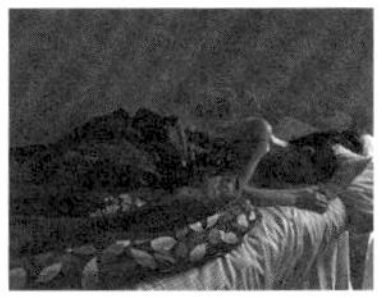

October 3, 2010
New York, NY
Pg. 286

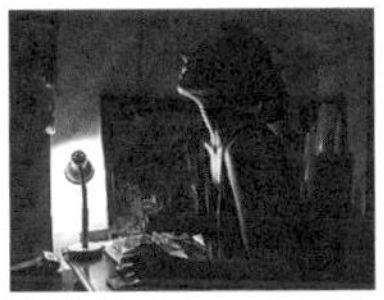

October 4, 2010
New York, NY
Pg. 287

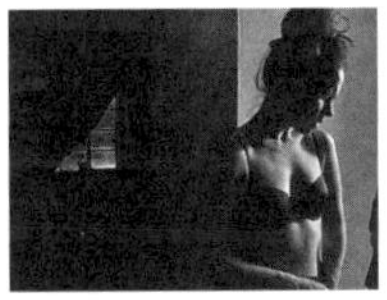

October 5, 2010
New York, NY
Pg. 288

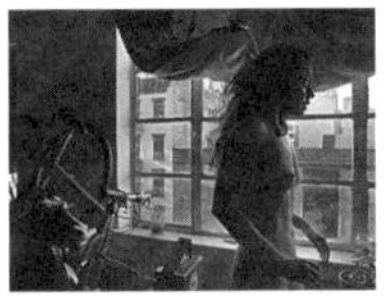

October 6, 2010
New York, NY
Pg. 289

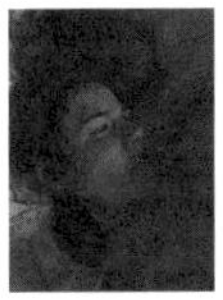

October 7, 2010
New York, NY
Pg. 290

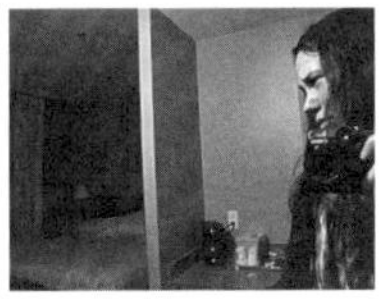

October 8, 2010
Toronto, Canada
Pg. 291

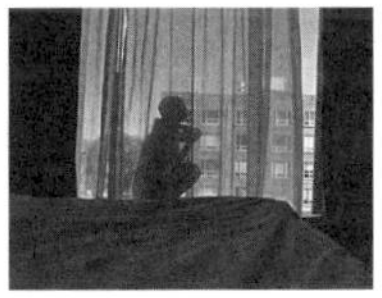

October 9, 2010
Toronto, Canada
Pg. 292

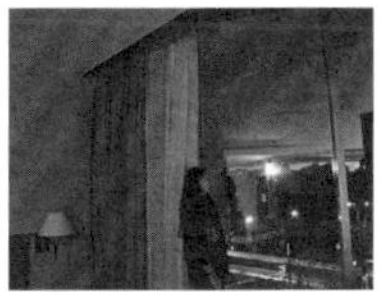

October 10, 2010
Toronto, Canada
Pg. 293

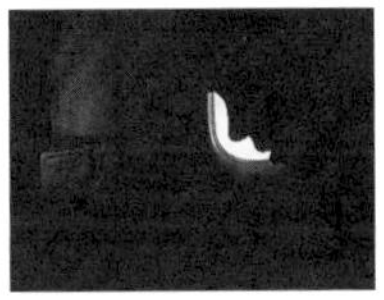

October 11, 2010
Somewhere above Toronto,
Canada
Pg. 294

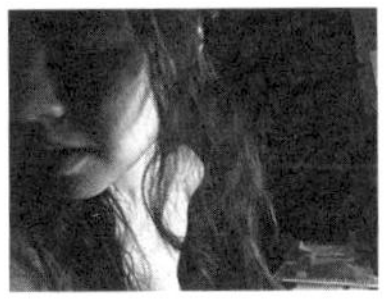

October 12, 2010
New York, NY
Pg. 295

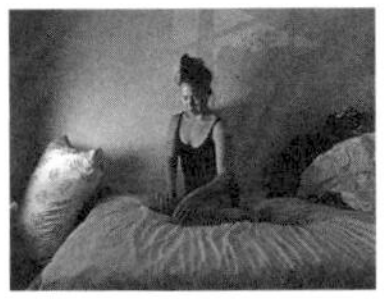

October 13, 2010
New York, NY
Pg. 296

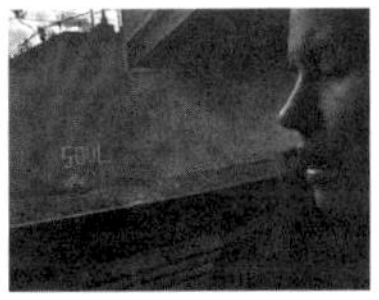

October 14, 2010
On Amtrak, outside
Philadelphia, PA
Pg. 297

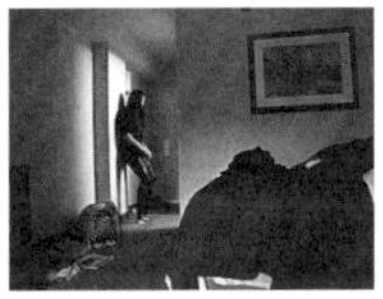

October 15, 2010
Philadelphia, PA
Pg. 298

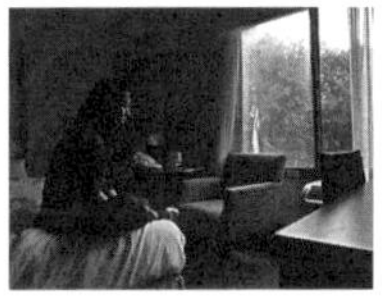

October 16, 2010
Philadelphia, PA
Pg. 299

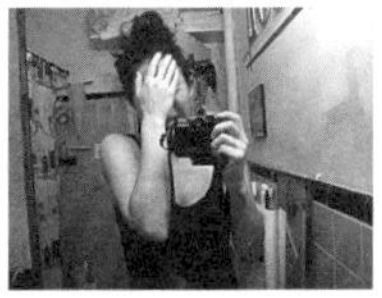

October 17, 2010
New York, NY
Pg. 300

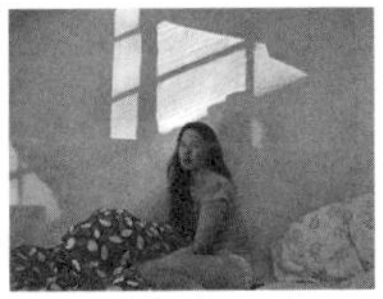

October 18, 2010
New York, NY
Pg. 301

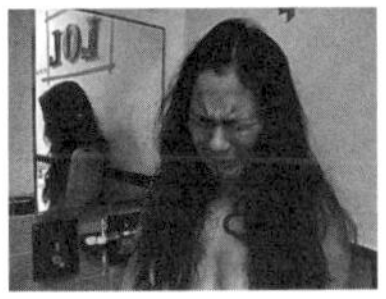

October 19, 2010
New York, NY
Pg. 302

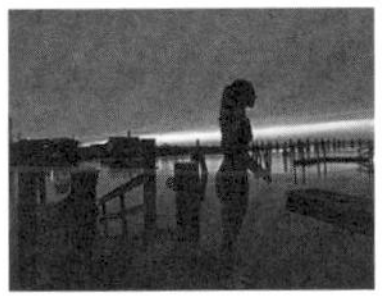

October 20, 2010
Fishers Island, NY
Pg. 303

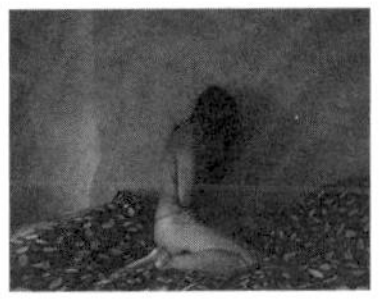

October 21, 2010
New York, NY
Pg. 304

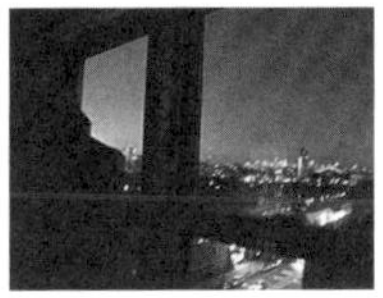

October 22, 2010
Brooklyn, NY
Pg. 305

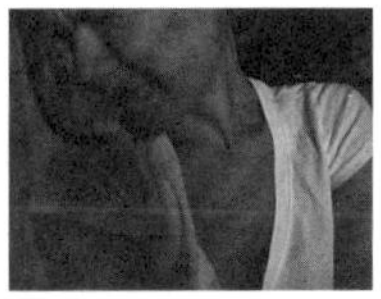

October 23, 2010
New York, NY
Pg. 306

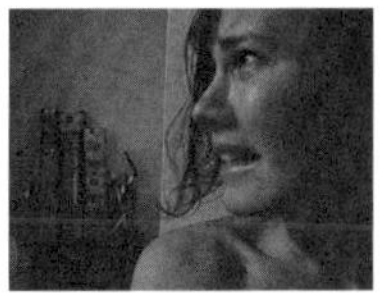

October 24, 2010
New York, NY
Pg. 307

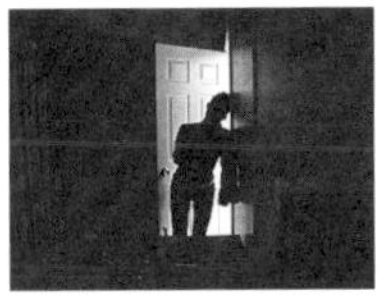

October 25, 2010
New Haven, CT
Pg. 308

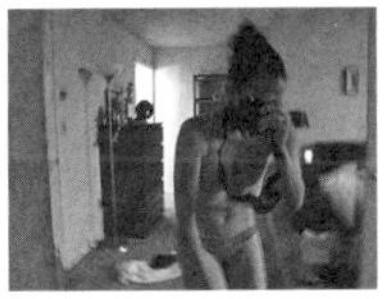

October 26, 2010
New Haven, CT
Pg. 309

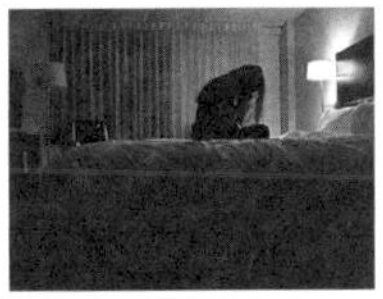

October 27, 2010
Somewhere over
New England
Pg. 310

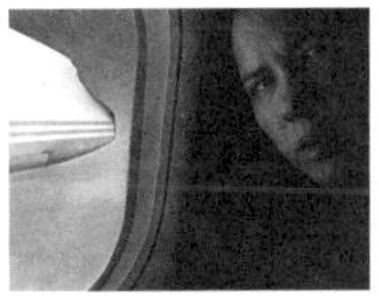

October 28, 2010
Ottawa, Canada
Pg. 311

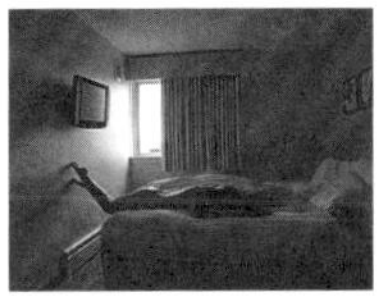

October 29, 2010
Ottawa, Canada
Pg. 312

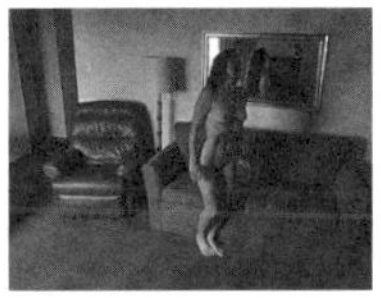

October 30, 2010
Ottawa, Canada
Pg. 313

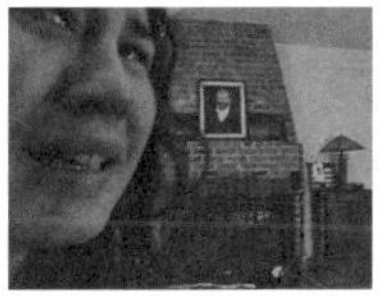

October 31, 2010
Fishers Island, NY
Pg. 314

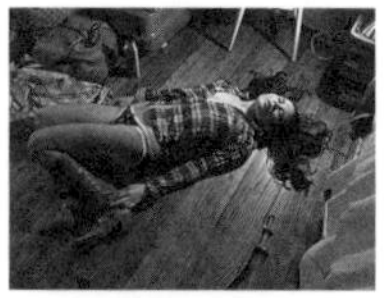
November 1, 2010
New York, NY
Pg. 315

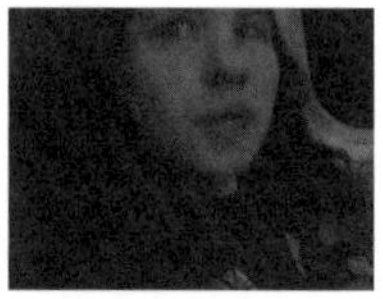
November 2, 2010
Somewhere over Iowa
Pg. 316

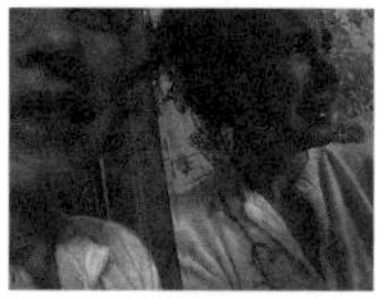
November 3, 2010
Ames, IA
Pg. 317

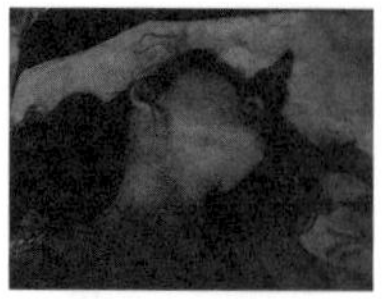
November 4, 2010
Ames, IA
Pg. 318

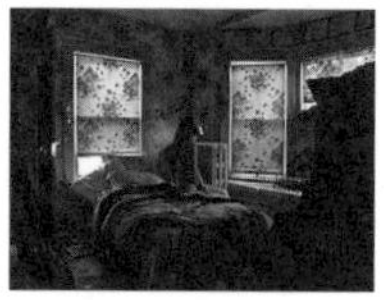
November 5, 2010
Ames, IA
Pg. 319

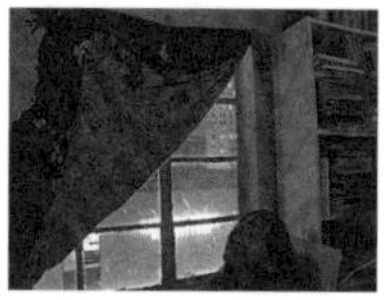
November 6, 2010
New York, NY
Pg. 320

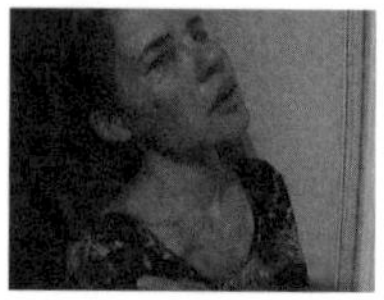
November 7, 2010
New York, NY
Pg. 321

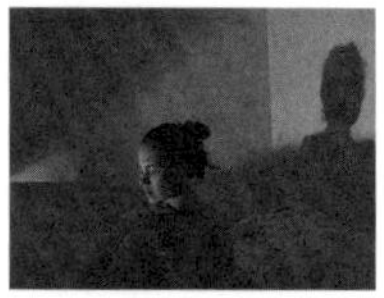
November 8, 2010
New York, NY
Pg. 322

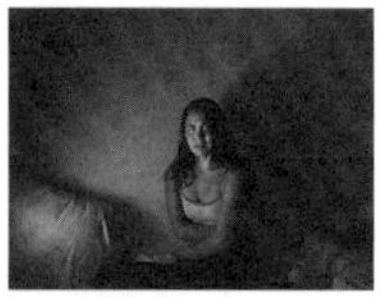
November 9, 2010
New York, NY
Pg. 323

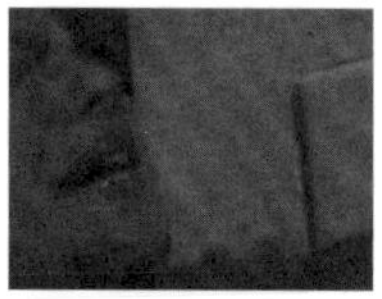
November 10, 2010
New York, NY
Pg. 324

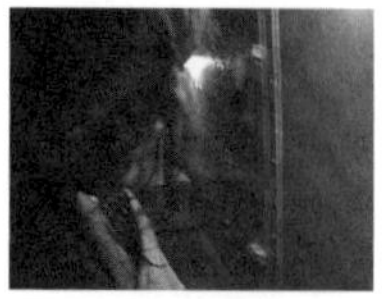
November 11, 2010
Off the coast of
New London, CT
Pg. 325

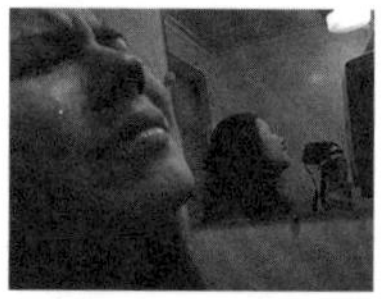
November 12, 2010
Off the coast of
Fishers Island, NY
Pg. 326

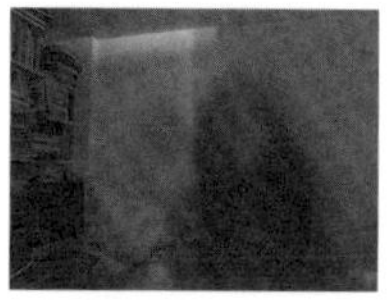
November 13, 2010
New York, NY
Pg. 327

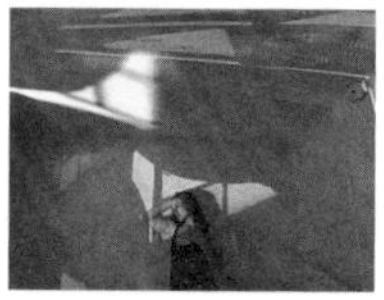
November 14, 2010
New York, NY
Pg. 328

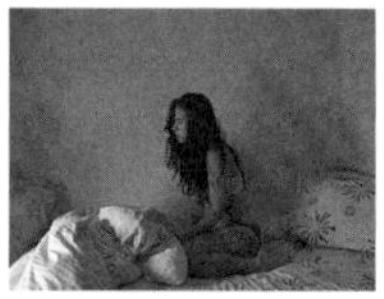
November 15, 2010
New York, NY
Pg. 329

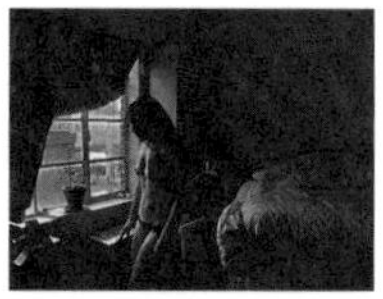
November 16, 2010
New York, NY
Pg. 330

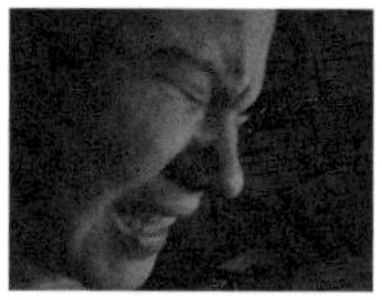
November 17, 2010
New York, NY
Pg. 331

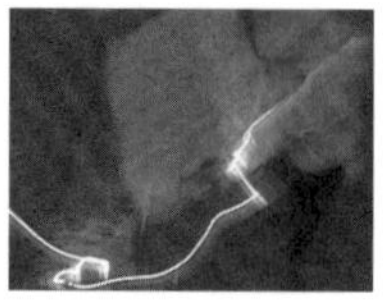
November 18, 2010
New York, NY
Pg. 332

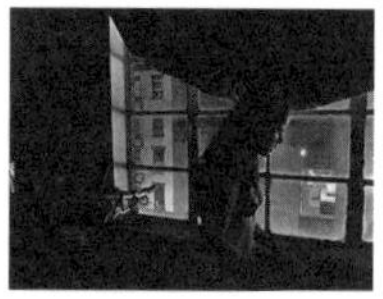
November 19, 2010
New York, NY
Pg. 333

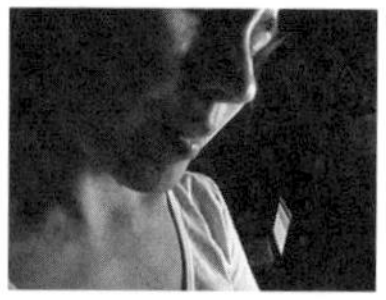
November 20, 2010
New York, NY
Pg. 334

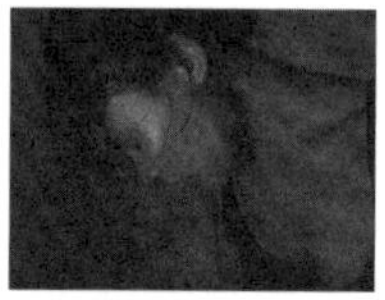
November 21, 2010
New York, NY
Pg. 335

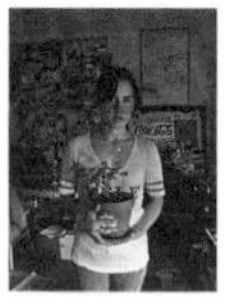
November 22, 2010
New York, NY
Pg. 336

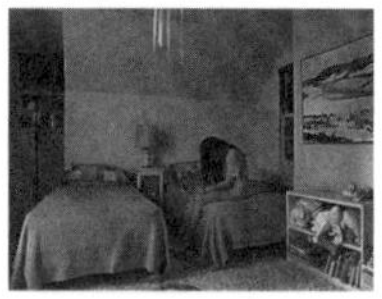
November 23, 2010
Fishers Island, NY
Pg. 337

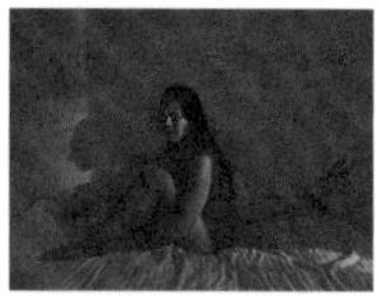
November 24, 2010
New York, NY
Pg. 338

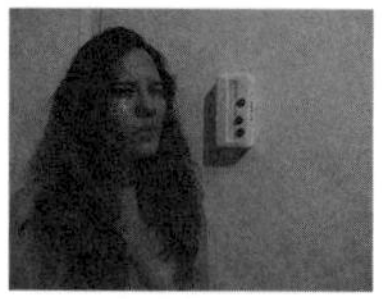
November 25, 2010
New York, NY
Pg. 339

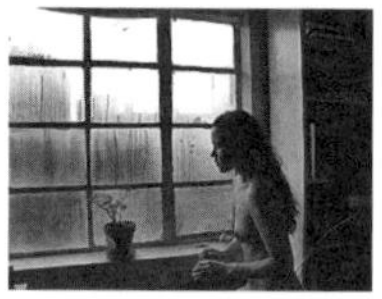
November 26, 2010
New York, NY
Pg. 340

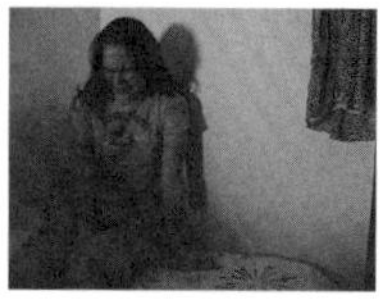
November 27, 2010
New York, NY
Pg. 341

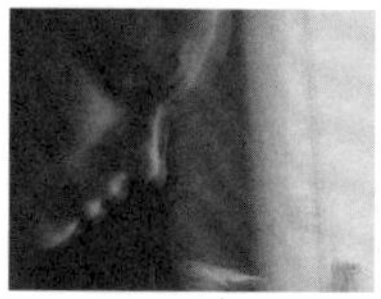
November 28, 2010
New York, NY
Pg. 342

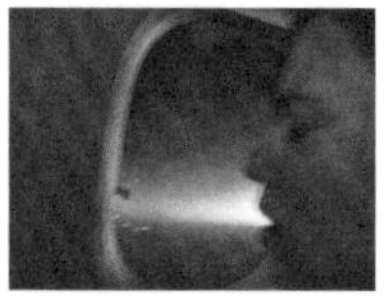
November 29, 2010
Somewhere over Nebraska
Pg. 343

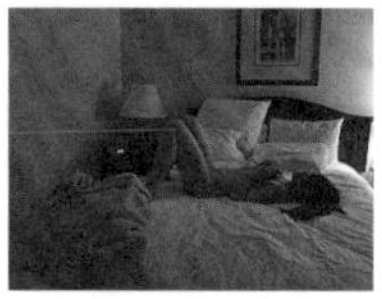
November 30, 2010
San Diego, CA
Pg. 344

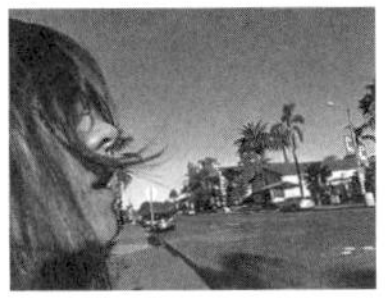

December 1, 2010
San Diego, CA
Pg. 345

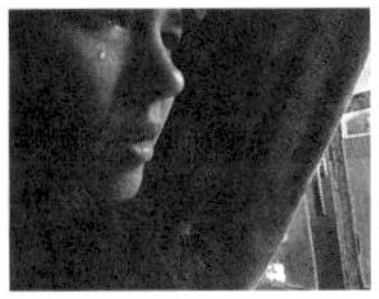

December 2, 2010
New York, NY
Pg. 346

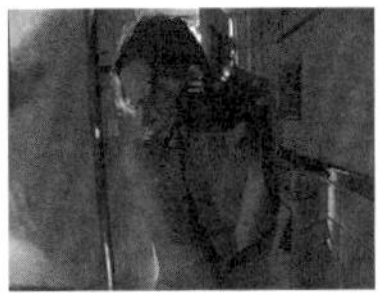

December 3, 2010
New York, NY
Pg. 347

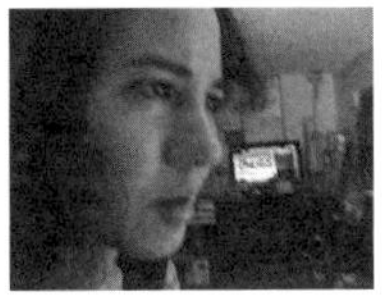

December 4, 2010
New York, NY
Pg. 348

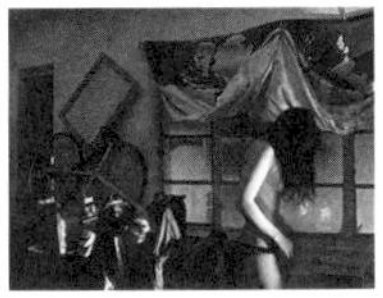

December 5, 2010
New York, NY
Pg. 349

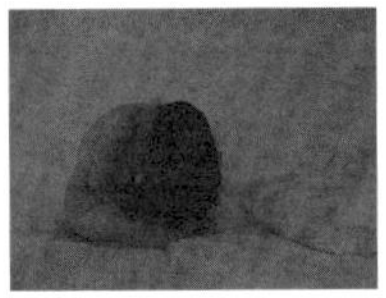

December 6, 2010
New York, NY
Pg. 350

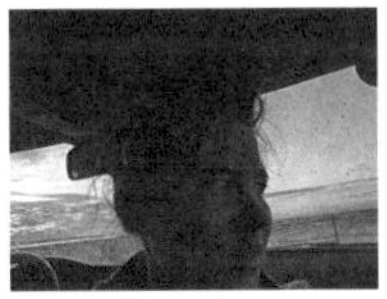

December 7, 2010
Off the coast of
Fishers Island, NY
Pg. 351

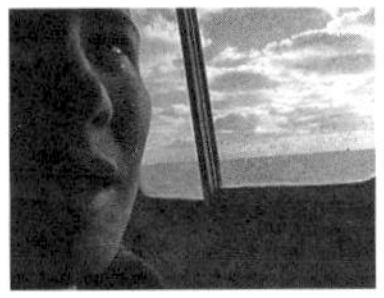

December 8, 2010
Off the coast of
Fishers Island, NY
Pg. 352

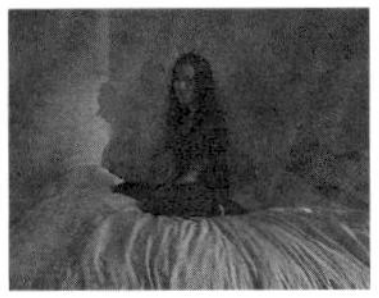

December 9, 2010
New York, NY
Pg. 353

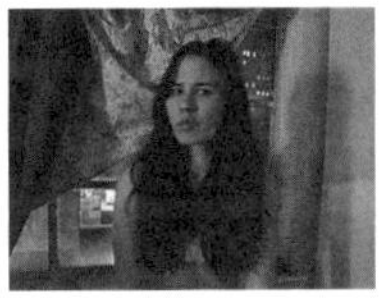

December 10, 2010
New York, NY
Pg. 354

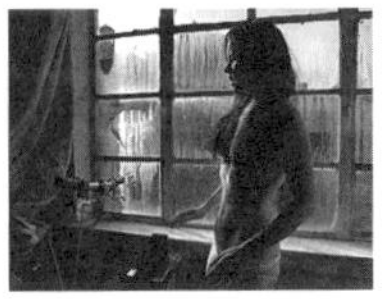

December 11, 2010
New York, NY
Pg. 355

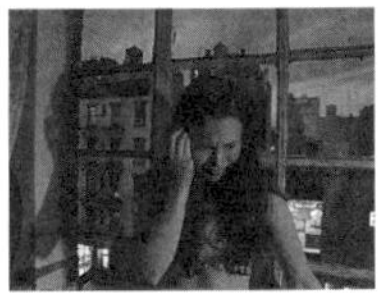

December 12, 2010
New York, NY
Pg. 356

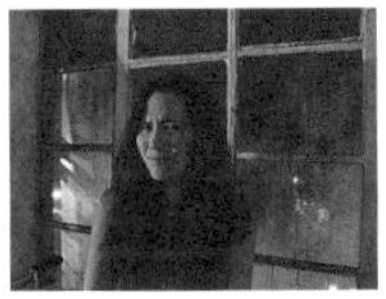

December 13, 2010
New York, NY
Pg. 357

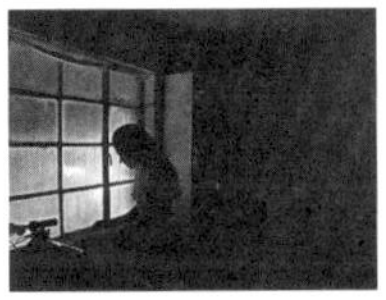

December 14, 2010
New York, NY
Pg. 358

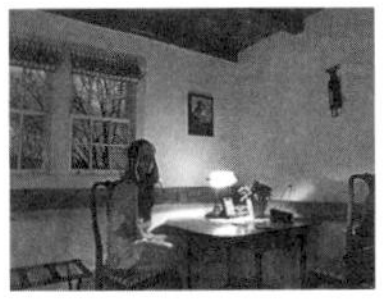

December 15, 2010
Hurley, NY
Pg. 359

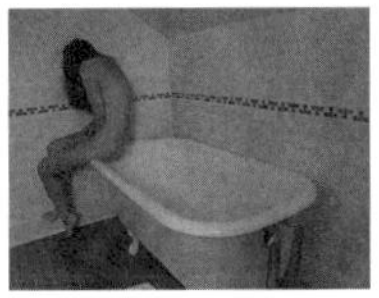

December 16, 2010
Hurley, NY
Pg. 360

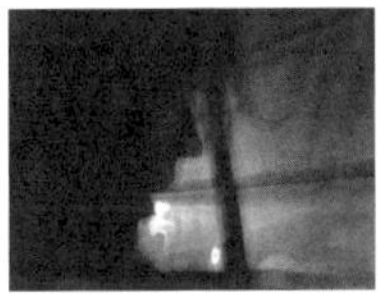

December 17, 2010
New York, NY
Pg. 361

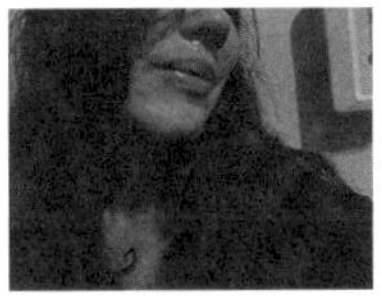

December 18, 2010
New York, NY
Pg. 362

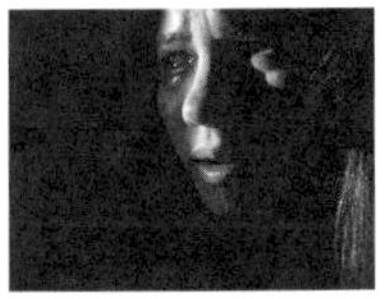

December 19, 2010
New York, NY
Pg. 363

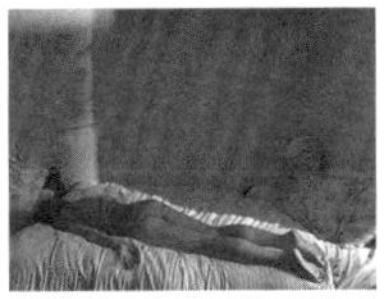

December 20, 2010
New York, NY
Pg. 364

December 21, 2010
New York, NY
Pg. 365

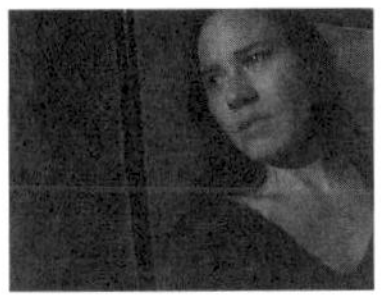

December 22, 2010
New York, NY
Pg. 366

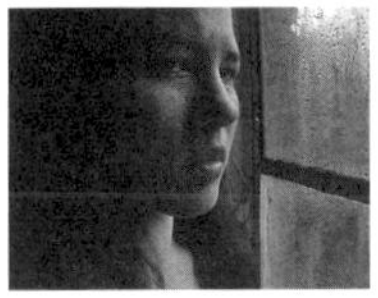

December 23, 2010
New York, NY
Pg. 367

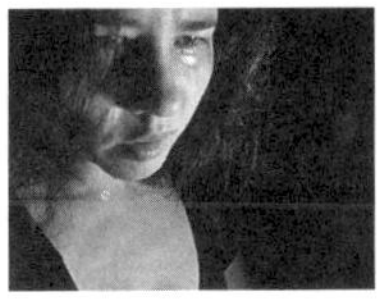

December 24, 2010
New York, NY
Pg. 368

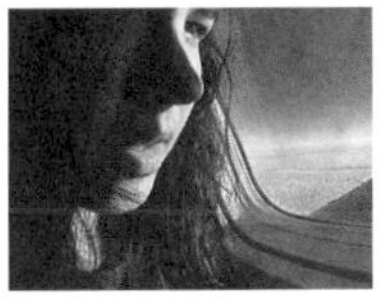

December 25, 2010
Somewhere over Indiana
Pg. 369

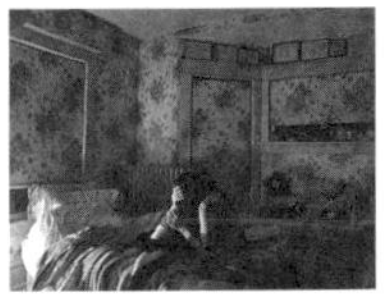

December 26, 2010
Ames, IA
Pg. 370

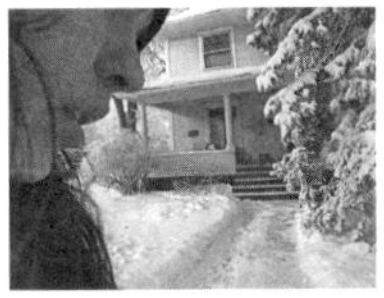

December 27, 2010
Ames, IA
Pg. 371

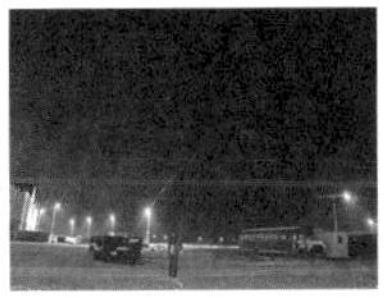

December 28, 2010
Ames, IA
Pg. 372

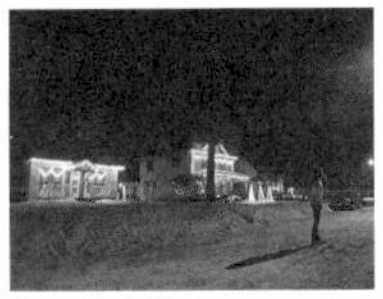

December 29, 2010
Ames, IA
Pg. 373

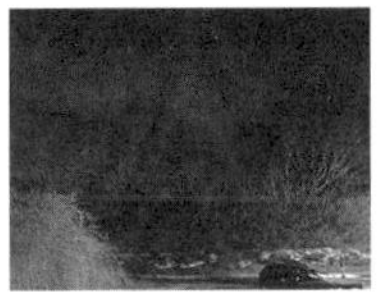

December 30, 2010
Fishers Island, NY
Pg. 374

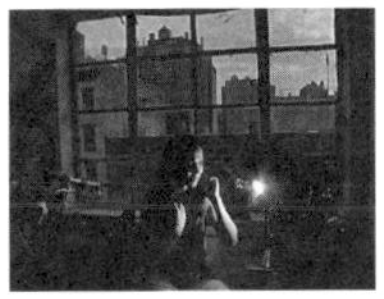

December 31, 2010
New York, NY
Pg. 375

Laurel Nakadate

Laurel Nakadate is known for powerful video, film, and photographic works in which the artist, her subjects, and the viewer are entangled in unsettling performances of seduction, power, trust, and tenderness.

Nakadate was born in Austin, Texas in 1975 and raised in Ames, Iowa. She received a Bachelor of Fine Arts from the School of the Museum of Fine Arts, Boston and Tufts University in 1998 and a Master of Fine Arts from Yale University in 2001. She has participated in solo and group exhibitions in major museums and galleries worldwide.

Her first feature film, *Stay the Same Never Change*, premiered at the 2009 Sundance Film Festival and has been screened at film festivals and museums throughout the U.S. and Europe. Her second feature film, *The Wolf Knife*, premiered at the 2010 Los Angeles Film Festival and was nominated for a 2010 Gotham Award and a 2011 Independent Spirit Award.

Works by Laurel Nakadate are in the collections of The Museum of Modern Art (MoMA); the Whitney Museum of American Art; the Yale University Art Gallery; the Princeton University Art Museum; the CCS Bard Hessel Museum of Art and distinguished private collections in the U.S. and Europe.

A ten-year survey of her work, *Laurel Nakadate: Only the Lonely*, curated by Klaus Biesenbach, ran from January to August of 2011 at MoMA PS1, Long Island City, New York.